Argentina
Uruguay & Paraguay
a travel survival kit

**Wayne Bernhardson
María Massolo**

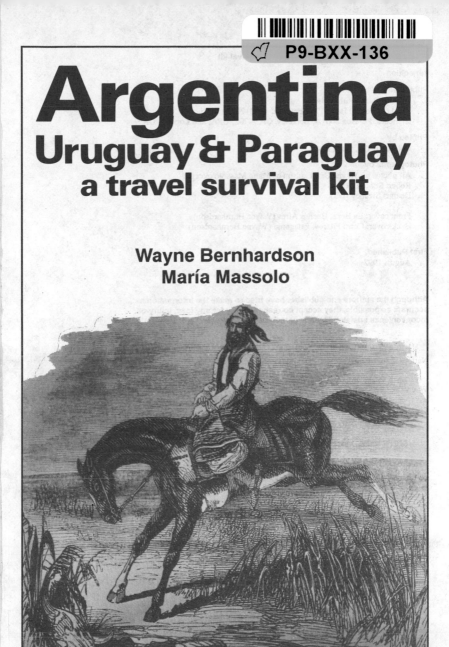

Argentina, Uruguay & Paraguay – a travel survival kit

1st edition

Published by
    Lonely Planet Publications
    Head Office: PO Box 617, Hawthorn, Vic 3122, Australia
    Branches: PO Box 2001A, Berkeley, CA 94702, USA, and London, UK

Printed by
    Colorcraft Ltd, Hong Kong

Photographs by
    All photos by Wayne Bernhardson or María Massolo except:
    Robert Strauss (RS)
    Deanna Swaney (DS)

    Front cover: La Boca, Buenos Aires (Wayne Bernhardson)
    Back cover: Cerro Fitzroy, Patagonia (Wayne Bernhardson)

First Published
    August 1992

National Library of Australia Cataloguing in Publication Data

Wayne Bernhardson.
    Argentina, Uruguay & Paraguay – a travel survival kit.

    1st ed.
    Includes index.
    ISBN 0 86442 140 0.

    1. Argentina – Description and travel –1981 – – Guidebooks. 2.
    Uruguay – Description and travel – 1981 – – Guidebooks. 3.
    Paraguay – Description and travel – 1981 – – Guidebooks. I. Massolo,
    María. II. Title.

989

Wayne Bernhardson

Wayne Bernhardson was born in North Dakota, grew up in Tacoma, Washington, and spent most of the past decade shuttling between North and South America en route to a PhD in geography from the University of California, Berkeley. In the process of doing so, he met co-author María Massolo in Bolivia, married her in Argentina, and fathered their daughter Clío in California. He has travelled extensively in Central and South America, and lived for extended periods in Chile, Argentina and the Falkland (Malvinas) Islands.

María Massolo

María Massolo was born in Olavarría, the 'cement capital' of Buenos Aires province, studied literature at the University of Buenos Aires and holds an MA in folklore from the University of California, Berkeley, where she is currently working toward a PhD in anthropology. She is proudest, though, of having worked for several months crushing and freezing crab legs in Stanley, capital of the Falkland (Malvinas) Islands. Wayne, María and Clío currently reside in Oakland, California.

From the Authors

We owe special thanks to Rodolfo and Mary Massolo of Olavarría, Buenos Aires province, who provided us with the vehicle in which we toured Paraguay, Uruguay and Argentina, and who kept Clío healthy and amused when we were unable to take her on the road. Also in Olavarría, thanks to Marcelo and María Estela Peruilh, and to Rodolfo and Viviano Massolo (hijo).

Many others in Argentina were exceptionally helpful and hospitable in the process of pulling this all together. The list could be even longer, but we mention especially Carlos Reboratti, Federico Kirbus, Mrs E F Grant and Joaquín Allolio of Buenos Aires; Pola and Gonzalo Sánchez Viamonte of La Plata; Eva Sanllorenti of Tandil, Buenos Aires province; Miguel Gutiérrez of Moreno, Buenos Aires province; Victor Centurión of Paraná, Entre Ríos; Sixto Vásquez Zuleta (Toqo) of Humahuaca, Jujuy; Dr Alfredo Bolsi and Juan José Coggan of Tucumán; María Marta and Raúl Balduzzi of Mendoza; Dr Raúl Manioloff of Resistencia, Chaco; Gustavo Gil and Diana Seijo de Gil of Neuquén; Jim and Ann Wood of Estancia Huechahue, Neuquén; Carlos Massolo and Laura Alvarez of Villa Regina, Río Negro; Marala Gregorini and Simo Guaña Benz of Puerto Madryn, Chubut; Arnold Ingram of

Comodoro Rivadavia, Chubut; Carlos Balestra of Monumento Natural Bosques Petrificados, Santa Cruz; and Juan Borrego of Chaltén, Santa Cruz. Varig officials in Buenos Aires and Río de Janeiro deserve credit for their willingness to haul the bulky, overweight boxes of books, papers and notes which accumulated in months of research.

Funmi Arewa of the American Consulate in Montevideo made an especially valuable contribution to both the Argentine and Uruguayan sections of the book. In Paraguay, we owe real gratitude to Antonio van Humbeeck of the Instituto Moisés Bertoni in Asunción, Alejandro Martínez Sánchez of the Asunción botanical garden, and Jacob and María Unger of Filadelfia, Chaco. In the Falkland Islands, where we spent more than a year, many people deserve our gratitude, but Graham Bound was most directly helpful in this specific project.

Foreign travellers were few in the time we spent in Argentina, Uruguay and Paraguay, but a few deserve special mention: Reiner Erben of Buenos Aires and Augsburg, Germany; Jacob Fjalland of Virum, Denmark; Jens Olander of Helsinki, Finland; and Béat Habegger of Tavannes, Switzerland. Thanks also to Bruce Caplan, for briefly joining us and for his observation that 'Patagonia is purgatory for contact lens wearers'.

Stateside, we owe real thanks to Roger Pacheco of Varig Brazilian Airlines in San Francisco. Special mention also goes to Eric Ketunen of Lonely Planet's Oakland office, whose faxes to Australia expedited many matters, including the check for our advance.

In Australia, Tony Wheeler showed great faith in our ability to complete this project, supporting it with additional funds when it became apparent that economic conditions had changed dramatically in Argentina. Peter Turner, Michelle de Kretser and Graham Imeson paid close attention to text and photo editing.

From the Publisher

This book was edited and proofed by Greg Alford. Thanks also to Michelle Coxall for her assistance with the editing of the Uruguay and Paraguay sections of the book. Glenn Beanland was responsible for mapping, design and production. Additional mapping was carried out by Graham Imeson, Greg Herriman and Chris Lee Ack. Thanks also to Vicki Beale for invaluable help with production.

This Book

This first edition of *Argentina, Uruguay & Paraguay – a travel survival kit* was researched and written by Wayne Bernhardson and María Massolo. It replaces LP's former title *Argentina – a travel survival kit* by Alan Samalgalski. Many readers wrote to us with helpful information and suggestions; a list of all your names can be found on page 606 of this book.

Warning & Request

Things change – prices go up, schedules change, good places go bad and bad places go bankrupt – nothing stays the same. So if you find things better or worse, recently opened or long since closed, please write and tell us and help make the next edition better!

Your letters will be used to help update future editions and, where possible, important changes will also be included as a Stop Press section in reprints.

All information is greatly appreciated and the best letters will receive a free copy of the next edition, or any other LP book of your choice.

Contents

TIERRA DEL FUEGO & CHILEAN PATAGONIA 407

FALKLAND ISLANDS

FALKLAND ISLANDS (ISLAS MALVINAS) 441

URUGUAY

FACTS ABOUT THE COUNTRY 469

FACTS FOR THE VISITOR 476

PARAGUAY

FACTS ABOUT THE COUNTRY 537

FACTS FOR THE VISITOR 549

GETTING THERE & AWAY 556

Map Legend

BOUNDARIES

— — — — — .... International Boundary

— — — .... Internal Boundary

+++++++++ .... National Park or Reserve

— — — — — .... The Equator

.... The Tropics

SYMBOLS

◉ NEW DELHI .... National Capital

● BOMBAY .... Provincial or State Capital

● Pune .... Major Town

● Borsi .... Minor Town

■ .... Places to Stay

▼ .... Places to Eat

▲ .... Post Office

✈ .... Airport

ℹ .... Tourist Information

☻ .... Bus Station or Terminal

66 .... Highway Route Number

☫ ✝ ♜ ...... Mosque, Church, Cathedral

∴ .... Temple or Ruin

✚ .... Hospital

※ .... Lookout

▲ .... Camping Area

⌒ .... Picnic Area

⌂ .... Hut or Chalet

▲ .... Mountain or Hill

.... Railway Station

.... Road Bridge

.... Railway Bridge

.... Road Tunnel

.... Railway Tunnel

.... Escarpment or Cliff

.... Pass

.... Ancient or Historic Wall

ROUTES

—————— .... Major Road or Highway

- - - - - - - .... Unsealed Major Road

——— .... Sealed Road

- - - - - - ..... Unsealed Road or Track

═══════ .... City Street

+++++++++ ....Railway

●————●— .... Subway

················ ....Walking Track

- - - - - - - .... Ferry Route

++++++++ .... Cable Car or Chair Lift

HYDROGRAPHIC FEATURES

.... River or Creek

.... Intermittent Stream

.... Lake, Intermittent Lake

.... Coast Line

...............................Spring

.... Waterfall

...............................Swamp

.... Salt Lake or Reef

OTHER FEATURES

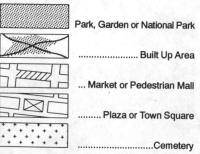

Park, Garden or National Park

.... Built Up Area

... Market or Pedestrian Mall

.... Plaza or Town Square

............................Cemetery

Note: not all symbols displayed above appear in this book

Introduction

Argentina, Uruguay and Paraguay comprise the bulk of the region commonly known as South America's 'Southern Cone', which stretches from the tropics to, by some accounts, the South Pole. Within this region are a remarkable variety of both natural and cultural attractions. The magnificent desolation of Patagonia and the high Andes contrast dramatically with the urban frenzy of Buenos Aires, one of the world's largest and most cosmopolitan cities.

For many travellers, the region's natural wonders will be the primary attraction. In the early 20th century, Argentina was the first South American country to embrace the national park idea. Its southern Andean cordillera offers a string of alpine parks where awesome glaciers spill icebergs into

blue-green lakes of incomparable beauty. The central cordillera features the highest peaks in the Western hemisphere, while the northern deserts are, in their own way, no less impressive. These thinly populated areas also contain unusual wildlife. In vivid contrast are the massive concentrations of sub-Antarctic wildlife on the southern Patagonian coastline. Argentina also shares the awesome Iguazú Falls with Brazil and Paraguay.

Because of the cultural domination of overseas immigrants, ecological historian Alfred Crosby has called Buenos Aires and its immediate hinterlands a 'neo-Europe', in which trans-Atlantic arrivals and their cultural baggage – domestic plants and animals, and weeds – transformed the natural environment and ensured the eventual demise of the way of life of the relatively few indigenous people who inhabited the area in the 16th century. According to Crosby, the most aggressive weeds were the Europeans themselves, whose overwhelming numbers created a society which never truly accepted either its New World uniqueness or its ultimately derivative nature. It did, however, maintain important economic and cultural links with Europe, feeding its parent with grains and beef, contributing to world literature through Borges and others, and exporting the tango to European salons. For such reasons, Argentina is one Latin American society in which Europeans, North Americans and Anglophones can feel at ease and inconspicuous.

Uruguay, whose economy and culture closely resemble those of Buenos Aires, is a political buffer between giant Brazil and Argentina, while isolated Paraguay is South America's 'empty quarter', a hot, sparsely populated, subtropical lowland best known, until recently, for the unusually durable military dictatorship of General Alfredo Stroessner. Historically, Uruguay is the most stable and democratic of the three countries, but the recent regional democratic revival has made all three countries more inviting destinations. There is still uncertainty whether democratic institutions will endure (Paraguay in particular still has far to go), but at present one can travel through all three countries without fear of arbitrary arrest and detention.

This was not the case through the 1970s and early 1980s, when Argentina's military government fought its infamous Dirty War against 'subversives' before losing both power and prestige in military confrontation with Britain in the South Atlantic war of 1982. Uruguay suffered a similar, only slightly less brutal, experience at the hands of its military, while Paraguay endured institutionalised authoritarian rule for decades until the ouster of General Stroessner and indications of a modicum of glasnost occurred in 1989.

Present-day Argentina also includes north-western areas with significant indigenous populations once more closely integrated with the pre-Columbian civilizations of Peru and Bolivia. Throughout the colonial era, when Buenos Aires was a near-forgotten backwater, cities like Tucumán and Salta provided mules and essential provisions for the vital mining economy of the central Andes.

In addition, only late in the 19th century, after a brutal war of extermination against mounted Indians and with the assistance of a new wave of European immigration, did the Argentine state incorporate enormous, thinly populated Patagonia into its effective orbit. These persistent regional distinctions contradict the ideal of a uniform Argentine nationality.

Even today, despite economic disorder, Argentina's relative prosperity attracts immigrants from adjacent lands like Chile and Bolivia. It also presents the visitor with a greater geographical and cultural diversity than one might expect. With Uruguay and Paraguay, it offers complementary natural and cultural attractions for an extended stay.

The Falkland (Malvinas) Islands are a special case. Politically, they are one of the world's last colonial relics, yet there is no doubt that the people, by and large, are content with their political status. Nearly inaccessible since the 1982 war between the UK and Argentina, the Islands can once again be reached from Punta Arenas, Chile, on the South American mainland.

While they have great historical interest, for most visitors the wild island landscapes and especially the tame, abundant and accessible wildlife will be their greatest attractions. Except for the nearly constant wind, the climate is surprisingly benign; yet short of Antarctica itself, there is no better place to see the birds and mammals characteristic of the world's most southerly regions.

Argentina

Facts about the Country

HISTORY
Pre-Colonial Era

Most histories portray Argentina as a homogeneous society based on European immigration, but the country's pre-Columbian and colonial past, as well as the present, are far more complex. When Europeans first arrived in South America in the 16th century, the continent presented a variety of economic and ecological adaptations ranging from the densely populated Andean civilisations to the semisedentary agricultural peoples of tropical and temperate forests to the totally nomadic hunters and gatherers of the Amazon and the Patagonian steppes.

On the eastern slopes of the central Andes, on the periphery of the civilisations of Peru and Bolivia, irrigated maize agriculture supported permanent villages of Diaguita Indians between present-day Salta and San Juan. Other groups, such as the Comechingones near Córdoba, practised a similar livelihood. To the east, in the forested Río Paraná delta across the Chaco scrubland, smaller Guaraní populations of shifting cultivators relied on maize, and tuber crops such as manioc (cassava) and sweet potatoes. In most of the region, though, highly mobile people hunted the guanaco (a wild relative of the Andean llama) and the rhea (a flightless bird resembling the ostrich) with bow and arrow or *boleadoras*, heavily weighted thongs. In the extreme south, groups like the Yahgans gathered shellfish and bird eggs.

Conquest of the New World

Ironically, even after a papal treaty ratified the Spanish-Portuguese division of the Americas in 1494, the structure of Indian societies more strongly influenced the economic and political structure of colonial society than the edicts of peninsular authorities. The primary goal of the Spanish conquistadores was the acquisition of gold and silver, and they ruthlessly appropriated precious metals through outright robbery when possible and by other, not always less brutal, means when necessary. El Dorado, the legendary city of gold, proved elusive, but the Spaniards soon realised that the true wealth of the west Indies consisted of the surprisingly large Indian populations which they encountered in Mexico, Peru, and elsewhere.

Adverse to physical labour themselves, the Spaniards exploited the indigenous populations of the New World through mechanisms such as the *encomienda*, best translated as 'entrustment', by which the Crown granted an individual Spaniard rights to Indian labour and tribute in a particular village or area. Institutions such as the Catholic Church also held encomiendas. In

PANAMA
GUYANA
VENEZUELA
SURINAME
FRENCH
GUIANA
COLOMBIA
ECUADOR
BRAZIL
PERU
BOLIVIA
PARAGUAY
ARGENTINA
CHILE
URUGUAY
ATLANTIC
OCEAN
PACIFIC
OCEAN
Falkland Islands
(Islas Malvinas)

Argentina

0   200   400 km

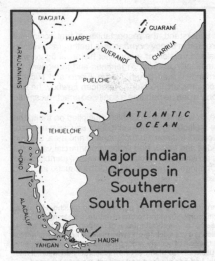

Araucanian Indians

theory, Spanish legislation at least required the holder of the encomienda to reciprocate with instruction in the Spanish language and the Catholic religion, but in practice imperial administration was inadequate to ensure compliance and avoid the worst abuses. Spanish overseers worked Indians mercilessly in the mines and extracted the maximum in agricultural produce.

In the most densely populated parts of the Americas, some *encomenderos* became extraordinarily wealthy, but the encomienda system failed when Indian populations declined rapidly. This was less because of overwork and physical punishment than because the Indians, isolated for at least 10,000 years from the diseases of the Old World, could not withstand the onslaught of smallpox, influenza, typhus and other microbial killers. In some parts of the New World, these diseases reduced the native population by more than 95%.

In most of Argentina and the other modern River Plate countries, the encomienda was less significant than in the Andes. Ironically, the most highly organised Indian peoples were the easiest to subdue and control, since they were accustomed to similar forms of exploitation. In hierarchical states like the Inca Empire, the Spaniards rather easily occupied the apex of the pyramid.

The semisedentary and nomadic peoples of the riverine lowlands and the southern Pampas, however, put up determined resistance. Indians routed Pedro de Mendoza's garrison at Buenos Aires within five years of its establishment in 1536, and even into the late 19th century, parts of the Pampas were not safe for white settlers. Abandoned Spanish livestock multiplied rapidly on the fine pastures of the Pampas, horses greatly aiding the Indians' mobility and ability to strike. Not until the so-called Conquista del Desierto, a de facto war of extermination against the Pampas Indians in the late 19th century, could Europeans relax their guard.

Colonial Period

Indian resistance discouraged early settlement of the lower River Plate. Potential settlers preferred Asunción, founded in 1537

The Rise & Romance of the Gaucho

No one could have predicted, and few completely understand, the respectability of that accidental icon, the Argentine gaucho. The modern gaucho, dressed in baggy *bombacha*, a leather *rastra* round his waist, and a sharp *facón* in his belt, is the idealised version of a complex historical figure who remains on the Argentine conscience. Directly or indirectly, to most Argentines and foreigners, he derives from the romantic portrayal of José Hernández' epic poem *Martín Fierro* and Ricardo Güiraldes' novel *Don Segundo Sombra*. Like his counterpart the North American cowboy, he has received elaborate cinematic treatment. Ironically, only when he became a sanitised anachronism did he achieve celebrity.

Without the rich pastures of the Pampas and the cattle and horses which multiplied on them, the gaucho could never have flourished. In a sense, he replaced the Pampas Indian; usually a mestizo, he hunted burgeoning herds of cattle just as the Querandí Indians did the guanaco and rhea. So long as cattle were many, people were few, and beef, hides and tallow had limited commercial value, his subsistence and independence were assured. This achieved, he could amuse himself gambling and drinking in the saloon or *pulpería*. Observers like Domingo Sarmiento thought the gaucho indolent, but grudgingly acknowledged that he led a good life:

Country life, then, has developed all the physical but none of the intellectual powers of the gaucho. His moral character is of the quality to be expected from his habit of triumphing over the forces of nature; it is strong, haughty, and energetic. Without instruction, and indeed without need of any, without means of support as without wants, he is happy in the midst of his poverty and privations, which are not such to one who never knew nor wished for greater pleasures than are his already. Thus if the disorganisation of society among the gauchos deeply implants barbarism in their natures, through the impossibility and uselessness of moral and intellectual education, it has, too, its attractive side to him. The gaucho does not labour; he finds his food and raiment ready to his hand.

Even as Sarmiento wrote, in the mid-19th century, the gaucho's independent, self-sufficient way of life was in decline. Just as the gauchos had replaced the Pampas Indians, so large landowners squeezed out the gauchos as the primitive livestock economy gave way to saladeros, which made use of a wider variety of products – processed hides, tallow and salted or jerked beef.

For their saladeros, landowners needed labour; the gaucho, with his horseback skills, was a desirable if unwilling source of manpower, but landowners were not reluctant to use their influence to coerce him. Classifying the gaucho as a 'lawless' element, discriminatory laws soon required internal passports, and men without jobs could no longer travel freely over the Pampas. Punishment for 'vagrancy' was often military conscription. As sheep replaced cattle on the Pampas, land was fenced and marked, forcing the gaucho to the fringes or onto the estancias.

Unlike the frontier, the estancia was not a democracy, and the gaucho was no longer his own master, even though his livestock skills were still in seasonal demand. He became instead a hired hand on an institution whose physical aspects bespoke hierarchy: the estanciero or his manager resided in the *casco* ('big house'), while, if fortunate, the peons and their families lived in hovels or isolated *puestos* ('outside houses') at the pleasure of the landowner – and the puestos themselves were a means of keeping an eye on remote properties. As European immigrants came to occupy many of these jobs, which often were detested by real gauchos, friction arose between gaucho 'natives' and Italian 'gringos' but, despite resistance, the day of the free-roaming gaucho was over by the late 19th century.

Ironically, about this time, Argentina discovered the gaucho's virtues. *Martín Fierro* romanticised the life of the independent gaucho at the very time when, like the open-range cowboy of the American West, he was disappearing. Hernández deplored both opportunistic strongmen like Juan Manuel de Rosas, who claimed to speak for the gaucho, and 'civilisers' like Sarmiento, who had no scruples about discarding the people of the countryside. The gaucho's fierce independence, so often depicted as lawlessness, became admirable, and Hernández almost single-handedly rehabilitated the image of the gaucho as Argentines sought an identity in a country being transformed by immigration and economic modernisation. Having fought alongside the gaucho, defended him in the public forums of his country, and pleaded for his integration into the country's future, Hernández was an eloquent spokesman for the positive gaucho values which even Sarmiento admitted – courtesy, independence, generosity. Urban Argentines soon elevated the gaucho to the status of myth, incorporating these values into their own system, but only after his fate was decided. ∎

in the upper Paraná, but the region's most significant early economic links were with silver-rich Alto Perú (now Bolivia), where the bonanza mine at Potosí financed Spanish expansion, and Lima, capital of the Viceroyalty of Peru, rather than directly with Spain. Although Spanish forces had re-established Buenos Aires by 1580, it long remained a backwater in comparison with Andean settlements like Tucumán (1571), Córdoba (1573), Salta (1582), La Rioja (1591), and Jujuy (1593). Spaniards from Chile settled the cities of Mendoza (1561), San Juan (1562), and San Luis (1596) in what became known as the Cuyo region. The Tucumán region provided mules, cloth and foodstuffs for Upper Peru; Cuyo produced wine and grain, while Buenos Aires languished.

The colonial decline of the Indian population in the North-West, and their relatively small numbers in the rest of the country, produced a maldistribution of land which resembled that in other parts of Latin America, but also had peculiarly Argentine characteristics. The appearance of *latifundios*, or large landholdings, came about after the virtual disappearance of the Indian pop-

ulation made the encomienda obsolete. Spanish immigrants and *criollos* (American-born Spaniards) responded by acquiring large tracts of the best land for agriculture and livestock; this new institution, the *hacienda*, bore some resemblance to its feudal Spanish namesake. As Indian populations gradually recovered, or merged with the Spanish to form a mixed-race *mestizo* population, they found that the best lands had been monopolised and that their only economic alternatives were cultivation of small plots *(minifundios)* on inferior lands, or dependent labour on the large estates.

Although the hacienda was never so important in Argentina as in Peru or Mexico, the livestock *estancia* came to play a critical role in the development of Argentine society. When the Spaniards returned to the estuary of the River Plate in the late 16th century, they found that the cattle and horses abandoned decades earlier had proliferated almost beyond belief as the primary agents in what Alfred Crosby has called 'ecological imperialism'. With commerce nearly prohibited except under Spanish mercantile restrictions, the inhabitants of colonial

Declaration of Independence, Tucumán, 1816

Buenos Aires looked to livestock for their livelihood. Without these livestock, the legendary gaucho of the Pampas could never have existed, but their growing commercial importance also brought about his extinction.

Growth & Independence

Though isolated and legally prohibited from direct European commerce for nearly two centuries, the people of Buenos Aires pursued a flourishing contraband trade with Portuguese Brazil and nonpeninsular European powers. When Buenos Aires became capital of the new Viceroyalty of the River Plate in 1776, it was explicit acknowledgment that the region had outgrown Spain's political and economic domination. Previously Buenos Aires had been governed as the tail end of a long, indirect supply line, via the Caribbean, Panamá and Peru. This was frustrating for the criollos, who wished to carry on direct trade between Buenos Aires and Spain.

Toward the end of the 18th century, the criollos became increasingly dissatisfied and impatient with peninsular authority in all parts of the continent, but the expulsion of British troops who briefly occupied Buenos Aires in 1806 and 1807 gave the people of the River Plate new confidence in their ability to stand alone, which they asserted in the revolution of 25 May 1810.

Independence movements throughout South America united to expel Spain from the continent by the 1820s. Under the leadership of General José de San Martín and others, the United Provinces of the River Plate, Argentina's direct forerunner, declared independence at Tucumán in 1816. Ironically, British financial and logistical support made it possible for Argentina and its allies to break the Spanish yoke. In the process, Bolivia and Paraguay became independent countries rather than remain with the former Viceroyalty of the River Plate.

After achieving independence, the United Provinces were united in name only. With no truly effective central authority, the regional disparities which Spanish rule had obscured came into the open. This resulted in the rise of the *caudillos*, or local strongmen, who resented and resisted Buenos Aires as strongly as Buenos Aires had resisted Spain. Argentine educator and President Domingo F Sarmiento, himself a product of the provinces, indicted the excesses of demagogic caudillos in his classic *Life in the Argentine Republic in the Days of the Tyrants*. At the same time the caudillos commanded great and often admirable personal loyalty – Charles Darwin observed that Juan Manuel Rosas 'by conforming to the dress and habits of the Gauchos...obtained an unbounded popularity in the country' and that he 'never saw anything like the enthusiasm for Rosas...'.

In theory, the great controversy in Argentine politics was between the Federalists of the interior, who advocated provincial autonomy, and Unitarists of Buenos Aires, who upheld central authority. The former, associated with conservative provincial landowners but supported by much of the rural working class, resented Buenos Aires as much as Madrid. The latter, led by intellectuals such as Bernardino Rivadavia, were more cosmopolitan and looked to Europe for capital, immigrants and ideas. For nearly two decades, bloody and vindictive conflicts between the two factions left the country nearly exhausted. A common salutation on documents of the period is 'Death to the Unitarist savages!'.

The Reign of Rosas

In practice, differences between Federalists and Unitarists often owed as much to convenience as conviction. Rosas came to prominence as a caudillo in Buenos Aires province, and undoubtedly represented the interests of rural elites whose power depended on their estancias and *saladeros* (tanneries and salting works). But he also helped centralise political power in Buenos Aires, and set other ominous precedents in Argentine political life, such as creating the *mazorca*, his ruthless political police, and institutionalising torture. According to Sarmiento:

the central consolidated despotic government of the landed proprietor, Don Juan Manuel Rosas...applied the knife of the gaucho to the culture of Buenos Ayres, and destroyed the work of centuries – of civilisation, law and liberty.

Even allowing for Sarmiento's partisan rhetoric, Rosas' opportunism and continual military adventures clearly required a large standing army, which consumed an increasing percentage of public expenditures, and forced overseas trade through the port of Buenos Aires rather than directly to the provinces.

Despite the efforts of the Federalists, Buenos Aires continued to dominate the new country. After the Unitarists and even some of his former allies finally forced Rosas from power in 1852, succeeding decades and economic developments confirmed the city's primacy. Rosas himself spent the last 25 years of his life in exile in Southampton, England.

The Roots of Modern Argentina

The expulsion of Rosas ushered in a new era in Argentine development. Sheep estancias, producing enormous quantities of wool to satisfy the almost inexhaustible demand of English mills, supplanted the relatively stagnant cattle estancias. According to the Argentine historian Hilda Sábato, the province of Buenos Aires was in the vanguard of this process, integrating Argentina into the global economy and, simultaneously, consolidating the country as a political entity. Steadily, European immigrants assumed important roles in crafts and commerce. In nearby areas of Buenos Aires province, small farms known as *chacras* supplied the city's food, but sheep displaced the semiwild cattle of the surrounding estancias. In the periphery of the province, however, cattle estancias operated much as before.

Politically, the Constitution of 1853, still in force today despite its frequent suspension, signified the triumph of Unitarism, even allowing the president to dissolve provincial administrations despite lip service to federal principles. The economic expression of Unitarism was Liberalism, an openness to foreign capital which even now raises the hackles of many Argentine nationalists.

According to historian David Rock, Liberalism had three main aspects: foreign investment, foreign trade and immigration. In the late 19th century, all three inundated the Humid Pampas, Mesopotamia and Córdoba, if barely lapping at the edges of some interior provinces. Basque and Irish refugees were the first shepherds, as both sheep numbers and wool exports increased nearly tenfold between 1850 and 1880. Some of these herders were independent family farmers on relatively small units, but the majority were sharecroppers and the land itself remained in the hands of traditional large landowners.

After 1880, Argentine agriculture became a major producer of cereal crops for export, which it remains today. The Humid Pampas were the focus of this development, whose origins lay in midcentury colonisation projects to attract European settlers. Estancieros rarely objected to occupation of lands which were nominally theirs because new settlers provided a buffer between themselves and the still troublesome Indians. Swiss, German, French and Italian farmers proved successful in provinces such as Santa Fe and Entre Ríos.

Such developments did not eliminate latifundios, as the government sold public lands at bargain prices to pay its debts. This encouraged speculators and reduced independent farming opportunities for immigrants, whose only agricultural alternatives were sharecropping or seasonal labour. Many remained in Buenos Aires, as the city's share of the country's population steadily increased.

British capital, amounting to one-third of Britain's total Latin American investment by 1890, dominated the Argentine economy. Most went to infrastructure improvements such as railroads, which rapidly made the cart roads of the Pampas obsolete. By the turn of the century, Argentina had a highly developed rail network, fanning out from Buenos Aires in all directions, but the economy was ever more vulnerable to international fluctuations, such as the depression which followed the Franco-Prussian war.

These conditions stimulated a debate over foreign investment which anticipated 20th-century controversies over 'dependence' and economic autonomy through industrial diversification and protectionism. In fact, the only industries to benefit from protection were agricultural commodities such as wheat, wine and sugar. These in turn benefited large landholders and encouraged further land speculation and concentration. Speculation led to a boom in land prices and paper money loans which depreciated in value, causing near collapse of the financial system toward the end of the century.

By reducing the opportunities for family farming, land speculation and commodity exports also encouraged urban growth. The port city of Buenos Aires, which rapidly modernised in the 1880s, nearly doubled its population through immigration. Urban services such as transportation, power, and water improved steadily. Because of its increasing importance, the capital became an administratively distinct federal zone (the Capital Federal), autonomous within its own boundaries. Outside the Pampas, uneven development exaggerated regional inequality.

From the mid-1890s until WW I, Argentina's economy recovered enough to take advantage of the enormous opportunities presented by beef, mutton and wheat exports. Because of inequities in land distribution, however, this prosperity was less broad-based than it might have been. Industry could not absorb all the immigrants and, with the onset of the Great Depression, the military took power under conditions of indecisive and ineffectual civilian government, and considerable social unrest. An obscure colonel, Juan Domingo Perón, was the first Argentine leader to try to come to grips with the economic crisis in a comprehensive manner.

Juan Perón & His Legacy

Born in Buenos Aires province in 1895, Juan Perón emerged from obscurity in the 1940s to become Argentina's most loved, and most hated, political figure. During his youth and rather mediocre military career, he came to know virtually the entire country from its subtropical north to its sub-Antarctic south. As Perón grew to maturity, Argentina was one of the world's most prosperous countries, but its prosperity was narrowly based on commodity exports such as meat, grain and wool.

The *oligarquía terrateniente*, or landed elite, benefited most from the export economy and resisted attempts to promote diversification through domestic industrialisation. Correctly or not, many Argentines came to perceive the country's agricultural sector as beholden to foreign, especially British, interests.

This was not an unreasonable interpretation. British capital built most of the railways which radiated from Buenos Aires like spokes from a wheel, bringing agricultural commodities to the capital for shipment to Europe. In return, inexpensive British manufactured goods flooded domestic markets and retarded local industry.

Perón associated a new economic order for Argentina with domestic industrialisation and economic independence. In this sense, he appealed to both conservative nationalists who distrusted the cosmopolitan landowning elite, and to radical working-class elements which objected to the role of foreign capital. Almost until his death, Perón avoided alienating either sector even as they conducted a virtual civil war with each other.

After being dislodged from his labour post and briefly incarcerated by jealous fellow officers, Perón stood for and won the presidency of Argentina in 1946 and again in 1952. Until his forced ouster in 1955, his reforms and programs benefited working-class interests in matters of wages, pensions, job security and working conditions. University education ceased to be the privilege of the elite, but instead became available to any capable individual. Many Argentines obtained employment in the expanding state bureaucracy.

Perón promoted industrialisation and economic self-sufficiency. Coming to power at a time of global crisis, just after WW II, he probably had no alternative but to foster state involvement since Europe, Argentina's traditional source of capital, was in economic ruin. In any event, his policies had broad support from both traditional working-class

---

Teniente General Juan Domingo Perón

Juan Perón (to whose supporters his name and rank are inseparable) is an Argentine enigma, embodying the contradictions of the country itself. Rising to power through the elitist institution of the military, he still enjoyed broad popularity among the public at large. Leader of a Roman Catholic country, he incited his followers to attack the church. Attracting people of intense and passionate convictions, he could appeal ambiguously to followers from across the political spectrum – for an equivalent in the English-speaking world, one would have to imagine Margaret Thatcher having resolute partisans ranging from Militant Tendency to the National Front. Irreconcilable factions within Perón's Justicialist party warred with each other, sometimes with words and often with bullets and bombs, while each ardently professed its allegiance to the man and his ideals.

Growing to maturity in the era of Argentina's greatest power and prestige, Perón saw the country's shortcomings as well as its strengths. When the Perón family relocated to Patagonia for an unsuccessful attempt at sheep farming, he saw first-hand the most unsavoury aspects of large, paternalistic sheep estancias, controlled almost exclusively by British interests. He treated the peons of the Pampas on a basis of equality, as he saw they were not far removed from his own humble origins. As a young military officer, he saw the miserable physical and educational state of rural conscripts, casualties of an inequitable social order. Sent to restore order in several labour disputes, he proved an attentive listener to working-class concerns, mediating labour settlements on the railways and sugar *ingenios* (factories) of the subtropical north.

Perón first came to national prominence after a military coup deposed President Ramón Castillo in 1943. Sensing an opportunity to assist the country's neglected working class, Perón settled for a relatively minor post as head of the National Department of Labour. In this post, his success at organising relief efforts after a major earthquake in the Andean city and province of San Juan earned praise throughout the country. In the process, he also met Eva Duarte, the actress who would become his second wife and make her own major contribution to Argentine history. Both occupy an enduring place in the country's political mythology.

During sojourns as Argentine military attaché in Fascist Italy and Nazi Germany, Perón had grasped the importance of spectacle in public life, and he had the personal charisma to put it into practice. With the equally charismatic 'Evita' at his side or on her own in the field, he transformed the country's political culture and economy, addressing massive rallies from the balcony of the Casa Rosada. Giving voice to the disenfranchised masses, the Peróns enlisted them in his cause and alienated traditionally powerful sectors of Argentine society. He created a powerful institution, the General Confederation of Labour (CGT), which overwhelmed rival labour organisations.

There was no disguising the Peron's demagoguery and ambition. Evita once wrote that 'There are two things of which I am proud: my love for the people and my hatred for the oligarchy'. Despite huge Congressional majorities, Perón's authoritarian tendencies led him to govern by decree rather than by consultation and consensus. His excessively personalistic approach created a political party, known formally as 'Justicialist' but universally as 'Peronist', which has never been able to transcend a stagnant reliance on its founder's charisma. He did not hesitate to use or condone intimidation and torture for political ends, although such activities never reached the level they did during the state terrorism of the late 1970s. Argentine literary great Jorge Luis Borges was among those who suffered Perón's caprice.

Yet during the decade they lived together, the Peróns also broadened the range and popular appeal of Argentine politics in many positive ways. Besides legitimising the trade union movement and extending political rights and economic benefits to working-class people, they managed to secure voting rights for women by 1947. Unfortunately, they could not or would not overcome the atmosphere of tension and confrontation which coloured Argentine politics for more than three decades after Evita's death in 1952. ∎

EVA PERON

supporters and a military which feared dependence on foreign sources for raw materials and munitions.

Economic shortcomings, including rising inflation, undermined the latter stages of this presidency. Perón also failed to disavow a virulent and often violent anticlerical campaign which divided the country towards the end of his first presidency. In late 1955, he himself was victim of a coup which sent him into exile and instituted nearly three decades of disastrous military government, with only brief interludes of civilian rule.

Perón's Exile & Return

After Perón left the country, Argentina's military government banned the Justicialist party, which split into several factions. Even to speak his name in public was suspect; Anglo-Argentines would often refer to 'Johnny Sunday', a gloss on Perón's Christian names 'Juan Domingo'. Perón himself wandered to Paraguay, Panamá (where he met his third wife, dancer María Estela Martínez, known better by her stage name of 'Isabelita'), Venezuela, the Dominican Republic, and eventually to Spain in 1961. He would remain there for another dozen years.

During exile, Perón and his associates constantly dreamed of and plotted their return to Argentina. Perón acquired a bizarre retinue of advisors, including his mysterious personal secretary José López Rega, a spiritualist and extreme right-wing nationalist who was Perón's Svengali or Rasputin. At Perón's modest house in Madrid, Evita Perón's embalmed body lay in state after being rescued from an anonymous grave in Italy in 1971. Reportedly, López Rega conducted rituals over the casket to imbue Isabelita with Evita's charismatic qualities.

In the late 1960s, increasing economic problems and political instability, including strikes, political kidnappings, and guerrilla warfare, marked Argentine political life. In the midst of these happenings, the opportunity to return finally arrived in 1973, when the beleaguered military relaxed their objections to the Justicialist party and loyal Peronist Hector Cámpora was elected President. Cámpora himself was merely a stalking horse for Perón and soon resigned, paving the way for new elections which Perón won handily.

After 18 years' exile, Perón once again symbolised Argentine unity, but there was no substance to his rule. His anticipated arrival at Ezeiza Airport, attended by hundreds of thousands of people on a dark winter's night, occasioned violent clashes between supporters across the broad spectrum of Argentine politics. Chronically ill, Perón died in mid-1974, leaving a fragmented country. His ill-qualified wife, elected as his literal running mate but under the influence of López Rega, inherited the presidency.

In this chaotic political climate, armed conflict was the rule rather than the exception. The urban Montoneros, a left-wing, anti-imperialist faction of the Peronist movement, went underground, kidnapping and executing their enemies, bombing foreign enterprises, and robbing banks to finance their armed struggle. The Ejército Revolucionario Popular (People's Revolutionary Army, known by its acronym ERP) undertook guerrilla warfare in the mountainous forests of Tucumán province. López Rega's Alianza Anticomunista Argentina (Argentine Anti-Communist Alliance or AAA) took the law into its own hands, assassinating labour leaders, academics, and others it perceived as 'subversive'.

The Dirty War, 1976-83

In March of 1976, unable to maintain civil order or control inflation, which sometimes exceeded 50% per month, Isabel Perón's government fell in a bloodless and widely anticipated military coup. Put under house arrest, she eventually went into Spanish exile, where her main interest appeared to be challenging Imelda Marcos and Nancy Reagan for the world's most extravagant wardrobe.

If the coup itself was bloodless, its aftermath was not. During the so-called Proceso de Reorganización Nacional, the new military government of General Jorge Rafael Videla instituted a reign of terror unparalleled since the days of Rosas. Military officers occupied nearly every position of political importance in the entire country.

In theory and rhetoric, the Proceso was a comprehensive effort at reforming the bloated state sector and stabilizing the economy by eliminating corruption, thus creating the basis for an enduring democracy; in practice, it was one more chapter in a history of large-scale government corruption in the name of development, accompanied by an orgy of state-sponsored or tolerated violence and anarchy.

The army's superior firepower quickly eliminated the naive and outmanned ERP in Tucumán. The more sophisticated and intricately organised Montoneros were a greater challenge, and were eventually eliminated only in the infamous Guerra Sucia (Dirty War), which claimed thousands of innocent victims. Operating with state complicity,

paramilitary death squads such as the AAA were responsible for many more casualties.

The 'Disappeared'

In eliminating the ERP and the Montoneros, the military dictatorship made little effort to distinguish among those who actively fought against it and gave the guerrillas assistance, those who openly or privately sympathised with the guerrillas without assisting them, or even those who expressed reservations about the indiscriminate brutality used to carry out the military's campaign. Only a few highly visible and courageous individuals and organisations publicly criticised the regime, at great personal risk.

During these years, to 'disappear' meant to be abducted, detained, tortured, and probably killed with no hope or pretence of legal process. The armed forces and police ran numerous illegal detention centres, the most notorious of which was the Navy Mechanics' School (ESMA) in an exclusive northern suburb of Buenos Aires. For anyone crossing the street, even at midday, the presence of a black Ford Falcon, without number plates but occupied by four men, was a symbol of outright terror.

The government almost never acknowledged illegal detention of individuals, although it sometimes reported their deaths in battles or skirmishes with the 'security forces'. Inexplicably, a few escaped or were released, but their stories gained more notoriety outside than within Argentina. A few courageous individuals and groups, such as Nobel Peace Prize winner Adolfo Pérez Esquivel and the famous 'Madres de la Plaza de Mayo', who paraded in front of Buenos Aires' Casa Rosada presidential palace every Thursday, kept the story in public view.

No one knows exactly how many people died during the Dirty War. In 1986 *Nunca Más*, the official report commissioned by civilian president Raúl Alfonsín, listed 9000 cases, but some estimates are three times greater. Ironically, the Dirty War really ended only when the Argentine military attempted a real military objective.

The Falklands War

In mid-1982, a cartoon in the Argentine magazine *Humor* depicted 'La Libertad Argentina' (a female figure equivalent to the American Statue of Liberty or England's Britannia) in a public park with her four children and their toys: an army general with a tank, an admiral with a destroyer, an air force brigadier with a jet fighter, and a smartly dressed civilian with a bridge. When another woman remarks how expensive it is to raise children, La Libertad responds 'You're telling me!'.

Despite public homage to economic growth and stabilisation, Argentina's economy continued to decline during military rule. On the one hand, the government enacted strict monetarist economic measures, including a fixed exchange rate to eliminate speculation on the dollar, but failed to reduce annual inflation below triple digits. It did, however, increase unemployment and undermine local industry through cheap imports. Its lip service to austerity brought in billions of dollars in loans which were invested in grandiose public works projects such as the nearly unused toll highway between downtown Buenos Aires and Ezeiza Airport, while public officials pocketed much of the money and sent it overseas to Swiss bank accounts. The military acquired the latest in European technology, including the deadly Exocet missile.

Under the weight of its import splurge and the burden of debt, the Argentine economy collapsed in chaos. Almost overnight, devaluation reduced the peso to a fraction of its former value, and inflation again reached astronomical, rather than merely high levels. The Proceso was coming undone.

In an orderly transition in early 1981, General Roberto Viola replaced General Videla as de facto president, but Viola's ineffectuality caused his replacement by General Leopoldo Galtieri before the end of the year. Under Galtieri, rapid economic deterioration and popular discontent, manifested in the first mass demonstrations at the Casa Rosada since before the 1976 coup, led to desperate measures. To stay in power, Galtieri launched an April 1982 invasion of the Falkland Islands, claimed by Argentina as the Malvinas for nearly a century and a half.

Overnight, the nearly unopposed occupation of the Malvinas unleashed a wave of nationalist euphoria which subsided almost as fast as it crested. Galtieri underestimated the determined response of British Prime Minister Margaret Thatcher, herself in political difficulties, and the ability of Britain's naval task force to absorb heavy losses to attain a remote goal. After only 74 days, Argentina's ill-trained, poorly motivated and ineffective forces surrendered ignominiously and the military meekly prepared to return government to civilian hands. In 1983, Argentines elected Raúl Alfonsín, of the Radical Civic Union, to the presidency.

For more information on the war, see the section on the Falkland Islands.

Aftermath

In his presidential campaign, Alfonsín pledged to try those military officers responsible for human rights violations during the Dirty War. Junta members, including Videla, Viola and Admiral Emilio Massera, were tried and convicted of kidnap, torture and homicide. Evidence uncovered by the commission which produced *Nunca Más* was critical in their convictions. Videla and Massera received life sentences, though in virtual luxury accommodation in a military prison.

When the government attempted to extend trials to junior officers, many of whom protested that they had been merely 'following orders', those officers responded with uprisings in several different parts of the country. These might have toppled the government, but if more forcefully resisted might have permanently subjugated the military to civilian control. The timid administration succumbed to military demands and produced a Law of Due Obedience which eliminated prosecutions of notorious individuals such as Navy Captain Alfredo Astíz (the 'Angel of Death'), who was implicated in the disappearance of a

Swedish-Argentine teenager and other crimes.

The Law of Due Obedience did not eliminate the divisive impact of the Dirty War on Argentine politics. Since 1987, the Argentine military has reasserted its role in Argentine politics despite internal factionalism. One especially disconcerting element has been the emergence of the overtly fascist *carapintada* movement of disaffected junior officers. In December 1990, prior to the visit of United States President George Bush, the carapintadas (so-called after their custom of painting their faces with camouflage markings) occupied army headquarters across from the Casa Rosada and elsewhere in Buenos Aires in the hope of encouraging the military establishment to join them in overthrowing President Carlos Menem, himself a prisoner of the military during the Dirty War.

Ironically, Menem himself contributed to the controversy. Just after Christmas of 1990, he pardoned Videla, Massera and others despite overwhelming evidence that the Argentine public opposed such measures. He also pardoned former Montonero guerrilla Mario Firmenich who, some speculated, still had access to substantial funds which might benefit Menem's Peronist party. At present, no one anticipates overt military domination of Argentina, but the spectre of military intervention has not disappeared.

GEOGRAPHY & CLIMATE

Argentina's total land area of about 2.8 million square km, excluding the South Atlantic islands and the Antarctic quadrant it claims as national territory, makes it the world's eighth-largest country, only slightly smaller than India. On the South American continent, only neighbouring Brazil is larger. From La Quiaca on the Bolivian border to Ushuaia in Tierra del Fuego is a distance of about 3500 km, about the same as from Havana to Hudson's Bay or from the Sahara to Scotland.

Argentine geographers acknowledge four major physiographic provinces: the Andes, the lowland North, the Pampas, and Patagonia. Each of these, however, has considerable variety in its own right, since altitude as well as latitude plays a major role in Argentine geography. Most of the country is a midlatitude lowland, but the Andean chain runs the length of the country's western border, diminishing in altitude in the south. The Andes isolate Argentina from Chile, while rivers form its borders with Uruguay, Brazil and Paraguay. Its relatively short Bolivian frontier has both mountainous and riverine areas.

The Andes

The Andean chain runs the length of Argentina from the Bolivian border before disappearing into the South Atlantic. Its greatest elevations present a formidable western barrier in that area colonised from Peru after the Spanish invasion of the New World. In this north-western region, there developed a string of oasis settlements from Jujuy and Salta southward to Mendoza, with communications links to Lima rather than to Buenos Aires. This area's colonial architecture, primarily but not exclusively ecclesiastical, is the most significant in Argentina. Here the mestizo population most closely resembles that of Peru and Bolivia, where indigenous traits are dominant.

Rainfall can be erratic, although rain-fed agriculture is feasible from Tucumán northwards. In most areas, perennial streams descending from the Andes provide irrigation water. In the extreme north is the southern extension of the Bolivian altiplano, a high plain between 3000 and 4000 metres altitude punctuated by even higher volcanic peaks, which is thinly populated. The inhabitants reside in scattered mining settlements and there are a few llama herders; the zone is too arid for the more valuable but delicate alpaca. Vegetation consists of sparse bunch grasses *(ichu)* and low, widely spaced shrubs, known collectively as *tola*. In the summer rainy season, travellers should be prepared for potential flash floods and even snow at higher elevations. Although days can be surprisingly hot (sunburn is a very serious hazard in the high altitude tropics), frosts occur almost nightly.

South of Tucumán, rainfall is inadequate for crops, but irrigation has brought prosperity to the wine-producing Cuyo region, consisting of the provinces of Mendoza, San Juan and San Luis. La Rioja and Catamarca are much less well-to-do. Much of this area resembles the Great Basin of the western United States, with north-south mountain ranges separated by salt flats or very shallow lakes.

On its far western limit is the massive Andean crest, featuring 6960-metre Aconcagua, the highest peak in South America. The area can be hot in summer, but pleasant the rest of the year despite cool winter nights. On occasion the Zonda, a dry wind descending from the Andes, causes dramatic temperature increases and serious physical discomfort.

The Chaco & Mesopotamia

East of the Andes and their foothills, northern Argentina consists of tropical and subtropical lowlands. In the arid western area, known as the Argentine Chaco and part of the much larger Gran Chaco region which extends into Bolivia, Paraguay and Brazil, open savannas alternate with almost impenetrable thorn forests. In the provinces of Santiago del Estero, Chaco, Formosa, and northern Santa Fe and Córdoba, summers are brutally hot.

Between the Paraná and Uruguay rivers, where the provinces of Entre Ríos and Corrientes comprise most of the area known as Mesopotamia, rainfall is sufficient to support swampy lowland forests as well as upland savanna. The province of Misiones, a politically important salient surrounded on three sides by Brazil and Paraguay, is even more densely forested and contains part of the awesome Iguazú Falls, which descend from the Paraná plateau of southern Brazil.

Rainfall decreases from east to west: Corrientes' annual average of about 1200 mm contrasts with Santiago del Estero's 500 mm, which is insufficient for rain-fed agriculture because evaporation is so high.

Shallow summer flooding is common throughout Mesopotamia and the eastern Chaco, while only the immediate river floodplains become inundated in the west. The Chaco has a well-defined winter dry season, which is even more pronounced the farther west one travels, while Mesopotamia's rainfall is more evenly distributed throughout the year.

The Pampas

Bordering the Atlantic Ocean and the Río de la Plata and stretching nearly to Córdoba and the central Andean foothills, the Pampas states are the political and economic heartland of modern Argentina. Argentine industry and agriculture are concentrated here; outside the federal capital of Buenos Aires and its industrial suburbs, most settlements are cookie-cutter farm towns resembling their counterparts in the American Midwest.

The Pampas are more properly subdivided into the Humid Pampas, along the littoral, and the Dry Pampas of the western interior and the south. More than a third of the country's population lives in and around Buenos Aires, whose humid climate resembles New York city's in the spring, summer and autumn. Annual rainfall exceeds 900 mm, but several hundred km westward it is less than half that. Buenos Aires' winters are humid, but relatively mild.

The Pampas are an almost completely level plain of wind-borne loess and river-deposited sediments, once covered by lush native grasses and now occupied by grain farms and cattle and sheep estancias. The absence of relief makes the area vulnerable to flooding from the relatively few, small rivers which cross it. Only the granitic Sierra de Tandil (484 metres) and the Sierra de la Ventana (1273 metres) in south-western Buenos Aires province, and the Sierra de La Pampa disrupt the otherwise monotonous terrain. The seacoast of Buenos Aires province features attractive, sandy beaches at resorts such as Mar del Plata and Necochea, which Porteños (inhabitants of the capital) overrun in January and February.

Patagonia & the Lake District

Patagonia is that region south of the Río Colorado, consisting of the provinces of Neuquén, Río Negro, Chubut and Santa Cruz. It is separated from Chilean Patagonia by the Andes, although their crest is much lower than in the north of the country; Cerro Tronador, at 3554 metres the highest peak in Parque Nacional Nahuel Huapi near Bariloche, dwarfs all surrounding summits by at least 1000 metres.

The cordillera is still high enough, though, that Pacific storms drop most of their rain and snow on the Chilean side. In extreme southern Patagonia, this rain shadow effect does not prevent the accumulation of sufficient snow and ice to form the largest southern hemisphere glaciers outside Antarctica. Hiking, trekking, skiing and mountaineering are common recreational activities, depending on the season. Outdoors enthusiasts should be prepared for changeable and inclement weather.

East of the Andean foothills, the cool, arid Patagonian steppes support huge flocks of sheep, almost all of whose wool is exported to Europe. In organisation and operation, Patagonian sheep estancias resemble their counterparts in New Zealand and Australia, although ecological conditions are very different. The Atlantic maritime influence keeps temperatures relatively mild even in winter, when more uniform atmospheric pressure moderates the strong gales which blow most of the year.

Except for urban clusters like Comodoro Rivadavia (the centre of the national petroleum industry) and Río Gallegos (wool and meat packing), Patagonia is thinly populated. Tidal ranges along the Atlantic coast are too great for major port facilities. In the valley of the Río Negro and at the outlet of the Río Chubut there is crop and fruit farming.

Tierra del Fuego

The southernmost permanently inhabited territory in the world, the Land of Fire consists of one large island (Isla Grande), unequally divided between Chile and Argentina, and many smaller ones, some of which have been objects of contention between the two Southern Cone powers. When Europeans first passed through the Strait of Magellan, which separates Isla Grande from the Patagonian mainland, the fires stemmed from the activities of the now almost extinct Yahgan Indians; nowadays, they result from the flaring of natural gas in the region's oilfields.

The northern half of Isla Grande resembles the Patagonian steppes and is devoted to sheep grazing for wool and mutton, while its southern half is mountainous and partly covered by forests and glaciers. Despite its reputation for inclemency, it would be more accurate to call the weather changeable. As in Patagonia, winter conditions are rarely extreme, although trekking and outdoor camping are not advisable except for experienced mountaineers. For most visitors, the brief daylight hours in winter may be a greater deterrent than the weather. Skiing is possible in Ushuaia, along with outstanding views of the famous Beagle Channel.

FLORA & FAUNA

Argentina's subtropical rainforests, palm savannas, high-altitude deserts and high-latitude steppes, humid temperate grasslands, alpine and sub-Antarctic forests and coastal areas all support distinctive biota (flora and fauna) which will be unfamiliar to most visitors, or at least to those from the northern hemisphere. To protect these environments, Argentina has created an extensive system of national parks, briefly described below. More detailed descriptions can be found in individual chapters.

National & Provincial Parks

For most visitors, Argentina's national parks are a major reason for visiting the country. One of the first national park systems in Latin America, Argentina's dates from the turn of the century when explorer and surveyor Francisco P Moreno donated 7500 hectares near Bariloche to the state in return for guarantees that it would be preserved for the enjoyment of all Argentines. This area is

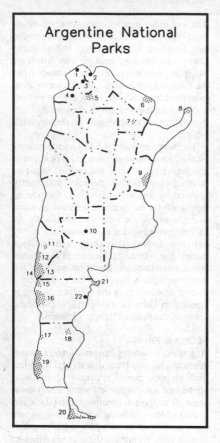

Argentine National Parks

1. Monumento Natural Laguna de los Pozuelos
2. Baritú
3. Calilegua
4. Los Cardones
5. El Rey
6. Río Pilcomayo
7. Chaco
8. Iguazú
9. El Palmar
10. Lihué Calel
11. Laguna Blanca
12. Lanín
13. Los Arrayanes
14. Nahuel Huapi
15. Lago Puelo
16. Los Alerces
17. Perito Francisco P Moreno
18. Monumento Natural Bosques Petrificados
19. Los Glaciares
20. Tierra del Fuego
21. Península Valdés Provincial Reserve
22. Punta Tombo Provincial Reserve

now part of Parque Nacional Nahuel Huapi, in the Andean Lake District.

Since then, the country has established many other parks and reserves, mostly but not exclusively in the Andean region. There are also many important provincial parks and reserves which do not fall within the national park system, such as Península Valdés, which deserve attention.

Before seeing the national parks, visitors to Buenos Aires should stop at the capital's national parks office for maps and brochures, which are often in short supply in the parks themselves. There may be a charge for some

of these. The address is Administración de Parques Nacionales, Santa Fe 690, Buenos Aires (☎ 311-1943).

Parque Nacional Iguazú In the northeastern province of Misiones, on the border with Brazil and Paraguay, this popular park contains the awesome Iguazú Falls, featured in the popular film *The Mission*. It also preserves nearly 55,000 hectares of subtropical rainforest, with abundant birds, mammals and reptiles.

Parque Nacional Río Pilcomayo On the Paraguayan border in the province of Formosa, this park preserves 60,000 hectares of subtropical marshlands and palm savannas which harbour birds, mammals and reptiles such as the caiman or *yacaré*.

Parque Nacional Chaco In Chaco province, this accessible but little-visited park offers 15,000 hectares of dense subtropical thorn forests, marshes, palm savannas and colourful birds.

Parque Nacional Baritú On the Bolivian border in Salta province and accessible by road only through Bolivia, this park contains 72,000 hectares of nearly virgin subtropical montane forest.

Monumento Natural Laguna de los Pozuelos This large, high-altitude lake in Jujuy province supports abundant bird life, including three species of flamingos, on its 16,000 hectares.

Parque Nacional Los Cardones Although its formal creation still awaits, this scenic montane desert park west of Salta protects the cardon cactus, which in the past has been used for timber and other purposes.

Parque Nacional Calilegua In Argentina's northerly province of Jujuy, this scenic unit of 76,000 hectares protects a variety of ecosystems, from *yungas* (transitional subtropical lowland forest) to humid, subtropical montane forest to subalpine grassland.

Parque Nacional El Rey In the eastern part of Salta province, this lush, mountainous park protects 44,000 hectares of subtropical and coniferous Andean forest.

Parque Nacional El Palmar Readily accessible from Buenos Aires, this 8500-hectare park on the Río Uruguay in Entre Ríos province protects the last extensive stands of *yatay* palm savanna, elsewhere destroyed or threatened by grazing. It is also an excellent place to see birds.

Parque Nacional Lihué Calel Relieving the desert monotony is this picturesque park in La Pampa province. Its salmon-coloured peaks and isolated valleys support a surprising range of fauna and flora, including pumas, guanacos, rheas and flowering cacti. There are also numerous Araucanian Indian petroglyphs in the park.

Parque Nacional Laguna Blanca Surrounded by ancient volcanos and lava flows near the city of Zapala in Neuquén province, this lake supports nesting colonies of black-necked swans, plus Andean flamingos and other distinctive birds. The lake and surroundings parklands cover more than 11,000 hectares.

Parque Nacional Lanín The snow-covered, symmetrical cone of the Lanín volcano is the centrepiece of this large (378,000 hectares) northern Patagonian park, near the mountain resort of San Martín de los Andes. Equally worthwhile, if less imposing, are the extensive forests of 'monkey puzzle trees' *(Araucaria* spp.) and southern beech *(Nothofagus* spp.). Fishing is a popular pastime.

Parque Nacional Los Arrayanes Surrounded on all sides by the much larger Parque Nacional Nahuel Huapi, this park on a small peninsula near the resort of Villa La Angostura protects pure stands of the unique *arrayan* tree, a member of the myrtle family.

Parque Nacional Nahuel Huapi Lake Nahuel Huapi, an enormous trough carved by Pleistocene glaciers and surrounded by impressive peaks, is the focus of this scenic, 758,000-hectare park. The city of Bariloche is the centre for visiting the park, the most highly developed in the Argentine system.

Península Valdés Although not part of the national park system, the provincial reserve of Península Valdés is an important destination for wildlife enthusiasts. Marine mammals, including whales, sea lions and elephant seals, are the main attraction, but there are also Magellanic penguins and other unusual seabirds. Along the Patagonian coast there are many smaller reserves with breeding colonies of seabirds and marine mammals.

Punta Tombo Also not part of the national park system, this scenic provincial reserve south of Trelew in Chubut has an enormous nesting colony of burrowing Magellanic penguins.

Parque Nacional Lago Puelo This aquamarine, low-altitude lake in north-western Chubut province, draining into the Pacific near the town of El Bolsón (Río Negro province), is surrounded by high Andean peaks. It covers 23,700 hectares along the Chilean border.

Parque Nacional Los Alerces Along the Andean crest in Chubut province, west of the city of Esquel, this very attractive park protects 263,000 hectares of the unique Valdivian forest ecosystem, which includes impressive specimens of the *alerce* tree, resembling the California redwoods.

Parque Nacional Perito Francisco P Moreno Named for the founder of the Argentine park system, this almost inaccessible unit of 115,000 hectares in north-western Santa Cruz province protects a series of awesome glacial lakes, surrounding alpine peaks and Andean-Patagonian forest. Wildlife includes herds of guanaco, the lowland counterpart of the domesticated llama of the central Andes. For real solitude, this park and Bosques Petrificados are best bets.

Monumento Natural Bosques Petrificados On the Patagonian steppe in northern Santa Cruz province, this isolated 10,000-hectare park features immense specimens of petrified *Proaraucaria* trees from an era when the region contained a dense, humid forest, before the building of the Andes.

Parque Nacional Los Glaciares One of Argentina's 'can't miss' attractions is the famous Moreno Glacier, one of few in the world that is currently advancing, but the awesome peaks of the Fitzroy range are no less impressive. Southern beech forests cover substantial zones of the 600,000-hectare park.

Parque Nacional Tierra del Fuego Argentina's only shoreline national park, this unit on the Beagle Channel stretches inland to envelop alpine glaciers and peaks within its 63,000 hectares. There are marine mammals, sea and shore birds, and extensive forests of southern beech.

GOVERNMENT

Since the end of military dictatorship in 1983, Argentina has returned to the Constitution of 1853, which established a federal system similar to that of the United States. There are separate executive and legislative branches, an independent judiciary, and a theoretical balance of power among the three. The president and the 254-member Chamber of Deputies are popularly elected, but provincial legislatures choose the 46-member Senate, the other branch of Congress. Provincial governors and legislatures are popularly elected.

In practice, the president is far more powerful than his American counterpart and frequently governs by decree without consulting Congress. He also can, and frequently does, intervene in provincial matters. In 1990, for instance, President Carlos Menem prevented Chubut province from exceeding its budget to pay employees of the provincial government, and also stepped in to ensure a complete investigation in a highly politicised murder case in which Catamarca provincial police and authorities were implicated.

Administratively, the country consists of a federal district, the city of Buenos Aires proper, plus 23 provinces and the territories of the South Atlantic islands (including the Falklands and South Georgia, under British administration) and the Argentine Antarctic (where territorial claims are on hold by international agreement).

Political Parties

Although personality is often more important than party, the spectrum of Argentine political parties is broad. At least 18 different ones are represented in Congress, but the most important parties are the Peronists (Justicialists) of the late Juan Perón and current President Carlos Menem and the somewhat misnamed Radicals of former

JUJUY

FORMOSA

SALTA

SANTIAGO
DEL
ESTERO

TUCUMÁN

CATAMARCA

CHACO

MISIONES

LA RIOJA

CORRIENTES

PACIFIC
OCEAN

SAN
JUAN

CÓRDOBA

SANTA
FE

ENTRE
RÍOS

SAN
LUIS

MENDOZA

BUENOS
AIRES

LA PAMPA

NEUQUÉN

ATLANTIC
OCEAN

RÍO NEGRO

CHUBUT

Provinces & Territories

0   200   400 km

SANTA
CRUZ

Falkland Islands
(Islas Malvinas)

TIERRA
DEL FUEGO

President Raúl Alfonsín, who generally represent middle class interests. Argentines of all classes actively participate in political discussion, which does not always constitute dialogue.

Until the 1940s, when Perón revolutionised Argentine politics by overtly appealing to labour unions and other underrepresented sectors of society, the Radicals vied against parties tied to traditional conservative landowning interests for electoral supremacy. Within the Peronist party, there are deeply opposed factions which, in the mid-1970s, even conducted open warfare against each other.

Currently these divisions are less violent, but there is still considerable friction between the official 'neoliberal' adherents of President Menem, who has attempted to reduce the role of the state in economic matters and limit the influence of militant labour, and leftist elements (known as the 'Group of Eight' in Congress) which see Menem's policies as capitulation to foreign institutions such as the World Bank and International Monetary Fund. Ultranationalist factions within the Justicialist Party are not much happier despite their loathing of the left.

Within the Menem government, the most important figure has been Economy Minister Domingo Cavallo, a Harvard-trained economist who has attempted to stabilise the Argentine currency and reduce the budget deficit by selling off unprofitable state enterprises. Defence Minister Erman González, Cavallo's predecessor, attempted the same goals until a run on the overvalued austral forced his resignation. Argentine presidents change economy ministers almost as often as their shoes.

Menem has forged an open association with the conservative Democratic Centre Union (UCD) and its leader Alvaro Alsogaray, whose counsel is a source of great irritation to the Group of Eight and its followers. Other parties, much less numerous and influential, include the Intransigent Party (PI), the Christian Democrats, the Movement Toward Socialism (MAS), and the Movement for Integration and Development (MID).

In some provinces, local political parties are especially important. In Neuquén, for instance, the Sapag family's Partido Popular Neuquino has been responsible for some of the most progressive social policies in the entire country.

The Military

Since 1930, when it overthrew Radical President Hipólito Yrigoyen, the military has played a crucial if not always public role in Argentine politics. Generals have often worn the presidential sash, most recently between 1976 and 1983. It is sometimes difficult to determine whether the frequent coups occur when the military feel themselves 'obliged' to intervene because of civilian incompetence, corruption, and disorder, or whether military activities themselves create conditions which undermine the civil order.

The military coup which overthrew constitutional President María Estela Martínez de Perón ('Isabelita') was bloodless, not unexpected and, even among moderate sectors of the populace, not unwelcome. After Juan Perón's death, people honestly yearned for relief from economic chaos and the erosion of public order, in which violent strikes, bombings and kidnappings were everyday occurrences.

In the aftermath of the coup, though, military rule was savage. The services operated dozens of clandestine detention centres, including that at the infamous Escuela de Mecánica de la Armada (ESMA or Naval Mechanics' School) in Buenos Aires, where opponents and presumed opponents of the government were tortured and frequently murdered under the ideology of the 'national security doctrine'.

The military themselves are a privileged sector in Argentine society. Second only to Brazil in size among Latin American powers, they number about 150,000, two-thirds of those in the army. More frequently used to control the civil population than to fight foreign enemies, the military failed miserably in confronting Britain during the

Falklands/Malvinas war of 1982, but soon recovered its technological capacity despite heavy material losses. The air force, which suffered the heaviest damage despite a creditable performance under difficult conditions, quickly replaced its lost hardware despite a grave economic crisis which foolish military action had made even worse.

Military service is compulsory for all males above the age of 18. Conscripts are poorly trained, maltreated, and paid almost nothing – at times they have been stationed near their homes so that their families will feed them rather than the army. During the Falklands war, for inexplicable reasons, the army sent conscripts to the front lines while leaving its crack units on the mainland. There is an embryonic movement to eliminate conscription.

Geopolitics

Besides the national security doctrine, one of the mainstays of military ideology and influence is the idea of geopolitics, a 19th-century European doctrine interpreted in a peculiarly Argentine way. According to this world view, first elaborated by German geographer Friedrich Ratzel and later exaggerated in National Socialist (Nazi) ideology in the 1930s, the state is akin to a biological organism which must grow (expand) or die. This means effective occupation of the territories which the state claims as its own, in which process the state comes into conflict with other states. Such thinking was clearly a major factor in General Galtieri's decision to invade the Falkland Islands in 1982.

Other South American countries, particularly Brazil and Chile, share this perspective. Chile's former dictator, General Augusto Pinochet, has even written a textbook entitled *Geopolítica*, while his Argentine and Brazilian counterparts expound on topics such as the 'Fifth Column' of Chilean immigrants (largely illiterate sheep shearers from the depressed island of Chiloé) in Patagonia or the justification of territorial claims in the Antarctic in accordance with each country's longitudinal 'frontage' on the icebound continent. In one instance, an

Argentine military government transported a pregnant woman to give birth in Antarctica in order to strengthen its case for 'effective settlement'.

The tenets of geopolitics are most popular among, but not restricted to, the military, who publish detailed articles in journals such as *Estrategia* (Strategy). Although some of these analyses are much more sophisticated than others, it would be a mistake to dismiss any of them too easily. Once, in an interview, an Argentine naval officer observed to one of the authors that, 'For us, the Malvinas are a pact sealed in blood'. So long as such attitudes persist, the militarisation of Argentine society is likely to endure.

ECONOMY

Nobody understands the Argentine economy, to which one could easily apply Mark Twain's apocryphal comment about the weather: 'Everyone talks about it, but nobody does anything about it'. Argentina's inability to achieve its potential, despite its abundant natural resources, and highly literate and sophisticated population, has mystified historians and foreign observers for decades. A country which, at the turn of the century, resembled now prosperous Australia and Canada has regressed instead of keeping pace with those countries. Now burdened with a monstrous foreign debt which is unlikely ever to be repaid, its middle class is shrinking, while the working class and the poor have little hope of advancement.

Ever since the colonial era, the basis of the Argentine economy has been reliance on agricultural export commodities – hides, wool, beef and grains – gleaned from the fertile Pampas. Self-sufficient in petroleum and other energy resources, the country has been unable to capitalise on these advantages despite a superficial prosperity. With a per capita income of US$2400, Argentina is one of the wealthiest countries in Latin America, but its economy is in a state of perpetual chaos. Crippling international debts of US$54 billion (thousand million) have nearly doubled since 1982.

Its borrowing binge of the 1970s and

1980s, encouraged by international institutions, funded gigantic, capital-intensive projects with no obvious economic advantages but myriad opportunities for graft and corruption. These undertakings, like the Yacyretá dam on the upper Río Paraná, encouraged economic speculation which contributed to the country's chronic inflation, which consistently exceeds 100% per annum and is often much higher.

One of Argentina's problems is the inequities in the rural sector, where Argentina's problems resemble those of other Latin American countries. The richest agricultural lands of the Pampas remained under control of relatively few individuals – unlike Canada or the United States, where family farmers benefited from a more broadly based prosperity. With other rural people relegated to marginal lands or a role as dependent labour on large estates, Argentina reproduced the classic Latin American pattern of latifundio versus minifundio. Institutions such as the powerful Sociedad Rural maintained the power of the landholding elite.

Perón's rise to power demonstrated that the structure of rural society was inadequate for broader prosperity, that Argentina needed to develop its industrial base, and that workers needed to share in the development of Argentine industry. At the time, there was probably no alternative to state involvement in industry, but its dominance over succeeding decades has outlived its usefulness.

The state sector remains the largest in the economy, but many if not most of its businesses are corrupt, inefficient or both. One need not be a Thatcherite to recognise that many state employees serve no useful function when, for example, the day after the announcement of the impending privatisation of ENTel, the state telephone company, so many people came to work that there were insufficient desks for all of them. Argentines refer to individuals who hold multiple government jobs as *ñoquis*, after the traditional potato pasta served in Argentine households on the 29th of each month – the implication is that they appear on the job just before their monthly paychecks are due.

The bloated public sector contributes greatly to the country's chronic inflation. The state railroad Ferrocarriles Argentinos, for example, loses US$3 million per day, while the government traditionally prints paper money to cover budget deficits. On the other hand, state domination has fostered a large informal sector which operates parallel to the official economy in providing goods and services. One recent study claimed that only 40% of Argentina's workers functioned in the 'official' economy – the remainder laboured independently, were often paid in cash, and avoided taxes entirely.

For non-Argentines it is sometimes difficult to comprehend what an inflation rate of, say, 585% (a figure reached between November 1983 and November 1984) means in practical terms. A plummeting national currency usually insulates foreigners from the most extreme fluctuations but, had the Argentine peso remained stable against the US dollar after 1979 at such rates of inflation, by 1984 a token for the underground would have cost US$154, a daily newspaper US$455, an *empanada* (meat pie) US$636, a pizza US$5000, and a 35 mm camera US$1.3 million!

Obviously such a situation cannot continue without adjustments, typically wage and price indexing. This in turn reinforces the inflationary spiral. For better or worse, the Menem administration has tried to break this spiral by reducing the public sector deficit, selling off inefficient state enterprises, and restricting the activities of militant labour unions. The side effects of such measures have included a major recession with major unemployment. Even though inflation subsided to only 2.6% for the month of July 1991, even this is a level intolerable by European or North American standards.

Many Argentine families deal with inflation by putting money into a stable currency, such as the US dollar. Unfortunately, but because they rightfully mistrust erratic government banking policies, middle class people hoard their dollar savings rather than invest them. Wealthier individuals safeguard their cash overseas – a cartoon in a Buenos Aires daily showed two businessmen in conversation, one saying that 'Under Alfonsín, I sent my dollars to Switzerland'. When his colleague inquires what he plans to do under Menem, he replies, 'I'm going to visit them'.

Whether the 'rationalisation' of the Argentine economy envisaged by Menem and his advisors will be successful is uncertain, but similar measures over the last 15 years have failed many times. The administration's pleas for austerity, its promises that things will get better, ring false when the president himself accepts a US$50,000 sports car gift from potential foreign investors, and a prominent labour leader admits that 'Nobody in Argentina ever got rich by working'. One of the side effects of privatisation has been increasing unemployment which the government sees as an essential structural adjustment but that ordinary people worry may be a more enduring problem.

The difference between these two views might be illuminated metaphorically by a popular joke during the 1990 holiday season. President Menem, dressed as Father Christmas, visits his native province of La Rioja and asks the local priest what sort of toys the children prefer. When the priest replies that 'Sir, here the children don't eat!', Menem exclaims, 'They don't eat? Well, then, no toys for them!'.

POPULATION & PEOPLE

Argentina's population of 32.3 million is unevenly distributed. More than a third reside in Gran Buenos Aires, which includes the Federal Capital and its suburbs in the province of Buenos Aires. More than 86 per cent live in urban areas; the other major population centres are Rosario in Santa Fe province, Córdoba, Tucumán, Mendoza, and Bahía Blanca in the province of Buenos Aires. South of the Río Colorado in Patagonia the population is very small and dispersed.

From the early 19th century, the Unitarist faction in Argentine politics had followed the dictum of Juan Bautista Alberdi, a native of Tucumán, who argued that 'to govern is to populate'. The Unitarists saw Europe as the model to which an independent Argentina should aspire, and did everything in their power to promote European immigration. Alberdi's ideas retain great appeal, surviving especially among geopoliticians who dream of filling the country's vast empty spaces, Patagonia and even Antarctica, with more Argentines.

Unlike the central Andean countries, which had large, urbanised Indian populations when Europeans appeared on the scene, the Pampas core of present-day Argentina was sparsely populated by hunting and gathering peoples. Except in the North-West, where early colonisation proceeded from Peru and Bolivia, European immigrants displaced relatively small numbers of indigenous peoples. From the mid-19th century, the trickle of Europeans became a flood, as Italians, Basques, Welsh, English, Ukrainians and other nationalities inundated Buenos Aires as they did New York. Italian surnames are even more common than Spanish ones, although Italo-Argentines do not constitute a cohesive, distinctive group in the way that Italian-Americans do in many cities in the United States.

Some groups have maintained a distinctive cultural identity, such as the Anglo-Argentines throughout the country and the Welsh in Chubut province (despite the eclipse of Welsh as a living language). In Buenos Aires, there is a significant Jewish community, although it does not approach the size of New York's. In some areas there are agricultural settlements with a definable ethnic heritage: the Germans of Eldorado in Misiones province, the Bulgarians and Yugoslavs of Roque Sáenz Peña in the Chaco, the Ukrainians of La Pampa.

Middle Eastern immigrants, though not numerous, have attained great political influence. The most obvious case is current President Carlos Menem, of Syrian ancestry, who rose to prominence in the province of La Rioja. Although a vocal and perhaps opportunistic Catholic (Catholicism is a formal requirement for the presidency), his marriage to his now estranged wife Zulema Yoma was arranged.

The Saadis in Catamarca and the Sapags in Neuquén province are other influential political families of Middle Eastern origins, while Colonel Mohammed Alí Seineldín is an imprisoned leader of the fascist carapintada movement in the army. Argentines refer indiscriminately to anyone of Middle Eastern ancestry (except Jews or Israelis) as a *turco* (Turk), sometimes but not always with racist connotations.

In the Buenos Aires suburb of Escobar, there is a notable Japanese community, but non-European immigrants have generally not been welcome – despite the upheavals in Asia over the past decade-plus, few immigrants from that region have entered the country. Many Chileans live in Patagonia, but their usual status as dependent labourers on sheep estancias marginalises their position in Argentine society. Bolivian highlanders often serve as seasonal labourers (*peones golondrinas* or 'swallows') in the sugar harvests of north-western Argentina; some have come to Buenos Aires, where they mainly work in the construction industry. Numerous Paraguayans and Uruguayans also reside permanently in Argentina.

Argentina's Indian population is small but increasingly visible and militant. The largest groups are the Quechua of the North-West and the Mapuche of northern Patagonia, but there are important populations of Matacos, Tobas and others in the Chaco and in north-eastern cities such as Resistencia and Santa Fe. The Alfonsín administration was surprisingly sympathetic to Indian issues, but the Menem government appears indifferent.

EDUCATION

Argentina's 94% literacy rate is one of the highest in Latin America. From the age of five to 12, education is free and compulsory, although the rate of attendance is low in some rural areas. The comprehensive secondary education system follows the French model, with no elective courses. Elite public secondary schools such as the Colegio Nacional Buenos Aires, where the teachers are also university instructors, are unequalled by other public or private institutions, although some bilingual schools are very prestigious.

Universities are traditionally free and open, but once students have chosen a career, their course of study is extremely rigid. Ready access to higher education has glutted Buenos Aires with large numbers of professionals, such as doctors and lawyers, who are not easily absorbed into the city's economy, but are reluctant to relocate to the provinces. Private universities exist, but the public universities such as Buenos Aires, Córdoba and La Plata are more prominent.

In addition to university education, there is a tertiary system for the preparation of teachers, who do not need a university degree. For individuals who are not academically oriented, there is vocational training.

ARTS

Art & Literature

Although derivative in many ways of European precedents, Argentine art and literature have been influential beyond the country's own borders. Argentine literature has produced writers of international stature, such as Jorge Luis Borges, Julio Cortázar, Ernesto Sábato, Manuel Puig, Osvaldo Soriano and Adolfo Bioy Casares. Much of their work is readily available in English translation. For suggested readings, see the section Books & Bookshops in the Facts for the Visitor chapter.

Many Argentine intellectuals have been educated in European capitals, particularly Paris. In the 19th and early 20th centuries Buenos Aires self-consciously emulated European, especially French, cultural trends in art, music and architecture. There are many important art museums and galleries.

Classical Music & Theatre

The palatial Teatro Colón, home of the Buenos Aires opera, is one of the finest facilities of its kind in the world. Classical music and ballet, as well as modern dance, appear here and at similar venues. The city has a vigorous theatre community, equivalent in its own way to New York, London or Paris. Even in the provinces, live theatre is an important medium of expression.

Cinema

Despite the limited funds with which directors must work, Argentine cinema has achieved international stature, especially since its renaissance after the end of the Dirty War. Many Argentine films, both before and after the Dirty War, are available on video.

La Patagonia Rebelde, which often plays university campuses and repertory houses in the USA, is an account of the Anarchist rebellion in Santa Cruz province at the turn of the century. *A Funny Dirty Little War* comically depicts the very serious matter of the consequences of a possible military coup in a small provincial town.

Several Argentine films portray the consequences of the Dirty War. One truly creepy one, which ironically depicts many amusing aspects of Porteño life, is the English-language film *Apartment Zero*, in which an Anglo-Argentine film buff takes a morbidly curious interest in his mysterious North American roommate. Films such as *Man Facing Southeast* and *The Official Story*, dealing with delicate themes like the adoption of the children of missing people by those responsible for their disappearance, have earned international acclaim. *The Night of the Pencils* also dealt with the Dirty War.

The commercial success *Kiss of the Spider Woman*, set in Brazil but based on the novel by Argentine Manuel Puig, was an intricate portrayal of the way in which the police and military abuse political prisoners and exploit informers. *Las Locas de la Plaza de Mayo* is a documentary tribute to the mothers and grandmothers who defied the military government of the Proceso by marching every Thursday in front of the Casa Rosada. Actress Norma Leandro has starred in English-language films in the United States.

Tango & Folk Music

Probably the best known manifestation of Argentine popular culture is the tango, both as music and dance, with important figures such as the legendary Carlos Gardel and the late Julio Sosa, and contemporaries like Susana Rinaldi, Eladia Blásquez, Astor Piazzola and Osvaldo Pugliese. Folk musicians, such as Mercedes Sosa, Atahualpa Yupanqui, Tarragó Ross, Leon Gieco and Conjunto Pro Música de Rosario are popular performers.

Popular Music

Argentine rock musicians such as Charly García (formerly a member of the important group Sui Generis) and Fito Páez have recorded overseas – García's version of the the Argentine national anthem does what Jimi Hendrix did for 'The Star-Spangled Banner'. After a judge dismissed a lawsuit which alleged that García lacked 'respect for national symbols', the *Buenos Aires Herald* editorialised that García's defence was a victory over 'extremist nationalist sectors' which had too long 'imposed their warped and often authoritarian views on the rest of society'.

Les Luthiers, an Argentine Bonzo Dog Band in tie and tails, satirise those sectors in the middle class and the military. Many performers are more conventional and derivative, but before you report an Elvis sighting in Buenos Aires, make sure it isn't Sandro, an Argentine clone of The King who is still very much alive.

CULTURE

English-speaking visitors will find Argentina more accessible than other Latin American countries because of its superficial resemblance to their own societies. In contrast to countries like Peru and Bolivia, with their large indigenous populations, foreign travellers are inconspicuous and can more easily integrate themselves into everyday life. Argentines are gregarious and, once you make contact with them, much likelier to invite you to participate in their regular activities than is, say, a Quechua llama herder in Bolivia.

One of these activities, which you should

never refuse, is the opportunity to *tomar un mate* (drink *mate*). Drinking *mate* (pronounced 'mah-tay'), or Paraguayan tea, is an important ritual throughout the River Plate countries and Chile, but especially so in Argentina. In the south, it is drunk bitter, but in the north people take it with sugar and *yuyos* (herbs).

Sport is extremely important to Argentines. Most people will know Argentine athletes through its World Cup soccer teams, featuring players such as Diego Maradona and Daniel Passarela, and tennis stars such as Guillermo Vilas and Gabriela Sabatini, but rugby, polo, golf, skiing and fishing also enjoy great popularity. Soccer, though, is the national obsession – River Plate and Boca Juniors, the latter based in Buenos Aires' immigrant Italian neighbourhood of La Boca, are nationwide phenomena.

RELIGION

Roman Catholicism is the official state religion but, as in many other Latin American countries, evangelical Protestantism is making inroads among traditionally Catholic believers. Even within the Catholic religion, popular beliefs diverge from official doctrine – one of the best examples is the cult of the Difunta Correa, based in San Juan province, to which hundreds of thousands of professed Argentine Catholics make annual pilgrimages and offerings despite an aggressive campaign by the Church hierarchy against her veneration.

Spiritualism and veneration of the dead have remarkable importance for a country which prides itself on European sophistication – novelist Tomás Eloy Martínez has observed that Argentines honour their national heroes, such as San Martín, not on the anniversary of their birth but of their death. Visitors to Recoleta and Chacarita cemeteries in Buenos Aires – essential sights for comprehending the Argentine character – will see steady processions of pilgrims communicating with cultural icons like Juan and Evita Perón, psychic Madre María, and tango singer Carlos Gardel by laying hands on their tombs and leaving arcane offerings.

Official Catholicism has provided Argentina with some of its most impressive monuments, from the modest but picturesque churches of the Andean North-West to the Jesuit missions of Mesopotamia, the colonial cathedral of Córdoba, and the neo-Gothic basilica of Luján in the province of Buenos Aires. Inattention to the role of religion will limit anyone's understanding of Argentine society.

Like other Argentine institutions, the Church has many factions. During the late 1970s and early 1980s, the official Church generally supported the de facto military government despite persecution, kidnapping, torture and murder of religious workers. These workers were, of course, adherents of the movement toward 'Liberation Theology', who often worked among the poor and dispossessed in both rural areas and the *villas miserias* (shantytowns) of Buenos Aires and other large cities. Such activism has resumed in today's more permissive political climate, but the Church hierarchy remains obstinate: the Archbishop of Buenos Aires, for example, has defended President Menem's pardon of the convicted murderers and torturers of the Proceso.

LANGUAGE

Spanish is official, but some immigrant communities retain their language as a badge of identity. Italian, representing the single largest immigrant group, is widely understood, while the Anglo-Argentine community retains a precise, clipped English – short-wave listeners who stumble onto Radio Argentina Al Exterior may briefly think they've found the BBC. In the province of Chubut, despite the persistence of many Welsh cultural traditions, the Welsh language itself has nearly disappeared.

No one should ignore the country's 17 native languages, though some are spoken by very few individuals. In the Andean North-West, Quechua speakers are numerous, although most are bilingual in Spanish. In the southern Andes, there are at least 40,000 Mapuche-speaking Indians. In north-eastern Argentina, there are about 15,000

Guaraní speakers, an equal number of Tobas, and about 10,000 Matacos.

Argentine Spanish

Spanish in Argentina, and the rest of the River Plate region, has characteristics which readily distinguish it from the rest of Latin America. Probably the most prominent are the usage of the pronoun *vos* (the *voseo* – see the Glossary) in place of *tu* (the *tuteo*) for 'you', and the trait of pronouncing the letters 'll' and 'y' as 'zh' (as in 'azure') rather than 'y' (like English 'you') as in the rest of the Americas – these will easily identify an Argentine elsewhere in Latin America or overseas. Note that in American Spanish, the plural of the familiar 'tu' or 'vos' is *ustedes* rather than *vosotros*, as in Spain. Argentines and other Latin Americans will understand continental Spanish, but may find it quaint or pretentious.

Every visitor to Argentina should make an effort to speak Spanish, whose basic elements are easily acquired. If possible, take a brief night course at your local university or community college before departure. Even if you can't speak very well, Argentines are gracious hosts and will encourage your Spanish, so there is no need to feel self-conscious about vocabulary or pronunciation. There are many common cognates, so if you're stuck try Hispanicising an English word – it is unlikely you'll make a truly embarrassing error. Do not, however, admit to being 'embarrassed' *(embarazada)* unless you are in fact pregnant!

Vocabulary

There are many differences in vocabulary between European and American Spanish, and among Spanish-speaking countries in the Americas. There are also considerable regional differences within these countries not attributable to accent alone – the language of Mesopotamia, for example, includes many words from the aboriginal Guaraní, while the speech of Buenos Aires abounds with words and phrases from the colourful slang known as *lunfardo*. Although you shouldn't use lunfardo words unless you are supremely confident that you know their *every* implication (especially in formal situations), you should be aware of some of the more common everyday usages. Check the glossary for some of these.

Argentines and other South Americans normally refer to the Spanish language as *castellano* rather than *español*.

Phrasebooks & Dictionaries

Lonely Planet's new *Latin American Spanish* phrasebook, by Anna Cody, is a worthwhile addition to your backpack. Another exceptionally useful resource is the *University of Chicago Spanish-English, English-Spanish Dictionary*, whose small size, light weight and thorough entries make it perfect for overseas travel.

Pronunciation

Spanish pronunciation is, in general, consistently phonetic. Once you are aware of the basic rules, they should cause little difficulty. Speak slowly to avoid getting tongue-tied until you become confident of your ability.

Pronunciation of the letters *f, k, l, n, p q, s* and *t* is virtually identical with English. Although *y* is identical in most Latin American countries when used as a consonant, most Argentines say 'zh' for it and for *ll*, which is a separate letter. *Ch* and *ñ* are also separate letters, with separate dictionary entries.

Vowels Spanish vowels are very consistent and have easy English equivalents.

a is like 'a' in 'father'.
e is like 'ai' in 'sail'.
i is like 'ee' in 'feet'.
o is like 'o' in 'for'.
u is like 'u' in 'food'. After consonants other than 'q', it is more like English 'w'. When the vowel sound is modified by an umlaut, as in 'Güemes', it is also pronounced 'w'.
y is a consonant except when it stands alone or appears at the end of a word, in which case its pronunciation is identical to Spanish 'i'.

Consonants Spanish consonants generally

resemble their English equivalents, but there are some major exceptions.

b resembles its English equivalent, but is undistinguished from 'v'. For clarification, refer to the former as 'b larga', the latter as 'b corta' (the word for the letter itself is pronounced like English 'bay').
c is like the 's' in 'see' before e and i, otherwise like English 'k'.
d closely resembles 'th' in 'feather'.
g is like a guttural English 'h' before Spanish 'e' and 'i', otherwise like 'g' in 'go'.
h is invariably silent. If your name begins with this letter, listen carefully when immigration officials summon you to pick up your passport.
j most closely resembles English 'h', but is slightly more guttural.
ñ is like 'ni' in 'onion'.
r is nearly identical to English except at the beginning of a word, when it is often rolled.
rr is very strongly rolled.
v resembles English, but see 'b', above.
x is like 'x' in 'taxi' except for very few words for which it follows Spanish or Mexican usage as 'j'.
z is like 's' in 'sun'.

Diphthongs Diphthongs are combinations of two vowels which form a single syllable. In Spanish, the formation of a diphthong depends on combinations of 'weak' vowels ('i' and 'u') or strong ones ('a', 'e', and 'o'). Two weak vowels or a strong and a weak vowel make a diphthong, but two strong ones are separate syllables.

A good example of two weak vowels forming a diphthong is the word *diurno* ('during the day'). The final syllable of *obligatorio* ('obligatory') is a combination of weak and strong vowels.

Stress Stress, often indicated by visible accents, is very important, since it can change the meaning of words. In general, words ending in vowels or the letters 'n' or 's' have stress on the next-to-last syllable, while those with other endings have stress on the last syllable. Thus *vaca* ('cow') and

caballos ('horses' both have accents on their next-to-last syllables.

Visible accents, which can occur anywhere in a word, dictate stress over these general rules. Thus *sótano* ('basement'), *América* and *porción* ('portion') all have stress on different syllables. When words appear in capitals, the written accent is generally omitted, but is still pronounced.

Greetings & Civilities

In their public behavior, Argentines are very conscious of civilities, sometimes to the point of ceremoniousness. Never, for example, approach a stranger for information without extending a greeting like *buenos días* or *buenas tardes*.

yes	*sí*
no	*no*
thank you	*gracias*
you're welcome	*de nada*
hello	*hola*
good morning	*buenos días*
good afternoon	*buenas tardes*
good evening	*buenas noches*
good night	*buenas noches*
goodbye	*adiós, chau*

I don't speak much Spanish.
   hablo poco castellano.
I understand.
   entiendo.
I don't understand.
   no entiendo.

Useful Words & Phrases

and	*y*
to/at	*a*
for	*por, para*
of/from	*de, desde*
in	*en*
with	*con*
without	*sin*
before	*antes*
after	*después*
soon	*pronto*
already	*ya*
now	*ahora*
right away	*en seguida*

here	aquí
there	allí
Where?	Dónde?
Where is...?	Dónde está...?
Where are...?	Dónde están...?
When?	Cuando?
How?	Cómo?
I would like...	Me gustaría...
coffee	café
tea	té
beer	cerveza
How much?	Cuanto?
How many?	Cuantos?

Countries

The list below only contains only countries whose spelling differs in English and Spanish.

Canada	Canadá
Denmark	Dinamarca
England	Inglaterra
France	Francia
Germany	Alemania
Great Britain	Gran Bretaña
Ireland	Irlanda
Italy	Italia
Japan	Japón
Netherlands	Holanda
New Zealand	Nueva Zelandia
Peru	Perú
Scotland	Escocia
Spain	España
Sweden	Suecia
Switzerland	Suiza
United States	Estados Unidos
Wales	Gales

Getting Around

airplane	avión
train	tren
bus	colectivo, micro, omnibus
ship	barco, buque
car	auto
taxi	taxi
truck	camión
pickup	camioneta
bicycle	bicicleta

motorcycle	motocicleta
hitchhike	hacer dedo

I would like a ticket to...
  Quiero un boleto/pasaje a...
What's the fare to...?
  Cuanto cuesta hasta...?
When does the next plane/train/bus leave for...?
  Cuando sale el próximo avión/tren/ómnibus para...?
Is there a student/university discount?
  Hay descuento estudiantil/universitario?
first/last/next
  primero/último/próximo
first/second class
  primera/segunda (or turista) clase
single/return (round trip)
  ida/ida y vuelta
sleeper
  camarote
left luggage
  guardería, equipaje

Accomodation

Below you will find English phrases with useful Spanish equivalents for Argentina, most of which will be understood in other Spanish-speaking countries.

hotel
  hotel, pensión, residencial
Is/Are there...?
  Hay ....?
single room
  habitación para una persona
double room
  habitación doble
What does it cost?
  Cuanto cuesta?
per night
  por noche
full board
  pensión completa
shared bath
  baño compartido
private bath
  baño privado
too expensive
  demasiado caro

discount
descuento
cheaper
mas económico
May I see it?
Puedo verla?
I don't like it.
No me gusta.
the bill
la cuenta

Around Town

tourist information
oficina de turismo
airport
aeropuerto
train station
estación de ferrocarril
bus terminal
terminal de buses
bathing resort
balneario
post office
correo
letter
carta
parcel
paquete
postcard
postal
airmail
correo aéreo
registered mail
certificado
stamps
estampillas
person to person
persona a persona
collect call
cobro revertido

Toilets

The most common word for 'toilet' is *baño*, but *servicios sanitarios* ('services') is a frequent alternative. Men's toilets will usually bear a descriptive term such as *hombres*, *caballeros* or *varones*. Women's restrooms will say *señoras* or *damas*.

Geographical Expressions

The expressions below are among the most common you will encounter in this book and in Spanish language maps and guides.

bay	*bahía*
bridge	*puente*
farm	*chacra*
glacier	*glaciar, ventisquero*
highway	*carretera, ruta*
hill	*cerro*
lake	*lago*
marsh	*estero*
mount	*cerro*
mountain range	*cordillera*
national park	*parque nacional*
pass	*paso*
ranch	*estancia*
river	*río*
waterfall	*cascada, catarata, salto*

Time

Telling time is fairly straightforward. Eight o'clock is *las ocho*, while 8.30 is *las ocho y treinta* (literally, 'eight and thirty') or *las ocho y media* ('eight and a half'). However, 7.45 is *las ocho menos quince* (literally, 'eight minus fifteen') or *las ocho menos cuarto* ('eight minus one quarter'). Times are modified by morning (*de la manaña*) or afternoon (*de la tarde*) instead of am or pm. It is also common to use the 24-hour clock, especially with transportation schedules.

Days of the Week

Monday	*lunes*
Tuesday	*martes*
Wednesday	*miércoles*
Thursday	*jueves*
Friday	*viernes*
Saturday	*sábado*
Sunday	*domingo*

Numbers

To deal with Argentina's inflationary epidemic, you will probably have to learn to count in very large numbers.

1	*uno*	70	*setenta*
2	*dos*	80	*ochenta*
3	*tres*	90	*noventa*
4	*cuatro*	100	*cien*
5	*cinco*	101	*ciento uno*
6	*seis*	102	*ciento dos*
7	*siete*	110	*ciento diez*
8	*ocho*	120	*ciento veinte*
9	*nueve*	130	*ciento treinta*
10	*diez*	200	*doscientos*
11	*once*	300	*trescientos*
12	*doce*	400	*cuatrocientos*
13	*trece*	500	*quinientos*
14	*catorce*	600	*seiscientos*
15	*quince*	700	*setecientos*
16	*dieciseis*	800	*ochocientos*
17	*diecisiete*	900	*novecientos*
18	*dieciocho*	1000	*mil*
19	*diecinueve*	1100	*mil cien*
20	*veinte*	1200	*mil doscientos*
21	*veintiuno*	2000	*dos mil*
22	*veintidós*	5000	*cinco mil*
30	*treinta*	10,000	*diez mil*
31	*treinta y uno*	50,000	*cincuenta mil*
40	*cuarenta*	100,000	*cien mil*
50	*cincuenta*	1,000,000	*un millón*
60	*sesenta*		

Facts for the Visitor

VISAS & EMBASSIES

Argentina has eliminated visas for many but not all foreign tourists. In theory, upon arrival all nonvisa visitors must obtain a free tourist card, good for 90 days and renewable for 90 more. In practice, immigration officials issue them only at major border crossings, such as airports and on the ferries and hydrofoils between Buenos Aires and Uruguay. Although you should not toss your card, losing it should not be a major catastrophe. At most exit points, immigration officials will provide immediate replacement; that is, the Argentine bureaucracy may require you to fill one in even though you're leaving the country.

Nationals of the USA, Canada and most Western European countries do not need visas to enter Argentina. Australians and New Zealanders, who do need them, must submit their passports with a payment of US$15. Ordinarily, the visa will be ready the following day. The consulate in Santiago, Chile, is particularly efficient.

Argentina has a wide network of embassies and consulates, both in neighbouring countries and overseas. Some of these are very accommodating, while others (most notably those in Colonia, Uruguay, and La Paz, Bolivia) act as if your visit is a major nuisance. Renewing a nearly expired visa at a consulate other than the one which issued it can be nearly impossible; it is easier to get a new passport from your own consulate and then request a new Argentine visa. As a result of the Falklands war, British passport holders still require visas, but Argentine consulates now issue them fairly routinely.

Individuals born in Argentina, even of foreign parents, are considered Argentines and may have difficulties entering the country with non-Argentine documents. In one instance, officials harassed a 50-year-old United States citizen born in Buenos Aires for lacking proof of completing obligatory military service in Argentina, even though he was a retired colonel in the US army. Argentine passports renewed overseas expire upon re-entry into Argentina, and renewing them with the federal police can be a tiresome experience on a short trip.

Very short visits to neighbouring countries do usually not require visas. Most importantly, you need not waste time obtaining a Brazilian visa to cross from the Argentine side of Iguazú Falls to Foz do Iguaçu if you return the same day, although you must show your passport. The same is true at the Bolivian border town of Villazón near La Quiaca, the Paraguayan crossing at Encarnación near Posadas, and others.

Argentine Embassies & Consulates

Argentina has diplomatic representation throughout Latin America, North America, Western Europe and many other regions, including Australia. The following are most likely to be useful to intending visitors. For more detailed information on overseas delegations, see Foreign Representatives in the Tourist Offices section.

Australia
    1st floor, MLC Tower, Woden, ACT 2606 (☎ (06) 282-4555)
Bolivia
    2nd floor, 16 de Julio 1486, La Paz (☎ 35-3089)
    cnr Bolívar and Ballivián, Tarija
Brazil
    2nd floor, Praia de Botafogo 228, Rio de Janeiro (☎ 551-5198)
Brazil
    8th floor, Rua Araújo 216, São Paulo (☎ 256-8555)
Canada
    Suite 620, 90 Sparks St, Ottawa, Ontario (☎ 236-2351)
Chile
    Vicuña Mackenna 41, Santiago (☎ 222-8977)
    2nd floor, Cauquenes 94, Puerto Montt
    21 de Mayo 1878, Punta Arenas
Paraguay
    Banco Nación, España at Perú, Asunción (☎ 60-0460)
    Cabañas and Mallorquín, Encarnación

UK
53 Hans Place, London SW1 XOLA (☎ (071) 584-6494, Consulate: 589-3104)
USA
1600 New Hampshire Avenue NW, Washington DC (☎ 939-6400)
Uruguay
Avenida G Flores, Colonia (☎ 2091)
Sarandí 3193, Fray Bentos (☎ 2638)
Río Branco 1281, Montevideo (☎ 90-0897)
Leandro Gómez 1034, Paysandú (☎ 2253)
Edificio Santos Dumont, Punta del Este (☎ 41106)

Visa Extensions

As mentioned, Argentine tourist cards are valid for 90 days. For a 90-day extension, you must go to the Immigration department in Buenos Aires (Avenida Antártida Argentina 1365) or provincial capitals, or to provincial delegations of the federal police. There is often a nominal charge. In areas where the police are unaccustomed to dealing with immigration matters, the process can be tedious and time-consuming.

If you wish to stay longer than six months, it is much easier to cross the border into a neighbouring country for a few days and then return. You can then stay an additional six months in Argentina. Although it is possible to obtain residence in Argentina, leaving the country then becomes problematical and you cannot take advantage of tourist regulations with respect to Argentine customs and duties.

Foreign Embassies in Argentina

Every European and South American country and many others throughout the world have embassies and consulates in Buenos Aires. The following list contains those most likely to be of use to independent travellers.

Australia
Santa Fe 846 (☎ 312-6841)
Bolivia
25 de Mayo 611 (☎ 311-7365)
Brazil
5th floor, Pellegrini 1363 (☎ 394-5260)
Canada
Suipacha 1111 (☎ 312-9081)

Chile
San Martín 439 (☎ 394-6582)
Denmark
Leandro N Alem 1064 (☎ 312-6091)
France
Santa Fe 1391 (☎ 311-8240)
Germany
Villanueva 1055 (☎ 771-5054)
Ireland
Santa Fe 1391 (☎ 44-9987)
Japan
Paseo Colón 275 (☎ 70-2561)
Netherlands
Maipú 66 (☎ 331-6066)
Perú
Tucumán 637 (☎ 392-1344)
Paraguay
Maipú 464 (☎ 322-6536)
Spain
Guido 1760 (☎ 41-0078)
Sweden
Corrientes 330 (☎ 311-3088)
Switzerland
Santa Fe 846 (☎ 311-6491)
UK
Dr Luis Agote 2412 (☎ 803-7070)
Uruguay
Las Heras 1907 (☎ 803-6030)
USA
Colombia 4300 (☎ 774-2282)

DOCUMENTS

Passports are required for all visitors except those from bordering countries. At present, Argentina still enjoys civilian government and the police and military presence are relatively subdued, but the police can still demand identification at any moment. It is advisable to carry your passport at all times, especially if there is political unrest. In general, Argentines are very document-oriented and your passport is essential for cashing travellers' cheques, checking into a hotel, and many other routine activities.

Motorists need an International Driving Permit to complement their national or state licences, but should not be surprised if police at the numerous roadside checkpoints do not recognise it or, worse, claim it is invalid and try to exact a bribe. Politely refer them to the Spanish translation.

CUSTOMS

Argentine customs officials generally defer

to foreign visitors, but if you cross the border frequently and carry electronic equipment such as cameras or a laptop computer, it is helpful to have a typed list of your equipment, with serial numbers, stamped by authorities. At Buenos Aires' Ezeiza Airport, you will likely be asked whether you are carrying such goods, which are much more costly in Argentina than overseas. Entering Argentina from Paraguay or Chilean Patagonia, where cheap electronics are also available, you may experience very thorough baggage checks.

Depending on where you have been, customs authorities focus on different things. Travellers coming south from the central Andean countries may be searched for drugs, while those from central Chile or from Brazil should know that fruit and vegetables are likely to be confiscated. Even after you have passed customs, which may be some distance from the actual border, you are subject to inspection by police at checkpoints which are usually at provincial borders or important highway junctions. *Never* carry firearms.

MONEY

For visitors unaccustomed to hyperinflation and without sufficient zeros on their pocket calculators, Argentine money can present real problems. When Argentine economists speak hopefully of single-digit inflation, they mean *per month*.

Currency

The present unit of currency is the new peso, ($) which replaced the *austral* on 1 January 1992. The austral replaced the *peso argentino* in 1985, which had replaced the *peso ley* in 1978, which had replaced the ordinary *peso* some years earlier. One new peso equals 10,000 australs, on a par with the US dollar.

New pesos come in 1, 2, 5, 10, 20, 50 and 100 denominations. One new peso equals 100 *centavos*; centavo coins come in 1, 5, 10, 25 and 50 denominations.

Exchange Rates

US dollars are by far the preferred foreign currency, although Chilean and Uruguayan pesos can be readily exchanged on the borders. Even when the dollar is relatively weak, only Buenos Aires will have a ready market for European currencies.

Exchange rates can be volatile. As of September 1991, for example, the rate for the previous currency was just below 10,000 australs per US dollar, but in mid-December of 1990 it had sunk below 5000 australs until a minor economic crisis and intensified domestic demand for dollars by Argentines planning overseas holidays drove the rate up dramatically. At present, there is no black market and you can change money freely, but visitors should stay aware of changes in the so-called 'parallel rate'. For the most up-to-date information, see *Ambito Financiero*, Argentina's equivalent of *The Wall Street Journal* or *Financial Times*, or the English-language daily *Buenos Aires Herald*.

Cash dollars can be exchanged at banks, *casas de cambio* (exchange houses), hotels and some travel agencies, and often in shops or on the street. At present, cash dollars earn a much better rate of exchange and avoid commissions of up to 10% levied on travellers' cheques, which are increasingly difficult to cash anywhere.

A$1	=	$0.74
US$1	=	$0.98
UK£1	=	$1.69
FFr1	=	$0.18
It£1000	=	$0.79
DM1	=	$0.59
UrgN$1000	=	$0.40
Par₡1000	=	$0.77
BraCr1000	=	$0.56
Chi$1000	=	$2.85
Bol$1	=	$0.26

Costs

At times of economic instability, which is often enough, Argentines panic and buy US dollars, the exchange rate collapses, and the country can become absurdly cheap for the visitor with hard currency. Presently, though, the economy is relatively stable due to strin-

gent monetarist policies and the country is nearly as expensive as Europe or North America. With a fixed exchange rate, inflation remains relatively high, so that prices in dollar terms are increasing faster than in local currency.

This does not mean it is impossible to travel in Argentina on a budget. Certain important costs, such as modest lodging, food and transportation, will be lower than in Europe or North America even if higher than in surrounding countries. After overcoming the initial shock, budget travellers arriving from countries like Bolivia should be able to spend a rewarding time in Argentina by adapting to local conditions. Still, you should probably allow a minimum of US$20 per day for food and lodging, and congratulate yourself if you can get by on less. Prices given in this book are subject to wild fluctuations.

Tipping

In restaurants, it is customary to tip about 10% of the bill, but in times of economic distress Argentines themselves frequently overlook the custom. In general, waiters and waitresses are poorly paid, so if you can afford to eat out you can afford to tip. Even a small *propina* will be appreciated.

Bargaining

Bargaining is not the way of life it is in Bolivia or Peru, but in the Andean North-West and in artisan's markets throughout the country it is customary. Even in Buenos Aires, downtown shops selling leather and other tourist items will listen to offers. Late in the evening, some hotels may give a break on room prices; if you plan to stay several days they almost certainly will. Many of the better hotels will give discounts up to 30% for cash payment.

Credit Cards

Credit cards can be very useful in a pinch. The most widely accepted are Visa and Mastercard (those with UK Access should insist on their affiliation to Mastercard), but American Express, Diner's Club and others are also valid in many places.

Credit card users should be aware of two complications. In the first place, because of inflation, many businesses add a surcharge *(recargo)* of 10% or more to credit card purchases because of the time between the purchase and their own receipt of payment. The flip side of this practice is that some merchants give a discount of 10% or more for cash purchases.

Second, the amount you pay depends upon the exchange rate at the time your purchase is posted to your overseas account, which can be weeks later. If the local currency is depreciating, your purchase price may be a fraction of the dollar cost you calculated at the time. On the other hand, a strong local currency may mean that your cost in dollars (or other foreign currency) will be greater than you thought. Thus you must always be aware of trends in the exchange rate.

WHEN TO GO

For residents of the northern hemisphere, Argentina offers the inviting possibility of two summers in the same year, but the country's great variety can make a visit worthwhile in any season. Buenos Aires' urban attractions transcend the seasons, but popular Patagonian destinations such as the Moreno Glacier in Santa Cruz province are best in summer. The Iguazú Falls in subtropical Misiones province are best in the southern winter or spring, when heat and humidity are less oppressive, at which time skiers could also visit the Andes.

WHAT TO BRING

Argentina is a mostly temperate, midlatitude country and seasonally appropriate clothing for North America or Europe will be equally suitable here. In the subtropical north, especially in summer, you will want lightweight cottons, but at higher elevations in the Andean North-West and the high latitudes of Patagonia you will want warm clothing even in summer.

There is no prejudice against backpackers in Argentina, and many young Argentines take to Patagonia and other remote parts of the country on a shoestring themselves. Cheaper Argentine outdoor equipment is generally inferior to that made in North American or Europe, so bring camping sup-

plies from home. Higher quality products will be very expensive.

TOURIST OFFICES

Almost every province and municipality has a tourist office, usually on the main plaza or at the bus terminal. Each Argentine province has its own tourist representation in Buenos Aires, which is usually an excellent source of information. Some municipalities, such as the Atlantic coastal resort of Villa Gesell in Buenos Aires province and the Patagonian city of Bariloche in Río Negro, have separate offices in Buenos Aires.

Provincial/Municipal Tourist Offices in Buenos Aires

The offices listed below are provincial unless noted otherwise.

Buenos Aires
    Callao 235 (☎ 40-7045)
Catamarca
    Córdoba 2080 (☎ 46-6891)
Chaco
    Callao 322 (☎ 45-0961)
Córdoba
    Callao 332 (40-0589)
Corrientes
    San Martín 333 (☎ 394-7432)
Entre Ríos
    Suipacha 844 (☎ 313-4599)
Formosa
    Bartolomé Mitre 1747 (☎ 45-1916)
Jujuy
    Santa Fe 967 (☎ 393-3174)
La Pampa
    Suipacha 346 (☎ 396-0511)
La Rioja
    Callao 745 (☎ 812-1662)
Mendoza
    Callao 445 (40-6683)
Misiones
    Santa Fe 989 (☎ 393-1615)
San Clemente del Tuyú (municipal)
    Bartolomé Mitre 1135 (☎ 38-0764)
Neuquén
    Perón (ex-Cangallo) 687 (☎ 49-6385)
Pinamar (municipal)
    2nd floor, Avenida Belgrano 520
Río Negro
    Tucumán 1916 (☎ 45-9931)
Salta
    Roque Sáenz Peña 933 (☎ 396-0130)

Santa Cruz
14th floor, Córdoba 1345 (☎ 42-0381)
Santa Fe
Montevideo 371 (40-1825)
San Juan
Sarmiento 1251 (☎ 35-7975)
San Luis
Azcuénaga 1083 (☎ 83-2425)
Santiago del Estero
14th floor, Florida 274 (☎ 46-9398)
Tierra del Fuego
4th floor, Sarmiento 745 (☎ 325-1791)
Tucumán
Bartolomé Mitre 836 (☎ 40-2214)
Villa Carlos Paz (municipal)
Florida 520, Local 38/39 (☎ 392-0348)
Villa Gesell (municipal)
Bartolomé Mitre 1702 (☎ 46-5098)

Foreign Representatives

The larger Argentine consulates, such as New York and Los Angeles, usually have a tourist representative in their delegation. Local representatives of Aerolíneas Argentinas often have similar information at their disposal. *Buenos Aires* *Registro de estado civil* *011-541-498441 or 467025*

Australia
1sr floor, MLC Tower, Woden, ACT 2606 (☎ (06) 282-4555
Canada
Suite 620, 90 Sparks Street, Ottawa, Ontario (☎ 236-2351)
Suite 605, 1010 Saint Catherine St West, Montréal, Québec(☎ 866-3810)
UK
53 Hans Place, London SW1 XOLA (☎ (071) 589 3104)
USA
1600 New Hampshire Avenue NW, Washington DC (☎ 939-6400)
12 West 56th Street, New York, NY (☎ 397-1400) *212-603-0400*
Suite 722, 25 SE Second Avenue, Miami, Florida (☎ 373-1889)
20 North Clark St, Suite 602 Chicago, Illinois (☎ 263-7435)
Suite 1810, 2000 S Post Oak Rd, Houston, Texas (☎ 871-8935)
Suite 1450, 3550 Wilshire Blvd, Los Angeles, California (☎ 739-9977)
Room 1083, 870 Market St, San Francisco, California (☎ 982-3050)

USEFUL ORGANISATIONS

ASATEJ (☎ 312-8476), the Argentine student travel agency, has offices on the 1st floor, Florida 833, 1005 Buenos Aires. You need not be a student to take advantage of their services. They are eager to encourage low-budget travellers in Argentina.

There is a small network of youth hostels throughout the country for which a youth hostel card is not imperative. Contact the Asociación Argentina de Albergues de la Juventud (☎ 45-1001) at 6th floor, Talcahuano 214, 1013 Buenos Aires.

Administración de Parques Nacionales (☎ 311-1943), the national parks office, is at Santa Fe 690 in Buenos Aires, at the north end of the Florida pedestrian mall. Another address of interest to conservationists is the wildlife organisation Fundación Vida Silvestre Argentina (☎ 331-4864), 6th floor, Defensa 245, Buenos Aires.

BUSINESS HOURS & HOLIDAYS

Traditionally, business hours in Argentina commence by 8 am and break at midday for three or even four hours, during which people return home for lunch and a brief siesta. After the siesta, shops reopen until 8 or 9 pm. This schedule is still common in the provinces, but government offices and many businesses in Buenos Aires have adopted a more conventional 8 am to 5 pm schedule in the interests of 'greater efficiency' and, especially in the case of government, reduced corruption.

There are numerous national holidays, on which government offices and businesses are closed. The following list does not include provincial holidays, which may vary considerably.

January 1
Año Nuevo (New Year's Day)
March/April (dates vary)
Viernes Santo/Pascua (Good Friday/Easter)
May 1
Día del Trabajador (Labour Day)
May 25
Revolución de Mayo (May Revolution of 1810)
June 10
Día de las Malvinas (Malvinas Day)
June 20
Día de la Bandera (Flag Day)

July 9
  Día de la Independencia (Independence Day)
August 17
  Día de San Martín (Anniversary of San Martín's
  death)
October 12
  Día de la Raza (Columbus Day)
December 25
  Navidad (Christmas Day)

POST & TELECOMMUNICATIONS

These are among the most intractable problems in modern Argentina. Both the post office and telephone services are traditionally corrupt and inefficient. Telephone infrastructure is almost hopelessly antiquated, although recent developments offer slight encouragement.

Postal Rates

Postal rates vary dramatically depending upon the rate of exchange. Recently, it cost nearly US$1 to send a postcard to North America, with letters being even more expensive, but subsequent devaluation of the currency brought costs down to par with their North American or European equivalent. Airmail packages are expensive, while surface mail is much cheaper but less dependable. International express mail services, including overnight, are expensive but dependable.

Sending Mail

ENCOTEL is the state postal and telegraph service. It is frequently paralysed by strikes and 'work-to-rule' stoppages, resulting in enormous accumulations of mail which never reach their final destinations. You should send essential overseas mail *certificado* (registered) to ensure its arrival. Mail is likely to be opened if it appears to contain money.

ENCOTEL also provides telegraph, fax and telex services.

Receiving Mail

You can receive mail via Poste Restante or Lista de Correos, both equivalent to general delivery, at any Argentine post office. Instruct your correspondents to address

letters clearly and to indicate a date until which the post office should hold them; otherwise they will be returned or destroyed.

Post offices have recently imposed charges on Poste Restante services, so if you can arrange to have mail delivered to a private address such as a friend or a hotel you will avoid this surprisingly costly and bureaucratic annoyance.

It is also worth remembering that Buenos Aires is often referred to as the 'Capital Federal' by Argentines, particularly in lists of addresses.

Telephone

President Carlos Menem's government has recently sold ENTel, the state-owned telephone company, to French and Spanish interests. The two new companies are Telecom, north of Buenos Aires, and Telefónica, south of the capital. Under ENTel, service was so difficult to obtain that Buenos Aires apartments with telephone would sell for many thousands of dollars more than those without, but the government claims that privatisation will improve the situation. Even so, decades are likely to pass before the antiquated phone system is even adequate.

Telecom and Telefónica have assumed control of most of ENTel's long-distance offices, although some provinces and smaller towns operate their own telephone cooperatives. If possible, make overseas calls outside costly peak business hours. You can make collect calls to North America or Europe from most but not all offices – be certain or you may have to pay the cost out of pocket. In major cities, you can make credit card calls to some countries, often on direct lines to overseas operators.

Because Argentina has no coins, most public telephones operate on tokens known as *fichas* or *cospeles*, which differ for local and long-distance service. In the unstable Argentine economy, these may be the only inflation-proof currency. They are available from street-corner kiosks as well as phone company offices. For local calls, one cospel gives you three minutes.

When calling or answering the telephone, the proper salutation is *'hola'* ('hello'). Exchange pleasantries before getting to the point of your conversation.

TIME
For most of the year, Argentina is three hours behind GMT, but this varies among provinces. The city and province of Buenos Aires observe daylight savings time (summer time), but most provinces do not. Exact dates for the changeover vary from year to year.

ELECTRICITY
Electric current operates on 220 volts, 50 cycles. In Buenos Aires, there is an electrical shop at Bolívar 488 (☎ 34-4288) which can help in adapting foreign appliances.

LAUNDRY
In recent years, self-service laundromats have become more common in both Buenos Aires and provincial cities, but they tend to be more expensive than their equivalent in the USA or Europe. Laverap has branches in most major cities. Most inexpensive hotels will have a place where you can wash your own clothes and hang them to dry. In some places maid service will be reasonable, but agree on charges in advance.

WEIGHTS & MEASURES
The metric system is universal and obligatory, but country folk commonly use the Spanish *legua* ('league', of about 5 km) to indicate distance. Hands are used to measure horses, while carpenters regularly use English measurements.

BOOKS & MAPS
There is a tremendous amount of literature on Argentina, so readers can afford to be selective. Many important Argentine writers, such as Jorge Luis Borges, Julio Cortázar, Adolfo Bioy Casares, Osvaldo Soriano and Manuel Puig have been translated into English.

Argentine Literature & Fiction
Borges is a world literary figure, best known for his short stories, but also an important poet. His erudite language and references sometimes make him inaccessible to readers without a solid grounding in the classics, even though his material often deals with everyday Porteño and rural life. Sábato's *On Heroes and Tombs* is a psychological novel which explores people and places in Buenos Aires. In the 1960s it was a cult favourite among Argentine youth. Try also *The Tunnel.*

Cortázar, while a Parisian resident, nevertheless emphasised clearly Argentine characters in novels such as the experimentally structured *Hopscotch* and *62: A Model Kit.* The famous 1960s film *Blow-Up* was based on one of his short stories. Manuel Puig's novels, including *Kiss of the Spider Woman*, *The Buenos Aires Affair* and *Betrayed by Rita Hayworth*, focus on the ambiguous role of popular culture in Argentina.

Bioy Casares's *The Invention of Morel* also deals with the inability or unwillingness to distinguish between fantasy and reality. His *Diary of the War of the Pig* is also available in translation. Osvaldo Soriano, perhaps the most popular novelist in Argentina today, wrote *A Funny Dirty Little War*, which was also made into a film (see below), and the recently translated *Winter Quarters*.

Foreign Literature

Writers from other countries have also dealt with Argentine themes. Although set in Lima, Peruvian novelist Mario Vargas Llosa's *Aunt Julia and the Scriptwriter*, banned by the military dictatorship of the Proceso, offers amusing but ironic and unflattering observations of what other Latin Americans think of Argentines. Graham Greene's *The Honorary Consul*, made into an atrocious film starring Richard Gere, is a semi-satirical account of the kidnapping of an insignificant British diplomat by a small but committed revolutionary group in the slums of Corrientes.

General History

For an account of early European exploration of Argentina and elsewhere in South America, see J H Parry's *The Discovery of South America* (London, Paul Elek, 1979). Although it does not focus specifically on Argentina, James Lockhart and Stuart Schwartz's *Early Latin America* (Cambridge, 1983) makes an unusual but persuasive argument that the structures of native societies were more important than Spanish domination in the cultural transitions of the colonial period. Uruguayan historian Eduardo Galeano presents a bitter indictment of European conquest and its consequences in *The Open Veins of Latin America: Five Centuries of the Pillage of a Continent* (Monthly Review Press, 1973). Do not miss Alfred Crosby's fascinating account of the ecological transformation of the Pampas in comparison with other mid-latitude lands settled by Europeans in *Ecological Imperialism: the Biological Expansion of Europe, 900-1900* (Cambridge, 1986).

For the South American wars of independence, including Argentina, a standard work is John Lynch's *The Spanish-American Revolutions 1808-1826* (W W Norton, New York, 1973). One of the best known contemporary accounts of postindependence Argentina is Domingo Faustino Sarmiento's *Life in the Argentine Republic in the Days of the Tyrants*, available in many editions, an eloquent but often condescending critique of the Federalist caudillos and their followers from the Unitarist perspective of the country's second constitutional president. Also worthwhile is Lynch's *Argentine Dictator: Juan Manuel de Rosas, 1829-1852* (Oxford, 1981). The conflict between Unitarism and Federalism is analysed in José Luis Romero's *A History of Argentine Political Thought* (Stanford, 1968).

For an account of Britain's role in Argentina's 19th-century development, see H S Ferns's *Britain and Argentina in the Nineteenth Century* (Oxford, 1960). James Scobie's *Argentina: A City and a Nation* (Oxford) has gone through many editions and is now a standard account of the country's development. The most up-to-date, comprehensive history of the country is David Rock's *Argentina 1516-1987: from Spanish Colonization to the Falklands War and Alfonsín* (University of California Press, 1987).

Several historians have compared Argentina, Australia and Canada from the perspective of exporters of primary products such as beef and wheat, and their subsequent economic development. These include Tim Duncan and John Fogarty's *Australia & Argentina – on Parallel Paths* (Melbourne, 1984), D C Platt and Guido di Tella's edited *Argentina, Australia and Canada – Studies in Comparative Development, 1970-1985* (MacMillan, 1985), and Carl Solberg's *The Prairies and the Pampas: Agrarian Policy in Canada and Argentina, 1880-1930* (Stanford, 1987).

For an interpretation of the role of the

gaucho in Argentine history, see Richard W Slatta's *Gauchos and the Vanishing Frontier* (University of Nebraska, 1983). More recently, Slatta has compared the gauchos with stockmen of other countries in the beautifully illustrated *Cowboys of the Americas* (Yale University Press, 1990).

A recent book, offering a kind of intellectual history of the country, is Nicholas Shumway's *The Idea of Argentina* (University of California Press, 1991).

Perón & His Legacy

A recent biography is Robert Alexander's *Juan Domingo Perón* (Westview Press, Boulder, Colorado, 1979). Another important book is Frederick Turner and José Enrique Miguens's *Juan Perón and the Reshaping of Argentina* (University of Pittsburgh, 1983). Also look at Joseph Page's *Perón: a Biography* (Random House, New York, 1983), and Robert Crassweller's *Perón and the Enigma of Argentina* (New York, W W Norton, 1987). A fascinating fictionalised version of Perón's life, culminating in his return to Buenos Aires in 1973, is Tomas Eloy Martínez's *The Perón Novel* (Pantheon Books, New York, 1988).

Eva Perón speaks for herself, to some degree, in her ghost-written biography *La Razón de Mi Vida*. V S Naipaul suggests that political violence and torture have long permeated Argentine society in his grim but eloquent essay *The Return of Eva Perón* (Knopf, New York, 1980). Try also J M Taylor's *Eva Perón: the Myths of a Woman* (University of Chicago, 1979).

Contemporary Argentine Politics

For an analysis of the contradictions in Argentine society, read Gary Wynia's *Argentina in the Post-War Era: Politics and Economic Policy-making in a Divided Society* (University of New Mexico, Albuquerque, 1978). A recent collection on the democratic transition is Monica Peralta-Ramos and Carlos Waisman's *From Military Rule to Liberal Democracy in Argentina* (Westview Press, Boulder, Colorado, 1987)

The Military, Politics & Geopolitics

One good general overview of the military in Latin America is John J Johnson's *The Military and Society in Latin America* (Stanford, 1964). Robert Potash has published two books on military interference in Argentine politics: *The Army and Politics in Argentina, 1928-1945: Yrigoyen to Perón* (Stanford, 1969), and *The Army and Politics in Argentina, 1945-1962: Perón to Frondizi* (Stanford, 1980). For an analysis of the notion of geopolitics in Argentina, see Philip Kelly and Jack Child's edited volume, *Geopolitics of the Southern Cone & Antarctica* (Lynne Rienner, London, 1988). A more general account, dealing with Chile, Brazil and Paraguay as well, is Cesar Caviedes' *The Southern Cone: Realities of the Authoritarian State* (Rowman & Allenheld, Totowa, N J, 1984).

The Dirty War

The classic first-person account of state terrorism in the late 1970s is Jacobo Timmerman's *Prisoner Without a Name, Cell Without a Number* (New York, Knopf, 1981). *Nunca Más*, the official report of the National Commission on the Disappeared, systematically details military abuses during the 1976-83 period. A good general account in English is John Simpson and Jana Bennett's *The Disappeared: Voices from a Secret War* (London, Robson Books, 1985). A highly regarded first novel on the Dirty War is the US writer Lawrence Thornton's *Imagining Argentina* (Bantam Books, 1988).

Geography

There are several readable texts which integrate Latin American history with geography. Try Arthur Morris's *South America* (Hodder & Stoughton, 1979), Harold Blakemore and Clifford Smith's collection *Latin America* (Methuen, 1983), which includes a detailed chapter on the River Plate countries, and *The Cambridge Encyclopedia of Latin America* (1985), which is rather broader.

Travel Literature

Argentina has inspired some excellent travel writing, most notably Bruce Chatwin's indispensable *In Patagonia* (New York, Summit Books, 1977), one of the most informed syntheses of life and landscape for any part of South America or the entire world. Avoid Paul Theroux's irritating and patronising *The Old Patagonian Express* (Penguin, 1980), whose author does everything possible to distance himself from the people he travels among.

American scientist George Gaylord Simpson's *Attending Marvels: a Patagonian Journal* (many editions) starts surprisingly with an account of the coup against President Hipólito Yrigoyen in 1930. British naturalist Gerald Durrell has written several lightweight but entertaining accounts of his travels in Argentina, from Jujuy to Patagonia, in *The Drunken Forest* and *The Whispering Land*, available in several inexpensive paperback editions. Make a special effort to locate Lucas Bridges' *The Uttermost Part of the Earth* about his life among the Indians of Tierra del Fuego. Bridges' father was one of the earliest missionary settlers from the Falkland Islands and compiled an important dictionary of the Yahgan language.

Don't ignore works of greater antiquity. Charles Darwin's *Voyage of the Beagle*, available in many editions, is as fresh as yesterday. His account of the gauchos on the Pampas and in Patagonia is a vivid evocation of a way of life which no longer really exists but to which Argentines still pay symbolic homage. William Henry Hudson's *Idle Days in Patagonia* is a romantic account of the 19th century naturalist's adventures in search of migratory birds. Also try his *Long Ago and Far Away*.

Travel Guides

Other guidebooks can supplement and complement this one, especially if you are visiting countries other than Argentina. One obvious endorsement is the latest edition of Lonely Planet's *South America on a Shoestring*, by Geoff Crowther, Rob Rachowiecki and Krzysztof Dydynski. LP also has travel survival kits for Ecuador & the Galápagos Islands, Peru, Colombia, Bolivia, Brazil, and Chile & Easter Island as well as a new phrasebook, *Latin American Spanish*.

If you're planning on doing some trekking, or even some short walks, you should take along LP's *Trekking in the Patagonian Andes* by Clem Lindenmayer, which is a detailed guide, including contour maps, for 24 walks in Chilean and Argentine Patagonia.

Since the 1920s *The South American Handbook* (Trade and Travel Publications, Bath, UK), now edited by Ben Box and updated annually, has been the standard guide to the continent. Its encyclopedic comprehensiveness and observant humour make it great armchair reading even though you can never visit every obscure destination it details. It appeals to travellers of every kind, but unfortunately and unavoidably, the area covered is so large that many sections are quickly outdated – some phrases persist that were written more than half a century ago. Since 1991, it no longer includes Mexico and Central America, which are now covered in a separate volume.

The *APA Insight Guides* series has volumes on Buenos Aires and Argentina which are excellent in cultural and historical analysis, with outstanding photographs, but weak on the nuts-and-bolts of everyday travel. The Argentine guide is marred by many typographical errors.

For Argentina's national parks, do not overlook William Leitch's beautifully written and comprehensive *South America's National Parks* (Seattle, 1990), which is superb on environment and natural history but much weaker on practical aspects of South American travel. Rae Natalie Prosser de Goodall's guidebook *Tierra del Fuego* was due for a new edition in late 1991.

Bookshops

Buenos Aires is a major publishing centre for Latin America and has many excellent bookshops on or near Avenida Corrientes, which is a delightful place to browse. For details, see the chapter on Buenos Aires.

Maps

The Automóvil Club Argentino (ACA), at Avenida del Libertador 1850 in Buenos Aires, publishes maps of the country and each province, which are regularly updated. You may also find them at specialist bookshops like Edward Stanford's in London or in the map rooms of major university libraries. They are not cheap, but they are indispensable for motorists and an excellent investment for any other traveller in Argentina. In most major Argentine cities, ACA has a service centre which sells these maps, although not all of them are equally well stocked.

Tourist offices in Buenos Aires and the provinces stock maps of considerable use to visitors – the province of Neuquén does an exemplary job. These vary in quality but are usually free. For members of the California State Automobile Association (CSAA) and its American Automobile Association (AAA) affiliates, there is a South American road map which is adequate for initial planning. Australian cartographer Kevin Healy's vivid three-sheet *South America* (ITM, Vancouver) is packed with information but not really suitable for taking along on a trip.

For topographic maps, the best source is the Instituto Geografico Militar, at Cabildo 381, reached by bus No 152 and open from 8 am to 1 pm.

MEDIA

Argentina is the most literate country in South America, supporting a wide spectrum of newspapers, magazines and book publishers despite its unceasing economic crisis. In recent years, the end of government monopoly in the electronic media has opened up the airwaves to a greater variety of programming than in the past. Argentine cinema does a great deal with limited resources.

Newspapers & Magazines

Both in the federal capital and the provinces, there is a thriving daily press with unambig-

uous political tendencies. The most important Porteño dailies are the venerable *La Prensa* and *La Nación* (the latter founded by President Bartolomé Mitre) and the middle-of-the-road tabloid *Clarín*, which has an excellent Sunday cultural section. *Página 12*, which does not publish on Mondays, provides a refreshing, intelligent leftist perspective and often breaks important stories which mainstream newspapers are slow to cover. Although not doctrinaire, it often succumbs to irritating, self-indulgent cleverness: continual references to President Menem's one-time economy minister as 'Sup-Erman González' quickly grew tiresome.

The English language daily *Buenos Aires Herald* covers Argentina and the world from an Anglo-Argentine perspective, with emphasis on business and commerce, but its perceptive weekend summaries of political and economic developments are a must for visitors with limited Spanish. It also has a well-deserved reputation for editorial boldness – during the Dirty War of the late 70s and early 80s, the *Herald* was so outspoken in condemning military and police abuses that its editor had to go into exile because of threats against himself and his family.

Ambito Financiero is the daily voice of Argentina's business community, centred around the Calle San Martín in Buenos Aires. *El Cronista Comercial* is its afternoon rival.

Magazines like *El Porteño* offer a forum for Argentine intellectuals and contribute greatly to the cultural life of the capital and the country. The monthly *Humor* caricatured the Argentine military during the Dirty War and even during the early nationalist hysteria of the Falklands conflict; in safer times, it has lost much of its edge, but is still worth reading. Avoid its soft-porn spinoff *Humor Sexo*.

Radio & TV

The most popular station, the nationwide Radio Rivadavia, is a combination of top 40 and talk radio, but there are many others on the AM band. In Buenos Aires, at least a dozen FM stations specialise in styles from classical to pop to tango.

Legalisation of nonstate television and the cable revolution have brought a wider variety of programming to the small screen. To be sure, there are countless game shows, dance parties and soap-opera drivel (novelas), but there is also serious public affairs programming on major stations at prime viewing times such as Sunday evening. Foreigners can tune in to CNN for news and ESPN for sports. Spanish and Chilean stations are also available.

FILM & PHOTOGRAPHY

The latest in consumer electronics is available in Argentina, but import duties make cameras and film very expensive, up to three times their cost in North America or Western Europe – one shop in Río Gallegos wanted US$20 for a lens cap which costs less than US$5 in the States. Developing is equally expensive. Bring as much film as you can; you can always sell anything you don't need to other travellers. Locally manufactured film is reasonably good, but no cheaper than imported.

Colour slide film can be purchased cheaply in Asunción, Paraguay, or in the free zones at Iquique and Punta Arenas, Chile. These are also good places to replace lost or stolen camera equipment, as prices are only slightly higher than in North America, even if the selection is not so great.

HEALTH

In general, Argentina presents few serious health hazards, although a few cases of cholera were reported after the major 1991 outbreak in Peru. For latest details, contact your country's consulate in Buenos Aires.

Travel Health Guides

For basic health information when travelling, a good source is Dr Richard Dawood's *Travellers' Health: How to Stay Healthy Abroad* (Oxford, 1989). Hilary Bradt and John Pilkington's *Backpacking in Chile and Argentina* (Bradt Enterprises, 1980) has a good section on the hazards of hiking and camping in the Southern Cone countries.

Predeparture Preparations

Argentina requires no vaccinations for entry from any country, but if you are visiting neighbouring tropical countries you should consider prophylaxis against typhoid, malaria and other diseases. Although it is better to leave home with a healthy mouth, Argentine dentists are excellent, especially in Buenos Aires. If the US dollar is strong against the peso, dental work can be an excellent bargain.

Health Insurance Relatively small costs can pay great benefits if you get sick. Look for a policy which will pay your return costs and reimburse you for your lost air tickets and other fixed expenses. Some policies exclude 'dangerous activities' such as trekking, skiing or mountain-climbing. Make sure your policy covers these activities if they're on your agenda.

Medical Kit All standard medications are available in well-stocked pharmacies. Many common prescription drugs can be purchased legally over-the-counter in Argentina. A possible kit list includes:

1. Aspirin or Panadol – for pain or fever.
2. Antihistamine (such as Benadryl) – useful as a decongestant for colds, allergies, to ease the itch from insect bites or stings or to help prevent motion sickness.
3. Antibiotics – useful if you're travelling well off the beaten track, but they must be prescribed and you should carry the prescription with you.
4. Kaolin preparation (Pepto-Bismol), Imodium or Lomotil – for stomach upsets.
5. Rehydration mixture – for treatment of severe diarrhoea, this is particularly important if travelling with children.
6. Antiseptic, mercurochrome and antibiotic powder or similar 'dry' spray – for cuts and grazes.
7. Calamine lotion – to ease irritation from bites or stings.
8. Bandages and Band-aids – for minor injuries.
9. Scissors, tweezers and a thermometer (note that mercury thermometers are prohibited by airlines).
10. Insect repellent, sunscreen, suntan lotion, chap stick and water purification tablets.

Basic Rules & Precautions
Food & Water North Americans, Europeans and Australasians who are not vegetarians will find Argentine food relatively bland and easy on the stomach. Salad greens and other fresh vegetables are safe to eat in virtually every part of the country. Although the aging water supply system of Buenos Aires has recently come under scrutiny for its chemical content, there is almost no danger of dysentery or similar ailments. In remote rural areas, where latrines may be close to wells, one should exercise caution. One geographical area of concern is the 'Impenetrable' of the central Chaco, north of Roque Sáenz Peña.

Medical Problems & Treatment
Altitude Sickness From the passes between Mendoza and Chile northwards to the Bolivian border, altitude sickness *(apunamiento* or *soroche)* represents a potential health hazard. In the thinner atmosphere above 3000 metres or even lower in some cases, look of oxygen causes many individuals to suffer headaches, nausea, shortness of breath, physical weakness and other symptoms which can lead to very serious consequences, especially if combined with heat exhaustion, sunburn or hypothermia.

Most people recover within a few hours or days as their body produces more red blood cells to absorb oxygen, but if the symptoms persist it is imperative to descend to lower elevations. For mild cases, everyday pain killers such as aspirin or *chachacoma*, an herbal tea made from a common Andean shrub, will relieve symptoms until your body adapts. In the Andean North-West, coca leaves are a common remedy, but authorities strongly frown upon their usage even by native peoples, who sell them surreptitiously in the markets of Jujuy, Salta and other towns. You should avoid smoking, drinking alcohol, eating heavily or exercising strenuously.

Cholera Although Argentina, Uruguay and Paraguay so far have been largely untouched by the cholera epidemic that has swept Peru and other South American countries, there's no reason to be complacent. In March 1992, an Aerolíneas Argentinas plane travelling from Buenos Aires to Los Angeles took contaminated food on board at the stopover in Lima, resulting in a serious cholera outbreak among the passengers. So far, the disease has not appeared among the general population of these three countries, but it would be wise to take minimum precautions.

The disease is characterised by a sudden onset of acute diarrhoea with 'rice water' stools, vomiting, muscular cramps and extreme weakness. Seek medical help fast - and treat for dehydration, which can be extreme. If there is an appreciable delay in getting to hospital then begin taking tetracycline (one 250 mg capsule four times daily for adults, ⅓ to ½ this dosage for childen).

While there is a vaccine for cholera it is not very effective, and is not required as a condition of entry to any country in the world.

Heat Exhaustion & Sunburn Although Argentina is mostly a temperate country, its northern provinces lie within the Tropic of Capricorn and the sun's direct rays and heat can be devastating, especially at high altitudes. In the western Chaco and other desert regions, where summer temperatures can exceed 40°C, dehydration is a very serious problem. Drink plenty of liquids and cover exposed parts of your body with light cotton clothing. Salt tablets, quality sunglasses, and a Panama hat or baseball cap are all excellent ideas.

Hypothermia At high altitudes in the mountains or high latitudes in Patagonia, cold and wet can kill. Changeable weather can leave you vulnerable to exposure: after dark, temperatures can drop from balmy to below freezing, while a sudden soaking and high winds can lower your own body temperature so rapidly that you may not survive. Disorientation, physical exhaustion, hunger, shivering and related symptoms are warnings that you should seek warmth, shelter and food. If possible, avoid travelling alone; partners are more likely to avoid hypothermia successfully. If you must travel alone, especially when hiking, be sure someone knows your route and when you expect to return.

Seek shelter when bad weather is unavoidable. Woollen clothing and synthetics, which retain warmth even when wet, are superior to cottons. A quality sleeping bag is a worthwhile investment, although goose down loses much of its insulating qualities when wet. Carry high-energy, easily digestible snacks such as chocolate or dried fruit, both of which are readily available in Argentina.

Sexually Transmitted Diseases Sexual contact with an infected sexual partner spreads these diseases. While abstinence is the only 100% preventative, using condoms is also effective. Gonorrhoea and syphilis are the most common of these diseases; sores, blisters or rashes around the genitals, discharges or pain when urinating are common symptoms. Symptoms may be less marked or not observed at all in women. Syphilis symptoms eventually disappear completely but the disease continues and can cause severe problems in later years. The treatment of gonorrhoea and syphilis is by antibiotics.

There are numerous other sexually transmitted diseases, for most of which effective treatment is available. However, there is no cure for herpes, and there is also currently no cure for AIDS. Using condoms is the most effective preventative. AIDS can also be spread by dirty needles – vaccinations, acupuncture and tattooing can potentially be as dangerous as intravenous drug use if the equipment is not clean. If you do need an injection it may be a good idea to buy a new syringe from a pharmacy and ask the doctor to use it.

AIDS certainly exists in Argentina, Uruguay and Paraguay, but it is not (yet) the disaster that it is in Brazil. Paraguay may be more under threat in the long term due to its large Brazilian population, but AIDS is not a major worry at present.

Women's Health
Gynaecological Problems Poor diet, lowered resistance due to the use of antibiotics for stomach upsets and even contraceptive pills can lead to vaginal infections when travelling in hot climates. Keeping the genital area clean, and wearing skirts or loose-fitting trousers and cotton underwear will help to prevent infections.

Yeast infections, characterised by a rash, itch and discharge, can be treated with a vinegar or even lemon-juice douche or with yoghurt. Nystatin suppositories are the usual medical prescription. Trichomonas is a more serious infection; symptoms are a discharge and a burning sensation when urinating. Male sexual partners must also be treated, and if a vinegar-water douche is not effective medical attention should be sought. Flagyl is the prescribed drug.

Pregnancy Most miscarriages occur during the first three months of pregnancy, so this is the most risky time to travel. The last three months should also be spent within reasonable distance of good medical care, as quite serious problems can develop at this time. Pregnant women should avoid all unnecessary medication, but vaccinations and malarial prophylactics should still be taken where possible. Additional care should be taken to prevent illness and particular attention should be paid to diet and nutrition.

WOMEN TRAVELLERS

For women travelling alone, Argentina is safer than Europe, the USA and most other Latin American countries, although you should not be complacent. Buenos Aires is more notorious than the provinces for annoyances such as unwelcome physical contact, particularly on crowded buses or trains. If you're physically confident, a slap or a well-aimed elbow should discourage any further contact. If not, try a scream, also very effective.

Other nuisances include vulgar language and *piropos*. Vulgar language, generally in the presence of other males, usually emphasises feminine physical attributes. If you respond aggressively ('Are you talking to me?'), you will probably put your aggressor to shame.

There is no good definition of the piropo, but most Argentine males would consider it the masculine art of approaching a woman, in public, commenting on her femininity or attractiveness. This is an idealised definition, because even though some are creative and even eloquent, piropos are most often vulgar. While irritating, such verbal aggression rarely becomes physical. On those occasions when persistent suitors trail you for blocks, the best means of discouraging their pursuit is to completely ignore them.

Single women checking in at low-budget hotels, both in Buenos Aires and the provinces, may find themselves objects of suspicion, since prostitutes often frequent such places. If you otherwise like the place, ignore this and it will evaporate. In the provinces, women travelling alone are objects of curiosity, since Argentine women generally do not travel alone. You should interpret questions as to whether you are running away from parents or husband as expressions of concern.

If you hitchhike, exercise judgment, but do avoid getting into a vehicle with more than one man. Argentine males will rarely find it necessary to demonstrate their machismo except in the company of other males.

DANGERS & ANNOYANCES

Although street crime appears to be increasing in Argentina, personal security is a minor problem compared with most other South American countries or with cities like New York or Washington DC. Violent crime is rare in Buenos Aires, and both men or women can travel in most parts of the city at any time of day or night without excessive apprehension. Take precautions against petty theft, such as purse snatching, especially on slow-moving trains, where thieves may grab your purse, run through the aisle and jump off while the train is still in motion. Temperley Station, in the suburbs of Buenos Aires, has a particularly bad reputation.

The police and military may be of more concern than common criminals. For motorists, frequent safety campaigns result in harassment for very minor equipment violations which carry very high fines – up to US$200 for an inadequate handbrake. In most cases, corrupt officers will settle for less expensive *coimas* (bribes), but this requires considerable caution and diplomacy on your part. A discreet hint that you intend to phone your consulate may limit or eliminate such problems – often the police depend on foreigners' ignorance of Argentine law. For further information, see the section on Driving in the Getting Around chapter.

The military retain considerable influence even under civilian government. Avoid approaching military installations, which often display the warning, 'No stopping or photographs – the sentry will shoot'. In event of a military coup or other emergency, state-of-siege regulations suspend all civil rights; carry identification at all times, and make sure someone knows your whereabouts. Contact your embassy or consulate for advice.

WORK

It is not unusual for visiting travellers to work as English-language instructors in Buenos Aires, but wages are much lower than they would be in the United States. Check the classified section of the *Buenos Aires Herald*. Residence and work permits are fairly easy to obtain, but the effort may not be worth it. Travellers can obtain work during the fruit harvests in areas like Río Negro valley and El Bolsón in Patagonia, but should not expect to do much more than break even.

Ideally, in Argentina and the rest of Latin America, there should be work for someone who can mend the fractured English which so often appears in brochure translations.

ACTIVITIES

Argentines are very fond of a variety of sports, both as participants and spectators, but the most widespread is soccer. In the villas miserias (shantytowns), children will clear a vacant lot, mark the goal with stones, and make a ball of old rags and socks to pursue their pastime, but even in exclusive country clubs the sport is popular. Argentine professional soccer is world-class, although many of the best athletes play in Europe because salaries are much higher. In 1978 and 1986, Argentina won the World Cup.

Other popular sports include tennis, basketball, auto racing, cycling, rugby, field hockey and polo. Some of these, especially rugby and polo, are confined to elite sectors. Skiing, although expensive, is gaining in popularity, as are other recreational activities like canoeing, climbing, kayaking, trekking, windsurfing and hang-gliding. Recently, paddle-ball has gained major popularity, with courts springing up around the country.

For the more sedate pastime of learning Spanish, there are many schools in Buenos Aires. See the Buenos Aires chapter for details.

Skiing

Although surprisingly little known to outsiders, Argentina offers some of the best skiing in the world. Most locations offer superb powder, good cover, plenty of sunny days and above all, cheap prices. Many fields are near large towns, so you don't even need to stay on the mountain, but can stay cheaply nearby. Many resorts have large ski schools with instructors from all over the world, so even language is not a problem. At some of the older resorts equipment can be a little antiquated, but in general the quality of skiing available more than makes up for it.

There are basically three areas in which ski fans can indulge themselves: the Mendoza region, featuring Las Leñas and Los Molles near Malargüe; the Lakes District, including the famous resort Bariloche with its Cerro Catedral complex, and Chapelco near San Martín de los Andes; and the most southerly commercial skiing in the world in Tierra del Fuego.

For more details, refer to the relevant chapters in this book. Ski tours can be booked through Aerolíneas Argentinas or with travel agents, especially adventure tour specialists; see the Getting There & Away chapter.

Trekking

Wilderness walks are very popular for both Argentines and foreigners alike, and there are plenty of vast, beautiful places to choose from. The most popular areas are the southern Andes, and the Andes west of Mendoza, both areas being on the border with Chile. The northern Andes around Valle de Humahuaca are also good, and plenty of Argentines enjoy the Sierras de Córdoba, and the Sierra de la Ventana in Buenos Aires province.

See the LP guide *Trekking in the Patagonian Andes* by Clem Lindenmayer for more information on southern Andean walks.

Climbing

Aconcagua, west of Mendoza, is naturally a magnet for climbers, but there are plenty of other huge peaks available in the Andes. The Fitzroy Range in Parque Nacional Los Glaciares, Santa Cruz province, is another popular destination, as are the mountains around Bariloche. The Sierra de la Ventana is a good area for technical climbing.

HIGHLIGHTS

For most visitors from overseas, Argentina's principal attractions will be of two utterly contradictory kinds: the sprawling capital of Buenos Aires, renowned for its European sophistication and the romantic image of the tango, and the country's awesome natural attractions like the Iguazú Falls of Misiones and the Moreno Glacier of Santa Cruz. The gaucho of the Pampas, a cultural icon and modern anachronism, is another enduring image, but Argentina has many other appealing features: the canyons of the Andean North-West, the fish-rich rivers of Mesopotamia and Patagonia, the soaring volcanos of the Andes and the Lake District, the unique wildlife of the Patagonian coast and the wild alpine scenery of Tierra del Fuego. Even the barren Patagonian steppes exercise a powerful hold on the imagination.

There are other cultural attractions: the

Indian peoples and the colonial Andean churches of the North-West, the monumental cathedrals of Luján and Córdoba, and the more offbeat appeal of features like the Difunta Correa memorial in San Juan province. Some of the country's most intriguing attributes are in its most remote corners.

ACCOMMODATION

The spectrum of accommodation in Argentina ranges from campgrounds to five-star luxury hotels. Where you stay will depend on your budget and your standards, where you are, and how thorough a search you care to make in an unfamiliar destination, but you should be able to find something reasonable by North American, European or Australian standards. You may also find yourself invited into Argentine homes, and should not hesitate to accept under most conditions. The remainder of this section details the alternatives from cheapest to costliest.

Camping & Refugios

If you're travelling on a budget, especially coming overland from the central Andean countries, you should not dismiss the idea of camping in Argentina – by doing so, you may be able to keep your expenses for accommodation at roughly what you have paid for hotels in Bolivia or Peru. Nearly every Argentine city and many smaller towns have municipal (or recently privatised) campgrounds where you can pitch a tent for about US$2 per night (most Argentines arrive in their own automobiles, but backpackers are welcome). These usually woodsy sites have excellent facilities – hot showers, toilets and laundry, a firepit for cooking, restaurant or confitería, a grocery, some even have swimming pools – and are often very central. In the city of Tucumán, for example, the municipal site in the Parque 9 de Julio is an easy 10 to 15-minute walk from the central plaza.

Although you should not tempt anyone unnecessarily by leaving around costly items such as cameras or cash, your personal possessions are generally secure; neither of us knows of anybody who has had anything stolen while camping, since attendants keep a watchful eye on the grounds.

There are drawbacks, though. Argentines are renowned *trasnochadores* ('night people'. During summer vacations, it is not unusual for them to celebrate their *asado* (barbecue) until almost daylight, so in extreme cases you may find sleep difficult unless you can isolate yourself on the margins of the campground. On the other hand, you may wish to join in with one of these gregarious groups. Otherwise, avoid the most popular tourist areas in the prime vacation months of January and February.

For comfort, invest in a good, dome-style tent with rainfly before you come to South America, where camping equipment is costly and inferior. A three-season sleeping bag should be adequate for almost any weather conditions you are likely to encounter. A good petrol or kerosene-burning stove is also a good idea, since white gas *(bencina)* is expensive and available only at chemical supply shops or hardware stores. Firewood is a limited and often expensive resource which, in any event, smudges your pots and pans. Bring or buy mosquito repellent, since many campsites are near rivers or lakes.

There are, of course, opportunities for more rugged camping in the national parks and their backcountry. Parks have both organised sites which resemble the ones in the cities and towns and more isolated, rustic alternatives. Some parks have *refugios*, which are basic shelters for hikers in the high country. For details, see the entries under the respective national parks.

Hostels

Sponsored by UNESCO, the non-profit Asociación Argentina de Albergues de la Juventud (☎ 451001) is at 2nd floor, Talcahuano 214, Buenos Aires. It's open weekdays from 11 am to 7 pm. There are youth hostels in Buenos Aires, Mar del Plata, San Fernando, Villa Gesell, Sierra de la Ventana, several in Córdoba province, Puerto Iguazú, Mendoza, Humahuaca, Calafate, Lago Puelo and Bariloche, but generally these are open in summer only. Most do not insist on a youth hostel card, but contact the association for more information.

Casas de Familia

During the tourist season, mostly in the interior, families rent rooms to visitors. Often these are excellent bargains, permitting access to cooking and laundry facilities, hot showers, and encouraging contact with Argentine hospitality. Tourist offices in most smaller towns, but even in cities as large as Salta or Mendoza, maintain lists of such accommodation.

Hospedajes, Pensiones & Residenciales

These offer cheap accommodation but the differences between them are sometimes ambiguous. Often all of them are called hotels. An *hospedaje* is usually a large family home which has a few extra bedrooms for guests (the bath is shared). Often they are not permanent businesses but temporary expedients in times of economic distress.

Similarly, a *pensión* offers short-term accommodation in a family home, but may also have permanent lodgers. Meals are sometimes available. *Residenciales*, which are permanent businesses, more commonly figure in tourist office lists. In general, they occupy buildings designed for short-stay accommodation, although some cater to clientele who intend only *very* short stays, say two hours or so. Occasionally prostitutes frequent them, but so do young Argentine couples with no other indoor alternative for their passion. Except for a little noise, such activities should not deter you, even if you have children.

Room and their furnishings are modest, usually including beds with clean sheets and blankets. Never hesitate to ask to see a room. While some have private bathrooms, more often you will share toilet and shower facilities with other guests.

Hotels

Hotels proper vary from one-star basic accommodation to five-star luxury, but you should not assume perfect correlation between these classifications and their standards. Many one-star places are better value than three-star and four-star lodgings. In general, hotels will provide a room with attached private bath, often a telephone, sometimes *música funcional* (elevator Muzak) or television. Normally they will have a *confitería* or restaurant; breakfast may be included in the price. In the top categories you will have room and laundry service, swimming pools, bar, shopping galleries and other luxuries.

Rental

House and apartment rentals can save money if you're staying in a place for an extended period. In resort locations, such as Mar del Plata, Bariloche or Paso de la Patria, you can lodge several people for the price of one by seeking an apartment and cooking your own meals. Check the tourist office or the newspapers for listings.

FOOD

Ever since Spanish livestock transformed the Pampas into enormous cattle ranches, Argentine cuisine has been renowned for its meat, but there is more ethnic and regional variety to Argentine food than most people expect. Most people will quickly recognise the influence of Italian immigrants in such pasta dishes as spaghetti, lasagna, canelloni and ravioli, but should not overlook the tasty *ñoquis* (gnocchi in Italian), an inexpensive staple when the budget runs low at the end of the month. Traditionally, ñoquis are a restaurant special on the 29th of each month, but in times of economic crisis people may joke that 'this month we'll have ñoquis on the 15th'.

Beef, though, is the focus of the diet; no meal is truly complete without it. In Argentina, the Spanish word *carne* (meat) is synonymous with beef – lamb, venison and poultry are all called something else. The most popular form is the *parrillada*, a mixed grill of steak and other cuts which no visiting carnivore should miss. A traditional parrillada will include offal such as *chinchulines* (small intestines), *tripa gorda* (large intestine), *ubre* (udder), *riñones*

A	B
C	D
E	F

A: Parque Provincial Talampaya
B: Guanacos
C: Flower, Parque Nacional Lanín
D: Parque Nacional Lanín
E: Children, Humahuaca
F: Gaucho, Chaco

A	B
C	D
E	F

A: King penguins, Saunders Island
B: Lago Cisne, Parque Nacional
   Los Alcerces
C: Quechua market seller
D: Hikers, Tierra del Fuego
E: Colonial governor, Stanley
F: Southern elephant seal

(kidneys), and *morcilla* (blood sausage), but don't let that put you off unless you're a vegetarian.

Since the early 1980s, health food and vegetarian fare have acquired a niche in the diets of some Argentines, but outside Buenos Aires and a few other large cities vegetarian restaurants are still uncommon. You will find Chinese food in the capital but not often outside; the quality is not outstanding but some offer *tenedor libre* ('all you can eat' for those on a budget. High cost and quality international cuisine is readily available if your budget is unlimited.

Some regions have very distinctive food. The Andean North-West is notable for spicy dishes, more closely resembling the food of the central Andean highlands than the bland fare of the Pampas. From Mendoza north, it is common to find Middle Eastern food. Argentine seafood, while not as varied as Chilean, deserves attention, even though Argentines are not big fish-eaters. In the Patagonian Lake District, game dishes such as trout, boar and venison are regional specialities, while river fish in Mesopotamia and the North-East are outstanding. In the extreme south, where wool and mutton are important commodities, lamb often replaces beef in the typical asado.

Places to Eat & Drink

There are different kinds of eating places in Argentina. If you're on a very low budget in the northern provinces, you may want to frequent the markets, where meals are often very cheap, but otherwise try the *rotiserías* (delis), which sell dairy products, roast chicken, pies, turnovers, and *fiambres* (processed meats). Such places often have restaurant-quality food for a fraction of the price.

Avoid fast-food clones such as *Pumper Nic*, which are neither as cheap nor even as good as their American cousins. For fast food, try bus or train terminal cafeterias or the common *comedor*, which usually has a limited menu, often including simple but filling fixed-price meals. Comedores also often serve *minutas* (short orders) such as

steak, eggs, *milanesa* (breaded steak), salad, and chips.

Confiterías serve mostly sandwiches, including *lomito* (steak), *panchos* (hot dogs) and hamburgers. *Restaurantes* are distinguished by their much larger menus – including pasta, parrillada, and fish – professional waiters, and often more elaborate decor. There is, though, a great difference between the most humble and the most extravagant.

Cafés & Bars

Cafés are the most important gathering places throughout Argentina. Everything from marriage proposals to business transactions to revolutions are born in them. Many Argentines spend hours on end over a single cup of coffee, although simple food orders are also available. Cafés also serve alcohol – beer, wine and hard liquor.

Bars are establishments where people go to drink alcohol. In large cities, gentrified bars may be called pubs, pronounced as in English. In small towns, bars are a male domain and the few women who go to them are likely to be prostitutes.

Breakfast

Argentines eat little or no breakfast. Most common is coffee, tea or yerba *mate* with *tostadas* (toast), *manteca* (butter) and *mermelada* (jam). In cafés, *medialunas* (small croissants), either sweet or *saladas* (plain) accompany your *café con leche* (coffee with milk). A midmorning breakfast may consist of coffee plus a *tostado*, a thin-crust toasted sandwich with ham and cheese, and a glass of fresh-squeezed orange juice.

Snacks

One of the world's finest snacks is the empanada, a tasty turnover filled with vegetables, hard-boiled egg, olive, beef, chicken, ham and cheese or other filling. These are cheap and available almost everywhere – buy them by the dozen in a rotisería before a long bus or train trip. Empanadas *al horno* (baked) are lighter than empanadas *fritas* (fried). Travellers coming from Chile will find Argentine empanadas very different.

Argentine pizza, a common snack in Argentine markets and restaurants, is one of the cheapest things you can find when purchased by the slice. In many pizzerías, it is cheaper to eat standing up at the counter than to take a seat. Toppings are standardised – not customised as in North America – but there are more options when buying an entire pizza rather than slices. For slices, try especially *fugazza*, a delicious cheeseless variety with sweet onions which is very cheap, or *fugazzeta*, which adds cheese. Mozzarella is the most popular cheese. Many Argentines eat their pizza with *fainá*, a dense chickpea (garbanzo) dough baked and sliced to match.

For Argentines at home or on the road, a common afternoon snack is *mate con facturas*, *mate* with sweet pastries. If you go to visit an Argentine family in the afternoon, stop by the bakery to bring some along.

Main Dishes

Argentines compensate for skimpy breakfasts with enormous lunches, usually begun about noon, and dinners, never earlier than 9 pm and often much later. Beef, in a variety of cuts and styles of preparation, is the most common main course.

An asado or parrillada (see above) is the standard, ideally prepared over charcoal or a wood fire and accompanied by *chimichurri*, a tasty marinade. Chips or salad will usually accompany it. Serious carnivores should not miss *bife de chorizo*, a thick, tender, juicy steak. *Bife de lomo* is short loin, *bife de costilla* or *chuleta* is T-bone steak, while *asado de tira* is a narrow strip of roast rib. *Vacío* is sirloin. *Matambre relleno* is stuffed and rolled flank steak, eaten cold as an appetizer or baked. Thinly sliced, it makes excellent sandwiches and is usually available at rotiserías.

Most Argentines like their beef *cocido* (well done), but on request restaurants will serve it *jugoso* (rare) or *a punto* (medium). *Bife a caballo* comes with two eggs and chips.

Carbonada is a beef stew with rice, potat-oes, sweet potatoes, maize, squash, chopped apples and peaches. *Puchero* is a slow-cooking casserole with beef, chicken, bacon, sausage, blood sausage, maize, peppers, tomatoes, onions, cabbage, sweet potatos, and squash. Sometimes the cook adds garbanzos or other beans. It is accompanied by rice cooked in the broth. *Milanesa*, a breaded steak usually fried but sometimes baked, is one of the cheapest and commonest short order items on the menu. The North American author is sick of it, but more elaborate versions are available – *milanesa napolitana* with tomato sauce and mozzarella, and *milanesa maryland*, made with chicken and accompanied by fried bananas and creamed corn.

Chicken dishes are good. *Pollo* sometimes accompanies the standard parrillada, but also comes separately with chips or salad. The most common fish is *merluza* (hake), usually fried in batter and served with mashed potatos. Spanish restaurants are good for well-prepared seafood.

Desserts

Fresh fruit is the most common *postre* in Argentine homes, where uncouth Americans and Australians will find that cultured Argentines peel their oranges and other fruit carefully with a knife. In restaurants, *ensalada de fruta* (fruit salad), *flan* (egg custard) or *queso y dulce* (cheese with preserved fruit, sometimes known as *postre vigilante* are frequent choices. The 'dulce' can be made of *batata* (sweet potato) or *membrillo* (quince). Flan will be topped with *crema* (whipped cream) or *dulce de leche*, a caramelised milk which is an Argentine invention. *Almendrado*, vanilla ice cream rolled with almonds, is also common. For more on ice cream, see below.

Ice Cream

Argentine *helado* (ice cream) deserves special mention. Coming from an Italian tradition, it is the best in South America and comparable to the best in the United States. Chains like *Massera*, found throughout the country, are not bad, but you will find the best Argentine ice cream at smaller *heladerías* which make their own in small batches on the premises or nearby – look for the words *elaboración propia* or *elaboración artesanal*. Often such places have many dozens of flavours, from variations on conventional vanilla and chocolate to common and exotic fruits and unexpected mixtures. Rarely will Argentine ice cream disappoint you, but only truly special shops are mentioned in the text.

DRINKS

Argentines consume a great variety of liquids, both nonalcoholic and alcoholic. Most famously Argentine is *mate*, a cultural bellwether described in detail below.

There are few drinking restrictions of any kind, although legally you must be 18 years old to drink alcohol in public.

Soft Drinks

Argentines drink prodigious amounts of soft drinks, from the ubiquitous Coca Cola to Seven-Up to the local tonic water, Paso de los Toros, which is probably your best choice. Mineral water, both carbonated *(con gas)* and plain *(sin gas)* is widely available, but tap water is potable almost everywhere. If there is no carbonated mineral water, ask for *soda*, which in small-town bars comes in large bottles with siphons. Soda is usually the cheapest thirst-quencher.

Fruit Juices & Licuados

Jugos are not so varied as in tropical South America. For fresh-squeezed orange juice, ask for *jugo de naranja exprimido* – otherwise you may get tinned juice. Oranges are extremely cheap in Argentina but, turned into fresh juice, miraculously increase their value tenfold. *Pomelo* (grapefruit), *limón* (lemon) and *ananá* (pineapple) are also common. *Jugo de manzana* (apple juice) is a speciality of the Río Negro region of Patagonia but available everywhere.

Licuados are milk-blended fruit drinks, but on request can be made with water. Common flavours are banana, *durazno* (peach), and *pera* (pear).

Coffee, Tea & Chocolate

Serious coffee drinkers will be delighted to find that even in the smallest town, your coffee will be an espresso (accompanied by enough packets of sugar to fuel a Brazilian Volkswagen). *Café chico* is a thick, dark coffee served in a very small cup. *Cortado* is a small coffee with a touch of milk, usually served in a glass – for a larger portion ask for *cortado doble*. *Café con leche (a latte)*, is similar but contains more milk, and is served for breakfast. Don't make the mistake of ordering it after lunch or dinner in a restaurant, when you should request a cortado.

Tea, produced domestically in the provinces of Corrientes and Misiones, is also a common drink. Usually it comes with lemon slices, but if you drink it with milk, do not order *té con leche*, which is a tea bag immersed in warm milk. Rather, ask the waiter for *un poquito de leche*.

Argentine chocolate can be delicious. For breakfast, try a *submarino*, a semisweet chocolate bar which dissolves in a glass of steamed milk. Prices vary greatly. Even *chocolate*, made with powdered cocoa, can be surprisingly good, especially in Bariloche.

Alcohol

Argentina's beer, wine, whiskey and gin should satisfy most visitors' alcoholic thirst, but don't refrain from trying *ginebra bols* (which differs from gin) and *caña* (cane alcohol), which are national specialities.

Quilmes, brewed in the Buenos Aires suburb but available everywhere, is an excellent beer. Bieckert is another popular brand. In bars or cafés, ask for the excellent *chopp* (draught or lager).

Argentine wines get less publicity abroad than Chilean ones, but they are not inferior. Reds *(tintos)* and whites *(blancos)* are both excellent. Especially at home, where jug wines are consumed at almost all meals, Argentines often mix their wine with soda water. When the prices on almost everything else skyrocket, wines miraculously remain reasonable. Often a bottle of good wine is cheaper than a litre of Coca Cola.

The major wine-producing areas are near Mendoza, San Juan, La Rioja and Salta. Wineries offer tours and tasting. Among the best known brands are Viñas de Orfila, Suter, San Felipe, Santa Ana and Etchart. Try to avoid cheap, boxed wines such as Termidor.

Mate

No other trait captures the essence of *argentinidad* ('argentinity') as well as the preparation and consumption of *mate* (pronounced 'mah-tay'), perhaps the only cultural practice which transcends barriers of ethnicity, class, and occupation. More than a simple drink like tea or coffee, *mate* is an elaborate ritual, shared among family, friends, and co-workers. In many ways, sharing is the point of *mate*.

Yerba mate is the dried, chopped leaf of *Ilex paraguayensis*, a wild relative of the common holly. Also known as 'Paraguayan tea', it became commercially important in the colonial era on the plantations of the Jesuit missions of the upper Río Paraná. Europeans quickly took to the beverage, crediting it with many admirable qualities. The Austrian Jesuit Martin Dobrizhoffer wrote that *mate*

provokes a gentle perspiration, improves the appetite, speedily counteracts the languor arising from the burning climate, and assuages both hunger and thirst...

Unlike many American foods and beverages, though, *mate* failed to make the trip back to Europe. After the Jesuits' expulsion in 1767 production declined, but since the early 20th century it has increased dramatically.

Argentina is the world's largest producer and consumer of *yerba mate*. Argentines consume an average of five kg per person per year, more than four times their average intake of coffee, although Uruguayans consume twice as much per capita as Argentines. It is also popular in Chile, southern Brazil and Paraguay.

Preparing *mate* is a ritual in itself. In the past, upper-class families even maintained a slave or servant for the sole purpose of preparing and serving. Nowadays, one person takes responsibility for filling the *mate* (gourd) almost to the top with yerba, heating but not boiling the water in a *pava* (kettle), and pouring it into the vessel. People sip the liquid from a *bombilla*, a silver straw with a bulbous filter at its lower end which prevents the leaves from entering the tube.

Gourds can range from simple calabashes to carved wooden vessels to the ornate silver museum pieces of the 19th century. Bombillas also differ considerably, ranging in materials from inexpensive aluminium to silver and gold with intricate markings, and in design from long straight tubes to short, curved ones.

There is an informal etiquette for drinking *mate*. The *cebador* (server) pours water slowly near the straw to produce a froth as he or she fills the gourd. The gourd then passes clockwise and this order, once established, continues. A good cebador will keep the *mate* going without changing the yerba for some time. Each participant drinks the gourd dry each time. A simple *gracias* will tell the server to pass you by.

There are marked regional differences in drinking *mate*. From the Pampas southwards, Argentines take it *amargo* (without sugar), while to the north they drink it *dulce* (sweet) with sugar and yuyos (aromatic herbs). Purists, who argue that sugar ruins the gourd, will keep separate gourds rather than alternate the two usages. In the withering summer heat, Paraguayans drink *mate* ice-cold in the form of *tereré*.

An invitation to *mate* is a sign of acceptance and should not be refused, even though *mate* is an acquired taste and foreign novices may find it bitter and very hot at first. On the second or third round, both the heat and bitterness will diminish. It is poor etiquette to hold the *mate* too long before passing it on, but it probably will not affect either your health or finances despite Dobrizhoffer's admonition that

by the immoderate and almost hourly use of this potation, the stomach is weakened, and continual flatulence, with other diseases, brought on. I have known many of the lower Spaniards who never spoke ten words without applying their lips to the gourd containing the ready-made tea. If many topers in Europe waste their substance by an immoderate use of wine and other intoxicating liquors, there are no fewer in America who drink away their fortunes in potations of the herb of Paraguay. ∎

ENTERTAINMENT
Cinemas
Traditionally, Argentines jam the cinemas, although outside Buenos Aires the video revolution has brought about the closure of many theatres which once counted on being the only show in town. Still, in the capital and larger cities, major theatres offer the latest films from Europe, the United States, and Latin America. Repertory houses, cultural centres and universities provide a chance to see classics or less commercial films you may have missed.

In Buenos Aires, the main cinema districts are along Lavalle, Avenida Corrientes, and Avenida Santa Fe. Prices have risen in recent years, but are still a bit lower than in North America; in midweek, most cinemas offer substantial discounts. On weekends, there are late night showings *(transnoches)* after midnight.

Theatres
Both in Buenos Aires and the provinces, live theatre is well attended and high quality, from the classics and serious drama to burlesque. Avenida Corrientes is Buenos Aires' Broadway or West End, but even in a place like Villa Regina, a small town in Río Negro province, there are several active theatre groups and venues for performances.

Discos
Argentines are fond of music and dancing. Clubs both in Buenos Aires and the provinces open late and close even later – nobody would go before midnight and things don't really jump before 2 am. After sunrise, when discos close, party-goers head to a confitería or home for breakfast before collapsing in their beds. This is nearly as common on weekdays as on weekends.

In the 1970s, clubs were good places to hear live music, but the best rock groups now play in stadiums and theatres instead. Recorded music is now the norm.

Nightclubs
Except in Buenos Aires, where there are good tango and jazz clubs, nightclubs tend to be disreputable places. Places listed in the *Buenos Aires Herald* as nightclubs usually mean the more respectable ones; but in a Spanish context, the word 'nightclub' tends to imply a fairly seedy place with bargirls who are thinly disguised prostitutes. So check out which type you're going to before you go!

Spectator Sports
By far, the most popular spectator sport is soccer. Its British origins are apparent from the names of many of the best teams: Boca Juniors, River Plate, Newell's Old Boys and others. Unfortunately, as in Britain, Argentine soccer has become prone to violence between partisans of opposing teams, even resulting in semi-accidental deaths.

Other popular spectator sports include automobile racing, horse racing, boxing, tennis and, increasingly, basketball. Many North American athletes unable to play professional basketball in the United States or Europe have come to Argentina, improving the quality of play.

THINGS TO BUY
As Argentine food is famous for beef, Argentine clothing is famous for leather. In Buenos Aires, many downtown shops cater to the tourist trade in leather jackets, handbags and shoes. Quality and prices can vary greatly, so shop around before you buy. Shopkeepers are aggressive but sometimes open to bargaining.

Argentines are very fashion-conscious, so if you're interested in the latest styles there is much to choose along Florida and Santa Fe in Buenos Aires and the main shopping streets in cities throughout the country. Bariloche is especially well known for woollen goods. You will find the best prices just before seasonal changes, as shops try to liquidate their inventory. Jewellery is another quality Argentine product, made frequently with 18-carat gold.

Mate paraphernalia make good souvenirs. Gourds and bombillas range from simple and inexpensive aluminium, often sold in street kiosks, to the elaborate and expensive gold and silver from jewellery stores or speciality shops. In the province of Salta, the distinctive *ponchos de Güemes* are a memorable choice.

In artisans' *ferias,* found throughout the country, it is often difficult to choose among a variety of handicrafts. There are good places in Buenos Aires (Plaza Francia), Mendoza, Bariloche and El Bolsón. In the summer, the Atlantic coast has many others.

Since the end of the military dictatorship, Buenos Aires has re-established itself as a publishing centre. Argentines are well read and interested in both national and world literature. Buenos Aires has a superb selection of general and special interest bookshops. Foreign and foreign-language books are very expensive, but there is a good selection at stores such as El Ateneo, including this and other Lonely Planet guides.

Getting There & Away

Argentina offers a multitude of land and river crossing points with the neighbouring countries of Uruguay, Brazil, Paraguay, Bolivia and Chile. All major and some minor connections are detailed below.

Argentina also has excellent air connections from North America, the UK, Europe and Australia/New Zealand to Buenos Aires' Ezeiza International Airport. There are feasible, if costly, routes from southern Africa across the Atlantic via Brazil. Another possibility is to fly to a neighbouring country such as Chile or Brazil and continue overland to Argentina. Be aware that international flights within South America tend to be very costly, unless they are part of a ticket purchased for intercontinental travel. One-way international tickets are usually very expensive.

Some travellers take advantage of Round the World (RTW) fares to visit widely separated countries, say in Asia and South America, on the same trip. One possibility is the Qantas/Aerolíneas Argentinas ticket which lets you circle the globe with stops in New Zealand, Europe and South-East Asia, but similar fares are available on other airlines.

AIR

From almost everywhere, South America is a relatively expensive destination, but discount fares can reduce the bite considerably. There are often significant seasonal discounts, so try to avoid travelling at peak times such as Christmas or New Year. Advance purchase of a ticket for a given period of time, usually less than six months, will usually provide the best and most flexible deal.

Advance Purchase Excursion (Apex) tickets must be bought well before departure, but can be a good deal if you know exactly where you will be going and how long you will be staying. Such tickets have minimum and maximum stay requirements, rarely allow stopovers, and are difficult or impossible to modify without monetary penalties.

Economy class (Y) tickets, valid for 12 months, have the greatest flexibility within their time period. However, if you try to extend beyond a year you'll have to pay the difference of any price increase in the interim period.

Miscellaneous Charges Orders (MCOs) are open vouchers for a fixed dollar amount, which can be exchanged for a ticket on any IATA (International Air Transport Association) airline. In countries that require an onward ticket as a condition for entry, such as Panamá or Colombia, this will usually satisfy immigration authorities. In a pinch, you can turn it into cash at the local offices of the airline from which you purchased it.

If you want to visit widely separate areas in Europe, the Americas and Asia, RTW tickets can be a great bargain. Generally valid for a year, these fares let you make numerous stopovers so long as you continue in the same direction.

For travellers starting in Australia or Argentina, one possibility is the combined ticket offered by Aerolíneas Argentinas and Qantas. Beginning from Sydney or Buenos Aires, you can stop in New Zealand, London, Paris, Bahrain, Singapore and other cities, although you must work out the details in advance. It does not, unfortunately, permit stopovers in North America, but similar fares are available in the United States and Canada. The price for the Aerolíneas/Qantas ticket is A$3569 in Sydney or US$3124 in Buenos Aires. The latter figure represents about 15% more than the former, so it is cheaper to buy in Australia.

Discounts on such fares are often available from travel agents, but usually not in Latin America, where discount ticketing is almost unknown. Standby can be a cheap way of getting from Europe to the United States, but there are no such flights to Argentina or other parts of South America.

Foreigners in Argentina *must* pay for all international air tickets in US dollars rather than local currency. If the new Argentine peso stabilises the economy (as officials hope but probably only fantasise), this could change, but there would then be no advantage in paying in local funds.

To/From the USA

From the USA, the principal gateways to South America are Miami, New York and Los Angeles. Aerolíneas Argentinas is the national carrier, although it has recently been purchased by Iberia. Other airlines which serve Buenos Aires from the United States include American, Avianca, Varig Brazilian, and Lloyd Aéreo Boliviano. Líneas Aéreas Paraguayas has bargain fares for stays up to three months via Miami; United States domestic carriers can make connections.

Most major airlines have ticket 'consolidators' which offer substantial discounts on fares to Latin America, but things change so frequently that even newspaper listings can be out of date within a very short time. Among the best sources of information on cheap tickets are the Sunday travel pages of major American newspapers, such as the *New York Times*, the *Los Angeles Times* or the *San Francisco Examiner*. If you're in a university town, look for bargains in the campus newspaper, such as *The Daily Californian* in Berkeley. There will usually be a listing for the local affiliate of American Student Council Travel or the Student Travel Network.

Student Council Travel The Student Council Travel agencies and the Student Travel Network have a range of interesting, cheap flight possibilities to various destinations, and you don't have to be a student to take advantage of their services. Student Council Travel offices are in the following locations:

Berkeley
    2511 Channing Way (☎ (510) 848-8604)
Boston
    Suite 201, 729 Boylston St (☎ (617) 266-1926)

La Jolla
    UCSD Student Center, B-023 (☎ (619) 452-0630)
Los Angeles
    1093 Broxton Ave (☎ (213) 208-3551)
New York
    205 E 42nd St (☎ (212) 661-1450)
    356 W 34th St (☎ (212) 239-4257)
San Diego
    4429 Cass St (☎ (619) 270-6401)
San Francisco
    312 Sutter St (☎ (415) 421-3473)
Seattle
    1314 NE 43rd St (☎ (206) 632-2448)

Student Travel Network You can find Student Travel Network in the following cities:

Dallas
    6609 Hillcrest Avenue (☎ (915) 360-0097)
Honolulu
    Suite 202, 1831 S King St (☎ (808) 942-7455)
Los Angeles
    Suite 507, 2500 Wilshire Blvd (☎ (213) 380-2184)
San Diego
    6447 El Cajon Blvd (☎ (619) 286-1322)
San Francisco
    Suite 702, 166 Geary St (☎ (415) 391-8407)

To/From Canada

There are direct services from Canada to South America as well as those via the United States. Aerolíneas Argentinas and LAN-Chile serve Montreal, while Aerolíneas Argentinas and Canadian Airlines International fly from Toronto.

Travel Cuts is the Canadian national student travel agency, with offices across the country. You don't need to be a student to make use of their services.

To/From the UK & Europe

Restoration of diplomatic relations between Britain and Argentina has meant resumption of direct air connections, but it is generally cheaper to fly to New York or Miami than to go directly to South America. British Airways and Aerolíneas Argentinas both offer service to Ezeiza. Aerolíneas Argentinas and other carriers serve other European capitals and major airports, including

Madrid, Paris, Rome, Zurich, London, Frankfurt and Amsterdam.

So-called 'bucket shops' in London and Amsterdam can provide some of the best deals. Try Trailfinders (☎ 938-3366) at 46 Earls Court Rd, London W8 or STA Travel at 74 Old Brompton Rd, London SW7 or 117 Euston Rd, London NW1.

To/From Australia & New Zealand

The most direct is Aerolíneas Argentinas' weekly transpolar route from Sydney via Auckland, which is an obvious connection for buyers of the Qantas-Aerolíneas RTW fare. From Argentina, the flight stops in Río Gallegos. Otherwise, LAN-Chile's trans-Pacific flights to Santiago have ready connections to Buenos Aires, but some travellers have found it cheaper to go via London or Los Angeles.

STA Travel STA Travel is a good place to inquire for bargain air fares; you don't need to be a student to make use of their services.

Adelaide
Level 4, the Arcade, Union House, Adelaide University (☎ (08) 223-6620)
Brisbane
Northern Security Building, 40 Creek St (☎ (07) 221-9629)
Canberra
Arts Centre, Australian National University (☎ (06) 470-800)
Hobart
Union Building, University of Tasmania (☎ (002) 233-825)
Melbourne
220 Faraday St, Carlton (☎ (03) 347-6911)
Perth
Hackett Hall, University of West Australia (☎ (09) 380-2302)
Sydney
1A Lee St, Railway Square (☎ (02) 212-1255)

To/From Neighbouring Countries

Air connections with Chile, Bolivia, Paraguay, Brazil and Uruguay are primarily but not exclusively via capital cities.

Chile Many airlines fly between Ezeiza and Santiago, Chile, but there are also Aerolíneas Argentinas flights from Santiago to Mendoza and Córdoba. The Chilean airline Ladeco goes to Mendoza. LAN-Chile also connects Mendoza to Santiago with flights each way on Tuesday and Sunday.

TAN, the regional airline of Neuquén province, connects Bariloche with Puerto Montt, Chile. There are projected Aerolíneas Argentinas flights between Jujuy and Iquique, Chile, in summer only. In the past, flights have connected Salta and Antofagasta.

Bolivia La Paz is the principal destination, but some flights continue to Santa Cruz de la Sierra. There are also flights from Salta to Santa Cruz.

Paraguay Asunción is the only airport connection with Buenos Aires; flights leave from both Aeropuerto Jorge Newbery (Aeroparque) and Ezeiza in Buenos Aires.

Brazil From Ezeiza, Río de Janeiro and São Paulo are the main destinations, but there are also flights from Bariloche via Aeroparque to São Paulo, and from Aeroparque to Porto Alegre.

Uruguay There are numerous flights from Aeroparque to Montevideo, while a few long-distance international flights continue from Ezeiza to Montevideo. From Aeroparque, the only other Uruguayan destinations are Punta del Este and Colonia del Sacramento.

LAND

There are multitudinous crossings from the neighbouring countries of Chile, Bolivia, Paraguay, Brazil and Uruguay. Some are very easy, some very difficult and time-consuming, but the latter are usually much more interesting.

To/From Chile

Andean Routes Except in Patagonia, every land crossing to and from Chile involves going over the Andes. Some are closed in winter. Only from Antofagasta to Salta is there any rail crossing, but that is not a regular passenger service.

Chilean visas (which are probably best to obtain in Buenos Aires) are required by citizens of the following countries: France, New Zealand, Mexico, Guyana, Haiti, Suriname, Kuwait, and African and Communist countries (the latter being a shrinking category, presumably). The rest usually only need a Chilean tourist card, which is obtainable at the border point. For some reason, French nationals can only get single-entry visas.

Salta to Antofagasta The 4275-metre Huaytiquina pass is usually open only from December to March. Buses Gemini and Atahualpa make the trip weekly in summer, but bookings are heavy. Automobile traffic is almost nonexistent, so forget about hitching. There may be an Argentine passenger train to the Chilean border at Socompa, but only freight service beyond, although it will sometimes take passengers. See the chapter on Salta for details.

San Juan to La Serena The 4779-metre Agua Negra pass, dynamited by the Argentine military during the Beagle Channel dispute of 1978-79, is now open again and bus service may commence soon. Check in La Serena or San Juan.

Buenos Aires & Mendoza to Santiago Many bus companies cover this most popular of crossing points between the two countries. See the Mendoza section of the Cuyo chapter for more details.

Going the other way, at the Terminal de Buses Norte on General Mackenna in Santiago, try Tas Choapa, Chile Bus, Igi Llaima, Fénix Pullman Norte or TAC. Taxi *colectivos*, which leave whenever they have five passengers, are faster, more comfortable and only slightly more expensive. Winter snow sometimes closes the route, but never for very long.

Lake District Routes There are a number of scenic crossings in the Argentine-Chilean Lake District, several of which involve bus-boat shuttles. These are popular routes during summer, so you should make bookings in advance whenever possible.

San Martín de los Andes to Temuco On the Argentine side, the road skirts the north slopes of Parque Nacional Lanín. There is a summer bus service, but the Tromen Pass is closed in winter. The road to Temuco passes Currarehue, Pucón and Lago Villarica via the pass (known to Chileans as Mamuil Malal).

San Martín de los Andes to Valdivia From San Martín you can take a ferry to Paso Hua Hum and Argentine customs. A local bus takes you to Pirehueico, from where a ferry across Lago Pirehueico lands at Puerto Fuy. From there, take a bus via Choshuenco and Panguipulli to Valdivia.

Bariloche to Osorno via Puyehue Pass This road crossing is the quickest land route in the Lake District, passing through Parque Nacional Nahuel Huapi on the Argentine side and Parque Nacional Puyehue on the Chilean side.

Bariloche to Puerto Montt, via Lago Todos los Santos This bus-boat combination is a very popular crossing in the summer; you can purchase a single through ticket or cross in stages via several scenic villages.

From Bariloche, there are frequent bus services to Llao Llao. Take the ferry from Puerto Pañuelo (Llao Llao) over Lago Nahuel Huapi to Puerto Blest, from where you take a short bus trip. After crossing Lago Frías by launch, go through Argentine immigration at Puerto Frías. A bus takes you over the Pérez Rosales pass to Peulla, from where you catch the ferry to Petrohué, at the west end of Lago Todos los Santos.

Southern Patagonian Routes Since the opening of the Carretera Austral (Southern Highway) beyond Puerto Aysén, it has become more common to cross between Chile and Argentina south of Puerto Montt. There are also several crossing points in extreme southern Patagonia and Tierra del Fuego.

Esquel to Puerto Cárdenas There are two possible crossings in this area. From Esquel there are colectivos to Futaleufú. Formerly you had to cross by *balsa* (barge) to the Chilean side. With the recent construction of a bridge and road here, the waterborne journey is unnecessary. This new road, to be opened in September 1992, connects Esquel with Chaitén, Chile. The road continues south-west to Puerto Ramírez and then turns north-west to Puerto Piedras. Then take the ferry to Puerto Cárdenas on Lago Yelcho.

The other crossing goes from Esquel via Trevelin and Corcovado (there is a bus service along this route) to Argentine customs at Carrenleufú. Soon after the border is the town of Palena; the road continues until it joins the road from Puerto Ramírez.

Comodoro Rivadavia to Coihaique There are three weekly buses, often heavily booked, from Comodoro Rivadavia to Coihaique via Río Mayo.

Los Antíguos to Chile Chico A bus from Los Antíguos (from which there are connections to the Patagonian coastal town of Caleta Olivia) goes to Chile Chico. From there you can continue to Puerto Ibañez on Lago Carrera (which is called Lago Buenos Aires on the Argentine side) by ferry.

Calafate & Río Turbio to Puerto Natales & Parque Nacional Torres del Paine There are frequent buses between Puerto Natales and the Argentine mining town of Río Turbio, where many Chileans work; from Río Turbio there are connections to Río Gallegos. Twice weekly or more in summer there are buses from Torres del Paine and Puerto Natales to Calafate, the gateway to Argentina's Parque Nacional Los Glaciares. By the time this is published, a new and shorter route may be open between Torres del Paine and Los Glaciares, bypassing Calafate over the Sierra de Baguales.

Río Gallegos to Punta Arenas There are many buses daily between Punta Arenas and Río Gallegos, a six-hour trip.

Tierra del Fuego to Punta Arenas From Río Grande, which has connections to Ushuaia, there are two buses weekly to Porvenir, in Chilean Tierra del Fuego. A three-hour ferry trip or a ten-minute flight takes you to Punta Arenas.

Ushuaia to Puerto Williams Every Saturday, there is a ferry from Puerto Williams on Navarino Island (reached by plane or boat from Punta Arenas) to Ushuaia. This ferry service, though, is frequently interrupted.

To/From Bolivia

There are one major and two minor crossing points between Argentina and Bolivia. There are both rail and road connections at La Quiaca/Villazón in the province of Jujuy, while the Aguas Blancas and Yacuiba crossings are in the province of Salta.

La Quiaca to Villazón From Jujuy and Salta, there are many daily buses to La Quiaca. Trains are cheaper but slower, less frequent, more undependable and uncomfortably crowded. You must walk or take a cab across the Bolivian border to catch a bus or train to La Paz.

Aguas Blancas to Bermejo From Orán, reached by bus from either Salta or Jujuy, you take a bus to Aguas Blancas and the Bolivian border town of Bermejo, where a bridge now crosses the river. From Bermejo, you can catch a bus to Tarija.

Pocitos to Yacuiba From Jujuy or Salta there are buses to Tartagal and on to the border at Pocitos/Yacuiba. From Yacuiba, there are trains to Santa Cruz de la Sierra.

To/From Paraguay

There are two direct border crossings between Argentina and Paraguay, plus one which requires a brief detour through Brazil. Another may open if the massive Yacyretá hydroelectric project on the Río Paraná is ever completed.

Clorinda to Asunción There are frequent bus services via the Puente Internacional Ignacio de Loyola between Asunción and Clorinda, in Formosa province, which is renowned for ferocious customs checks.

Posadas to Encarnación Frequent bus service across the Paraná has facilitated this crossing on the new international bridge, although it is still possible to take a launch between the river docks, at least until the Yacyretá dam floods the low-lying parts of both cities.

Puerto Iguazú to Ciudad del Este Frequent buses connect Puerto Iguazú in Misiones province to the Brazilian city of Foz do Iguaçu, with easy connections to Ciudad del Este (ex-Puerto Presidente Stroessner).

To/From Brazil
The most common overland crossing is between Puerto Iguazú and Foz do Iguaçu, but you can also go from Paso de Los Libres, in Corrientes province, to Uruguaiana, Brazil, and on to Porto Alegre. A direct bus service connects Buenos Aires with Río de Janeiro and São Paulo.

To/From Uruguay
For those who get seasick on the ferry or hydrofoil, there are direct buses from Buenos Aires to Montevideo, but these are less convenient than the land/river combinations across the Río de La Plata, which are detailed below. All other land connections are across the Río Uruguay in Entre Ríos province.

Gualeguaychú to Fray Bentos There are three buses a day across the Puente Internacional Libertador General San Martín, with good connections to Montevideo from Mercedes, the first town beyond Fray Bentos.

Colón to Paysandú The Puente Internacional General José Gervasio Artigas links these two cities, south of Parque Nacional El Palmar.

Concordia to Salto The bridge across the Salto Grande hydroelectric complex, north of Concordia, unites these two cities, north of Parque Nacional El Palmar. There are also direct launches across the river.

RIVER
From Buenos Aires, there are many ways to Uruguay which involve ferry and hydrofoil, often requiring combinations with buses. The main companies are Ferrytur, at Florida 780 in Buenos Aires, and Río Branco 1368 in Montevideo; ONDA, at Florida and Lavalle in Buenos Aires, and at San José 1145 in Montevideo; and Buquebus, at Suipacha 776 in Buenos Aires.

Buenos Aires to Colonia Ferrytur and ONDA have morning and evening sailings to Colonia from Buenos Aires. The trip costs US$20 and takes four hours. From Colonia, you can make direct bus connections to Montevideo, a three-hour trip. Hydrofoils, which cost about the same but have luggage limitations, leave from the new terminal at Dársena Sud. Tickets can be purchased at ONDA. See the Buenos Aires chapter for more details.

Tigre to Carmelo There are launches across the estuary of the Río de la Plata from the Buenos Aires suburb of Tigre, reached from Retiro Station or via the No 60 bus ('Tigre') from Avenida Callao. Services leave the Estación Fluvial daily at 8 am. From Carmelo there are good connections to Montevideo.

TOURS
Myriad companies offer tours to Argentina, but most of them focus on the attractions of Buenos Aires, Iguazú Falls and the Moreno Glacier, a few including Ushuaia and Tierra del Fuego. Other parts of the country get short shrift, so if you're interested in those areas, you may have to make arrangements in Buenos Aires.

Increasingly, both Argentine and foreign companies have become involved in nature-oriented tourism (known as *turismo ecológico* or *turismo aventura*. In Buenos Aires, Patagonia Wilderness operates climbing and hiking trips, some of them very challenging, such as Cerro Torre and Aconcagua. They will design custom trips, with knowledgeable local guides. Contact them at 8th floor, Avenida Julio A Roca 610, 1067 Buenos Aires (☎ 334-5134).

North American companies which operate in Argentina include Wilderness Travel (☎ 548-0420 or toll-free at 1-800-247-6700), 801 Allston Way, Berkeley, California 94710; and Mountain Travel Sobek (☎ 527-8100 or 1-800-227-2384), 6420 Fairmount Ave, El Cerrito, California 94530. Both have lavishly illustrated catalogues of their numerous excursions to Patagonia and the Andean Lake District, which range from easy day hikes, staying at hotels and campgrounds, to strenuous treks and climbs, bivouacking in the back country. For visitors with limited time, especially in areas like Patagonia where logistics can be difficult, these trips may be ideal.

Similar companies exist in Europe and Australia. Journey Latin America (☎ (081) 747-8315), 16 Devonshire Rd, Chiswick, London W4 2HD, takes smallish groups to Latin America. It specialises in tours for one or two people. Explore Worldwide (☎ (0252) 34-4161), 1 Frederick St, Aldershot, Hants GU11 1LQ, and Melia Travel (☎ (081) 491-3881), 12 Dover St, London W1X 4NS, are also Latin American specialists.

In Australia, try Peregrine Bird Tours (☎ (03) 726-8471), 2 Drysdale Place, Mooroolbark, Victoria 3138, or World Expeditions (☎ (02) 261-1974), 3rd floor, 377 Sussex St, Sydney 2000.

LEAVING ARGENTINA
Departure Tax
International passengers leaving from Ezeiza Airport must pay a US$10 departure tax. On flights of less than 300 km to neighbouring countries, such as to Uruguay, the tax is only about US$4. These taxes may be paid in local currency, but it is usually slightly cheaper to pay in US dollars. There is no tax for land or sea departures.

Getting Around

AIR

There are three principal Argentine airlines: Aerolíneas Argentinas handles domestic as well as international routes, Austral domestic routes only, while Líneas Aéreas del Estado (LADE) serves mostly Patagonian destinations. There are smaller regional airlines in Patagonia, most notably Transportes Aéreos Neuquén (TAN). Aerolíneas and Austral have recently been privatised, while LADE belongs to the Argentine Air Force, and TAN to the provincial government of Neuquén. Generally, fares are lower on the state-owned airlines, but there are worthwhile discounts on all of them if you persist.

In Patagonia, flying with LADE or TAN is sometimes cheaper than covering the same distance by bus, but summer demand is heavy and flights are often booked, usually overbooked, well in advance. With polite insistence and a convincing story, you can often get a seat on a LADE flight in town, but in desperation do not hesitate to go to the airport. Often you will find a plane with tens of empty seats.

Fares

The cost of flying in Argentina has risen dramatically in recent years. Fortunately, Aerolíneas Argentinas is introducing a new series of discounted fares which should make air travel more reasonable despite some significant restrictions. Consult the accompanying chart for the most recent standard airfare structure.

Domestically, Aerolíneas Argentinas and Austral offer comparable prices and services. LADE, TAN and other small lines offer lower fares, but operate smaller, slower aircraft on fewer routes. One low-cost alternative on all airlines is *banda negativa*, in which limited seats on an arbitrarily selected list of flights every month are available for discounts of 40% or so. Often, but not always, these are night flights and require advance purchase, but they are excellent bargains.

Air Passes

For short-term visitors, the most popular possibility is Aerolíneas Argentinas' 'Visit Argentina' fare, which lets you fly anywhere served by the airline so long as you make no more than one stop in any city except for an immediate connection. The minimum of four flight coupons would enable you to fly, for example, from Buenos Aires to Ushuaia, Ushuaia to Puerto Iguazú, Puerto Iguazú to Salta (via Buenos Aires) and Salta to Buenos Aires. Since the one-way flight to Ushuaia would cost almost as much if purchased separately, this is a tremendous bargain for anyone visiting widely separated parts of the country on a brief trip.

Four flight coupons cost US$359 and are valid for 30 days. There are options for six coupons (US$409) and eight coupons (US$459). Theoretically the pass must be purchased overseas, but some LP correspondents claim to have done so in Buenos Aires.

Timetables

Aerolíneas, Austral and the other airlines publish detailed timetables to which they adhere very closely. You should know that LADE will sometimes leave early if the flight is full or nearly full, so don't be getting to the airport late. You will find central airline offices in the Buenos Aires chapter, and regional offices in each city entry.

Departure Tax

Argentine domestic flights carry a departure tax of about US$2.50, which is not included in the price of the ticket.

BUS

Long-distance Argentine buses are generally large, comfortable, and sometimes faster than you might like. Most have toilets and serve coffee or snacks, while a few provide

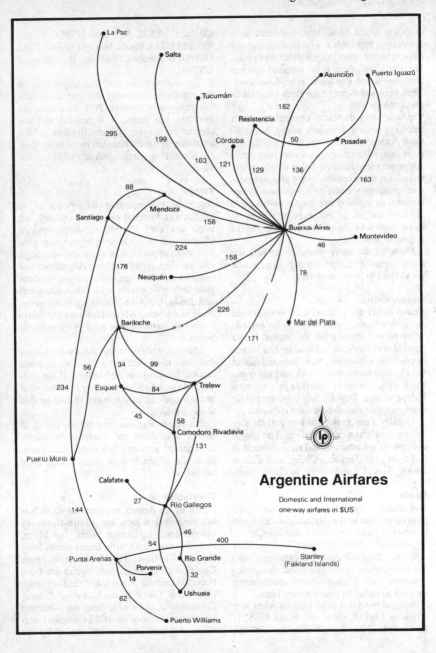

Argentine Airfares

Domestic and International
one-way airfares in $US

on-board meals. Most Argentine cities have central bus terminals at which each company has a separate office, although in some cities, like Bariloche, there is no terminal and bus companies are clustered near downtown. Most companies post their fares and schedules prominently.

Some long-distance companies offer reclining seats at premium prices, but ordinary Argentine buses on main routes are more than adequate even on very long rides. Although some offer on-board meal service, most stop at reasonably good and inexpensive restaurants. Local or provincial services (known as *comun*) are likely to be more crowded and sometimes make very frequent stops and take much longer than direct (*expreso*) services.

Buses reach more destinations and are more dependable than the railroads, which are subject to frequent strikes.

Reservations
Reservations are generally unnecessary on Argentine buses, but during holiday periods or on routes where seats are limited it is a good idea to buy your ticket as far in advance as possible. Christmas, New Year and Easter are obvious times, but you should not overlook the winter holidays around Independence Day (9 July), when public transportation can also be very crowded.

Usually a trip to the bus terminal the day before you travel will suffice. The major exceptions are international services such as Salta to Antofagasta, Chile, and Caleta Olivia, Santa Cruz province, to Chile Chico.

Costs
Bus fares in Argentina are considerably more expensive than in the Andean countries and somewhat more expensive than in Chile - figure on about US$0.05 per kilometre. This will vary depending on the exchange rate, but bus services are private rather than state-operated and fares respond much more quickly to inflation than do train fares.

Sample bus fares from Buenos Aires are: Rosario US$16, Mar del Plata US$21, Paraná US$22, Bahía Blanca US$29, Córdoba US$35, Mendoza US$54, Puerto Iguazú US$57, Puerto Madryn US$64, Salta US$69, Bariloche US$80 and Río Gallegos US$96.

Travellers should note that, depending on the company, university students and teachers frequently receive 20% discounts on intercity bus fares. It is helpful to have student or university identification, which need not be up-to-date, but more often than not just asking for the discount will be sufficient.

TRAIN
Argentina has extensive rail services in the northern and central part of the country, but none south of Esquel, in north-western Chubut province. On long trips, trains give you more opportunities to stretch your legs, visit the dining car, and meet Argentines and other travellers. At regular intervals, vendors pass through each car with sandwiches and soft drinks, but it is best to bring along something like a dozen empanadas from a rotisería – this will be better than what you can get on board.

Train trips are often but not always longer than bus trips, and are subject to frequent delays, breakdowns and strikes. If the railroads do go on strike, you may find that your ticket is useless, although you should be able to get a refund.

Passenger services may be privatised, in which case there are likely to be major changes in service, schedules and fares, since the railroads now receive large state subsidies.

Timetables
Ferrocarriles Argentinos operates six different railroads which are administratively independent. In Buenos Aires, the Mitre, Belgrano and San Martín lines operate from Retiro Station, the Roca line from Constitución Station, the Urquiza line from Federico Lacroze Station, and the Sarmiento line from Once Station. From Retiro, Constitución and Once, there are suburban commuter services as well as intercity services. All four stations are served by the

underground (Subte). For information and reservations in Buenos Aires, contact Ferrocarriles Argentinos (☎ 30-7220) at Maipú 88.

The Mitre line goes to the larger cities of north-western Argentina, such as Córdoba, Santiago del Estero and Tucumán. The Belgrano line, which is older, slower and less comfortable than the Mitre, goes to Salta, Jujuy and the Bolivian border at La Quiaca. The San Martín line goes to Mendoza, while the Roca line serves the Atlantic beach resort of Mar del Plata, other destinations in Buenos Aires province, and northern Patagonia, where it bifurcates. One branch goes to Zapala, in Neuquén province, while the other goes to Bariloche, in Río Negro province. From Ingeniero Jacobacci, on the southern Roca branch, there is a picturesque narrow-gauge railway to Esquel.

The Urquiza line goes to destinations in Mesopotamia and north-eastern Argentina, such as Paraná, Corrientes and Posadas. The Sarmiento line is primarily a commuter line.

Classes

There are four classes of service on Ferrocarriles Argentinos, not all of which are found on every train. *Coche cama*, a sleeper compartment, is the costliest but most comfortable on long journeys such as Retiro-Mendoza or Constitución-Bariloche. *Pullman* is considerably cheaper, with air-conditioning and reclining seats which are somewhat larger than those in *primera* (first class). However, primera is very acceptable in almost all circumstances, especially since the price differential with the rigid bench seats of *turista* (tourist or second class) is minimal. For trips of more than a few hours, and especially overnight, avoid turista class.

Reservations

Because they are so much cheaper than buses, Argentine trains can be very crowded. During holiday periods such as Christmas and around Independence Day (9 July), it is very important to buy your tickets as far in advance as possible. On their honeymoon in July of 1981, the authors neglected to do so

and had to travel in hard-backed turista carriages jammed with students, and with army conscripts who travel free in standing room but quickly dart into any available seat.

At most major stations, ticket purchases are now computerised and your ticket will show date of travel *(fecha)*, departure time *(sale)*, carriage number *(coche)* and seat *(asiento)*. Argentines, especially when travelling with friends or family, pay little attention to seat assignments, but do not hesitate to insist on your proper seat or even call the conductor to straighten out any problems.

Costs

Argentine train fares are much lower than bus fares, but privatisation could eliminate state subsidies and raise prices. Presently the train fare for the 24-hour trip from Constitución to Bariloche, for example, is US$100 in a sleeper, US$76 in Pullman, US$48 in primera and US$38 in turista. Ferrocarriles' Argenpass offers unlimited travel for 30, 60, and 90 days – ask for details.

TAXI

In areas such as Patagonia, where public transportation can be scarce, it is possible to hire a cab with driver for the day to visit places off the beaten track. If you bargain, this can be cheaper than a rental car, but negotiate the fee in advance.

CAR & MOTORBIKE

Because Argentina is such a large country, and even though the public transport system is very extensive, many parts are easily accessible only by motor vehicle. Especially in Patagonia, where distances are great and buses can be infrequent, you cannot easily stop for something interesting at the side of the road and then continue on your merry way by public transport.

Unfortunately, operating a car in Argentina is expensive. Although Argentina is completely self-sufficient in oil, the price of *nafta* (petrol) has risen to world levels at nearly US$1 per litre, although *gas-oil* (diesel fuel) is only about half that. Distances are comparable to those in the United States, driving costs even higher unless shared by several people. Except in Buenos Aires, though, there are few security problems, and you should not drive in Buenos Aires anyway.

Formally, you must have an International or Inter-American Driving Permit to supplement your national or state driver's license. In practice, police rarely examine these documents closely and generally ignore the latter. They do not ignore automobile registration and tax documents, which must be up to date.

Although motorbikes have become fashionable among many Argentines, they are very expensive. In addition, the authors have never seen a hire place that rents motorbikes in Argentina.

Road Rules

Once, in the province of Buenos Aires, an Argentine driver passed us at very high speed *on the left side* of a traffic island separating one-way lanes at a major T-intersection. In another instance, in the province of Salta, an enormous lorry blithely ignored a red light to pass us at an intersection where dozens of schoolgirls were crossing the highway on their way home for lunch.

These are not atypical incidents. Anyone considering driving in Argentina should know that Argentine drivers are reckless and even wilfully dangerous, ignoring speed limits, road signs and even traffic signals. Theoretically all Argentine highways have an 80 km/h speed limit, but hardly anybody pays attention to this or any other regulation. In the summer of 1991, Argentine President Carlos Menem drove his Ferrari Testarossa, a dubious gift from two Italian industrialists, to the Atlantic coast resort of Pinamar, a distance of about 400 km, in a little over three hours.

Argentine police contribute little toward highway safety. Shortly before Menem's excursion, the Buenos Aires provincial police had announced a major summer safety campaign, but were directed *not* to interfere

with a red Ferrari travelling at high speed to the Atlantic coast. In fact you will rarely see police patrolling the highways, where high-speed, head-on crashes are common, but you will meet them at major intersections and checkpoints where they conduct meticulous document and equipment checks. A particularly bad place is the intersection of national Rutas 9 and 14 at Zárate, in Buenos Aires province, and provincial borders also are frequently sites for these annoying inspections.

Equipment violations, such as a defective turn signal, brake light or handbrake, carry fines up to US$200 but are most commonly opportunities for graft. The police may claim that you must pay the fine at a local bank which may not be open until the following day or, on a weekend, until Monday. If you are uncertain about your rights, state in a very matter-of-fact manner your intention to contact your embassy or consulate. Offer a coima only if you are confident that it is appropriate and unavoidable.

If you drive in Argentina, especially with your own car, it may be worthwhile to become a member of the Automóvil Club Argentino (ACA), which has service stations and garages throughout the country, offering free road service and towing in and around major cities. It has excellent maps and insurance services. Membership costs about US$30 per month, and brings discounts on accommodation, camping, tours and other services. Members can purchase petrol and other supplies with credit cards at ACA stations.

Rental

Major international rental agencies such as Hertz, Avis and A-1 have offices in Buenos Aires and in major cities and other tourist areas throughout Argentina. To rent a car, you must have a valid driver's licence and be 25 years of age. It may also be necessary to present a credit card such as Mastercard or Visa.

Even at smaller agencies, rental charges are now very high, the cheapest and smallest vehicles going for about US$20 per day plus

US$0.20 per km. When you add on the cost of insurance and petrol, operating a vehicle becomes very pricey indeed unless you have several people to share expenses. Although unlimited mileage deals are possible they only apply to weekly or longer periods and are very expensive.

If you camp out – feasible in or near most cities as well as the countryside – rather than staying in hotels, you may offset a good part of the difference.

Purchase

If you are spending several months in Argentina, purchasing a car is an alternative worth exploring, but it has both advantages and disadvantages. On the one hand, it is more flexible than public transport and is likely to be cheaper than rentals which can easily reach US$100 per day. If you resell it at the end of your stay, it may turn out even more economical. On the other hand, any used car can be a risk, especially on the rugged back roads of Patagonia. When the gearbox gave out on our Peugeot pickup, we were fortunate enough to be in Bariloche, where it was easily but not cheaply repaired.

If you purchase a car you must deal with the exasperating Argentine bureaucracy. Be sure you have the title (tarjeta verde or 'green card') and that licence tax payments are up-to-date. As a foreigner, you may find it very useful to get a notarised document authorising your use of the car, since the bureaucracy does not move quickly enough to change the title easily. In any event, Argentines rarely do so because of the expense involved – even vehicles 30 years old or more often bear the original purchaser's name.

As a foreigner you may own a vehicle in Argentina but, in theory at least, you may not take it out of the country even with a notarised authorisation, although certain border crossings, such as Puerto Iguazú, appear to be more flexible. On the other hand, at Gualeguaychú, Entre Ríos province, Argentine customs were adamant in refusing permission for temporary export even with

the legal owner's permission. Contact your consulate for assistance and advice.

Argentina's domestic automobile industry, based in Córdoba, has left a reserve of decent used cars in the country. The most popular models are Peugeot 404s and Ford Falcons. Parts are readily available. You should not expect to find a dependable used car for much less than about US$2000. Prices will be higher for a gasolero, a vehicle which uses cheaper diesel fuel.

BICYCLE

Bicycling is an interesting and inexpensive alternative for travelling around Argentina – if you camp it could make your trip nearly as cheap as in the Andean countries. Racing bicycles are suitable for paved roads, but on the gravelled roads in the Andean Northwest or Patagonia you would be better off with a mountain bike (todo terreno). Argentine bicycles are inferior to their counterparts in Europe or the United States.

There are many good routes for bicycling, especially around the Patagonian Lake District and in the North-West – the highway from Tucumán to Tafí del Valle, the direct road from Salta to Jujuy and the Quebrada de Cafayate would be exceptionally beautiful rides on generally good surfaces. Bicycling is an increasingly popular recreational activity among Argentines.

There two major drawbacks to bicycling in Argentina. One is the wind, which in Patagonia can slow your progress to a crawl. Argentine motorists, with total disregard of anyone but themselves, are the other. On the country's straight, narrow, two-lane highways, they are a real hazard to bicyclists.

HITCHING

Along with Chile, Argentina is probably the best country for hitching in all of South America. The only drawback is that Argentine vehicles are often stuffed with families and children, but truck drivers will frequently take backpackers. At the servicentros at the outskirts of large Argentine cities, where truckers gas up their vehicles, it is often worthwhile soliciting a ride.

Women can and do hitchhike alone, but should exercise caution and especially avoid getting into a car with more than one man. In Patagonia, where distances are great and vehicles few, hitchers should expect long waits and carry warm, wind-proof clothing. A water bottle is also a good idea, especially in the desert north. Carry some snack food.

There are a few routes where we would discourage hitching. National Ruta 40, from Calafate to Perito Moreno and Río Mayo, carries almost no automobile traffic and is virtually hopeless. The scenic route from Tucumán to Cafayate is very difficult past Tafí del Valle. The Andean crossing from Salta to Antofagasta, Chile, is utterly futile.

BOAT

There are few opportunities for boat or river travel in Argentina, except for the international services across the Río de la Plata to Uruguay, across the Andean lakes to Chile, or from Ushuaia to Puerto Williams, Chile, in Tierra del Fuego.

There is a passenger ferry from Rosario, Santa Fe province, across the Río Paraná to Victoria, Entre Ríos. There are also numerous boat excursions around the River Plate delta from Tigre, a suburb of Buenos Aires. Every winter, there is a river cruise up the Paraná to Asunción, Paraguay. Ask for details at travel agencies in the capital.

LOCAL TRANSPORT
To/From the Airport

In most Argentine cities, each airline has a minibus which operates in tandem with the flight schedule; sometimes Aerolíneas Argentinas and Austral combine their operations. There is also usually a city bus which stops at the airport.

In Buenos Aires, there are a variety of ways to get to either the domestic airport Aeroparque or the international airport at Ezeiza. See the chapter on Buenos Aires for details.

Bus

Even small Argentine cities have extensive public transportation networks, usually bus systems. Except when conducting 'work-to-rule' stoppages, Buenos Aires' bus drivers go for speed before safety. The sight of one barrelling down a narrow street with his elbows on the wheel as he counts and sorts reams of inflated pesos is likely to be one of your unforgettable memories of the capital. Hang on tight!

Buses are clearly numbered and usually carry a placard indicating their final destination. Since many identically numbered buses serve slightly different routes, pay attention to these placards. When you board a bus, tell the driver your final destination and he will tell you the fare and give you a ticket. Do not lose this ticket, which may be checked en route. A few cities, such as Tucumán and Córdoba, use tokens rather than cash.

Train

Ferrocarriles Argentinos operates an extensive system of commuter trains from Constitución, Retiro, Once and Lacroze stations to the suburbs of Buenos Aires. There are also trains between Rosario and its suburbs. During railroad strikes, which are frequent, these operate on severely reduced schedules.

Underground

Buenos Aires is the only Argentine city with a subway system. Although it has seen better days, it is still an excellent way of getting around the city centre. For details, see the Buenos Aires chapter.

Taxi

Like New Yorkers, the Porteños of Buenos Aires make frequent use of taxis, which are reasonably priced. Cabs are metered, but because Argentine currency is so unstable, each driver carries a photocopied list of codes which translates into the appropriate fare. Drivers are generally polite and honest, but there are exceptions. It is customary to leave small change as a tip.

Outside Buenos Aires, meters are less common, so it is wise to agree upon a fare in advance if possible.

Buenos Aires

To Porteños, Buenos Aires is virtually synonymous with Argentina. Nearly 40% of the country's 33 million citizens live in Gran Buenos Aires (Greater Buenos Aires), which includes suburbs like Avellaneda and Quilmes. Residents of the provinces, especially those from large and important cities like Córdoba and Rosario, are the most openly critical of the capital's primacy, yet almost everyone acknowledges the undesirability of the concentration of political and economic power in the capital.

Even so, when the Radical government of President Raúl Alfonsín proposed moving the seat of government to the small northern Patagonian city of Viedma, Río Negro province, entrenched opposition forced him to abandon the plan. Probably the project

would have been no less expensive and no more successful than Brazil's experiment in reducing the importance of Río de Janeiro and São Paulo by the creation of Brasilia, but his failure vividly illustrated the persistent dominance of Buenos Aires.

HISTORY

Buenos Aires dates from 1536, when an expedition of 16 ships and nearly 1600 men, headed by the Spanish explorer Pedro de Mendoza, camped on a bluff overlooking the Río de La Plata, possibly at the site of present-day Parque Lezama. This oversized expedition arrived too late in the summer to plant crops, and the few Indians in the area proved hostile when the Spaniards forcibly recruited them to find food. Lacking adequate provisions and facing incessant Indian pressure, part of the expedition sailed up the Río Paraná to found the city of Asunción among the more sedentary Guaraní peoples, who were friendlier and more inclined to share their sustenance with the Spaniards. Within five years, despite some reluctance, the Spaniards completely abandoned Buenos Aires to the Querandí Indians.

More than four decades passed before the Spaniards of Asunción, led by Juan de Garay, re-established themselves on the west bank of the Río de la Plata. Even then, being at the terminus of a tenuous supply line which stretched from Madrid via Panama and Lima, Buenos Aires was clearly subordinate to Asunción, and the Spaniards in Buenos Aires survived but did not flourish. Garay himself died at the hands of the Querandí only three years later.

Over the next two centuries, Buenos Aires slowly grew on the basis of the enormous herds of cattle and horses which had proliferated on the Pampas and, with the decline of the bonanza silver mine at Potosí, Lima's colonial primacy also declined. With this growth came frustration at Spain's colonial restrictions, as merchants began to trade for contraband from Portuguese and British vessels on the river. In 1776 the promotion of Buenos Aires to the status of capital of the new Viceroyalty of the River Plate, including Potosí within its boundaries, was palpable recognition that the adolescent city had outgrown Spain's parental authority.

In the late colonial history of Buenos Aires and the country, the British invasions of 1806 and 1807 were a major turning point, when criollo forces repelled British forces after first seeming to cooperate with them. Only three years later, influential criollos, on the pretext that Spain's legitimate government had fallen, confronted and deposed Viceroy Cisneros at the Cabildo. As described by the American diplomat Caesar Rodney, the architects of the revolution and the people of the city showed remarkable restraint and maturity:

At some periods of the revolution, when the hands of authority were relaxed, the administration actually devolved into the hands of the inhabitants of the city. Hence, it might have been imagined, endless tumult and disorder would have sprung up, leading directly to pillage and bloodshed. Yet no such disturbances ever took place; all remained quiet...The people have in no instance demanded victims to satisfy their vengeance; on the contrary, they have sometimes, by the influence of public opinion, moderated the rigour with which their rulers were disposed to punish the guilty.

Six years later, the United Provinces of the River Plate declared independence in Tucumán. Only gradually achieved in fact, independence did not resolve the conflict between two elite sectors: the landowners of the interior provinces, who were concerned about preserving their economic privileges, and the residents of Buenos Aires (not yet the capital), who maintained an outward orientation toward commerce and ideas. After more than a decade of violence and uncertainty, the Federalist caudillo Juan Manuel de Rosas asserted his authority over Buenos Aires.

When Charles Darwin visited Buenos Aires in 1833, shortly after the ruthless Rosas took power, he was impressed that the city of 60,000 was

...large; and I should think one of the most regular in the world. Every street is at right angles to the one it crosses, and the parallel ones being equidistant, the houses are collected into solid squares of equal dimensions, which are called quadras. On the other hand the houses themselves are hollow squares; all the rooms opening into a neat little courtyard. They are generally only one story high, with flat roofs, which are fitted with seats, and are much frequented by the inhabitants in summer. In the centre of the town is the Plaza, where the public offices, fortress, cathedral, &c., stand. Here also, the old viceroys, before the revolution had their palaces. The general assemblage of buildings possesses considerable architectural beauty, although none individually can boast of any.

Rosas lasted nearly three decades more, during which time (ironically) Buenos Aires' influence grew despite his perhaps opportunistic Federalist sympathies. After his overthrow, the city was opened to European immigration, and the population grew from 90,000 in 1854, to 177,000 in 1869, to 670,000 by 1895. By the turn of the century, it was the largest city in Latin America, with a population of more than a million.

In the 1880s, when the city became the official federal capital, the indignant authorities of Buenos Aires province moved their government to a new provincial capital, La Plata. Still, as the country's agricultural exports boomed and imports flowed into the country, the port city became even more important. According to British diplomat James Bryce, none of the leaders of Glasgow, Manchester or Chicago

...shewed greater enterprise and bolder conceptions than did the men of Buenos Aires when on this exposed and shallow coast they made alongside their city a great ocean harbour.

Immigration and growth brought problems of course, as families crowded into substandard housing, merchants and manufacturers kept wages low, and labourers became increasingly militant. In 1919, under pressure from landowners and other elite sectors, the Radical government of President

Buenos Aires

0   2   4 km

To Tigre

To Córdoba &
Mendoza

Bmé Mitre

To Córdoba &
Mendoza

Rio de la Plata

Avenida del Libertador

Maipú

Ruta Panamericana

Avenida Cabildo

Avenida General Paz

Avenida Pres. Alcorta

Aeroparque Jorge
Newbery

de los Incas

Aliscafos

Lacroze Station

PALERMO

Avenida del Libertador

Estación Maritima

see Central
Buenos Aires
map

Avenida San Martín

Avenida Corrientes

Santa Fe

Retiro Station

Avenida Diaz Velez

Avenida Juan B Justo

Avenida Gaona

Plaza
de Miserere
(Once)

Avenida
9 de Julio

Paseo Colón

To Luján,
Córdoba &
Mendoza

Primera
Junta

Avenida San Juan

Avenida Rivadavia

J B Alberdi

Constitución Station

Parque
Lezama

Avenida E Castro

Avenida Perito Moreno

Avenida La Plata

Entre Rios

Avenida A Alcorta

M A Montes de Oca

La Boca

To Bahía Blanca,
Bariloche &
Patagonia

Avenida Directorio

Avenida

Avenida General Paz

Autopista General Luis T Dellepiane

27 de Febrero
Rio Riachuelo

Avenida Pavón

Avenida Mitre

A Debenedetti

To Ezeiza
International Airport

Avenida Paz

To Mar del Plata

Hipólito Yrigoyen ordered the Army to suppress a metalworkers' strike in what became known as La Semana Trágica, the Tragic Week, which set an unfortunate precedent for the coming decades.

In the 1930s, ambitious governments undertook a massive modernisation program in the city centre, where major avenues like Santa Fe, Córdoba and Corrientes obliterated narrow colonial streets. Since WW II, sprawling Gran Buenos Aires has absorbed many once-distant suburbs and now holds more than a third of the country's population. Though surpassed by Mexico City and São Paulo as Latin America's largest city, it remains the country's dominant economic, political and cultural centre. But a city which once prided itself on its European uniqueness now shares the same problems as many other Latin American cities – pollution, noise, decaying infrastructure and declining public services, unemployment and underemployment, and spreading shantytowns whose residents have little access to those benefits that most Argentines have traditionally enjoyed.

Not all signs are negative. Since the restoration of democracy in 1984, Buenos Aires is once again a lively place, where political and public dialogue are freewheeling, the publishing industry has rebounded, and the arts and music flourish within the limits of economic reality. Fewer foolish public works projects, such as the motorway to Ezeiza Airport, are being built. Buenos Aires may have seen its best days, but it should survive to offer the visitor a rich and unique urban experience.

ORIENTATION

At first glance, Buenos Aires seems as massive and imposing as New York or London, but a brief orientation will suffice to explore the city's compact, regular centre and accessible neighbourhoods on foot, except on brutally hot and humid summer days, when bus, underground and taxi services are good alternatives.

In downtown Buenos Aires, the Plaza de Mayo is the traditional focus of activity,

where hundreds of thousands of Argentines have rallied to cheer Perón or jeer Galtieri. Both the Cathedral and the remaining portions of the original Cabildo are also here, at the east end of Avenida de Mayo. At the west end is the Plaza del Congreso, and the stately but now rather drab Congress building, the result of years of neglect and disuse.

The broad Avenida 9 de Julio (actually encompassing Cerrito and Carlos Pellegrini north of Avenida de Mayo, and Lima and Bernardo de Irigoyen south of Avenida de Mayo) forms a second, north-south axis. It runs from Plaza Constitución to the Avenida del Libertador, leading to the city's exclusive northern suburbs and their spacious parks.

One of the most popular tourist zones is north of the Avenida de Mayo and east of 9 de Julio, an area which includes the Florida and Lavalle pedestrian malls, Plaza San Martín and the important commercial and entertainment areas along Avenidas Corrientes, Córdoba and Santa Fe. Florida is a *peatonal* in its entire length from Plaza San Martín to Diagonal Roque Sáenz Peña, while Lavalle is a *peatonal* (pedestrian mall) only between Carlos Pellegrini and Florida. Beyond Avenida Santa Fe are the chic Recoleta and Palermo suburbs, while south of the Plaza de Mayo are the colourful, working-class San Telmo and Boca neighbourhoods.

Street numbering is fairly simple. Numbers on east-west streets start from zero near the waterfront, while those on north-south streets climb on each side of the Avenida de Mayo. Only outside the centre do things get any more complicated.

INFORMATION
Tourist Offices

The Dirección Nacional de Turismo (☎ 312-2232), at Avenida Santa Fe 883, is open weekdays from 9 am to 5 pm, but for most purposes the municipal tourist kiosks are more helpful, with excellent pocket-sized maps of the city centre. These kiosks, on Florida between Avenida Córdoba and Paraguay and at the intersection of Florida and Diagonal Roque Sáenz Peña, are open weekdays from 8.30 am to 8.30 pm, and Saturdays from 9 am to 7 pm.

For more detailed information on Buenos Aires, visit the city's Dirección General de Turismo (☎ 45-3612), in the Centro Cultural San Martín, 5th floor, Sarmiento 1551.

Money

Dozens of exchange houses crowd Calle San Martín, Argentina's equivalent of Wall Street or the City of London, south of Avenida Corrientes. There are many more north of Avenida Corrientes, along Avenida Corrientes itself, and on the Florida mall. Rates, prominently posted in the windows, are slightly better than in banks, but no cambio in this area pays consistently higher rates than any other. More than a few blocks from here, cambios pay less for your dollars.

Hours are generally 9 am to 6 pm weekdays, but a few are open Saturday mornings. Try Cambio Corprend, Florida 627, or the cubbyhole on the south side of Avenida Corrientes near Calle San Martín. On weekends rates will drop, so try to change by Friday afternoon.

Holders of Mastercard and Visa can get cash advances at many downtown banks. Try Banco de la Nación at Bartolomé Mitre 361, Banca Nazionale del Lavoro at Florida 40, or Banco Mercantil at Avenida Corrientes 629. Bank hours are generally 10 am to 4 pm.

If arriving at Ezeiza Airport, do not change more than necessary at its branch of Banco de la Nación, which gives much poorer rates than downtown cambios.

Post

The Correo Central, Sarmiento 189, occupies an entire block along Avenida Leandro Alem between Avenida Corrientes and Sarmiento. It's open weekdays from 9 am to 7.30 pm. There is a useful branch station near the Congress, at Solís and Hipólito Yrigoyen, and many others scattered throughout the city.

For international parcels weighing more than one kg, you must go to the Correo Postal Internacional, on Antártida Argentina, near Retiro Station. Opening hours are weekdays from 11 am to 5 pm.

When writing to places in Buenos Aires, bear in mind that Argentines often refer to the city as the 'Capital Federal'. This particularly applies to addresses. Porteños often shorten this term further to 'la capital'.

Telephones

Despite signs of improvement, the legacy of ENTel's inept monopoly will be apparent for many decades, and making a phone call in Buenos Aires will continue to be a challenge and a frustration. In theory, local calls should be simple enough, but you will often find that, even if your call gets through, the person at the other end will be unable to hear you. When our own telephone in Buenos Aires gets no dial tone, we have to leave the apartment, find a pay phone, and call in so that we can return to the apartment and call out (with no guarantee, of course, that our call out will be successful!). Repairs can take weeks.

To make a local call from a pay phone, purchase cospeles (tokens) from almost any kiosk or newsstand. Should you be so fortunate as to get through, you will only be able to speak for about two minutes, so carry a pocketful. There are different cospeles for local and long-distance calls.

To make a long-distance call, go to any of Telefónica's long-distance phone offices – the most convenient and efficient is the one at 701 Avenida Corrientes, corner of Maipú, which is open 24 hours and has 44 booths. When you enter, an attendant will give you a priority number and, when your priority number is called, a cashier will give you a ticket for a booth – do not lose this ticket, since you cannot leave the building without it. Once in the booth, you can either dial directly or an operator will make the connection, but once your call is complete, you must return to pay the cashier.

In this office and in some others around the country, there are booths with direct connections with operators in North America, Japan, Europe and neighbouring countries, greatly simplifying the task of making a collect or credit card call. However, you still need your ticket to leave the building.

Long-distance offices are usually very busy places, especially during the evening and weekend discount hours when overseas calls are most economical. Check to see how these hours have changed, since telephone rates are now among the highest in the world and such hours have been reduced since privatisation.

Telegrams, Telex & Fax
International telegrams, telexes and faxes can be sent from ENCOTEL, which is still a state monopoly, at Avenida Corrientes 711 next door to the main telephone office.

Foreign Embassies
For diplomatic representatives from overseas and neighbouring countries, see the Facts for the Visitor chapter.

Cultural Centres
The high-rise Centro Cultural San Martín is one of the best resources in all of Buenos Aires, with art galleries, live theatre, lectures and absurdly inexpensive films at the Sala Leopoldo Lugones. Officially, the address is Sarmiento 1551, but most people enter from Avenida Corrientes. On the Sarmiento side, there is a shaded alcove where free concerts are often held on summer weekends.

Also downtown, the Centro Cultural Islas Malvinas, Florida 983, gives exhibitions of Argentine and foreign artists. At Junín 1930, the Centro Cultural Recoleta offers free or inexpensive events, such as art exhibitions and outdoor films on summer evenings.

The United States Information Agency's Lincoln Center, Florida 935, has an excellent library which receives *The New York Times*, *The Washington Post* and English-language magazines. The Center also has satellite TV transmissions from the States and often shows free, sometimes very unconventional, films. You need not be an American citizen, but you must show identification before being admitted. Hours are Monday, Tuesday, Thursday and Friday from 10.30 am to 6.15

pm, and Wednesday from 5 pm to 9.30 pm. It is closed on weekends and US holidays.

The Goethe Institute, 1st floor, Avenida Corrientes 319 near Florida, offers German-language instruction, lectures and films.

Travel Agencies
ACA (☎ 802-6061) is at Avenida del Libertador 1850. This is the club's central office and it has a wealth of member services and a complete selection of provincial road maps.

One of Buenos Aires' best known and most convenient travel agencies is Turismo ONDA (☎ 392-5011), Florida 502 at the corner of Lavalle, which is also an exchange house. This is the best place to book a passage to Uruguay. Another big agency is Lloydtur (☎ 393-7894), Arenales 1123. American Express, Arenales 707 north of Plaza San Martín, will cash its own travellers' cheques without additional commission, but also has many other services.

ASATEJ (☎ 312-8476), Argentina's non-profit student travel agency, is on the 1st floor, Oficina 104, at Florida 835. Open weekdays from 11 am to 7 pm, it has a list of discount offers at hotels, restaurants and other businesses for holders of international student cards, and has tried to establish a meeting place for young travellers. See the Entertainment section for details.

Bookshops
Buenos Aires' largest and best known bookshop is El Ateneo, which occupies a classic building at Florida 340, with an excellent selection of travel books in the basement, including Lonely Planet guides. Besides its emphasis on Argentine history and literature, it also stocks foreign language books, although they are expensive. Try also Librería ABC at Avenida Córdoba 685 (which has cheap, used English paperbacks at the back of the store), and Hachette at Avenida Córdoba 936. Avenida Corrientes, between Avenidas 9 de Julio and Callao, is a popular place to browse for books.

Visiting academics and just plain curiosity seekers should explore the stacks at Platero,

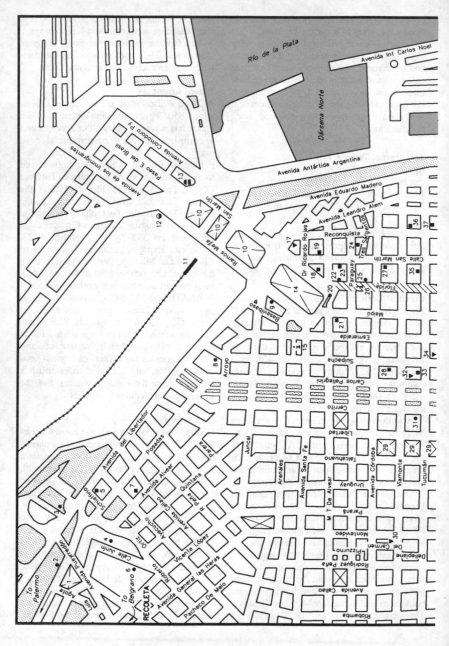

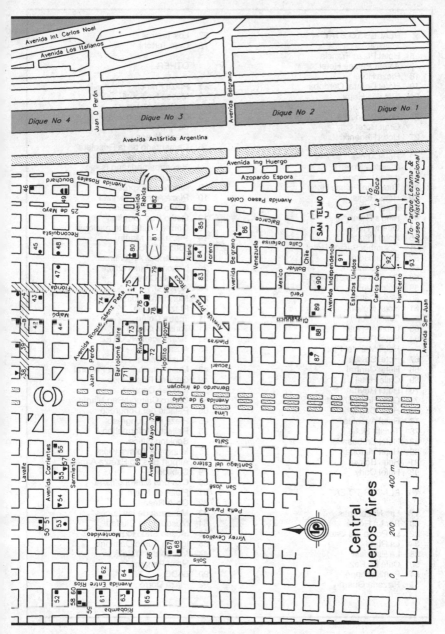

■ PLACES TO STAY

5 Hotel Plaza Francia
7 Alvear Palace Hotel
18 Plaza Hotel
19 Hotel Central Córdoba
21 Elevage Hotel
23 Hotel Diplomat
24 Hotel Waldorf &
Gran Hotel Orly
27 Hotel Phoenix
28 Petit Hotel Goya
33 Hotel Apolo
35 Claridge Hotel
36 Italia Romanelli
37 Tucumán Palace Hotel
39 Hotel Regis
40 Hotel O'Rei
43 King's Hotel
44 Liberty Hotel
46 Hotel Plaza
51 Columbia Palace Hotel
52 Bauen Hotel
56 Hotel Bahía
58 Gran Hotel Sarmiento
59 Hotel Lyon
60 Hotel Callao
61 Hotel Molino
62 Savoy Hotel
63 Lourdes Hotel
64 Hotel Plaza &
Hotel Mar del Plata
67 Hotel Sevilla
68 Hotel Central
69 Chile Hotel
70 Hotel Reyna
71 Gran Hotel Argentino
74 Hotel Continental
77 Hotel Avenida
78 Turista Hotel
88 Hotel Embasador
89 Hotel Victoria
91 Hotel Bolívar
93 Hotel Carly

▼ PLACES TO EAT

17 Las Nazarenas
30 Bar La Robla
32 La Posta del Gaucho
34 La Rural
38 La Estancia
50 Café La Paz
54 Parrilla Pippo
55 Pizzería Guerrín
57 Los Teatros
72 Café Tortoni

OTHER

1 Plaza Francia
2 Museo Nacional
de Bellas Artes
3 Centro Municipal
de Exposiciones
4 Plaza Alvear
6 Cementario de la Recoleta
8 Museo de Arte
Hispanoamericano Isaac
Fernández Blanco
9 American Express
10 Plaza Arrea Argentina
11 Retiro Train Station
12 Retiro Bus Terminal
13 Correo Postal Internacional
14 Plaza San Martín
15 Tourist Office
16 Aerolíneas Argentinas
20 National Parks Office
22 Lincoln Center
25 ASATEJ
26 Municipal Tourist Kiosk
29 Plaza Lavalle
31 Teatro Colón
41 Turismo ONDA
42 Telefónica/ENCOTEL
45 Austral
47 Museo Mitre
48 Museo de la Policia Federal
49 General Post Office
(Correo Central)
53 Centro Cultural San Martín
65 Palacio del Congreso
66 Plaza del Congreso
73 Railways Information &
Booking Office
75 Municipal Tourist Kiosk
76 Airport Bus (to Ezeiza Airport)
79 Cabildo
80 Catedral Metropolitana
81 Plaza de Mayo
82 Casa Rosada
83 Manzana de las Luces
84 Museo de la Ciudad
85 Museo San Roque
86 Iglesia Santo Domingo
87 Museo del Traje &
Hotel Panamá
90 LADE
92 Plaza Dorrego

Talcahuano 485, perhaps the best bookstore in the entire city, with an extraordinary selection of new and out-of-print books about Argentina and Latin America. Ask to see the basement. The staff is knowledgeable in almost every field of interest, and trustworthy and efficient in packaging and sending books overseas. Nearby, on Plaza Lavalle, there are good used bookstalls.

Maps

The tourist kiosks on Florida have an excellent, detailed pocket-size map, the *Plano Turístico de la Ciudad*, of downtown Buenos Aires and the San Telmo, Recoleta, Boca and Palermo neighbourhoods. It also contains a useful diagram of the underground (Subte).

ACA's *Carta Vial de Buenos Aires y Alrededores* is very useful beyond the city centre, and its detailed provincial road maps are imperative for motorists and useful for anyone else. Obtain them at ACA's central office (see Travel Agencies above). Another worthwhile acquisition is the *Guía Peuser*, available at nearly all of downtown's multitudinous newsstands, with a good Subte map and street-by-street routes of the capital's sometimes Byzantine bus system.

Film & Photography

Kinefot, Talcahuano 262, has fast, high-quality developing of E-6 slide film, but is not cheap. For prints, try Le Lab at Viamonte 612 or Laboclick at Esmeralda 444.

For minor camera repairs, visit Gerardo Föhse, Florida 890, Local 26 (☎ 311-1139). For fast, dependable service on more complex problems see José Norres (☎ 490963), 4th floor, Oficina 403, Lavalle 1569, who accepts payment in US dollars only.

Medical Services

Buenos Aires' Hospital Municipal Juan Fernández (☎ 801-5555) is at Avenida Cerviño 3356, but there are many others, including Hospital Güemes (☎ 89-1675) at Avenida Córdoba 3933 and the British Hospital (☎ 23-1081) at Perdriel 74.

BARRIOS OF BUENOS AIRES

Most Porteños 'belong' to a *barrio* (neighbourhood) where they have spent almost all their lives. Tourists will rarely explore most of these, but five fairly central ones contain most of the capital's major attractions. These are described below – the boundaries indicated are more convenient than precise, but should help you get around to the most important public buildings, parks and museums.

Plaza de Mayo & Central Buenos Aires

Juan de Garay founded Buenos Aires for the second time in 1580, just north of Mendoza's encampment near Parque Lezama. In accordance with Spanish law, he laid out the large Plaza del Fuerte (Fortress Plaza), later called the Plaza del Mercado (Market Plaza), then the Plaza de la Victoria after victory over the British invaders in 1806 and 1807. It acquired its present name of **Plaza de Mayo** after the month of the Revolution of 1810.

The major public buildings were located here, including the **Cabildo**, part of which still exists, and the church, whose site is now occupied by the **Catedral Metropolitana**. Inside the Cathedral is the tomb of the repatriated San Martín, who died in France.

In the centre of the Plaza is the **Pirámide de Mayo**, a small obelisk built around an earlier monument, around which the Madres de la Plaza de Mayo still march every Thursday afternoon in their unrelenting campaign for a full accounting of the atrocities of the Dirty War.

At the east end of the Plaza the **Casa Rosada** presidential palace, begun during the presidential term of D F Sarmiento, occupies the site on which early colonial fortifications once stood along the riverbank – today, after filling, it is more than a km inland. From the balcony of the Casa Rosada, Juan Perón, General Leopoldo Galtieri, Raúl Alfonsín and other Argentine politicians have convened throngs of impassioned Argentines when they felt it necessary to demonstrate public support. In 1955, naval aircraft attacked the Casa Rosada and other government buildings in the so-called Revolución Libertadora which toppled Perón.

Most of the remaining public buildings in this area belong to the 19th century, when the Avenida de Mayo first connected the Casa Rosada to the **Plaza del Congreso** and the **Palacio del Congreso**, unfortunately obliterating part of the historic and dignified Cabildo in the process. Bryce, though, found these developments symbols of progress:

One great thoroughfare, the Avenida de Mayo, traverses the centre of the city from the large plaza in which the government buildings stand to the still larger and very handsome plaza which is adorned by the palace of the legislature. Fortunately it is wide, and being well planted with trees it is altogether a noble street, statelier than Piccadilly in London, or Unter den Linden in Berlin, or Pennsylvania Avenue in Washington...

The streets are well kept; everything is fresh and bright. The most striking new buildings besides those of the new Legislative Chambers, with their tall and handsome dome, are the Opera-house, the interior of which equals any in Europe, and the Jockey Club, whose scale and elaborate appointments surpass even the club-houses of New York.

Bryce might be surprised by modern Buenos Aires' faded elegance and failure to keep pace with European and North American capitals, but visitors to the area can still glimpse visions of the city's 'Belle Epoque', even though the focus of downtown activities has moved north along streets like Florida, Lavalle, and Avenidas Corrientes, Córdoba and Santa Fe.

In the early part of the century **Florida**, which is closed to motor vehicles between noon and 1.30 pm, was the city's most fashionable shopping street, a status it has since lost to **Avenida Santa Fe**. Today both Florida and **Lavalle** are pedestrian malls. The wide avenues of **Corrientes** (the city's theatre district), **Córdoba** and Santa Fe were created by demolition of older buildings. The even wider **Avenida 9 de Julio**, with its famous **Obelisco** at the intersection with Avenida Corrientes, is a pedestrian's worst nightmare. Fortunately, there is also a tunnel underneath it.

At the north end of downtown, just beyond **Plaza San Martín** and its magnificent *ombú* tree, is the famous **Torre de los Ingleses**. This replica of Big Ben testifies to the partial truth of the aphorism that 'an Argentine is an Italian who speaks Spanish, wishes he were English, and behaves as if he were French'. Ironically, since the 1982 Falklands war the plaza in which it stands, opposite Retiro Station, is now the **Plaza Fuerza Aérea Argentina** (Air Force Plaza).

Museo del Cabildo Modern construction has twice truncated the Cabildo, which dates from the mid-18th century, but there remains a representative sample of the arches which once ran the breadth of the Plaza de Mayo. The two-storey building itself is more interesting than the scanty exhibits, which include mementos of the British invasions of the early 19th century, some modern paintings in colonial and independence era styles, and religious art from missions of the Jesuits and other orders, plus fascinating early photographs of the Plaza. Since the museum was being reorganised at the time of writing, these exhibits may improve.

At Bolívar 65, the museum is open Thursday to Sunday from 2 to 6 pm. Admission costs US$1. There is an attractive interior patio with a modest confitería.

Catedral Metropolitana Also on the Plaza de Mayo, built on the site of the original colonial church but not finished until 1827, Buenos Aires' cathedral is not only an important religious landmark but an even more important national historical site, containing the tomb of José de San Martín, Argentina's most revered historical figure. In the chaos following Argentine independence, San Martín chose exile in France, never returning alive to Argentina even though, in 1829, he reached the shores of Buenos Aires before retreating, disillusioned, to Montevideo.

Casa Rosada Off limits during the military dictatorship of 1976-83, the presidential palace is no longer a place to avoid – you can even photograph the grenadiers who guard

Top: Congreso Nacional, Buenos Aires
Left: Tango musicians, La Boca, Buenos Aires
Right: Tomb of President Nicolás Avellaneda, Recoleta Cemetery

Top Left: Billboard of Carlos Gardel, Buenos Aires
Top Right: Basilica of Luján, Buenos Aires Province
Bottom: Fountain, Plaza del Congreso, Buenos Aires

the main entrance. Its recently reopened basement museum, entered at Hipólito Yrigoyen 218, exhibits the personal effects of Argentine presidents. Opening hours are Tuesday to Friday from 9 am to 6 pm and Sunday from 3 to 6 pm.

Palacio del Congreso In costing more than twice its original budget, the national Congress set a precedent for modern Argentine public works projects. Modelled on the Capitol Building in Washington, DC, and completed in 1906, it faces the Plaza del Congreso, which features the **Monumento a los Dos Congresos**, honouring the Congresses of 1810 in Buenos Aires and 1816 in Tucumán which led to Argentine independence. Its enormous granite steps symbolise the high Andes, while the fountain at its foot represents the Atlantic Ocean. On Sundays, Ravel's *Bolero* usually blares from the loudspeakers.

In the waning days of the military dictatorship, the monument was blanketed in graffiti, but regular sand-blasting has since kept it clean.

Museo Mitre Bartolomé Mitre was a soldier, journalist, and Argentina's first legitimate president under the Constitution of 1853, although his term ran from 1862-68. After leaving office he founded the influential daily *La Nación*, still a Porteño institution.

At Calle San Martín 366, the museum is an enormous colonial house, plus additions, in which Mitre resided with his family – a good reflection of upper-class Argentine life in the 19th century. A side exit led directly to *La Nación*'s offices. Take a look at the library, which holds more than 80,000 volumes. Hours are Tuesday to Friday from 1 pm to 6 pm, Sunday from 2 to 6 pm. Admission is US$1.

Teatro Colón For decades, visitors to Buenos Aires have marvelled at the Colón Theatre, a world-class facility for opera, ballet and classical music, which opened in 1908 with a presentation of *Aida*. Occupying an entire block bounded by Libertad,

Tucumán, Viamonte and Cerrito (Avenida 9 de Julio), the seven-storey building has seating for 2500 spectators and standing room for another 1000. There are presidential command performances on the winter patriotic holidays of 25 May and 9 July.

In the theatre there is a popular museum with exhibits of costumes, instruments and photographs of performers and performances. It's open weekdays from noon to 6 pm. Inquire about free guided tours. Dress well, since it is a very formal place.

Other Downtown Museums The **Museo de Arte Moderno**, in the Centro Cultural San Martín at Avenida Corrientes 1530, 9th floor, has works by Dali and Picasso, among others. It's open daily except Monday, from noon to 8 pm. A bit farther away, at Sarmiento 2573, is the **Museo del Cine** (film museum), open weekdays from 9 am to 4 pm.

The **Museo de la Policía Federal**, in the heart of the financial district at Calle San Martín 353, 7th floor, is open Tuesday to Friday, 2 to 6 pm. As if Argentina needed one, there is a **Museo de Armas** (weapons museum) at Maipú 1030, corner of Avenida Santa Fe. It's open Wednesday, Thursday and Friday from 3 to 7 pm.

San Telmo
South of the Plaza de Mayo, San Telmo is one of the most interesting neighbourhoods in Buenos Aires, not dominated by the rampant gentrification of areas like Recoleta and Palermo. To some degree, it is still an artist's quarter, where Bohemians can find large spaces at low rents.

It is also famous for the rugged street fighting which took place when British troops, at war with Spain, invaded the city in 1806 and occupied it until the following year, when covert Porteño resistance became open. When a second British force advanced up narrow Calle Defensa, the impromptu militia, supported by women and slaves pouring cauldrons of boiling oil and water from the rooftops and firing cannons from the balconies of the house at **Defensa 372,** routed the British back to their ships. Victory gave the Porteños confidence in their ability to stand apart from Spain.

In this area, the most interesting sight is the **Manzana de las Luces** (Block of Lights), bounded by Calles Alsina, Bolívar, Perú and Moreno, which includes the Jesuit **Iglesia San Ignacio**, the oldest colonial church in Buenos Aires. At Defensa and Humberto Primo is **Plaza Dorrego**, site of a weekly flea market, the Feria de San Telmo. A few blocks beyond, at Defensa and Brasil, is **Parque Lezama**, the presumptive site of Pedro de Mendoza's original foundation of the city.

Until the late 19th century, San Telmo was a fashionable part of the city, but after a yellow fever epidemic hit the low-lying area, the Porteño elite evacuated to higher ground west and north of downtown. When immigrants began to pour into Argentina, many of the older houses became *conventillos*, tenements which housed European families in cramped, divided quarters with inadequate sanitary facilities.

Despite the neighbourhood's historic colour, these conditions still exist. According to the Buenos Aires daily *Clarín*, over the past decade squatters have occupied more than 120 abandoned houses in San Telmo, selling 'places' to their successors as they find permanent housing. In one former single family house, 22 persons from six families resided in one room each.

Museo Histórico Nacional Appropriately located in Parque Lezama, this historical museum offers a panorama of the Argentine experience from its shaky beginnings to independence and the present. Its Sala de la Conquista, with paintings depicting the Spanish domination of wealthy, civilised Peru and Columbus' triumphant return to Spain, could not offer greater contrast with the Mendoza expedition's struggle to survive on the shores of the River Plate. There is also a map of the Buenos Aires of Juan de Garay's second founding of the city, four decades later.

In the Sala de la Independencia and other rooms, there are portraits of major figures of the independence and republican periods, such as Simón Bolívar, his ally and rival San Martín both in his youth and the disillusionment of old age, and Rosas and his bitter but eloquent enemy Sarmiento, the latter with his perpetual scowl. There are also portrayals of the British invasions of 1806 and 1807, and of late 19th-century Porteño life.

At Defensa 1600, the museum is open Wednesday, Thursday, Friday and Sunday, from 2 to 6 pm. Take the No 86 bus from Plaza Congreso.

Other San Telmo Museums The **Museo de la Ciudad** (Museum of the City), at 1st floor, Alsina 412, has both permanent and temporary exhibitions on Porteño life and history. It's open weekdays from 11 am to 7 pm and weekends from 3 to 7 pm.

The **Museo del Traje** (Museum of Dress & Uniforms), Chile 832, displays civilian and military clothing from colonial times to the present. At the time of writing it was closed for repairs, but its library is open Tuesday to Friday from 1.30 to 5.30 pm.

For religious art from the colonial period, visit the **Museo San Roque** at the Basílica San Francisco, Alsina 340. The **Museo de la Basílica del Rosario**, in the Santo Domingo church on the corner of Defensa and Belgrano, contains relics of the British invasions and the wars of independence. Opening hours are 9 am to 1 pm and 4.30 to 8.30 pm daily.

La Boca

Literally Buenos Aires' most colourful neighbourhood, La Boca was settled and built up by Italian immigrants along the **Riachuelo**, a small waterway lined by meat packing plants and warehouses which separates Buenos Aires proper from the industrial suburb of Avellaneda. Part of its colour comes from the brightly painted houses and corrugated iron roofs of the **Caminito**, a popular pedestrian walk which was once a rail terminus and takes its name from a popular tango. The rest comes from petroleum and other waste which tints the waters of the Riachuelo, where rusting hulks and dredges lie offshore and rowers strain to take passengers who prefer not to walk across the high girder bridge to Avellaneda. When the rains are heavy and tides are high, flood waters submerge most of the area.

Once, areas like La Boca were places where immigrants could find a foothold in the country, but they were less than idyllic. Bryce described them as

...a waste of scattered shanties...dirty and squalid, with corrugated iron roofs, their wooden boards gaping like rents in tattered clothes. These are inhabited by the newest and poorest of immigrants from southern Italy and southern Spain, a large and not very desirable element among whom anarchism is rife.

In fact, before the Italians, the first settlers of La Boca were French Basques. Today the area is partly an artists' colony, the legacy of local painter Benito Quinquela Martín, but still a flourishing working-class neighbourhood. The symbol of the community's solidarity is the Boca Juniors soccer team, once the club of disgraced superstar Diego Maradona.

Tourists also come to Boca to savour the atmosphere of **Calle Necochea**, which is lined with pizzerías and garish cantinas. When these places were still brothels, the tango was not the respectable, middle-class folk phenomenon it is today. The No 86 bus from the Plaza del Congreso is the easiest route there.

Museo de Bellas Artes de La Boca

Once the home and studio of Quinquela Martín, the Boca Fine Arts Museum exhibits his work and that of other modern Argentine artists. At Pedro de Mendoza 1835, it's open daily from 9 am to noon and 3 to 6 pm.

Recoleta

North-west of downtown, Recoleta is one of the most fashionable areas in Buenos Aires. It takes its name from the Franciscan convent which dates from 1716, but is best known for the astonishing necropolis of **Cementerio de la Recoleta** (Recoleta Cemetery) where,

in death as in life, generations of the Argentine elite have rested in ornate splendour.

The **Iglesia de Nuestra Señora de Pilar**, a colonial church consecrated in 1732, is a national historical monument. Also in the same area are the important **Centro Cultural Recoleta**, the **Museo Nacional de Bellas Artes** (fine arts museum), and the **Centro Municipal de Exposiciones**, which hosts book fairs and other cultural events.

Recoleta was among the areas to which the upper-class Porteños of San Telmo relocated after the yellow fever epidemic of the 1870s. It has many attractive public gardens and open spaces, including **Plaza Alvear**, **Plaza Francia** (which on Sundays holds the largest crafts fair in Buenos Aires), and several other parks which stretch into the neighbourhood of Palermo.

Museo Nacional de Bellas Artes Unquestionably the country's most important art museum, this museum houses paintings of European masters like Renoir, Rodin, Monet, Van Gogh and Picasso, as well as Argentine artists of the 19th and 20th centuries. There are also significant sculptures and wood carvings. At Avenida del Libertador 1473, just north of Recoleta Cemetery, it's open daily except Monday from 9 am to 1 pm and 3 to 7 pm.

Museo de Arte Hispanoamericano Isaac Fernández Blanco Containing an exceptional collection of colonial art, including silverwork, painting, costumes and antiques, this museum occupies a restored colonial house at Suipacha 1422. Opening hours are daily, except Monday, from 2 to 7 pm.

Museo José Hernández Named for the author of the gaucho epic *Martín Fierro*, this museum has a comprehensive collection of Argentine folk art from prehistory through the colonial period to the present. It's open weekdays from 8 am to 7 pm and weekends from 3 to 7 pm, at Avenida del Libertador 2373.

Other Recoleta Museums The **Museo**

Eduardo Sivori, a museum of Argentine art at Calle Junín 1930 in the Centro Cultural Recoleta, is open Tuesday to Friday from 3 to 8 pm, weekends from 10 am to 8 pm. Sivori was an Italo-Argentine painter who studied in Europe but later returned to Argentine themes, mainly associated with rural life on the Pampas.

Two museums share the same building at Avenida Libertador 1902. The **Museo de Arte Decorativo** (Museum of Decorative Arts) is open daily except Tuesday from 3 to 7 pm, while the **Museo de Arte Oriental** (Museum of Oriental Art) is open Wednesday to Sunday from 3 to 7 pm.

Palermo

Ironically, perhaps the most positive legacy

Life & Death in Recoleta & Chacarita

Death is an equaliser, except in Buenos Aires. When the arteries harden after decades of dining at Au Bec Fin and finishing up with coffee and dessert at La Biela or Café de la Paix, the wealthy and powerful of Buenos Aires move ceremoniously across the street to Recoleta Cemetery, joining their forefathers in a place they have visited religiously all their lives. Perhaps no place else says more about Argentina and Argentine society.

According to Argentine novelist Tomás Eloy Martínez, Argentines are 'cadaver cultists' who honour their most revered national figures not on the date of their birth but of their death. Schoolchildren repeat their last words. Nowhere is this obsession with mortality and corruption more evident than at Recoleta, where generations of the elite repose in the grandeur of ostentatious mausoleums – it is a common saying and only a slight exaggeration that 'it is cheaper to live extravagantly all your life than to be buried in Recoleta'. Traditionally, money alone is not enough: you must have a surname like Anchorena, Alvear, Aramburu, Avellaneda, Mitre, Martínez de Hoz or Sarmiento. The remains of Evita Perón, secured in a subterranean crypt, are an exception which infuriates the presumptive aristocracy.

One reason for this is that the defunct often play a peculiar, and more than just symbolic, role in Argentine politics. Evita rests in Recoleta only after an odyssey which took her embalmed body (an unusual practice in Argentina) from South America to an obscure cemetery in Milan and to Perón's house in exile in Madrid before its return to Buenos Aires. The man responsible for her 'kidnapping' was General Pedro Aramburu, a bitter political enemy of the Peróns who reportedly sought the Vatican's help in sequestering the cadaver after Perón's overthrow in 1955.

Aramburu himself was held for 'ransom' by the left-wing Peronist Montoneros *after* his assassination in 1970 – only after the military government of General Alejandro Lanusse ensured Evita's return to Perón in Madrid did Aramburu's body reappear to be entombed in Recoleta, now only a few short 'blocks' from Evita. Juan Perón himself lies across town, in the much less exclusive cemetery of Chacarita, which opened in the 1870s to accommodate the yellow fever victims of San Telmo and La Boca.

Although more democratic in conception, Chacarita has many tombs which match the finest in Recoleta. One of the most visited belongs to Carlos Gardel, the famous tango singer. Plaques from around the world cover the base of his life-size statue, many thanking him for favours granted – like Evita, Perón and others, Gardel is a near-saint to whom countless Argentines feel a quasi-religious devotion. The steady procession of pilgrims reveals the pervasiveness of spiritualism in a country which prides itself on European sophistication.

One of the best places to witness this is the Chacarita tomb of Madre María Salomé, a disciple of the famous healer Pancho Sierra. Every day, but especially on the 2nd of each month (she died on 2 October 1928), adherents of her cult leave floral tributes – white carnations are the favourite – and lay their hands on her sepulchre in rapt supplication.

Organised tours regularly visit Recoleta Cemetery, open daily from 7 am to 6 pm on Calle Junín across from the Plaza Alvear, but it is fine to wander about on your own. For Evita's grave, ask directions to the relatively modest tomb of the 'Familia Duarte' (her maiden name), but do not overlook the monuments to Mitre, Sarmiento and other elite families.

To visit Chacarita, which is not a major tourist attraction like Recoleta, take Línea B of the Subte to the end of the line at Federico Lacroze, from which it is a short walk. Look for the tomb of 'Tomas Perón', but do not miss those of Gardel, Madre María, aviator Jorge Newbery, tango musician Aníbal 'Pichuco' Troilo, and comedian Luis Sandrini. Hours are identical to those at Recoleta. ■

of dictator Juan Manuel de Rosas is the wide open spaces of Palermo, beyond Recoleta on both sides of Avenida Libertador. Once Rosas' private retreat, the area became public parkland after his fall from power. One measure of the dictator's disgrace is that the man who overthrew him, Entre Ríos caudillo and former ally Justo José de Urquiza, sits here astride his mount in a massive equestrian monument on the corner of Sarmiento and Figueroa Alcorta. Domingo F Sarmiento, another who detested Rosas, was president of the country when development resumed.

When Bryce visited Buenos Aires after the turn of the century, he marvelled at the opulence of the Porteño elite who frequented the area:

On fine afternoons, there is a wonderful turnout of carriages drawn by handsome horses, and still more of costly motor cars, in the principal avenues of the Park; they press so thick that vehicles are often jammed together for fifteen or twenty minutes, unable to move on. Nowhere in the world does one get a stronger impression of exuberant wealth and extravagance. The Park itself, called Palermo, lies on the edge of the city towards the river, and is approached by a well-designed and well-planted avenue.

Now a major recreational area for all Porteños, Palermo contains the city's **Jardin Botánico Carlos Thays** (the botanical gardens, now swarming with feral cats), **Jardin Zoológico** (the zoo, currently a focus of controversy over its proposed lease to a political crony of the Peronist mayor of Buenos Aires), **Rosedal** (rose garden), **Campo de Polo** (polo grounds), **Hipódromo** (racetrack) and **Planetarium**. As you might guess, some of these uses were not really for the masses, but elite sectors no longer have the park to themselves.

Museo del Instituto Nacional San-martiniano In Palermo Chico, in a small plaza at the junction of Calles Aguado, Elizalde, Castilla and Sánchez de Bustamante, this museum is a replica of San Martin's home-in-exile at Boulogne-Sur-Mer, France. It's open weekdays from 9 am to noon and 2 to 5 pm, weekends from 2 to 5 pm only.

Other Museums in Buenos Aires
Outside the city centre and close-in barrios most frequented by tourists, there are several other significant museums. The **Museo Sarmiento**, Cuba 2079 in Belgrano, was once the site of the Congress and executive offices, but now contains memorabilia of Domingo F Sarmiento, one of Argentina's most famous statesmen and educators. Despite the look of perpetual indignation on his face, the classically educated Sarmiento was an eloquent writer who analysed 19th-century Argentina from a cosmopolitan, clearly Eurocentric, point of view. The museum is open Tuesday to Friday from 3 to 7 pm and Sundays from 4 to 7 pm. From Congreso or Avenida Callao, take bus No 60, disembarking at Cabildo and Juramento.

Nearby, at Juramento 2291, is the **Museo Larreta**, the private art collection of Hispanophile novelist Enrique Larreta. It's open Monday, Tuesday, Wednesday and Friday from 9 am to 1 pm and 3 to 7.45 pm, weekends only from 3 to 7.45 pm. A few blocks away, at O'Higgins 2390, is the **Casa de Yrurtia**, the former residence of sculptor Rogelio Yrurtia. Hours are Wednesday to Sunday, 3 to 7 pm.

Also in Belgrano, at 3 de Febrero 1370, is the **Museo del Instituto Nacional de Antropología**. Opening hours are weekdays from 2 to 7 pm.

LANGUAGE COURSES
There are many opportunities for Spanish language instruction in Buenos Aires. Consult the Sunday classified section of the *Buenos Aires Herald*, which offers several columns' worth of possibilities, as well as opportunities for teaching English.

One place to try is the Instituto de Lengua Española para Extranjeros (☎ 49-8208), Oficina E, 3rd floor, Lavalle 1619. It has conversation-based courses at basic, intermediate and advanced levels. Private classes cost US$15 per hour, group lessons are US$11 an hour. The institute can also arrange accommodation in a private home for US$300 per month.

ORGANISED TOURS

Many agencies offer half-day and full-day city tours, but unless your time is very limited try to get around on your own. It may be worthwhile checking to see if the municipal tourist office in the Centro Cultural San Martín still offers free guided tours of the city's neighbourhoods.

One destination that may justify a guided tour is the historic island of Martín García, site of an important naval battle during the wars of independence and later a penal colony. Cacciola (☎ 322-0026), in downtown on the 1st floor at Florida 520, or in the riverside suburb of Tigre (☎ 749-2369), at Lavalle 520, runs enclosed catamarans to the island on weekends.

PLACES TO STAY

Places to Stay – bottom end

Hostels The Buenos Aires hostel (☎ 362-9133) is at Brasil 675, near Constitución Station, easily reached by the Subte. It closes between noon and 6 pm. There is a privately run hostel (☎ 771-4449) in Belgrano, at José Ortega y Gasset 1782. Prices run about US$6 per person.

Hotels The best located budget hotel is *Hotel O'Rei* (☎ 393-7186), Lavalle 733 near Maipú, just a block from Florida. Quiet (except for the rooms that front directly onto Lavalle), clean and very friendly, it has singles/doubles with shared bath for US$7/10, with good laundry facilities. Almost equally cheap is *Petit Hotel Goya* (☎ 392-9269) at Suipacha 748.

Another recommended place is *Hotel Bahía* (☎ 35-1780), at Avenida Corrientes 1212. *Hotel Apolo* (☎ 393-6970), Tucumán 951, is acceptable but less than ideal.

In San Telmo, the slightly musty *Hotel Panamá* (☎ 40-0072), Chile 838 near the Museo del Traje, charges about US$6 per person with shared bath, US$7 with private

bath. Slightly better would be the nearby *Hotel Embajador* (☎ 362-6617) at Chacabuco 747 or *Hotel Victoria* at Chacabuco 726. *Hotel Bolívar* (☎ 361-5105), Bolívar 886, is comparable in price and standard. Close to the colourful Plaza Dorrego is *Hotel Carly* (☎ 361-7710), Humberto Primo 464. Try also *Hotel Zavalia* (☎ 362-4845) at Juan de Garay 474 or *Hotel Washington* (☎ 361-4738) at Juan de Garay 340, both near Parque Lezama.

Returning from Mar del Plata or Patagonia, try the neighbourhood around Constitución Station (although some accommodation in this area rents on an hourly basis). Possibilities include *Hotel La Casita* (☎ 27-0250) at Constitución 1549, *Hotel Atlas* (☎ 27-9587) at Perú 1681, or *Hotel Miramar* (☎ 23-9069) at Salta 1429.

In a slightly higher category, try *Hotel Alba* (☎ 27-4303) at Juan de Garay 1381, *Hotel Carlos I* (☎ 26-3700) at Carlos Calvo 1463, *Hotel Esquel* (☎ 23-5722) at Brasil 1319, or *Hotel Autopista* (☎ 26-1634) at Salta 1444. Other places include *Hotel Central* (☎ 23-3783) at Brasil 1327 and *Hotel Brasil* (☎ 23-5141) at Brasil 1340.

Congreso is a good place to look for inexpensive lodging. Certainly one of the cheapest in town is the funky but passable *Hotel Plaza* (☎ 40-9747) at Rivadavia 1761, across from the Plaza del Congreso, with singles with shared bath for US$4, only slightly more with private bath (and unlikely to be confused with the exclusive Plaza Hotel in Barrio Norte). *Hotel Central* (☎ 49-8785), Alsina 1693, has rooms with private bath for US$9/13.

Hotel Callao (☎ 45-3534), in an interesting building at Avenida Callao 292, has singles with shared bath for US$10, and rooms with private bath for US$12/18. A good choice is the friendly *Gran Hotel Sarmiento* (☎ 45-2764), on a quiet block at Sarmiento 1892, where rates are US$14/22 with private bath. *Hotel Sevilla* (☎ 45-8447), also near Plaza del Congreso at Solís 138, is very convenient.

If wandering around the Congreso area,

avoid *Gran Hotel Oriental*, Bartolomé Mitre 1840, whose astonishingly rude manager will probably drive you out in a day anyway.

For reasonable accommodation in a lively university area, try *Hotel Rich* (☎ 83-7942), at Paraguay 2080 near the Facultad de Medicina of the Universidad de Buenos Aires. Nearby is *Hotel Oviedo* (☎ 84-0852), Paraguay 2313.

Places to Stay – middle

There are many midrange hotels around the Avenida de Mayo. *Chile Hotel* (☎ 34-5664), Avenida de Mayo 1297, has rooms with bath for US$17/25. Although the street noise is considerable, its corner rooms have huge balconies with great views of the Congress and the Casa Rosada. Try also the once-elegant *Hotel Reyna* (☎ 37-2664) at Avenida de Mayo 1120, near Avenida 9 de Julio.

The spacious air-conditioned rooms at the newly remodelled *Hotel Avenida* (☎ 331-4341), at Avenida de Mayo 623, are among the best value in town at US$15/22 with private bath. *Turista Hotel* (☎ 331-2281), Avenida de Mayo 686, is slightly more expensive but so central that, according to one reader, 'you can practically see President Menem in his Casa Rosada office interviewing the next Minister of Finance' – a frequent enough occurrence. On the other hand, another called the hotel very unfriendly, as they refused even to show him a room.

Closer to downtown, there are conflicting reports on the convenient *Hotel Phoenix* (☎ 312-4845), Calle San Martín 780, which has undoubtedly declined from the days when the Prince of Wales once stayed there. Friendly, it still has a shabby charm to its turn-of-the-century woodwork and balconies despite the loss of part of its ground floor to a restaurant, but one critical LP reader called it 'filthy, noisy and depressing'. Rooms are US$12/21 with shared bath, US$16/26 with private bath. *King's Hotel*, Avenida Corrientes 623, is comparably priced. *Hotel Central Córdoba* (☎ 311-1175) is modest but friendly and pleasant, and also very central at Calle San Martín

1021, but some of the rooms are small. Rates are US$24/31.

Other possibilities are *Hotel Plaza Roma* (☎ 311-1679), Lavalle 110 near Leandro Alem, and *Hotel Regis* (☎ 393-5131), Lavalle 813. *Hotel Waldorf* (☎ 312-2071), Paraguay 450, and *Hotel Diplomat*, Calle San Martín 918, are a bit dearer. Try also *Tucumán Palace Hotel* (☎ 311-2298) at Tucumán 384.

Near the Plaza del Congreso, *Hotel Mar del Plata* (☎ 40-0072), Rivadavia 1777, charges about US$18/22 with shared bath, US$21/26 with private bath. Rates are almost identical at *Lourdes Hotel* (☎ 48-3087), Avenida Callao 44. A reader strongly recommends the centrally located *Promenade Hotel* (☎ 312-5681), Alvear 444, which charges about US$25 per person per night. *Hotel Molino* (☎ 46-8961), Avenida Callao 164, charges US$28/37 for rooms with air-conditioning, private bath and telephone.

Places to Stay – top end

Top-end hotels usually quote their prices in dollars but do accept Argentine currency. All of them take credit cards.

Prices start around US$35/50 at places like the *Liberty Hotel* (☎ 325-0261) at Avenida Corrientes 632, the *Italia Romanelli* at Reconquista 647, the *Gran Hotel Argentino* (☎ 35-3071) at Pellegrini 37, and *Gran Hotel Orly* (☎ 312-5344) at Paraguay 474.

In the heart of the theatre district, the *Columbia Palace Hotel* (☎ 49-1906), Avenida Corrientes 1533, charges US$39/54. A bit farther away, *Hotel Lyon* (☎ 45-0100), Riobamba 251, has rooms with private bath for US$45/60, while the *Savoy Hotel* (☎ 814-3592), Avenida Callao 181, has doubles for US$70. Rates at the very central *Hotel Continental* (☎ 49-3251), Avenida Roque Sáenz Peña 725, are US$60/70.

A traveller heartily recommends the four-star *Hotel Regidor*, Tucumán 451, which is about half the price of other four-star places at US$38 per night, including breakfast.

Few places can match the Old World charm of *Hotel Plaza Francia* (☎ 804-9631),

Eduardo Schiaffino 2189 in Recoleta, where doubles cost about US$90. The prestigious *Bauen Hotel* (☎ 804-1600), Avenida Callao 360 near Avenida Corrientes, charges US$110 for a double. Other five-star downtown hotels include the *Plaza Hotel* (☎ 311-5011) at Florida 1005, which has an interesting Dutch dining room, and the *Elevage Hotel* (☎ 313-2082) at Maipú 960.

The venerable, dignified *Claridge Hotel* (☎ 322-7700), conveniently central at Tucumán 535, has very comfortable rooms with cable television and other amenities starting at US$125/140. The modern *Sheraton Hotel* (☎ 311-6330) at Calle San Martín 1225 is less central and convenient, with doubles upwards of US$150. If you're going to stay that far away and pay that much, you're better off at the revered and elegant *Alvear Palace Hotel* (☎ 804-4031), at Avenida Alvear 1891 in Recoleta, where doubles can reach $200 or more. It may affect your decision to know that Chile's General Pinochet stays here when he visits Buenos Aires.

PLACES TO EAT
Food in Buenos Aires ranges from the cheap and simple to the costly and sophisticated. In some places you may find decent fixed-price meals for less than US$3, but if you order a la carte you will find that side orders, such as chips and soft drinks, can drive the price up considerably. Rather than downtown, you might find better bargains in San Telmo and La Boca.

In run-of-the-mill restaurants, which are often very good, the standard fare is basic pasta, short orders like milanesa, and the more economical cuts of beef, plus fried potatoes, green salads, and desserts. By spending just a little more, you can eat the same sort of food with better ingredients. More cosmopolitan meals are available at the capital's innumerable high-class restaurants, but these can be very costly indeed. One good place to catch up on the latest in Buenos Aires *haute cuisine* is the weekly 'Good Living' section in the Sunday *Buenos Aires Herald*, where Dereck Foster also

offers the latest on Argentine wines, but you should be aware that by his criteria 'inexpensive' meals can easily cost US$15. The tourist office's English-language freebie, *Where in Buenos Aires*, also has a list of suggestions.

Meals in Argentine restaurants are generally relaxed affairs. Breakfasts are negligible, but other meals can last for hours. Lunch starts around midday, but dinner starts later, much later, than in English-speaking countries. Almost nobody eats before 9 pm, and it is not unusual for people to dine after midnight even on weeknights.

An important part of the meal, whether at home or in the restaurant, is the *sobremesa*, dallying at the table to discuss family matters or other events of the day. No matter how long the lines outside, no Argentine restaurateur would even dream of nudging along a party which has lingered over its coffee long after the food itself is history.

Parrillas
When Charles Darwin rode across the province of Buenos Aires in the 1830s, he could not contain his astonishment at the gauchos' diet, which he himself followed of necessity:

I had now been several days without tasting any thing besides meat: I did not at all dislike this new regimen; but I felt as if it would only have agreed with me with hard exercise. I have heard that patients in England, when desired to confine themselves exclusively to an animal diet, even with the hope of life before their eyes, have scarce been able to endure it. Yet the Gaucho in the Pampas, for months together, touches nothing but beef...It is, perhaps, from their meat regimen that the Gauchos, like other carnivorous animals, can abstain long from food. I was told that at Tandeel, some troops voluntarily pursued a party of Indians for three days, without eating or drinking.

Even many Argentines admit that a diet so reliant on beef is unhealthy, but sedentary Porteños continue to consume it in large quantities at parrillas. So long as you don't make it a way of life, you can probably indulge yourself on the succulent grilled meat, often stretched on a vertical spit over red-hot coals in the picture windows of the capital's most prestigious restaurants. Even though we rarely eat red meat at home in California, we can't resist when we visit Argentina.

If you visit only one parrilla in Buenos Aires, overlook the hired tourist gauchos at *La Estancia*, Lavalle 941, and focus on their excellent food at moderate prices. Other highly regarded, but pricier, downtown places include *La Cabaña* at Entre Ríos 436, *La Chacra* at Avenida Córdoba 941, *La Rural* at Suipacha 453, *Las Nazarenas* at Reconquista 1132, *La Posta del Gaucho* at Carlos Pellegrini 625, and *Los Troncos* at Suipacha 732.

One LP correspondent called *Dora*, on Reconquista near Paraguay, 'the best restaurant we found in Argentina', with outstanding seafood and pasta in addition to its parrilla, plus 'incredible' desserts. A bit away from the centre, but worth the trip on bus No 37 or No 60, is *El Ceibal*, Las Heras 2265, which has excellent atmosphere and service as well as outstanding food.

Bar La Robla, Viamonte 1613, has both excellent seafood and standard Argentine dishes, in a pleasant environment at moderate prices. Although it is a chain, the food is well prepared and far from monotonous. Other branches are at Avenida Alvarez Thomas 1302, Gascón 1701, Lambaré 807, and Montevideo 194. Another good, popular and reasonable chain is *El Palacio de la Papa Frita*, at Lavalle 735, Lavalle 954, and Avenida Corrientes 1612. *Cervantes II*, Perón 1883, has enormous serves of standard Argentine fare, but is often so crowded that you may wish to take your food away instead of eating there.

There are countless cheaper but ordinary downtown parrillas, such as *Don Pipón*, Esmeralda 521. Traditionally, one of the most popular and economical is *Pippo*, at Paraná 356 with another entrance on Montevideo.

Cafés & Confiterías

Café society is a major force in the life of Argentines in general and Porteños in particular – they spend hours solving their own problems, the country's and the world's over

a chessboard and a cheap cortado. Some cafés double as bookstores.

Undoubtedly the most famous is the *Café Tortoni*, at Avenida de Mayo 829, which was founded in 1858 but has occupied its present site only since 1893. Oozing its 19th-century atmosphere out of the woodwork and onto the sidewalk, it showcases traditional jazz bands on weekends, and you can play billiards in the back. The ornate, almost rococo interior at *Confitería del Molino*, Avenida Callao 20 near Plaza del Congreso, also merits a visit from anyone seeking turn-of-the-century ambience. The sweets for afternoon tea are exquisite.

Avenida Corrientes is a favourite hangout for Argentine intellectuals. Famous for Bohemian atmosphere is the spartan *Cafe La Paz*, Avenida Corrientes 1599. *Café Pernambuco*, Avenida Corrientes 1680, has a good atmosphere for drinking a cup of coffee or a glass of wine.

Downtown cafés include the *Young Men's Bar* at Avenida Córdoba 800, and the funky, informal *Bar-o-bar* or *Bár-baro* at Tres Sargentos 451. The always-crowded *Florida Garden*, at Florida 899, is popular among politicians, journalists and other influential people. Another possibility is the *Richmond*, Florida 468.

Some of the Porteño elite while away the hours on caffeine from *La Biela*, Quintana 598 across from the famous Recoleta Cemetery. The rest exercise their purebred dogs nearby, so watch your step as you cross the street to *Café de la Paix*, Quintana 595. Another elegant place is the *Winter Garden* at the Alvear Palace Hotel.

Italian

Despite the abundance of Italian surnames in Argentina, most Italian food is hybrid Italo-Argentine. Exceptions to this rule tend to be pricey, but try *La Casona del Nono* at Lavalle 827. Definitely upscale are *Cicerón* at Reconquista 647, *Tommaso* at Junín 1735, *A'Mamma Liberata* at Medrano 974, *Robertino* at Vicente López 2158 in Recoleta, or *La Zí Teresa di Napoli*, Las Heras 2939. *Subito*, at Posadas 1245 and with several other branches scattered around town, is another possibility.

Pizzerías

Buenos Aires has great pizza. In our experience, consistently best has been the unsung *Pizzería Guerrín*, Avenida Corrientes 1372, which sells individual slices of superb fugazza, fugazzeta and other specialities, plus excellent empanadas, cold lager beer to wash it all down, and many appealing desserts. It is cheaper to buy at the counter and eat standing up, but there is a much greater variety of flavours if you decide to be seated and served. The traditionally excellent *Pizzería Serafín*, nearby at Avenida Corrientes 1328, wasn't up to snuff on our last visit but we wouldn't write it off either. Their chicken empanadas are always good.

Los Idolos, Suipacha 436, is popular but its atmosphere and service are better than its food. Ditto for *Pizza Cero* at Cerviño 3701. *Los Inmortales*, renowned for its gigantic billboard of Carlos Gardel along Avenida Corrientes, has branches at Lavalle 746, Avenida Callao 1165, and Avenida Alvear 1234.

Another recommended pizzería is *Las Marias II*, at Bolivar 964-66 in San Telmo. A reader described it as 'the best pizza I tasted in Buenos Aires', and staff are friendly and efficient.

Spanish

Los Teatros, Talcahuano 360 between Sarmiento and Avenida Corrientes, has outstanding seafood, chicken and pasta dishes. Among seafood restaurants, *El Pulpo*, Tucumán 400, is considered the city's best. Try also *Antigua Casca de Cuchilleros* at Carlos Calvo 319, *El Hispano* at Salta 20, *Cantabria* (seafood) at Avenida Callao 1235, *Villarosa* at Hipólito Yrigoyen 1389, or *Meson Español*, Caseros 1745, San Telmo. For Basque food, try *Laurak Bat* at Belgrano 1144 or *Taberna Baska* at Chile 980.

French

Widely acknowledged as one of the best restaurants in Buenos Aires, *Au Bec Fin*, Vicente López 1825 in Recoleta, has prices to match. *Hippopotamus*, Junín 1787, which includes a popular but very formal disco/nightclub, is in the same category; a reader endorses it's US$18 'executive menu'. Try also *Catalinas*, at Reconquista 875. Across the street is *Flo*, Reconquista 878. Other choices include *Chez Moi* at San Juan 1223, *El Gato Que Pesca* at Rodríguez Peña 159, and *Cien Años* at Amenábar 2075, Belgrano.

European/International

If price is no object, check out Recoleta institutions like *Estilo Munich* at Roberto Ortiz 1878, the nearby *Gato Dumas* at Ortiz 1813, or *Clark's* at Ortiz 1777. *La Mosca Blanca*, Avenida Libertador 901, also has a good reputation and more reasonable prices. For Swiss cuisine, try *La Petit*, Salta 2158. There is a classy international restaurant in the Sheraton Hotel.

An open secret is the popular smorgasbord at the *Swedish Club* (☎ 334-1703), 5th floor, Tacuarí 143. Theoretically open to members only, it takes place the third Wednesday of every month, but you can 'request' an invitation by phone.

For cheaper fare, try the hole-in-the-wall *Restaurant San Francisco*, at Defensa 177 near Plaza de Mayo.

Chilean

If you can't cross the Andes, there is good Chilean seafood and other national dishes at *Restaurant Los Chilenos*, Suipacha 1042.

Vegetarian

After you've beefed up for a few days, you may want to take a break at one of these surprising places – since the mid-1980s, there has been a vegetarian boom in carnivorous Buenos Aires. Some places failed because their food was monotonously bland, but many have survived, like the self-service *Ratatouille*, Sarmiento 1810. For about US$5, it is tenedor libre. One reader endorses *Giardino*, with locations at Suipacha 429 and Lavalle 835.

In addition to being one of the most enduring vegetarian places in Buenos Aires, *La Esquina de las Flores*, Avenida Córdoba 1599, also has a health-food store. Other places worth trying include *Granix*, with branches at Florida 126 and 461, and *La Huerta*, Paraguay 445.

Asian

One of our most memorable bilingual menus came from a Chinese restaurant near Congreso, where an unusually creative mistranslation turned *camarones a la plancha* into 'ironed shrimp'. Despite this vivid image, most Asian food in Argentina is standard and unimaginative Cantonese, but a recent boom in all-you-can-eat restaurants, with meals for about US$3, is a good option for low-budget travellers. Quality is ordinary, but if you choose wisely it's good enough. Most also have salad bars, whose ingredients are excellent. There is little difference among these places, but try *Macau*, Suipacha 477, *Restaurant Doll*, Suipacha 544, *La Fronda*, Paraná 342, or *Han Kung*, Rodríguez Peña 384.

For better quality Chinese food, try *La Cantina China* at Maipú 976, *La Casa China* at Viamonte 1476, or *Oriente* at Maipú 512. Recently a new Korean restaurant, *Yong Bin Kwan*, has opened at Rivadavia 2030, a couple of blocks west of Congreso.

Fast Food

In general, Argentine fast food restaurants are no cheaper and much inferior to standard inexpensive eating places, but if you can't leave it at home, there are nine *McDonald's* in Buenos Aires, the most central at Lavalle and Carlos Pellegrini and on the Florida peatonal. *Kentucky Fried Chicken* is at Roberto Ortiz 1815 in Recoleta, and the indigenous *Pumper Nic* at many locations throughout the city. In quality, these fall just short of *vomitivo*, a term which should need no explanation.

Among the cheapest places to eat is the basic *Supercoop* chain – the most convenient branches are at Sarmiento 1431, and at Rivadavia and Piedras. For an adequate, nutritious budget meal try the basement

cafeteria at *Restaurant Islas Malvinas*, downtown at Reconquista 335. A reader has recommended *La Lecherísima*, on Avenida Corrientes between Suipacha and Esmeralda, which has a variety of large salads, sandwiches and pasta.

Ice Cream

For ice cream lovers, Buenos Aires is paradise. Our favourite is the unpretentious *Heladería Cadore*, at Avenida Corrientes and Rodríguez Peña, distinguished by the outline map of Italy over its entrance. Chocolate fans should not miss their exquisite chocolate amargo (semisweet chocolate) and chocolate blanco (white chocolate), but everything is good. In Recoleta, try *Heladería Freddo* at Ayacucho and Quintana.

During winter, when Argentines rarely eat ice cream, the best places offering homemade (elaboración propia) specialities often close.

ENTERTAINMENT

Cinemas

Buenos Aires is famous for its cinemas, which play first-run films from around the world, but there is also an audience for unconventional and classic films. The main cinema districts are along the Lavalle peatonal, west of Florida, and on Avenidas Corrientes and Santa Fe, all easy walking distance from downtown. The price of cinema tickets has risen dramatically in recent years, but many theatres offer substantial discounts at midweek showings, usually Tuesdays, Wednesdays and Thursdays. It is also common to buy discount tickets from agencies along Avenida Corrientes.

There are two excellent, inexpensive repertory cinemas, which change their program almost daily and are good places to catch up on films you may have missed. Both the Cinemateca Hebraica, Sarmiento 2255, and the Teatro General San Martín, Avenida Corrientes 1530, regularly offer thematic foreign film cycles as well as reprises of outstanding commercial films.

Gardel & the Tango

In June 1935, a Cuban woman committed suicide in Havana, while a woman in New York and another in Puerto Rico tried to poison themselves, all over the same man whom none of them had ever met. The man whose smiling photograph graced their rooms had himself just died in a plane crash in Medellín, Colombia. On his long odyssey to his final resting place in Argentina, Latin Americans thronged to pay him tribute in Colombia, New York, Río de Janeiro and Montevideo. Once in Buenos Aires, his body lay in state at Luna Park stadium before a horse-drawn carriage took him to Chacarita Cemetery. The man was tango singer Carlos Gardel, *El Zorzal Criollo*, the songbird of Buenos Aires.

Born around 1880, only a decade before Gardel, the tango was the vulgar dance and music of the capital's *arrabales* or fringes, blending gaucho verse with Spanish and Italian music. Gardel created the *tango canción*, the tango-song, taking it out of the brothels and tenements and into the salons of Buenos Aires, but only after a roundabout odyssey to New York and Paris, where its acceptance legitimised it to the Argentine elite.

It was no accident that the tango grew to popularity when it did. In the late 19th century, the *Gran Aldea* (Great Village) of Buenos Aires was becoming an immigrant city, where frustrated and melancholic Europeans displaced gaucho rustics, who retreated gradually to the ever more distant countryside. The children of those immigrants would become the first generation of Porteños, and the tango-song summarised the new urban experience.

Permeated with nostalgia over a disappearing way of life, the tango-song expressed the apprehensions and anxieties of individuals, ranging from mundane pastimes like horse racing and other popular diversions to more profound feelings towards the changing landscape of neighbourhood and community, the figure of the mother, betrayal by women, and friendship or other important personal concerns. One tango compares the inevitable transformations of La Boca's 'Caminito' with those in the singer's own life:

Caminito que entonces estabas
bordeado de trébol y juncos en flor...
una sombra ya pronto serás,
una sombra, lo mismo que yo...

Caminito of what you once were
Bordered by clover and flowering rushes
A shadow you soon will be
A shadow just like me.

Although born in France, Gardel came to epitomise the Porteño. When he was three, his poor and single mother brought him to Buenos Aires, where he passed his formative years in a neighbourhood near the Mercado de Abasto (central produce market). In his youth, he worked at a variety of menial jobs, but he also entertained neighbours with his singing. His performing career began after he became friends with Uruguayan-born musician José Razzano, forming the popular duo Gardel-Razzano, which lasted until Razzano lost his voice.

From 1917, Gardel became a solo performer. His voice, his singing and his personal charisma made him an immediate popular success in Argentina and other Latin American countries, although the Argentine elite still despised the music and what it stood for – the rise of a middle class which challenged its monopoly on power. Building on this popularity, Gardel appeared regularly on the radio and soon became a recording star. To broaden his appeal, he travelled to Spain and France, where widespread acceptance finally made him palatable even to the elite sectors of Argentine society, which once were scandalised by the tango's humble origins and open sensuality. Later, he began a film career which was cut short by his death in Medellín.

In a sense, Gardel's early death rescued him from aging and placed him in an eternal present, where his figure is an icon which still dominates Argentine popular culture. One measure of this immortality is the common saying that 'Gardel sings better every day'. Photographs of Gardel, with his unmistakeable smile, are everywhere – one laboratory in Buenos Aires sold more than 350,000 pictures in the first two decades after his death. There is a devoted community of Gardel followers, known as Gardelianos, who cannot pass a day without listening to his songs or watching his films.

Daily, there is a steady procession of pilgrims to his plaque-covered tomb in Chacarita Cemetery where, often, a lighted cigarette rests in the hand of his life-sized statue. On 11 December 1990, the centenary of his birth, it was smothered in floral tributes. Within a few days those flowers wilted, but Gardel's legend does not. ■

Since the Spanish translations of English-language film titles are often very misleading, check the *Buenos Aires Herald* to be certain what's playing. Foreign films are almost always in the original language with Spanish subtitles.

Theatre

Live theatre enjoys great popularity. Avenida Corrientes, between Avenidas 9 de Julio and Callao, is the capital's Broadway or West End, but there are many other venues. One of the best places is the Teatro General San Martín, Avenida Corrientes 1530, which has several auditoriums and frequent free events.

Other important locations include the Teatro President Alvear at Avenida Corrientes 1659, Teatro Blanca Podestá at Avenida Corrientes 1283, Teatro La Plaza at Avenida Corrientes 1660, Teatro del Sur at Venezuela 1286, Teatro El Vitral at Rodríguez Peña 344, and Teatro Esmeralda at Esmeralda 425. For complete theatre listings, consult the *Buenos Aires Herald* or the entertainment section of *Clarín*.

Clubs & Discos

Argentina's nonprofit student travel agency ASATEJ has a club for young travellers on Wednesdays at Bár-baro, Tres Sargentos 415, which has a pleasant funky decor. La Porteña jazz band plays there on Thursdays.

Discos tend to the exclusive and expensive, such as Trump's at Bulnes 2772, Hippopotamus at Junín 1787, Africa at Alvear 1885 in the Alvear Palace Hotel, Le Club at Quintana 111, and the Elevage Hotel at Maipú 960.

Tango

Finding the real, spontaneous tango is not easy, but plenty of places portray Argentina's most famous cultural export, for prices up to US$40 per show in the San Telmo and Boca neighbourhoods. Try La Casa Blanca at Balcarce 868, El Viejo Almacén at Balcarce and Independencia, Bar Sur at Estados Unidos 299, and Taconeando, Balcarce 725. Among the least formal are A Media Luz at Chile 316 and Los Dos Pianitos at Giuffra

and Balcarce. The latter, a reader alleges, is very lively and goes to all hours of the morning.

La Casa de Carlos Gardel (in fact, once Gardel's home) is at Jean Jaurés 735, in the Abasto neighbourhood. Downtown tango spots include Caño 14 at Talcahuano 975 and Tanguería Corrientes Angosta at Lavalle 750.

For an excellent account of Gardel's life, in English, see Simon Collier's *The Life, Music, and Times of Carlos Gardel* (University of Pittsburgh Press, 1986), a serious biography which avoids the most romantic exaggerations of Gardel's fanatical devotees.

Spectator Sports

As an American, one of the authors has struggled to appreciate a game in which you run around for 90 minutes only to settle for a scoreless tie, but Argentine soccer is world-class and the fans are no less rabid than in Europe. Wear a hard hat if you attend a soccer game at Boca Juniors stadium, where a hostile visiting fan killed an innocent spectator by throwing a broken guard rail from the upper stands.

THINGS TO BUY

Compulsive shoppers will love Buenos Aires. The main shopping zones are downtown, along the Florida peatonal and the more fashionable and more expensive Avenida Santa Fe, although Recoleta is another worthwhile area. One of the most interesting districts is San Telmo, whose fascinating flea market, the Feria de San Telmo, takes place every Sunday from 10 am to about 5 pm on Plaza Dorrego. There are good restaurants, and often spontaneous live entertainment from buskers and mimes. Prices have risen considerably at the gentrified antique shops.

Buenos Aires' best buys are jewels, leather goods, shoes, and typical souvenirs like *mate* paraphernalia. Among the many leather shops, you can try Kerguelen at Santander 747, Rossi y Carusso at Santa Fe 1602, Chiche Farrace at Avenida de Mayo 963,

Carteras Italianas at Alvear 720, Campanera Dalla Fontana at Reconquista 735, or Jota U Cuero at Tres Sargentos 439. Celina Leather, Florida 971, gives 15% discounts to holders of student cards.

You can look just about anywhere along Avenida Corrientes or Florida for shoes, but try Andrea Carrera at Maipú 943 or Celine at Florida 793 for women's footwear. For men's shoes, try Guante at Florida 271 or Delgado at Florida 360.

For typically Argentine souvenirs, check out places like Artesanías Argentinas at Montevideo 1386, Friend's at Avenida Santa Fe and Esmeralda, or Iguarán at Libertad 1260. Other places, offering student discounts, include Rancho Grande at L N Alem 564 and Patagonia at Avenida Córdoba 543. Several provincial tourist offices, especially those along Avenida Santa Fe and Avenida Callao, have small but worthwhile selections of regional crafts.

GETTING THERE & AWAY
Air

Most major international airlines have Buenos Aires offices or representatives. The following list includes the most important ones.

Aerolíneas Argentinas
  Perú 2 (☎ 362-5008)
Aeroflot
  Avenida Santa Fe 822 (☎ 312-5573)
Aero Perú
  Avenida Santa Fe 840 (☎ 311-6431)
Air France
  Avenida Santa Fe 800 (☎ 311-9863)
American Airlines
  Avenida Córdoba 657 (☎ 392-8849)
British Airways
  Avenida Córdoba 657 (☎ 393-9090)
KLM
  Suipacha 1109 (☎ 311-9821)
LAN-Chile
  Avenida Córdoba 879 (☎ 311-5334)
Líneas Aéreas Paraguayas
  Cerrito 1026 (☎ 393-1000)
Lloyd Aéreo Boliviano
  Carlos Pellegrini 141 (☎ 35-3505)
Lufthansa
  Avenida Alvear 636 (☎ 312-8171)

PLUNA
  Florida 1 (☎ 34-7000)
Swissair
  Avenida Santa Fe 846 (☎ 312-0669)
United Airlines
  Avenida Alvear 590 (☎ 312-0664)
Varig
  Florida 630 (☎ 35-3014)

The major domestic carriers are Aerolíneas Argentinas (☎ 30-8551), with offices at Perú 2 and elsewhere throughout the city, and Austral (☎ 325-0777), at Avenida Corrientes 485. Both serve nearly every major Argentine city between Bolivia and the Beagle Channel.

Líneas Aéreas del Estado (LADE) (☎ 361-0583), the Argentine Air Force's commercial service, is at Perú 710. It serves exclusively Patagonian destinations from Buenos Aires.

To Uruguay, regional air services from Aeroparque Jorge Newbery are cheaper and more efficient than the major international airlines which operate from Ezeiza. Aerolíneas Uruguayas (☎ 313-3331) at Paraguay 617 charges US$46 return to Colonia, US$74 return to Montevideo, and US$110 return to Punta del Este. Fares are comparable on Líneas Aéreas Privadas Argentinas (LAPA) (☎ 812-3322), 2nd floor, Avenida Santa Fe 1970, which serves only Colonia and Montevideo.

Bus

Buenos Aires' massive Retiro bus terminal is at Avenida Antártida Argentina and Ramos Mejía, a short distance from Retiro train station. Each company has a desk resembling an airline ticket counter, from which it issues tickets to both national and international destinations. By presenting anything remotely resembling a student ID card, you can get a discount of 20% on any fare except for special promotions.

ONDA (☎ 313-3192), Buses de la Carrera and General Urquiza (☎ 313-2771) have daily buses to Montevideo for US$20 single. La Internacional (☎ 313-3164) has regular buses to Asunción, Paraguay, via Formosa and Clorinda for US$49 regular, US$68 for the more comfortable *Servicio Diferencial*. Nuestra Señora de la Asunción and Chevallier Paraguaya (☎ 313-2349) have comparable service and prices.

Pluma (☎ 313-3836) goes to Brazilian destinations, including Foz do Iguaçu (US$49), Porto Alegre (US$54), Florianópolis (US$64), Camboriú (US$66), Curitibá (US$70), São Paulo (US$79) and Río de Janeiro (US$88).

Cocorba has buses to Córdoba (US$35) and Catamarca (US$58). Colta serves the Sierras de Córdoba. ABLO (☎ 313-2385) goes to Rosario (US$15), Córdoba and its Sierras, and La Rioja. Chevallier (☎ 312-3297) has very extensive routes to Rosario, Córdoba, Catamarca, Santiago del Estero, Corrientes, Mendoza, San Luis, and Santiago, Chile (US$60). Fénix Pullman Norte (☎ 313-0134) and Ahumada also go to Santiago, with connections to the Peruvian border at Arica. El Rápido Internacional and Ormeño both have good connections to Lima.

TAC has buses to Mendoza (US$52) and Santiago de Chile (US$60). Autotransportes San Juan has buses to Río Cuarto (US$27), Villa Mercedes (US$30), San Luis (US$34) and San Juan (US$42).

La Estrella and El Trébol go to Termas de Río Hondo, Santiago del Estero and Tucumán (US$55). La Unión also goes to Rosario and Tucumán. La Veloz del Norte goes to Salta (US$65) and to the Bolivian border at Pocitos. La Internacional also goes to Salta and Jujuy.

El Rápido serves the littoral cities of Santa Fe, Paraná (US$20) and Corrientes. El Turista and El Norte bis go to Resistencia and Reconquista. Expreso Río Paraná and La Encarnación follow similar routes. TATA (☎ 313-3836) has buses to the Mesopotamian cities of Gualeguaychú, Colón and northerly destinations, passing Parque Nacional El Palmar. Expreso Singer (☎ 313-2355) has buses to Posadas (US$40) and Puerto Iguazú (US$54).

Empresa Pehuenche goes to Santa Rosa in La Pampa province, and Neuquén. El Cóndor and La Estrella have buses to Neuquén and Bariloche (US$76). El Valle goes to Bariloche and to San Martín de los Andes.

La Estrella serves many destinations within the province of Buenos Aires. Empresa Argentina goes to Mar del Plata and the province's other beach resorts. Micro Mar (☎ 313-3128) also does the Atlantic coast.

Costera Criolla/Don Otto (☎ 313-2503) is the major Patagonian carrier. It has routes to Tandil (US$11), Mar del Plata (US$20), Necochea (US$26) Bahía Blanca (US$28), Puerto Madryn (US$61), Comodoro Rivadavia (US$72) and Río Gallegos (US$91). La Estrella also runs these routes as far as Comodoro Rivadavia.

Train

Ferrocarriles Argentinos' main information and ticket office (☎ 30-7220) has moved from its former location on Florida to new offices at Maipú 88.

There are three principal train stations. From Retiro Station, near downtown Buenos Aires, the San Martín, Mitre and Belgrano railways serve western and northern destinations such as Mendoza, Rosario, Córdoba, Tucumán, Salta and Jujuy. From Lacroze Station, the superannuated Urquiza railway serves north-eastern Argentine destinations in Mesopotamia, while the Roca line serves southern Buenos Aires and Patagonia from Constitución Station, south of downtown. The Sarmiento railway, from Once Station, has only very limited passenger services.

Trains are cheaper than buses and often very crowded, especially during holiday periods. Buy tickets as far in advance as possible, but remember that long, bitter strikes and 'work-to-rule' stoppages are common.

Car Rental

No sane person would recommend driving in Buenos Aires but, for a price, all the standard agencies will let you take your chances. Try Alamo (☎ 40-2523), 5th floor, Uruguay 367, Budget (☎ 313-8169) at Carlos Pellegrini 977, Hertz (☎ 312-0787) at

Esmeralda 985, and National (☎ 312-4318) at Esmeralda 1084.

River

From Buenos Aires, there are regular ferry and hydrofoil *(aliscafo)* services to Colonia, Uruguay, with bus combinations to Montevideo – check ONDA at Florida and Lavalle. The ferry-bus combination Buquebus (☎ 393-0174) at Suipacha 776 has three departures daily, charging US$20 single, US$35 return to Montevideo. The trip takes six hours.

GETTING AROUND
To/From the Airport

Buenos Aires has two major airports. All domestic flights and some to neighbouring countries leave from Aeroparque Jorge Newbery (☎ 771-2071), only a few km north of the city centre. Aeropuerto Internacional Ezeiza (☎ 620-0271), the international airport, is about 35 km south of downtown.

To Aeroparque, take the No 33 bus ('Ciudad Universitaria') opposite Retiro Station. The fare is only about US$0.25. To Ezeiza, the cheapest way is to catch the No 86 bus, (be sure it says 'Ezeiza', since not all No 86s go to the end of the line) which starts in La Boca and comes up the Avenida de Mayo past the Plaza del Congreso. To be assured of a seat, take the more comfortable 'Servicio Diferencial', which will cost about US$2. Theoretically neither will allow very bulky luggage, although normal backpacks and suitcases should be permitted, but for a judicious tip you should be able to take almost anything. Because of heavy traffic, figure on 1½ hours to Ezeiza.

Manuel Tienda León (☎ 396-2078), in the Hotel Colón at Carlos Pellegrini 509, runs a comfortable and efficient service to Ezeiza in buses and minibuses, depending on demand. These leave every half-hour between 5.30 and 10 am, every 20 minutes between 10 am and 5 pm, and every half-hour again until 10 pm. The one-way fare is US$12. The hours for return services from Ezeiza are identical. The trip takes about 30 to 45 minutes, depending on the traffic.

Taxis are expensive for individuals, costing about US$40, but may be cheaper than Manuel Tienda León if you have a group of three or four – negotiate with the driver.

Bus

Buenos Aires has a large and complex bus system which serves the entire federal district and Gran Buenos Aires. For novices, the best guide is the *Guia Peuser*, sold at nearly all kiosks and bookstores, which details nearly 200 different routes, accompanied by a fold-out map. However, not all No 60 buses, for example, go all the way to Tigre, nor do all No 86 buses go to Ezeiza Airport – you must check the sign in the window to know their ultimate destinations.

You will find, though, that Porteños have memorised the system and can instantly tell you which bus to take and where to get off for a particular destination. Unlike the Subte, fares depend on distance – when you board, tell the driver where you're going and he will charge you accordingly. Although burdened with negotiating Buenos Aires' narrow streets and chaotic traffic, and making change from reams of low-value banknotes, drivers are usually polite enough to give warning of your stop. If not, or if you find yourself standing at the back of a crowded bus, ask any other passenger for advice and assistance. Anyone taller than Napoleon will have to bend over to see out the windows.

Like other motorists in the capital, bus drivers are fast and ruthless. Hang on tight!

Train

Local rail services serve most of Gran Buenos Aires from Retiro, Constitución, Lacroze, Once and Lacroze stations. Retiro and Constitución are by far the most important.

Underground

On Buenos Aires' oldest Subte line, starting at the Plaza de Mayo, the tarnished elegance of the tiled stations and the worn vintage woodwork of the cars offer a distant glimpse of the city's 'Belle Epoque'. Despite its age, the Subte is still fast and efficient, but it reaches only certain parts of a city which is many times larger than when the system opened in 1913.

The Subte consists of five lines, each identified alphabetically (Líneas A, B, C, D and E). Four of these run from downtown to the capital's western and northern outskirts, while the other connects the two major train stations of Retiro and Constitución. The lines and their termini are:

Línea A runs from Plaza de Mayo, under Avenida Rivadavia, to Primera Junta.

Línea B runs from L N Alem, under Avenida Corrientes, to Federico Lacroze, the station for the Urquiza railway.

Línea C runs between the major train stations of Retiro and Constitución, with transfer stations for all other lines.

Línea D runs from Catedral, on the Plaza de Mayo, to the suburb of Palermo.

Línea E runs from Bolívar, on the Avenida de Mayo, to Plaza de los Virreyes.

Fichas for the Subte cost about US$0.20. To save time and trouble, buy a pocketful, since

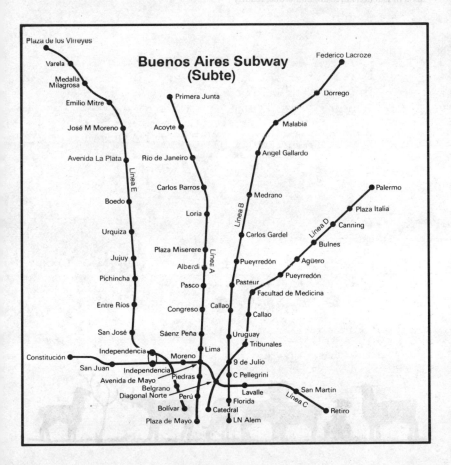

Buenos Aires Subway (Subte)

the lines get very backed up during rush hour and even at other times. Trains operate from 5.30 am to 1.30 am and are frequent on weekdays, but on weekends waiting time can be considerable. Backpacks and suitcases are permitted, allowing convenient connections between the train stations. At a few stations, like Alberdi, you can only go in one direction – in this case toward Primera Junta rather than Plaza de Mayo, so you may have to backtrack to reach your ultimate destination.

Taxi

Taxis in Buenos Aires are numerous, readily identified by their black and yellow paint jobs, and reasonably priced. All are metred, but since the Argentine currency is so unstable, each driver carries an approved, photocopied list of fares which correspond to the metre reading. Almost all drivers are honest, but check to be certain the metre is set at zero. Taxi drivers do not expect a big tip, but it is customary to let them keep the change so long as it is a modest amount.

When it rains, taxis can be hard to find, and you may have to wait out the storm in a confitería.

Atlantic Coast

For Porteños and others from the province of Buenos Aires, summer means the beach, while the beach means the Atlantic coast in general and Mar del Plata in particular. Every summer millions of Argentines take a vacation from their friends, families and co-workers, only to run into them on the beaches. Those who can't make it in person participate vicariously in the beach scene every afternoon through television.

Beach access is unrestricted in Argentina, but *balnearios* (bathing resorts) are privately run, so access to toilets and showers is limited to those who rent tents. Legally, balnearios must have life guards, medical services, toilets and showers. Most also have confiterías, paddle-ball courts (a current fad in Argentina), and even shops.

Even by Argentine standards, prices are hard to pin down, since they rise every two weeks from December 15 to February 15, and then decline slowly until the end of March, when most hotels and residenciales close. Those that stay open year-round lower their prices considerably after summer ends.

North of Mar del Plata to Cabo San Antonio, gentle dunes rise behind the generally narrow beaches of the province. South-west from Mardel to Miramar, steep bluffs highlight the changing coastline, although access is still good for bathing. Beyond Miramar, towards Monte Hermoso, the broad sand beaches delight bathers, fishing enthusiasts and windsurfers.

MAR DEL PLATA

When Juan de Garay, the founder of Buenos Aires, sailed along the Atlantic Coast in 1581 he described the shoreline around present-day Mar del Plata as *'muy galana'* ('very beautiful'), but Europeans were slow to occupy the area. Nearly two centuries later, in 1747, Jesuit missionaries tried to evangelise Indians from the southern Pampas, but the only remainder of their efforts is the body of water known as Laguna de los Padres.

More than a century later Portuguese investors established a small town, El Puerto de Laguna de los Padres, with a pier and a saladero. Beset by economic problems in the 1860s, they sold the land to Patricio Peralta Ramos, who founded Mar del Plata proper in 1874.

Ramos helped develop the area not just as an important commercial and industrial centre, but later as a beach resort. By the turn of the century, most upper-class Porteño families owned a villa or summer residence in the city, some of which still grace the exclusive Barrio Los Troncos.

Since the 1960s Mardel, as it is popularly known, has become the main holiday destination for middle-class Porteños, who outnumber the local population three to one

Northern Beaches, Atlantic Coast

```
0          50        100 km
```
Approximate Scale

BUENOS AIRES

ATLANTIC

OCEAN

La Plata

215

20

2   11

Bahía Samborombón

Punta Rasa

San Clemente del Tuyú

Las Toninas
Santa Teresita
Partido   Mar del Tuyú
de la   Costa del Este
Costa   La Lucila
              San Bernardo
              Mar de Ajó

56

11

Pinamar
Ostende
Valeria del Mar
Villa Gesell

2

11

To   Laguna
Tandil   Mar Chiquita

Mar Chiquita
Mar de Cobo
226   Santa Clara del Mar
      Mar del Plata
      Chapadmalal
Miramar

during the summer. Multitudinous skyscrapers have risen as local authorities have failed to enforce building codes, leaving many of the finest beaches in the shade for much of the day. As the 'Pearl of the Atlantic' has lost its exclusivity, its architectural character and its calm, the Argentine elite have sought refuge in more exclusive resorts like Pinamar or in Punta del Este, Uruguay.

Mar del Plata still has many appealing qualities, but unless you are a very gregarious person, you may want to visit in spring or fall, when prices are lower and the area's natural beauty encourages relaxation.

Orientation

Mar del Plata, 400 km from Buenos Aires, sprawls along eight kilometres of beaches, as ceaseless construction adds new neighbourhoods. The downtown area, containing most points of interest for visitors, is bound by Avenida J B Justo, running roughly west from the port, Avenida Independencia, which runs roughly north-south, and the sea.

On street signs, the road running along the water is called Avenida Peralta Ramos, but it is generally referred to as Blvd Marítimo. San Martín and Rivadavia are both pedestrian streets during summer evenings.

Information

Tourist Office The main municipal tourist office (☎ 21777, 20853) is at Blvd Marítimo 2267. Since Mar del Plata gets very crowded in summer, it processes tourists almost like an assembly line, but its computerised information system is very efficient, with good maps and descriptive brochures. There is also a provincial tourist office (☎ 25340) in the Rambla del Hotel Provincial, Blvd Marítimo 2500, Local (shop) 60.

Money There are several cambios along San Martín and Rivadavia. Jonestur has branches at San Martín 2574 and Avenida Luro 3191. Try also La Moneda at Rivadavia 2625, Mar del Plata Cambio at Santiago del Estero 1732, or Mar del Plata at Luro 3071.

Post & Telecommunications ENCOTEL

has several branches: the Correo Central is at Avenida Luro 2460, while others are at Avenida Luro 7099, 12 de Octubre 3346 and Sarmiento 2710. Telefónica has offices at Avenida Luro 2554, Olavarría 2495, the train station, the bus terminal and the airport.

Cultural Centres The Sociedad de Cultura Inglesa is at San Luis 2498.

Travel Agencies ACA (☎ 22096) is at Avenida Colón and Santa Fe. There are several travel agencies at the bus terminal: Turismo Esplanada (☎ 51-2636), Local (shop) 27; Turismo La Plata (☎ 51-2153), Local 12; and Zenit Turismo (☎ 51-8733), Local 11.

Medical Services Centro de Salud Municipal No 1 (☎ 20568) is at Avenida Colón 3294. Hospital Mar del Plata (☎ 22021) is at Castelli 2460.

Walking Tour
A stroll past some of Mar del Plata's mansions offers vivid insights into the city's upper-class origins and its relatively recent past when it was still the exclusive playground of wealthy Argentines. Built in 1919, **Villa Normandy,** at Avenida Colón and Viamonte, is one of few examples of that French style which survived the renovation craze of the 1950s. On the hilltop, at Almirante Brown and Viamonte, is **Iglesia Stella Maris,** with its impressive marble altar. Its virgin is the patron saint of local fishers. On the highest point of this hill, at Falucho and Mendoza, is the 88-metre **Torre Tanque.** The view from its *mirador* (viewpoint) justifies the climb.

After descending Viamonte to Rodriguez Peña, walk toward the ocean to the corner of Urquiza, where the **Chalet Los Troncos** gave its name to this distinguished neighbourhood. The timber of the gate and fence are *quebracho* and *lapacho* hardwoods from the province of Salta. Walking along Urquiza, Quintana, Lavalle, Rodríguez Peña, Rivas and Almafuerte you'll see examples of more recent but equally elite design.

To return to the centre, you may want to take the longer route along Avenida Peralta Ramos, which offers beautiful views of the city from **Cabo Corrientes.**

Museo Municipal de Arte Juan Carlos Castagnino
Lovers of both art and architecture should visit this museum at Avenida Colón 1189, in the Villa Ortiz Basualdo, the summer residence of a prominent Argentine family. Built in 1902, its exterior resembles a Loire Valley castle, while the interior decor comes from Belgium. The museum exhibits paintings, drawings, photographs and sculptures by Argentine artists.

Opening hours are Tuesday to Sunday from 6 to 11 pm. Bus No 221 or 592 will take you there.

Museo Archivo Histórico Municipal
A superb collection of turn-of-the-century photographs, plus other exhibits, recalls Mardel's rich past in this museum in Villa Mitre, once also a summer residence of the Argentine oligarchy. At Lamadrid 3870, it's open daily from 3 to 7 pm. Take bus No 523 to get there.

Museo de Ciencias Naturales
Paleontological, archaeological, geological and zoological pieces are on exhibit in this museum at Libertad 2999, on Plaza España. The ground floor aquarium has local fresh and salt water species. Opening hours are 3 to 7 pm daily.

Banquina de Pescadores
Mar del Plata is one of the most important fishing ports and seafood processing centres in the country. At the port's picturesque wharf, busy fishers and stevedores on colourful wooden boats follow their daily routine, monitored by sea lions who have established a large – mostly male – colony on one side of the pier.

In the early morning, unfazed by the chill sea breeze, the fishers load their nets and crates before leaving to spend all day at sea. The lions follow suit. At about 5 pm, the pier

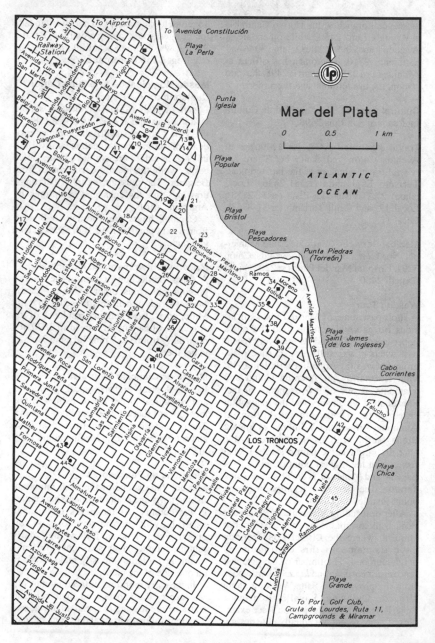

Mar del Plata

■ PLACES TO STAY

1	Hotel Traful
3	Hotel España
7	Hotel Bologna
13	Gran Hotel Iruna
14	Hotel Astor
19	Hotel Aragón
23	Gran Hotel Provincial
25	Hospedaje San Francisco
26	Hospedaje Star
27	Hotel Boedo
28	Hospedaje
30	Youth Hostel/Hotel Pergamino
31	Hospedaje Lamadrid
32	Hotel Aguila Blanca
33	Hotel Alsina
34	Chateau Frontenac
37	Hospedaje Colonial
40	Gran Hotel Pelayo
41	Hostería la Madrileña
42	Hotel Champs Eliseés

▼ PLACES TO EAT

2	Restaurant Comedor Naturista
11	Restaurant Ambos Mundos

15	Parrila El Rey del Bife
17	Restaurant Tía Pepina
24	Restaurant La Biblioteca

OTHER

4	Centro de Salud No 1
5	Plaza San Martín
6	Catedral de San Pedro
8	Telefónica
9	Banco de la Provincia
10	Banco de la Nación
12	Post Office
16	Plaza Mitre
18	ACA
20	Tourist Office
21	Casino
22	Plaza Colón
29	Hospital
35	Museo Municipal de Arte Juan Carlos Castagnino
36	Bus Terminal
38	Iglesia Stella Maris
39	Torre Tanque
43	Villa Victoria
44	Museo Archivo Histórico Municipal
45	Parque San Martín

gets noisy and hectic as the returning fishers sort and box the fish, bargain for the best price, and tidy up their boats and tools. The sea lions return to seek or fight over a spot to rest.

There are excellent opportunities for photography, and you can end the day in one of the port complex's great restaurants or, more cheaply in one of the standing-room seafood cafeterias. Local bus Nos 511, 522, 551, 561, 562, 593 and 221 go there from the centre.

Gruta de Lourdes
Only 10 blocks from the port, at Magallanes 4100, exuberant vegetation covers this replica of the French grotto. It contains an image of Nuestra Señora de Lourdes, and a trail with the stations of the cross, which includes a kitschy model of Jerusalem with waterfalls, sound and light show, and mobile figures.

To reach the grotto from the port, walk along 12 de Octubre, the main commercial street in the area, to the 4100 block. Magallanes is the next block east. Bus No 522 also goes there.

Mar del Nácar
At San Luis 1771, this is an incredible permanent exhibition of shells, consisting of 52,000 pieces representing 6000 species. Opening hours are Monday to Saturday from 4 to 8 pm.

Catedral de San Pedro
At San Martín and San Luis, this turn-of-the-century neo-Gothic building features gorgeous stained glass, an impressive central chandelier from France, tiled floors from England and a tiled ceiling from other European countries.

Villa Victoria
At Matheu 1851, this is an example of the prefabricated homes built in Norway and imported during Mar del Plata's *belle*

epoque. Its owner Victoria Ocampo, a prominent Argentine writer, hosted literary salons here, attended by prominent intellectuals of the 1920s and 1930s. She was also the founder of *Sur*, Argentina's most important literary journal between the wars. It's open daily from 6 pm to midnight, and on cloudy days from 3 pm.

Organised Tours
Turimar offers boat rides from the Banquina de Pescadores, at the port. For city tours, Micros de Excursión (tour buses) leave from Plaza Colón and from San Martín. Ask at the tourist office for details.

Festivals
Mar del Plata's Festival Internacional de Cine (International Film Festival) takes place every two years in March. In season, there are national golf and tennis tournaments and regattas.

Places to Stay – bottom end
It is worth reiterating that prices climb considerably from month to month during summer and fall in the off season, when many hotels and residenciales close their doors. Prices included here are from the beginning of the high season.

Camping There are several campgrounds, all of them crowded in summer, south of the city along provincial Ruta 11. Bus Rápido del Sud goes to all of them. *Los Horneros* has relatively large plots, clean showers and washing facilities. *Acuario* is also on Ruta 11, about 7½ km south of the lighthouse. Further along in the tranquil locality of La Serena is the shady, well-kept *Camping Suizo*, Calle 11 and Calle 20. Bus Nos 221 and 511 ('Serena') go there from the centre.
At the northern entrance of town, in the beautiful multi-use Parque Camet is *Camping El Bosque de Camet*, at Williams and Villalobo. Bus Nos 221 and 541 go there.

Hostels, Hospedajes & Hosterías The cheapest accommodation is near the bus terminal. A few blocks away is the youth hostel,

Albergue de la Juventud (☎ 27927), which functions in a wing of Hotel Pergamino at Tucumán 2728. They have rooms with shared bath for about US$4 and with private bath at US$9 per person.
At Sarmiento 2268 there is an unnamed hospedaje, in a beautiful colonial-style house, with a friendly owner. A room for four, with a huge, clean, shared bath is about US$4 per person. Another excellent place is *Hostería La Madrileña*, Sarmiento 2955, which has clean, modest doubles with private bath for US$5 per person.
Other cheap accommodation includes *Hospedaje San Francisco* (☎ 37509), Tucumán 2316 near Plaza Colón. Also near the bus terminal are *Hospedaje Lamadrid* (☎ 25456) at Lamadrid 2518, *Hospedaje Colonial* (☎ 51-1039) at Olavarría 2663, and *Hospedaje Star* (☎ 25044) at Falucho 1949.

Places to Stay – middle
At these one-star and two-star hotels, prices range from US$22 to US$32 per person. At the lower end are *Hotel Alsina* (☎ 51-4465) at Alsina 2368, *Hotel Aragón* (☎ 23064) at Buenos Aires 1933, and *Hotel Boedo* (☎ 24695) at Almirante Brown 1771. *Gran Hotel Pelayo* (☎ 51-3579), Sarmiento 2899, is good value at US$14 per person with breakfast.
Costlier two-star hotels include *Hotel Bologna* (☎ 43369) at 9 de Julio 2542, *Hotel Champs Eliseés* (☎ 51-2692) at Rawson 233, *Hotel España* (☎ 20526) at Avenida Luro 2964, *Hotel Aguila Blanca* (☎ 51-9582) at Sarmiento 2455, and *Hotel Traful* (☎ 36650) at Yrigoyen 1190.

Places to Stay – top end
In high season, rooms in this category range between US$45 and US$61 per person. The most luxurious is the enormous *Gran Hotel Provincial* (☎ 24081), Boulevard Marítimo 2500, with its famous casino, restaurant and commercial gallery. Others include *Hotel Sasso* (☎ 84-0031), Avenida Martínez de Hoz 3545; *Chateau Frontenac* (☎ 51-9828), Alvear 2010, with an excellent but expensive restaurant; and *Hotel Hermitage* (☎ 51-

9081), Boulevard Marítimo 2657, which is usually frequented by Argentine showbiz people.

Gran Hotel Iruna (☎ 24037) is at Alberdi 2270. At the lower end of the price range, *Hotel Astor* (☎ 23051), Entre Ríos 1649, is also good. *Hotel Benedetti* (☎ 30031), is at Colón 2198, while *Hotel Presidente* (☎ 28810) is at Corrientes 1516.

Places to Eat

Although Mar del Plata's numerous restaurants, pizzerías and snack bars usually hire extra help between December and March, they have a hard time keeping up with impatient crowds of tourists. As a result, there are always waiting lines. Food is generally good, and at the restaurants in the Nuevo Complejo Comercial Puerto (the renovated old port) seafood is invariably excellent, though costly. Around the bus terminal you can find very cheap minutas or sandwiches.

For standard Argentine food, try *Tía Pepina*, Yrigoyen 2645, *La Biblioteca*, Santa Fe 2633, or *Ambos Mundos*, Rivadavia 2644; the latter serves abundant minutas and good puchero de gallina for moderate prices. *La Cantina de Armando*, San Lorenzo y Catamarca, is also reasonable. *Don Pepito*, on Blvd Marítimo across from the Casino, is very reasonable and serves large portions.

The few vegetarian restaurants are all good value. Try *Comedor Naturista*, Salta 1571, or *El Jardín* at Plaza San Martín.

There are many pizzerías, which also have good lager beer. *Joe*, at Lamadrid and Rawson, serves super pizza and calzone. *Manolo*, Rivadavia 2371, has a variety of tasty pizzas. Try also *La Casona* at Rivadavia 2598, and *Strega* at Rivadavia 2320.

Of course there are many parrillas. Although a bit expensive, *Trenque Lauquen*, Mitre 2807, is excellent. *La Marca*, Almafuerte 253, is similar. *El Rey del Bife*, Colón 2863, and *Rincón de los Amigos*, Córdoba 2588, are more economical.

Italian cuisine is very popular among beachgoers. A small, moderate place with good dishes is *Teresa*, San Luis 2089. *Il Vero Napoli*, Belgrano 3408, has superb lasagna. *Trattoria Napolitana*, 3 de Febrero 3160, has costly but excellent food, while *La Strada*, Entre Ríos 2642, is more moderate in price.

Alfajores, biscuit sandwiches filled with chocolate, dulce de leche or fruit, are delicious for afternoon tea or *mate*. Havanna is a very popular brand.

Entertainment

Cinemas & Theatre When Buenos Aires shuts down in January, many shows come from the capital to Mar del Plata. Theatres mostly cater to vacationers with comedies that range from *café concert* (stand-up comedy) to vulgar but popular burlesque. There are also several cinemas downtown.

Discos After a leisurely day at the beach, Argentines like to stay up all night dancing and socialising. Mar del Plata has a lot to offer disco goers along Avenida Constitución, nicknamed Avenida del Ruido (Avenue of Noise), where discotheques and nightclubs line both sides of the street. Bus No 551 runs all night.

Casino Unlike its flashy counterparts in Las Vegas or Reno, the Casino at Mar del Plata's Hotel Provincial is an elegant, black-tie venue at night, but is more informal during the daytime. It's busy all day, but especially active after midnight.

Things to Buy

Mar del Plata is famous for sweaters and jackets. Shops along Avenida J B Justo, nicknamed 'Avenida del Pullover', have competitive, near-wholesale prices. To go shopping there, take bus No 561 or 562. For the fashion-conscious, there is a multitude of boutiques along San Martín and Rivadavia.

Getting There & Away

Air Aeropuerto Camet is 10 km north of the city. Both Aerolíneas Argentinas (☎ 45626) and Austral (☎ 23085), with offices at the Gran Hotel Provincial, Blvd Marítimo 2300,

have several daily flights to Buenos Aires.
Fares are about US$80.

Bus The busy bus terminal (☎ 51-5406) is
very central at Alberdi 1602. Costamar
(☎ 51-2843), Costera Criolla (51-2963),
Chevallier (☎ 51-8447), El Cóndor (51-
2110) and El Rápido (☎ 51-0874) have
several buses daily to Buenos Aires in the
summer. El Rápido Argentino (☎ 51-1516)
travels to La Plata twice daily. Expreso
Córdoba-Mar del Plata (☎ 51-8733) serves
Córdoba, while Empresa Pampa (☎ 51-
6223) goes to Bahía Blanca, where you can
make connections to Patagonia. TAC (☎ 51-
0014) and TIRSA (☎ 51-3507) travel to
Mendoza and other northern destinations.

Typical fares are: Buenos Aires US$16, La
Plata US$10 and Bahía Blanca US$19.

Train The train station (☎ 72-9553) is at
Avenida Luro 4599, about 20 blocks from
the beach. Ferrocarriles Argentinos also has
downtown offices open daily until 9 pm, at
San Martín 2300 (☎ 23059), and at the bus
terminal (☎ 51-2501). During the summer
the tourist train *El Marplatense* travels three
times daily to Buenos Aires. Reservations
should be made far in advance, since it
remains booked solid through the season.
Fares are: turista US$6.50, primera US$8,
and pullman US$10.

Car Rental Try Avis (☎ 37850), Blvd
Marítimo 2451, Alquilauto (☎ 37400) at
Bolívar and San Luis, or Angel Car
(☎ 25234) at Rivadavia 2547, Local 55.

Getting Around
Mar del Plata is a sprawling city but has
excellent public transportation. Buses are
frequent and reach just about every place in
town. For local destinations, the tourist
office can help.

MAR CHIQUITA
Along provincial Ruta 11, 34 km north of
Mar del Plata, is the peaceful resort of Mar
Chiquita, a paradise for swimming, fishing
and windsurfing. Its lagoon, unique in the
country, is sheltered by a chain of sand
dunes. Fed by creeks from the Sierras de
Tandil, the lagoon alternately drains into the
ocean or absorbs sea water, depending on the
tides. Bus Rápido del Sur goes eight times
daily to Mar Chiquita from the casino in Mar
del Plata. There are several campgrounds
and hotels.

VILLA GESELL
This recently developed resort was the vision
of merchant, inventor and nature-lover
Carlos Gesell, who created a town of zigzag,
unpaved streets lined with acacias, poplars,
oaks and pines to stabilise its sand dunes.
The town has a very small stable population
and is much more sedate than Mar del Plata,
although it attracts many summer visitors.
Middle and working-class people perceive
Villa Gesell as exclusive and stay away, but
backpackers and campers can pursue both
traditional beach-oriented activities and less
conventional ones like horseback riding.

Orientation
Villa Gesell is 100 km north of Mar del Plata,
and about 450 km south of Buenos Aires.

Avenida 3, the only paved road in town, parallels the beach and runs from Avenida Buenos Aires, at the edge of Barrio Norte suburb, south to the bus terminal and most of the campgrounds.

With few exceptions, streets in Villa Gesell are numbered rather than named. Outside Barrio Norte, the town centre consists of 10 Alamedas, running east-west, and 145 Paseos, running north-south. Barrio Norte lies between the beach in the east and Circunvalación in the west, and between Avenida Buenos Aires in the south and Calles 307 and 312 in the north.

Avenida 3, with its pedestrian mall, is the shopping and entertainment centre of Villa Gesell, with tea houses, specialised bakeries, and high-class restaurants, plus artisan shops, boutiques and video arcades. Everything is within walking distance, and the concentration of hotels and restaurants would probably dismay its founder.

Information

Tourist Office The tourist office (☎ 68569), at Avenida Buenos Aires and Circunvalación, has friendly staff and good maps. There are also several booths throughout the city with information on accommodation, places to eat, and bus schedules. ACA (☎ 62272) is on Avenida 3, between Paseos 112 and 113.

Things to See & Do

The European country-style **Playa Hotel**, Alameda 205 and Calle 304 in Barrio Norte, established Villa Gesell as a vacation resort. Every summer, the Sociedad Camping Musical organises chamber music concerts in its auditorium. Other musical events, such as the Encuentros Corales (a gathering of choirs from around the country) take place at the town's **Anfiteatro** (amphitheatre).

At the **Muelle de Pesca**, at Playa and Paseo 129, the 15-metre pier offers year-round fishing for mackerel, rays, shark and other fish.

Riding is a popular activity in Villa Gesell, at places like the **Escuela de Equitación**

San Jorge, where you can rent horses or take guided trips.

Organised Tours El Trencito de Villa Gesell, which is actually a bus, leaves from Avenida 3 and Paseo 110 bis (the second Paseo 110) at 10 am and 5 and 7 pm, for a two-hour excursion past the Casa de Don Carlos Gesell, the pine forest, the amphitheatre, the pioneer houses, the pier and the bus terminal. It costs US$4 per person, but is free for children under five.

Agencia Playa Médanos (☎ 63118), Avenida 3 and Paseo 111, runs trips to Faro Querandí, the local lighthouse. The trip takes up to 10 passengers in American army 4WD jeeps on a 30-km trip over dunes, stopping along the way for photography, swimming and exploring. The lighthouse itself, one of the highest and most inaccessible in the country, soars impressively above the surrounding dense forest. The four-hour trip, leaving daily in both the morning and afternoon, costs US$16 per person.

Places to Stay – bottom end

Camping Camping is the cheapest accommodation only if you are part of a group of four, since campgrounds have a minimum group rate of about US$16. With one exception, all close at the end of March.

On the north end of town, both *Camping Africa* (☎ 68507), Avenida Buenos Aires and Circunvalación, and *Camping Caravan* (☎ 68259), Paseo 101 and Circunvalación, have swimming pools. *Camping California* (☎ 68346) is on Avenida Buenos Aires and Circunvalación, while *Campamento del Sol* (☎ 68001), Blvd Silvio Gesell and Paseo 102, is open until April. Nearby *Camping El Faro* is on Blvd Silvio Gesell and Paseo 101.

Among the campgrounds on Avenida 3 at the south end of town are *Camping Casablanca*, *Camping Mar Dorado*, and *Camping Monte Bubi* at Avenida 3 and Paseo 168.

The youth hostel/campground *El Coyote* (☎ 68448), is at Alameda 212 and Calle 304 bis.

Hospedajes & Hotels In Villa Gesell there is no such a thing as an inexpensive, basic hospedaje with shared bath. Most accommodation includes a private bathroom and even a telephone. Figure on about US$12 to $US20 for singles/doubles in places like *Hospedaje Aguas Verdes* (☎ 62040), at Avenida 5 between Paseos 104 and 105, and *Hospedaje Sarimar*, Avenida 3 between Paseos 117 and 118. The enormous *Hospedaje Inti Huasi*, Alameda 202 and Avenida Buenos Aires, has rooms with private bath and includes breakfast.

Hospedajes open all year include *Hospedaje Villa Gesell* (☎ 62393) at Avenida 3 and Paseo 108, *Hospedaje Mariel* on Avenida 5 between Paseos 104 and 105, and *Hospedaje Bellavista* (☎ 62293) at Paseo 114 between Avenidas 1 and 3. The small *Hospedaje Viya* (☎ 62757), Avenida 5 between Paseos 105 and 106, includes breakfast. *Hospedaje Antonio* (☎ 62246), Avenida 4 between Paseos 104 and 106, has some rooms with shared bath and some with private bath.

Among the slightly more expensive one-star hotels are *Hotel Torremolinos* (☎ 62389) at Paseo 111 and Playa, and *Hotel Maracas* (☎ 68779) at Avenida 1 and Paseo 103. Both *Hotel Cantábrico* (☎ 62835), Avenida 2 and Paseo 102, and *Hotel Demi* (☎ 62658), Avenida 3 and Paseo 111, remain open all year.

Places to Stay – middle
There are several two-star hotels, with prices from about US$20/30, but only three are open all year. *Hotel Romadrid* (☎ 68368) is at Paseo Costanero between Avenida Buenos Aires and Alameda 201, *Hotel El Loco Chávez* (☎ 62452) is at Avenida 3 and Paseo 125, and *Hotel Colón* (☎ 62310) is at Avenida 4 and Paseo 104.

Places to Stay – top end
The most expensive hotels in the city start at about US$30 per person. Try *Hotel Coliseo* (☎ 62955), Avenida 1 and Paseo 107, or *Hotel Terrazas Club* (☎ 62181), Avenida 2 between Paseos 104 and 105, both of which

have swimming pools. *Hotel Gran Internacional* (☎ 68672) is on Paseo 103 between Avenida 1 and Paseo Costanero.

Places to Eat
There is a wide variety of restaurants in Villa Gesell, mostly along Avenida 3, catering to all tastes and budgets. *La Jirafa Azul*, on Avenida 3 between Avenida Buenos Aires and Paseo 102, has long had a reputation for being cheap and good. It serves a standard menu. The owner-operated *Cantina Arturito*, Avenida 3 between Paseos 126 and 127, serves large portions of exquisite home-made pasta, as well as shellfish, and home-cured ham, at medium to expensive prices. Also costly, but serving exotic game and international cuisine amidst very pleasant decor is *Restaurant El Establo* at Avenida 3 and Avenida Buenos Aires.

For tasty seafood go to the *Marisquería El Gallego*, Avenida 3 between Paseos 108 and 109. It has good but not cheap paella.

For good sandwiches and hamburgers and super friendly attention by the owners, try *Sangucheto*, Paseo 104 between Avenidas 3 and 4. Also good and family-attended, with some health food and drinks, is *La Martona*, Paseo 107 between Avenidas 2 and 3. For moderately priced takeaway food try the rotisería *El Faro* at Avenida 3 and Paseo 119.

Getting There & Away
Air Aerolíneas Argentinas (☎ 68228), at Avenida Buenos Aires and Avenida 10 in town, has flights to/from Villa Gesell daily in summer.

Bus The bus terminal (☎ 66058) is at Avenida 3 and Paseo 140, on the south side of town. Some long-distance buses stop at the Mini Terminal (☎ 62340) at Avenida 4, between Paseos 104 and 105.

Empresa Río de la Plata (☎ 62224), a block from the Mini Terminal, has several direct buses daily to Buenos Aires in summer, as does Antón (☎ 63215), Paseo 108 between Avenidas 3 and 4.

PINAMAR

Architect Jorge Bunge, of a well-known elite Argentine family, founded and designed the sophisticated resort of Pinamar in 1944 as a tranquil, elegant refuge for upper-class Porteños. Its beautiful beaches, extensive forests, sandy streets, luxury homes and hotels, chic shops and posh restaurants have made Pinamar the 'in' place for Argentines who needn't work for a living.

Bathed by a tropical current from Brazil, its waters are pleasantly warm and its clean beaches slope gradually into a sea with abundant fish. Other adjacent resorts, like Ostende and Valeria del Mar, differ little but offer more moderate prices. Cariló, also nearby, has a very exclusive, country-club atmosphere but merits a visit for its insight into upper-class Argentine life. Do not let the security gates deter you from entering, although you will probably be asked to leave your name.

Orientation

Pinamar, 120 km north of Mar del Plata, and 400 km south-east of Buenos Aires, was planned around an axis formed by Avenida Libertador, running parallel to the beach, and Avenida Bunge, running perpendicular to the beach. In the areas on either side of Bunge, the streets in the original city plan form two large fans which make orientation a bit tricky at first. The newer parts of town follow a conventional grid pattern.

Pinamar's commercial area is very compact, since residents are zealous about zoning codes. Most shops, restaurants, and hotels are on or within a few blocks of Avenida Bunge, the main thoroughfare.

Information

Tourist Office The busy tourist office (☎ 82749), Avenidas Bunge and Libertador, has a good map with useful descriptions of Pinamar, Valeria, Ostende and Cariló.

Things to See & Do

Pinamar is another great outdoor centre where, besides sunbathing and swimming, people practise a variety of water sports, including surfing, windsurfing, water-skiing, kayaking, and of course fishing. Also popular are golf, on the city's attractive course, horseback riding, tennis, paddleball, and hiking in the woods. Unfortunately, dune buggies, both on the beach and even along nature trails, are also popular.

Places to Stay

There is no cheap accommodation in Pinamar. There is a youth hostel in nearby Ostende. There are only a few hospedajes, but plenty of hotels, motels, and hosterías. They are invariably full during the season, so reservations are a must.

Other long-stay options include house rentals (information is available at the tourist office or at Casa de Pinamar in Buenos Aires), and apart-hotels. We have emphasised categories rather than prices, which are comparable to those in Villa Gesell.

Places to Stay – bottom end

Camping Three campgrounds serve the area between Ostende and Pinamar. *Autocamping Moby Dick* (☎ 86045), on Avenida Víctor Hugo and Tuyú in Ostende, has a dense tree canopy. *Camping Saint Tropez*, at Quintana and Nuestras Malvinas, Mar de Ostende, has a good beachfront location, but is small. *Camping Ostende* is on Cairo and Avenida La Plata in Ostende.

Hostels The youth hostel, on Quintana and Nuestras Malvinas, Ostende, is a friendly place, with dormitories and kitchen facilities, in an interesting building at the beach.

Hospedajes & Hosterías Hospedajes in Pinamar include *Hospedaje Acacia* (☎ 82522) at Del Cangrejo 1358, *Hospedaje Rose Marie* (☎ 84799) at De las Medusas 1381, and *Hospedaje Valle Fértil* at Del Cangrejo 1110.

Among one-star hotels are *Hotel Berlin* (☎ 82320) at Rivadavia and Artes, *Hotel Sardegna* (☎ 82760) at Avenida Bunge and Marco Polo, and *Hotel Yacanto* (☎ 82367) at Rivadavia and Simbad el Marino.

Places to Stay – middle

Posada del Rey (☎ 82267), at Del Tuyú and Odiseo, offers an optional continental breakfast in its pleasant surrounding garden. *Hotel San Marco* (☎ 82424) is at Rivadavia and Robinson Crusoe, *Hotel Zita* (☎ 82241) at Constitución and Robinson Crusoe, and *Hotel Riviera* (☎ 82334) at Del Tuyú and Avenida del Mar.

Places to Stay – top end

The most expensive in this group are the four-star, ultramodern *Hotel del Bosque* (☎ 22480), at Avenida Bunge and Júpiter, and *Hotel Algeciras* (☎ 85550), Avenida Libertador between Del Tuyú and Jonas.

Hotel La Golondrina (☎ 82240) is at Constitución and Robinson Crusoe. The *Hotel El Bufón del Rey* (☎ 82323), Delfines and Odiseo, has an intriguing French sculpture of a jester with twins in his arms, who supposedly helps those who desire children. The owners welcome visits from non-guests.

Places to Eat

From the local rotiserías to the most exclusive restaurants, food in Pinamar is superb but costly. *Parrilla Las Marías*, Avenida Bunge and Marco Polo, serves great pork and chivito a la parrilla (grilled kid goat). For good paellas, cazuelas and empanadas tucumanas, try *El Negro B* at Jason and Robinson Crusoe.

International cuisine is the highlight at *Matarazzo Party*, Avenida Bunge and Júpiter, with unusual Italian food including a variety of cheeses and cantimpalo (a special salami), dips with smoked venison and toasted almonds for hors d'oeuvres, great salads, and the famous spaghetti Matarazzo, with nine different sauces. Since it is tenedor libre, you can take your choice. The dessert list includes vanilla ice cream with hot strawberry sauce. Since it is always crowded, you may need reservations. *Mamma Liberata*, Avenida Bunge and Simbad el Marino, and *Club Italiano*, Eneas and Cazón, also offer tasty pasta.

El Vivero, Avenidas Bunge and Libertador, is an enormous but high-quality vegetarian restaurant. Despite its name *Paxapoga*, Avenidas Bunge and Libertador, is a parrilla and pasta place open all year.

Pizzería La Reja, Jason and Robinson Crusoe, offers 25 varieties of pizza, and great empanadas including traditional ones with hand-chopped beef, either to eat there or to go.

German cooking, mostly breads and cakes, can be found at *Tante*, De las Artes 35, and *Zur Tanne*, Rivadavia and De las Artes.

Getting There & Away

Air Aerolíneas Argentinas (☎ 83299) flies to Pinamar in summer.

Bus The bus terminal is at Avenida Shaw and Del Pejerrey. Empresas Antón (☎ 82378) and Río de la Plata (☎ 82247) service Buenos Aires. Costamar (☎ 82885) connects the beaches.

SAN CLEMENTE DEL TUYÚ

Partido de la Costa, a county 320 km southeast of Buenos Aires, is the closest resort area to the capital. It consists of 11 localities, the northernmost of which, San Clemente del Tuyú, is a few kilometres from Punta Rasa, the southern tip of Bahía Samborombón.

These beaches are less attractive than those further south and much less exclusive. While they also receive large numbers of tourists in summer, visitors are mostly working-class people who arrive by public transportation and enjoy traditional beach activities such as sunbathing or fishing. Housing is modest and the towns, with a few exceptions, are undistinguished, but all have very enthusiastic people working to promote tourism.

San Clemente stands out from the rest of the Partido de la Costa. Not only is the city quite attractive with its large wooded park El Vivero, but its location near Cape San Antonio puts it on the flyway for migrating birds from as far away as Alaska and Canada. Mundo Marino, a theme park with a serious commitment to the conservation of marine life, attracts youngsters and adults alike.

Orientation

The streets in San Clemente are mostly numbered, with east-west Avenidas running perpendicular to the beach and north-south Calles running parallel to it, but the city plan is irregular and confusing. North of the ACA campground, roughly in the middle of town, streets fan out from the beach. Some Avenidas have Roman numerals rather than Arabic numerals.

Information

Tourist Office Turismo (☎ 21478), at Calle 2 and Avenida 1, is friendly but has few maps or brochures.

Mundo Marino

Mundo Marino, the third most popular tourist destination in the country in terms of annual visitors, reflects the commitment of the Méndez family to marine wildlife conservation. Mundo Marino rescues, treats and in some circumstances keeps orcas ('killer whales'), sea lions, dolphins, sea otters and seabirds. Their research, education and conservation-oriented park is well designed and immaculately maintained, with spacious enclosures. The US$4 entry fee is reasonable for what you get.

The park is on the north end of town, at Avenida X No 157. All shows take place in the open, so bring sun protection. Local bus No 500 goes there from every city of Partido de la Costa.

Estación Biológica de la Fundación Vida Silvestre

This research station in Punta Rasa is an interesting place for birdwatchers. For details ask at the tourist office.

Places to Stay – bottom end

Camping There are several campgrounds at the entrance of San Clemente, all of which charge about US$2 per person and US$2 per tent per day. These include *Camping Kumelcan 1*, Calle 48 and Avenida 7, *Camping Kumelcan 2*, Calle 50 and 33 bis, and *Camping El Tala*, Calle 9 bis and 72. All are some distance from the beach.

Right downtown is the shady *Camping del ACA*, Avenida II No 96, which is mostly for members but you can 'join' on the spot. Rates are about US$12 for up to four people, tent and car, including electricity. The bathroom and washing facilities are excellent.

Hospedajes & Hotels San Clemente has a number of reasonably priced, comfortable hotels. *Hotel Rivera*, Calle 21 No 312, and *Hotel Avenida*, Calle 5 No 1561, are both good value at about US$6 per person. *Hospedaje Pereira*, Calle 13 No 90, is slightly more expensive but includes breakfast. *Hotel Acuario*, Avenida San Martín 444, charges US$8 per person.

Places to Stay – middle

Two-star *Hotel Correa*, Talas del Tuyú 2883, has rooms for US$12 per person with breakfast. *Hotel Savoia*, Avenida San Martín 267, charges US$15 with 'normal' breakfast and US$18 with 'abundant' breakfast.

At *Hotel Casino*, Calle 16 No 71, rates are US$29 per person with breakfast but US$36 with half-pension. There is a 10% discount for cash.

Places to Stay – top end

Hotel Morales (☎ 21207), Calle 1 No 1856, charges US$35 double, but for twice that you can have all meals included. *Hotel Fontainbleu*, Costanera and Calle 3 Sur, is the most expensive and luxurious hotel in the city at US$49 per person with breakfast. The nearby *Hotel Altair* is equally comfortable but more reasonably priced.

Places to Eat

Restaurant Oraya, Calle 1 between Avenidas 13 and 14, has reasonable prices and a good pollo al ajillo (chicken with tomato sauce). *Restaurant-Parrilla La Quebrada*, Calle 1 between Avenidas 13 and 22, is family oriented, basic and cheap. *Pizzería Gugupu*, Calle 1 No 2426, has tasty pizza. *El Rey del Calzón* specialises in Neapolitan calzone.

Getting There & Away

Bus Empresa Río de la Plata (☎ 31340), Calle 3 between Avenidas 1 and 15, has daily buses to Buenos Aires. Empresa Costamar, Avenida San Martín and Calle 3, goes to Buenos Aires, Pinamar, Villa Gesell and Mar del Plata. El Rápido, Calle 21 No 132, also has a service from Buenos Aires to Mar del Plata which stops at every resort.

Alvarez Hermanos, Calle 15 and Avenida 20, connects Greater Buenos Aires with the beaches to Villa Gesell, as does CAT, San Martín 157, which goes all the way to Miramar.

MIRAMAR

From Cabo Corrientes in Mar del Plata, car-clogged national Ruta 11 follows spectacular cliffs past the summer presidential residence at Chapadmalal and holiday complexes belonging to different trade unions (a legacy of Perónism), before finally arriving at Miramar.

This small, pleasant family resort, nick-named La Ciudad de los Niños (City of Children), dates from the turn of the century but did not attract mass tourism until the 1950s. Lacking nightlife and entertainment despite the presence of a casino, its safety and friendliness attract families with young children. Vacationers spend most days relaxing on the clean, gently sloping beaches.

Bicycling is safe and pleasant, so that children and adults alike use bicycles both in town and in the Vivero Municipal F Ameghino, a densely forested park covering 500 hectares.

Orientation

Miramar is 45 km south-west of Mar del Plata, 450 km from Buenos Aires and 102 km from Necochea. Its city plan mimics that of La Plata, with numbered streets and diagonals starting at the central plaza and ending at peripheral plazas, allowing easy access to places and smoothly flowing traffic. Even-numbered streets run parallel to the sea in a roughly east-west direction, while odd-numbered streets run north-south.

Common practice has imposed the use of names for some arterial roads: Avenida B Mitre (Avenida 23), Calle 9 de Julio (Calle 21), Calle Legarra (Calle 19), Avenida H Yrigoyen (Avenida 9), Diagonal Fortunato de la Plaza to the north, Diagonal Illia to the east, Diagonal R Mitre to the south, and Diagonal J Dupuy to the west.

Information

Tourist Office The Dirección Municipal de Turismo (☎ 20190), Calle 28 at Calle 21, sells a very thorough city guide for about US$2. It also has good free brochures and a useful map.

Money Cambio Ibertur is on Calle 21, between Calles 18 and 20. Banco de la Nación is at the corner of Calles 23 and 30, Banco Provincia at Calles 21 and 24 and Banco del Tandil is on Calle 30 between Calle 21 and 23.

Post & Telecommunications ENCOTEL is on Calle 17 at Calle 32. Telefónica is at Diagonal F de la Plaza 1451.

Travel Agencies ACA (☎ 61-0682) is at Diagonal Fortunato de la Plaza 1733. There are two other travel agencies in Miramar: Anuschka Tours (☎ 21119) at Calle 21 No 787, and Droppy Tours (☎ 20735) at Calle 24 No 1130.

Medical Services The Hospital Municipal (☎ 20837) is at Diagonal Dupuy 1150.

Places to Stay – bottom end

There is a great variety of accommodation in Miramar. Rates are generally lower than those of other resorts.

Camping *Camping El Durazno* is on provincial Ruta 11 to Mar del Plata, two km from the centre. It has clean plots, with electricity and sanitary facilities, for about US$2.50 per person per day. There are other campgrounds in nearby Mar del Sud – *Camping Mar del Sud* charges about US$2 per person.

Top: Iguazú Falls, Misiones Province
Bottom: Parque Nacional El Palmar, Entre Ríos

Top Left: Jesuit Church of La Compañía, Córdoba city
Top Right: Cathedral, Paraná city
Bottom: Sierras de Córdoba

Hospedajes & Hotels There are several inexpensive hospedajes, starting at about US$8 per person. These include *Hospedaje Familia* (☎ 20788) at Calle 23 No 1701, nearby *Hospedaje Dorimar* (☎ 21109) at Calle 24 No 839, and *Hospedaje España* at Calle 14 No 1046. *Hospedaje Laurana* (☎ 22462), Calle 11 No 1728, is clean and pleasant.

One-star hotels offer rooms with private bath for about US$10 to US$15 per person. Try *Hotel Santa Eulalia II* (☎ 20091), Calle 15 at Calle 20; *Hotel Miramar* (☎ 21617), Calle 21 No 974; *Hotel Ideal* (☎ 20259), Calle 21 No 632; *Hotel Cervantes* (☎ 20387), Calle 24 No 1110; and *Hotel Castilla* (☎ 20938), Calle 21 No 1032.

Places to Stay – middle
Two-star hotels in this category run to about US$14 to $18 per person. Possibilities are *Hotel Montecarlo* (☎ 20469) at Calle 16 No 1050, *Hotel Carolina* (☎ 20925) at Calle 11 No 1114, *Hotel Domani* (☎ 20978) at Avenida 9 No 1034, and *Hotel Continental* (☎ 20895) at Calle 19 No 1168.

Places to Stay – top end
There are several three-star hotels, including *Hotel América* (☎ 20847) at Diagonal Mitre 1114, and the *Grand Hotel* (☎ 20358) at Calle 29 No 586. Both charge around US$20 to US$25 per person. *Hotel Palace* (☎ 20258), at Calle 23 No 774, includes meals.

Places to Eat
Food in Miramar is considerably less expensive than in Mar del Plata or most other beach resorts. *Círculo Italiano*, Avenida 9 between Calles 30 and 28, serves abundant Italian dishes, as does *Río Nápole*, on Calle 21 at Calle 30. *Restaurant El Aguila*, Calle 19 No 1461, has a standard Argentine menu. *El Estribo*, Calle 30 between Calle 19 and 21, has good parrillada. For seafood, especially shellfish, try *El Muelle*, Costanera at 37, and *Mesón Español*, Avenida 26 No 1351.

Restaurante Punto y Banca, F de la Plaza 1426, offers good seafood and pasta.

Parrilla Rancho Grande, Calle 23 No 1022, has a good tenedor libre. *La Posta de Facundo*, Avenida 9 No 1053, is good but closes in winter. Good rotiserías with food to go include *Katty*, Calle 21 No 780, *Popeye*, Avenida 26 between Avenidas 19 and 21, and *Valeria*, Calle 25 No 620.

Getting There & Away
Air Miramar has flights to Buenos Aires during summer only. Aerolíneas Argentinas (☎ 21553) is at 9 de Julio 710, while Austral (☎ 20735) is at Calle 24 No 1130.

Bus For a small town, Miramar has excellent bus connections despite its lack of a central terminal. Several companies have their offices (☎ 23359) at Avenida Mitre 1701 and others are located at Calle 32, at the corner of Calle 19. Companies at Mitre include El Rápido del Sur, which has buses to Mar del Plata. CAT travels to different areas of Greater Buenos Aires, and Micromar goes to the Capital Federal also.

Costera Criolla (☎ 20747), Calle 32 at Calle 19, travels to Necochea, while El Pampa, at the same office, goes to Bahía Blanca. Fares to Buenos Aires cost about US$22.

Train The Ferrocarril Roca (☎ 20657) is on Avenida 40, between Calles 13 and 15, with daily service to Buenos Aires.

NECOCHEA
Famous for wide, sandy beaches, dunes and its casino, Necochea is a popular, tranquil, family-oriented resort. Among its permanent population there is a substantial Danish colony.

Orientation & Information
Necochea is 500 km from Buenos Aires and 125 km south-west of Mar del Plata. The south-flowing Río Quequén divides the city in half. East of the river, all streets are numbered 500 and above, while west of the river street numbers run from 2 to the low 100s in the centre. Even-numbered steets run parallel to the sea, while odd numbers run perpendicular.

During the tourist season Calle 83, the main commercial street, is a pedestrian mall.

Things to See & Do
One of the city's more attractive features is the **Parque Miguel Lillo**, a large green space along the beach. Its dense pine woods are widely used for bicycling, riding or picnicking. The Río Quequén, rich in rainbow trout and mackerel, also allows for adventurous canoeing, particularly around the falls at Saltos del Quequén.

At the village of **Quequén**, at the mouth of the river, several stranded shipwrecks offer good opportunities for exploration and photography below sculpted cliffs. The **Faro** (lighthouse) is another local attraction.

Tourist brochures assert that the **Casino** is 'irresistible'.

Places to Stay – bottom end
Camping The *Camping Municipal* is in Parque Lillo. There are several privately owned campgrounds along the beach.

Hospedajes & Hotels Most accommodation in Necochea is downtown, relatively close to the beach. The most reasonable are hospedajes such as *Hospedaje Bayo* (☎ 23334) at Calle 87 No 338; *Hospedaje Colón* (☎ 24825) at Calle 62 No 3034; *Hospedaje Necomar* (☎ 22689) Calles 20 and 79 bis; *Hospedaje Regis* (☎ 25870) at Avenida San Martín 626; *Hospedaje Pleno Mar* (☎ 22674), at Calle 87 No 250; and *Hospedaje Lanus* (☎ 25729) at Calle 79 bis No 675. Expect to pay about US$8 per person.

One-star hotels cost about US$10 to US$15 per person. Try *Hotel Lido* (☎ 23508) at Calle 81 No 328, *Hotel Flamingo* (☎ 20049) at Calle 83 No 333, or *Hotel María Paula* (☎ 23903) at Calle 4 No 3927. *Hotel Suizo* (☎ 24008) is at Calle 22 No 4235.

Places to Stay – middle
There are numerous two-star hotels, like *Hotel Argentino* (☎ 23661) at Calles 87 and 6; *Hotel Trocadero* (☎ 22589) at Calle 81 No 275; *Hotel Bahía* (☎ 23353) at Avenida San Martín 731; *Hotel Corona* (☎ 22646) at Avenida 75 No 371; *Hotel Internacional* (☎ 24587) at Calle 81 No 232; and *Hotel Necochea* (☎ 22062) at Avenida 79 No 217. Prices are about US$14 to US$18 per person.

Places to Stay – top end
Three-star hotels include *Hotel Presidente* (☎ 23800) at Calle 4 No 4040; *Hotel León* (☎ 24800) at Avenida 79 No 229; *Hotel Peruggia* (☎ 22020) at Calle 81 No 288; *Hotel San Miguel* (☎ 25155) at Calles 85 and 6; and *Hotel Tres Reyes* (☎ 22011) at Calle 4 bis No 4112. All charge about US$25 to US$35 per person.

Places to Eat
Parrilla El Palenque, Avenida 79 and Calle 6, has good food and reasonable prices.

Getting There & Away
Bus The bus terminal is at Avenida 47 and Calle 582, near the river. Both El Cóndor and Costera Criolla have several buses daily to Buenos Aires.

Train The Ferrocarril Roca has trains between Necochea and Constitución Station in Buenos Aires three times weekly in each direction.

CLAROMECÓ
This tranquil village, with only 1000 permanent residents, has attractive beaches for sunbathing, swimming, surfing and waterskiing, but is most famous for its fishing. Nicknamed 'Fisherman's Paradise', Claromecó holds a 24-hour fishing tournament every February which attracts aficionados from all over the province. One year the winning entry was a 48-kg *corvina negra*.

Claromecó is off the main coastal routes at the mouth of the Arroyo Claromecó, 565 km from Buenos Aires at the end of provincial Ruta 73, 68 km from Tres Arroyos on national Ruta 3, and 260 km from Bahía Blanca.

It has several campgrounds and hotels,

plus good and relatively inexpensive food. There are bus connections to Buenos Aires, Necochea, Bahía Blanca and Mendoza.

MONTE HERMOSO

With a stable population of 5000 people, Monte Hermoso has an interesting past tied to the 19th-century colonisation of Buenos Aires province and the displacement of native peoples. In 1897 Don Esteban Dufaur, exiled by his father to develop the 4000-hectare El Recreo cattle estancia, blundered along with ex-convict labour for years before even finding a site where the shifting dunes would not cover the main house. Local Indians, not accepting his ownership, resisted establishment of the estancia, but by the turn of the century Dufaur's position was stable and the village of Monte Hermoso developed nearby. By 1917 Dufaur built its first hotel from a jettisoned cargo of lumber which washed up on the beach, and the village opened up for tourism.

Orientation & Information

The southernmost beach resort in Buenos Aires province, Monte Hermoso is 106 km from Bahía Blanca and 633 km from Buenos Aires, situated on provincial Ruta 78 a short distance off national Ruta 3. The main commercial street is Dufaur.

Tourist Office The friendly Oficina de Turismo (☎ 8223) is open all year at the bus terminal. It offers an English version of its tourist guide to Monte Hermoso (for a charge), and good free maps and brochures.

Things to See & Do

Warm currents, broad sandy beaches and relative quiet attract vacationers to Monte Hermoso. It is also cheaper and less crowded than the more fashionable resorts to the north, with a good but not overwhelming tourist infrastructure, including several shady, spacious campgrounds and good if standard restaurants and pizzerías. Beaches, especially those toward the lighthouse on the east end of Avenida Costanera, are wide

enough to accommodate large-court beach games such as *paleta* (beach tennis).

The beaches closest to the lighthouse are used almost exclusively for fishing, walking or jogging. The lighthouse itself, 73 metres and 327 steps high, merits a visit for the panorama of the town, beaches, dunes and the ocean.

Swimmers should note occasional water temperature changes which can bring hordes of stinging jellyfish. Although these invasions do not last long, it happens every summer – to avoid awful discomfort, stay out of the ocean at these times.

Places to Stay

Camping Monte Hermoso has several campgrounds, including two highly recommended ones. The village-like *Camping Americano* (☎ 81149), right on the beach west of town, has a swimming pool, store, and recreation facilities, but is not cheap at US$4 per person, US$3 for the tent and US$2 for electrical hookup. The well-maintained *Autocamping Nuevo Montemar* (☎ 81183) is on Dufaur, about 1½ km away from the beach, with friendly owners who charge US$2.50 per person, and US$1.50 for electricity. There are ACA discounts available there.

Hospedajes & Hosterías Hospedajes at Monte Hermoso, charging an average of about US$7 per person, include: *Hospedaje Ambar*, Dufaur and Valle Encantado; *Hospedaje Rambla* (☎ 81015), Dufaur 67; *Hospedaje Pec-Mar* (☎ 81195), Río Colorado 445; *Hospedaje Mari-Car* (☎ 81223), Avenida Costa 58; and *Hospedaje Ripoll* (☎ 81237), Los Pinos and Traful.

More expensive is *Hostería La Goleta* (☎ 81142), Avenida Costanera at Calle 10, with singles/doubles at about US$18/30. *Nauta Motel* (☎ 81083), Dufaur 635, has similar prices and service.

Places to Eat

Monte Hermoso has reasonably priced restaurants such as *Parrilla La Rueda*, Los Pinos and Traful, which also prepares food to go. *Marisquería Rincón Basko*, Perón 50, has superb pollo al ajillo and shellfish dishes. The sidewalk *Pizzería Las Carabelas*, Dufaur and Costanera, also serves good food.

Getting There & Away

The bus terminal is at Valle Encantado and Mendoza. La Estrella connects Monte Hermoso with Buenos Aires, and La Acción goes to Bahía Blanca several times daily.

The Pampas

Argentina's famous Pampas are monotonously, almost unrelentingly flat except for their extensive coastline, several small mountain ranges and the delta of the Río de la Plata. These features give some variety to the country's agricultural heartland which comprises the provinces of Buenos Aires, La Pampa and major parts of Santa Fe and Córdoba. Within this area are a surprising number of tourist attractions.

Buenos Aires province contains several important cities, particularly its capital of La Plata and the Atlantic port of Bahía Blanca. The colonial city of Luján is one of the most important religious centres in all of South America.

Rosario, a vital port for Argentina's agricultural exports, lies up the Río Paraná in Santa Fe province and vies with Córdoba for the status of 'second city' in the republic even though it is not even the capital of its own province – the colonial city of Santa Fe retains that position.

History

The aboriginal inhabitants of the Pampas were Querandí hunter-gatherers, less numerous and more dispersed than the sedentary, civilised peoples of the North-West or even the semisedentary Guaraní of the upper Paraná basin. Although they lacked both the plough and the domestic draft animals to cultivate the fertile Pampas, the Querandí had no real need for them, hunting guanaco and rhea with boleadoras (also known as *bolas*) – accurately thrown, they would become entangled in the animal's legs and make it easy prey. Hunting was a communal rather than individual activity, and so long as game remained abundant on the Pampas' boundless pastures, the hard labour of cultivation was pointless.

The Querandí were hostile to the Spanish presence, besieging early settlements and preventing the Spaniards from establishing any foothold in the area for more than half a century. Even after the definitive founding of the city of Buenos Aires in 1580, settlement of the Pampas proceeded slowly, only in part because Spain's mercantile policy favoured already populous Peru and constrained potential rivals to Lima's political and economic primacy.

In many ways, feral animals accomplished what Madrid's early colonial policy actually discouraged, the spontaneous Europeanisation of the Pampas. When the Spaniards abandoned their first settlement at Buenos Aires for the pleasures of Paraguay, they also left behind cattle and horses, which multiplied prodigiously in their absence.

During the centuries and even millennia before the arrival of the Spanish, aboriginal peoples had transformed the Pampas environment through hunting and, especially, through fire. Frequent burning, a hunting technique to flush out game, prevented the re-establishment of *monte* (scrub forest) and directly benefitted the grasses, which recuperated much more quickly. In turn, the new, succulent native grasses could support even more game.

Or more cattle. In 1619, according to ecological historian Alfred Crosby, less than 40 years after the re-establishment of Buenos Aires, colonial officials informed Madrid that a harvest of 80,000 cattle per year for hides would not diminish the herds. One 18th-century visitor estimated the number of cattle south of modern Paraguay and north of the Río Negro at 48 million. Even granting the impossibility of a truly accurate estimate, numbers were obviously very great.

Horses were also numerous. Like the Plains Indians of North America, Araucanians on both sides of the Andes quickly learned to tame and ride them, aiding their resistance to the invasion of their territories as late as the 19th century. Mobile on horseback rather than on foot, they were much more formidable opponents for the forces of imperial Spain and even independent Argentina, but as European immigration increased, their options were fewer and the Pampas eventually fell to the cattle producers and farmers.

The wild cattle and horses left two enduring and related legacies: the culture of the gaucho, who persisted for many decades as a neohunter-gatherer and then as a symbol of argentinidad, an extreme but romantic Argentine nationalism; and environmental impoverishment, as grazing and opportunistic European weeds altered the native grasslands. Nineteenth-century observers such as Darwin and William Henry Hudson remarked on the rapid displacement of native plants by European artichokes and thistles in parts of the Pampas. Darwin wrote that in one area

...very many (probably several hundred) square miles are covered by one mass of these prickly plants, and are impenetrable by man or beast. Over the undulating plains, where these great beds occur, nothing else can now live...I doubt whether any case is on record of an invasion on so grand a scale of one plant over the aborigines.

Unpremeditated introductions of European biota, then, were at least as important as European force in undermining indigenous resistance and opening the frontier to overseas immigrants.

Upon Argentine independence, the country's doors opened fitfully to foreign commerce. The Pampas' saladeros yielded only hides, tallow and salt beef, products with limited overseas markets. This trade, in turn, benefited only the relatively few estancieros with the luck to inherit or the foresight to grab large tracts of land. Some landowners did not survive the fall of Rosas, whose policies had encouraged the alienation of public lands for grazing establishments, but others prospered as Buenos Aires experienced a wool boom in the latter half of the 19th century.

From shortly after midcentury, the railroads, built largely with British capital, made it feasible to export wool and then beef, but the meat from rangy, unimproved criollo cattle did not appeal to British tastes. Improved breeds required more succulent feed, such as alfalfa, but the estancieros could not produce this on their enormous holdings with the skeletal labour force available to them. Consequently, their traditional opposition to immigration declined as they sought to attract tenant farmers to their holdings.

Although the estancieros had no intention of relinquishing their lands, the development of arable farming was an indirect benefit of the intensification of stock-raising. Cultivation of alfalfa required preparatory cultivation, so landowners rented their properties to *medieros* (sharecroppers), who raised wheat for four or five years before moving elsewhere, and thus benefited both from their share of the wheat crop and from their new alfalfa fields. Still, shortly after the turn of the century, agricultural exports such as maize, wheat and linseed exceeded the

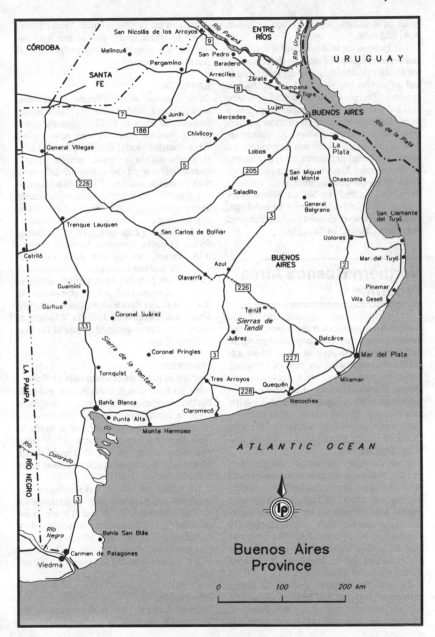

Buenos Aires Province

0   100   200 km

value of livestock products such as hides, wool and meat.

The Pampas are still famous for their beef and the estancias still dominate the economy, but smaller landholdings have made inroads and Argentina has remained a major grain exporter. The province of Santa Fe, where rain-fed maize is the principal crop, has a more democratic structure of land ownership, but almost everywhere agriculture is now highly mechanized and dependent on petroleum-based fertilizers and pesticides. In this sense, Argentina resembles other major grain-producing areas such as Australia, Canada and the United States. Near Buenos Aires and other large cities, though, there is intensive cultivation of fruit and vegetables, as well as dairying.

Northern Buenos Aires Province

Buenos Aires province is the largest, richest, most populous and most important province in the country. Its area of 307,000 sq km makes it nearly twice the size of Uruguay, while its population, even excluding the federal district of the city of Buenos Aires, is more than triple Uruguay's three million. Its wealth lies in its soil, whose yields of hides, beef, wool and wheat for global markets placed an independent Argentina on the map in the 19th century.

From the mid-19th century, the province and city of Buenos Aires were the undisputed political and economic centre of the country, but Buenos Aires' de facto secession as a federal zone subjugated the powerful province to national authority without completely eliminating its influence. By 1880, the province responded by creating its own model city, La Plata, on the design of the United States' capital of Washington, DC.

Outside the Capital Federal, a dense network of railroads and highways connects the agricultural towns of the Pampas, forming an astonishingly symmetrical pattern on the provincial map. Most of these towns resemble each other as much as one part of the almost endlessly flat Pampas resembles another.

LA PLATA

After Buenos Aires became the federal capital of Argentina, Governor Dardo Rocha founded La Plata in 1882 to give the province of Buenos Aires its own new capital. After detailed study, Rocha selected Pedro Benoit's elaborate plan, which greatly resembled that of Washington, DC, with major avenues and broad diagonals connecting its public buildings and numerous plazas. For two years, an army of labourers worked day and night to bring the plan to fruition.

La Plata's grandiose public buildings reflect Benoit's intention to build a great urban centre, but the city does not overwhelm the human dimension. As envisioned, the city has become an important administrative, commercial and cultural centre. Rocha was the first rector of its university, which was founded by Joaquín V González and widely acknowledged as one of the best in the country.

Orientation

La Plata is just 56 km south-east of Buenos Aires. Its basic design is a conventional grid, but the superposition of numerous diagonals forms a distinctive diamond pattern, connecting the plazas and permitting traffic to flow smoothly between them. While most public buildings are on or around Plaza Moreno, the commercial centre is near Plaza San Martín.

All streets are named and numbered, but residents use numbers only to identify locations. Avenidas 1, 7 and 13 are main thoroughfares which run north-south, while Avenidas 44, 51, 53, and 60 run east-west. On each block, street numbers run in groups of 50 rather than the customary 100 per block.

Information

Tourist Office The Subsecretaría de Turismo (☎ 21-6894) is on the 13th floor of the municipal tower at Calle 12 and Avenida 53. It has excellent descriptive brochures and a good map.

Money Most banks and cambios are in the area bounded by Calles 6 and 8, and 46 and 50. Banco de la Nación is at Avenida 7 and Calle 49, and Banco de la Provincia is on Avenida 7 and Calle 47.

Post & Telecommunications ENCOTEL is at Calle 4 and Avenida 51. Telefónica (☎ 21-9908) is at Calle 47 No 680.

Cultural Centres The Pasaje Dardo Rocha, Calle 50 between Calle 6 and Avenida 7, is La Plata's most important cultural centre. It has display galleries, a library, and facilities for theatre, concerts, movies and lectures. The building itself is worth seeing.

Travel Agencies ACA (☎ 30161) is at Calle 9 and Avenida 51. Titán Turismo (☎ 40495) is at Calles 43 and 6, while Turismo San Martín is at Avenida 51 between Avenida 7 and Calle 8.

Medical Services The Hospital Español (☎ 21-0191) is on Calle 9 between Calles 35 and 36.

Plaza Moreno

La Plata's **founding stone of 1882** in the middle of Plaza Moreno, which is between Calles 12 and 14 and Avenidas 50 and 54, marks the city's precise geographical centre. On Calle 14 between Avenidas 51 and 53, visit the unfinished neo-Gothic **Cathedral**, inspired by its medieval counterparts in Cologne and Amiens, with fine stained glass and polished granite floors. Dardo Rocha and his wife are buried here.

On the opposite side of the Plaza is the **Palacio Municipal** designed in German Renaissance style by the Hannoverian architect Hubert Stiers. Not far away, on Calle 6, is the provincial **Casa de Gobierno**, built in Flemish Renaissance style.

Paseo del Bosque

Plantations of eucalyptus, gingko, palm, and subtropical hardwoods cover this 60-hectare park at the north-east edge of town. It houses the **Anfiteatro Martín Fierro**, an open air facility which hosts summer drama festivals, the **Museo de Ciencias Naturales**, the **Observatorio Astronómico**, the symbolic United Nations of the **Jardín de la Paz** (Garden of Peace), a small zoo, and several university departments.

Museo de Ciencias Naturales

When Buenos Aires became the federal capital, provincial authorities built this museum, in the spacious park known as Paseo del Bosque, to house the archaeological and anthropological collections of lifetime director Francisco P Moreno, the famous Patagonian explorer.

Finished in 1889, the building itself consists of an attractive oval with four storeys and a mezzanine with showrooms, classrooms, workshops, laboratories, offices, libraries and storage. Its exterior mixes Corinthian columns, Ionic posterior walls and Hellenic windows, with pre-Columbian Aztec and Inca embellishments. Since 1906, the university's school of natural sciences has functioned there.

Despite the quality and abundance of materials, the archaeological and anthropological exhibits from South America and Argentina suffer from an outdated form of presentation. The extensive zoology collection, although it has some good pieces, is also unimaginative. More innovative is the recently opened botany room, which displays 'economic' plants (those useful to the indigenous inhabitants in the past and the largely immigrant population of the present) in their geographical context.

The museum is open daily, except for 1 January, 1 May and 25 December, from noon to 6 pm weekdays and 10 am to 6 pm weekends and holidays. Admission is US$2.

La República de los Niños

Evita Perón sponsored this scale reproduction of a city for the education and enjoyment

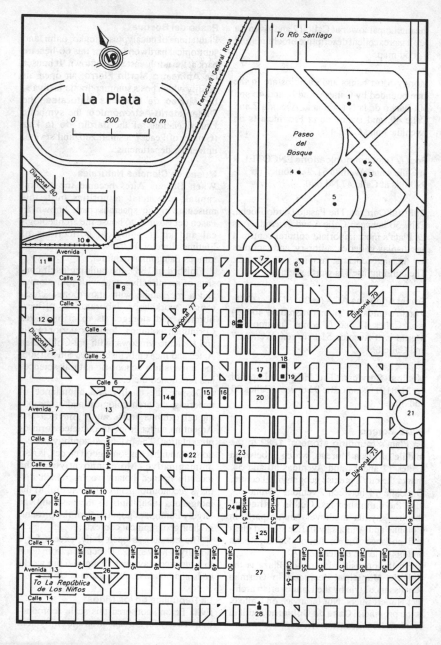

■ PLACES TO STAY

6	Hotel Roga
9	Hotel Plaza
11	Hotel Roca
18	Hotel San Marcos
19	Hotel Corregidor
24	Hotel La Plata

OTHER

1	Observatorio Astronómico
2	Museo de Ciencias Naturales
3	Jardín de la Paz
4	Zoo
5	Anfiteatro Martín Fierro
7	Plaza Rivadavia
8	Post Office
10	Train Station
12	Bus Terminal
13	Plaza Italia
14	Banco de la Provincia
15	Banco de la Nación
16	Pasaje Dardo Rocha
17	Government Palace
20	Plaza San Martín
21	Plaza Rocha
22	Telefónica
23	ACA
25	Municipality/Tourist Office
26	Plaza Passo
27	Plaza Moreno
28	Cathedral

of children, completed shortly before her death in 1952. A fascinating architectural hodgepodge, inspired by medieval European and Islamic styles and Grimms' and Andersen's fairy tales, it includes a civic centre with church, a (working) post office, courts and police station, shops, supermarket, restaurants, factories and museum, plus an artificial lake.

From the Plaza de la Amistad, a steam train circles the city, even passing through tunnels.

It also contains a zoo, an aquarium and an educational farm, plus the captivating **Museo Internacional del Muñeco**, a doll museum with domestic and imported dolls and puppets, open daily from 10 am to 6 pm.

República de los Niños is on Camino General Belgrano km 7, north of La Plata in the suburb of Gonnet. From the centre, take bus No 518 or 273.

Places to Stay

Since visitors to La Plata are often government officials on per diem, hotels price their rooms accordingly. One of the few budget hotels, the friendly but run-down *Hotel Roca*, Avenida 1 at Calle 42, has singles/doubles at US$12/18 with private bath, and doubles at US$14 with shared bath.

The one-star *Hotel Roga* (☎ 21-9553) at Calle 54 No 334, has clean, comfortable rooms with private bath at US$26/34 including breakfast. Similar in price and standard is *Hotel Plaza* (☎ 24-3109), near the train station at Avenida 44 No 358. Rooms are US$22/33 without breakfast, but there is a budget double room on the third floor for US$26.

At the top end are three-star hotels like *Hotel San Marcos* (☎ 42249) at Calle 54 No 523; *Hotel La Plata* (☎ 21-1365), which has a nice restaurant, at Avenida 51 No 783, near the Cathedral and Municipalidad; and *Hotel Cristal* (☎ 24-1043) at Avenida 1 No 620. All charge about US$35/50.

The luxurious *Hotel Corregidor* (☎ 25-6800), Calle 6 No 1026, has everything for US$61/76.

Places to Eat

Among the cheapest restaurants are *Everton*, Calle 14 between Calles 63 and 64, and *Club Matheu*, Calle 63 between Avenida 1 and Calle 2. Both offer limited but good menus at affordable prices. A bit more pricey but very pleasant is the *Restaurant Club Hípico* in the Paseo del Bosque.

For a good parrillada try *El Chaparral*, Avenida 60 and Calle 117, which has excellent mollejas (sweetbreads). On Plaza Passo is *El Quijote*; it is in an undistinguished building but has delicious food, particularly the ensalada de frutos de mar (seafood salad). According to a local lawyer, the best food in town is at the *Colegio de Escribanos*, Avenida 13 between Calles 47 and 48.

Highly recommended is omelette surprise for dessert.

The quintessential La Plata experience is the 85-year-old *Cervecería Modelo* or simply *La Modelo*, at the corner of Calles 54 and 5. On a warm summer night, you can pass hours at their sidewalk tables, with excellent *cerveza tirada* (lager beer) and complimentary peanuts – for something more substantial, try a lomito with chips. In winter there is plenty of space inside.

Getting There & Away
Bus The bus terminal (☎ 21-2182) is at Calles 4 and 42. Río de la Plata (☎ 38537) has buses every half hour to Once, Constitución and Retiro in Buenos Aires. It also has a beach service to Pinamar and Villa Gesell. Long-distance bus companies include Costera Criolla (☎ 31185) which serves Mar del Plata, Miramar, Necochea, and Tandil, and El Cóndor (☎ 44456) which goes to Bahía Blanca via Olavarría and Sierra de la Ventana. Liniers goes daily to Santa Rosa, La Pampa province, while Pampa goes to Tandil and Necochea. Fare to Buenos Aires is about US$2.

Train The turn-of-the-century train station (☎ 21-9377), at Avenida 1 and Calle 43, features an interesting Art Nouveau dome and wrought-iron awning. There are hourly trains to Constitución via Quilmes or Temperley.

Getting Around
Buses to different places in the city stop by the train station.

AROUND LA PLATA
Río Santiago
At the end of the Roca line past La Plata is Río Santiago, where ghost factories haunt the port. The most notable is the Swift meat packing plant, which employed 24,000 workers at its peak. The train is usually packed with soldiers coming and going from the military academy that functions there.

From the Río Santiago train station, it is also possible to take a boat to picturesque

Isla Paulino, rarely visited by tourists, whose inhabitants cultivate grapes in the well-known *viñedos de la costa* (coastal vineyards). Bus Nos 307 ('Ensenada') and No 214 ('Berisso') also go to the port.

LUJÁN
Buenos Aires' second founder, Don Juan de Garay, granted the lands around the Río Luján to Spanish pioneers, but constant Indian attacks and the distance from Buenos Aires deterred settlement until the 17th century, when the settlement by the Río Luján became an important stop on the cart road west.

According to legend, in 1630 a wagon containing a Virgin sent from Brazil to a Portuguese farmer would not budge until the gauchos removed her image. The image's devoted owner cleared the site and built a chapel where the Virgin had chosen to stay, about five km from present-day Luján. This image took the name of La Virgen de Luján and became Argentina's patron saint, now occupying the neo-Gothic basilica, one of the city's two main tourist attractions. The other is a colonial historical museum complex.

Orientation
Luján is 65 km from Buenos Aires on national Ruta 7, and many people come from the capital for the day. Most places of interest, as well as hotels, are near the church.

Information
Tourist Office There is an Oficina de Turismo (☎ 20032) at the bus terminal, but the central office (☎ 20453) at Edificio La Cúpula, at the west end of Lavalle, is more knowledgeable and better provided with information and brochures.

Basílica Nuestra Señora de Luján
Every year four million people from all over Argentina visit Luján to pay homage to the Virgin for intercession in matters of peace, health, forgiveness and consolation. The terminus of all pilgrimages is the huge neo-Gothic basilica, where the 'Virgencita'

(she is known by the affectionate diminutive) occupies a *camarín* (chamber) behind the main altar. Devotees have covered the stairs with plaques thanking her for her favours.

Every October, since the days of the Dirty War, a massive Peregrinación de la Juventud (Youth Pilgrimage) originates in Buenos Aires' Once Station, 62 km away. In the days of political repression, when any mass demonstration was forbidden, this walk had tremendous symbolic importance. Since the restoration of democracy it has become more exclusively devotional. The other large gathering of believers takes place on 8 May, the Virgin's day.

Near the basilica is the **Museo Devocional**, which houses *ex-votos* (gifts) to the Virgin, including objects of silver, wood and wax, musical instruments, and icons from all over the world. It's open Tuesday to Friday from 1 to 6 pm, weekends from 10 am to 6 pm.

Complejo Museográfico Enrique Udaondo

Bounded by Calles Lezica y Torrezuri, Lavalle, San Martín and Parque Ameghino, this museum complex occupies three full hectares. It includes the 30 rooms of the **Museo Colonial e Histórico**, housed in beautiful colonial buildings such as the **Cabildo**, and the so-called **Casa del Virrey** (no viceroy ever actually lived there). The exhibits cover the area's history from pre Columbian times to 1953. The **Museo de Transporte** has four showrooms, plus a patio with colonial wagons, a windmill and a horse-powered mill.

Museum hours are Wednesday from 12.30 to 4.30 pm, Thursday and Friday 11.30 am to 4.30 pm, and weekends from 10.45 am to 6 pm. The combination library and archive is open weekdays from 9.30 am to 6 pm, but closes in January.

Places to Stay

Camping For about US$2 per person per day, *Camping 7* on Ruta 7 (Avenida Carlos Pellegrini) across the Río Luján is basic and

less than perfectly maintained. There is another more expensive campground along the river near the Dirección Municipal de Turismo at Edificio La Cúpula. Informally, pilgrims camp just about anywhere they feel like it.

Hospedajes & Hotels Several low budget hotels cater to the pilgrims who come throughout the year. On the north side of the basilica is the friendly *Hospedaje Carena* (☎ 21287), Calle Lavalle 114, with singles/doubles at US$6/12 with private bath. Similar in price and standard is *Hotel Santa Rita* (☎ 20335), on Calle Lezica y Torrezuri, with small, musty but clean rooms with private bath for US$8/12. Opposite the bus terminal, *Hospedaje Royal* (☎ 21295), 9 de Julio 696, has small rooms at US$12/21.

Also nearby is the dark and run-down but clean and friendly *Venezia Hotel*, at Calle Almirante Brown and Lezica y Torrezuri, which has small rooms, with private baths and fans, at US$10/15. Rates are similar at the *Hotel Victoria* (☎ 20582), Lavalle 136. South of the basilica is the once-elegant *Hotel de la Paz* (☎ 24034), 9 de Julio 1054, which is now worn around the edges. The owners are friendly and the rooms are acceptable at US$14/23.

The only two-star hotel, the *Real Hotel Luján* (☎ 20054), Avenida Nuestra Señora de Luján 816, is good value at US$15/19, including private bath and telephone. For the most unexpected hotel name in this major devotional centre, we nominate *Hotel Eros* (☎ 20797), San Martín 129. Very clean, small rooms with no exterior windows cost US$20/25 with private bath.

Places to Eat

There is a slew of cheap, fixed-menu restaurants near the basilica along Avenida Nuestra Señora de Luján, with very aggressive waiters trying to lure tourists. Off the central plaza, the quiet *Restaurant Don Diego*, Colón 964, has excellent but pricey Argentine food. *Restaurante Match Point*, San Martín 199, is cheaper but portions are small. There are discounts for ACA members.

Getting There & Away

Bus The bus terminal is at Avenida de Nuestra Señora del Rosario, four blocks north of the basilica. Transporte Luján (Línea 52) goes to Plaza Miserere in Buenos Aires, Transportes Atlántida (Línea 57) connects Luján with Palermo. TALSA goes frequently to Once for US$3.

There are also long-distance services. Empresa Argentina has three buses daily to Mar del Plata (US$18), while Atlántida has similar but costlier services to Mardel (US$22), Pinamar and Villa Gesell. La Estrella goes to San Juan (US$43) and to San Rafael, with connections to Mendoza, for US$46. General Urquiza serves Rosario (US$12) and Córdoba (US$26).

Train Ferrocarril Sarmiento has daily trains from Once Station (Plaza Miserere Subte) in Buenos Aires.

Southern Buenos Aires Province

BAHÍA BLANCA

In an early effort to establish military control on the margins of the Pampas, Colonel Ramón Estomba built the pompously named Fortaleza Protectora Argentina at the natural harbour of Bahía Blanca in 1828. In 1884 the railway connected the area with Buenos Aires, but another 11 years passed before it officially became a city. Only in this century has the city flourished in commerce and industry, on the base of agriculture and petrochemicals.

Because of its location, Bahía Blanca is the southern gateway to Buenos Aires province, the Atlantic outlet for the produce from the Río Negro valley, and the coastal entrance to Patagonia. It is an important crossroads more than a tourist city per se, being home to South America's largest naval base at Puerto Belgrano, and also to the prestigious Universidad Nacional del Sur.

Orientation

Bahía Blanca is 653 km south of Buenos Aires, 530 km east of Neuquén, and 278 km north of Viedma. Plaza Rivadavia is the centre of its conventional grid. Street names change on either side of the Plaza.

Information

Tourist Office The tourist office functions in the Municipalidad (☎ 20114), Alsina 65, across from Plaza Rivadavia. It has few brochures, but you can photocopy material from their files.

Money Cambios keep fairly short hours, most closing by 4 pm. Try Cambio Pullman at San Martín 171, Iberotur at Soler 144, or Florida at Belgrano 187.

Banco del Sud, next to the Municipalidad, has a cambio which opens from 10 am to 3 pm. Banco de la Nación is at Estomba 52, and Banco de la Provincia is at Chiclana and Undiano. Bank schedules are 8 am to 2 pm in summer, 10 am to 4 pm in winter.

Post & Telecommunications ENCOTEL (☎ 22376) is at Moreno 34. Telefónica (☎ 22710) is at O'Higgins 203.

Foreign Consulates The Chilean Consulate (☎ 25808) is at Güemes 102.

Travel Agencies ACA (☎ 20076) has offices at Chiclana 305, with a reasonable, members-only parking garage.

Other agencies include Viajes Bahía Blanca (49767) at Drago 63, Toa (☎ 49150) at San Martín 108, and Turmundo (☎ 49150) at Soler 156.

Medical Services The Hospital Italiano (☎ 29048) is at Necochea 675, while the Hospital Municipal (☎ 30242), is at Estomba 968.

Places to Stay – bottom end

Camping There is a basic municipal campground at *Balneario Maldonado* (☎ 29511), four km from the centre at the south-western end of town. Open all year, it has salt water swimming pools, but hot water and electricity are available in summer only. Fees are US$1 per person. *Camping Cala Gogó*, on Sarmiento km 4 in Aldea Romana, east of Bahía Blanca, is open all year.

Hospedajes & Hotels There are several cheap but run-down hospedajes across from the train station, charging about US$5 per person. Try *Hospedaje Molinari* (☎ 22871) at Cerri 719, *Hospedaje Los Vascos* (☎ 29290) at Cerri 747, or *Hospedaje Roma* (☎ 38500) at Cerri 759. Four blocks away is *Hospedaje Victoria* (☎ 20522), at General Paz 84.

On Chiclana, closer to the plaza, accommodation is better but slightly more expensive, at about US$6 to US$10 per person. *Hospedaje Los Angeles*, Chiclana 367, is very clean. *Hotel Argentino* (☎ 33507), at Chiclana 466, is basic but has a restaurant. *Hotel Bayón* (☎ 22504) is at Chiclana 487. Surprisingly, there are no hotels by the bus terminal.

Places to Stay – middle
Hotel Chiclana (☎ 30436), Chiclana 370, and *Hotel Canciller* (☎ 38270), Brown 667, have singles/doubles at US$12/17 with private bath. The friendly *Hotel Muñiz* (☎ 20021), O'Higgins 23, has rooms at US$18/23. The pleasant *Hotel Italia* (☎ 201210), Drown 181, has nice rooms with bath at US$20/32, and a good restaurant.

Places to Stay – top end
Prices and standards are very similar at top-end hotels. *Hotel Austral* (☎ 20241), Avenida Colón 159, has comfortable rooms with TV and telephone at about US$34/58. *Hotel Argos* (☎ 40001) is at España 149.

Places to Eat
There are several acceptable restaurants in Bahía Blanca, although none are really memorable. *El Cholo*, Ruta 3 South, km 696, is

the most popular truck stop in the province. Food is basic, abundant and inexpensive. Also cheap is *La Cigala*, across from the train station at Cerri 757.

Taberna Baska, Lavalle 284, and *La Española*, Zelarrayán 51, serves appetising, reasonably priced Spanish food. *El Aljibe*, Donado and Thompson, offers a conventional Argentine menu but is somewhat pricey. There are several parrillas and pizzerías in the centre.

For breakfast, try *Bar Lácteo La Barra*, Chiclana 155. It has good fresh orange juice and tasty grilled sandwiches.

Getting There & Away
Air Aerolíneas Argentinas (☎ 38323), San Martín 298, flies to Buenos Aires directly every day, with other flights via Santa Rosa, La Pampa province. Tuesday, Thursday and Sunday flights go to Río Gallegos and Ushuaia.

Austral (☎ 21383), Colón 59, has two daily flights to Buenos Aires, except Sunday when there is only one. Daily, except Sunday, there are flights to Comodoro Rivadavia, Río Gallegos, Río Grande and Ushuaia.

Bus The comfortable bus terminal (☎ 29616), Estados Unidos and Brown, is about two km from the plaza. Costera Criolla (☎ 21075), La Estrella (☎ 34846) and El Cóndor (☎ 34846) serve Buenos Aires several times daily. Pampa (☎ 24121) goes to Mar del Plata and Necochea, while El Valle (☎ 30134) travels to Neuquén and Zapala, via the Río Negro valley, four times daily. Don Otto (☎ 22505) has buses to coastal Patagonian destinations daily at 8 am, and to Río Gallegos on Wednesdays. TICSA (☎ 30152) serves San Luis and San Juan daily. La Acción (☎ 30152) goes to Monte Hermoso. TUP and TUS (☎ 49245) have buses to Córdoba.

Typical fares are: Buenos Aires US$17, Río Gallegos US$62, Mar del Plata US$19, Neuquén US$16.

Train The once-seigneurial Ferrocarril Roca

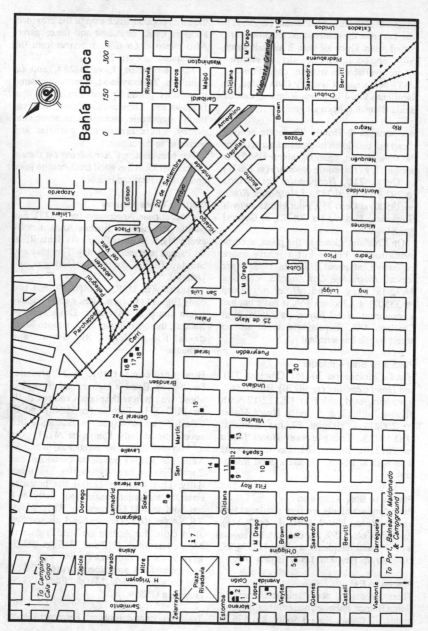

■ PLACES TO STAY

3 Hotel Austral
4 Hotel Muñiz
6 Hotel Italia
10 Hotel Argos
11 Hospedaje Los Angeles
12 Hotel Argentino
13 Hotel Bayón
14 Hotel Chiclana
15 Hospedaje Victoria
16 Hospedaje Roma
17 Hospedaje Los Vascos
18 Hospedaje Molinari
20 Hotel Canciller

OTHER

1 Post Office
2 Banco de la Nación
5 Telefónica
7 Tourist Office
8 Aerolíneas Argentinas
9 ACA
19 Railway Station
21 Bus Terminal

---

station (☎ 21168), Cerri 750, is run down and lacks any comfortable place to wait for connections. There are two trains daily from Constitución Station in Buenos Aires via Las Flores, Azul and Olavarría. One of these continues to Bariloche via the Río Negro valley. Fares to Buenos Aires are US$11 for primera and US$14 for pullman.

Car Rental Try AT (☎ 23705) at Colón 177, Alquilauto (☎ 24444) at Güemes 14, or Rent a Car (☎ 40200) at Colón and Brown.

Hitching Hitching both to Buenos Aires and to Neuquén is fairly easy, as large numbers of trucks pass through the port all year. To hitch south, go to El Cholo, a popular truck stop on Ruta 3 South, km 696, where you can directly approach truckers at the gas station or restaurant. For hitching to Buenos Aires, go either to Ruta 3 North or to provincial Ruta 51.

Getting Around
To/From the Airport Aeropuerto Bahía Blanca (☎ 21665) is 15 km east of the city on the Espora naval base, Ruta 3 Norte, km 674. Bus No 10 goes to the airport.

Bus Bus Nos 505, 512, 514, 516 and 517 go to the bus terminal from downtown. Bus No 514 along Avenida Colón goes to Balneario Maldonado.

SIERRAS OF BUENOS AIRES PROVINCE
In only two parts of Buenos Aires province does granitic bedrock emerge from the deep sediments of the Pampas. Tandilia and Ventania, low mountain ranges trending from north-west to south-east, disrupt the monotony of the almost endlessly flat terrain. The easterly Sierras de Tandil are low, rounded hills whose peaks, not exceeding 500 metres, take the names of the counties they cross – Olavarría, Azul, Tandil and Balcarce. The westerly Sierra de la Ventana, its jagged peaks reaching above 1300 metres in places, is more' scenic and attracts hikers and climbers. Between the two ranges is a generally level area which slopes only gradually towards the bluffs and sandy beaches of the Atlantic coast, between Mar del Plata and Claromecó.

TANDIL
On a plain surrounded by a horseshoe-shaped range of hills, Tandil (population 81,000) developed from Fuerte Independencia, a military outpost established in 1823 by Martín Rodríguez. Today it serves an important agricultural and livestock area and is a manufacturing centre for cement, limestone and dairy products. The local campus of the Universidad del Centro de la Provincia de Buenos Aires is well known for its agronomy and computer science departments.

Tandil traditionally attracts masses of tourists during Easter Week to Calvario, a hill which resembles the site of Christ's crucifixion at Golgotha, but the town has many other features worth seeing.

Orientation

Tandil is 384 km from Buenos Aires via national Rutas 3 and 226, and 170 km from Mar del Plata. The downtown area is bound by Avenidas Rivadavia in the west, Avellaneda in the south, Buzón in the east, and del Valle in the north. Street names change at the intersections of Avellaneda/Estrada and Rivadavia/Dorrego. The main commercial streets are Rodríguez and 9 de Julio.

Information

Tourist Office The Subsecretaría de Turismo (☎ 25661) is at 9 de Julio 555. They have a city map and some useful brochures, including a guide to points of interest, with directions on reaching them by public transport.

Post & Telecommunications Both ENCOTEL and Telefónica are at Rodríguez 630.

Travel Agencies ACA (☎ 25463) is on Rodríguez 399.

Medical Services Hospital Ramón Santamarina (☎ 22011) is at Paz 1406.

Things to See

Parque Independencia offers good views of the city, particularly at night. The **Dique del Fuerte**, two km from the city, is a huge artificial lake, where the Balneario Municipal has three swimming pools.

For many years, a 300-ton boulder balanced precariously atop the legendary **Cerro La Movediza** before falling, but the site still attracts visitors. In the early 1870s, it gained notoriety from one of the most notorious incidents in provincial history, when a group of renegade gauchos, followers of an eccentric healer named Tata Dios, gathered here to distribute weapons before going on a murderous rampage against European settlers and recent immigrants.

Places to Stay

Camping On the way to the Dique del Fuerte, clean and shady *Camping Municipal Pinar de la Sierra* charges US$2 per tent (for up to four people) per day. It has a grocery and hot showers. Some but not all No 500 (yellow) buses go there – ask the driver.

Hospedajes & Hotels The friendly, modest and tidy *Hotel Kaiku* (☎ 23114), Mitre 902, is good value at US$4/8 a single/double with breakfast. *Hotel Cristal* (☎ 25951), Rodríguez 871, is very basic but also cheap at US$5 per person. *Hospedaje Savoy* (☎ 25602), Alem and Mitre, is an old-fashioned family hotel, with a confitería for breakfast or snacks, whose congenial owner charges US$8/14 for rooms with bath. At *Hotel Royal* (☎ 25606), 9 de Julio 725, rates are US$9/16 for rooms with private bath, but the friendly señora offers discounts to tourists upon request.

The more upscale *Hotel Dior* (☎ 21901), Rodríguez 471, charges US$15/19 with breakfast. Across from the main plaza is the very pleasant *Plaza Hotel* (☎ 27160), General Pinto 438, where rooms with private bath, telephone and TV cost US$26/35 with breakfast. Its confitería serves the best coffee in town and its restaurant is also highly regarded. Except in an emergency, avoid *Hotel Crillón* (☎ 22068), San Martín 455, whose unpleasant owner might do better in another business.

Places to Eat

Probably the cheapest place to eat is the *Comedor Universitario*, a stone house at the corner of Maipú and Fuerte Independencia. For great pollo a la piedra try *Restaurant El Nuevo Don José*, Avenida Monseñor De Andrea 269. *Restaurant El Estribo*, San Martín 759, has tasty pork. At *La Farola*, Pinto 681, the dish to order is El gran pejerrey, a tasty mackerel. For parrillada, go to *Parada 4*, Rodríguez and Constitución.

Getting There & Away

Bus The bus terminal (☎ 25585) is at Avenida Buzón and Portugal. La Estrella (☎ 26018) and Río Paraná (☎ 24812) go to Buenos Aires three times daily. TAC

(☎ 25275) serves the west to Córdoba and San Juan. El Rápido (☎ 26171) travels to Mar del Plata every two hours.

Train Ferrocarril Roca (☎ 23002), Avenida Machado and Colón, has one daily train to Buenos Aires.

Getting Around
Tandil has an excellent public transportation system which reaches every important area. Bus No 500 (yellow) goes to Dique del Fuerte and the municipal campground. No 501 (red) goes to the bus terminal and train station, while No 503 (blue) goes to La Movediza, the university and the bus terminal.

AROUND TANDIL
Estancia Acelain
On the wealthy estancias of the province of Buenos Aires, there remain many opulent cascos. This one, 54 km north-west of Tandil, belonged to the writer Enrique Larreta (1875-1961), whose erudite historical novels made him famous. Built in 1924 with local stone, it features furnishings and ornaments which, following Larreta's love for the Old Country, were brought from Spain. The chapel has beautiful stained glass made in Germany.

Dense woods surround the buildings of the estancia, which also has a natural lagoon with good fishing for mackerel.

SIERRA DE LA VENTANA
Only a short distance from Bahía Blanca but resembling the Sierras of Córdoba, this charming village is gaining popularity among tourists. It has conventional facilities, such as a casino, golf links and swimming pools, but also offers opportunities for less traditional activities such as hiking, climbing, riding, bicycling and kayaking. Its two rivers offer good fishing. There is comfortable if limited accommodation and good food.

Orientation
Sierra de la Ventana is 125 km north of Bahía

Blanca via national Ruta 33 to Tornquist, and provincial Ruta 76. It is 602 km from Buenos Aires via national Ruta 3 to Azul, national Ruta 226 to Olavarría, and provincial Ruta 76.

The village itself consists of two sectors divided by the railway: Sierra de la Ventana, with government offices and businesses, and the residential Villa Arcadia by the golf links. Avenida San Martín is the main street, with most services near the train station. Street names are generally ignored.

Information
Tourist Office The tourist office (☎ 91-5032) is at Roca and Avenida San Martín, near the train station. It has a useful packet of maps and flyers.

Parque Provincial Ernesto Tornquist
The elegant iron gates which guard the entrance of this scenic 6700-hectare park belonged to the Tornquist family, original owners of the lands. Although small, the park has an informative visitors centre with a well-organised display on local ecology, supported by a terrific audiovisual presentation. There are also corrals with local fauna, mostly deer and guanaco, and a forestry station.

Hiking is a popular activity, both independently and with rangers. In summer there are daily five-km guided walks to the corral at 11 am, and 4.30 and 7 pm; to other parts of the reserve on Fridays and Sundays at 6.30 pm; and four-hour trips to the gorge at Garganta del Diablo (Devil's Throat) on Saturdays at 8.30 am, and by request on weekdays. You can also hike on your own.

Cerro de la Ventana is the best hike in the park. From the trailhead, it takes about two hours to the treeline and two to three hours more to the 1136-metre summit, which gives a spectacular view of the surrounding hills and the distant Pampas.

Other worthwhile sights are the Indian caves at Las Cuevas del Toro de Corpus Cristi and the gorge at Garganta Olvidada. Opening hours for the visitors centre are 9 am to 12.30 pm, and 4 to 8.30 pm daily. An audiovisual presentation is given daily at 10.30 am and at 4.30 and 6.30 pm. There is a designated campground with toilets but no showers, for a charge of US$1.50 per person.

Places to Stay – bottom end
Camping There are several free campsites along the river, but if you prefer an organised campground try *Autocamping* (☎ 91-5100), on Diego Meyer, which has good facilities at US$3 per adult, US$1.50 per child. *Camping Yamila*, at the balneario, charges US$1.50 per person.

Motel & Hotels Sierra de la Ventana has good, reasonably priced accommodation. *Hotel Argentino*, on Roca, and *Hospedaje La Perlita* (☎ 91-5020), Malvinas and Pasaje 3, charge US$7 per person. ACA's *Motel Maitén* (☎ 91-5073), on Iguazú, is good value at US$11 per person for members and US$14 for nonmembers, with breakfast. Similarly *Hotel Pillahuinco* (☎ 91-5024), Rayces and Punta Alta, Villa Arcadia, has rooms for US$8 per person, US$9 with breakfast, and US$20 with all meals.

Hotel Carlitos (☎ 91-5011), at Coronel Suárez and Punta Alta, Villa Arcadia, has doubles for US$12. *Hotel Atero* (☎ 91-5002), Avenida San Martín and Güemes, has singles at US$12 with breakfast.

Places to Stay – middle
Hotel La Península has singles at US$30 with all meals. *Hotel Anay-Ruca*, Rayces and Punta Alta, Villa Arcadia, has singles at US$16 with breakfast and US$24 with half-board. *Hotel Silver Golf* (☎ 91-5079), at Barrio Parque Golf, has singles at US$30 with meals.

Hotel El Mirador, 22 km from the village near Cerro de la Ventana, has rooms at US$22/34 with breakfast.

Places to Stay – top end
The most expensive accommodation is the luxurious *Hotel Provincial* (☎ 91-5025), on Drago, with singles/doubles at US$40/60 with breakfast.

Places to Eat
Besides those restaurants in the hotels, try *Restaurant Irupé*, on Avenida San Martín, *Restaurant Espadaña* on Ruta 76 (one km from the village), *Restaurant Las Sierras*, Drago and Alberdi (which has great homemade desserts), and the great and only parrilla *Rali-Hue*, on Avenida San Martín.

Getting There & Away
From Constitución in Buenos Aires, there is one train daily to Sierra de la Ventana on the Roca line. La Estrella has daily buses to Buenos Aires for US$25. There are also regular buses between Bahía Blanca and Sierra de la Ventana.

AROUND SIERRA DE LA VENTANA
Villa Ventana
This friendly, small village, 17 km north of Sierra de la Ventana, has shady lanes, a riverside balneario with a municipal campground, and an excellent tea house, *Casa de Heidi*, that alone justifies the trip if you're in the area.

Cerro Tres Picos
Although it is not part of the park, 1239-metre Cerro Tres Picos, seven km west of Sierra de la Ventana, is a great choice for a backpacking trip. The tourist office in Sierra de la Ventana can provide more details.

Santa Fe Province

Along with the province of Buenos Aires, Santa Fe province is the heartland of the Humid Pampas, an agricultural area of phenomenal fertility even though its northernmost areas are part of the drier, less fertile Chaco. Many hostile groups of Indians, including the Toba and Mocoví, disrupted early Spanish settlement.

Marginal during the colonial period, Santa Fe grew dramatically after Argentine independence and especially with the expansion of the railroads. Unlike the province of Entre Ríos, a virtual island on the opposite bank of

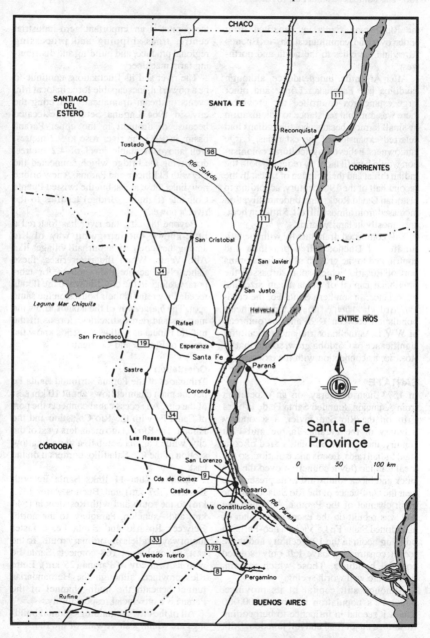

Santa Fe
Province

0   50   100 km

the Río Paraná, Santa Fe benefited from better overland communications to Buenos Aires and the cities to the north and north-west.

After Argentine independence, although caudillos like Estanislao López and other large estancieros controlled the province, there was minimal resistance to colonisation by small farmers because hostile Indians had deterred expansion of the estancias. Large landowners believed agricultural colonisation would benefit them by reducing both the Indian threat and their burden of taxes. In the second half of the 19th century, according to historian David Rock, land under cultivation increased from almost nil to 1.5 million hectares, mostly in family farms.

This contrasted dramatically with the latifundios of Buenos Aires province and contributed to the growth of the Río Paraná port of Rosario, which soon surpassed the provincial capital of Santa Fe in size and importance. In southern Santa Fe, the cultivation of wheat helped double the province's population between 1895 and the outbreak of WW I. As the industrial and agricultural significance of Córdoba grew, so did that of Rosario, its connection with the exterior.

SANTA FE

In 1573 Juan de Garay, on an expedition from Asunción, founded Santa Fe de la Vera Cruz on the Río San Javier, a secondary tributary of the Paraná. In the mid-17th century, though, the Spaniards tired of constant Indian raids, floods and isolation, so the local Cabildo (town council) moved the city stock and block southward to its present site near the confluence of the Río Salado and the main channel of the Paraná. Although the city was rebuilt on the exact urban plan of abandoned Santa Fe La Vieja, a neo-Parisian building boom in the 19th century and more recent construction have left only isolated colonial buildings. Those which remain, though, are well worth seeing.

Although still capital of its province, Santa Fe's population of about 500,000 leaves it second in influence to burgeoning Rosario, a major road and rail junction. Still,

the capital is an important agro-industrial centre, trans-shipping and processing regional produce, and building and distributing farm machinery.

The river and its fluctuations continue to be a powerful, inescapable force in local life, events upstream dramatically affecting the city. In 1964 Laguna Setúbal desiccated because of drought in the upper Paraná basin; in 1983 the river rose to 9.2 metres, well above its stable level of 4.2 metres, destroying the bridge which connected the city with El Rincón and Paraná. A new bridge now links these areas, but the twisted Puente Colgante (Hanging Bridge) testifies to the river's power.

Beyond the city, the river has fostered a little-known but intriguing way of life among the people of 'suburban' villages like Alto Verde. When the river rises, these fisherfolk evacuate their houses for temporary refuge in the city, but when the floods recede they rebuild their houses on the same spot. The *baqueanos* of the islands know the marshes and dense, trackless forests of the middle Paraná as well as Porteños know the corner of Florida and Corrientes.

Orientation

Tributaries of the Paraná surround Santa Fe but the main channel flows about 10 km east of the city. An access canal connects the port of Santa Fe with the Río Colastiné and the Paraná. The Río Salado meanders west of the city, while Laguna Setúbal, a wide, shallow section of the Río Saladillo, borders it on the east.

National Ruta 11 links Santa Fe with Rosario (167 km) and Buenos Aires (475 km) to the south and with Resistencia (544 km) and Asunción, Paraguay, to the north. Between Rosario and Santa Fe, a faster motorway parallels the ordinary route. To the east, national Ruta 168 connects Santa Fe with its twin city of Paraná (25 km), Entre Ríos province, although the Hernandarias tunnel beneath the main channel of the Paraná is a provincial responsibility.

All of the city's remaining colonial buildings are within a short walk of the Plaza 25 de Mayo, the functional centre of the town. Avenida San Martín, north of the Plaza, is the major commercial street; between Juan de Garay and Catamarca, it is an attractive *peatonal* (pedestrian mall).

Information

Tourist Office The exceptionally well-informed, motivated and helpful Dirección Municipal de Turismo (☎ 30982) is at the bus terminal, Belgrano 2910, north of downtown. It has maps, loads of brochures, and much other detailed information in looseleaf binders, which you can consult.

Money Try Cambio Bica at Avenida San Martín 2453. Banco de la Nación and Banco de la Provincia are on opposite sides of Avenida San Martín at Tucumán.

Post & Telecommunications The post office is at Avenida 27 de Febrero 2331. Long-distance telephone services are both here and upstairs at the bus terminal.

Cultural Centres The Teatro Municipal Primero de Mayo at Avenida San Martín 2020, constructed in the French Renaissance style so common in turn-of-the-century Argentina, offers drama and dance performances.

Travel Agencies ACA (☎ 43999) is at Avenida Rivadavia 3101, near Suipacha. There is another branch (☎ 31949) at Pellegrini and Avenida San Martín. For standard travel services, inquire at the Asociación Santafesina de Agencias de Viajes (☎ 40090), at Avenida San Martín 2231.

Medical Services The Hospital Provincial (☎ 21001) is at Lisandro de la Torre and Freyre, west of downtown.

Historic Buildings

Although Santa Fe is one of the oldest cities in Argentina, the 20th century has changed its face – in 1909, for example, the French Renaissance-styled **Casa de Gobierno** (Government House) replaced the demolished colonial Cabildo on Plaza 25 de Mayo. Many remaining colonial buildings are museums, although several revered churches still serve their original functions. One is the **Templo de Santo Domingo**, at 3 de Febrero and 9 de Julio, which dates from the mid-17th century but has been modified several times. Its interior is Ionian, while the exterior is a combination of Ionian and Roman styles, topped by a pair of symmetrically placed bell towers and a dome.

The exterior simplicity of the Jesuit **Iglesia de la Compañía**, on the plaza at Avenida San Martín and Avenida General López, masks a much more ornate interior. Dating from 1696, it is the best preserved colonial church in the province.

The **Casa de los Aldao**, Buenos Aires 2861, is a restored two-story house from the early 18th century. Like others of the period, it has a tiled roof, balconies and metre-thick walls.

Museums are generally open from 8 am to noon and from 3 to 7 pm, but usually closed Sunday mornings and Mondays.

Convento y Museo de San Francisco

This is Santa Fe's single most outstanding historical landmark. Built in 1680, the church's walls are more than a metre thick, supporting a roof whose Paraguayan cedar and hardwood beams are held together with fittings and wooden spikes rather than nails. Like many other colonial churches, its floor plan duplicates the Holy Cross. The doors are the original, hand-worked ones, while the baroque pulpit is laminated in gold. Besides these architectural features, the church contains many works of important colonial art.

Note the tomb of Father Magallanes, killed by a jaguar which, driven from the shores of the Paraná during the floods of 1825, took refuge in the church. The church also contains the coffins of the Santa Fe caudillo Estanislao López and his wife. Parts of the interior patio are open to the public, but do not go beyond into the cloisters.

Adjacent to the church is an intriguing historical museum which covers both secular

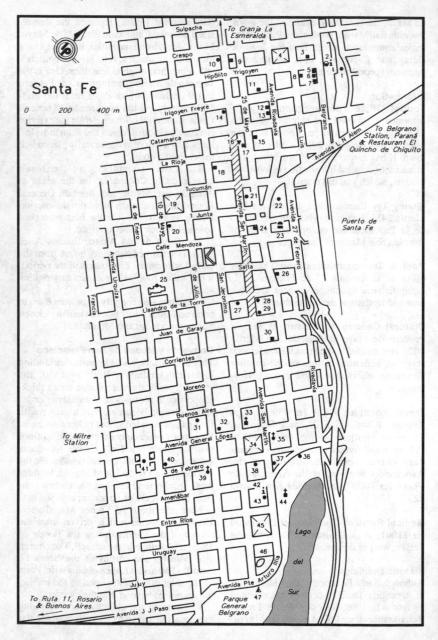

Santa Fe

0   200   400 m

and religious subjects from both colonial and republican eras. One interesting exhibit is the Sala de los Constituyentes, containing wax figures of the representatives to the assembly which wrote the Argentine Constitution of 1853.

The church is at Amenábar 2257 near Avenida San Martín, just south of the Plaza 25 de Mayo.

Museo Histórico Provincial

In a damp but well-preserved building from the late 17th century, this museum contains permanent exhibits on the civil wars of the 19th century, provincial governors (and caudillos), period furnishings and religious art, as well as a room which alternates displays on more contemporary themes.

At San Martín 1490, the museum is closed on Mondays, but may open on request – try

knocking on the door or standing around looking lost.

Museo Etnográfico Colonial

The most interesting single display in this museum is a scale model of the original settlement of Santa Fe La Vieja. Besides the excellent collection of Spanish colonial artefacts from the excavations at the former site near present-day Cayastá, there are native basketry, Spanish ceramics, and coins and money. The staff is very patient and helpful in explaining details of the exhibits. It's at 25 de Mayo 1470.

Museo del Indígena

Not a museum in the narrow sense, this is a hybrid institution staffed by local Indians, which does offer exhibits on the history and contemporary situation of Argentina's indigenous peoples, but also serves as an informational and cultural centre and meeting place for them and for others interested in indigenous issues. It displays and sells Indian crafts (mostly Mocoví, but also Toba), educates school children about native peoples, and presents other short talks and lectures daily. The staff are exceptionally friendly and eager to speak with foreign visitors.

According to the staff, there are about 4000 Mocoví dispersed throughout the province of Santa Fe. The largest concentration is in Recreo, a small village of sharecroppers and artisans 17 km north of Santa Fe. There are other indigenous communities in Helvetia and San Javier, north-east of Santa Fe.

There is no admission charge to the museum, which is in the Galería Via Macarena, Avenida San Martín 2945. Opening hours are weekdays from 9.30 am to 1 pm and from 3.30 to 7.30 pm. In the same Galería is the Casa de Cultura Indo-Afro-Americana, which offers classes and also a selection of local handicrafts.

Granja La Esmeralda

On the northern outskirts of Santa Fe, this experimental farm also contains a worthwhile zoo which concentrates on fauna native to the province, mostly in spacious enclosures. The most interesting specimens are tropical birds such as toucans, big cats such as pumas and jaguars, and the giant anteater.

Admission is US$1, and opening hours are 8 am to 6 pm. You can reach the zoo by bus No 10 Bis which crosses Avenida San Martín at the peatonal.

Places to Stay – bottom end

Camping There is no formal campground in Santa Fe proper, but the city tolerates free camping along the Lago del Sur in Parque General Belgrano, at the south end of Avenida San Martín. Look for Argentine campers. The nearest formal campground is at San José del Rincón, 12 km east of Santa Fe across the bridge, reached by bus No 19.

Hotels Several inexpensive places are exactly opposite the bus terminal or a very short distance away. The cheapest is *Hotel Gran Terminal* (☎ 32395), at Belgrano 2837, where rooms with shared bath cost US$6 per person, while those with private bath cost US$8/14 for singles/doubles. The comparably priced *Hotel Apolo* (☎ 27984), almost next door at Belgrano 2821, is clean but dark. *Hotel Bristol* (☎ 35044), Belgrano 2859, has air-conditioned rooms for US$9/15 with shared bath, US$12/18 with private bath. Friendly but dingy *Luka's Hotel*, Hipólito Yrigoyen 2222, has rooms with private bath for US$10/15, but its restaurant is better than its accommodation.

There are a few budget choices slightly closer to the centre. *Mini Hotel Uruguay*, Avenida Rivadavia 2719, has singles with private bath for US$8, but the staff is likely to be surprised if you come alone and stay for more than two hours. The modern and undistinguished *Hotel California*, 25 de Mayo 2190, is very friendly but has only 12 rooms, all with private bath. Rates are US$10/18.

Places to Stay – middle

A good choice is *Hotel Niza* (☎ 22047), at Rivadavia 2755, where rooms with private bath, air-conditioning and telephone cost US$15/24. An even better choice, and the best value in town, is *Hotel Emperatriz* (☎ 30061), which is in a remodelled private house which once belonged to an elite Santa Fe family. It's quiet, friendly and dignified for US$18/27 with private bath.

Places to Stay – top end

The large, impersonal and rather noisy *Castelar Hotel* (☎ 20141), 25 de Mayo 2349, has rooms for US$27/36. Some bigger rooms are slightly more expensive. A better choice is the unpretentious *Gran Hotel España* (☎ 21016), 25 de Mayo 2647, where rates are US$30/45.

If you have money to burn, the owners of the Gran Hotel España will happily accept it across the street at the *Conquistador Hotel* (☎ 40195), 25 de Mayo 2676, which is more modern but no better at US$50/70. Similarly priced, and probably superior, is the *Hostal Santa Fe de la Vera Cruz* (☎ 51740), Avenida San Martín 2954.

Places to Eat
There are several very good, inexpensive places on Belgrano, across from the bus terminal, which serve basic Argentine foods such as empanadas, pizza and parrilla. For a downtown treat, try *Restaurant España* at Avenida San Martín 2642.

Tourists flock to *El Quincho de Chiquito*, which is some distance north of downtown at Almirante Brown and Obispo Vieytes, but so do locals. Because of its enormous size, the service is rather impersonal, but it has earned its reputation for outstanding grilled river fish such as boga and sábalo and exceptional hors d'ouevres such as fish empanadas. In practice, if not in theory, it is all you can eat for about US$7 plus drinks. It may be a splurge, but a very worthwhile splurge. Take bus No 16 on Avenida Gálvez.

Things to Buy
For local crafts, visit the Asociación de Artesanos Santafesinos at Avenida San Martín 1389. See also the listing for the Museo del Indígena, above.

Getting There & Away
Air Aerolíneas Argentinas (☎ 20713) is at Lisandro de la Torre 2633. It has nonstop flights to Buenos Aires on weekday mornings and every evening. The one-hour trip costs US$70.

Bus The bus terminal (☎ 40698) is at Belgrano 2940. Services are almost identical to those from Paraná, although Chevallier has more extensive routes. The information kiosk posts all fares for destinations throughout the country, so it is not necessary to run from window to window for comparison.

Train There are two train stations in Santa Fe. The Ferrocarril Mitre (☎ 22342), at Avenida General López 3600, goes to Rosario, with connections to Buenos Aires.

The Ferrocarril Belgrano (☎ 40116), at Gálvez 1100, goes south to Buenos Aires and north to Resistencia and Roque Sáenz Peña.

AROUND SANTA FE
Alto Verde
Shaded by enormous willows and other trees, Alto Verde is a picturesque fishing village on Isla Sirgadero, accessible only by canoe for most of the year. In really wet years, when the Paraná floods and destroys their houses, fishing families abandon the island for Santa Fe, returning and rebuilding when the flood waters recede. To reach the village, catch a canoe from Puerto del Piojo, in the port complex at the east end of Calle Mendoza in Santa Fe.

San José del Rincón
The shady earthen roads of San José del Rincón still offer a few colonial buildings and an excellent **Museo de la Costa** (Museum of the Coast). Many Santafesinos maintain weekend homes here, where camping and fishing are popular pastimes. Local gardeners cultivate ornamental flowers, such as gladiolus bulbs, for sale in the city.

Bus No 19 from Santa Fe goes directly to Rincón.

Cayastá
Cayastá, the site of Santa Fe La Vieja, is 78 km north-east of Santa Fe on provincial Ruta 1. The Río San Javier has eroded away part of the original site, including half of the Plaza de Armas, but recent excavations have revealed the sites of the Cabildo, and the Santo Domingo, San Francisco and Merced churches. Authorities have built external structures to protect the remains of these buildings. For educational purposes, they have also reconstructed a typical period house with furnishings.

The excavations have also uncovered numerous artefacts from the colonial period, some of them exhibited in the nearby **Museo Fundacional Argentino**, and others in the Museo Etnográfico in present-day Santa Fe.

There is a regular bus service from the capital.

ROSARIO

Arguably the second city of the republic (a status disputed by Córdoba), Rosario sits on a bluff above the west bank of the main channel of the Río Paraná, 320 km upstream from Buenos Aires. Never formally founded as a city, its first European inhabitants settled informally around 1720 without sanction from the Spanish Crown. After Argentine independence it quickly superseded Santa Fe as the economic powerhouse of the province, but the northerly capital held on to political primacy, a source of some irritation to Rosarinos – between 1869 and 1914 the city's population multiplied nearly tenfold to 223,000, easily overtaking the capital in numbers.

The reason for this growth was Rosario's position as port of entry for agricultural colonists from Europe, assisted by the fact that the first trunk railway in the country connected it with Córdoba and, later, Mendoza and Tucumán. The Central Argentine Land Company, an adjunct of the railroad, was responsible for bringing in colonists.

Some Argentines refer to Rosario as the 'Chicago of Argentina' because of its role in exporting the produce of a large agricultural heartland and its industrial importance. The port can accommodate ocean-going vessels as easily as Buenos Aires, despite its distance up the Paraná.

Orientation

Rosario's size and port status make it a node for several major highways and railroads. National Ruta 9 passes through Rosario en route to Córdoba. A major motorway also connects it with the Buenos Aires. National Ruta 11 heads north to Santa Fe, while national Ruta 178 goes south to the prosperous farm zone around Pergamino, in Buenos Aires province. National Ruta 33 heads south-west to Venado Tuerto. Motorists can bypass the city on the Avenida Circunvulación.

Rosario displays a very regular grid pattern except where the curvature of the bluffs above the river channel dictates otherwise – much of this area is open space, with excellent views of the river. Traditionally, the focus of urban activities is the Plaza 25 de Mayo, but the pedestrian streets of San Martín and Córdoba are the centres of commerce. The centre's shady plazas offer relief from the heat, while outside the centre streets are tree-shaded and the many new plantings of palms are signs of municipal vigour. There are some 70 square blocks of open space in Parque Independencia, south-west of downtown.

Information

Tourist Office The municipal Dirección de Turismo (☎ 24-8382) is in the Centro Cultural Rivadavia at San Martín 1080, but it's not easy to locate – it occupies a tiny cubicle in a very large building and the staff is not geared to dealing with independent visitors. Once you find it, they're helpful and supply a decent city map but little other information.

Money The numerous cambios along San Martín and Córdoba will change cash and travellers' cheques, the latter with the usual discount and commission. Try Bonsignore at San Martín 998 or Exprinter at Córdoba 960.

Post & Telecommunications The post office is at Córdoba 721, on the Plaza 25 de Mayo. Telecom is at San Luis 936 between Maipú and San Martín.

Cultural Centres The Centro Cultural Rivadavia, San Martín 1080, is a good place to find out what's happening in Rosario. It shows free or inexpensive films, and sometimes has rather incongruous displays: one photographic exhibition depicted the achievements of 45 years of Albanian socialism, juxtaposed with highly erotic woodcuts by a local woman.

Travel Agencies ACA (☎ 41278) is at Blvd Oroño and 3 de Febrero.

Historical Museums

Rosario is a 19th-century city with no colonial pretensions, but it displays many French Renaissance buildings typical of turn-of-the-century Argentine architecture. It also has many museums which deserve at least passing mention. The local art community is very active.

The **Museo Histórico Provincial** in Parque Independencia contains some pre-Colombian and colonial materials, but concentrates on postindependence materials. It's open Tuesday to Friday from 9 am to 12.30 pm and 3 to 6.30 pm, weekends from 3 to 6.30 pm. Another historical museum is the municipal **Museo de la Ciudad**, Blvd Oroño 1540, open Wednesday to Sunday from 9 am to noon and 3 to 7 pm.

Arts Museums

The fine arts **Museo Municipal de Bellas Artes**, at Avenidas Pellegrini and Oroño, is open Wednesday to Sunday from 11 am to 7 pm. The **Museo Barnes de Arte Sacro** exhibits sculptures from the man responsible for parts of the Monument to the Flag. It's open Thursday from 4 to 6 pm.

There are wider-ranging art collections at the **Museo de Arte Decorativo**, at Santa Fe 748. Opening hours are Wednesday to Friday from 4 to 8 pm, weekends 2 to 8 pm.

Science Museums

Those interested in environment and wildlife may wish to visit the **Museo Provincial de Ciencias Naturales** at Moreno 758, open Tuesday to Friday from 9 am to 12.30 pm and Tuesday, Friday and Sunday from 3 to 6 pm.

Those interested in more distant environments can visit the planetarium at the **Complejo Municipal Astronómico Educativo Rosario** (Municipal Observatory) in Parque Urquiza. It has shows on Saturday and Sunday from 5 to 6 pm. On Tuesday and Thursday, from 9 to 10 pm, visitors can view the austral skies through its 2250 mm refractor telescope and 4500 mm reflecting telescope.

Monumento Nacional a la Bandera

Rosario's biggest claim to fame is the patriotic hubris of architect Angel Guido's colossal Monument to the Flag, which occupies 10,000 square metres in the shape of a boat whose bow contains the crypt of General Manuel Belgrano, the flag's designer. Every June, Rosario celebrates **La Semana de la Bandera** (Flag Week), climaxed by ceremonies on 20 June, the day of Belgrano's death.

The monument is topped by a 78-metre tower. Heroic sculptures by Alfredo Bigatti and José Fioravanti and bas-reliefs by Eduardo Barnes symbolically represent the regions of the country and various patriotic figures. The museum, containing the original flag embroidered by Catalina de Vidal, is open daily from 7 am to 7 pm, except Mondays when it is open from 1 pm to 7 pm. There are good views of the Paraná waterfront from the monument, which is located at the foot of Calle Córdoba.

Museo del Paraná y Las Islas

Life on the river – flora, fauna and people – is the focus of this museum on the 1st floor of the Estación Fluvial on the waterfront. It has very limited opening hours: Wednesday from 2.30 to 4 pm and Sunday from 4 to 6.30 pm. But go at any time to see the romantic but fascinating murals of local painter Raúl Domínguez: *Recorrido del Paraná* (Exploring the Paraná), *Cortador de Paja'* (Thatch Cutter), *El Paraná y Sus Leyendas* (The Paraná and Its Legends), *El Nutriero* (The Otter Trapper), *Creciente* (In Flood), *Bajante* (In Drought), and others. Don't miss it if you're in Rosario.

Festivals

Besides La Semana de la Bandera, Rosario holds its own **Semana de Rosario** in the first week of October and the national **Encuentro de las Colectividades**, a tribute to the country's immigrants, in November or December.

In October of 1990, Rosario held its first **traditional jazz festival**, an event municipal

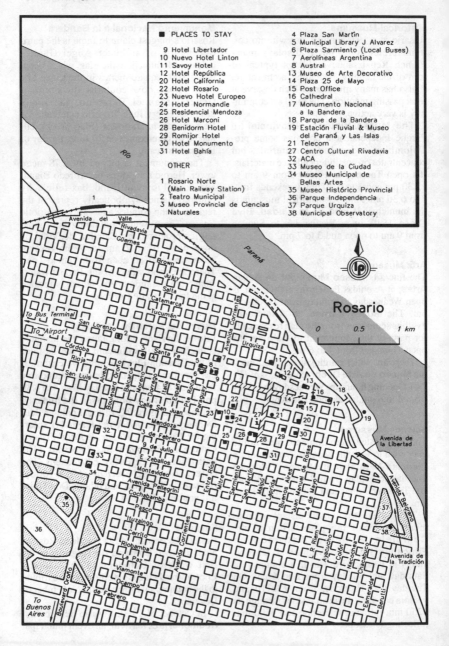

■ PLACES TO STAY

9 Hotel Libertador
10 Nuevo Hotel Linton
11 Savoy Hotel
12 Hotel República
20 Hotel California
22 Hotel Rosario
23 Nuevo Hotel Europeo
24 Hotel Normandie
25 Residencial Mendoza
26 Hotel Marconi
28 Benidorm Hotel
29 Romijor Hotel
30 Hotel Monumento
31 Hotel Bahía

OTHER

1 Rosario Norte
    (Main Railway Station)
2 Teatro Municipal
3 Museo Provincial de Ciencias
    Naturales

4 Plaza San Martín
5 Municipal Library J Alvarez
6 Plaza Sarmiento (Local Buses)
7 Aerolíneas Argentina
8 Austral
13 Museo de Arte Decorativo
14 Plaza 25 de Mayo
15 Post Office
16 Cathedral
17 Monumento Nacional
    a la Bandera
18 Parque de la Bandera
19 Estación Fluvial & Museo
    del Paraná y Las Islas
21 Telecom
27 Centro Cultural Rivadavia
32 ACA
33 Museo de la Ciudad
34 Museo Municipal de
    Bellas Artes
35 Museo Histórico Provincial
36 Parque Independencia
37 Parque Urquiza
38 Municipal Observatory

Rosario

authorities hope to repeat, with bands from around the country and from Uruguay.

Places to Stay – bottom end

Camping Rosario is one of very few cities in Argentina without any really suitable place for camping. You can try the small site around the Ciudad Universitaria at the south end of Avenida Belgrano, near its intersection with Boulevard 27 de Febrero.

Hotels *Hotel Normandie* (☎ 21-2694), Mitre 1030, is friendly and inexpensive. Singles/doubles are US$6/9 with shared bath, US$8/11 with private bath. The very friendly *Hotel Bahía* (☎ 21-7271; the phone is actually located in the Santa Rosa restaurant across the street) at Maipú 1254 is comparable. *Nuevo Hotel Linton* (☎ 21-1426), at Entre Ríos 1043 across from the noisy Plaza Sarmiento, has attractive balconies on many of its rooms.

Romijor Hotel (☎ 21-7276), Laprida 1050, has quiet patio rooms for US$10/15. For about the same price at *Residencial Mendoza* (☎ 24-6544), Mendoza 1246, breakfast is included. Fans are provided but air-conditioning is extra.

Hotel Buenos Aires, Buenos Aires 1063, rents most of its rooms to long-term occupants, but may have occasional rooms for men only at US$10/15.

Places to Stay – middle

At the *Hotel Marconi* (☎ 49115), San Juan 1077, rates are US$20/30 with private bath. The nearby *Benidorm Hotel* (☎ 21-9368) at San Juan 1049 is comparably priced. The *Savoy Hotel* (☎ 60071), San Lorenzo 1022, maintains a shabby dignity for about US$25/40. At *Hotel California* (☎ 24-7715), San Luis 715, rooms with phone, air-conditioning, colour TV and parking included are US$30/45 with a 15% discount for payment in cash. The dark but friendly *Hotel Monumento* (☎ 46446), Buenos Aires 1020, is a bit costlier.

Places to Stay – top end

Top of the line places start at about US$40/50, such as *Hotel República* (☎ 24-8580) at San Lorenzo 955, and *Nuevo Hotel Europeo* (☎ 21-1514) at San Luis 1364. The best in town is *Hotel Libertador* (☎ 24-1005), which charges US$50/65.

Places to Eat

Italian or Italian-derived food is big in Rosario. One of the best places is a great, great deli alongside *Restaurant Rich*, San Juan 1031 near the Centro Cultural Rivadavia. *Casablanca*, Córdoba 1471, serves typical Italo-Argentine food at reasonable prices, such as about US$2 for items like canneloni and ravioli, along with cold lager beer.

Despite its self-consciously Italian name, *Il Nuovo Pavarotti* at Laprida 988 is a medium-priced parrilla. *Restaurant Il Gatto*, San Martín 533, does have more strictly Italian specialities, with a good fixed-price lunch. The *Centro Gallego*, Buenos Aires 1127, serves fixed-price all-you-can-eat meals. *Restaurant Hans*, Mitre 775, has economical fixed-price meals.

Confitería *Café de La Paz*, at Sarmiento and San Lorenzo, draws big crowds. For an upscale dinner, try *Borgo Antico* at Ricardone 131.

Things to Buy

For regional handicrafts, check out Regionales Tilcara at Ricardone 130.

Getting There & Away

Air Aerolíneas Argentinas (☎ 24-9332) is at Santa Fe 1410. On every weekday it has two flights to Buenos Aires, but only one each day on Saturday and Sunday. The fare is US$60.

Austral (☎ 64041), at Paraguay 731, has two flights to Buenos Aires every weekday. On Sundays it has a flight to Bariloche (US$250).

Bus The bus terminal (☎ 39-6011) is at Cafferata 702, near Santa Fe. Bus No 101 from Calle San Juan goes there.

Chevallier has services south to Buenos Aires (US$15, four hours), west to Córdoba, and on to Bariloche. ABLO passes through Rosario en route from Buenos Aires to Córdoba and on to La Rioja. El Rápido connects Buenos Aires, Rosario and Santa Fe, while ESAP goes to Buenos Aires, La Plata and Mar del Plata. La Unión serves Santiago del Estero and Tucumán, while TAC has buses to Mendoza.

Rosario has international services with La Internacional to Asunción (Paraguay), and Pluma to Porto Alegre and Río de Janeiro (Brazil).

Train The Ferrocarril Mitre no longer uses Rosario Central Station for intercity passenger services; instead, go to the station at Rosario Norte (☎ 39-2429), Avenida del Valle 2700. Bus No 120 from Calle San Juan and Mitre will take you there.

Car Rental Try Avis (☎ 25-4144) at Corrientes 725 or Ovalle (☎ 21-6592) at Santa Fe 837.

Boat Daily at 1.30 pm (Sundays only at 2 pm) there is a launch across the Paraná to the city of Victoria from the Estación Fluvial (☎ 62136) at Avenida Belgrano and Rioja. There are also river excursions on Saturdays at 4.30 pm and Sundays at 2 pm and 4.30 pm.

Getting Around

To/From the Airport Both Austral and Aerolíneas Argentinas run direct buses to Fisherton Airport, eight km west of town.

Bus Rosario has a very extensive public bus system. Most leave from the local bus station around Plaza Sarmiento. The Ferrocarril Mitre also runs local trains to suburbs such as Fisherton.

La Pampa Province

For most Argentines, the province of La Pampa is like the Great Plains or the Prairies for North Americans and Canadians – a place you cross to get somewhere else. Primarily an agricultural zone, it was settled later than the province of Buenos Aires because hostile Indians resisted European incursions much longer, and because its erratic rainfall made agriculture more unpredictable than in the Humid Pampa toward the Atlantic. It borders five other provinces: Río Negro, Mendoza, San Luis, Córdoba and Buenos Aires.

No one would visit Argentina just to go to La Pampa, even though its capital city of Santa Rosa is an attractive administrative and service centre, but its little-known Parque Nacional Lihué Calel more than justifies a detour from the standard routes to and from Patagonia. Travellers returning from Neuquén to Buenos Aires should find its tranquil granitic peaks a very interesting alternative.

Despite the monotony implied by its name, La Pampa offers a variety of other environments, including rolling hills with native *caldén* forests, desert zones with saline lakes which support flamingos and other birds, and extensive native grasslands.

SANTA ROSA

In the midst of the Pampas, 600 km from Buenos Aires, Santa Rosa de Toay was not legally founded until 1892. Although French, Spanish and Italian immigrants arrived with the expansion of the railroads at the turn of the 19th century, one measure of its continuing isolation and insignificance was that the surrounding area was a territory rather than a province – La Pampa did not acquire provincial status until 1951. Santa Rosa is now a clean, pleasant city of about 75,000.

Orientation

Santa Rosa is only 80 km from the Buenos Aires provincial border on national Ruta 5, which is paved all the way from the Federal Capital. National Ruta 35 goes north to Córdoba and south-east to Bahía Blanca.

North of Avenida España, the city consists of a standard grid pattern centred on Plaza San Martín and its surrounding streets, where most businesses are located. A more recent focus of activity is the modern Centro

Top: Pilgrims bringing presents to Difunta Correa, San Juan Province
Left: Parque Provincial Talampaya, La Rioja Province
Right: Pucará fortifications, Tilcara, Jujuy Province

Cerro Torre, Parque Nacional Los Glaciares, Santa Cruz Province

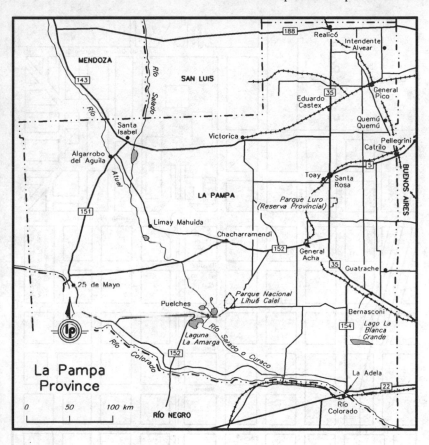

La Pampa Province

Cívico on Avenida Pedro Luro, seven blocks east. One km west, Laguna Don Tomás is a major recreational resource for city residents. In the quadrant south-west of the junction of Avenida España and Avenida Pedro Luro, streets trend north-west to south-east, rather than north-south.

Information
Tourist Office The enthusiastic and helpful Dirección Provincial de Turismo (☎ 25060) is at Avenida Pedro Luro and Avenida San Martín, directly across from the bus terminal. They have maps, brochures and an interesting selection of local handicrafts in the Mercado Artesanal (see below). Opening hours are weekdays from 7 am to 8 pm, weekends from 9 am to 1 pm and 6 pm to 10 pm.

Money Several banks will change money, though not travellers' cheques. Banco de la Nación is at Avenida Roca 1, at the south-east corner of Plaza San Martín. There are several others along Avenida Pellegrini, one block west of the plaza.

Post & Telecommunications ENCOTEL is

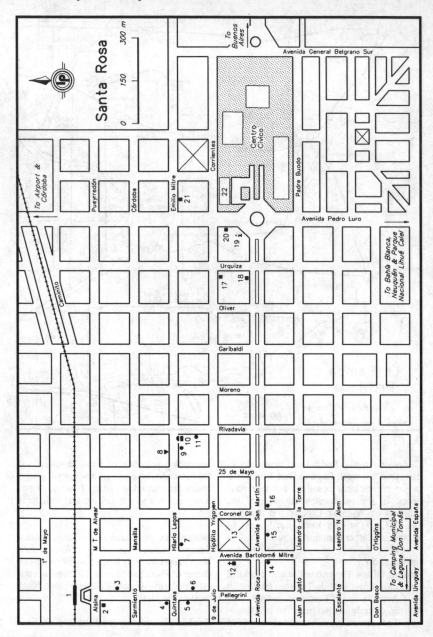

at Hilario Lagos 258 near Rivadavia. Telefónica is next door.

Travel Agencies ACA (☎ 22435) is at Avenida San Martín 102, on the corner of Coronel Gil. There are several other travel agencies, the most central of which is Turindio (☎ 26753) at Pellegrini 253.

Medical Services The Hospital de Zona (☎ 27033) is at Raúl P Diaz and Pilcomayo, two km north of downtown.

Museo Provincial
At Pellegrini 190, the provincial museum contains natural science, archaeological, historical, artisanal and fine arts collections. Opening hours are 7 am to 1.30 pm and 4 to 9 pm in summer. In winter, when hours are more limited, it does not close at midday.

Places to Stay
Camping One of Argentina's last remaining free campgrounds is the comfortable site at Laguna Don Tomás, at the west end of Avenida Uruguay. From Plaza San Martín, take bus No 25 or 26.

Facilities are excellent, including picnic tables, parrillas, a swimming pool, hot showers and shade trees, but the mosquitos can be ferocious – bring some repellent. There is a fitness course for joggers.

Hospedajes, Hosterías & Hotels Except for camping, really cheap accommodation is hard to find. The most reasonable is *Hospedaje Mitre* (☎ 25432), a short distance from the bus terminal at Emilio Mitre 74. Singles/doubles are US$8/13 with shared bath, while those with private bath are about US$10/16. *Hostería Santa Rosa* (☎ 23868), at Hipólito Yrigoyen 696, charges about the same. At *Hostería Río Atuel* (☎ 22597), conveniently across from the bus terminal at Avenida Pedro Luro 356, rooms with private bath are slightly costlier.

The central *Hotel San Martín* (☎ 22549), Alsina 101, has rooms with private bath for US$18/29. The uncontested top of the line is the high-rise *Hotel Calfucurá* (☎ 23608), at San Martín 695, distinguished by the enormous mural of the Indian *cacique* (chief) which climbs the sides of the building. Prices are US$55/77.

Places to Eat
The *Club Español* at Hilario Lagos 237 has excellent Argentine and Spanish food, outstanding service and reasonable prices. For regional specialities, try *Rancho de Pampa Cuatro*, opposite the bus terminal. There are several parrillas along Avenida Pedro Luro and a number of confiterías around Plaza San Martín.

Things to Buy
For traditional gaucho-style handicrafts and similar goods, don't miss the Mercado Artesanal in the tourist office, with its excellent selection, including horse gear, silverwork, woollen goods, and wood carv-

ings from the caldén trees which cover large areas of the province. Another place to check out is El Matrero at Pellegrini 86.

Getting There & Away
Air Aerolíneas Argentinas (☎ 24707), on Rivadavia between Hilario Lagos and Hipólito Yrigoyen, has Monday, Wednesday and Friday flights from Buenos Aires, which continue to Bahía Blanca and back to Buenos Aires in a counter-clockwise pattern. On Tuesday, Thursday and Sunday, the circuit is repeated clockwise. The fare to Bahía Blanca is US$66, to Buenos Aires US$100.

Bus The bus terminal (☎ 22592) is at the Centro Cívico, Avenidas Pedro Luro and San Martín. Chevallier has four buses daily to Buenos Aires for US$21, taking nine hours. There is one bus daily to San Martín de los Andes and Bariloche, for US$50, which takes 21 hours. TUS has services to the Mesopotamian littoral, while TUP goes to Comodoro Rivadavia and Caleta Olivia. Andesmar has buses to Mendoza.

Train The Ferrocarril Sarmiento (☎ 22451) is at Alsina and Pellegrini, but services have declined and are much slower and less convenient than buses.

Car Rental This is a good alternative for visiting Parque Nacional Lihué Calel. Try Alquilauto (☎ 26513) at 9 de Julio 227.

AROUND SANTA ROSA
Parque Luro
Originally a private hunting reserve, this 7500-hectare park, 35 km south of Santa Rosa, now belongs to the province of La Pampa. Dr Pedro Luro, an influential early resident, imported exotic game species such as Carpathian deer and European boar into its pastures and native caldén forests. He also built an enormous lodge for foreign hunters, formerly known as The Castle, which is now a museum.

With the decline of sport hunting by the European aristocracy during and after WW I, followed by the Great Depression, the reserve fell into disrepair, and the animals escaped through holes in its fences. During and after WW II, another landowner exploited its forests for firewood and charcoal, grazed cattle and sheep, and bred polo ponies. Since its acquisition by the province in 1965, it now constitutes a recreational and historical resource for the people of La Pampa.

Parque Luro is closed on Mondays and Tuesdays. Besides the museum, there are picnic areas, a small zoo, and a collection of turn-of-the-century carriages. Camping is possible. There is a modest admission charge.

PARQUE NACIONAL LIHUÉ CALEL
Like the Sierras de Tandil and the Sierra de la Ventana in Buenos Aires province, Parque Nacional Lihué Calel (a Pehuenche phrase meaning Sierra de la Vida or the Range of Life) is a series of small, isolated mountain ranges and valleys in an otherwise nearly featureless landscape, situated 226 km south-west of Santa Rosa. Its salmon-coloured, exfoliating granites, resembling parts of the Joshua Tree National Monument in California's Mojave Desert, do not exceed 600 metres but still offer a variety of subtle environments, which change with the season and even with the day, and a refuge from the monotony of the Pampas.

Though Lihué Calel is a desert, receiving only about 400 mm rainfall per annum, water is an important factor in the landscape. Sudden storms can bring flash floods or create spectacular, temporary waterfalls over the granite nickpoints near the visitor centre. Even when the sky is cloudless, the subterranean streams in the valleys nourish the monte, a scrub forest with a surprising variety of plant species. Within the park's 10,000 hectares, there exist 345 species of plants, nearly half the total found in the entire province.

In this thinly populated area survives wildlife which is now extinct in the humid Pampas farther east. Park rangers have seen puma (Felis concolor), although the large cats are not common. Other cats are more

Puma

through a dense thorn forest of characteristic caldén *(Prosopis caldenia,* a local species of a common worldwide genus), and similar trees, along an intermittent stream. This trail leads to a site with petroglyphs, unfortunately vandalised since 1927. The exceptionally friendly and knowledgeable rangers will accompany you if their schedule permits.

During and after rainstorms, the granite boulders on the upper streamcourse briefly form spectacular waterfalls. There is a marked trail to the 589-metre peak which bears the unwieldy name of **Cerro de la Sociedad Científica Argentina,** but the climb is gradual enough in any direction that you can choose your route. Watch for flowering cacti such as *Trichocereus candicans* between the boulders, but be advised that the granite is slippery when wet. From the summit, there are outstanding views of the entire Sierra and its surrounding marshes and salt lakes, like Laguna Urre Lauquen to the south-west.

If you have time or a vehicle, hike or drive to the **Viejo Casco,** the big house of the former Estancia Santa María before the provincial government expropriated the land, which was later transferred to the national park system. It is possible to make a circuit via the **Valle de las Pinturas,** where there are more, undamaged petroglyphs. Ask the rangers for directions.

likely to be seen, including Geoffroy's cat *(Felis geoffroyi)* and the yaguarundi *(Felis yagouaroundi).* There remain other large mammals like the guanaco *(Lama guanicoe),* which is more common on the Patagonian steppe, and smaller species like the *mara* or Patagonian hare *(Dolichotis patagonicum)* and *vizcacha (Lagostomus maximus),* a wild relative of the domestic chinchilla.

The wide variety of birds includes the rhea or *ñandú (Rhea americana)* and many birds of prey including the *carancho* or crested caracara *(Polyborus plancus).* Although you not likely to encounter them, you should be aware of the highly poisonous pit vipers commonly known as *yarará (Bothrops spp.).*

Until General Roca's so-called Conquest of the Desert, Araucanian Indians successfully defended the area against European invasion. Archaeological evidence, including numerous petroglyphs, still remains of their presence and of that of their ancestors. Lihué Calel was the last refuge of the Indian cacique Namuncurá, who hid for several years before surrendering to Argentine forces.

Things to See & Do
From the park campground, there is an excellent signed nature trail along a stream

Places to Stay
Near the visitor centre, there is a very comfortable campground with shade trees, picnic tables, firepits, cold showers (summer weather is hot enough, anyway), and many, many birds. There is no charge, but bring food – the nearest available supplies are at the town of Puelches, 35 km south. On the highway, it is possible to stay at the *ACA Hostería,* which also has a restaurant.

Getting There & Away
Cooperativa Alto Valle's service from Neuquén to Santa Rosa will drop you at the ACA station, near the park entrance, shortly after midnight after leaving Neuquén at 9.15

pm Tuesdays, Thursdays and Saturdays. The fare is US$7. Buses from Rosario to Neuquén via Santa Rosa will take you to the park, but charge full fare from Santa Rosa to Villa Regina because it is an express service.

Mesopotamia, Misiones & the North-East

Mesopotamia is that part of Argentina between the Paraná and Uruguay rivers, consisting of the provinces of Entre Ríos, Corrientes and Misiones. Historically, the winding channels and sandbars of these rivers made navigation difficult above present-day Rosario (Santa Fe province), while their breadth made cross-river communications no less awkward. In effect, Mesopotamia was an island. The area between and along the rivers is commonly known as the littoral.

Subtropical Misiones province, north-east of Corrientes, is Argentina's politically strategic peninsula between the Paraná and Uruguay, nearly surrounded by the countries of Paraguay and Brazil. Its most spectacular attraction is the Iguazú Falls, the setting for the successful film *The Mission*. Corrientes borders both Brazil and Uruguay to the east, and the provinces of Chaco and Santa Fe to the west. The province of Formosa lies between Chaco and Paraguay.

History

In history and geography, Mesopotamia and the North-East differ greatly from the Argentine heartland. Nomadic hunter-gatherers populated the temperate Pampas when Europeans first arrived, but the Guaraní peoples, from northern Entre Ríos through Corrientes and into Paraguay and Brazil, were semisedentary agriculturalists, raising sweet potatoes, maize, manioc and beans. River fish also played an important role in their diet.

Rumours of wealthy Indian civilisations first drew Europeans into the region. Pedro de Mendoza led the earliest expedition to the Río de la Plata, the estuary formed by the two rivers, but his founding of Buenos Aires in 1536 proved ephemeral when his sick, starved and ill-prepared men were eventually driven out by Querandí Indians, who prevented the city's re-establishment for nearly half a century. The following year, Mendoza's lieutenant Pedro de Ayolas established a beachhead in the upper Paraná at Asunción, where the Spanish could obtain food and supplies from the friendlier Guaraní. Settlement thus proceeded southward from Asunción rather than northward from Buenos Aires. Corrientes was founded in 1588, Santa Fe about the same time. For further information on early Spanish settlement in the upper Paraná, see the Paraguay part of this book.

Jesuit missionaries helped colonise the upper Uruguay and Paraná rivers, concentrating the native Guaraní populations in settlements which at least approximated the

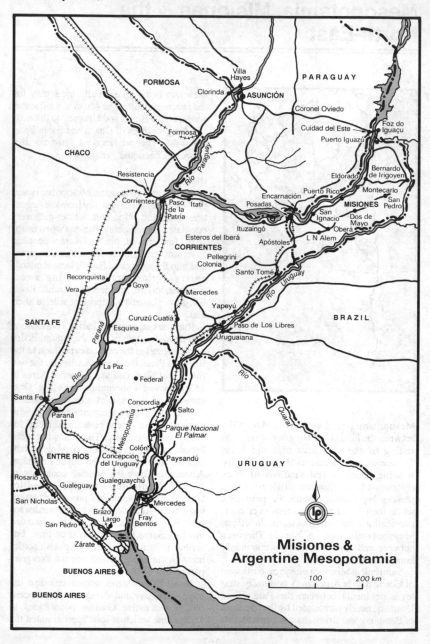

Misiones & Argentine Mesopotamia

0   100   200 km

Spanish ideal of reciprocal rights and responsibilities in dealing with native peoples in the Americas. To be sure, the Jesuit fathers exploited native labour on their *yerba mate* (Paraguayan tea) plantations, but they also conscientiously taught the Spanish language, Catholic religion and other European customs to their charges. Jealousy of the missions' economic success and their monopolisation of the Indian labour force led to expulsion of the Jesuits and the disintegration of mission communities, but their ruins, second only to Iguazú Falls in attracting visitors to Misiones province, are a monument to an extraordinary period of history. Perhaps 15,000 Guaraní remain in the region, their legacy including many place names and linguistic survivals such as the common usage of words such as *gurí*, meaning 'child', by the general populace.

Settlement of the Argentine Chaco came much later. Oppressive summer heat, hostile Indians, and poisonous snakes discouraged exploration of its dense thorn forests. After the middle of the 19th century, though, woodcutters from Corrientes entered the forest to exploit the valuable quebracho (axe-breaker) tree, a source of natural tannin used to process leather. These activities opened the area to agricultural exploitation, which has primarily taken the form of cotton and cattle production.

Entre Ríos Province

This province's name literally describes its location between the two major rivers. Covered by rolling grasslands, with forests along its riverbanks, it has always supported livestock enterprises but is also an important agricultural centre. Fiercely independent from Buenos Aires, once declaring itself an independent republic, it ironically became a Unitarist stronghold after Rosas took power. Local caudillo Justo José Urquiza, commanding an army comprised of provincial loyalists, Unitarists, Brazilians and Uruguayans, was in large part responsible for the demise of dictator Juan Manuel de Rosas and the eventual adoption of Argentina's modern constitution.

The provincial economy formerly resembled that of Buenos Aires. Large landowners, including Urquiza himself, controlled extensive cattle estancias. Like their Buenos Aires counterparts, these estancias salted their beef and prepared hides for export at riverside locations. By the 1880s, European colonisation schemes managed to settle 15,000 immigrant farmers in the province, including Russo-Germans south of Paraná and Russian Jews near Basavilbaso.

Until the early years of the 20th century, Entre Ríos' cattle were the native creole type, but improved breeds eventually displaced these. Rail connections with Buenos Aires, not established until 1908 and even then via ferry rather than bridges, retarded economic modernisation. After meat freezer plants were built locally, the province enjoyed greater prosperity. Since construction of a bridge across the Río de la Plata delta to Zárate, in Buenos Aires province, much of the livestock processing industry has moved south.

For the visitor, the principal attractions of Entre Ríos are the rivers and their recreational opportunities. These include camping and fishing in winter, spring and autumn when the weather is not oppressively hot. Parque Nacional El Palmar, established to protect the region's declining native palm forests, is only a few hours north of Buenos Aires on the Río Uruguay. There are several bridges across the river to the neighbouring republic of Uruguay.

PARANÁ
One of the oldest cities in Mesopotamia, Paraná is also the provincial capital. Although it has no official founding date, most residents associate it with the establishment of the Parroquia (parish) del Rosario de la Bajada in 1730. Between 1853 and 1861, it was capital of the short-lived Argentine Confederation, but eventually lost its primacy to Buenos Aires.

Paraná is a pleasant modern city whose

Paraná

0   250   500 m

Orientation

Paraná sits on a high bluff on the east bank of the Río Paraná. Its city plan is more irregular than most Argentine cities, with numerous diagonals, curving boulevards and complex intersections. Plaza Primero de Mayo is the town centre, along which Calle San Martín is a peatonal for six blocks. On Saturday mornings, the entire town congregates for a *paseo* (outing) here.

Except for Calle San Martín, street names change on all sides of the plaza. At the west end of Calle San Martín, Parque Urquiza extends more than a kilometre along the

major attraction is the river itself, along which there are large public parks and campgrounds with river access. Most of the important public buildings were built during the 19th century. In recent years, Paraná and neighbouring Santa Fe, across the river, take pride in having built the subfluvial Hernandárias tunnel which connects the two cities, despite apathy and, later, active opposition from the national government. Interestingly, Paraná is a hotbed of interest in North American softball, having entertained national and international tournaments.

■ PLACES TO STAY

1   Camping Balneario Thompson
15 Gran Hotel Alvear
19 Plaza Hotel
20 Gran Hotel Paraná
28 Hotel Super Luxe
29 Hotel 9 de Julio
31 Hotel City
35 Hotel Bristol

▼ PLACES TO EAT

27 Restaurant Florentino

OTHER

2   Provincial Tourist Office
3   Softball Stadium
4   Monument to Urquiza
5   Casino
6   Museo de Ciencias Naturales y
    Antropológicas Dr Antonio Serrano
7   Plaza Carbo
8   Casa de Gobierno
9   Plaza Mansilla
10 Museo Bellas Artes
11 ACA
12 Plaza Alvear
13 Aerolíneas Argentinas
14 Museo Histórico de Entre Ríos Martín
    Leguizamón & Museo de Bellas
    Artes Pedro E Martínez
16 Telecom
17 Teatro 3 de Febrero
18 Museo y Mercado Provincial de
    Artesanías
21 Plaza Primero de Mayo
22 Cathedral
23 Plaza Alberti
24 Post Office
25 Municipal Tourist Office
26 Central Market
30 Train Station
32 Plaza R Sáenz Peña
33 Hospital
34 Plaza M Fierro
36 Bus Terminal

riverfront and the bluffs above it. Many other attractive parks and plazas are scattered throughout the city.

Information
Tourist Office The municipal tourist office

(☎ 22-1632) is at 25 de Mayo 44, on the main plaza, with a branch at the bus terminal. Hours are weekdays from 8 am to 8 pm, Saturdays from 8 am to 1 pm and 3 to 8 pm, and Sundays from 9 am to 1 pm and 4 to 8 pm. There is a provincial tourist office (☎ 24-2601) at the exit from the Santa Fe-Paraná tunnel.

Money Tourfe, the local cambio, and Banco de Entre Ríos, both on the Calle San Martín peatonal, are as good as any. There are street changers, but their rates are no better.

Post & Telecommunications The post office is at 25 de Mayo and Monte Caseros, while the long-distance phone office is at Calle San Martín 735, on the peatonal.

Travel Agencies ACA (☎ 21-1522) is at Buenos Aires and Laprida. For other agencies, see specific activities below.

Medical Services The public hospital (☎ 21-3459) is at Presidente Perón 450, near Gualeguaychú.

Walking Tour
You can see most of Paraná's important buildings in a short walk beginning at the Plaza Primero de Mayo, where the post office occupies the former site of **General Urquiza's residence**. The current **Iglesia Catedral** (Cathedral) has been on the plaza since 1730, although the current building dates only from 1885; its museum is open from 5 to 7 pm daily. When Paraná was capital of the Argentine Confederation, the Senate deliberated at the present **Colegio del Huerto**, behind the Cathedral at 9 de Julio and 25 de Mayo.

A block west, at Corrientes and Avenida Urquiza, are the **Palacio Municipal** (1889) and the **Escuela Normal Paraná** (Paraná Normal School), the first of its kind in the country, founded by the famous educator and President D F Sarmiento. Across Calle San Martín, at 25 de Mayo 60, is the **Teatro Municipal Tres de Febrero** (1908). At the west end of the Calle San Martín peatonal is the **Plaza Alvear**, around which are several important museums. A block south, bounded by Córdoba, Laprida and Santa Fe, is the **Centro Cívico**, which contains provincial government offices. Farther south, along the diagonal Avenida Rivadavia, is the provincial library **Biblioteca de Entre Ríos**.

You can continue to **Parque Urquiza**, walk the length of the park and double back at the foot of Calle San Martín to return to the plaza. The park has a number of important monuments, including a statue of Urquiza.

Museo Histórico de Entre Ríos Martín Leguizamón

This modern, well-arranged museum at the Plaza Alvear, Laprida and Buenos Aires, flaunts the regional pride of Entrerrianos. The knowledgeable but somewhat patronising guides go to rhetorical extremes to emphasise the importance of provincial caudillos and their role in Argentine history. There are excellent collections of portraits and 19th-century artefacts of provincial life.

Admission charges are nominal. Hours are Tuesday to Friday 8 am to 1 pm and 4 to 8 pm, Saturday 8 am to noon and 4 to 6 pm, and Sunday 9 am to noon.

Museo de Bellas Artes Pedro E Martínez

Oil paintings, illustrations and sculptures by provincial artists are displayed in this subterranean museum, just off the Plaza Alvear at Buenos Aires 355, adjacent to the historical museum. Morning hours are Tuesday to Sunday, 9 am to noon all year. Winter afternoon hours are 3 to 6 pm Tuesday to Saturday; in summer, afternoon hours are 5 to 8 pm.

Museo y Mercado Provincial de Artesanías

At Avenida Urquiza 1239, this combined crafts centre and museum displays and sells handicrafts from throughout the province. Materials include wood, ceramics, leather, metal, bone, iron and others. Hours are 8 am to noon and 5 to 9 pm Monday to Saturday, 9 pm to noon Sunday.

Museo de Ciencias Naturales y Antropológicas Dr Antonio Serrano

From late 1990, much of this museum at Avenida Rivadavia 462 was closed for repairs, but things may improve when those parts reopen. The natural history specimens were in poor condition, while the anthropological exhibits were mediocre. Hours are Tuesday to Sunday 9 am to noon; Tuesday to Saturday, 3 to 6 pm in winter and 4 to 7 pm in summer.

Túnel Subfluvial Hernandárias

Until the opening of this tunnel beneath the Río Paraná in 1969, the provincial capitals of Paraná and Santa Fe had to rely on ferry boats for interurban transport. The national government, at the time building a bridge between Buenos Aires province and southern Entre Ríos, refused even to allow the two provinces to build a bridge, a right reserved to Buenos Aires. This forced the provinces into the more difficult alternative of the 2.4 km tunnel under the main channel of the Paraná, which cost US$60 million.

Hourly guided tours include a film and visit to the control centre. Any bus to Santa Fe will drop you at the tunnel entrance. Hours are daily from 8 am to noon all year; winter afternoon hours are 2 to 6 pm, summer afternoon hours from 3 to 9 pm.

Motorists should know that they are likely to encounter irritating document checks from the police at each end of the tunnel.

Activities

Fishing River fishing is a popular local pastime, and tasty local game species such as *boga*, *sábalo*, *dorado* and *surubí* reach considerable size. Licences are available through the Dirección Provincial de Recursos Naturales at Monte Caseros 195. Equipment is available at El Ciervo (☎ 21-3991), Alem 886. For more detailed information, see the section on Paso de la Patria, Corrientes province, below.

Water Sports Boating, water-skiing, windsurfing and swimming are popular pastimes for much of the year. Sporting goods are available at Los Deportes (☎ 21-3991), 9 de Julio 178 or Calle San Martín 732. For boat excursions on the river, contact Turismo Fluvial (☎ 22-1632) on Calle San Martín and the costanera Avenida Laurencena.

Festivals
Every January, Paraná hosts the **Fiesta Provincial Música y Artesanía Entrerriana**, which features regional folk music. In October, the **Fiesta Provincial del Inmigrante** acknowledges the contribution of immigrants to provincial development.

At Diamante, 44 km south of Paraná, the January **Fiesta Nacional de Jineteada y Folklore** celebrates gaucho culture and music. Diamante also is the site of the **Fiesta Provincial del Pescador** (Provincial Fisherman's Festival) in February.

Places to Stay – bottom end
Camping There are numerous campgrounds in and around Paraná. Closest to the centre is the shady *Camping Balneario Thompson*, which can be noisy on weekends when locals come there for all-night asados. The cold showers are of no concern in the summer, but you may want to choose your time in more changeable spring and autumn weather. Beware of *jejénes*, annoying biting insects, along the river in summer. Sites are US$4 per vehicle. Bus Nos 1 and 6, with the sign 'Thompson', go between the campground and the centre.

There are other good campgrounds at Toma Vieja, the old waterworks, a few km outside town but accessible by bus No 5, and at Los Arenales, reached by bus No 1 (red).

Hotels Compared to Santa Fe, accommodation in Paraná is fairly limited in all categories. The best low budget place is *Hotel City* (☎ 21-0086) at Racedo 231, directly opposite the train station, with a wonderful patio garden and cool rooms with high ceilings. Singles/doubles are about US$7/12 with shared bath, US$10/16 with private bath. Prices are similar at *Hotel 9 de Julio* (☎ 21-3047), 9 de Julio 674, half a block from the train station. *Hotel Bristol*

(☎ 21-3961), near the bus station at Alsina 221 between Ruiz Moreno and Avenida Echagüe, is more expensive but very clean and attractive.

Places to Stay – middle
The crumbling but interesting *Plaza Hotel* (☎ 21-0720), Calle San Martín 916 at Avenida Urquiza, has rooms at US$15/20 with shared bath, US$16/23 with private bath. Several have balconies with views of the plaza. The modern *Hotel Super Luxe* (☎ 21-2787), Villaguay 162 between 9 de Julio and Monte Caseros, has rooms with bath at $20/26.

Places to Stay – top end
Gran Hotel Alvear (☎ 22-0000), at Calle San Martín 637, and *Gran Hotel Paraná* (☎ 22-3900), at Urquiza 976 on the plaza, have rooms with private baths and many other conveniences for about US$26/37.

Places to Eat
River fish is the local speciality. *Restaurant Florentino*, at Gualeguaychú 186 between 9 de Julio and Monte Caseros, serves good surubí and other fish in season. Also try *Los Quinchos* at Bravard 280, near Balneario Thompson.

Comedor Centro Comercial, upstairs on 25 de Mayo across from the Plaza Primero de Mayo, serves a very inexpensive parrillada and other typical Argentine food. For ice cream, go to *Costa Azul*, Calle San Martín 1059. Ice cream shops on the littoral invariably have water coolers, a welcome relief in the often oppressive heat.

Entertainment
Teatro 3 de Febrero The municipal theatre at 25 de Junio 60 has exhibitions of local art, inexpensive films, and other activities.

Casino If you have money to spare, you can gamble at the casino at Etchevehere in Parque Urquiza. Winter hours are from 9 pm to 3 am, summer hours from 9.30 pm to 3.30 am.

Nightclubs If your Spanish is good enough Lloyd, Avenida Urquiza 1001 on the plaza, offers stand-up comedy. La Belle Epoque is an Art Deco-style club on Avenida Urquiza, next to the Plaza Hotel.

Softball In 1989, Paraná attracted crowds as large as 5000 people for the third annual Panamerican Softball Championships at its new ballpark, Estadio Ingeniero Nafaldo Cargnel, but the sport has been popular since the 1960s. From the number of children and teenagers walking around the town in softball uniforms, you might think you were in a small town in the American Midwest on a summer weekend.

Youth and adult leagues play on the city's eight fields, three of which are lit. Both slow and fast pitch versions are popular. The quality of play varies considerably, but can be excellent. There are games, free of charge except for special events such as regional or national championships, almost every night at the stadium, near the entrance to the Hernandárias tunnel to Santa Fe.

Getting There & Away
Air Aerolíneas Argentinas has offices on Calle San Martín, across from the Plaza Alvear, between Colón and La Paz, but flights leave from Santa Fe's airport at Sauce Viejo. See Getting There & Away for Santa Fe for details.

Bus The bus terminal (☎ 21-5053) is at Echagüe and Ramírez. Paraná is a centre for provincial bus services, but Santa Fe is more convenient for longer distance trips.

About every half-hour throughout the day, buses leave for Santa Fe for US$2. Empresa Tata goes to northern littoral destinations between Paraná and Corrientes, including La Paz, Esquina and Goya. Chevallier also goes to Esquina and Corrientes, as well as Patagonian destinations. El Rápido has seven buses daily to Rosario (US$8, three hours) and five to Buenos Aires (US$18, eight hours).

Empresa Kurtz offers service to Puerto Iguazú on Monday, Tuesday and Friday afternoons. El Litoral also goes to Puerto Iguazú via Posadas. El Serrano goes to Córdoba and TAC to Mendoza. International services include Cora, which goes to Montevideo, Uruguay, and Singer, which travels to Porto Alegre, Brazil.

Train The Ferrocarril Urquiza station (☎ 21-7505) is on Racedo, at the east end of Calle San Martín. From Paraná, there are trains to Buenos Aires' Lacroze Station on Tuesdays, Thursdays and Sundays at 7.30 pm. There are services to Concepción del Uruguay daily at 1.30 pm and to Concordia twice daily, at 4.35 am and 3 pm.

LA PAZ
On the east bank of the Paraná, about 160 km north-west of the provincial capital, La Paz is known for its excellent fishing and good camping. In February it celebrates the **Fiesta Nacional de Pesca Variada de Río** (national river fishing festival). It also has a regional museum.

The tourist office is on Larrea, at the eastern entrance to town. For inexpensive accommodation, try *Residencial Las Dos M* (☎ 21303) at Urquiza 825.

GUALEGUAYCHÚ
Founded in 1783, Gualeguaychú (population 85,000) is the first city of any size after entering the province of Entre Ríos from Buenos Aires. While not a major tourist destination, it has some historical interest and leads to the most southerly bridge crossing into Uruguay.

Orientation
Gualeguaychú is located on the east bank of the Río Gualeguaychú, a tributary of the Río Uruguay, about 13 km east of national Ruta 14. It has a very regular grid pattern centred on the Plaza San Martín, which occupies four square blocks. National Ruta 136 bypasses the city centre en route to the San Martín toll bridge to the Uruguayan city of Fray Bentos.

Information
Tourist Office The municipal tourist office

(☎ 3668) is on Avenida Costanera near the bridge across the Río Gualeguaychú. It's open 8 am to 10 pm in summer and 8 am to 8 pm in winter, and has good brochures and a list of accommodation, but poor quality maps.

Money Casa Goyo, on Ayacucho near Calle San Martín, will change cash dollars at reasonable rates, but not travellers' cheques. It's open weekdays from 8 am to noon and 4 to 7.30 pm, Saturdays from 8 am to noon. You can also change, but with much more bureaucracy, at Banco de la Nación or at Banco de la Provincia, both on 25 de Mayo near España.

Post & Telecommunications The post office is at Urquiza and Angel Elías, while long-distance telephones are at Urquiza 910. There are also long-distance phone services at the bus terminal.

Foreign Consulates Uruguay has a consulate (☎ 6168) at Rivadavia 510.

Travel Agencies ACA (☎ 6088) is at Urquiza 1000, on the corner of Chacabuco.

Medical Services The Hospital Centenario (☎ 7831) is at 25 de Mayo and Pasteur.

Things to See
A few colonial buildings remain in Gualeguaychú, plus several others important in Argentine political and literary history. The **Museo Haedo**, at San José 105 just off the main plaza, is the oldest house in town and is the municipal museum, open daily from 8 am to noon and 7 to 9 pm. The colonial **Casa de Andrade**, at Andrade and Borques, now contains the Centro Artesanal San José, with a good selection of handicrafts. In the mid-19th century it belonged to Entrerriano poet and journalist Olegario Andrade.

Casa de Fray Mocho, at Fray Mocho 135, is the birthplace of José Álvarez, founder of the influential satirical magazine *Caras y Caretas* at the turn of the century.

Fray Mocho was his pen name. The **Casa de la Cultura**, an unusual building at 25 de Mayo 734, has occasional public exhibitions.

The **Museo Ferroviario** is an open-air exhibit of steam locomotives, dining cars, and other hardware from provincial rail history. It's at the train station, at the end of Maipú on Tala.

Festivals
Gualeguaychú is a party town, with several important festivals. Its **Carnaval** has a national and even international reputation, so if you can't go to Río or Bahía, make a stop here. Every October for the past 30 years, high school students have built and paraded floats through the city for the **Fiesta Provincial de Carrozas Estudiantiles**.

Other celebrations include the folkloric **Abrazo Celeste y Blanco** (after the colours of the Argentine flag) and numerous *jineteadas* (rodeos) throughout the course of the year.

Places to Stay
Camping There are good facilities at *Camping La Delfina*, in Parque Unzué on the far side of the river, but take plenty of mosquito repellent in summer. Fees are US$4 for two people, US$5.50 for four.

Hospedajes & Hotels Most reasonably priced hotels are near the bus station. The cheapest is the clean and friendly *Pensión Gualeguaychú*, 25 de Mayo 456 near Nieves, where rooms with shared bath are US$5 per person. At *Hospedaje Mayo* (☎ 7661), on Bolívar 550 at 3 de Febrero, singles/doubles with private bath cost US$10/13. *Residencial Marina* (☎ 7159), 25 de Mayo 1031, has quiet, spacious rooms with good beds for US$10/22.

Several places charge about US$20/26, including *Hotel Brutti* (☎ 6048), Bolívar 571 and *Hotel Abadia* (☎ 7675), Calle San Martín 588. At *Hotel Berlin* (☎ 6085), Bolívar 733, rooms are about US$29/42. Closest to luxury is the three-star *Hotel*

Gualeguaychú

0   250   500 m

Embajador, at Calle San Martín and 3 de Febrero, which also has a casino.

Places to Eat

Most restaurants are along 25 de Mayo, but try also the *Círculo Italiano* at Calle San Martín and Pellegrini.

Getting There & Away

The bus terminal is very central at Bolívar and Chile. Buenos Aires is three hours plus and US$10 away, with frequent services by San José, El Rápido, and El Tata lines. Ciudad de Gualeguay has five buses daily to

Paraná via Larroque, Gualeguay and Victoria. The trip take six hours and costs US$13. Three times a week, El Serrano goes to Córdoba (US$32, 11 hours) via Santa Fe. Ciudad de Gualeguaychú has daily buses to Corrientes.

From Monday to Saturday, ETA has three buses to Fray Bentos, Uruguay, two of which continue to Mercedes. Fares are US$3 to Fray Bentos and US$4 to Mercedes. For Montevideo, you can make connections in Fray Bentos.

There are no passenger trains to Gualeguaychú now, only freight services.

1	Uruguayan Consulate
2	Museo Haedo
3	Church
4	Casa de Fray Mocho
5	Municipalidad
6	ENTel
7	Banco de la Nación
8	Banco de la Provincia
9	ACA
10	ENCOTEL
11	Residencial Marina
12	Casa Goyo (Exchange)
13	Hotel Berlin
14	Hotel Abadia
15	Pensión Gualeguaychú
16	Tourist Office
17	Camping La Delfina
18	Casa de Andrade
19	Hotel Embajador
20	Hospedaje Mayo
21	Bus Terminal
22	Hotel Brutti
23	Train Station & Museo Ferroviario

COLÓN

One of three major border crossings in Entre Ríos, Colón sits on the west bank of the Río Uruguay, connected to the Uruguayan city of Paysandú by the General Artigas bridge. Founded in 1863, Colón is an attractive tourist destination due to its beautiful riverine landscape, and fine beaches

It's also worth visiting the nearby village of **San José**, 5 km to the west, where in 1857 European pioneers established the second agricultural colony in the country. There is an interesting regional museum with tools and memorabilia from the pioneer era.

Four km from Colón is the **Molino Forclaz** building, the first flour mill in the area. From Colón you can also catch a bus to the entrance of Parque Nacional El Palmar.

The tourist office (☎ 21233) is at Emilio Gouchon and the Costanera. For cheap lodging, try *Residencial Ver-wei* (☎ 21972) at 25 de Mayo 10.

PARQUE NACIONAL EL PALMAR

On the west bank of the Río Uruguay, midway between Colón and Concordia,

8500-hectare Parque Nacional El Palmar is one of the most visited parks in the Argentine system. It preserves the last extensive stands of native yatay palm *(Syagrus yatay)* on the Argentine littoral. In the 19th century, these palms covered large parts of Entre Ríos, Uruguay and southern Brazil, but the intensification of agriculture, ranching and forestry throughout the region destroyed much of the palm savannas and inhibited the reproduction of the species. The park itself was once a cattle estancia, but was acquired by the state in 1966.

Most of the palms which remain in El Palmar are relics, some more than two centuries old, although under protection from grazing and fire they have once again begun to reproduce themselves. They reach a maximum height of about 18 metres, with a trunk diameter of 40 cm. The larger specimens clustered throughout the park accentuate a striking and soothing subtropical landscape which lends itself extremely well to photography. The grasslands and the gallery forests along the river and creeks shelter much wildlife, including birds, mammals and reptiles.

To see wildlife, go for walks along the watercourses or through the palm savannas, preferably in early morning or just before sunset. The most conspicuous bird is the ñandú, or rhea *(Rhea americana)*, but there are also numerous parakeets, cormorants, egrets, herons, storks, caracaras, woodpeckers and kingfishers. Among the mammals, the *carpincho* or capybara, a semiaquatic rodent weighing up to 60 kg, and the vizcacha, a relative of the chinchilla, are frequently seen, but there are also foxes, raccoons and wild boars.

Vizcachas inhabit the campground at Arroyo Los Loros, where their nocturnal squeaks and reflective eyes sometimes disturb campers, but they are harmless. The same is not true of the yarará, a highly poisonous pit viper which inhabits the savannas. Bites are not common, but you should watch your step and wear high boots and long trousers when hiking. Even reptile-lovers will probably prefer the river turtles. The

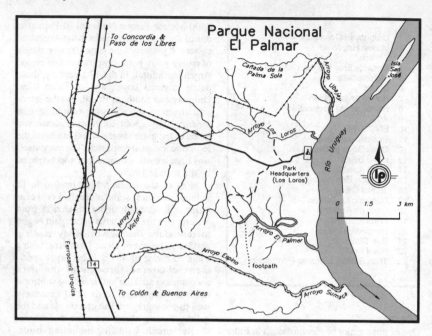

Parque Nacional El Palmar

gigantic toads which invade the showers and toilets at night are harmless.

Things to See & Do
El Palmar is remarkably tranquil and undeveloped, despite its proximity to population centres. Thus most activities will be oriented towards the park's natural attractions.

Centro de Interpretación
Across from the campground at Los Loros, the visitor centre has displays on the park's natural history, including a small herpetarium (reptile house), and offers slide shows in the evening. Unfortunately, many of the excellent colour blowups of landscape, flora and fauna have faded over the years and badly need replacement. There is a confitería next door at which you can get food and drink. The park administration *(intendencia)* was once the big house (casco) of the estancia.

Río Uruguay
There is excellent access to the river for swimming and boating from the Arroyo Los Loros campground. You can rent canoes at the campground store.

Arroyo Los Loros
A short distance by gravel road from the campground, this is a good place to observe wildlife.

Arroyo El Palmar
Five km from Los Loros campground is Arroyo El Palmar, a pleasant stream with a beautiful swimming hole, accessible by a good gravel road. It is a good place to see birds, and crossing the ruined bridge, you can walk for several km along a palm-lined road now being reclaimed by savanna grasses.

Places to Stay
Thankfully, there are no hotels in the park and your only alternative is to camp at Los Loros, which has good sites, hot showers, a store and a confitería. Sites are US$2 per person. There are hotels in Concordia, about

50 km north of the park entrance on national Ruta 14, and in Colón, about the same distance south.

Getting There & Away

El Palmar is 360 km north-west of Buenos Aires on Ruta 14, a major national highway, so there are frequent north-south bus services. Any bus from Buenos Aires, Gualeguaychú, Concepción del Uruguay or Colón to Concordia will drop you at the park entrance. There is no public transport to the visitor centre and camping area, but hitching should not be difficult. Park entry costs US$1.50 per person.

CONCORDIA

This agricultural and livestock centre offers the most northerly border crossing to Uruguay in the province of Entre Ríos, via the Salto Grande hydroelectric project to the Uruguayan city of Salto. There are also launches across the river. In December there is a national citrus festival in Concordia.

The tourist office (☎ 21-2137) is at Mitre 64. For cheap lodging, try *Residencial La Terminal* (☎ 21-1758) at Irigoyen 1313.

Corrientes Province

Like Entre Ríos, Corrientes traditionally has been an isolated province with a strong regional identity. The low, rolling terrain of its south, with its productive agriculture, greatly resembles Entre Ríos. The alluvial grasslands of the north, however, support mostly livestock except where interrupted by marshes such as the Esteros del Iberá, a potential national park with wildlife comparable to the better known Brazilian Pantanal. Gallery forests are common along the many watercourses, but plantations of exotic conifers also flourish in the warm, humid climate. Winter and early spring are the best times for a visit. Summer can be oppressively hot.

During the colonial era, settlement in Corrientes advanced southward from Paraguay. Indian resistance discouraged a permanent Spanish presence in the area until 1588, with the founding of the city of Corrientes. Jesuit priests were the region's most effective colonisers until their expulsion from South America in 1767; their most southerly mission, at Yapeyú on the Río Uruguay, was also the birthplace of Argentina's greatest hero, General José de San Martín.

Since Argentine independence, Corrientes' economy has relied on livestock: first cattle and more recently sheep. The province's isolation and distance from markets reduced any incentive to improve its cattle breeds until well into the 20th century. In recent years, forestry and timber processing have become important industries. Attempts to encourage provincial industry through large-scale energy development such as the trouble-plagued hydroelectric project at Yacyretá have been unsuccessful so far.

For visitors, the Río Paraná and its fishery may be the province's greatest attraction. Both the city and province of Corrientes also hold the most notable celebrations of Carnaval in the country. The city has many historic buildings dating back to the colonial era.

CORRIENTES

Just below the confluence of the Río Paraná and the Río Paraguay, the provincial capital of Corrientes is 850 km from Buenos Aires. Founded by Spaniards moving south from Asunción in 1588, it is one of the oldest cities in the country. Road connections from Buenos Aires are good, but the train system is antiquated and much less direct. On the opposite bank of the Paraná is Resistencia, capital of Chaco province.

Orientation

As one of the oldest cities established in the area, Corrientes has an extremely regular grid plan centred around the Plaza 25 de Mayo, although major public buildings are more dispersed than in most Argentine cities. There are several other important plazas, including Plaza La Cruz and Plaza Cabral. Between Salta and Catamarca, Calle Junín is

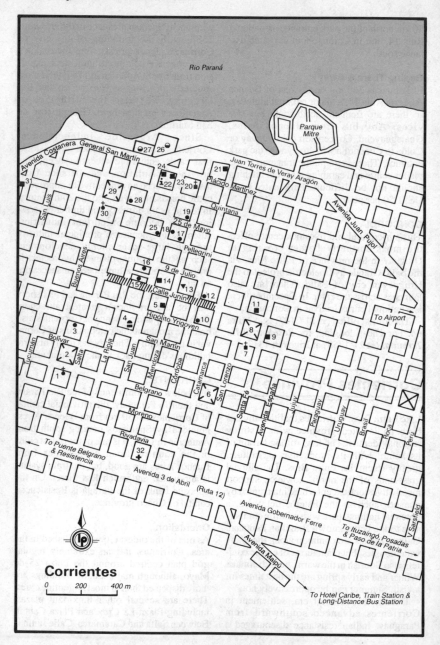

Corrientes

0   200   400 m

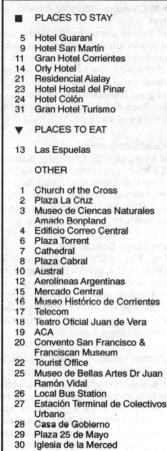

■ PLACES TO STAY

5 Hotel Guaraní
9 Hotel San Martín
11 Gran Hotel Corrientes
14 Orly Hotel
21 Residencial Aialay
23 Hotel Hostal del Pinar
24 Hotel Colón
31 Gran Hotel Turismo

▼ PLACES TO EAT

13 Las Espuelas

OTHER

1 Church of the Cross
2 Plaza La Cruz
3 Museo de Ciencas Naturales Amado Bonpland
4 Edificio Correo Central
6 Plaza Torrent
7 Cathedral
8 Plaza Cabral
10 Austral
12 Aerolíneas Argentinas
15 Mercado Central
16 Museo Histórico de Corrientes
17 Telecom
18 Teatro Oficial Juan de Vera
19 ACA
20 Convento San Francisco & Franciscan Museum
22 Tourist Office
25 Museo de Bellas Artes Dr Juan Ramón Vidal
26 Local Bus Station
27 Estación Terminal de Colectivos Urbano
28 Casa de Gobierno
29 Plaza 25 de Mayo
30 Iglesia de la Merced
32 Hospital Escuela San Martín

a peatonal along which most commercial activities are concentrated.

Calle Junín and most other areas of interest to the tourist are within a triangle formed by Avenida Costanera General San Martín, the north-south Avenida España, and Avenida 3 de Abril, a westward extension of Avenida Gobernador Ferre, which is also national Ruta 12 to Resistencia. To the east,

Ruta 12 parallels the course of the Paraná to Ituzaingó and to Posadas, the capital of Misiones province.

Information
Tourist Office The tourist office (☎ 23054) has recently moved to La Rioja 475, half a block from the costanera. It is friendly and helpful but rather disorganised, with only limited information on hotels and few brochures or maps, but by the time this is published the situation may have improved. It's open weekdays from 7 am to 1 pm and from 3 to 9 pm.

Money There are no cambios in town but numerous banks, such as Banco de la Provincia, at San Juan and 9 de Julio, Banco Francés, at Mendoza and Pellegrini, and Banco del Iberá at 9 de Julio 1002.

Post & Telecommunications The post office is at the corner of San Juan and Avenida San Martín. Telecom has long-distance services at Pellegrini 1175, between Mendoza and San Juan.

Foreign Consulates There is a Paraguayan consulate on San Juan, between 9 de Julio and Pellegrini.

Cultural Centres The Teatro Oficial Juan de Vera, named after the city's colonial founder, offers classical music concerts and other cultural events at San Juan 637.

Travel Agencies ACA (☎ 24545) is at 25 de Mayo and Mendoza. There are several other travel agencies in the downtown area, such as Turismo Taragui (☎ 22236) at La Rioja 730.

Medical Services The Hospital Escuela San Martín (☎ 65041, 65047, 65049) is at Avenida 3 de Abril 1251, between Mendoza and Córdoba.

Walking Tour
Because of Corrientes' stifling heat, early morning or late afternoon hours are best for

walking around town. A good starting point is the **Convento de San Francisco**, Mendoza 450, a colonial church beautifully restored in 1939. Dating from the founding of Corrientes, it has a museum which is open from 8 am to noon and 5 to 9.30 pm weekdays.

From there you can stroll to Parque Mitre and then back along the tree-lined Costanera, past the small but interesting zoo, beyond which there are excellent views of the **Puente Belgrano**, the bridge which crosses the Paraná to Resistencia. Returning by Edison and Bolívar, stop at the **Santuario de la Cruz del Milagro**, which contains a 16th-century cross that, according to legend, defied all efforts of hostile Indians to burn it.

Continue along Bolívar and up San Lorenzo to the **Cathedral** on the Plaza Cabral, which contains the mausoleum and statue of local hero Colonel Genaro Berón de Astrada. From Plaza Cabral, return along the Calle Junín pedestrian walk to Salta and back toward the river, passing Plaza 25 de Mayo.

Museo Histórico de Corrientes

The city's historical museum, at 9 de Julio 1044, has exhibits of weapons, antique furniture, and coins, as well as religious and civil history. There is also a library here.

Museo de Bellas Artes Dr Juan Ramón Vidal

The fine arts museum, at San Juan 634 opposite the Teatro Vera, emphasises sculpture but has frequent special exhibitions. Opening hours are Tuesday to Saturday 9 am to noon and 6 to 9 pm.

Zoological Gardens

On the costanera at the foot of Calle Junín, the Jardín Zoológico has a small selection of provincial wildlife, including caimans, capuchin monkeys, toucans, pumas and Geoffrey's cat. The enclosures are small, but most of the animals appear healthy. Hours are 10 am to 6 pm daily.

Museo de Ciencias Naturales Amado Bonpland

Founded by and named for Alexander von Humboldt's naturalist companion, who spent much of his life in the province and is buried at Paso de Los Libres, this natural history museum at Avenida San Martín 850 has some good fossils but is otherwise unexceptional. Opening hours are weekdays from 9 am to noon and 4 to 9 pm.

El Carnaval Correntino

Inspired by immigrants from the provincial town of Paso de Los Libres on the Brazilian border, Corrientes has had a riotous carnival for most of the past 30 years. It now appears to be in decline, but if you're in the area it may be worth a visit.

Places to Stay – bottom end

Camping The only campground in Corrientes is the privately owned site belonging to the telephone company, near the bus terminal and train station. They sometimes allow nonmembers, but the municipal sites in Paso de la Patria and Resistencia are more dependable.

Hotels Accommodation is relatively scarce and expensive in Corrientes, and generally inferior to that in nearby Resistencia. Most reasonable is the basic but friendly *Hotel Colón* (☎ 24527) at La Rioja 437, a few doors down from the tourist office. Singles/doubles with shared bath are US$9/13, while rooms with private bath are slightly higher. It is near the city's pleasant riverfront parks.

Places to Stay – middle

Gran Hotel Turismo, in attractive parklike grounds on the Avenida Costanera General San Martín at 25 de Mayo, is good value at US$20/30. It has a swimming pool, restaurant and bar. Slightly more expensive is *Gran Hotel Corrientes* (☎ 65019), at Calle Junín 1549 on Plaza Cabral, with similar facilities. The *Orly Hotel* (☎ 27248), San Juan 867, charges about US$28/40 for rooms that are rather small and frayed about the edges, but spotlessly clean.

Other in this category include *Hotel Caribe* (☎ 69045) at Maipú 2590, which is close to the bus and train stations; and *Hotel San Martín* (☎ 65004) at Santa Fe 955.

Places to Stay – top end
At the high-rise *Hotel Hostal del Pinar* (☎ 69060), on the riverfront at Plácido Martínez and San Juan, rooms with private bath are about US$35/50.

Places to Eat
Las Espuelas, at Mendoza 847, is an outstanding parrilla with reasonable prices. At lunchtime, you may wish to take advantage of its air-conditioning, but the outdoor patio would be more pleasant for dinner. For surubí and other river fish, try *Rancho Grande* at 3 de Abril 935. A reader has recommended *Parrilla Los Troncos* on Hipólito Yrigoyen, between Córdoba and Catamarca.

The Calle Junín peatonal has many cafés and confiterías, but is always completely deserted during the midday heat. You can eat cheaply in and near the Mercado Central (central market) on Calle Junín between La Rioja and San Juan.

Things to Buy
Local crafts can be purchased at the Museo de Artesanía Folklórica, in a colonial house at Salta and Quintana. Opening hours are 7.30 am to 12.30 pm and 2 to 6 pm weekdays, except Tuesdays (when it is closed), and on Saturdays 9 am to noon and 3 to 6 pm.

Getting There & Away
Air Aerolíneas Argentinas (☎ 23918) is at the corner of Calle Junín and Córdoba. It has daily flights, except Sunday, to Buenos Aires, and daily flights from Resistencia. The fare to Buenos Aires is about US$100, but there are discounts of up to 40% on some flights.

Austral (☎ 22570), Córdoba 983 at Hipólito Yrigoyen, has direct service to

Buenos Aires on Monday, Wednesday and Friday; on other days, its flights leave from Resistencia.

Bus Resistencia is a better place for bus connections than Corrientes, especially to the west and north-west. Local buses to Resistencia leave from the local bus terminal, on Avenida Costanera General San Martín at La Rioja, at frequent intervals throughout the day.

Empresa Ciudad de Posadas has regular services to Posadas, the capital of Misiones province, where there are connections to the former Jesuit missions and to Puerto Iguazú. Chevallier has buses to Paraná, Santa Fe, Rosario and Buenos Aires. El Rápido runs the same route, and also has service to Córdoba. Fares to Buenos Aires are about US$40.

There are also services to Paso de Los Libres, on the Brazilian border, via the interior city of Mercedes, which has good access to the Esteros del Iberá.

Train The Urquiza railway leaves daily from Corrientes to Buenos Aires' Lacroze Station at 3.30 pm. The trip lasts 21 to 22 hours and costs about US$24 primera, double that in a sleeper.

Car Rental For visiting remote places such as the Esteros de Iberá, you can arrange car rentals through Turismo Taragui (☎ 22236), La Rioja 730.

Getting Around
To/From the Airport Local bus No 8 goes to Corrientes airport, while Aerolíneas Argentinas runs a minibus to Resistencia airport in accordance with flight schedules.

Bus & Train The Estación Terminal de Transporte Gobernador Benjamín S González combines the train station (☎ 63954) and the long-distance bus terminal. From the local bus station, take bus No 6. Central Corrientes is sufficiently compact that walking suffices for most things.

PASO DE LA PATRIA
This small, quiet resort, about 30 km north-east of Corrientes at the confluence of the Paraguay and Paraná rivers , has a national and international reputation for sport fishing, making tourism the backbone of the local economy. High season is July to September; early October to early March is the closed season. Only the main street is paved, so it can be very muddy when it rains. Paso de la Patria can be very expensive, it but offers outstanding opportunities for dedicated fisherfolk.

Information
Tourist Office The tourist office (☎ 94007) is at 25 de Mayo 462.

Fishing
Besides the famous dorado, local sport fish include the surubí, which weighs up to 70 kg, the exceptionally tasty *boga*, *sábalo*, *pejerrey*, *pacú*, *patí*, *manduví*, *manduve*, *mangrullo*, *chafalote* and *armado*. Methods of capture include trolling, spinning and fly casting. Night fishing is possible.

Prices for fishing holidays start at about US$60 per person per day, which includes boat, guide, and an evening parrilla to feast on the day's catch. For further information on fishing holidays, contact Luís Maríns (☎ 94218), 25 de Mayo 470, 3904 Paso de la Patria, Corrientes.

Fiesta Nacional e Internacional de Pesca de Dorados
This annual festival lasts four days in mid-August, with a competition for the largest specimens of dorado *(Salminus maxiliosus)*, with a minimum allowable catch size of 75 cm. Entry costs US$60 for two persons, with prizes for the five largest fish. This carnivorous species, known as the 'tiger of the Paraná' for its fighting nature, weighs up to 25 kg.

Places to Stay
There is not much budget accommodation in Paso de la Patria, but several campgrounds charge about US$3 per person per night, with

all facilities. Many Correntinos have weekend houses here, and often rent them to visitors. Prices for a two-bedroom house start at about US$30 per day for up to six persons. For more information, contact the tourist office.

One alternative for local accommodation is *Le Apart Hotel* (☎ 94174), 25 de Mayo 1201, which charges US$90 per day with breakfast for up to four persons.

Getting There & Away
There is frequent bus service between Corrientes and Paso de la Patria.

ESTEROS DEL IBERÁ
The marshes of the Esteros del Iberá, a nearly trackless wilderness which occupies 13,000 sq km of the north central part of the province, are a wildlife area comparable to the Brazilian Pantanal of Mato Grosso. Although plans for a national park are on hold, the marshes are a cornucopia of plant and animal species which deserve a visit despite difficult access.

Aquatic plants and grasses dominate the marsh vegetation, while trees are relatively few. The most notable wildlife species are reptiles such as the cayman, mammals such as the capybara and pampas and swamp deer, and some 280 species of birds. At the settlement of Colonia Pellegrini, on Laguna Iberá, it is possible to organise canoe trips into the marshes.

There are no hotels, but camping is possible on the site. The best place to purchase supplies is the town of Mercedes, 107 km south-east of Colonia Pellegrini.

Getting There & Away
Colonia Pellegrini, 353 km from Corrientes and 241 km from Paso de Los Libres, is the best centre for visiting the Esteros. There is regular public transportation between Paso de Los Libres and Corrientes which stops at Mercedes, where provincial Ruta 40 leads north-west to Colonia Pellegrini. The Urquiza railway between Buenos Aires and Corrientes also stops at Mercedes.

There is occasional truck transport

between Mercedes and Colonia Pellegrini, and it may be possible to hitch. Taxis with drivers can be hired, but Corrientes is the only place to hire a car without driver. For all-inclusive tours, contact Turismo Operativo Misionero at Junín 2472, Posadas (☎ 38373), or at Corrientes 753, Buenos Aires (☎ 393-3476).

PASO DE LOS LIBRES

Paso de Los Libres is a town of 5000 people on the Río Uruguay, about 700 km north of Buenos Aires and 370 km south of Posadas on national Ruta 14. It has the only international border crossing in the province, to the much larger Brazilian city of Uruguaiana on the opposite bank of the river. Brazilians come here to load up on trinkets.

Due to Brazilian influence, Paso de Los Libres is known as the Cradle of the Carnaval of Corrientes. Emigrants to the provincial capital established a carnival tradition there which, however, has weakened in recent years.

Orientation

Located on the west bank of the river, Paso del Los Libres has a standard rectangular grid, centred on the Plaza Independencia. The principal commercial street is Avenida Colón, a block away. Most points of interest are nearby, but the international bridge to Uruguaiana is about 10 blocks south-west.

Information

Tourist Office There is no tourist office in the town centre; for information, try the facilities at the entrance to the international bridge to Uruguaiana.

Money Alhec Tours, Avenida Colón 901 at Juan Sitja Min, will change cash but not travellers' cheques.

Post & Telecommunications The post office is at General Madariaga and Juan Sitja Min. Telecom is at General Madariaga 854, half a block off the Plaza. Collect calls overseas must be routed through Rosario and can be very time consuming.

Travel Agencies ACA is at the entrance to the international bridge.

Medical Services The hospital (☎ 21404) is on the Plaza España.

Bonpland's Tomb

Paso de Los Libres is the final resting place of Amado (also known as Aimé) Bonpland, the famous naturalist and travel companion of Alexander von Humboldt. Bonpland eventually settled in Corrientes, where he founded the province's first natural history museum.

The frequently visited tomb is in the Cementerio de la Santa Cruz, just beyond the bus station, about 10 blocks from the centre via Avenida San Martín. Ask the attendant for directions to 'El sabio Bonpland'.

Places to Stay

The cheapest place in town is *Residencial Colón Hotel*, at Avenida Colón 1065, which charges US$7 per person for a room with private bath. The shabby but comfortable *Hotel Buen Comfort* (☎ 21848), at Coronel López 1091, has rooms with bath and very welcome air-conditioning for US$12/18.

Getting There & Away

Air Aerolíneas Argentinas (☎ 21017) is at Juan Sitja Min 1118. There are three flights weekly to Buenos Aires with a stopover at Concordia. There is a larger airport on the Brazilian side of the border.

Bus The bus terminal (☎ 21608) is at Avenida San Martín and Santiago del Estero. Expreso Singer and Cruzero del Norte pass through Paso de Los Libres three times daily en route between Buenos Aires and Posadas.

There are daily buses to Paraná and Santa Fe, service daily to Rosario except Thursdays, and three daily to Posadas. Daily except Thursday, Paso de Los Libres is a stopover between Córdoba and Puerto Iguazú.

Provincial bus services run three times daily to Corrientes, twice daily to Goya,

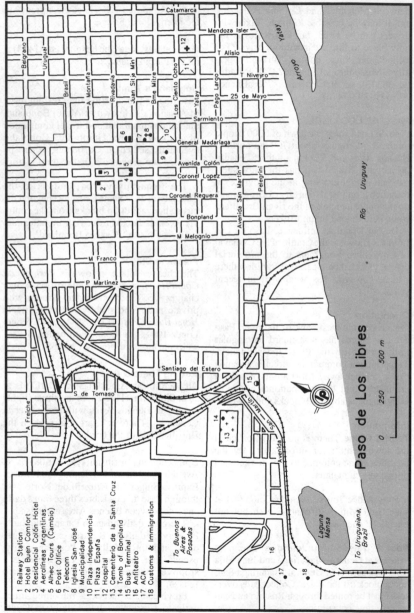

Paso de Los Libres

1 Railway Station
2 Hotel Buen Comfort
3 Residencial Colón Hotel
4 Aerolíneas Argentinas
5 Alhec Tours (Cambio)
6 Post Office
7 Telecom
8 Iglesia San José
9 Municipalidad
10 Plaza Independencia
11 Plaza España
12 Hospital
13 Cementerio de la Santa Cruz
14 Tomb of Bonpland
15 Bus Terminal
16 Anfiteatro
17 ACA
18 Customs & Immigration

twice daily to Santo Tomé via Yapeyú, and daily to Sauce via Curuzú Cuatiá.

Train The Urquiza railway connects Paso de Los Libres with Buenos Aires daily at 3.15 am, and with Posadas daily at 12.20 am.

YAPEYÚ

Yapeyú has two major claims to historical interest: it was the southernmost of the Jesuit missions, and the birthplace of Argentina's greatest national hero, General José de San Martín. It is also a charming riverside village of 1500 people which, at least out of season, may be the quietest place in Argentina.

Founded in 1626, Yapeyú once had a population of more than 8000 Guaraní Indians who tended as many as 80,000 cattle until the Jesuit expulsion in 1767. The Indians dispersed and the mission fell into ruins, but in 1778 San Martín was born in a modest house whose ruins still exist in a protected site. Many other houses are built of red sandstone blocks from the mission buildings.

Orientation

On the west bank of the Río Uruguay, Yapeyú is 55 km north of Paso de Los Libres, several km off national Ruta 14. Everything in town is within easy walking distance of the central plaza.

Information

Tourist Office The tourist office is just inside the portal at the entrance to town. The staff are helpful but have no maps and few brochures.

Museo de Cultura Jesuítica

This museum on the plaza, consisting of several modern kiosks built on the foundations of mission buildings, has an interesting photographic display which is a good introduction to the mission zone. A sundial and a few other mission relics are also here.

Casa de San Martín

In 1938 the Argentine government completed a pretentious temple to protect the modest birthplace of the country's greatest hero. The interior is covered with tributary plaques, including one from General and de facto President Jorge Rafael Videla, a convicted but pardoned Dirty War lifer, attesting to his 'most profound faith' in San Martín's ideals of liberty.

Museo Sanmartiniano

Next door to San Martín's birthplace, in a house dating from the Jesuit era, this museum contains a number of artefacts and documents from San Martín and his family. Opening hours are erratic.

Places to Stay & Eat

There is little accommodation in Yapeyú. The most reasonable place is the municipal campground near the river, where sites cost US$3, with hot showers. Insects can be abundant.

El Parador Yapeyú (☎ 93056), at the entrance to town, has bungalows for US$15/22 for singles/doubles. *Hotel Paraíso* is comparable.

Restaurant Bicentenario has well-prepared food, reasonable prices and extremely friendly and attentive service. There is an another adequate restaurant on the plaza.

Getting There & Away

The small bus station is two blocks south of the plaza. Services are similar to those to and from Paso de Los Libres.

SANTO TOMÉ

Another stop on the Jesuit mission circuit, Santo Tomé is 140 km north of Yapeyú. The **Museo Histórico Regional**, Navajas 844, is open Monday to Friday from 8 to 11 am and 5 to 7 pm. It also has a library.

There is an ACA hotel (☎ 20162), at Patricio Bertrán and Belgrano, but no formal campground; with permission from the municipality, you can camp in the plaza.

Misiones Province

On the map of Argentina, Misiones is the strategically important narrow peninsula surrounded by the ocean of Brazil and Paraguay. Its outstanding natural feature is the Iguazú Falls on the upper Río Paraná, one of the major natural attractions in all of South America, but the historic cultural landscape of ruined Jesuit missions also draws many visitors every year.

Unlike the rest of Argentine Mesopotamia, Misiones is mountainous. The Sierra Central, separating the watersheds of the two major rivers, reaches elevations up to 800 metres, although it rarely exceeds 500 metres. The natural vegetation is mostly subtropical forest, although there remain some large stands of native Araucaria pines.

Economically, Misiones is the country's largest producer of *yerba mate*, the staple drink of Argentines and of many Uruguayans, Paraguayans and Brazilians. Most yerba plantations are just east of the provincial capital of Posadas. The province's central uplands also support large tea plantations. In recent years forestry has become important, with large plantations of northern hemisphere pines replacing the native Araucarias.

History

Misiones is best known for the Jesuit settlements *(reducciones* or *congregaciones)* for which the province is named. From 1607, after finding the nomadic Indians of the Chaco poor candidates for missionary instruction, the Jesuits established 30 missions among the semisedentary Guaraní in the upper Paraná, in present-day Argentina, Brazil and Paraguay. Perhaps as many as 100,000 Indians lived in these settlements, which resembled other Spanish municipalities but operated with a political and economic independence the envy of other Iberian settlers, who resented the missions' wealth and their monopoly on Indian labour which made that wealth possible. The missions competed with secular producers in the cultivation and sale of *yerba mate*, the region's only important commodity.

The conflict between the Jesuits and other Iberians, both Spanish and Portuguese, is the background for the popular film *The Mission*. Non-Jesuit settlers in the region, where the encomienda was never as important as elsewhere in colonial America, correctly saw that they could never effectively match the Jesuits unless they could persuade the Spanish crown to grant them Indian labour. The Jesuits resisted these efforts politically and even militarily, but their success eventually undermined their own position; Spanish concerns that they were becoming an autonomous state-within-a-state resulted in their expulsion from Spanish America in 1767.

The Jesuits' high degree of organisation is apparent in ruins such as San Ignacio Miní, with its enormous plaza, imposing church and extensive outbuildings. Unlike most secular Spaniards and many other monastic orders, they took seriously their obligation to instruct indigenous peoples in the Spanish language and Catholic religion, but they also taught music, literature and the arts. Much of the elaborate sandstone statuary which embellishes the Jesuit ruins is the work of indigenous sculptors.

Long before expulsion, the missions had begun to suffer *malocas* (Portuguese slave raids) and other setbacks – despite their good intentions, the Jesuits' concentration of Indians in fixed settlements made them more vulnerable to epidemics like smallpox. In the political vacuum after 1767 the mission communities disintegrated rapidly and much of the area lapsed into virtual wilderness. Densely forested areas became a refuge for Indians lacking the protection of the missions but unwilling to submit to the demands of secular Spaniards.

During the 19th century Argentina, Brazil and Paraguay contested the territory, but after the War of the Triple Alliance (1865-70) between Paraguay, on the one hand, and Argentina, Uruguay and Brazil on the other, Argentina took definitive control. Precise boundaries were not

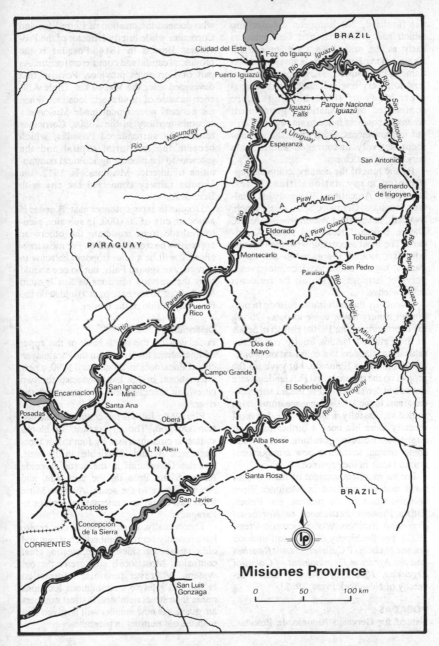

Misiones Province

0   50   100 km

yet finalised, but European colonisation which had proceeded from Corrientes as early as the mid-1850s soon intensified. Exploitation of wild *yerba mate* spurred settlement, but resulted in large concessions of land to a very few individuals and companies. Many of these holdings were confiscated by the national government when their owners failed to survey and carry out improvements. Soon after, the government actively encouraged small-scale agricultural settlement.

By the turn of the century, colonists represented many nationalities: Poles, Brazilians, Argentines, Paraguayans, Italians, Russians, Germans, Spaniards, French, Swedish, unspecified Asians, Swiss, Arabs, Danes, British, Greeks and North Americans. The most successful were the German colonists around Eldorado on the upper Paraná, but the entire province preserves a polyglot heritage which all its residents acknowledge.

Potentially the most ironic episode in provincial history never came to pass. During the depression of the 1930s, British officials in the Falkland Islands briefly considered relocating Islanders to a colonisation project at Victoria, near Eldorado, but gave up the project on the rationale that Falklanders were not suited for settlement in humid subtropical areas. In the 1950s, Japanese immigrants settled successfully in the province, but most recently there has been a further influx of Brazilians. Besides agriculture, forestry and some mining, tourism is now a major economic factor in the province.

For an excellent account of the environment and colonisation in Misiones from colonial times to the present, see Robert Eidt's *Pioneer Settlement in Northeast Argentina* (University of Wisconsin Press, 1971). For the history of the Jesuit mission era, see Nicholas P Cushner's *Jesuit Ranches and the Agrarian Development of Colonial Argentina, 1650-1767* (Albany State University of New York Press, 1982).

POSADAS

Named for Gervasio Antonio de Posadas, who decreed the creation of Entre Ríos and Corrientes while briefly Director of the Provincias Unidas in 1814, Posadas is the provincial capital and commercial centre. As part of Corrientes province, Posadas first developed after the War of the Triple Alliance because of its strategic location. When the national government made Misiones a separate territory in the 1880s, Corrientes reluctantly surrendered Posadas, which became the territorial capital and the gateway to the pioneer agricultural communities of interior Misiones. In 1912, the Urquiza railway connected the city with Buenos Aires.

Despite its recent pioneer past, Posadas is a modern city of 200,000. In summer, plentiful shade trees moderate the otherwise oppressive heat and humidity. For most travellers, it will be a brief stopover en route to Paraguay or Iguazú Falls, but no one should miss the restored missions at San Ignacio Miní, about 50 km east, or at Trinidad on the Paraguayan side of the border.

Orientation

Posadas is on the south bank of the upper Paraná, across the river from the Paraguayan city of Encarnación. Since April 1990, a new international bridge has connected the two cities, but launches still operate across the river.

Plaza 9 de Julio is the centre of Posadas' standard grid. The city centre, 14 blocks square, is circumscribed by four major thoroughfares: Avenida Corrientes in the west, Avenida Guaycurarí in the north, Avenida Roque Sáenz Peña on the east side, and Avenida Mitre to the south. Avenida Mitre leads east to the new international bridge to Paraguay.

Theoretically, all streets in the city centre have recently been renumbered, but new and old systems exist side-by-side, creating great confusion. Most locals still prefer the old system. Wherever possible, information below will refer to unambiguous locations rather than street numbers. If street numbers are given, the new number will be given first with the old number in parentheses.

Information

Tourist Office The exceptionally helpful and well-informed tourist office (☎ 30504) is on Colón between Córdoba and La Rioja. It has numerous maps and brochures, and is open weekdays from 6.30 am to 12.30 pm, and from 2 to 8 pm. Holiday and weekend hours are 8 am to noon and 4 to 8 pm.

Money You can change cash at Banco de la Nación, on Avenida Azara between Bolívar and Córdoba, or at Banco de la Provincia, corner of Avenida Azara and Bolívar. Turismo Posadas, on Colón just south of the plaza, and Cambio Mazza, on Bolívar between San Lorenzo and Colón, will change travellers' cheques. Hours are 8 am to noon and 3.30 to 7.30 pm weekdays, 8 am to noon on Saturdays.

Post & Telecommunications The post office is at Bolívar and Ayacucho. Telecom is at Colón and Santa Fe, but there are additional long-distance telephones on Junín between Bolívar and Córdoba, open from 7 am to midnight.

Foreign Consulates Paraguay has a consulate (☎ 27421) on San Lorenzo between Santa Fe and Sarmiento, open weekdays from 8 am to noon. It's friendly and has a few brochures and basic maps.

Brazil has a consulate (☎ 2601) at Mitre 1242 (631), near the entrance to the Encarnación bridge. If you need a visa, it offers same-day service and does not insist on a photograph. Hours are weekdays 9 am to 1 pm and 4 to 6.30 pm.

Travel Agencies ACA (☎ 36955) is at Córdoba and Colón. To arrange tours to nearby sights, try Turismo Operativo Misionero (☎ 38373), on Junín between Tucumán and Santiago del Estero.

Bookshops Librería Ediciones Montoya, on the corner of La Rioja and Ayacucho, concentrates on natural sciences, prehistory, history and the literature of the province.

Medical Services The regional hospital is about one km south of the centre, at Avenida Torres and Avenida Cabred.

Museo de Ciencias Naturales e Históricas

This museum, on San Luis between Córdoba and La Rioja, is very worthwhile. Its natural history section focuses on invertebrates, vertebrates, and the geology and mineralogy of the province, while its historical section stresses prehistory, the Jesuit missions and modern colonisation. In addition, it has an excellent serpentarium, an aviary and an aquarium. Normal hours are Tuesday to Friday from 8 am to noon and 3 to 7 pm, weekends 9 am to noon. During winter holidays, hours are 9 am to noon and 3 to 8 pm, daily except Monday. Every July morning at 10 am, there is a demonstration of venom extraction.

Museo Regional de Posadas

At the north end of Alberdi near Parque República do Paraguay, this museum has an interesting collection of stuffed natural history specimens, ethnographic artefacts and historical relics.

Places to Stay – bottom end

Camping The campground at the Balneario Municipal on the river is cramped, noisy and expensive at US$4 per person. It's not recommended, but there is no nearby alternative.

Residenciales & Hotels There is a wide selection of relatively inexpensive accommodation in Posadas. One popular place is *Residencial Misiones* (☎ 30133), on Avenida Azara between La Rioja and Córdoba, where singles/doubles with private bath are US$8/15. It's very friendly, with an attractive patio. The *Savoy Hotel* (☎ 24430), on the corner of Colón and Sarmiento, has rooms at US$10/17 and a gigantic adjacent billiard hall which is open 24 hours if the street noise gives you insomnia.

Other budget recommendations include *Hotel Familiar* (☎ 24113), near the Expreso

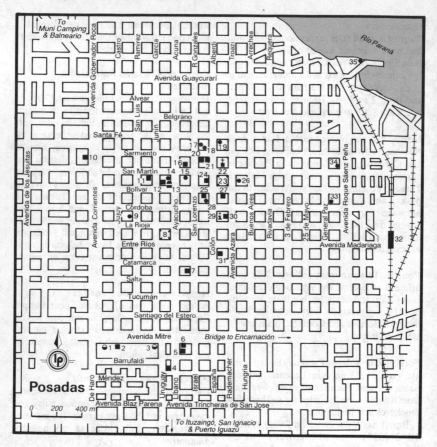

Posadas

0 200 400 m

Singer bus terminal; *Hotel Horianski* (☎ 22673) at Avenida Mitre and Líbano (where the owner will change money in a pinch); *Residencial Nagel* (☎ 25656) at Méndez and Uruguay; and the *Plaza Hotel* on San Martín between San Lorenzo and Ayacucho. You can only guess what goes on at the forbidding *Pensión Argentina*, on Sarmiento near San Lorenzo.

Places to Stay – middle

Visually pleasant but distinctly unfriendly is *Residencial Colón* (☎ 25085), on Colón between Entre Ríos and Catamarca, where

singles with bath are US$14. Despite its impersonal appearance, the high-rise *Hotel de Turismo Posadas* (☎ 37401), at Bolívar and Junín, is much friendlier and its balconies have excellent river views. *City Hotel* (☎ 33901), on Colón opposite the main plaza, is comparable. *Gran Hotel Misiones* (☎ 22777), Líbano at Barrufaldi near the bus terminal, also has a restaurant.

Places to Stay – top end

Hotel Continental (☎ 38966), on Bolívar opposite the plaza, and *Hotel Canciller* (☎ 30401), at Junín and San Martín, have

■	PLACES TO STAY
2	Hotel Familiar
4	Residencial Nagel
5	Gran Hotel Misiones
6	Hotel Horianski
7	Hotel Libertador
10	Residencial Marlis
11	Hotel Canciller
12	Hotel de Turismo Posadas
16	Plaza Hotel
20	Pension Argentina
21	Savoy Hotel
24	City Hotel
25	Posadas Hotel
27	Hotel Continental
30	Residencial Misiones
31	Residencial Colón

	OTHER
1	Expreso Singer Terminal
3	Main Bus Station
8	Plaza San Martín
9	Museo de Ciencias Naturales e Históricas
13	Post Office
14	Austral
15	Aerolíneas Argentinas
17	Paraguayan Consulate
18	Teatro El Desván
19	Telecom
22	Cathedral
23	Plaza 9 de Julio
26	Casa de Gobierno
28	ACA
29	Tourist Office
32	Train Station
33	Museo Argueológico
34	Municipal Market
35	Launches to Paraguay

rooms with private bath for US$25/35. At the top-of-the-line *Posadas Hotel* (☎ 30801), on Bolívar between Colón and San Lorenzo, rooms with bath and breakfast are US$40/50. *Hotel Libertador* (☎ 36901), on San Lorenzo between Catamarca and Salta, offers similar prices and services.

Places to Eat

Parrillas are the standard, and there are several excellent ones. The spiffiest is *La*

Querencia on Bolívar, across from the plaza. *El Tropezón*, on San Martín between Colón and San Lorenzo, is in the same price range.

La Gran Alegría, a sidewalk pizzería with good lager beer on Colón just north of the plaza, is worth a visit. There are many interchangeable, inexpensive places along San Lorenzo west of the plaza.

Entertainment

Theatre Teatro El Desván, a provincial theatre company on Sarmiento between Colón and San Lorenzo, offers works by major Spanish-language playwrights such as García Lorca. There is also a children's theatre.

Things to Buy

Posadas has a good selection of artisanal products. Try La Barraca, next door to Teatro El Desván, or El Payé, around the corner on Colón, where there is a good selection of *mate* paraphernalia (gourds and bombillas), basketry, wood carvings and ceramics. La Casa de Mendoza, next door to the tourist office at Colón and La Rioja, sells produce of the Cuyo region, including wines and dried and canned fruits.

Getting There & Away

Air Aerolíneas Argentinas (☎ 22036), on San Martín between Ayacucho and San Lorenzo, has daily flights to and from Buenos Aires, but there is no longer any service to Puerto Iguazú.

Austral (☎ 32889), on the corner of Ayacucho and San Martín, flies daily except Sunday between Posadas and Buenos Aires, and weekdays to Puerto Iguazú and back.

Bus The main bus terminal is at Avenida Mitre and Uruguay, but Tigre and Expreso Singer have a separate terminal three blocks west. There are excellent regional and long-distance services.

Expreso Singer has a daily service to Buenos Aires (US$45) and intermediate points, and to Córdoba and Asunción. To Puerto Iguazú, Martignoni, COTAL and Tigre take 5½ hours on the express but much longer on the local (stopping) bus. Fares are about US$15. Tigre's earliest reasonable bus to San Ignacio Miní leaves at 6.10 am, then hourly thereafter.

Ciudad de Posadas has buses to Corrientes and Resistencia, with connections across the Chaco to north-western Argentina.

Since the opening of the international bridge, there are buses from downtown Posadas to Encarnación, Paraguay, every 15 minutes for US$1. Including border formalities, the trip can take an hour, but is often quicker.

Train There are daily trains between Posadas and Lacroze Station in Buenos Aires. The station (☎ 24602) is on Avenida Madariaga, at the east end of Entre Ríos.

Boat Launches across the Paraná to Encarnación continue to operate despite the new bridge, although they will probably cease when the reservoir behind Yacyretá dam floods the low-lying parts of the two cities. For the moment, they leave from the dock at the east end of Avenida Guaycurarí.

Car Rental There are several car rental agencies. Try Avis (☎ 23483), across from ACA at Córdoba and Colón, or A1 (☎ 36901), on San Lorenzo between Catamarca and Salta.

Getting Around
To/From the Airport Both Aerolíneas Argentinas and Austral have their own minibuses to the airport, but the No 8 bus from Plaza San Martín also goes there.

AROUND POSADAS
Posadas is more a stopover than a destination, but it has some worthwhile sights which make either feasible daytrips or overnights. The Jesuit missions, especially San Ignacio Miní, are a colourful historical attraction, and the Yacyretá hydroelectric project is a different sort of monument.

Santa Ana
Buses from Posadas will drop you at the clearly marked turnoff to the ruins at Santa Ana (founded 1637), which are mostly covered by the luxuriant rain forest and strangler figs, but the outlines of settlement are clear. The walk from the junction is about one km.

Loreto
Buses from Posadas will also stop here, but the distance from the highway to the ruins is greater. The mission was founded in 1632.

Yacyretá Dam
A vivid lesson in foreign debt, this gigantic hydroelectric project is actually in Corrientes province near the town of Ituzaingó, but is more accessible from Posadas. When and if completed, it will form a monstrous reservoir of 1800 sq km which will submerge the Paraná more than 200 km upstream, including low-lying areas of Posadas and Encarnación, requiring the relocation of nearly 40,000 people. Presumably it will provide energy for industrial development in Argentina's northern provinces, and at capacity it will increase Argentine and Paraguayan electricity supplies by 50%.

Argentine President Carlos Menem himself has called the project, first planned in 1973 during Juan Perón's last government, 'a monument to corruption' which may cost eight times the original estimate of US$1.5 billion (thousand million). Despite Menem's publicly stated intention of stopping the project, his government has solicited further loans to continue construction.

At Ituzaingó, 1½ hours from Posadas by bus, the Argentine-Paraguayan Entidad Binacional Yacyretá maintains a public relations office which tries to put this boondoggle in the best possible light. They offer free tours at 9, 10 and 11 am, and at 3.30 and 4.30 pm. Tours leave from the public relations office, at Entre Ríos and Ingeniero Roque Carranza, where there is also a museum with artefacts unearthed in the process of construction and a scale model of the project. You can also see the enormous city built to house the dam workers. The

The Jesuit Missions

After the Spaniards realised that America was not a storehouse of precious metals, they sought their wealth through the encomienda, a grant of native labour which also assigned them the responsibility of cathechising 'their' Indians and teaching them Spanish. Although Spaniards rarely lived up to their part of the bargain, in settled, densely populated areas such as Mexico and Peru, the encomienda successfully overcame problems of economic organisation, at least until the Indians died out from smallpox and other introduced diseases. But where the Indians were less sedentary and their political organisation less centralised, the encomienda was ineffective. This was the case on the upper Paraná of Paraguay and Argentina, where Spanish encomenderos controlled only very small amounts of Indian labour.

Into this setting stepped the Jesuit order, whose history differed greatly from the mendicant orders of the Middle Ages. Unhindered by vows of poverty and with a genius for organisation, the Jesuits brought about a major political, economic and cultural transformation among the semisedentary Guaraní. Their remarkable success also aroused envy and intrigue against them.

The Jesuits began their activities in eastern Paraguay, an area largely overlooked by secular Spaniards, in 1607. Sixteen of the 30 missions which operated in the 18th century were in present-day Argentina, mostly in Misiones but a few in Corrientes, while the remainder were equally distributed between modern Paraguay and Brazil. Their organisational principle was reducción or congregación, the common Spanish practice which concentrated the Indians, breaking their nomadic habits and reorganising their political structure. Because the area was so isolated, the Jesuits had little competition until the success of their enterprise became apparent.

The first challenge to the Jesuits came from the Portuguese slave raiders of São Paulo, known as *paulistas* or *bandeirantes*. Only two decades after their establishment, 11 of the first 13 missions were destroyed and their native inhabitants abducted. The Jesuits responded by moving operations westward and raising an army to repel any further incursions. The evacuation of the missions was an epic event as the Jesuits and Indians rafted down the Paraná to the precipitous Guairá Falls (now inundated by the Brazilian-Paraguayan Itaipú dam), descended to their base, and built new rafts to continue the journey. Thousands of Indians perished, but the Jesuits successfully re-established themselves at new sites.

Slavers were not the only menace. Some local caciques (chiefs) resented the Jesuit conversion of their peoples, while the physical concentration of the Indians accelerated the spread of European diseases to which they had little natural immunity. Between 1717 and 1719, for example, an epidemic killed off nearly a sixth of the mission population. Travel between missions spread the contagion. In succeeding decades, discontent among secular Spaniards *(comuneros)* in Corrientes led to invasions just as devastating as those of the bandeirantes. Eventually, these disturbances and exaggerated rumours of Jesuit intrigue resulted in the order's expulsion in 1767.

The physical organisation of the Jesuit missions was nearly identical to that of Spanish secular municipalities. Spanish colonial ordinances had dictated the Roman grid system based upon a central square from which all streets extended at right angles. The Jesuits imitated this form but usually enclosed the plaza with buildings whose function was religious rather than secular – the church, priests' quarters and classrooms. This pattern is obvious in the plan of San Ignacio Miní, the best restored of the Argentine missions. Often earthworks or a trench surrounded the settlement for purposes of defence.

The mission economy was largely agricultural and diversified. The Indians raised their own subsistence crops (maize, sweet potatoes and cassava) but also laboured on communal fields. *Yerba mate* was the most important plantation crop, but cotton, citrus and tobacco were also important. Within the settlement itself, intensive vegetable gardening yielded carrots, tomatoes, beans, peas, radishes and beets. Outside the settlement, native herders tended the mission's numerous livestock. When the Jesuits were expelled San Ignacio Miní had a human population of 3200 but possessed ten times that many cattle and more than twice that many sheep and goats.

Life on the reducción was probably less idyllic than portrayed in *The Mission*, but the labour was certainly less odious than elsewhere. The Jesuits closely regulated many aspects of everyday life such as education and dress, but their exuberant approach to work made mission residence sufficiently attractive that many Indians willingly chose it over the grim certainties of the encomienda. With the aid of skilled German priests, the Guaraní learned crafts and trades such as weaving, baking, carpentry, cabinet-making and even the building of musical instruments. Unfortunately, these skills served them little in the post-mission world. ∎

guides are well-rehearsed, but the bus rarely slows and never stops for photographs.

Upon completion, the highway across the dam will connect Ituzaingó with the Paraguayan city of Ayolas in a new border crossing.

SAN IGNACIO & SAN IGNACIO MINÍ

You can visit the ruins of San Ignacio Miní on a day trip from Posadas, but lodging in the appealing village of San Ignacio will give you more time to explore. San Ignacio is 56 km east of Posadas via national Ruta 12.

From the junction of Ruta 12, the broad Avenida Sarmiento leads about one km to Calle Rivadavia, which leads four blocks east to the ruins.

There are other things to see besides the ruins, including the house of Uruguayan writer Horacio Quiroga and the provincial museum. The town is very small and everything is within easy walking distance.

San Ignacio Guazú, founded in 1609 but abandoned after repeated attacks by the bandeirantes, was the forerunner of San Ignacio Miní, which was founded in 1632 on the Río Yabebiry and later shifted a short distance away. At its peak, in 1733, it had an Indian population of nearly 4000. Its ruins, rediscovered in 1897 and restored after 1943, are among the most impressive in the region, although Trinidad and Jesús on the Paraguayan side of the river have more imposing sites.

San Ignacio's architecture belongs to a style known as 'Guaraní baroque'. Designed by the Italian Jesuit architect Juan Brasanelli, the enormous red sandstone church, 74 metres long and 24 metres wide with walls two metres thick at their base, was the focus of the settlement. Adjacent to the tile-roofed church, which was embellished with bas-relief sculptures by Guaraní artisans, were the cemetery and the priests' cloisters. In the same complex were classrooms, a kitchen, dining room and workshops. On all sides of the Plaza de Armas were the Indians' living quarters.

Centro de Interpretación San Ignacio

This interesting building has been closed for repairs since late 1990, but may merit a visit when it reopens.

Museo Provincial Miguel Nadasdy

On Avenida Sarmiento near the turnoff to the

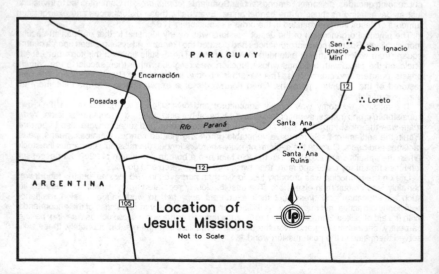

Location of
Jesuit Missions
Not to Scale

ruins, this museum displays the archaeological and ethnological collections of a dedicated Romanian immigrant. Focus on the exhibits, which include stone tools, a complete dugout canoe and 19th-century weapons, and try to overlook the caretaker's rather bizarre theories of local prehistory. Opening hours are 7.30 am to noon and 3.30 to 7 pm daily.

Casa de Horacio Quiroga
Uruguayan-born of Argentine parents, Quiroga was a poet and novelist who also dabbled in other activities – he took some of the earliest photographs of the rediscovered ruins at San Ignacio and was also an unsuccessful cotton farmer in the Chaco. He lived in San Ignacio from 1910-17, when his wife committed suicide. The house is open daily from 8.30 am to 7.30 pm.

Places to Stay & Eat
Camping At the free site just beyond the entrance to the ruins, there are no sanitary facilities and your sleep may be disturbed by the urchins who hang out there. Try instead

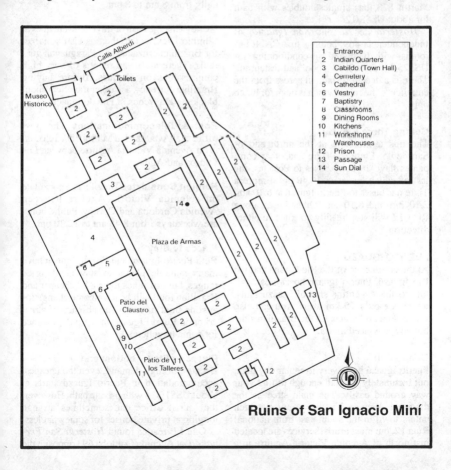

1	Entrance
2	Indian Quarters
3	Cabildo (Town Hall)
4	Cemetery
5	Cathedral
6	Vestry
7	Baptistry
8	Classrooms
9	Dining Rooms
10	Kitchens
11	Workshops/ Warehouses
12	Prison
13	Passage
14	Sun Dial

Ruins of San Ignacio Miní

Hospedaje Los Salpeterer (see below), where two can pitch a tent on the grounds for US$3.

Hospedajes, Hosterías & Hotels There are several reasonable places to stay in San Ignacio. The cheapest is the German-run *Hospedaje Los Salpeterer* at Sarmiento and Centenario, a short walk from the bus terminal. It has rooms with shared bath for US$4 per person. Another possibility is *Hospedaje El Descanso*, a bit farther from the ruins at Pellegrini 270. *Hotel San Ignacio*, San Martín 823, has singles/doubles with bath for about US$8/12.

Hostería de Turismo San Ignacio, at Independencia 469, belongs to ACA. It has rooms with bath and air-conditioning for US$25/30, as well as a pool and restaurant. There is a decent restaurant across from the entrance to the ruins, which is open for lunch only.

Getting There & Away
The bus terminal is at the north end of Sarmiento. Empresa Tigre and other companies have 26 daily buses to Posadas, the last of which leaves at 10.40 pm. Empresa Tigre has buses to Puerto Iguazú at 6.10 am, 2.10 pm and 8.10 pm. Other buses along Ruta 12 will stop readily en route in either direction.

PUERTO IGUAZÚ
At the confluence of the Río Paraná and the Río Iguazú, Puerto Iguazú hosts most visitors to the Argentine side of Iguazú Falls, which are only 15 km away. You can also stay at Foz do Iguaçu, on the Brazilian side, but you may need a visa.

Orientation
Puerto Iguazú has a very irregular city plan, but fortunately is small enough to find your way around easily. The main street is the diagonal Avenida Victoria Aguirre, which enters town in the south-east from national Ruta 12, but most tourist services are located just north of Avenida Victoria Aguirre in a rabbit warren of streets which cross each other at odd angles.

From the Hito Argentino, at the confluence of the river at the end of Avenida Tres Fronteras, you can see both Brazil and Paraguay. (The Hito Argentino is the Argentine landmark; all three countries have a landmark on their side of the Paraná and Iguazú river junction.)

Information
Tourist Office The tourist office (☎ 20800), at Avenida Victoria Aguirre 396, is open daily from 8 am to 8 pm.

Money Change cash or travellers' cheques at Cambio Dick, where there is also a market for Brazilian cruzados and Paraguayan guaranis. There are some reports of very high commissions on cheques. Before buying Brazilian currency, ask other travellers about black market trends in Foz do Iguaçu.

Post & Telecommunications The post office is at Avenida San Martín 780. Telecom is on Avenida Victoria Aguirre between Los Cedros and Aguay.

Foreign Consulates Brazil has a consulate on Avenida Victoria Aguirre between Avenida Córdoba and Curupy. Public hours are weekdays from 8.45 am to 12.30 pm.

Places to Stay
Both Puerto Iguazú and Foz do Iguaçu have many suitable places to stay in all price ranges, but Foz tends to be a bit cheaper and Brazilian food will be a welcome change for anyone tired of beef. The absence of street crime in Puerto Iguazú may tip the balance for some travellers.

Places to Stay – bottom end
Because of high demand, even the cheapest accommodation in Puerto Iguazú starts at about US$10/14 with private bath. However, the tourist office can sometimes arrange lodging at private houses for somewhat less.

One LP reader found *Hostería San Fernando*, at Avenida Córdoba 693 opposite the bus terminal, more convenient than clean, with real mosquito problems (which is virtually universal in Puerto Iguazú). *Residencial Arco Iris* (☎ 20236) at Curupy 152 is popular with travellers. Others in this category include *Residencial Iguazú* at Bonpland 285, and *Residencial Paquita* at Avenida Córdoba 731. *Residencial Cataratas* (☎ 20610) at Uruguay 251 is probably a good choice. One LP correspondent called *Hotel King* (☎ 20917) at Avenida Victoria Aguirre 916, 'great value', with its attractive grounds and a swimming pool.

Residencial Río Selva (☎ 20592) at Perito Moreno 333 is slightly dearer, as is *Hotel Paraná* (☎ 20399) at Brasil 367, a noisy street. *Residencial Gloria* (☎ 20323) at Uruguay 344 is a better bargain. *La Cabaña* (☎ 20564) is farther out, on Avenida Tres Fronteras 434 at Urquiza, and is probably quieter. Another inexpensive choice is *Hotel Misiones* (☎ 20917), at Avenida Victoria Aguirre 916 near Avenida Brasil.

Places to Stay – middle
Residencial Tierra Colorada (☎ 20649), at El Oro 265, charges US$15/20 for rooms with private bath. Perhaps the best deal in this category is the comparably priced *Hostería Los Helechos* (☎ 20338) on Almirante near Fray Luis Beltrán.

Comparable but somewhat costlier are *Hotel Turismo Iguazú* (☎ 20154) at Paraguay 372, *Hotel Alexander* (☎ 20249) at Avenida Córdoba 665, and the perennial favourite *Hotel Saint George* (☎ 20633), at Córdoba 745, which includes breakfast; it also has a swimming pool. The declining *Hotel Libertador* (☎ 20758) at Bonpland 475 has slipped from the top-end category it probably once occupied. Rates are US$30/40.

Places to Stay – top end
For in-town luxury, go to *Hotel Esturión* (☎ 20020), at Avenida Tres Fronteras 650, where singles cost US$80. For just a little more, you can indulge yourself at the hideously misplaced *Hotel Internacional Iguazú*, near the visitor centre at Parque Nacional Iguazú, a short walking distance from the falls themselves. For reservations, write to them at Avenida Eduardo Madero 1020 P B, 1106 Buenos Aires, Argentina.

Places to Eat
There are many places to eat in Puerto Iguazú, but there is also rapid turnover. For cheap eats, walk around the triangle formed by Avenida Brasil, Perito Moreno, and Ingeniero Eppens.

La Estancia, a recommended parrilla at the bus terminal, is now known as *Toma's*. Another good parrilla is *Charo* at Avenida Córdoba 106. There are wildly contradictory opinions of *Restaurant Saint George* at Avenida Córdoba 745, which one traveller praised as a 'superb French restaurant' with especially good surubí (local river fish), while another indignant LP correspondent called it 'the only seriously bad restaurant we encountered', which served instant coffee and chocolate mousse.

Getting There & Away
Air Aerolíneas Argentinas (☎ 20237), at Brasil 404, has frequent service to Buenos Aires and daily international service to and from São Paulo. Austral (☎ 20144), at Avenida Victoria Aguirre 272, also has frequent flights to Buenos Aires with intermediate stops. If you are coming from Brazil, flights to Foz do Iguaçu airport will be cheaper than international flights.

Bus The bus terminal is at Avenidas Córdoba and Misiones. The major companies, with services to and from Posadas, are Martignoni, COTAL, Empresa Iguazú and Empresa Tigre. Expreso Singer has direct service to Buenos Aires for US$60.

There are provincial services to the sierra immigrant town of Oberá with Empresa Capital del Monte.

Car Rental Try Avis (☎ 20020) at the Hotel Esturión, Avenida Tres Fronteras 650, or A1 (☎ 20748) at the Hotel Internacional Iguazú.

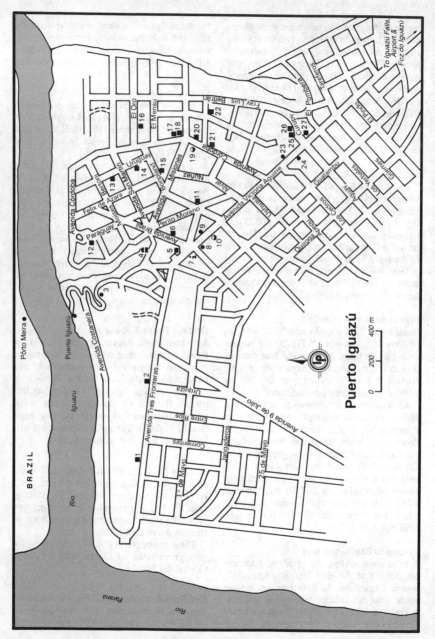

Puerto Iguazú

Getting Around

To/From the Airport Turismo Caracol's airport bus charges US$6 per person for a very short trip; you can do it more cheaply by sharing a cab with several other people.

Bus Buses to Parque Nacional Iguazú leave from Avenida Victoria Aguirre between Brasil and Bonpland. If you catch an early one, you can avoid the hordes of tour buses which swarm around the falls about 11 am, when noisy Brazilian helicopters also begin their flights.

PARQUE NACIONAL IGUAZÚ

Near the visitor centre at Parque Nacional Iguazú, a plaque credits Alvar Nuñez Cabeza de Vaca with discovery of the awesome Iguazú Falls in 1541, but he was at best the first European to view them. For the Guaraní Indians of the region and their predecessors, these impressive falls had been the source of legend for millennia.

According to Guaraní legend, the falls originated when an Indian warrior named Caroba incurred the wrath of a forest god by escaping down the river in a canoe with a young girl named Naipur, with whom the god had become infatuated. Enraged, the god caused the riverbed to collapse in front of the lovers, producing a line of precipitous falls over which Naipur fell and, at their base, turned into a rock. Caroba survived as a tree overlooking his fallen lover.

The geological origins of the falls are simpler and more prosaic. In southern Brazil, the Río Iguazú passes over a basaltic plateau which ends abruptly just east of the confluence with the Río Paraná. Where the lava flow stopped, at least 5000 cubic metres of water per second plunges more than 70 metres into the sedimentary terrain below – during flood, the volume can be many times greater. Prior to reaching the falls, the river divides into many channels with hidden reefs, rocks and islands, which separate the many visually distinctive falls which together form the famous *cataratas*. The falls themselves are more than two km across.

You can see many of the falls up close via a system of *pasarelas* (catwalks) which offer unmatchable views. The most awesome is the semicircular *Garganta del Diablo* (Devil's Throat), a deafening and dampening but indispensable part of the experience.

Parque Nacional Iguazú occupies a total area of about 55,000 hectares, of which 6000 hectares constitute a Reserva Nacional which allows commercial development in the immediate area of the falls. Above the falls, the river itself is suitable for canoeing, kayaking and other water sports.

Other attractions are well worth seeing, including substantial areas of subtropical rain forest, with unique flora and fauna – there are thousands of species of insects, hundreds of species of birds, and many mammals and reptiles.

To Curitiba 650 km &
São Paulo 1050 km

BRAZIL

Aeropuerto de
Foz do Iguaçu

Itaipú
Dam

Foz do Iguaçu

Rio   Paraná

Rio   Iguazú

Iguazú Falls

Ciudad
del Este

Pòrto Meira

Puente Tancredo
Neves

Puerto Iguazú

PARAGUAY

ARGENTINA

To Asunción

Around Iguazú Falls
Not to Scale

To Posadas 300 km &
Buenos Aires

Iguazú Falls

Before seeing the falls themselves, have a quick look around the visitor centre, which has a small museum and, depending on the budget, information brochures. The tower near the visitor centre offers a good overall view, but walking around is the best way to see the falls. Plan your hikes before or after the midmorning influx of tour buses. At midday, you can take a break from the heat at the restaurant and confitería here.

Formerly, an interconnected series of catwalks led to all the falls from the visitor centre, but floods in 1983 destroyed a section and isolated those which go to Garganta del Diablo, the single most impressive cascade. You can still reach Garganta del Diablo by a good dirt road which goes to Ñandú, where there is a confitería and, a bit farther on, a rudimentary campground. Beyond the confitería, the road may not be passable to ordinary cars after heavy rain.

You can see most of the falls by roaming at will on the trails and catwalks around the visitor centre; descending to the river, you can take a launch across to Isla Grande San Martín for US$5 return. Although the trip takes only a few minutes, the island offers views not available elsewhere and does insulate you from the masses on the mainland. Swimming and picnicking are popular activities. After returning to the mainland, you can catch a bus or taxi to Ñandú, where another catwalk leads across the river to the Garganta del Diablo.

Of all the sights on earth, the Garganta del Diablo must come closest to the experience of sailing off the edge of the flat earth imagined by early European sailors. On three sides, the deafening cascade plunges to a murky destination; the vapour which soaks the viewer blurs the base of the falls. It is difficult to abandon a site of such menacing attraction, where you can still sense the awe which native peoples must have felt. Faced with this spectacle, early Spaniards showed only a practical indifference: Cabeza de Vaca reported that

...the current of the Yguazú was so strong that the canoes were carried furiously down the river, for near this spot there is a considerable fall, and the noise made by the water leaping down some high rocks into a chasm may be heard a great distance off, and the spray rises two spears high and more over the fall. It was necessary, therefore, to take the canoes out of the

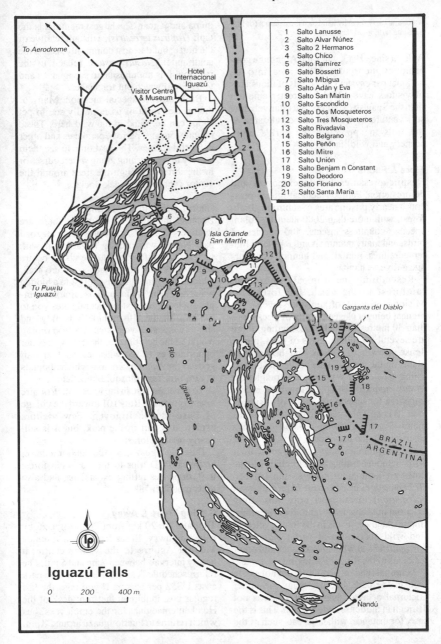

1	Salto Lanusse
2	Salto Alvar Núñez
3	Salto 2 Hermanos
4	Salto Chico
5	Salto Ramírez
6	Salto Bossetti
7	Salto Mbigua
8	Salto Adán y Eva
9	Salto San Martín
10	Salto Escondido
11	Salto Dos Mosqueteros
12	Salto Tres Mosqueteros
13	Salto Rivadavia
14	Salto Belgrano
15	Salto Peñón
16	Salto Mitre
17	Salto Unión
18	Salto Benjam n Constant
19	Salto Deodoro
20	Salto Floriano
21	Salto Santa María

To Aerodrome

Hotel Internacional Iguazú

Visitor Centre & Museum

Isla Grande San Martín

Tu Puerto Iguazú

Río Iguazú

Garganta del Diablo

BRAZIL
ARGENTINA

Nandú

Iguazú Falls

0   200   400 m

water and carry them by hand past the cataract for half a league with great labour...

At least since 1943, when the Argentine government incorporated the area into its national park system, hundreds of thousands of visitors have felt much greater emotion than the Spanish explorers, but relatively few still venture beyond the immediate area of the falls to appreciate the park's other scenery and wildlife.

Flora & Fauna
Despite pressures for development and deforestation, Parque Nacional Iguazú presents a nearly pristine area of subtropical rain forest, with more than 2000 identified plant species, countless insects, 400 species of birds, and many mammals and reptiles. High temperatures, rainfall and humidity encourage a diverse habitat.

Resembling the tropical Amazonian rainforest to the north, the forests of Misiones consist of multiple levels, the highest being a closed canopy of trees more than 30 metres in height. Descending, there are several additional levels of trees, plus a dense growth of shrubs and herbaceous plants on the ground. One of the most interesting species is the *guapoy* or strangler fig *(Ficus monckii)*, an epiphyte which uses a large tree for support until it finally asphyxiates its host. This species covers the ruins of many abandoned Jesuit mission buildings elsewhere in the province.

Other epiphytes take advantage of their hosts without harming them. Orchids use the limbs of large trees such as the lapacho *(Tabebuia ipe)* or *palo rosa (Aspidosperma polyneuron)* for support only, absorbing essential nutrients from rainfall or the atmosphere. At lower levels in the forest, you will find wild specimens of *yerba mate (Ilex paraguariensis)* which Argentines and other residents of the River Plate region use for tea.

Mammals and other wildlife are not easily seen in the park, because many are either nocturnal or avoid humans – which is not difficult in the dense undergrowth. This is the case, for instance, with large cats such as the puma and jaguar. The largest mammal is the tapir *(Tapirus terrestris)*, a distant relative of the horse, but the most commonly seen is the coatimundi *(Nasua nasua)*, related to the raccoon. It is not unusual to see iguanas and you should watch out for snakes.

Birds deserve special mention. Many of the species most of us normally see in pet shops can be found in the wild here. These include toucans, parrots, parakeets and other colourful species. The best time to see them is early in the morning along watercourses or in the forest, although the trees around the visitor centre do not lack flocks.

Hiking, Bicycling & Rafting
Because the forest is so dense, there are relatively few trails, but walks along the road past Ñandú will usually reward you with views of wildlife. Close to the visitor centre is the park service's Macuco nature trail, which leads through dense forest to a hidden waterfall. The main trail is almost completely level, but a steep lateral takes you to the base of the falls, which is muddy and slippery – watch your step. Early morning would be the best time for the trip, with better opportunities to see wildlife. Another trail goes to the *bañado*, a marsh which abounds in bird life. Take mosquito repellent.

To get elsewhere in the forest, hitch or hire a car to go out on Ruta 101 toward the village of Bernardo de Irigoyen. Few visitors explore this part of the park, but it is still nearly pristine forest.

Floating Iguazú, at the visitor centre, arranges 4WD trips to the Yacaratia forest trail, organises rafting excursions, and also rents mountain bikes.

Getting There & Away
The falls are 20 km from Puerto Iguazú by paved highway. Buses leave from Avenida Victoria Aguirre to the visitor centre at hourly intervals between 7 am and 5 pm. The return schedule is similar. Entry to the park costs US$2 per person. If you miss the last regular bus, inquire at the front desk of the Hotel Internacional for the employees' bus which returns to Puerto Iguazú around 8 pm.

PARQUE NACIONAL FOZ DO IGUAÇU (BRAZIL)

To reach the Brazilian side of the falls, take a Singer or Tigre bus from Puerto Iguazú over the Puente Internacional Tancredo Neves, which commemorates the popular Brazilian President-elect who died before he could take office in 1985. The trip takes about half an hour and costs US$1.

If you are only crossing for the day, border formalities are minimal; you do not need a Brazilian visa, but you do need your passport, though neither Argentine nor Brazilian authorities should stamp it unless you are remaining in Brazil (in which case you may need a visa, depending on your nationality). A reader has reported that Australian and US citizens need a visa to cross to Foz do Iguaçu, so check in advance.

The bus will drop you at the bus terminal at the city of Foz do Iguaçu, from which you can catch the Transbalan bus marked 'Cataratas' to the falls. There is an admission charge of US$2 to the park. The bus drops you at the park's complex of hotels and parking lots, from which a hillside catwalk leads to the falls themselves. There is an excellent overview of the falls, but you cannot approach them as closely as on the Argentine side.

The Brazilian side of the falls is more commercial than the Argentine side, but the hotels fit better into the landscape than the Argentine constructions. Below the parking lot there is a helicopter pad, with rides over the falls for about US$25 per person, but you should know that Argentine park officials have complained that low-flying choppers have disturbed wildlife, including nesting birds.

Chaco & Formosa Provinces

The Gran Chaco is a lowland of savannas and thorn forests which extends from about 30° south latitude into Paraguay, eastern Bolivia and western Brazil. Together, Chaco and Formosa provinces comprise the bulk of the Argentine Chaco, although parts of the region also fall with in the boundaries of the western provinces of Salta and Santiago del Estero, as well as the northern edges of Santa Fe and Córdoba. Summer is brutally hot, but there are occasional winter frosts. Rainfall is high in the east, on the border with Corrientes, but declines towards the west, where irrigation is essential for agriculture. The area is little visited – the mostly roadless western half of Chaco province is popularly known as El Impenetrable, a term whose translation would be superfluous.

Traditionally, the region's economy depends on agriculture and forestry, particularly the exploitation of the famous quebracho tree *(Quebrachia lorentzii)* an unequalled source of tannin for leather processing. The *quebracho colorado*, a different species, is an important resource for timber, firewood and charcoal. Presently, there is accelerating forest clearance for rain-fed agriculture in which cotton and oil crops, especially sunflowers, have become more important. Petroleum exploration is proceeding in the area north of Castelli, along the border between the two provinces.

History

In the colonial era, there was little to attract Europeans to the hot, desolate Chaco. The few hunter-gatherer peoples who lived there were hostile and not sufficiently numerous to justify their pacification for encomiendas. There remain about 20,000 Guaycurú (Toba, Mocoví) and Mataco peoples, both in the interior of the Chaco and in urban areas.

The earliest probable Spanish settlement in the region was Concepción del Bermejo, founded in 1585 but abandoned in 1632 under Indian pressures and rediscovered only recently, 75 km north of present-day Roque Sáenz Peña. After the mid-18th century, Jesuit missionaries had some success among the Abipone nation, but their expulsion from the Americas in 1767 again delayed the inevitable European settlement.

Only after 1850, with the exploitation of

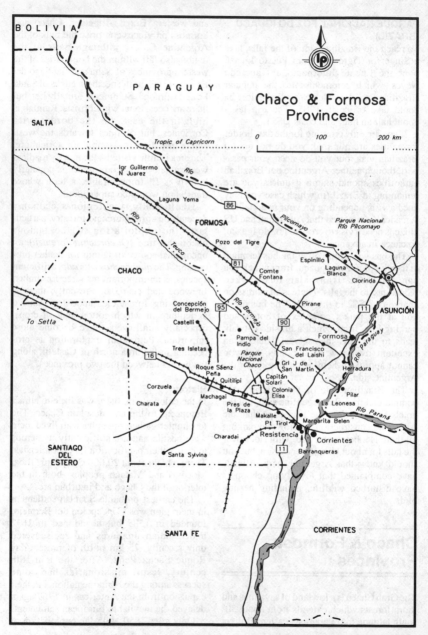

Chaco & Formosa Provinces

0   100   200 km

quebracho forests, did colonisation proceed, via immigration from the province and city of Corrientes. Resistencia, founded in 1750 as the Jesuit reducción of San Fernando del Río Negro, was the jumping-off point for woodcutters, who literally cleared the way for graziers and then agriculture. The two railroads built across the Chaco have made it easier to get logs to Resistencia and Formosa, where there is sufficient water to process the tannin.

Most of the region's agricultural development took place after 1930, when Argentine cotton production increased rapidly. New settlers of mostly central European origin – Austrians, Bulgarians, Czechs, Russians, Yugoslavs and some Spaniards – came via the Humid Pampa. The agricultural frontier continues to expand westward, and the quebracho forests are being cleared for wood and charcoal, although the erratic rainfall in the western Chaco makes rain-fed agriculture risky.

RESISTENCIA

Linked to Corrientes by the Belgrano bridge across the Paraná, Resistencia is the capital of Chaco province. First settled in 1750, it grew rapidly with the growth of the tannin industry and subsequent agricultural progress. Surprisingly, for a town which developed on the frontier, it is proudest of its fine arts tradition – it prefers to be known as the 'city of sculptures' or 'the open-air museum' for the many statues which can be seen in virtually every public space. There is an important university and many museums here.

Orientation

Resistencia does not front directly on the Paraná, to which it is connected by road to the small port of Barranquera. Plaza 25 de Mayo, occupying four square blocks, is the focus of the city centre. Street names change on each side of the plaza.

Avenida Sarmiento is the main street from national Ruta 16, which leads east to the Belgrano bridge and west to Roque Sáenz Peña and across the Chaco to Salta and San-

tiago del Estero. To the west, Avenida 25 de Mayo leads to national Ruta 11, which goes north to Formosa and the Paraguayan border at Clorinda. Ruta 11 also goes south to Reconquista and Santa Fe.

Information

Tourist Office The tourist office (☎ 23547) is upstairs at Juan B Justo 135, so poorly marked it's easy to miss, but the staff are friendly and well-informed. It's open weekdays from 6.30 am to 7.30 pm. There is also a tourist kiosk on the plaza.

Money There are no cambios, but except for limited hours, changing money is easier than in Corrientes. Banco de la Provincia del Chaco, at Güemes and H Yrigoyen, is open between 10 am and 1 pm, but takes a minimum commission of US$8 on travellers' cheques regardless of the amount. Banco de la Nación is directly on the plaza at Avenida 9 de Julio. Caja Nacional de Ahorros y Seguros, also on the plaza, changes cash only between 10.30 am and noon.

Post & Telecommunications The post office faces the plaza at Sarmiento and H Yrigoyen. Telecom is at the corner of J M Paz and Juan B Justo, a block from the plaza.

Travel Agencies For motorists, ACA (☎ 70507) is at Avenida 9 de Julio and Avenida Italia, three blocks from the plaza. For general purposes, try Organización Espinosa (☎ 23004) at Güemes 182.

Medical Services The Hospital Ferrando (☎ 25050) is on Avenida 9 de Julio near Mena.

Sculptures

There is insufficient space to detail the numerous sculptures in the city, but the tourist office has a map, with addresses, of 75 of them which makes a good introduction to the city. Walk around early in the morning, before the suffocating summer heat. The **Museo Provincial de Bellas Artes**, which

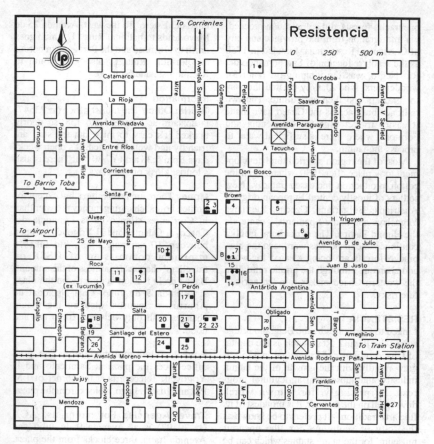

concentrates on sculpture, is at 9 de Julio 254.

One sculpture deserves special explanation. The shattered monument in Plaza 25 de Mayo, near the corner of Alvear and Avenida Sarmiento, was a memorial to a guerilla group massacred by the army in 1976 after surrendering and laying down their weapons in the village of Margarita Belén, 17 km north of Resistencia. Erected in 1986 with the concurrence of all major political parties, it was vandalised within a few days of its placement. Nearby graffiti charge that the building opposite the mem-

orial was used for torture during the Dirty War. The current elected governor of the province was a military official during the Proceso.

El Fogón de los Arrieros

This privately owned museum (☎ 26418), at Brown 350, is famous for its eclectic collection of art objects from around the Chaco, Argentina and the world, but it also features the wood carvings of local artist Juan de Diós Mena.

It's open from 8 am to noon Monday to Saturday, with a bar, renowned for its ambience, open in the evenings. There is an admission charge of US$2.

Museo Policial

Before dismissing the idea of visiting the police museum, be assured you can ignore the grisly photos of auto accidents and the predictable drug-war rhetoric and focus on the fascinating exhibits on *cuatrerismo* (cattle rustling, still common in the province today) and social banditry – one elaborate display is a surprisingly sympathetic presentation of the careers of two outlaws of the late 1960s who, after killing a policeman, lived for five years on the run, helped by the *humildes* (poor rural people) of the province. The museum is at Roca 233, between

Nechochea and Vedia. Hours are 9 am to noon and 6 to 8 pm Tuesday to Friday, and 6 to 9 pm Sunday and holidays. A police officer will guide you around, but avoid the place during a military coup or state-of-siege.

Barrio Toba

Toba Indians inhabit this modern government *reducción* which appears to be cohesive and well-maintained, if impersonal in appearance.

At the Cooperativa de Artesanos, some of the ceramics are very cheap and gaudy, but the traditional *yisca* (string bag) and other goods show traditional skills. You can reach the barrio by bus No 2 from the Plaza 25 de Mayo.

Centro de Ofidiología Resistencia

Reptile-lovers will be unable to resist a visit to this centre which specialises in the study of snakes which eat other snakes. It's open Monday to Saturday from 2.30 to 8 pm, at Santiago del Estero 490.

Museo Regional de Antropología Juan Alfredo Martinet

This focus of this museum at the Universidad Nacional del Noroeste, at Avenida Las Heras 727, is archaeological, with special emphasis on the failed Spanish settlement at Concepción del Bermejo. There are ethnographic exhibits as well, but acceptance of the low estimates for the aboriginal population of the Americas at European contact by Argentine scholar Angel Rosenblat, whose work has been largely superseded, point up the difficulties which provincial universities have in keeping up with more recent research. It's open weekdays from 9 am to noon.

Museo Histórico Regional Ichoalay

The provincial history museum, at Donovan 475 opposite the Plaza 9 de Julio, is open weekdays from 1.30 to 6 pm. Named for an Indian cacique who negotiated a peace settlement with the Spanish governor of Corrientes in 1750, it features ethnographic materials relating to Chaco Indians and exhibits on European colonisation.

Museo de Ciencias Naturales
Located at Pellegrini 745, this museum has a good collection of stuffed birds of the region but is otherwise unexceptional, although it has a friendly and dedicated staff. It's open weekdays from 8 am to 12.30 pm and from 2 to 8 pm.

Festivals
In August, Resistencia hosts the **Exposición Nacional de Ganadería** (National Livestock Show).

Places to Stay – bottom end
Camping *Camping Parque 2 de Febrero*, 15 blocks from the centre at Avenida Avalos 1100, has excellent facilities but may be a bit crowded and noisy in high season. Fees are reasonable at US$2 per person, and the staff are very friendly and helpful.

Residenciales, Hospedajes & Hotels
Resistencia has a wider selection of reasonable accommodation than nearby Corrientes. Cheapest place in town is the rather depressing *Hospedaje Anita*, at Santiago del Estero 45, where a single/double with shared bath costs US$6. *Residencial Aragon*, Santiago del Estero 154, is only slightly more expensive but is rather unfriendly and claims to have no singles.

Despite a run-down exterior, *Residencial Alberdi*, at Alberdi 317 between Ameghino and Obligado, has decent rooms with shared bath for US$8 per person, but it's often full. *Residencial San José* (☎ 26062), at Rawson 304, is funky but clean, with one truly enormous room.

Three other places charge about US$10/15 with private bath: *Residencial El Diamante* (☎ 22866) at Avenida Belgrano 383; *Residencial Marconi* (☎ 21978) at Perón (ex-Tucumán) 332; and *Residencial Hernandarias* (☎ 27088) at Avenida Hernandarias 215. *Residencial Celta* (☎ 24861) at Alberdi 210 is a bit dearer. *Hotel Alfil* (20822), at Santa María de Oro,

is good value but charges extra for air-conditioning.

Places to Stay – middle
Midrange hotels, like *Hotel Esmirna* (☎ 22898) at H Yrigoyen 83 on Plaza 25 de Mayo, start about US$20/26. Others are slightly higher, including *Hotel Colón* (☎ 22861) at Santa María de Oro 149, and *Hotel Lemirson* (☎ 22277) at Rawson 167.

Places to Stay – top end
There is no real luxury lodging in Resistencia, but try *Hotel Covadonga* (☎ 22875), at Güemes 200, which charges US$35/50. *Hotel Sahara* (☎ 22970), at Güemes 160, is a bit more expensive but no better.

Places to Eat
El Círculo at Güemes 350 has decent fixed-price meals with huge portions. Most restaurants are parrillas, like *La Estaca* at Güemes 202, but for variety try *Por la Vuelta* at Obligado 33 or *Trattoria Italiana* at H Yrigoyen 236. For a wide selection of ice cream, try *Helados San José* at Pellegrini and Saavedra.

Entertainment
For nightowls, Caffé Concert Cabaret at Obligado 185 opens at 11 pm and doesn't shut the doors till 5 am.

Things to Buy
Besides the artisans' cooperative at Barrio Toba (see above), check out Bogado, at Güemes 154, for a good selection of Indian and non-Indian handicrafts, including hammocks, yiscas, etc. For leather goods, go to Chaco Cueros at Brown 81.

Getting There & Away
Air Aerolíneas Argentinas (☎ 22854), at Juan B Justo 136, has four flights weekly to and from Buenos Aires. Austral (☎ 25921), at Rawson 99, has flights to and from Buenos Aires on Tuesday, Thursday, Saturday and Sunday.

For both Aerolíneas Argentinas and

Austral, see also the schedule for nearby Corrientes.

Bus The bus terminal is at Santa María de Oro and Santiago del Estero, just three blocks from the plaza. Resistencia is an important hub of bus travel for destinations in all directions.

La Internacional (☎ 26924) goes south to Reconquista, Santa Fe, Rosario and Buenos Aires, west to Roque Sáenz Peña, and north to Formosa and Asunción, Paraguay. El Norte Bis (☎ 24522) serves the same routes to the south, goes twice weekly to Mar del Plata, and also east to Posadas.

La Estrella (☎ 25221) connects with Roque Sáenz Peña and also goes to the village of Capitán Solari, near Parque Nacional Chaco. La Estrella and Cacorba (☎ 21521) alternate daily service to Córdoba.

Godoy SRL (☎ 20730) heads north to Formosa, the border town of Clorinda, and Asunción. Central Sáenz Peña (☎ 21521) has four daily buses to Roque Sáenz Peña and alternates with La Velóz del Norte in crossing the Chaco to Salta daily, while El Rayo (☎ 21123) takes a more southerly route to Santiago del Estero and Tucumán. Cotal (☎ 21521) serves Mendoza and San Juan twice weekly via Catamarca and La Rioja. Ciudad de Posadas (☎ 20730) goes to Posadas (three buses daily) and Puerto Iguazú (daily).

Train The Ferrocarril Belgrano (☎ 22689) is fairly central at Lisandro de la Torre and Avenida Rodríguez Peña. It connects Resistencia with Buenos Aires and Roque Sáenz Peña, with only primera and very uncomfortable turista class services. It no longer carries passengers across the Chaco to Salta.

Getting Around
Resistencia airport is six km from the centre of town, via bus No 2 from the post office on the plaza. Godoy Resistencia buses make the rounds between Corrientes and Resistencia at frequent intervals throughout the day.

PARQUE NACIONAL CHACO
This very accessible but little-known park, 115 km north-west of Resistencia, preserves 15,000 hectares of the humid eastern Chaco. Although the park has abundant bird life, the primary reason for its creation in 1954 was the preservation of its surprisingly diverse ecosystems, which depend on subtle differences in relief, soils and rainfall.

Flora & Fauna
Ecologically, Parque Nacional Chaco falls within the 'estuarine and gallery forest' sub-region of the Gran Chaco, but the park encompasses a variety of marshes, open grasslands, palm savannas, scrub forest and denser gallery forests. The most widespread system is the *monte fuerte*, where mature specimens of quebracho, *algarrobo* and lapacho reach above 20 metres, while lower stories of immature trees and shrubs provide a diversity of habitats at different elevations.

Scrub forests form a transitional environment to seasonally inundated savanna grasslands, punctuated by *caranday* and *pindó* palms. More open grasslands have traditionally been maintained by human activities, including grazing and associated fires, but this is disappearing. The marshes and gallery forests cover the smallest areas, but are biologically the most productive. The meandering Río Negro has left several shallow oxbow lakes in which dense aquatic vegetation flourishes.

Mammals are few and rarely seen, but birds are abundant, including the rhea, jabirú stork, roseate spoonbill, cormorants, common caracaras and other less conspicuous species. The most abundant and widely distributed animal species is the mosquito, so plan your trip during the relatively dry, cool winter and bring insect repellent.

Activities
Hiking and birdwatching are the principal activities, and are best in early morning or around sunset. Park service personnel are extremely hospitable and will accompany visitors if their duties permit. Some inundated areas are accessible only by horseback;

inquire for horses and guides in Capitán Solari, six km from the park.

Places to Stay & Eat

At Capitán Solari, you may find basic accommodation, but camping is the only alternative at the park itself. Fortunately, there are numerous shaded sites with clean showers (cold water only) and toilets, despite many ants and other harmless *bichos* (creatures). A tent or other shelter is essential. There are firepits, picnic tables, plenty of wood lying around for fuel and no fees, but beware of Panchi, the rangers' pet monkey, who will steal anything not tied down.

Weekends can be crowded with people from Resistencia, but at other times you are likely to have the park to yourself. Sometimes on weekends a concessionaire (snack bar licensee) from Resistencia sells meals, but you should bring everything you need from Resistencia or Capitán Solari.

Getting There & Away

Capitán Solari is 2½ hours from Resistencia with La Estrella, which has four buses daily, at 6.30 am and 12.30, 5.30 and 8 pm. From Capitán Solari, you will have to walk or catch a lift to the park entrance. Avoid walking in the midday heat.

ROQUE SÁENZ PEÑA

Properly speaking, this city of 75,000 people, located 168 km west of Resistencia, goes by the rather clumsy name of Presidencia Roque Sáenz Peña, after the term of the Argentine leader responsible for the adoption of electoral reform and universal male suffrage in 1912. Primarily a service centre for cotton and sunflower growers, its major tourist attraction is the thermal baths complex in the city centre. It has one of the country's better zoos, and is the gateway to the 'Impenetrable' of the central Chaco. There are several immigrant communities with their own clubs, including Italians, Yugoslavs and Bulgarians.

Orientation

Roque Sáenz Peña lies directly on national

1	Plaza Ramos Mejías
2	Hotel Gualok
3	Termas de Sáenz Peña (Mineral Thermal Baths)
4	Plaza Leandro Alem
5	Residencial El Colono
6	Post Office
7	Hotel Premier
8	ACA
9	Hotel Avenida
10	Telecom
11	Hotel Augustus
12	Hotel Asturias
13	Tourist Office
14	Plaza San Martín
15	Cathedral
16	Train Station
17	Plaza J B Justo

Ruta 16, which connects Resistencia with Salta. It has a regular grid plan centred on willow-shaded Plaza San Martín. Avenida San Martín is the principal commercial street. It is very hot in summer and, except around the plazas, almost treeless.

Information

Tourist Office The tourist office (☎ 22135) is at Avenida San Martín and 9 de Julio.

Money Try Banco Nordecoop, Avenida San Martín and Avellaneda, or Banco del Chaco, Pellegrini 439.

Post & Telecommunications The post office is at Belgrano 602, on the corner of Mitre. Telecom is at Rivadavia 435 between 9 de Julio and 25 de Mayo.

Travel Agencies ACA (☎ 20471) is at 25 de Mayo 725. A regular tourist agency is Tobas Tour, 9 de Julio 479.

Medical Services Hospital 4 de Junio (☎ 21404) is at Malvinas 1350.

Termas de Sáenz Peña

Consciously developed for tourism, this complex of saunas, mineral baths and

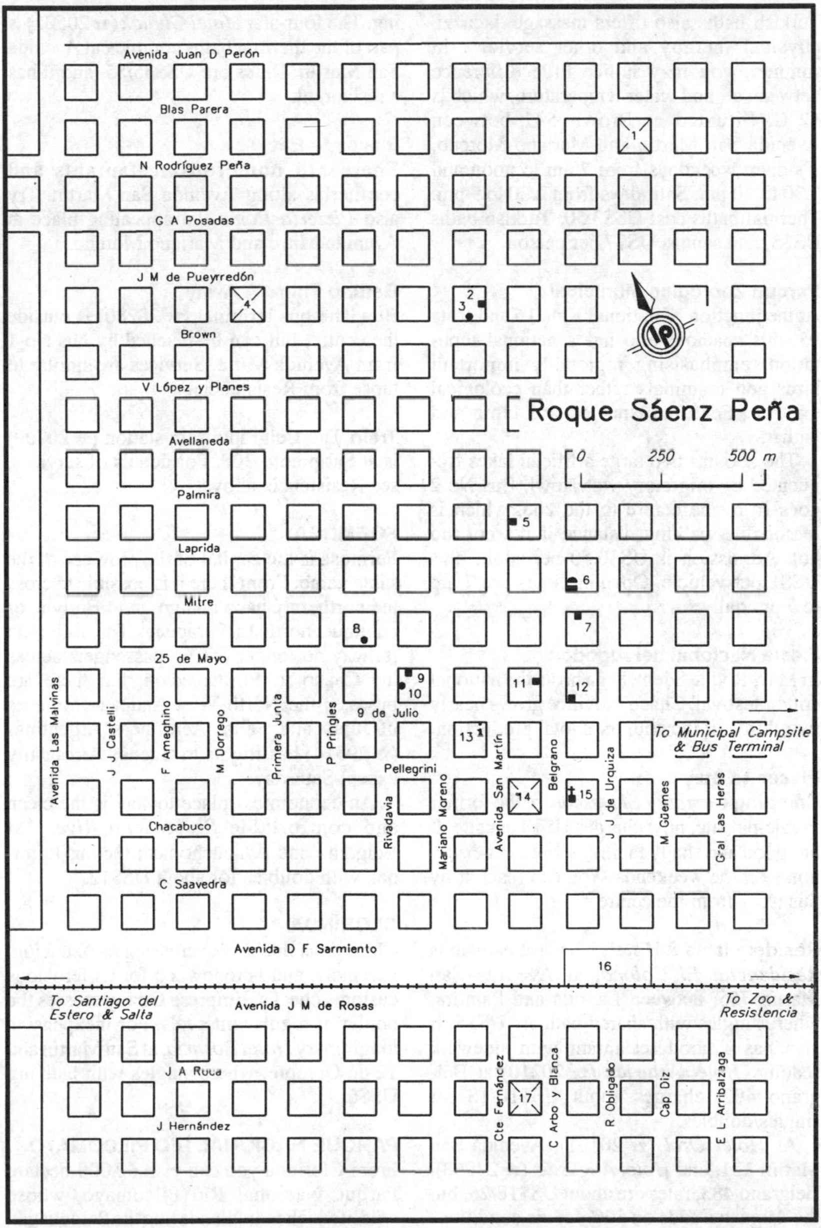

Roque Sáenz Peña
0
250
500 m
Avenida Juan D Perón
Blas Parera
N Rodríguez Peña
G A Posadas
J M de Pueyrredón
Brown
V López y Planes
Avellaneda
Palmira
Laprida
Mitre
25 de Mayo
9 de Julio
Pellegrini
Chacabuco
C Saavedra
Avenida D F Sarmiento
Avenida J M de Rosas
J A Roca
J Hernández
Avenida Las Malvinas
J J Castelli
F Ameghino
M Dorrego
Primera Junta
P Pringles
Rivadavia
Mariano Moreno
Avenida San Martín
Belgrano
J J de Urquiza
M Güemes
Gral Las Heras
Cte Fernández
C Arbo y Blanca
R Obligado
Cap Diz
E L Arribalzaga
To Municipal Campsite & Bus Terminal
To Santiago del Estero & Salta
To Zoo & Resistencia
1
2
3
4
5
6
7
8
9
10
11
12
13
14
15
16
17

Turkish baths also offers massage, jacuzzi, physical therapy and other services. In summer, you may notice little difference between air and water temperature, which is 42°C. Situated at Brown 541 between Avenida San Martín and Mariano Moreno, it's open weekdays from 7 am to noon and 3.30 to 10 pm, Saturdays from 2.30 to 9 pm. Thermal baths cost US$3.50, Turkish baths US$5, and saunas US$7 per person.

Parque Zoológico Municipal
At the junction of national Ruta 16 and Ruta 95, this spacious zoo has a national reputation, emphasising regionally important birds and mammals rather than ecological exotics. Featured species are tapir and jaguar.

The zoo has two large artificial lakes frequented by migratory waterfowl. Bus No 2 goes from the centre to the zoo, which is reasonable walking distance if it's not too hot. Admission is US$0.50 per adult, plus US$1 per vehicle. Opening hours are 7 am to 7 pm daily.

Fiesta Nacional del Algodón
In May, Roque Sáenz Peña hosts the national cotton festival. Chaco province grows nearly two-thirds of the country's total production.

Places to Stay
Camping *Camping El Descanso*, the former municipal site, now charges US$4 per site. It has good and shady facilities, but can be very noisy on the weekends. You can reach it by bus No 1 from the centre.

Residenciales & Hotels The best bargain is *Residencial El Colono*, at Avenida San Martín 755, between Laprida and Palmira, where singles with shared bath are US$5. It also has a good restaurant with sidewalk seating. *Hotel Asturias* (☎ 20210) at Belgrano 402, charges about US$10/18 for singles/doubles.

At *Hotel Orel* (☎ 20101), Avenida San Martín 131, and *Hotel Augustus* (☎ 22068), Belgrano 483, rates are about US$18/25, but the Augustus adds on 50% for air-condition-

ing. The four-star *Hotel Gualok* (☎ 20521) is part of the thermal baths complex at Avenida San Martín. Rates are US$35/55, and it has a restaurant.

Places to Eat
There are numerous restaurants and confiterías along Avenida San Martín. Try also *Pizzería Roma*, an appealing place at Avenida Mitre and Mariano Moreno.

Getting There & Away
Bus The bus terminal (☎ 20280) is outside the centre, but can be reached by bus No 1 from Avenida Mitre. Services are similar to those from Resistencia.

Train The Belgrano train station (☎ 20709) is at Sarmiento 300. For details of services, see Resistencia above.

FORMOSA
Formosa is the capital of the province of the same name. From there it is possible to cross the northern Chaco and go on to Bolivia, or continue north to Paraguay. The Belgrano railway no longer carries passengers across the Chaco to Embarcación, but there are buses to the North-West Andean provinces of Jujuy and Salta. Aerolíneas Argentinas (☎ 29314) has flights to Buenos Aires daily except Saturday.

An economical place to stay is the clean and comfortable *Residencial Rivas*, at Belgrano and Ayacucho near the bus terminal, with doubles for about US$12.

CLORINDA
Clorinda is the border crossing to Asunción, Paraguay, and is renowned for its ferocious customs checks. Empresa Godoy crosses the border at regular intervals. For inexpensive lodging, try *Hotel Rosario*, at San Martín and 12 de Octubre, where singles with bath are US$6.

PARQUE NACIONAL RÍO PILCOMAYO
From Clorinda you can visit 60,000-hectare Parque Nacional Río Pilcomayo, whose wildlife-rich marshlands hug the Paraguayan

border. There is a bus service along national Ruta 86 beyond Laguna Naick-Neck, where there is there is a well-marked turnoff to the ranger station at Laguna Blanca.

Public transport will take you only as far as the turnoff, from where you will have to hike or hitch the last 5 km to Laguna Blanca. It has camping facilities and pasarelas from which you can view the wildlife. At the town of Laguna Blanca, 11 km beyond the turnoff, there is lodging available at *Hotel Guaraní*.

Córdoba

Córdoba, a transitional province between the Andes and the Pampas, is a very popular destination for Argentine tourists even if almost overlooked by foreigners. Excluding Patagonia, it lies in the virtual centre of the country, bound by the Andean provinces to the north-west, Cuyo to the south-west, the Chaco to the north-east, and the Pampas to the south-east. Most of the province is agricultural, but its major attractions are the city of Córdoba and its scenic mountain hinterland, the Sierras de Córdoba.

The city of Córdoba, capital of the province, holds a special place in colonial and modern Argentine history. It is Argentina's second city and long a rival with Buenos Aires for political, economic and cultural supremacy. From the early 17th century, its churches and universities were among the best in Latin America, while Buenos Aires languished at the end of Spain's circuitous mercantile supply route. Today, it is one of Argentina's most important industrial centres, especially important as the heart of the Argentine automotive industry.

The geologically complex Sierras, consisting of three longitudinal ranges reaching as high as 2800 metres, stretch 500 km from north to south, separating the Pampas from the Andes. Giving birth to several east-flowing rivers, prosaically named Primero (First), Segundo (Second), Tercero (Third) and Cuarto (Fourth), they bring visitors the year round to dozens of small towns and villages dedicated to the tourist trade. In the north-east of the province, the Río Primero drains into the Laguna Mar Chiquita, a shallow inland sea.

Many of the province's features appeal to conventional tastes, but there are also opportunities off the beaten track. Historical resources are especially abundant, varied and appealing.

History

Prior to the arrival of the Spaniards, the sedentary Comechingones Indians occupied the area around Córdoba. Like their counterparts farther north, they were maize cultivators, but also herded llamas and collected the fruit of the algarrobo tree. Proficient warriors, for a brief period they actively and effectively resisted the Spanish – by one account they shot a Spaniard so full of arrows that he 'looked like San Sebastián', a famous Christian martyr.

The Spaniards also found that the local Indians lacked the hierarchical political structure which made others ideal for tribute and coerced labour under the encomienda:

It is notorious that no village which has a cacique is the subject of another cacique or pueblo. These people are in such anarchy that in all the encomiendas which

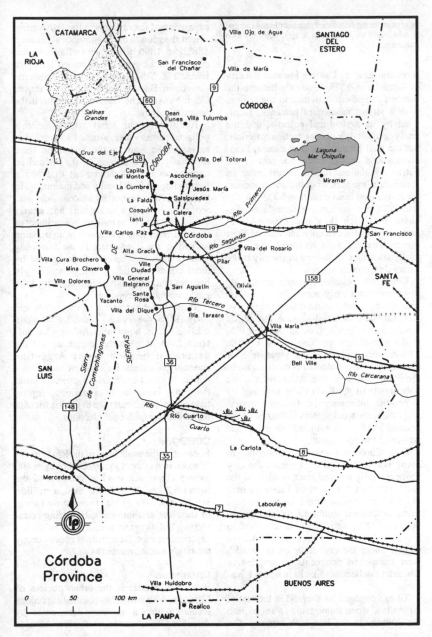

Córdoba
Province

0   50   100 km

exist or are being established each pueblo and cacique is mentioned by itself even if there are only two Indians.

Jerónimo Luis de Cabrera founded the city of Córdoba in 1573. It quickly became the centre for Spanish activities in the region, with a strong missionary presence, facilitated by its agricultural potential and the ready accessibility of construction materials, but the well-intentioned Dominicans, Franciscans and Jesuits could not protect the native population. In the century after its foundation, the number of Indians in encomienda declined from more than 6000 to fewer than 500, due primarily to introduced diseases to which they had little natural immunity. Little evidence remains of their presence except in place names – the major mountain range south-west of the city is the Sierra de Comechingones.

Córdoba's ecclesiastical importance made it an important early centre for education, fine arts and architecture. Many impressive colonial monuments still grace the centre where, on weekends when the bustling auto traffic diminishes, you can still absorb the 17th-century ambience and visualise how Buenos Aires depended on its connections to the north. However, with the creation of the Viceroyalty of the River Plate, followed by Argentine independence, Córdoba underwent the same reorientation as the rest of the country and became subject to the economic whims of the port capital.

Still, Córdoba asserted its autonomy in many ways. Royalist forces from the city unsuccessfully resisted Buenos Aires in the early years of the wars of independence, although it benefited from increased foreign trade thereafter, doubling its population between 1840 and 1860. In contrast to Buenos Aires, Córdoba's conservative clergy, under the cry 'Religion or Death', were outspoken opponents of progressive Unitarist intellectuals like Bernardino Rivadavia.

Things changed, as they did in the rest of Argentina, when immigrants swarmed into the country in the late 19th century. The expansion of the railways in the 1870s stimulated the growth of the province – between 1882 and 1896, the number of agricultural colonies in the province increased from just five to 176. Still, because of the phenomenal growth in Buenos Aires and the Pampas, Córdoba experienced a relative decline in the national picture.

Eventually, the local establishment's political conservatism aroused so much dissatisfaction among the populace that, especially in the university, it spawned an aggressive reform movement that had a lasting impact both locally and nationally. In the late 1960s, university students and auto workers forged a coalition that nearly unseated the de facto military government of General Juan Carlos Onganía in an uprising known as the *cordobazo*. In the following years many such insurrections, ignited by local conditions but growing increasingly broader and more radical in their aims, took place around the country.

Today, after the chaos of the 1970s and early 1980s, the region's economy has again declined as the automobile industry has suffered from its obsolete equipment and the general stagnation in the Argentine economy. Renault, for example, has abandoned the city. Provincial Governor Eduardo Angeloz, however, is a national figure, having lost a difficult race to Carlos Menem in the 1989 presidential elections.

CÓRDOBA

Located on the south bank of the Río Primero (also known as the Suquía), Córdoba sits 400 metres above sea level at the foot of the Sierra Chica. With more than a million inhabitants, the city has sprawled well north of the river and into the surrounding countryside, but its centre is compact and readily explored on foot. Its industrial zones occupy the city's southern suburbs.

Orientation

Plaza San Martín is the urban nucleus of Córdoba, with most of its colonial attractions located within a quadrant demarcated by Avenida Olmos on the north side, Avenida

Maipú to the east, Blvd Junín to the south and Avenida General Paz on the west side. The commercial centre is just north-west of the Plaza, where the pedestrian streets 25 de Mayo and Indarte cross each other. Calle Obispo Trejo, just south of the Plaza, has the finest concentration of colonial buildings.

Just south of downtown, Parque Sarmiento offers some relief from the densely built and bustling downtown, but the largest open space is Parque General San Martín, on the banks of the river on the north-west outskirts of town.

Information
Tourist Office The provincial Subsecretaría de Turismo (☎ 44027), inside a gallery at Tucumán 25, is open weekdays from 7 am to 2 pm, but it is less helpful than the municipal office (☎ 35031) at Centro Obispo Mercadillo, downstairs at Calle Rosario de Santa Fe 39, on Plaza San Martín. The latter is open weekdays from 8 am to 9 pm, and weekends from 9 am to noon and 5 to 8 pm.

There is also a branch of the provincial tourist office (☎ 34169) at the bus terminal, Avenida Perón (ex-Reconquista) 380. Its hours are weekdays from 7.30 am to 8.30 pm, weekends 8 am to 8 pm. If arriving by bus or at the nearby train station, look here first for latest information on hotels.

Money For changing cash or travellers' cheques (the latter with a hefty commission), try Exprinter at Rivadavia 39 or Barujel at San Martín 37.

Post & Telecommunications ENCOTEL is at Avenida General Paz 201. Telecom is at Avenida General Paz 36, but just before its privatisation, service was at best indifferent, sometimes openly hostile, and very time-consuming. Theoretically, it is possible to make an international call from the phones outside on the street, but formerly no operators would answer the line. To make a collect call, you need your passport.

Travel Agencies ACA (☎ 44636) is at Avenida General Paz and Humberto Primo,

eight blocks north of Plaza San Martín. For tours around Córdoba, try Oceania (☎ 36082) at Calle Rivadavia 86 or Aeroturis (☎ 21872) at Avenida Olmos 351.

Medical Services The Hospital de Urgencias (☎ 40243) is at Catamarca and Blvd Guzmán.

Historical Buildings
The centre of Córdoba is a treasure of colonial buildings and other historical monuments. Besides specific buildings mentioned below, you should see the **Cabildo** on Plaza San Martín, now occupied by the police and currently being restored; the **Casa del Obispo Mercadillo** at Rosario de Santa Fe 39; the **Universidad Nacional de Córdoba** (1613) at Calle Obispo Trejos 242, and the nearby **Colegio Nacional de Monserrat** (1782).

Iglesia Catedral
Begun in 1577, Córdoba's cathedral was the work of several architects, including Jesuits and Franciscans, over more than two centuries. Consequently, it shows a mixture of styles, crowned by its Romanesque dome. It's on Calles Independencia and 27 de Abril, at the south-west corner of Plaza San Martín.

Iglesia de La Compañía
Designed by the Flemish Padre Philippe Lemaire, the Jesuit church at Calle Obispo Trejos and Caseros dates from 1645. It has a modest exterior, while the interior is ornate but tasteful. It was not completed until 1667-71, with the successful execution of the design of Lemaire's timber roof, in the form of an inverted ship's hull. The altarpiece is carved of Paraguayan cedar.

Museo Histórico Provincial Marqués de Sobremonte
At Calle Rosario de Santa Fe 218, this claims to be one of the most important historical museums in the country, with collections of religious paintings, Indian and gaucho weapons, musical instruments, leather and wooden trunks, furniture and

Córdoba

0   100   200 m

other miscellanea. Built in the 18th century, the house once belonged to the colonial governor of Córdoba and has 26 rooms and five interior patios, but the most notable feature is a wrought-iron balcony supported by carved wooden brackets. It's open Tuesday to Friday from 8.30 am to 1.30 pm.

Museo de la Ciudad
Not quite what it implies, this museum features modern painting. At Entre Ríos 40, it has erratic opening hours.

Club Andino Córdoba
For information on climbing or exploring the Sierras de Córdoba, contact the Club Andino de Córdoba at Duarte Quiros 1591 or Calle Obispo Trejos 658. It's open Wednesdays from 8.30 to 11 pm and Saturdays from 11 am to 1 pm.

Festivals
Córdoba celebrates the foundation of the city on 6 July.

Places to Stay – bottom end
Camping The nearest site is in Parque General San Martín, 13 km from downtown but easily reached by city bus No 31 from Plaza San Martín. This leaves you at the Complejo Ferial, an exhibition and entertainment complex about one km from the campground, so you'll have to walk or hitch the last stretch.

The campground itself is spacious but shade is at a premium. Showers and toilets are funky and the water supply is undependable, but it's a passable place to stay. Charges are about US$2 per site.

Hospedajes, Residenciales & Hotels As usual, economy lodging is found around the bus terminal and the train station. Without a doubt, the cheapest in town is *Residencial La Soledad* at Calle San Jerónimo 479, near Calle Paraná. Quiet, friendly and basic but not really bad, it costs just US$2 per person with shared bath. The spotlessly clean *Hospedaje Suzy*, Entre Ríos 528, has no singles but doubles are only US$5 with shared bath. The indifferent *Residencial El Crishsol* (not to be confused with Hotel Gran Crisol), Calle San Jerónimo 581, is bottom-of-the-barrel accommodation at about the same price. Try instead *Hotel Lady* at Calle Balcarce 324.

Hospedaje Dory's, San Jerónimo 327, is dark and dingy but quiet, with rooms at US$7/11 with private bath. *Residencial Central* (☎ 46667), Avenida Perón 150 near the train station, is also dingy but the rooms are very clean. It is slightly more expensive than Dory's. Other inexpensive alternatives include *Residencial Mallorca* at Avenida Balcarce 73, *Hotel Florida* at Calle Rosario de Santa Fe 459, and *Residencial San Francisco* at Buenos Aires 272; all charge about US$10/16. At the comparably priced *Residencial Gran Bristol*, Pasaje Corrientes 64 (also called Pasaje Tomás Oliver), the air-conditioning appears not to work.

A step up in this category, if not quite equal to its Buenos Aires namesake, is *Hotel Claridge*, 25 de Mayo 218, which has rooms with a balcony and air-conditioning on a quiet pedestrian street for US$12/20. The friendly *Hotel Entre Ríos* (☎ 30311), at Entre Ríos 567, has rooms with shared bath for US$12/18, but add a private bath and it costs US$18/26.

Places to Stay – middle

The modern *Hotel Termini*, near the train station at Entre Ríos 687, has rooms for US$20/32. *Hotel Riviera*, Calle Balcarce 74, is close to the train and bus terminals, and charges about the same. *Hotel Viña de Italia*, San Jerónimo 611, is modern but inviting at US$30/40. More central is the very attractive and well-maintained *Hotel Garden*, 25 de Mayo 35, for about US$20/30.

Places to Stay – top end

Hotel Sussex (☎ 22907), a beautiful building at San Jerónimo 125, has rooms for US$80/120. The modern high-rise *Hotel Nogaró* (☎ 22-4001), next door at Calle San Jerónimo 137, lacks its character but is somewhat cheaper. *Hotel Crillon* (☎ 46093), at Calle Rivadavia 85, is comparable. A bit away from the centre is the wood, brick and concrete *Hotel de la Cañada* (☎ 37569) at Avenida Alvear 580 near San Luis.

Places to Eat

The municipal Mercado Norte at Calle Rivadavia and Oncativo has excellent inexpensive eats – pizza, empanadas and lager beer. There are many other inexpensive places to eat on Avenida Perón, near the train and bus terminals, and on streets like Calle San Jerónimo, where numerous video bars serve meals – the evening's shows are posted outside, taking precedence over the food. *Pizzería Italiana*, at Calle San Jerónimo 610, is a decent choice despite its unimpressive appearance.

Bar Montserrat, a confitería at Duarte Quiros and Calle Obispo Trejos, has the best croissants in Argentina – fresh, hot and reasonably priced. It's a big hangout for students from the Universidad Nacional de Córdoba. For lunch, *Parrilla Acapulco* at Calle Obispo Trejos 169 has a good selection of reasonable, fixed-price meals as well as other more elegant dishes. There are many other good, reasonable restaurants in this area.

Things to Buy

For indigenous crafts of the Wichí, Toba, Pilagá, Colla and Calchaquí peoples of the northern provinces, check out Mundo Aborígen (☎ 37924), 25 de Mayo 73, which is also a research and information centre.

Getting There & Away

Air The airport is at Pajas Blancas, 15 km from town. From the bus terminal, take the Empresa Ciudad de Córdoba bus, marked 'Salsipuedes', which enters the airport.

Aerolíneas Argentinas (☎ 46041) is at Avenida Colón 520. Its early Wednesday flight from Buenos Aires continues to Mendoza and Santiago, Chile, while its Sunday flight reverses that itinerary. There are 28 other weekly flights to and from the federal capital, four others to Mendoza and one to San Juan. Another Sunday flight to Mendoza continues to Bariloche.

Austral (☎ 34883) is at Buenos Aires 59. It has 23 weekly flights from Buenos Aires, a daily flight to Mendoza, and two weekly to Tucumán and Río Hondo.

Bus Rarely is a bus terminal an attraction in its own right, but the Nueva Estación Terminal de Omnibus de Córdoba (NETOC) (☎ 34169, 30532) at Avenida Perón 380 deserves a visit even if you're not taking a trip. Its facilities include two banks, an automatic teller, a pharmacy, a travel agency, public telephones, a post office, a day care centre, first aid, a photo lab, and more than 40 shops, restaurants, and other utterly unexpected services.

It also has 42 different bus companies which serve local, provincial, national and international destinations. To Buenos Aires, Costera Criolla (☎ 34100), ABLO (☎ 34095), General Urquiza (☎ 40711) and Cacorba (☎ 22-5973) take 10 hours and charge US$40. Check for discounts.

COTIL (☎ 39011) and Chevallier (☎ 22-5898) have buses to Catamarca for US$20. SOCASA (☎ 35469) goes to San Juan twice weekly, with a 20% discount on return fares. Uspallata (☎ 22-4091) and TAC (☎ 37666) charge US$35 to Mendoza, with connections to Santiago, Chile.

Veloz del Norte (☎ 39011) goes to Salta and Orán, near the Bolivian border. Balut serves Salta and Jujuy, while Panamericano (☎ 22-3569) goes to Tucumán and continues to the Bolivian border crossings at La Quiaca and Pocitos.

La Estrella (☎ 22-6927) crosses the Chaco to Roque Sáenz Peña, Reconquista and Resistencia three times a week. El Serrano (☎ 22-9751) has buses to Santa Fe and Corrientes. Expreso Singer (☎ 35379) offers through buses to Puerto Iguazú for US$85. CORA (☎ 22-4222) serves Montevideo four times weekly for US$60, with connections to Brazil.

Train The Mitre train station (☎ 24168) is on Avenida Perón at the east end of San Jerónimo, just north of the bus terminal. There are evening services to Retiro, Buenos Aires, at 8 pm and 8.45 pm daily, and on Tuesday and Sunday at 7.40 am. Fares are about US$25 pullman, US$20 primera and US$18 turista.

Car Rental Try Avis (☎ 22483) at Corrientes 452. For the circuits in the Sierras de Córdoba, a car would be extremely useful.

Getting Around
Córdoba has an extensive public transportation system. Recently, the city was planning to bring in a computerised pass system to replace the unwieldy tickets and large amounts of cash with which drivers have to deal. Why this costly high-tech approach is preferable to Tucumán's traditional system of fichas is not immediately apparent.

Sierras de Córdoba

The Sierras de Córdoba offer literally hundreds of small towns and even tinier villages whose attractions range from the reservoirs, beaches and casinos of resorts like Villa Carlos Paz to more sedate places like Cosquín or Candonga. The area is very picturesque, with many sites of historical interest. Outside the peak summer season, prices for accommodation can be much lower and you can benefit greatly from bargaining, but many places close by the end of March. The Sierra's dense network of roads, many well paved but some gravelled, make it a good candidate for bicycle touring – Argentine drivers here seem a bit less ruthless than elsewhere in the country. A mountain bike is still the best choice, but a racing bike would suffice if you plan your itinerary well.

LA CALERA
Just 18 km west of downtown Córdoba, this is an easy day trip to La Calera's simple 17th-century Jesuit chapel (which has been restored and modernised). There are many parrillas, a municipal campground, and dozens of roadside stands selling regional specialities like salami and fresh bread for your picnic. Stop at places whose handmade signs advertise *salami casero* and *pan casero*.

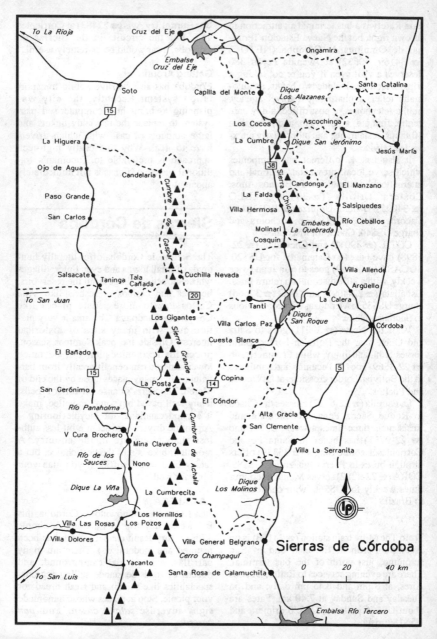

Sierras de Córdoba

VILLA CARLOS PAZ

Only 36 km from Córdoba on Lago San Roque (in fact a large reservoir), Villa Carlos Paz is popular among Argentines but is really only a minor-league, freshwater Mar del Plata. There are many expensive hotels, such as *Hostería Alpenrose* (☎ 25595), *Hotel Portal del Lago* (☎ 24931), and *Hotel Alfil* (☎ 22184).

There is a tourist office (☎ 21624) at the bus terminal. ACA's Centro Turístico (☎ 22132), which includes a campground, is on the shores of the lake at Avenida San Martín and Nahuel Huapi. There is a municipal campground at Alfonsina Storni and A Magno.

Getting There & Away

COTIL and COTAP have frequent buses between Córdoba and Villa Carlos Paz. Some long-distance buses start and end their Córdoba routes here.

COSQUÍN

Cerro Pan de Azúcar, east of town, offers good views of the Sierras and, on a clear day, the city of Córdoba. Hitch or walk (there are few buses) five km to a saddle where there is an *aerosilla* (chairlift) to the top, although a steep 25-minute walk to the 1260-metre summit will save you US$4. At the saddle there is also a confitería whose owner, a devotee of Carlos Gardel, has decorated his business with Gardel memorabilia and built a mammoth statue of the great man.

For the past 31 years in January, Cosquín has held a folklore festival, recently adding classical music and ballet performances.

Places to Stay

During the summer, try the youth hostel at the *Grand Sierras Hotel* (☎ 52120), San Martín 733. The owner-operated *Petit Hotel* (☎ 51311), A Sabattini 739, is very friendly and quiet, with an attractive patio with a parrilla for asados. In season, prices are about US$25 double, but out of season may be barely half that. At Santa María de la Punilla, just south of Cosquín, there is a good campground.

Getting There & Away

La Capillense and La Capilla run buses from Córdoba to Cosquín.

LA FALDA

This woodsy resort, 78 km from Córdoba beneath the precipitous Sierra Chica, may be the most pleasant town in the immediate area. Both its **Museo de Trenes en Miniatura** (Miniature Train Museum) and the **Museo Arqueológico Ambato** (archaeological museum) are worthwhile. The narrow zigzag road across the Sierra Chica to Salsipuedes, Río Ceballos and back to Córdoba climbs to 1500 metres at Cerro El Cuadrado, but the best views are back to the west. There are no buses over this route, but enough auto traffic that hitching should be possible in high season. Dedicated joggers can get an excellent workout.

ACA has a service station (☎ 22674) at Avenidas España and Edén. Wella Viajes, Avenida Edén 412, No 12, arranges hiking and trekking in the Sierras.

Places to Stay & Eat

Hotel El Piccolo (☎ 23343), Uruguay 51 near Avenida Edén, charges US$10 per person with private bath. It is very friendly, quiet and clean, doing a great deal of repeat business. *Old Garden Residencial*, Capital Federal 28, has a pool and beautiful gardens but is slightly more expensive. Try also *Hotel de la Ciudad* (☎ 51376), only half a block from the bus station at Salta 726. In nearby Villa Hermosa, there is a municipal campground, plus an historical museum in the old train station.

There are a number of decent restaurants along Avenida Edén, such as *Confitería Kattak* at Edén 444.

Things to Buy

Avenidas Eden and España are the main shopping district, with crafts at Taller Artesanal del Cristal, Avenida España 199 and woollens at Martex, Avenida España 446.

Getting There & Away

La Capillense and El Cóndor have buses from Córdoba.

CANDONGA

Candonga's 18th-century Jesuit chapel is a minor masterpiece in a very picturesque, isolated canyon. At one time it was part of the Estancia Santa Gertrudis, whose overgrown ruins, including buildings, a large stone wall, and an aqueduct can still be seen. While there is no public transport direct to the site, there is enough traffic that you should be able to hitch from El Manzano, 40 km north of Córdoba (try Empresa Ciudad de Córdoba or Sierras de Córdoba).

A day trip is worthwhile, but there is good accommodation at Isabel Souto's *Hostería Candonga* (☎ 71-1092 in Córdoba for reservations). For US$20 per person you get a room plus all meals, including Argentine and regional specialities like *asado con cuero*, locro, empanadas and homemade desserts.

JESÚS MARÍA

Jesús María, 51 km north of Córdoba, was one of the finest Jesuit estancias, with a diverse economy based on irrigated vineyards, orchards and croplands, livestock, and ancillary industries. The church and convent are now a museum.

Ciudad de Córdoba has buses to and from the town of Jesús María. Five km away is the colonial posthouse of Sinsacate, site of a wake for the murdered La Rioja caudillo Facundo Quiroga in 1835.

SANTA CATALINA

About 12 km north of Ascochinga, but more easily reached from Jesús María, this Jesuit estancia was perhaps the richest and most elaborate in the region. It is now in private hands, but can be visited.

ALTA GRACIA

Only 35 km south-west of Córdoba, Alta Gracia's most notable attraction is the former Jesuit church and estancia, which supplied food and other provisions for the Jesuits in the city until their expulsion in 1767. One of its owners was Santiago Liniers, one of last officials to occupy the post of Viceroy of the River Plate. Although he was a hero in the British invasion of 1806, Liniers was executed for his loyalty to Spain and resistance to independence for Argentina. He is now buried in his native France; the house is a museum.

There is also a museum in the house occupied by the late Spanish composer Manuel de Falla.

Getting There & Away
SATAG has regular bus services between Córdoba and Alta Gracia.

VILLA GENERAL BELGRANO
About 90 km south-west of Córdoba, Villa General Belgrano flaunts its Teutonic origins as a settlement of unrepatriated survivors from the sunken German battleship *Graf Spee* near Montevideo during WW II. Its Oktoberfest is the *Fiesta Nacional de la Cerveza*.

There are two youth hostels, *El Rincon* (☎ 6323) and *Estancia Alta Vista* (☎ 6299), plus more upscale accommodation at the *Hotel Edelweiss* (☎ 6317) and *Hotel Bremen* (☎ 6133). In the more remote, scenic village of La Cumbrecita, try *Hotel Las Verbenas* (☎ 98405).

Getting There & Away
Valle de Calamuchita and COLTA both serve Villa General Belgrano from Córdoba.

CANDELARIA
Only the church and casco remain of this late 17th-century estancia east of La Higuera. In a remote part of the Sierra, their thick walls and buttresses, iron-clad algarrobo doors and hideaways give evidence of defensive functions in an area of hostile Indians. The estancia is 218 km from Córdoba by the most direct route.

MINA CLAVERO
Mina Clavero's therapeutic mineral waters began to attract vacationers from Córdoba in the late 19th century, when Doña Anastasia Fabre de Merlo opened the first guest house on the advice of the famous 'gaucho priest' José Gabriel Brochero, who had gotten to know the area in the course of his evangelical activities. A century later Mina Clavero is an important resort with hotels, campgrounds, restaurants, plus vacation homes along the Río de los Sauces. The clear streams, rocky waterfalls and verdant, idyllic mountain landscapes provide a relaxing environment in which visitors can leave the faster-paced life of Córdoba and Buenos Aires behind.

Orientation
Mina Clavero is 170 km south-west of Córdoba along the splendid Nuevo Camino de las Altas Cumbres (Ruta 15). It sits at the confluence of Río de Los Sauces and Río Panaholma, in the Valle de Traslasierra between the eastern Sierras Grandes and Cumbres de Achala and the western Sierra de Pocho. Below the confluence, both streams become the Río Mina Clavero, which divides the town.

Avenida San Martín is the principal street on both sides of the river. Since the town is very compact, walking is the main means of transportation.

Information
Tourist Office The Dirección de Turismo (☎ 70171) is an Avenida San Martín 1464, near the bridge.

Money Banco de la Nación, Avenida San Martín 898, and Banco de la Provincia, Avenida San Martín 1982, will change cash US dollars.

Post & Telecommunications The post office is at Avenida San Martín and Pampa de Achala. Telecom is at Avenida San Martín and Intendente Vila.

Travel Agencies ACA (☎ 70197) is at Córdoba and Ramón Carcano.

Places to Stay
Camping *Autocamping El Faro*, three km south of Mina Clavero towards Nono, is the only one that remains open all year. It has very pleasant, shady grounds along the river, with impeccable bathrooms, hot showers and good laundry facilities. Daily charges are US$5 per group of four, including vehicle and electricity.

Hospedajes & Residenciales For a complete list of the many hospedajes and residenciales, check at the tourist office, but note that there is little accommodation after the end of March, when the town almost rolls up the sidewalks. Try *Hospedaje Italia* (☎ 70232) at Avenida San Martín 1176, *Hospedaje Las Moras* (☎ 70704) at Urquiza 1353, *Hospedaje Franchino* (☎ 70395) at Mitre 1544, *Residencial El Parral* (☎ 70005) at Intendente Vila 1430, *Residencial Aire y Sol* (☎ 70226) at Rivadavia 551, and *Residencial El Colonial* (☎ 70292) at Urquiza 1596.

Hosterías, Hotels & Motels Most one-star hotels in town include breakfast, private bath and similar services. Unless otherwise indicated, prices are for doubles in late season, but may be higher in midseason.

The reasonable *Hotel Agüero* (☎ 70439), 12 de Octubre 1166, and *Hotel Milac Navira* (☎ 70278), Oviedo 1407, charge US$12. *Hotel Coronado* (☎ 70225), Avenida San Martín 1495, has nice rooms for US$16, while the rates at *Hotel España* (☎ 70123), Avenida San Martín 1687, are US$20. *Hostería Champaquí* (☎ 70393), Oviedo 1429, is excellent value with singles at US$10 with half pension.

A bit more upscale are *Hotel Aguirre* (☎ 70239) at Avenida San Martín 1148, *Hotel La Morenita* (☎ 70347) at Urquiza 1138, and *Hotel Marengo* (☎ 70224) at Avenida San Martín 598; all with rooms for about US$23. *Hotel Los Aromos* (☎ 70200), at Mitre 1640, and *Hotel Rossetti* (☎ 70012), at Mitre 1434, charge US$25. *Hotel Molino Blanco* (☎ 70124), Urquiza 1266, has rooms at US$28. The fancy *Motel du Soleil* (☎ 70066), at Mitre and La Piedad at the entrance to town, has doubles at US$45 with breakfast.

Places to Eat
Parrilla La Costanera, on Avenida Costanera by the river, has a good *diente libre* (all-you-can-eat) deal. *Restaurant Lo de Jorge*, on Poeta Lugones, serves good, abun-

dant dishes at reasonable prices. *Restaurant La Nona*, Mitre 1600, has tasty pasta.

Getting There & Away
The bus terminal is at Mitre 1191. Empresas El Petizo and Pampa de Achala have several daily buses to Córdoba and Villa Dolores. TAC has a daily bus to Merlo, San Luis, and Buenos Aires. Chevallier goes to Buenos Aires daily. The fare to Buenos Aires is US$38.

AROUND MINA CLAVERO
Museo Rocsen
Operated by J J Bouchon, an anthropologist, curator and collector who first came to Argentina in 1950 as cultural attaché in the French Embassy, this eclectic museum displays more than 11,000 pieces ranging from European furniture and Pacific seashells to Peruvian mummies and musical instruments. While these materials might sound incompatible, the collection is so well presented that individual exhibits truly recreate the ambience of a rural rancho or German bedchamber. Particularly well done are the entrance's Rincón del Oligarca de Campo (Rural Landowner's Corner) and Rincón del Oligarca de Ciudad (Urban Elite Corner).

The museum is in the pastoral village of Nono, a one-time Indian settlement, nine km south of Mina Clavero. Opening hours are from 10 am to 6 pm daily. The museum shop sells beautiful ceramic reproductions of artefacts at very reasonable prices.

VILLA LAS ROSAS
Further south along the Altas Cumbres highway is a district with several small villages. Charming Villa Las Rosas stands out, since it provides the most direct route to the summit of 2887-metre Cerro Champaquí, the highest peak in the province. In the Municipalidad, the tourist office (☎ 94407) can give you a map with a list of local people who can be hired as guides.

For accommodation; try *Hostería Las Rejas, Hotel Sierras Grandes, Hotel Vila* or *Hotel Micheletti*. There is also a campground. *Restaurant Los Horcones* serves typical regional food.

YACANTO

Further south of Villa Las Rosas is the village of Yacanto, site of the *Golf Club and Hotel Yacanto*, which merits a special trip even if you can't afford the US$58 per person for full lodging. This turn-of-the-century build-

ing and its surrounding manicured parkland once belonged to the British railways. Hiking, tennis and horseback riding are the other popular activities here, where business people from Córdoba and Buenos Aires take a break from stressful city life.

In nearby San Javier, you can stay a bit more cheaply at *Hostería San Javier*, for US$38 with all meals.

Cuyo

The Cuyo region consists of the Andean provinces of Mendoza and San Juan, and adjacent San Luis. Settled from and once part of Chile, the area still retains a strong regional identity and its considerable mestizo population differs from the people of Buenos Aires and the Pampas. The term 'Cuyo' derives from the Huarpe Indian *cuyum*, meaning 'sandy earth'.

The formidable barrier of the Andes is the backdrop for the one of Argentina's most important agricultural regions – which produces grapes and wine mostly for the internal market, rather than beef and grain for export. Aconcagua, at 6960 metres the highest peak in the Americas, towers over the area. Cuyo lies in the rain shadow of the massive Andean crest, but enough snowfall accumulates on the eastern slopes to sustain the rivers which make the irrigation of extensive vineyards possible. Because of these advantages, Mendocinos, the inhabitants of the province of Mendoza, call their home La Tierra de Sol y Buen Vino (Land of Sun and Good Wine).

With its variety of terrain and climate, Cuyo offers outdoor recreation the year round. Possible summer activities include climbing, trekking, riding, hang-gliding, canoeing, fishing, water-skiing, windsurfing and sailing. In winter, skiing is a popular if costly pastime. Most people visit Mendoza in travelling between Santiago (Chile) and Buenos Aires, but you should not overlook the other provinces, particularly San Juan, for off-the-beaten-track experiences.

Mendoza Province

Despite the physical barrier of the Andes, for most of its history Mendoza has been isolated from both the other Andean provinces and the distant Pampas. In large part this resulted from an accident of history, the settlement of Cuyo from Chile.

Like their counterparts in the Tucumán region, the Huarpe Indians of Cuyo practised irrigated agriculture. Their population was large enough to encourage Spaniards to cross the 3850-metre Uspallata pass from Santiago to establish encomiendas, but the impossibility of traversing the mountains during winter stimulated economic independence and encouraged political initiative. Still, trans-Andean communications were the rule, with links to Lima via Santiago rather than northward to Tucumán and Bolivia. Buenos Aires was a remote backwater.

Vineyards first became important during the colonial period, but after Argentine independence the economy declined with the closing of traditional outlets for their produce. Only after the arrival of the railroad

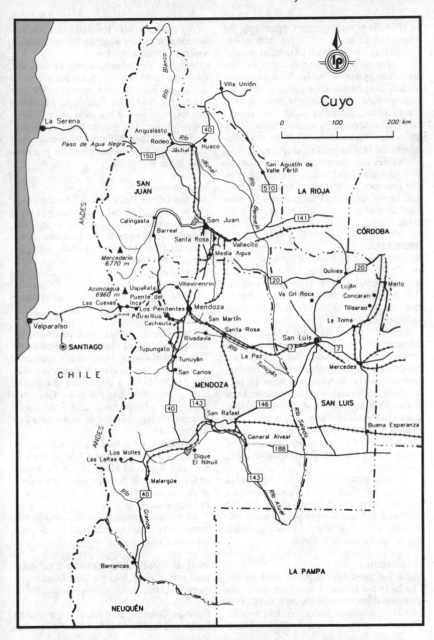

in 1884 did prosperity return, permitting the expansion of grape and olive cultivation, plus alfalfa for livestock. Provincial authorities promoted modernisation of the irrigation system to assist the agricultural sector. Despite the centralisation of water management, the vineyards remain relatively small, owner-operated enterprises, most not exceeding 50 hectares. Since 1913, the annual Fiesta de la Vendimia has celebrated the famous provincial wines.

Besides the towering Andean landscape and its poplar-lined vineyards and orchards, the province offers several nature reserves and important thermal baths. It is a popular destination for both summer and winter holidays.

MENDOZA

Founded in 1561 and named for the governor of Chile, the provincial capital sits 761 metres above sea level in the valley of the Río Mendoza, east of the Andes. Earthquakes have often shaken the city, most recently in 1985.

Except during its long siesta hours, Mendoza is a lively city, its bustling downtown surrounded by tranquil neighbourhoods where, every morning, meticulous shopkeepers and housekeepers swab the sidewalks with kerosene to keep them shining. The *acequias* (irrigation canals) along its tree-lined streets are visible evidence of the city's indigenous and colonial past, even where modern quake-proof construction has replaced fallen historic buildings.

With a population exceeding half a million, Mendoza is the most important administrative and commercial centre in the province. It has also an important state university and a growing industrial base, supported by nearby oilfields.

Orientation

Plaza Independencia occupies four square blocks in the centre of town; on weekends there are often open-air concerts there. Two blocks from each of its corners, four smaller plazas are arranged in a virtual orbit. Beau-

tifully tiled, recently restored Plaza España deserves particular attention for its Saturday morning artisans' market.

Avenida San Martín, which crosses the city from north to south, has many sidewalk coffee houses. Briefly on weekdays but almost religiously on Saturdays, Mendocinos socialise here; it is a good place to meet local people. The poplar-lined Alameda, beginning at the 1700 block of Avenida San Martín, was a traditional place for promenades in the 19th century.

Information

Tourist Office The provincial tourist office (☎ 24-2800), at Avenida San Martín 1143, is open weekdays from 7 am to 9 pm. The friendly staff operate an excellent computerised information system, but you should have specific questions to ask them. They have good maps, but no other brochures.

There is also a tourist information booth (☎ 25-9709) in the bus terminal.

Money There are several cambios on Avenida San Martín between Garibaldi and Lavalle, and also on Espejo and Catamarca. Cambio Santiago in Galería Tonsa, Avenida San Martín 1177, is one of the few places open Saturdays, until 8 pm. American Express is at Rivadavia and 9 de Julio. Exprinter, a large cambio, is on Avenida San Martín 1198.

Citibank, at Avenida San Martín 1099, changes currency between 7.30 and 10.30 am only. Banco de Mendoza, on the corner of Gutiérrez and 9 de Julio, also has a branch at the bus terminal. Banco de la Nación is at Necochea and 9 de Julio.

At the bus terminal, there is a cambio that opens early in the morning and offers good rates for Chilean pesos.

Post & Telecommunications The main post office is at Avenida San Martín and Avenida Colón. Telecom is at Chile 1574.

Foreign Consulates Chile has a consulate (☎ 25-5024) at Emilio Civit 296. Those who need visas should have no problem getting one here.

Cultural Centres The Instituto Cultural Argentino Norteamericano (☎ 24-1719) is at Chile 985. There are also branches of the Alianza Francesa (☎ 23-4614) at Chile 1754 and the Instituto Dante Alighieri (☎ 25-7613) at Espejo 638. The Instituto Goethe (☎ 24-9407), at Morón 275, often shows German films.

Travel Agencies ACA (☎ 24-4900) is at Avenida San Martín and Amigorena.

Several commercial travel agencies organise trips in both the city and the province. These include Turismo Mendoza (☎ 25-7743) at Las Heras 559, Turismo Cóndor (☎ 23-4019) at Las Heras and Perú (near the train station), Hunuc Huar Expeditions at España 1340, 8th floor, and Agencia de Turismo Mamb (☎ 23-0646) at Espejo 391. For details of services, see the Organised Tours section below.

Terraza Mirador
Mendoza is more spread out than most Argentine cities, so you will need to walk or learn something about the bus system to get around. A good place to start is the Terraza Mirador, the rooftop terrace of the Municipalidad, 9 de Julio 500, which offers a panoramic view of the city and surroundings. It's open Monday and Friday from 8 am to 12 noon, and Tuesday, Thursday and Saturday from 4 to 7 pm.

Ruinas de San Francisco
Located in the Old Town, at the corner of Ituzaingó and Fray Luis Beltrán, these misnamed ruins, which occupy the entire block, belong to a Jesuit-built church/school dating from 1638. After the Jesuits' expulsion in 1767, the Franciscans, whose own church was demolished in the 1782 earthquake, took over.

Acuario Municipal
The aquarium, at Ituzaingó and Buenos Aires, contains both local and exotic fish.

Particularly interesting are the species from the Río Paraná. The trolley 'Dorrego' takes you there. It opens daily from 10 am to noon, and from 3 to 9 pm.

Iglesia, Convento y Basílica de San Francisco
This church possesses the image of the Virgin of Cuyo, patron of the people of Cuyo and of San Martín's Army of the Andes, which many people consider miraculous since it survived the devastating 1968 earthquake. In the Virgin's semicircular *camarín* (chamber), visitors leave tributes to her and to San Martín. There is also a mausoleum with the remains of San Martín's daughter, son-in-law and granddaughter, which were repatriated from France in 1951. Public hours are Monday to Saturday, 10 am to noon.

Parque San Martín
Bus No 11 ('Favorita') from around Plaza Independencia or Plaza España takes you to this 420-hectare park west of the city centre, which has 50,000 trees of about 700 different species. Designed by architect Carlos Thays in 1897, it was donated to the provincial government by Emilio Civit. The main gates, originally designed for the Turkish Sultan Hamid II, were imported from England. The park is popular for weekend family outings and other activities.

Bus No 11 continues to the **zoo**, in an impressive hillside setting in the park. It's open Tuesday to Sunday from 9 am to 7 pm.

Also in the park, the famous **Cerro de la Gloria** features a monument to San Martín's Army of the Andes for their liberation of Argentina, Chile and Peru from the Spanish. On a rare clear day, views of the valley make the climb worthwhile.

Museo del Pasado Cuyano
At Montevideo 544, this historical museum opens weekday mornings from 9 am to noon, and Tuesday and Friday afternoons. There are guided tours at 11 am.

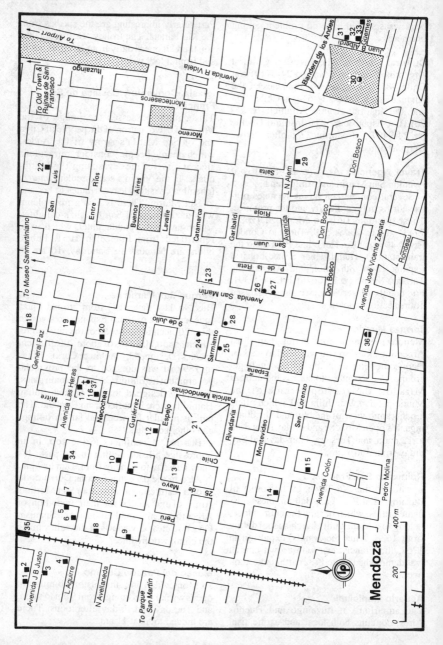

Mendoza

0   200   400 m

■ PLACES TO STAY

1 Hotel Margal
2 Hotel Penitentes
3 Hotel Marconi
4 Hotel Laerte
5 Hotel Presidente
6 Hotel Vigo
7 Hotel Petit
8 Hotel Savoy
9 Hotel Provincial
10 Hotel Horizonte
11 Hotel Castelar
12 Hotel Argentino
13 Plaza Hotel
14 Hotel Aconcagua
15 Hotel Lucense
16 Hotel Necochea
17 Hotel Balbi
18 Hotel Vecchia Roma
19 Hotel Royal
20 Hotel El Nevado
22 Hotel Escorial
29 Hotel Center
31 Hotel Terminal
32 Residencial Evelyn
33 Residenciales 402, San
   Fernándo & Betty
34 Hotel Rincón Vasco

OTHER

21 Plaza Independencia
23 Provincial Tourist Office
24 LAN-Chile
25 Ladeco
26 ACA
27 Austral
28 Aerolíneas Argentinas
30 Bus Terminal
35 Railway Station
36 Main Post Office
37 Iglesia de San Francisco

Enoteca Giol
Those without time to visit the wineries outside Mendoza should see this wine museum, at Peltier 611 in the civic centre. It's open Monday to Saturday from 9 am to 7 pm.

Museo Bellas Artes Casa de Fader
This art museum is on national Ruta 40 (called M Drumond in town), in the suburb of Luján de Cuyo. The house itself justifies the trip, but the exhibition of paintings and sculptures by Argentine artists, particularly Mendocinos, adds flavour to it. Take bus No 20 from the centre.

Museo Sanmartiniano
Dedicated to General José de San Martín, whose name graces parks, squares and streets everywhere in Argentina, this historical museum is at Remedios Escalada de San Martín 1843. San Martín is especially dear to Mendoza, where he resided with his family and recruited and trained his army to cross into Chile. It's open weekdays from 9 am to noon and 5 to 8 pm.

Organised Tours
The city and the popular tourist areas west of Mendoza, toward the Chilean border, are suitable for day trips or for a circuit through areas of scenic river valleys, foothills, soaring mountains and medicinal thermal springs.

Several travel agencies (see above for addresses and telephone numbers) organise trips to these areas. Turismo Mendoza offers tours of the city, the wineries and Dique Cipoletti three days a week, to Potrerillos and Vallecitos daily, to Villavicencio twice weekly and the highlands daily via Puente del Inca, Cristo Redentor and Aconcagua. They also organise ski trips. Turismo Cóndor also has good tours of the city and surroundings.

Since Mendoza is becoming an adventure travel centre, agencies like Hunuc Huar organise expeditions to Aconcagua and the high cordillera for climbers, trekkers or hikers. Agencia de Turismo Mamb organises rafting trips along Río Mendoza, trekking in Potrerillos, and pack trips on horseback. All these begin at Gran Hotel Potrerillos.

Festivals
Mendoza's biggest annual event is the **Fiesta Nacional de la Vendimia** (wine harvest festival), lasting about a week from late February to early March. There is a parade with floats from each department of the

province on Avenida San Martín, as well as numerous concerts and folkloric events, terminating with the coronation of the festival's queen in the amphitheatre of Parque San Martín.

Bicyclists may wish to participate in the provincial equivalent of the Tour de France, the **Vuelta Ciclística de Mendoza**, in February. In July and August, the **Festival de la Nieve** features ski competitions.

Places to Stay – bottom end
Camping The closest campgrounds to the city of Mendoza are *El Challao*, six km from town, and *Parque Suizo*, nine km from town in Las Heras. Bus No 11 goes to both campgrounds; they each have clean showers, laundry facilities, electricity, and a grocery store. Charges are US$1.50 per person and US$1.50 per tent per day.

Hotels & Residenciales Near both the train station and the bus terminal there are several inexpensive hotels. Those near the train station are closer to downtown, but travellers to Chile or Argentine destinations other than Buenos Aires will find hotels by the bus terminal more convenient. The tourist office also keeps a list of casas de familia, with accommodation for about US$6 to US$10 a single.

Hotel Center (☎ 24-1184), at Alem 547 near the bus terminal, is basic but cheap, with singles/doubles at US$6/10. There are quite a few comparable hotels on Güemes, such as *Residencial Betty*, Güemes 456, and the nearby *Residencial San Fernando*; *Residencial 402* at, surprisingly, Güemes 402; and *Residencial Evelyn* at Güemes 294.

The modest, friendly *Hotel Lucense* (☎ 24-5937), at Chile 759, has rooms with shared bath for about US$8. *Hotel Vigo* (☎ 25-0208), also central at Necochea 749, is perhaps one of the best inexpensive hotels in town, with a nice garden and a good restaurant. Rates are US$6/10 for singles/doubles. Also very pleasant and clean is the *Hotel Escorial* (☎ 25-4777), San Luis 263, for about US$8/11 with bath.

Near the train station, *Hotel Penitentes*

(☎ 23-0208) at J B Justo 67, has good rooms with bath at US$7/10, with hot water, heating and a snack bar. *Hotel Dardex*, Perú 1735, is friendly and has rooms for US$5/8.

Places to Stay – middle
There is a wide price range for hotels in this category. The cheapest are the *Hotel Alcázar* (☎ 23-4808), Perú 1469, and *Hotel Horizonte* (☎ 25-3998), Gutiérrez 565, which has good heating and air-conditioning. Both have singles/doubles for US$12/17 with bath. *Hotel Terminal* (☎ 31-3893), Juan B Alberdi 261 near the bus terminal, is very clean and relatively comfortable but the rooms, for US$13/17 with bath, are rather small.

Hotel San Remo (☎ 23-4068), at Godoy Cruz 477 near the train station, is friendly and convenient. Rooms are US$17/19 with bath. A block and a half from the station, *Hotel Petit* (☎ 23-2099), at Perú 1459, is clean, with a friendly staff. Rooms are US$21/29. Across the street is the *Hotel Presidente*. Enthusiastically recommended is the *Hotel Laerte* (☎ 25-5041), a modern but homey place near the train station at Leonidas Aguirre 19, which has rooms for US$20/28.

In the old part of town, *Hotel Royal* (☎ 38-0675) at Avenidas Las Heras 145 is good value, with rooms at US$21/34. Also good and central is *Hotel Rincón Vasco* (☎ 23-3033) at Las Heras 590, which is slightly cheaper but with air-conditioning extra.

Similar prices and quality are available at *Hotel Necochea* (☎ 25-3501), at Necochea 541, which is very central and has comfortable rooms. *Hotel Margal* (☎ 25-2013), at Avenida J B Justo 75 near the train station, has good air-conditioned rooms. Rooms are US$20/25.

One step beyond in price are *Hotel Castillo* (☎ 25-7370) at Gutiérrez 572, *Hotel Castelar* (☎ 23-4245) at Gutiérrez 598, Hotel Vecchia Roma (☎ 23-1515) at España 1619, and *Hotel Provincial* (☎ 25-8284) at Belgrano 1259, only a short walk from the train station. Try also *Hotel San Martín* (☎ 38-0677) at Espejo 435, or the nearby

Hotel Argentino (☎ 25-4000) at Espejo 455 (with a nice patio, and breakfast included), or *Hotel América* (☎ 25-6514) at J B Justo 812. All have singles/doubles for US$24/33, and very similar standards.

Places to Stay – top end
There are several hotels in this category, starting at about US$32/42 with *Hotel El Nevado* (☎ 25-6200) at España 1433-39. The price includes continental breakfast. *Hotel Balbi* (☎ 23-3500), Las Heras 340, has singles/doubles for US$35/48.

The stylish *Plaza Hotel* (☎ 23-3000), in a beautiful neocolonial building at Chile 1124, is good value with rooms for US$52/69. *Gran Hotel Huentala* (☎ 24-0766), at P de la Reta 1007, has rooms for US$58/69. *Hotel Aconcagua* (☎ 24-2321), at San Lorenzo 545, charges US$70/81.

Places to Eat
Mendoza has good food in a variety of restaurants, pizzerías, cafés and snack bars. Although many are in the centre, you should not hesitate to look elsewhere.

Middle Eastern immigrants have left an imprint on the province. *Al Arab*, at Perú and Rivadavia, serves both Middle Eastern and Argentine dishes, with live entertainment. Try also the *Sociedad Libanesa* at Necochea 538.

Several places specialise in pasta. *Montecatini* at General Paz 370 near the train station, is good and reasonable. *Trevi*, at Las Heras 68, has superb lasagna. There are two locations for *Il Tuco*: Emilio Civit 556 and Sarmiento 68. They both have excellent food and low prices. *Vecchia Roma*, next to the hotel of the same name on Avenida España 1619, has superb Italian cuisine, good service, and medium to high prices.

Parrilladas are of course ubiquitous. *Azul* has a pleasant setting on Avenida Las Tipas and Ortega, in Parque San Martín. Despite their Italian names, *Boccadoro*, Mitre 1976, and *Trattoria Aveni*, 25 de Mayo 1163, are parrillas, the latter with some interesting fish dishes.

Vieja Recova, Avenida San Martín 924, emphasises seafood, while the *Centro Andaluz* at L Aguirre 35 has tasty paella. *Club Español* at España 948 has typical Spanish food, with moderate fixed-price meals.

There are two vegetarian restaurants. *Covindas* at San Juan 840 and *Línea Verde* at Montecaseros 1177 are good, wholesome and reasonable.

El Dragón de Oro, 25 de Mayo 1553, serves basic but tasty Chinese food. *Pampi* on España 1581 serves good grilled chicken.

Things to Buy
Even if you're not buying, you should see the provincial handicrafts at the Mercado Artesanal at Avenida San Martín 1133, next to the tourist office. There is a superb display of vertical loom weavings (Huarpe-style) from the north-west of the province and horizontal looms (Araucanian-style) from the south. You'll also see baskets woven in Lagunas del Rosario, and braided, untanned leather horse gear. The staff is very knowledgeable and eager to talk about crafts and the artisans, who receive the proceeds directly. Prices are reasonable. A must-see, the market is open weekdays from 8 am to 1 pm.

Getting There & Away
Air Aerolíneas Argentinas (☎ 24-9585), at Sarmiento 82, has morning flights to Buenos Aires daily except Sunday, and also in the afternoon on Monday, Wednesday, Thursday, Saturday and Sunday, some via Córdoba. There are twice-weekly services to Bariloche and to Santiago, Chile.

Austral (☎ 24-9101, 29-3167), at Avenida San Martín 921, has two afternoon flights daily to Buenos Aires, except Saturdays when there is only one. The early afternoon flights stop over in Córdoba.

Ladeco (Lineas Aéreas del Cobre), a private Chilean airline, is at Sarmiento 144 (☎ 24-2778), while LAN-Chile is at 9 de Julio 1126 (☎ 23-0404). LAN-Chile also flies to and from Santiago on Tuesday and Sunday.

Typical fares are: to Buenos Aires

US$160; to Córdoba US$70; to Bariloche US$158; to Santiago, Chile US$88.

Bus TAC has daily buses to Buenos Aires, Rosario, Bariloche, Córdoba, La Rioja, Mar del Plata, and to Santiago, Valparaíso and Viña del Mar in Chile.

La Estrella and Libertador have daily buses to San Juan, La Rioja, Catamarca and Tucumán.

Empresa del Sur y Media Agua has six buses a day to San Juan (two hours), while La Veloz del Norte has a daily bus to Salta via San Juan.

Central Argentino stops at all northern beach resorts in Buenos Aires province en route to Villa Gesell, three times weekly during summer, and goes daily to Rosario.

Empresa Jocolí has a daily bus to Buenos Aires via San Luis. Empresa COTAL has buses to Posadas and Puerto Iguazú three times weekly.

Colta has daily service to Cordoba via the Altas Cumbres route. In summer it has two buses a day at 10 am and 11 pm. Turismo Uspallata takes the same route to Córdoba, and also has two daily buses to Las Cuevas.

Andesmar has daily service to Caleta Olivia via Neuquén and Puerto Madryn, continuing Tuesday and Thursday to Río Gallegos. It also travels to Salta via Tucumán four times weekly. During the summer it has buses to destinations on the southern coast of Buenos Aires province: Monte Hermoso, Necochea, Miramar and Mar del Plata. Empresa Alto Valle has daily buses to Neuquén.

Typical fares from Mendoza are: to Buenos Aires US$68, to Bariloche US$61, to Mar del Plata US$70, to Santa Fe US$39, to Rosario US$40, to Córdoba US$31, to San Luis US$13, to San Juan US$9, to Malargüe (Las Leñas) US$10, and to San Rafael US$6.

Train The Ferrocarril San Martín (☎ 23-3840) is at Las Heras and Perú. There are three trains from Mendoza to Buenos Aires: the best and fastest is *El Libertador*, which replaces rugged tourist class with a comfortable bar, cinema lounge, air-conditioning

and good steward service. Buy tickets in advance for its Monday and Friday 8 pm departures. The more modest *El Aconcagua* leaves Mendoza daily at 4 pm, while the 'take-it-only-in-desperation' *El Cóndor* goes once weekly.

Car Rental Try National (☎ 23-1420), Sarmiento 127, or Avis (☎ 25-7802), Espejo 228.

Hitching It is very easy to hitch a ride to the Chilean border, walk across and catch another lift towards Santiago. Take a local bus to the outskirts of Godoy Cruz and wait at the gas station. For lifts to San Juan, take bus No 6 to the airport and hitch from the entrance.

Getting Around

To/From the Airport Plumerillo Airport is eight km from the centre. Bus No 6 ('Aeropuerto') from San Juan and Avenida L N Alem goes to the terminal. Departure taxes are US$1.50 for local flights, US$3 for regional flights and US$10 for international flights.

Bus The modern and very busy bus terminal is on Avenida Gobernador Ricardo Videla and Alberdi, just beyond the city limits. To get there, take the local trolley marked 'Villa Nueva' from Lavalle, between Avenida San Martín and San Juan. Bus Nos 5, 6 and 9 connect the bus terminal and train station.

AROUND MENDOZA

There are varied sights and recreational opportunities in and near Mendoza. Almost all of them can be done as daytrips, but some of the more distant ones would be more suitable for at least an overnight trip.

Wineries

Most of the wineries near Mendoza offer tours and tasting. **Bodega Giol**, at Ozamis 1040 in Maipú, is open weekdays 9 am to noon and 3 to 8 pm, Saturdays from 9 am to noon. Take bus No 15 or 16 from the centre.

Bodega Peñaflor, on N Mayorga in

Coquimbito, Maipú, is open weekdays 9 am to 4 pm. Buses Nos 17A, 17B, and 17C go there. Also in Coquimbito is **Bodega La Rural**, on Montecaseros, whose Museo Francisco Rutini displays wine making tools used by 19th-century pioneers, as well as colonial religious sculptures from the Cuyo region. It opens weekdays from 10 am to noon and 3 to 6.30 pm.

Bodega Toso, at Alberdi 808, San José, Guaymallén, opens weekdays from 7 am to 6 pm. Bus No 2 and trolley 'Dorrego' take you there.

Bodega Santa Ana, at Roca and Urquiza, Villa Nueva, Guaymallén, opens weekdays 8.30 to 11 am and 2.30 to 3.30 pm. Bus No 2 ('Buena Nueva via Godoy Cruz') goes there.

Calvario de la Carrodilla

A national monument since 1975, this church in Carrodilla, Godoy Cruz, houses an image of the Virgin of Carrodilla, the patron of vineyards, brought from Spain in 1778. A centre of pilgrimage for Mendocinos and other Argentines, it also has a sampling of indigenous colonial sculpture. Reached by bus Nos 1 and 20, it's open weekdays from 10 am to noon and 5 to 8 pm.

Cacheuta

In the department of Luján de Cuyo, 45 km from Mendoza, Cacheuta (altitude 1237 metres) is famous for its medicinal thermal waters and pleasant microclimate. Since 1986, the facilities have undergone modernisation. There is a restaurant, *Mi Montaña*, and campground on national Ruta 7, km 39. You can make reservations at Centro Termal Cacheuta (☎ 25-9000), Buenos Aires 536, Mendoza.

Potrerillos

The road to the Andean resort of Potrerillos (altitude 1351 metres), 56 km from Mendoza, passes through a typical precordillera landscape along the Río Blanco, the main source of drinking water for the capital. Birdwatching is excellent in summer.

There are two hotels, the luxury *Gran* *Hotel Potrerillos* (☎ 23-3000) and the more modest *Hotel de Turismo*. There is also an ACA campground, on Ruta 7 at km 50, which costs US$4 per site for members, and US$5 for nonmembers. The town also contains the restaurant *Armando* and a gas station.

On Sundays and holidays a tourist train leaves Mendoza for Potrerillos at 8.45 am, stopping at Canota (Maipú department), Paso de Los Andes (Chacras de Coria), Blanco Encalada and Cacheuta (Luján). It arrives at Potrerillos at 10.30 am and makes the return trip to Mendoza at 6.20 pm.

Uspallata

This village 105 km west of Mendoza, at an altitude of 1751 metres, lies in an exceptionally beautiful valley surrounded by polychrome mountains. There are two hotels: the upscale *Hotel Uspallata* (☎ 35539), and the simpler *Hostería Los Cóndores* (☎ 25539), which is very friendly. There is also a campground (☎ 20009) which charges US$3 per site. There is also a gas station in town.

Villavicencio

Panoramic views make the *caracoles* (winding road) to Villavicencio (altitude 1800 metres), 51 km from Mendoza, an attraction in itself. Mineral water from the region is sold throughout the country. The *Gran Hotel de Villavicencio*, located in a spectacular mountainous setting, has thermal baths. There is hang-gliding in the area.

Aconcagua

The highest peak in the Americas at 6960 metres, Aconcagua is called the 'roof of the Americas'. Its name has two possible indigenous sources: in Aymara, *Acon-Cagua* means New Mountain, while the Quechua *Ackon-Cahuac* means Sentinel or Stone Watch. There are several routes to the summit; four local guides lead trips of 13 to 15 days along the north route. Even if you're not a climber, you can still trek to a refugio at the permanent snow line; see the section

Trekking in Parque Provincial Aconcagua below.

Puente del Inca

This natural stone bridge over the Río Mendoza, 2720 metres above sea level and 177 km from Mendoza, is one of Argentina's natural wonders. From there you can hike to the base of Aconcagua, to the pinnacles of Los Penitentes (so-named because they resemble a line of monks), or to Tupungato (6650 metres), an impressive volcano partly covered by snowfields and glaciers. The very pleasant *Hostería Puente del Inca* is cheaper in the off season.

Cristo Redentor

Nearly 4000 metres above sea level on the rugged Argentine-Chilean border, battered by chilly but exhilarating winds, the high Andes make a fitting setting for this famous monument, erected after settlement of a territorial dispute between the two countries in 1902. The view is a must-see either with a tour or in your own car (since the road is no longer a border crossing into Chile). However, the first autumn snowfall closes the hairpin road to the top. At Las Cuevas, 10 km before the border, you can stay at *Hostería Las Cuevas*.

Ski Resorts

The snow still brings people to Mendoza province, while wine ages in the barrels, the soil becomes bare and the poplars stand leafless. Four ski resorts, particularly the fashionable Las Leñas, attract skiers from Argentina and overseas. Two of them are covered here; for Las Leñas and Los Molles, see the relevant section under Malargüe below.

Vallecitos At 2900 metres in the Cordón del Plata, only 80 km from Mendoza, Vallecitos has only six downhill runs. Open between early July and early October, it is the least expensive ski resort in the area.

Hostería La Canaleta has four-bunk rooms with private bath, as well as a restaurant and snack bar. The cheapest

accommodation is *Refugio San Antonio* which has rooms with a shared bathroom, and a restaurant. Since the resort is so close to Mendoza, most skiers stay there.

Los Penitentes At 2580 metres, 165 km from Mendoza, Los Penitentes has 21 runs for downhill and nordic skiing. The scenery and snow cover are excellent. Lifts and accommodation are very modern.

Hostería Los Penitentes (☎ 23-1200) has double and quadruple rooms with private bath, plus a restaurant and bar. Another resort is the new, three-star *Hostería Ayelén*. Five apartment buildings in Los Penitentes offer maid service, bar and reception. *Confitería La Herradura* is a skiers' hangout. A small market is open from 8 am to 10 pm. For more information, contact the Los Penitentes office (☎ 24-1770) at Rufino Ortega 644, Mendoza.

Water Sports

Two important reservoirs provide the setting for water sports in Mendoza province. **Dique El Carrizal**, 54 km south-west of the city, gathers the waters of the Río Tunuyán mainly for irrigation; its proximity to the city has made it a major recreation and camping area. To the south, **Dique El Nihuil** is 64 km from the city of San Rafael, on the Río Atuel (see the San Rafael section).

Trekking in Parque Provincial Aconcagua

Also called turismo aventura in Argentina, the first trekking trips were organised by experienced mountain climbers who wanted to share some of their experiences with unconventional travellers. Today several agencies specialise in this type of travel.

Aconcagua South Face Operadores Mendoza (☎ 25-3334, 23-1883) at Las Heras 420, Mendoza, has trips of three and six days from Puente del Inca, partly by horse or mule. It follows the route that climbers attempting the difficult south face of Aconcagua must traverse.

Aconcagua Cerro Aconcagua itself is in Parque Provincial Aconcagua. Sol Andino (☎ 29-1544) at Martínez de Rosas 489, Mendoza, offers treks to the mountain, starting from Hostería Ayelén in the village of Los Penitentes, and rafting on the Río Mendoza.

Several guides from the Asociación de Guías de Montaña lead two-week trips to Aconcagua: Alejandro Randis, Soler 721, Mendoza; Daniel Rodríguez, Cervantes 1697, Godoy Cruz; and Daniel Burrieza, Fader 383, Mendoza. They leave from Mendoza by bus to Puente del Inca, then follow the northern route, partly on mule. Departures are twice monthly between December and March, and should be booked 30 days in advance, with a 20% advance payment.

If you prefer independent climbing, Club Andino Mendoza, Lemus between Rioja and Salta, will help with paperwork.

In San Martín's Footsteps You can cross the high Andes route taken by part of San Martín's Andean army on an eight-day pack trip with guides from Turismo Masnú Barros (☎ 22444), at Sarmiento and Echeverría in Tunuyán.

SAN RAFAEL

Founded as a military outpost, San Rafael is now a modern commercial and industrial centre of 80,000 people. Its vineyards, particularly Suter, Bianchi and Lávaque, have earned a national and international reputation. Like Mendoza, its acequias remind the visitor that the area is a desert, irrigated by the Río Atuel and the Río Diamante, and surrounded by scenic mountains. Its clean, tree-lined streets, sidewalks and parks are a local pride. The city has recently made special efforts to attract tourists.

Information

Tourist Office The tourist office (☎ 24217), at the corner of Avenida H Yrigoyen and Avenida Balloffet, has helpful staff and great brochures and maps. It opens from 7 am to 8.30 pm, and to 11 pm during summer.

Post & Telecommunications ENCOTEL is at San Lorenzo and Barcala, and Telecom is at San Lorenzo 131.

Travel Agencies Agencies that arrange local excursions include Alue Tour (☎ 22732), at Cmte Salas 51, and Buttini Hermanos (☎ 21423), at Corrientes 495.

Things to See

Worthwhile city sights are the parks, the **Catedral**, and the **Museo de Historia Natural**, six km from the centre on an island, the Isla Río Diamante.

Places to Stay – bottom end

On Isla Río Diamante, there is an ACA campground (☎ 24286).

Hospedaje Ideal (☎ 22301), Avenida San Martín 184, is the cheapest in town at US$9/16 for singles/doubles. Other inexpensive places are *Hospedaje La Esperanza* (☎ 22382) at Avellaneda 263, and *Hospedaje Cerro Nevado* (☎ 28209) at H Yrigoyen 376, both with singles/doubles for US$10/17. *Hotel Turis* (☎ 28090), at Alvarez Condarco 340, is basic but clean, with rooms for US$11/19. *Hospedaje Rex* (☎ 22177) at H Yrigoyen 56 has rooms for US$12/20.

Places to Stay – middle

Hotel España (☎ 24055), at Avenida San Martín 270, has rooms with bath for US$15/24 in its *sector económico* (cheap wing). A block away *Hotel Tonín* (☎ 22499), Avenida San Martín 327, has rooms for US$16/29. *Hotel Millalén* (☎ 22776), at Ortíz de Rosas 198, is good value for US$18/30 with breakfast, with a 10% discount for cash. *Hotel Regine* (☎ 21470), Independencia 623, has rooms for US$14/24 with breakfast, also with cash discounts.

Places to Stay – top end

The most expensive hotels are the *Hotel Kalton* (☎ 22568) at H Yrigoyen 120, with rooms for US$22/40; and the more exclusive *sector celeste* at the *Hotel España*, which has rooms for US$19/31. *Hotel San Rafael*

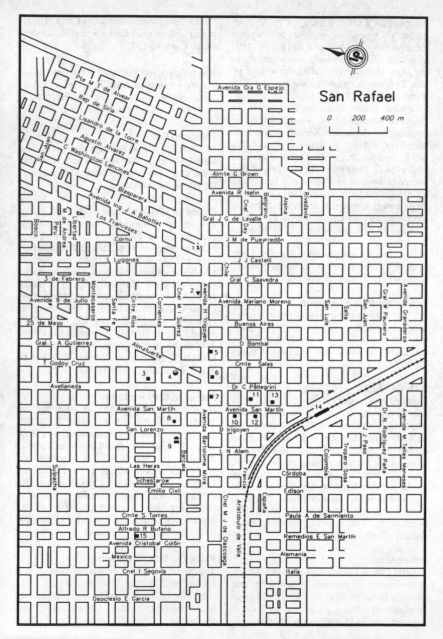

San Rafael

0   200   400 m

Avenida Gra G Espejo
Almte G Brown
Avenida R Iselin
Gral J G de Lavalle
J M de Pueyrredón
J J Castelli
Gral C Saavedra
Avenida Mariano Moreno
Buenos Aires
D Bombal
Cmte Salas
Dr C Pellegrini
Avenida San Martín
B Irigoyen
L N Alem
Córdoba
Edison
Paula A de Sarmiento
Remedios E San Martín
Alemania
Italia

Pte M T de Alvear
Rep de Siria
Lisandro de la Torre
Agustín Alvarez
C Washington Lencinas
Blasparera
Avenida Ing J A Balloffet
Los Franceses
Cornu
L Lugones
3 de Febrero
Avenida 9 de Julio
25 de Mayo
Gral L A Gutierrez
T Godoy Cruz
Avellaneda
Avenida San Martín
San Lorenzo
Las Heras
Schestarow
Emilio Civil
Cmte S Torres
Alfredo R Bufano
Avenida Cristobal Colón
Mexico
Cnel I Segovia
Deoclesio E Garcia

Bosco
Perú
M de Andrea
Libertad
Montecaseros
Santa Fe
Entre Ríos
Corrientes
Cnel M I Suárez
Almafuerte
Avenida H Yrigoyen
Avenida Bartolome Mitre
Barcala
Supacha
Cnel M J de Olascoaga
Aristobulo de Valle
Francia
España

Cnel Day
Belgrano
Chile
San Luis
Salta
San Juan
Alsina
Rivadavia
Gral W Paunero
Avenida Granaderos
Dr N Rodriguez Peña
Avenida M Telles Meneses
J J Paso
Tropero Sosa
Colombia

1	Tourist Office
2	ACA Restaurant
3	Hospedaje La Esperanza
4	Bus Terminal
5	Hospedaje Cerro Nevado
6	Hotel Kalton
7	Hospedaje Rex
8	CAT
9	Post Office
10	Hospedaje Ideal
11	Hotel San Rafael
12	Hotel España
13	Hotel Tonín
14	Railway Station
15	Hotel Regine

(π 28251), at Day 30, has rooms for US$29/46 with breakfast.

Places to Eat
Try *Restaurant ACA* at H Yrigoyen 3522, *Club Español* at Cmte Salas and Day, *Jockey Club* at Belgrano 338, or *El Encuentro* at Coronel Plaza (the eastward continuation of Santa Fe) and P Mendocinas. The local parrillas are on Avenida H Yrigoyen: *El Cortijo* at No 999, *El Pancho* at No 1110, and *Estancia Chica* at No 366.

Getting There & Away
Air Aerolíneas Argentinas (π 21500), at Day and Pellegrini, flies to Mendoza and Buenos Aires three times weekly. The fare is US$165 one-way.

Bus The bus terminal is on Coronel Suárez between Avellaneda and Almafuerte. San Rafael is served by most of the same bus lines as Mendoza. Alto Valle has daily buses to Neuquén. Andesmar goes daily to Comodoro Rivadavia via Puerto Madryn, and to Río Gallegos on Tuesdays.

Empresa Del Sur y Media Agua goes daily to San Juan. Expreso Uspallata goes daily to

Córdoba, and to Las Leñas on weekends and holidays.

TAC has two buses weekly to San Luis, and frequent buses to Mendoza, seven a day to Malargüe and three weekly to Las Leñas.

La Estrella and TAC go nightly to Buenos Aires.

Car Rental Cars can be rented at Avis (π 22515), at Day 28; and at Sánchez Ariel (π 21189), at Avenida Bartolomé Mitre 1178.

AROUND SAN RAFAEL
Cañón del Atuel
South along the Río Atuel, towards El Nihuil, a winding road takes you through a spectacular, multicoloured ravine which locals compare to the Grand Canyon of the Colorado. But much of Cañón del Atuel has been submerged by three hydroelectric dams. The road crosses the Sierra Pintada, where there are interesting petroglyphs on the Cuesta de los Terneros, 32 km from San Rafael.

Dique El Nihuil
El Nihuil, 79 km from San Rafael, is one of the main water sports centres in the province. The 9600-hectare reservoir, Dique El Nihuil, has a constant breeze which makes it particularly good for windsurfing and sailing; other activities include swimming, canoeing and fishing. The *Camping Club de Pescadores* (π 24286) has a restaurant and store, plus some bungalows for rent. In El Nihuil there are more restaurants and a gas station. Empresa TAC has buses from San Rafael at 5.30 am, 10 am and 6 pm.

GENERAL ALVEAR
An agricultural town of 41,000 on the banks of the Río Atuel, Alvear is the south-western entrance to Mendoza province. In the late 19th century, General Diego de Alvear acquired the rich valley lands that originally belonged to the Indian cacique Goico and populated them with immigrants to form an agricultural colony. Among the main products are wine, fruits, vegetables, fodder,

timber and olives. You can visit the wineries along the poplar-lined roads around town.

Orientation
The main streets, Avenida Libertador and Avenida Alvear, divide the town into quadrants. Street names are modified by directional indications.

Information
Tourist Office The Municipalidad, on Avenida Alvear Oeste 550, provides tourist information.

Places to Stay & Eat
There are a few cheap hotels along Avenida Alvear. The friendly *Hotel Avenida*, Avenida Alvear Este 254, has triple rooms for US$4 per person, with a bath shared between every two rooms. Bathrooms are a bit run down but have hot water. Downstairs is a comedor where you can have large portions of basic food for very little money. Other inexpensive places are *Hotel Grosso* (☎ 2392) at Ingeniero Lange 31, and *Hotel Salamanca* on Avenida Alvear Este near República del Líbano.

Other places in town are the *Hotel Buenos Aires* (☎ 2393) at Lange 54, *Hotel Alhambra* (☎ 2706) at Sarmiento 55, and *Hotel San José* at Paso de los Andes 125.

There are confiterías and pizzerías along Avenida Alvear.

Things to Buy
Wine is the thing to buy, from wine shops or supermarkets. Some wine shops are: Vinería Blanco at Avenida San Martín 463, Vinería El Turista at Mitre 2576, and Vinería Favimar at Avenida San Martín 235.

MALARGÜE
Malargüe comes from a Mapuche word meaning either Place of Rocky Mesas or Place of Corrals. The Spaniard Villagra reached the valley in 1551, but until then it had been home to the Pehuenche Indians, who hunted and gathered in the area. As in most regions of the country, the advance of European colonists in the 19th century displaced and dispossessed the original inhabitants. Today petroleum is the main industry, followed by uranium processing for the Comisión Nacional de Energía Atómica.

Malargüe also has a wealth of archaeological and palaeontological sites, but unfortunately the cave paintings and petroglyphs are closed for study. There are two fauna reserves nearby, Payén and Laguna Llancanelo. In winter Las Leñas offers excellent skiing and in summer there is pleasant hiking.

Information
Tourist Office The tourist office is at F Inalicán and N Uriburu.

Places to Stay & Eat
Camping Municipal Malargüe is on Alfonso Capdeville, as is *Camping Polideportivo*.

Three of Malargüe's four hotels are on Avenida San Martín. *Hotel Bambi* (☎ 71237) is at Avenida San Martín 410, *Hotel Theis* (☎ 71429) at Avenida San Martín 938, and *Hotel Turismo* (☎ 71042) at Avenida San Martín 224. *Hotel Rioma* (☎ 71065) is at Fray Inalicán 68.

The Hotel Turismo has a restaurant, called *Puli-Huen*.

Getting There & Away
Transportes Diego Berbel, at Emilio Civit and Cmte Salas, has buses to Las Leñas and other destinations. J A Barros, at Avenida San Martín 997, has tours to Caverna de Las Brujas, and guides for hire. Chaltén Aventura, at Avenida San Martín 113, has smaller vehicles for guided tours or excursions.

AROUND MALARGÜE
Cave & Petrified Trees
The **Caverna de Las Brujas** is a limestone cave on Mt Moncol, eight km from Bardas Blancas along national Ruta 40, 72 km from Malargüe. The nearby **Bosques Petrificados de Llano Blanco** contains petrified

Araucaria trees over 120 million years old. It is six km from the village of Llano Blanco.

Las Leñas

Designed primarily to attract wealthy foreigners, Las Leñas is the most self-consciously prestigious ski centre in Argentina, but despite the glitter it is not totally out of the question for budget travellers. Since opening in 1983, it has attracted an international clientele to its 33 runs.

Las Leñas is located 400 km south-west of Mendoza, 200 km from San Rafael and only 70 km from Malargüe. Its altitude is 2200 metres at the base, but the slopes reach up to 3430 metres. It is open June to October, with international competitions every year. One of the runs has lights and music twice a week.

Las Leñas has a small village with four luxury hotels. *Piscis* is the most extravagant, with wood-burning stoves, a gymnasium, sauna, swimming pool, restaurant, bar, casino and shops. The town also has self catering 'apart-hotels', dormitories with five to eight beds and shared bathrooms, a restaurant *(El Brasero)* and a supermarket. You can stay much more cheaply at Malargüe, 70 km away.

For further information contact the Skileñas office (☎ 23-1628) in Mendoza at Galería Caracol, room 70, Avenida San Martín 1233. In Buenos Aires, contact Skileñas (☎ 312-2104) on the 3rd floor, Reconquista 585. In the USA, call Ski International Reservations System (☎ 864-7545, or toll-free 1-800-862-7545), 2nd floor, 9592 Harding Ave, Surfside, Miami, Florida 33154.

Los Molles

Los Molles is a small, quiet resort 55 km north-west of Malargüe set in a transverse Andean valley. A small number of lifts carry you up to the relatively gentle slopes. The thermal baths are a local attraction. Los Molles is easily accessed from Malargüe, being on the same road as Las Leñas. There is one hotel and a couple of guest houses available. It is much cheaper to stay at Los Molles and ski at Las Leñas.

San Juan Province

SAN JUAN

Founded in 1562 by Juan Jufré de Loaysa y Montesso, San Juan de la Frontera is 170 km north of Mendoza and 1140 km from Buenos Aires. Juan Perón first became a major public figure for his relief efforts after the massive 1944 earthquake, which necessitated complete reconstruction of the city. It stood relatively unharmed in the 1977 earthquake that destroyed Caucete, 30 km away, and which was even felt in Buenos Aires.

Modern construction, wide tree-lined streets and exceptional tidiness characterise the city centre. Full-time custodians sweep the sidewalks and water and patrol the parks and plazas, keeping people off the manicured lawns. As in Mendoza, people swab the sidewalks with kerosene to keep them shining.

For a provincial capital, San Juan preserves the rhythm and cordiality of a small town. With an annual average of nine hours of sun daily, its nickname is Residencia del Sol (Residence of the Sun). El Zonda, the famous north wind, often brings extreme heat and very high pressure, slowing the pace of local activities. As in Mendoza, the streets are empty during siesta hours, between noon and 4 pm.

Orientation

National Ruta 40 from Mendoza passes through San Juan from south to north. Like most Argentine cities, San Juan's grid pattern makes orientation very easy. The addition of cardinal points to street addresses helps even more. East-west Avenida San Martín and north-south Calle Mendoza divide the city into quadrants. The functional centre of town is south of Avenida San Martín.

Information

Tourist Office The Direccion de Turismo (☎ 22-7219), at Sarmiento 24 Sur near

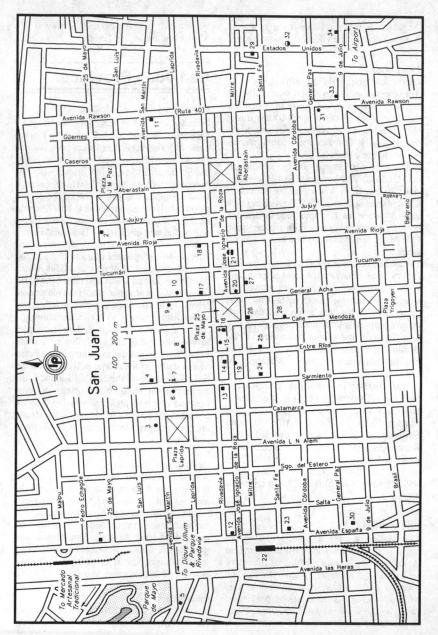

■ PLACES TO STAY

1   Residencial El Mendocino
2   Hotel Jardín Petit
4   Residencial Jessy Mar
11 Residencial Embajador
12 Residencial San
    Francisco
13 Residencial Lara
14 Hotel Nogaró
17 Hotel Alhambra
18 Hotel Selby
23 Residencial Sussex
24 Hotel Plaza
25 Hotel Bristol
26 Hotel Capayán
27 Pensión Central
29 Residencial Hispano
    Argentino
30 Pensión España
34 Hotel América

OTHER

3   Museo de Ciencias
    Naturales
5   Casino Provincial
6   Casa de Sarmiento
7   Tourist Office
8   San Martín's Cell
9   Austral Airlines
10 Casa de Cambio
15 Banco de San Juan
16 Catedral
19 Telecom
20 Bolsa de Comercio
21 ENCOTEL
22 Train Station
28 Aerolíneas Argentinas
31 Museums
32 Bus Terminal
33 ACA

Avenida San Martín, has a good map of the city and its surroundings. They also have useful information and brochures on the rest of the province, particularly Parque Provincial Ischigualasto, also known as Valle de la Luna (Valley of the Moon). Opening hours are 8 am to noon and 4 to 8 pm.

If you are interested in tours, the friendly and knowledgeable staff will provide a list of guides throughout the province. At the entrance, artisanal pottery, crafts, wines and dried fruits are for sale.

Money Money can be changed at Banco de San Juan at Rivadavia 44 Este, Bolsa de Comercio at General Acha 278 Sur, Cambio Cash at Tucumán 210 Sur, and at Cambio Santiago at General Acha 52 Sur. Many travel agencies also exchange cash.

Post & Telecommunications The main post office (ENCOTEL) is at Avenida Ignacio de la Roza 259 Este. Telecom is at Ignacio de la Roza 123 Oeste.

Travel Agencies Several travel agencies organise trips to the interior or to other provinces. Try Yafar Turismo (☎ 22-6176) at Aberastain 102 Sur, Yanzón Viajes y Turismo (☎ 22-2420) at Calle Mendoza 322, Mario Agüero Turismo (☎ 22-3652) at General Acha 17 Norte, and Turismo Sol Sanjuanino (☎ 22-6018) at Avenida España 33 Norte.

Casa de Sarmiento
This colonial house is the birthplace of Domingo Faustino Sarmiento, the Argentine educator, Governor of San Juan and President of the Republic from 1868 to 1874. He was the first president from the interior provinces.

Sarmiento's prolific writing as politician, educator and journalist made him a major public figure both within and beyond Argentina. Exiled in Chile during the government of Rosas, he wrote the famous polemic *Life in the Argentine Republic in the Days of the Tyrants*, readily available in English translation and still used in many South American history courses. A fierce critic of caudillos like Buenos Aires' Rosas and his gaucho followers, Sarmiento argued that Unitarism embodied 'civilisation' on the European model, while Federalism represented unprincipled 'barbarism', resulting in

...the final formation of the central consolidated despotic government of the landed proprietor Don Juan Manuel Rosas, who applied the knife of the gaucho to the culture of Buenos Ayres, and destroyed the work of centuries – of civilisation, law and liberty.

Ironically, most of Sarmiento's knowledge of the Pampas and their gauchos was second-hand, as he did not cross the country overland until after the fall of Rosas.

Sarmiento's *Recuerdos de Provincia* recounted his childhood in this house and his memories of his mother, Doña Paula Albarracín, who paid for part of the house's construction by weaving cloth in a loom under the fig tree which still stands in the front patio. The house is at Sarmiento 21 Sur and is open daily except Monday.

Museo de Bellas Artes Franklin Rawson
Named after the local 19th-century painter, this museum at General Paz 737 Este offers a good overview of Argentine art. Its valuable collection includes paintings, sculptures, drawings and engravings by famous artists such as Prilidiano Pueyrredón, Monvoisin, Rawson, De la Córcova, Berni, Soldi, Spilimbergo, Petorutti, Forner and others.

Museo Histórico Provincial Agustín Gnecco
In the same building as the Museo de Bellas Artes, this museum has an important collection of historical material related to San Juan's colonial life and political development. It also has some archaeological artefacts, and a great coin collection assembled by the historian for whom it is named.

Convento de Santo Domingo
At Avenida San Martín and Entre Ríos, the present Dominican convent, constructed after the 1955 earthquake, lacks the grandeur of the 17th-century original, the order's richest in the territory.

The only part of the old building to survive the quake was the cell occupied by San Martín during his visits to San Juan in 1815, which has a small museum at Laprida 96 Oeste. San Martín held meetings here, soliciting political and financial support for his army, one local division of which liberated

Coquimbo and La Serena, Chile. The original furnishings and some other materials are displayed. It's open Tuesday to Sunday.

Iglesia Catedral
The modern cathedral, at Calle Mendoza and Rivadavia across the street from Plaza 25 de Mayo, was inaugurated in 1979. Italian artists designed and sculpted the bronze doors and the main ornaments inside.

Museo de Ciencias Naturales
At Avenida San Martín and Catamarca, this museum has an interesting collection of plants, animals, minerals and rocks from the province. The museum has conducted studies of important palaeontological sites at Ischigualasto and Ullum, with a comprehensive collection of fossils.

Mercado Artesanal Tradicional
Inaugurated in 1985 to promote local handicrafts, the market is in the Parque de Mayo, at 25 de Mayo and Urquiza, beneath the Auditorio Juan Victoria. Particularly attractive are the brightly coloured *mantas* (shawls) of Jáchal, and the warm ponchos. Besides textiles, there are pottery, riding gear and basketry, as well as traditional silver knife handles, *mate* gourds and key chains. The market is open weekdays.

Wineries
Visit the Bragagnolo winery (☎ 21-1305), on Ruta 40 and Avenida Benavídez in the suburb of Chimbas, for a sample of the region's famous *blanco sanjuanino* (white wine). Besides table and reserve wines, the winery produces excellent dessert wines, such as *mistela* and *moscato dulce* (muscatel), and other products such as juices, raisins, and the regional speciality *arrope de uva*, a sort of grape jam.

Places to Stay – bottom end
Camping *Camping El Pinar*, the municipal site, is on Avenida Benavídez Oeste, six km from the centre, reached by Empresa de la Marina buses. It has a small artificial lake, a swimming pool and a forest plantation.

Charges are US$1 per person and US$1 per tent. There are other sites west of the city, where Avenida San Martín becomes a highway to Dique Ullum and Parque Rivadavia. Take bus No 23 or No 29.

Residenciales & Pensions There are several conveniently located, inexpensive places to stay in San Juan, most of which rent rooms by the hour. Near the train station is *Residencial San Francisco* (☎ 22-3760), Avenida España 248 Sur, with modest but clean singles/doubles for US$8/14. Similar in price and standard are *Residencial El Mendocino* (☎ 22-5930) at España 234 Norte, and *Residencial Sussex* at España 402 Sur. *Pensión España* (☎ 22-2350), also near the train station at España 612 Sur, is a quiet, friendly place with some permanent residents. Singles are US$7 with shared bath.

There are several more near the bus terminal. The small rooms at friendly *Residencial Hispano Argentino*, Estados Unidos 381 Sur, cost US$5 per person with shared bath. *Residencial Embajador* (☎ 22-5520), Avenida Rawson 25 Sur, has nice, clean rooms at US$8 per person.

With a well-established reputation for cleanliness, *Pensión Central* (☎ 22-3174) at Mitre 131 Este is the best inexpensive accommodation in town; it's central but quiet, has firm beds, and costs US$7 per person with shared bath. At *Residencial Jessy Mar* (☎ 22-7195), Sarmiento 8 Norte, the owner is friendly and the clean but tiny rooms cost US$5 per person. *Residencial Lara* (☎ 22-7973), Rivadavia 213 Oeste, is a bargain at US$3 per person but somewhat run down. Since there are resident families with children, it can get noisy.

Places to Stay – middle
There is more variation in price than in standard and services of hotels in this category. All offer telephone, heating, air-conditioning and parking garage. Some have a restaurant or confitería.

The cheapest in the category are *Hotel América* (☎ 21-4514), 9 de Julio 1052 Este, which charges US$15/28 with private bath,

and *Hotel Plaza* (☎ 22-5179), Sarmiento 344 Sur, where rates are US$18/30.

Hotel Alhambra (☎ 22-8280), General Acha 180 Sur, has rooms for US$24/32. In the same range are *Hotel Selby* (☎ 22-4777), Avenida Rioja 183 Sur, and *Hotel Bristol* (☎ 22-2629), Entre Ríos 368 Sur. *Hotel Jardín Petit* (☎ 21-1825), 25 de Mayo 345 Este, has rooms for US$25/40.

Places to Stay – top end
The costliest hotels in San Juan are comfortable but not as luxurious as those in Mendoza. *Hotel Capayán* (☎ 22-5122), Mitre 31 Este, has rooms for US$31/42, while *Hotel Nogaró* (☎ 22-7501), at Ignacio de la Roza 132 Este, has rooms for US$40/54.

Places to Eat
Like Mendoza, San Juan has a varied international cuisine at private clubs operated by different cultural associations. *Club Sirio Libanés*, Entre Ríos 33 Sur, serves Middle Eastern food in a very pleasant environment of beautifully conserved tiles and woodwork. Prices are moderate. *Comedor Español*, at Rivadavia 32 Este, is rather sombre, with ordinary food and erratic service.

La Nona María, at Avenida San Martín and P Moreno, has excellent pasta. *El Rincón Cuyano*, at Sarmiento 394 Norte, has a standard Argentine menu, but the food is good, service is friendly and prices are reasonable. Near the outskirts of town, on Avenida Circunvalación near Avenida San Martín, *Wiesbaden* has good German food.

There are two vegetarian restaurants: *Xe Lu Cher* at San Martín 1653 Oeste, and *Soychu* at Ignacio de la Roza 223 Oeste. The restaurant of the *Hotel Nogaró* is rather expensive but good.

There are several parrillas on Avenida Circunvalación; *La Bodega del 800* at Tucumán is recommended. *Nahuel* is at Salta, while *Bona Nit* and *Mikonos* are on Avenida San Martín. There are others near the city centre, mostly along Avenida San Martín, such as *El Gordo* (corner of Alvear) and *Las Cubas* (corner of P Moreno). *Bigotes*, Las Heras and Ignacio de la Roza, has tenedor libre beef, chicken and salads for a reasonable price.

For a good inexpensive lunch, try *Restaurant Avenida* on 9 de Julio Este, half a block from the ACA. For fast food, try the lomo (steak sandwich) at *Lomos al Tiro*, on Calle Mendoza and Avenida San Martín. Pizzería *Un Rincón de Napoli*, Rivadavia 175 Sur, has a wide selection of toppings and good beer.

Getting There & Away
Air Both Aerolíneas Argentinas (☎ 22-0205), Mendoza 468 Sur, and Austral, General Acha 19 Sur, have daily flights to Buenos Aires. Las Chacritas Airport (☎ 25-0486) is on national Ruta 20, 13 km south-east of town.

Bus The bus terminal (☎ 22-1604) is at Estados Unidos 492 Sur. Empresa Del Sur y Media Agua has four daily buses to Mendoza and daily service to Rosario and Neuquén. Autotransportes San Juan has three afternoon buses to Buenos Aires, and also goes to Mar del Plata daily at noon.

Empresa SOCASA has two buses daily to Córdoba, one direct and the other via La Rioja. Buses 20 de Junio also goes to Córdoba, but takes the scenic Altas Sierras route. La Estrella has direct buses to Tucumán, Catamarca and La Rioja.

TICSA buses travel daily to Bahía Blanca and three times weekly to General Roca, Neuquén and Zapala. On Wednesday a bus also goes to San Martín de los Andes, and on Friday and Sunday to Bariloche. Wednesday and Friday mornings it has buses to Viedma, and on Tuesdays and Fridays to Santiago de Chile.

TAC has daily service to Chile (Santiago, Valparaíso and Viña del Mar), plus five buses to Mendoza. It also serves northern San Juan, (Jáchal and Pismanta), Bariloche to the south, and the eastern destinations of San Luis, Merlo and Paraná.

Empresa Iglesia travels to provincial destinations only. It goes daily to Baños,
Talacasto, Iglesia, Las Flores, Pismanta, Tudcun, Rodeo and Angualasto. Empresa Vallecito has a daily bus to Caucete, the Difunta Correa shrine, and San Agustín del Valle Fértil.

Typical one-way fares are: to Córdoba US$25, Buenos Aires US$43, Mar del Plata US$56, Bariloche US$72, San Luis US$12, Neuquén US$48, Chile US$22, Pismanta US$9, and to Vallecito (Difunta Correa) US$2.50.

Train The train station (☎ 22-6254) is on Avenida España between Mitre and Santa Fe. Ferrocarril San Martín's *El Aconcagua* train goes daily to San Juan via Mendoza. It arrives at San Juan 2½ hours after reaching Mendoza. Going to Buenos Aires, it departs at 1.30 pm.

AROUND SAN JUAN
Dique Ullum
Only a short distance west of San Juan, this reservoir is a centre of nautical sports – swimming, fishing, water-skiing and windsurfing.

Museo Arqueológico La Laja
Focusing on the prehistory of San Juan and part of the province's university, this museum is 25 km north of downtown San Juan in the village of La Laja. Seven showrooms, organised chronologically from the Fortuna culture of 6500 BC to the Incas and their trans-Andean contemporaries, display mummies, basketry, tools of many different materials, sculptures, petroglyphs and remains of cultivated plants.

Outdoors, there are reproductions of natural environments, farming systems, petroglyphs and house types, all built to scale. The building itself, in a Moorish style of large stone blocks, was once a hotel which featured thermal baths, which are still in use. After your visit, have a hot soak.

To reach the museum, take bus No 20 ('Albardón') from Avenida Córdoba in San Juan. Only three a day, at 8 am and 1 and 4 pm, go all the way. If you miss any of those, take any No 20 'Albardón' to Las Piedritas

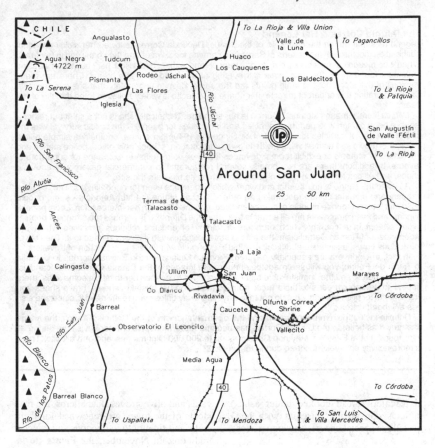

Around San Juan

and hitch the last five km with trucks or other vehicles which go to the quarry across from the museum.

DIFUNTA CORREA SHRINE

At Vallecito, about 60 km east of San Juan, the shrine of the popular saint Difunta Correa is one of the most fascinating, offbeat cultural attractions in all of Argentina. While patronising, Sarmiento's commentary on Argentine rural religion in the 19th century can give you some idea what to expect:

To this, that is, to natural religion, is all religion reduced in the pastoral districts. Christianity exists, like the Spanish idioms, as a tradition which is perpetuated, but corrupted; coloured by gross superstitions and unaided by instruction, rites, or convictions.

Places to Stay & Eat

There is one inexpensive hostería, but accommodation is much better in San Juan. Like the pilgrims, you can camp almost anywhere. There is good street food and a decent restaurant in the village. Be sure to visit the kiosk of lively and personable Doña María, at the foot of the stairs to the shrine, for tortas

The Difunta Correa & Her Legend

Legend tells that during the civil wars of the 1840s, Deolinda Correa followed her sickly conscript husband on foot through the deserts of San Juan, carrying food, water and their baby son in her arms. When her meagre supplies ran out, thirst, hunger and exhaustion killed her, but when passing muleteers found them, the infant was still nursing at the dead woman's breast. There are many versions of this story, but the main points are the same, despite uncertainty that she ever existed. Commemorating this apparent miracle, her shrine at Vallecito is widely believed to be the site of her death.

Difunta literally means 'defunct'; Correa is her surname. Technically she is not a saint but rather a 'soul', a dead person who performs miracles and intercedes for people – the child's survival was the first of a series of miracles attributed to her. Since the 1940s her shrine, originally a simple hilltop cross, has grown into a small village with its own petrol station, school, post office, police station and church. At 17 chapels or exhibit rooms, devotees leave *ex-votos* (gifts) in exchange for supernatural favours. In addition, there are two hotels, several restaurants, a commercial gallery with souvenir shops, and offices for the non-profit organisation which administers the site.

A visit to the shrine is an unusual and worthwhile experience even for nonbelievers. The religious imagery and material culture resembles no other Christian shrine in Latin America – some people build and leave elaborate models of homes and cars obtained through her intercession. Local people, pilgrims and even merchants are all eager to talk about the Difunta. It is perhaps the strongest popular belief system in a country which harbours a variety of unusual religious practices which are independent of Roman Catholicism, the official state religion, even if clearly related to it. They tell of miraculous cures, assistance at difficult childbirth, economic windfalls and protection of travellers.

In fact, truck drivers are especially devoted. From La Quiaca, on the Bolivian border, to Ushuaia in Tierra del Fuego, you will see roadside shrines with images of the Difunta Correa, wax candles, small banknotes, and the unmistakable bottles of water left to quench her thirst. At some sites, there appear to be enough parts to build a car from scratch – do not mistake wheels, brake shoes and crankshafts for piles of trash – but do not take anything away unless you really need it, since she also has a vengeful streak.

Despite lack of government support and the open antagonism of the Catholic Church, the shrine has grown as belief in the Difunta Correa has become more widespread. People visit the shrine all year round, but at Easter, 1 May and Christmas up to 200,000 pilgrims descend on Vallecito. There is more activity on weekends than during the week. ∎

---

al rescoldo (bread cooked under ashes), tabletas con arrope (biscuits with jam), quesillo (a special cheese) and empanadas.

Getting There & Away

Empresa Vallecito goes daily from San Juan to the shrine. Any bus going east, toward La Rioja or Córdoba, will drop you at the site. Another alternative is to take a bus to Caucete, midway between San Juan and Vallecito, and go to the offices of Fundación Cementerio Vallecito, where you can catch a lift with the water trucks which serve the shrine.

JÁCHAL

Founded in 1751 and known as the Cuna de la Tradición (Cradle of Tradition), Jáchal is a charming, small town surrounded by vine-yards and olive groves. Jachalleros, the residents of the town, are renowned for their crafts and fidelity to indigenous and gaucho traditions. In November, the **Fiesta de la Tradición** pays homage to this way of life and reinforces it.

Jáchal contains a mix of older adobe buildings and more contemporary brick architecture. In their patios, you can still see the 19th-century looms on which weavers make the famous Jachallero ponchos and blankets. Across from the main plaza, the **Iglesia San José**, a national monument, houses the *Cristo Negro* (Black Christ) or *Señor de la Agonía* (Lord of Agony), a leather image with articulated head and limbs, brought from Potosí in colonial times.

There are several campgrounds in and around Jáchal.

AROUND JÁCHAL

A day trip on national Ruta 40, north of San Juan, passes through a beautiful landscape of rich folkloric traditions, which foreigners rarely see.

East of Jáchal, the road climbs the precipitous **Cuesta de Huaco**, with a view of Los Cauquenes dam, arriving a bit later at the village of **Huaco**, birthplace of the poet Don Buenaventura Luna, who put the Jachallero culture in the map. The 200-year-old flour mill justifies the trip.

Backtracking to national Ruta 150, you cross the **Cuesta del Viento** and pass through the tunnels of Rodeo west of Jáchal to the department of Iglesia, home of the precordillera thermal baths of **Pismanta**. Its waters, at 42°C are recommended for rheumatic ailments, blood circulation and general cleansing and relaxation. The *Hotel Termas de Pismanta* has rooms with bath, a restaurant/confitería, and a swimming pool.

Ruta 150 continues westwards to La Serena and Coquimbo, both in Chile, via the recently re opened **Paso de Agua Negra** (altitude 4722 metres).

South of Pismanta, provincial Ruta 436 returns to Ruta 40 and San Juan. Another worthwhile stop is **Iglesia**, a small Andean town where people cultivate fruit (mostly apples), make goat and cow cheeses, and weave unique guanaco blankets, ponchos and saddlebags.

SAN AGUSTÍN DE VALLE FÉRTIL

The department of Valle Fértil presents a different landscape to that of the Jáchal area. Rather than the Andes, it is among the Sierras Pampeanas, which are low sedimentary mountains cut by impressive canyons. The colourful hills, the rivers, and the exuberant flora and varied fauna make the place a special tourist attraction.

Founded in 1788, the town of San Agustín de Valle Fértil, containing 6000 people and located 314 km from San Juan, has a temperate climate and high rainfall. The main activities are agriculture and animal husbandry, and mining of quartz, mica and marble, plus smaller quantities of granite, gold and iron. Señor Américo Cortés of the tourist office is exceptionally helpful, providing general information, chatting about the town's traditional artists, and recommending walks along the river.

The town is small enough that people pay little attention to street addresses. Ask directions or use the map.

Things to See & Do

A day by the river is pleasant and relaxing, for fishing, sunbathing or walking. About 300 metres west of it, you can see the petroglyphs of **Piedra Pintada**. About 500 metres farther on there are Indian mortars. The village of **La Majadita**, 7 km from San Agustín by mule or cart, is only possible to reach during the winter dry season, since the road crosses the river several times. You can find lodging at a local rancho, where you can eat kid goat, goat cheese, and have fresh milk in the morning.

Places to Stay & Eat

The *Camping Municipal* is a giveaway, charging US$0.40 per person, US$0.40 per tent and US$0.20 per vehicle. *Camping del ACA* is a great place, with excellent facilities for US$3 per group per day. Given its popularity among Sanjuaninos, it gets very crowded during long weekends and holidays.

The cheapest and most pleasant places are private homes. Four families all charge about US$5/8 for singles/doubles with shared bath: *Pensión Patrocinio Romero, Pensión Doña Zoila, Pensión Nicolás Mercado* and *Pensión Villalón*.

There are also three hospedajes: *Hospedaje San Agustín* has rooms at US$8/13 with private bath and hot water; it also has a restaurant/confitería. Similar in price, but with shared baths, is *Hospedaje Los Olivos*. At *Hospedaje Santa Fe* rooms with shared bath cost US$7/11.

The costliest place is the spectacularly sited *Hostería del ACA*, which has great

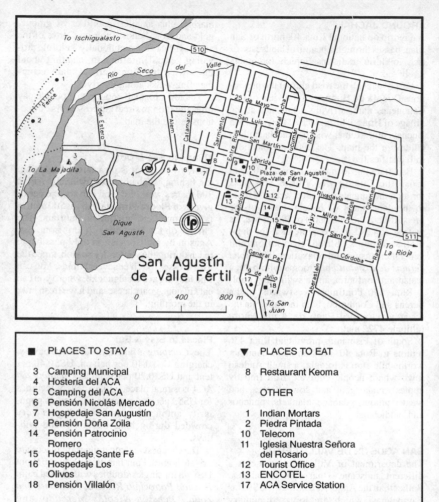

San Agustín de Valle Fértil

■	PLACES TO STAY
3	Camping Municipal
4	Hostería del ACA
5	Camping del ACA
6	Pensión Nicolás Mercado
7	Hospedaje San Augustín
9	Pensión Doña Zoila
14	Pensión Patrocinio Romero
15	Hospedaje Sante Fé
16	Hospedaje Los Olivos
18	Pensión Villalón

▼	PLACES TO EAT
8	Restaurant Keoma

	OTHER
1	Indian Mortars
2	Piedra Pintada
10	Telecom
11	Iglesia Nuestra Señora del Rosario
12	Tourist Office
13	ENCOTEL
17	ACA Service Station

views of the valley and the reservoir. It also has a good restaurant and confitería. Singles/doubles cost US$15/23 for members and US$22/34 for nonmembers.

Besides the hotel restaurants, try *Restaurant Keoma*, a pleasant parrilla owned and attended by a very friendly family, who will also change money.

Getting There & Away
From San Juan, take Empresa Vallecito buses or hitch a ride with the mining trucks.

PARQUE PROVINCIAL ISCHIGUALASTO
Valles de la Luna (Valleys of the Moon) may seem a dime a dozen if you spend much time

in South America, but they are usually worth seeing. One of them is San Juan's Parque Provincial Ischigualasto, named for an ancient Indian culture and comparable to North American national parks like Bryce Canyon or Zion. It has yielded a wealth of fossils, some 180 million years old from the Triassic period, exposed by the persistent action of water over time.

Ischigualasto is a desert valley between two sedimentary mountain ranges, the Cerros Colorados in the east and Cerro Los Rastros in the west. Over millennia, at every meander in the canyon, the waters of the nearly Río Ischigualasto have carved distinctive shapes in the monochrome clays, red sandstones and volcanic ash. Predictably, some of the these forms have acquired popular names: Cancha de Bochas (The Ball Court), Lámpara de Aladino (Aladdin's Lamp), El Loro (The Parrot), and El Gusano (The Worm). The desert flora of algarrobo trees, shrubs and cacti complement the eerie landforms.

Getting There & Away

Ischigualasto is about 75 km north of San Agustín. Given its size and isolation, the only practical way to visit the park is by vehicle. After you arrive at the visitor centre and pay the US$0.80 entrance fee, one of the park rangers will accompany your vehicle on a two-hour circuit through the park.

If you have no vehicle, ask in the tourist office at San Agustín for people who will be making the trip. Alternatively, contact the park in advance so that the park ranger off duty during your visit can be hired as a guide, using their vehicle. The ranger will pick you up at the police checkpoint at Los Baldecitos on provincial Ruta 510, reached by the COTIL bus to La Rioja. Write to them at the following address: Sr Pereira or Sr Villafañe, Parque Provincial Ischigualasto, (5449) San Agustín del Valle Fértil, San Juan.

Camping and hiking are possible, but there are no clear rules. With persistence, if you can prove you are an experienced hiker, the rangers will let you pitch your tent by the Visitor Centre and will supply water. There is a small confitería there.

San Luis Province

SAN LUIS

San Luis is the eastern gateway to Cuyo, being 260 km from Mendoza via national Ruta 7, 456 km from Córdoba via national Ruta 148, and 832 km from Buenos Aires. A small but lively city of 80,000 people, this provincial capital was founded in 1594. During the 1970s and 1980s, San Luis grew and attracted industry through a program of industrial promotion and tax incentives.

Orientation

The commercial centre is along the parallel streets of San Martín and Rivadavia between Plaza Pringles in the north and Plaza Independencia in the south.

Information

Tourist Office The Dirección Provincial de Turismo, open weekdays only, is at San Martín 555. It has flashy brochures with little information, but the staff can provide more thorough material, including a fairly complete list of hotels with budget alternatives.

Money You can exchange money at the Banco de la Nación, Banco Provincia, Banco Hipotecario, and Banco Nacional de Desarrollo, all around Plaza Pringles. Alituris, at Junín 868, also changes dollars and Chilean pesos weekdays from 8 am to noon, and Saturdays from 8.30 to 12.30.

Post & Telecommunications The post office is at Arturo Illia and San Martín. The telephone office is at Colón and Lavalle.

Travel Agencies Besides Alituris, try Dasso Viajes, at Jofré 590 or Turismo La Cumbre at Colón 950.

Iglesia Catedral

Across from Plaza Pringles, on Rivadavia, is

San Luis

0   200   400 m

To Beazley &
Mendoza

To Zanjitas

■ PLACES TO STAY

1 Residencial Rivadavia
2 Residencial 17
3 Residencial Los Andes
4 Hotel Iguazú
5 Residencial San Antonio
8 Hotel Quintana
9 Hotel Aiello
11 Hotel San Luis
12 Hotel Mitre
13 Hotel España
15 Hotel Regidor
17 Residencial Royal
18 Hotel Retana
20 Hotel Dos Venados
23 Hotel Castelmonte
25 Hotel Grand Palace
27 Hotel Comesa
30 Hotel Huarpes
32 Residencial María Eugenia
33 Residencial Buenos Aires

OTHER

6 Bus Terminal
7 Railway Station
10 ACA
14 Post Office
16 Telecom
19 Palacio de Gobierno
21 Iglesia Catedral
22 Plaza Pringles
24 Banco de la Nación
26 Banco de San Luis
28 Intendencia Municipal
29 Tourist Office
31 Plaza Independencia

the 19th-century cathedral, built of provincial woods like algarrobo for windows and frames, local white marble for steps and columns, sand from Montevideo and French tiles.

Iglesia de Santo Domingo

This church and convent are across from Plaza Independencia. The present church, built in the 1930s, replaced its 17th-century predecessor but conserved its Moorish style. Part of the old church can be seen next door, inside the historical archives on 25 de Mayo, whose algarrobo doors alone justify a visit.

Mercado Artesanal

Run by Dominican friars, and located next to the Santo Domingo church on 25 de Mayo, this market sells gorgeous handmade wool rugs as well as ceramics, onyx crafts, and weavings from other parts of the province. It's open weekdays from 7 am to 1 pm.

Places to Stay – bottom end

The cheapest hotel in San Luis is *Residencial María Eugenia*, 25 de Mayo 741, with large, very clean rooms with shared bath atUS$5/8 for singles/doubles. Since the all rooms front onto an enclosed hall, it can be a bit noisy during the day, but it's quiet at night. *Residencial Royal* (☎ 22022), at Colón 878, has rooms for US$7/13.

Similar in price and standard are *Residencial Casablanca* (☎ 23206), Belgrano 1046; *Residencial 17* (☎ 23387), at Estado de Israel 1475; and *Residencial Rivadavia* (☎ 22437), across the street at Estado de Israel 1470. The latter two are both near the bus terminal.

Residencial Los Andes (☎ 22033), Ejército de los Andes 1180, has singles for US$9. Nearby *Residencial San Antonio* (☎ 22717), on the corner of Avenida Ejército de los Andes and Avenida España, is slightly cheaper. *Residencial Buenos Aires* (☎ 24062), at Buenos Aires 834, has modest but adequate rooms for US$9/17. At *Hotel Cesar* (☎ 20483), Falucho 163, rates are US$8/14.

Places to Stay – middle

Hotels in this category are similar in price, appearance and services. *Hotel Iguazú* (☎ 22129), Ejército de los Andes 1582, has rooms for US$11/17. *Hotel Mitre* (☎ 24599) at Mitre 1045 has identical prices. *Hotel Grand Palace* (☎ 22059), at Rivadavia 657, has a pleasant atmosphere and nice rooms for US$12/19. At the *Hotel Retana* (☎ 24432), Maipú 874, rates are US$14/22.

A bit more expensive are *Hotel Comesa* (☎ 22996) at Colón 667 and *Hotel Huarpes* (☎ 25597) at Belgrano 1568, with rooms for US$16/23. *Hotel Castelmonte* (☎ 24963), at Chacabuco 769, charges US$16/19.

Places to Stay – top end

One good-value place is the pleasant *Hotel España* (☎ 25051), at Arturo Illia 300, with rooms at US$20/27 including breakfast. A block away are *Hotel Aiello* (☎ 25609), Illia 431, and *Hotel San Luis* (☎ 22881), Illia 470, both with rooms for US$23/31. Try also *Hotel Dos Venados* (☎ 22312), at Sucre and República del Líbano, which has a good restaurant and confitería.

The most expensive hotels are *Hotel Regidor* (☎ 24756) at San Martín 804, with rooms for US$32/41, and *Hotel Quintana* (☎ 29548), at Illia 546, with rates of US$36/50. The latter has a good restaurant and confitería.

Places to Eat

There are many restaurants doing good business in San Luis. Traditional dishes include *locro* (a thick maize soup), empanadas de horno (baked empanadas), and cazuela de gallina (chicken soup). For desert, try quesillo con arrope or figs.

La Taberna Vasca, at Colón and Bolívar, has mostly Spanish cuisine. Try their seafood dishes. *El Colonial*, at Pedernera 1460, has a pleasant setting and moderate prices. *La Porteña* is at Junín 696. *El Triángulo*, at Illia and Caseros, has a varied menu and acceptable prices.

Restaurant Argentino at Illia 352 serves large portions of good pasta. *Restaurant San Antonio*, next door to the Hotel Iguazú, is good value. *El Abuelo*, at J Roca and General Paz, has good lunches at moderate prices.

There are also a few parrillas on Ruta 20 and some in the town centre. *El Fogón* is at J Roca 1515, *El Chacho* at Miramar and San Juan, and *Patio Quieto* at Uriburu and Rivadavia.

A good breakfast place is the confitería at the bus terminal. They open early in the morning, and serve terrific café con leche with croissants.

Getting There & Away

Air Aerolíneas Argentinas (☎ 23407) has two flights a week to Buenos Aires via Río Cuarto, Córdoba province .

Bus The bus terminal is on España between San Martín and Rivadavia.

Autotransportes San Juan travels daily to San Juan, four times daily to Buenos Aires via Villa Mercedes and Río Cuarto, and to Mar del Plata. Chevallier has three buses nightly to Buenos Aires. TAC has hourly buses to Mendoza, three daily to Córdoba, one to Rosario, buses to Villa Mercedes every two hours, and two daily to Villa Dolores.

Empresa del Sur y Media Agua goes to Rosario and San Juan. TICSA travels to Bariloche (via the Río Negro valley and Neuquén) four times weekly.

Jocolí goes to Mendoza, Buenos Aires, Mar del Plata and Santa Rosa. It also covers provincial destinations: Villa Mercedes, Merlo, San Martín, Unión, Trapiche, Florida and Pozo de los Funes.

Colta has buses to Córdoba, Río Cuarto, Villa Mercedes, La Falda, Cosquín, Carlos Paz and Mendoza. They also have a direct bus to Santiago de Chile.

Empresa Dasso travels to small provincial towns, and also organises fortnightly excursions to the Difunta Correa on Sundays at 12.45 am if they get a minimum of 30 people.

Typical one-way fares are: Buenos Aires US$40, Mar del Plata US$45 and Chile US$30.

Train *El Aconcagua*, on the San Martín line, travels daily to Buenos Aires at 8 pm. It has turista, primera, pullman and sleeper coaches. The primera fare is US$17.

MERLO

In the Sierras de Comechingones, 180 km from San Luis and 900 metres above sea level, Merlo's mountainous locale and gentle climate make it a popular resort, but it is less frequented than the better known Sierras de Córdoba. Founded in 1797, its church, plaza and other buildings still impart a colonial atmosphere which struggles against the modern architecture of private homes, restaurants and hotels.

Orientation & Information

The local tourist office, on the plaza, has complete information on hotels and campgrounds, but little on outdoor activities. The woman at the confitería next door, a native of Merlo, is most helpful in this regard. Banco Provincia, also on the plaza, will change cash at better rates than most hotels.

Places to Stay – bottom end

Camping There are several campgrounds in Merlo, mostly in El Rincón about two km from the town centre. The shady and tidy *Camping Municipal* has superb views of the Sierra. They charge US$3 a day per site. You can get there by bus with Empresa Virgen del Valle.

Residenciales, Hotels & Motels For a town its size, Merlo has an abundance of hotels. The cheapest is *Residencial Oviedo*, (☎ 75193) at Coronel Mercau 799, where singles/doubles with bath cost US$3/6. Try also *Residencial Egle* (☎ 75168) at Poeta Lugones in Barrio Pellegrini. *Residencial El Castaño* (☎ 75327), on the elegant Avenida del Sol, charges US$5/9. A bit costlier, but excellent, is *Hotel Mirasierras* (☎ 75043) at Avenida del Sol and Pedernera.

Several places charge about US$8/14: *Hotel La Llegada* at Sarmiento 405, *Hotel El Molino* on Rincón del Este, and *Residencial Chiquita* (☎ 75218) at Coronel Mercau 479. *Motel 27 de Abril*, which belongs to the auto

workers union, has an incredible setting and is open to the public if space is available.

Other possibilities are *Hotel Castelar* (☎ 75206), Comechingones 21; *Residencial Villegas*, at Avenida de los Césares 1406 in El Rincón; and *Residencial Amancay* (☎ 75311), Avenida del Sol 500.

Places to Stay – middle

The very intimate *Posada Ignali* (☎ 75274), at Avenida San Martín 684, has rooms with bath for US$16/25 with breakfast. *Residencial Planetario*, at Avenida del Sol and Marte, is comparably small, and has rooms with bath for US$10/16. *Hotel Conyilo* (☎ 75293) is very good value at US$10/16 with bath and breakfast.

Residencial Sierras Verdes (☎ 75340), Avenida del Sol 458, and *Residencial Piscu Yaco* (☎ 75187), at Avenida del Sol 231, have rooms with bath for US$16/21. *Motel Algarrobo* (☎ 75208), at Avenida del Sol 1120, has identical prices. *Hotel Casablanca* (☎ 75084), at Avenida del Sol 50, is dearer at US$21/33 with breakfast.

Places to Stay – top end

The most expensive hotels are *Parque Hotel* (☎ 75110), Avenida del Sol 821, with singles at US$42; and *Hotel Clima 3* (☎ 75297), at Av del Sol 416, where the same price includes all meals.

Places to Eat

There is a good, very inexpensive restaurant called *Restaurant Plaza* near the Casa del Poeta and the ACA station.

Getting There & Away

Empresa Jocolí buses connect Merlo with San Luis.

The Andean North-West

The most 'traditional' part of Argentina, the Andean North-West consists of the provinces of Jujuy, Salta, Tucumán, La Rioja, Catamarca and Santiago del Estero, all of which had thriving cities when Buenos Aires was still an insignificant backwater. The region's highly visible pre-Hispanic and colonial past make the trip south from Peru and Bolivia to the Argentine heartland a journey through time as well as space.

History

In pre-Columbian times, the North-West was the most densely populated part of what is now Argentina, containing perhaps two-thirds of the population. Several indigenous groups, the largest of which was the Diaguita, practised irrigated maize agricul-

ture in the valleys of the eastern Andean foothills, and also cultivated a variety of complementary crops, such as potatoes, beans, squash and *quinoa* (a native Andean grain) at different altitudes. While their numbers were smaller and their political organisation less complex than the native civilisations of Peru and Bolivia, they could mobilise sufficient labour to build agricultural terraces and military fortifications. Other groups included the Lule to the south and west of present-day Salta, the Tonocote around Santiago del Estero, and the Omahuaca of Jujuy.

Some decades before the European invasion, the Inca Empire began to expand its influence among the Diaguita and other southern Andean peoples, but the area was only peripheral to the Andean civilisations. Its orientation, though, was toward the agricultural peoples of the north rather than to the hunters and gatherers of the Pampas. When the Spaniards replaced the Incas at the apex of political authority, they reinforced this trend, founding cities as they advanced south.

The first Spaniard to visit the region was Diego de Almagro, whose expedition from Cuzco to Santiago, Chile, travelled the eastern side of the Andes before crossing the heights of the Puna de Atacama. En route, Almagro and his men passed through present-day Jujuy and Salta, but it was decades before the Spaniards established permanent settlements in the region, which was known by the name of Tucumán. The Spaniards hoped that Indian populations would be sufficiently large to provide substantial encomiendas, but the area never provided the wealth of labour and tribute that Peru did.

The earliest city, founded in 1553, was Santiago del Estero. Hostile Indians destroyed several others before the successful founding of San Miguel de Tucumán (1565), Córdoba (1573), Salta (1582), La

Rioja (1591), and San Salvador de Jujuy (1593). The Cuyo region, including the cities of Mendoza and San Juan, was settled from Santiago, Chile, across the Andes about the same time as Tucumán, while Catamarca was founded more than a century later.

These settlements were not impressive in their infancy – according to historian David Rock, the number of Spaniards in the Tucumán region did not exceed 700 at the end of the 16th century. Still, they established the basic institutions and visible features of Spanish colonial rule which still survive in many modern Argentine cities: the cabildo or town council, the church, and the rectangular plaza around which clustered important public buildings. The governor or the members of the cabildo distributed rights to the Spanish landowners for the labour of local Indians, but as the Indians fell to European diseases and Spanish exploitation over the next century, encomiendas lost most of their economic value. In Santiago del Estero, for example, there were 48 encomiendas with 12,000 Indians in 1582, while in 1673 the remaining 34 encomiendas had only 3358 Indians.

During the colonial period, Tucumán was in the economic orbit of the bonanza silver mine at Potosí, in modern Bolivia. Spanish economic activities in the region started with the provision of mules and the cultivation of cotton and production of textiles, but as the region recovered from the 17th-century depression (due largely to labour shortages), sugar cane eventually became the dominant factor. In part, the Spaniards had no alternative to this northward orientation, since the crown's mercantile policy decreed that commerce between Spain and the colonies had to pass through Lima, by sea to Panamá, and across the isthmus to the Caribbean and then across the Atlantic.

Only after creation of the Viceroyalty of the River Plate in 1776 did this orientation change, as Buenos Aires began to emerge from the shadow of Lima. Opening of the Atlantic to legal shipping towards the end of the colonial period, followed by political independence, relegated the provinces of Jujuy and Salta to economic marginality, but the adoption of sugar monoculture reversed Tucumán's economic orientation and increased its importance in the new country.

Even today, the northern provinces resemble the Andean countries as much or more than they do the cultural core of the Argentine Pampas. Quechua Indian communities can be found as far south as Santiago del Estero.

Jujuy Province

Jujuy is one of Argentina's smallest and poorest provinces. To the north, it is bound by Bolivia, to the west by Chile, and to the south and east by Salta province. Geographically, it resembles the high arid steppe (altiplano) of Bolivia, with saline lakes *(salares)* above 4000 metres in the west, punctuated by soaring volcanic peaks. To the east, a lower range of foothills gives way to deeply dissected river valleys, opening onto subtropical lowlands toward the Gran Chaco. The river valleys, such as the Quebrada de Humahuaca of the Río Grande, have exposed spectacular desert landforms.

Most budget travellers are likely to approach Jujuy from Bolivia via the border complex of Villazón/La Quiaca en route to Salta, although some take the trans-Chaco highways from Resistencia or Formosa. For approaches from the south, see the section on Salta below.

If you do enter Argentina from Bolivia, Argentine prices are likely to be an unpleasant shock. Before you panic and dash back across the border, look at the alternatives for cheaper lodging, food and transportation which are suggested in this chapter and elsewhere in the book.

Jujuy has numerous wildlife and fauna reserves, though access to most of them is difficult.

JUJUY
At the southern end of the Quebrada de Humahuaca, where the valley broadened and

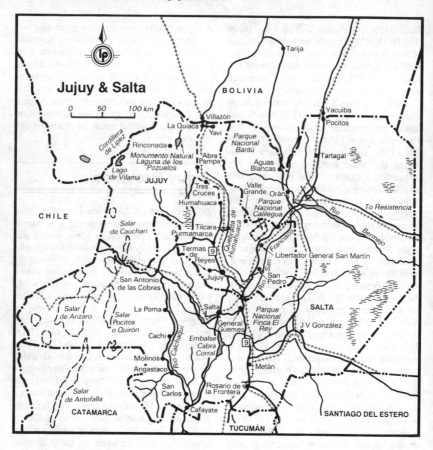

the climate was perpetually spring-like at 1200 metres, the Spaniards founded Jujuy, the most northerly of their colonial cities. During the colonial era, Jujuy was an important way station for mule traders en route to Potosí, but it also gained a certain prosperity through the cultivation of sugar cane under the aegis of Jesuit missions and, well after independence, of British investors.

The province is rich in archaeological resources. Jujuy's name may be evidence of Inca influence, since according to the Inca noble Guamán Poma de Ayala, designated Inca governors in the region went by the Quechua title of *Xuxuyoc*, a word Hispanicised as 'Jujuy' by early European residents. There are several other explanations, including the Spanish corruption of the name of the Río Xibi Xibi. The town's proper name of San Salvador de Jujuy distinguished it as a Spanish settlement and also avoided confusion with nearby San Pedro de Jujuy.

During the wars of independence, both the city and the province were the scene of many historic events. In one instance, under the direction of General Manuel Belgrano, the residents of Jujuy evacuated the city to avoid falling into royalist hands; every August,

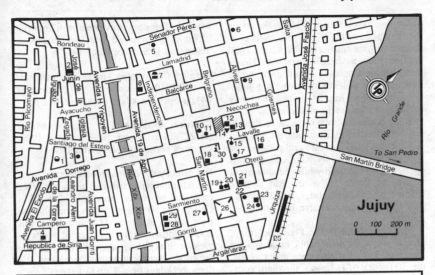

■ PLACES TO STAY

2   Residencial Río
    de Janeiro
4   Residencial Los
    Andes
8   Residencial 19
    de Abril
12 Hotel Augustus
13 Residencial Lavalle
16 Residencial Chungking
18 Hotel Sumay
21 Hotel Internacional
23 Residencial Norte
28 Hotel Fenicia
29 Hotel Avenida

▼ PLACES TO EAT

14 La Rueda

OTHER

1   Bus Terminal
3   Mercado del Sur
5   Telecom
6   Teatro Mitre
7   Post Office
9   Central Market
10 Austral
11 Museo Histórico
    Provincial
15 San Francisco Church
17 Aerolíneas Argentinas
19 Cathedral
20 Artisans' Market
22 Cabildo (Museo Policial)
24 Dirección General de
    Fauna y Parques
25 Railway Station
26 Plaza Belgrano
27 Casa de Gobierno
30 Tourist Office

there is a week's celebration of the *éxodo jujeño* (Jujuy exodus).

Except for the colonial remains around the Plaza Belgrano, Jujuy has relatively few distinguished buildings. It will repay some exploration outside the centre, but most sites of interest are in the provincial countryside, especially the villages of the Quebrada de Humahuaca.

Orientation

At the mouth of the Quebrada de Humahuaca, Jujuy (population 170,000) sits above the floodplain of the Río Grande at its confluence with the smaller Río Xibi Xibi, 1650 km from Buenos Aires. National Ruta 9 leads north up the Quebrada Humahuaca, while national Ruta 66 leads south-east to a junction with national Ruta 34, the main highway to Salta, though not the most direct.

Jujuy consists of two main parts: the old city between the Río Grande and the Río Xibi Xibi, with a fairly standard grid pattern, and a newer part south of the Xibi Xibi which is sprawling up the nearby hills. Shantytowns crowd the floodplain of the Río Grande below the San Martín bridge, which leads to San Pedro by an attractive but little-used route.

The city centre is the Plaza Belgrano, around which the main public buildings are clustered. Between Necochea and Lavalle, the 700 block of Belgrano, the main commercial street, is a pedestrian mall.

Information
Tourist Office The tourist office (☎ 28153) is at Belgrano 690. The staff are surprisingly indifferent to visitors, but have an abundance of maps, brochures and other materials. Weekday hours are 7 am to 9 pm, weekends 8 am to 8 pm. There is a satellite office at the bus terminal, open 8 am to noon and 3 to 8 pm.

Money There are several banks, but the cambios are efficient and will cash travellers' cheques (commission is substantial). Try Cambio Dinar, Belgrano 731, or Noroeste Cambio, almost next door at Belgrano 711.

The governments of Jujuy, Salta and Tucumán sometimes issue *bonos* (bonds) which circulate as legal tender within each province. There is sometimes a black market in bonos which does not exist in national currency; but you should be aware that bonos are invalid outside the province in which they are issued, cannot be used for some purchases such as air tickets or petrol, and have expiration dates beyond which they are worthless. If you pay in bonos, you will normally receive your change in them.

Post & Telecommunications The post office is at Lamadrid and Independencia. Telecom is at Senador Pérez 141.

Foreign Consulates The Bolivian consulate (☎ 22010), which has moved to Arenales 641, is open weekdays from 8 am to 1 pm.

Cultural Centres The Teatro Mitre (☎ 22782) at Alvear 1009, built in 1901, sponsors plays and other cultural events.

National Parks & Reserves Office
For information on national parks and other reserves, go to the provincial Dirección General de Fauna y Parques, opposite the train station at Alvear 412, upstairs. It has good information on the state of roads to parks such as Calilegua and El Rey, plus free information publications and brochures. It's open weekdays from 7 am to 1 pm.

Travel Agencies ACA (☎ 22568) is at Senador Pérez and Alvear. For excursions, try Tea Turismo (☎ 22357) at 19 de Abril 485, or Dinar SRL (☎ 25353) at Belgrano 731.

Medical Services The Hospital Pablo Soria (☎ 22025) is at Güemes and General Paz.

Iglesia Catedral
On Plaza Belgrano, Jujuy's Cathedral dates from 1763, when it replaced one destroyed by Calchaquí Indians during the 17th century. Its outstanding feature is the Spanish Baroque pulpit, built and laminated in gold for the original church, and salvaged for its replacement. Local artisans probably built the pulpit under the direction of a European master. In the shaded colonnade along the side entrance on Belgrano, there is an lively and interesting artisans' market, with excellent pottery.

Cabildo (Museo Policial)
Also on the plaza and in the process of restoration, the building deserves more attention than the contents. The museum, an uncritical homage to authority with grisly

photographs of crimes and accidents, is open weekdays from 10 am to 1 pm and 3 to 9 pm, Saturday from 10.30 am to 12.30 pm and 6.30 to 9 pm, and Sunday from 6.30 to 9 pm.

Museo Histórico Provincial

This colonial house at Lavalle 256, between Belgrano and San Martín, has seven large rooms dedicated to distinct themes in provincial history, including the independence period, religious and colonial art, the original owners of the house, provincial governors, 19th-century dress, the evacuation of Jujuy and the death of General Juan Lavalle. He was a hero of the wars of independence who became a victim of the civil wars, reportedly struck by a bullet through the house's impressive wooden door.

The museum is open daily, including weekends, from 9 am to 12.30 pm and 4 to 8 pm. There is a nominal admission charge.

Iglesia Santa Barbara

This colonial church at Lamadrid and San Martín contains several paintings from the well-known Cuzco school.

Mercado del Sur

Jujuy's lively southern market, opposite the bus terminal, is a real Indian market where Quechua men and women swig *mazamorra* (a pasty maize soup, served cold) and surreptitiously peddle illegal coca leaves, which is unofficially tolerated for native people.

Festivals

Jujuy's biggest event, in August, is the weeklong **Semana de Jujuy** which celebrates Belgrano's evacuation of the city during the wars of independence. The next largest, on October 7, is the pilgrimage to the **Virgin of Río Blanco & Paypaya**. The March harvest festival is called **Festival de la Humita y El Folclor**, while in May the town honours the mining industry through the **Fiesta de la Minería**. In September, there is a student celebration, the **Fiesta Nacional y Latinoamericana de los Estudiantes**.

Places to Stay – bottom end

Camping You can reach the municipal campground, three km north of Parque San Martín on Avenida Bolivia, opposite Motel Huaico, on bus No 4 from the centre. It's friendly, the facilities are clean and there is occasional hot water, but not much shade until the newly planted trees take over. Charges are US$3.50 for vehicle, tent and up to four persons.

Residenciales There is ample budget accommodation in Jujuy, mostly near the train station and bus terminal. The cheapest in town is *Residencial Río de Janeiro* (☎ 23700), west of the bus terminal at José de la Iglesia 1356, at US$3 per person with shared bath. *Residencial Los Andes* (☎ 24315), a few blocks east of the terminal at Republica de Siria 456, is bit costlier.

One recommended cheapie is *Residencial Norte* (☎ 22721), opposite the train station at Alvear 444, with singles/doubles at US$5/8 and a decent restaurant. Comparably priced is *Residencial 19 de Abril* (☎ 23224), at Avenida 19 de Abril 943, but rooms with private bath are slightly higher. *Residencial Aramayo* (☎ 23207), west of the train station at Salta 1058, charges US$5/8 with shared bath, slightly more with private bath.

Residencial El Quijote, Güemes 1151, has rooms for US$3.50 per person, but you may have to share with another person – most rooms are rented by the month. It has exceptionally cordial management and a good and very inexpensive restaurant – freshsqueezed orange juice costs a tiny fraction of what it does anywhere else in the country.

Other reasonable alternatives, all about US$10/13 with shared bath, include *Residencial Lavalle* (☎ 22698) at Lavalle 372, *Residencial Chungking* (28142) at Alvear 627, and *Residencial San Carlos* (☎ 22286) at Republica de Siria 459.

Places to Stay – middle

Midrange accommodation starts at about US$20/30 with bath. Two recommendations are *Hotel Avenida* (☎ 22678) at Avenida 19 de Abril 469, and *Hotel Asor's* (☎ 23688) at

Urquiza 462. Slightly more expensive are *Hotel Fenicia* (☎ 27492) at Avenida 19 de Abril 427, and *Hotel Sumay* (☎ 22554) at Otero 232.

Places to Stay – top end
Rooms at *Hotel Augustus* (☎ 22390), Belgrano 715, run about US$30/50. *Hotel Internacional* (☎ 22004) at Belgrano 501 charges about US$50/70, while rates at the four-star *Hotel Panorama*, Belgrano 1295, are US$70/100. Across from the municipal campground *Motel Huaico* (☎ 22274), at Bolivia 3901, has rooms for US$35/50 on quiet, attractive grounds.

Places to Eat
Check the bottom-end hotels for good, cheap food. *Restaurant Club Teléfono*, Alvear 1050, also has basic but nourishing four-course meals for very little money.

Upstairs at the central market, Alvear and Balcárce, several restaurants serve regional specialities which are generally spicier than in the rest of Argentina – try chicharrón con mote (stir-fried pork with boiled maize). Another local favourite is the modest-looking but interesting *La Sucreña*, on Leandro Alem east of the bus terminal, which serves a spicy sopa de mani.

There is also, of course, standard Argentine food at parrillas like *La Rueda*, Avenida Lavalle 329. On Belgrano, on and around the pedestrian mall, there are numerous confiterías and excellent ice creameries.

Getting There & Away
Air Aerolíneas Argentinas (☎ 22619), Otero 310, has four flights weekly to and from Buenos Aires. In summer, it may have flights across the Andes to Iquique, Chile. Austral (☎ 22384), at San Martín 735, has Tuesday, Thursday and Saturday flights to Buenos Aires. One-way fares to Buenos Aires are about US$200. Air connections are better from Salta.

Both Aerolíneas Argentinas and Austral run minibus services to El Cadillal Airport, which is 32 km south-east of town.

Bus The bus terminal, at Dorrego and Iguazú, has provincial and long-distance services, but Salta has more alternatives. Panamericano goes south daily to Tucumán and Córdoba and north to destinations in the Quebrada de Humahuaca as far as the Bolivian border, plus isolated *puna* settlements like El Moreno, Susques and Olaroz Chico. COTA Norte also goes to Humahuaca. Atahualpa's Salta to La Quiaca service also stops in Jujuy.

Empresa Balut goes to Nuevo Orán and the other Bolivian border crossing at Pocitos.

Empresa Itatí crosses the Chaco weekly to Corrientes and Iguazú.

Train The antiquated Belgrano railway from Buenos Aires' Retiro Station connects Jujuy with La Quiaca, on the Bolivian border, three times a week. In the summer rainy season, flooding of the low-lying track in the Quebrada de Humahuaca may delay or eliminate service. The trip to La Quiaca takes nearly 10 hours and costs US$9 primera, US$8 turista. To Buenos Aires, fares are about US$35 primera and US$30 turista.

Car Rental A1 (☎ 29697), at Senador Pérez 398, rents Fiat 147s and other vehicles, starting at about US$60 per day, plus petrol plus mileage.

AROUND JUJUY
Termas de Reyes
Don't leave Jujuy without a visit to these thermal baths, on the slopes of the scenic canyon of the Río Reyes, reached easily and cheaply from the bus terminal. Rustic facilities are free, but for US$5 you can wallow in the enormous, comfortable tubs at *Hostería Termas de Reyes* (☎ 24600), whose room rates of US$30/40 a single/double include in-room facilities. Although the hostería's public baths were not constructed for the view, it's still a worthwhile experience. The hostería serves only a costly fixed-price lunch, so take along some food.

QUEBRADA DE HUMAHUACA

The long, narrow Quebrada de Humahuaca, north of Jujuy, is an artist's palette of colour, splashed on barren hillsides which dwarf the hamlets where Quechua peasants scratch a living from irrigated agriculture and scrawny livestock. Whether you come south from La Quiaca or head north from Jujuy, there's something interesting every few kilometres on this colonial post route between Potosí and Buenos Aires.

The main settlement in the valley is Humahuaca, 130 km from Jujuy, and there are so many worthwhile sights that the convenience of an automobile would be a big plus if you have a group to share expenses. Otherwise, buses are frequent enough that you should be able to do the canyon on a 'whistle-stop' basis, flagging down a bus when you need one. There is excellent accommodation available in Tilcara, only 88 km from Jujuy, if things go more slowly than expected.

Because this area was colonised from Peru in the early decades of Spanish rule, the area has many cultural features which recall the Andean countries, particularly the numerous, historic adobe churches. Earthquakes have levelled many, but they were often rebuilt in the 17th and 18th centuries. They have thick walls, simple bell towers, and striking doors and panelling constructed from the wood of the unusual *cardón* cactus.

Purmamarca

A few km off the main highway, the polychrome Cerro Colorado is the backdrop for a noteworthy 17th-century colonial church in this tiny village.

La Posta de Hornillos

This beautifully restored way station, part of a chain which ran from Lima to Buenos Aires during Viceregal times, is 11 km north of the Purmamarca turnoff. During the wars of independence it was the scene of several important battles. The informal but informative guided tours make this an obligatory stop on the way up the Quebrada.

Maimará

From the highway, only a few km south of Tilcara, you pass the astounding hillside cemetery of this picturesque valley settlement, a can't-miss photo opportunity. The town also has a worthwhile museum.

Uquía

The 17th-century **Iglesia de San Francisco de Paula** in this roadside village displays a restored collection of paintings from the Cuzco school, featuring the famous *Angeles harquebuseros*, angels armed with Spanish colonial weapons.

TILCARA

Tilcara, at an elevation of 2461 metres, fea-

tures a classic Andean *pucará*, a fortification commanding unobstructed views of the Quebrada de Humahuaca in several directions. Its many museums and other interesting features, including its reputation as an artists' colony, make for a highly desirable stopover.

Orientation
Tilcara is on the east bank of the Río Grande, connected by a bridge to national Ruta 9, which leads south to Jujuy and north to Humahuaca and La Quiaca. Its central grid is irregular beyond the village nucleus. As in many small Argentine villages, people pay little attention to street names and numbers.

Information
Tourist Office There is little formal information available, but El Antigal, a hotel and restaurant, distributes a small, useful brochure.

Telecommunications The telephone cooperative is on the ground floor of the Hotel de Turismo, Belgrano 590.

El Pucará
Stretching up through the sediments of the Río Grande valley, an isolated hill provided a place for this pre-Columbian fortification, one km from the centre of the village. Admission is US$1.50. There are even better views from the hill on the road which leads to the fort. From the south end of the bridge across the Río Huasamayo, it's an easy 15-minute climb to the top.

Museo Arqueológico Dr Eduardo Casanova
The University of Buenos Aires operates this outstanding, well-displayed collection of regional artefacts. Located in a beautiful colonial house, it's open daily from 9 am to 6 pm; admission is US$1.50, but free on Tuesdays.

Museo Ernesto Soto Avendaño
Ernesto Soto Avendaño was a sculptor from Olavarría, in the province of Buenos Aires, who spent most of his life in Tilcara and

designed the monument to the heroes of Argentine independence in Humahuaca. This collection of his work is open Tuesday to Saturday from 9 am to noon and from 3 to 6 pm.

Museo José Antonio Terry
Also located in a colonial building, this museum features the work of a Buenos Aires-born painter whose themes were largely rural and indigenous – his oils depict native weavers, market and street scenes, and portraits. Hours are Tuesday to Sunday, 9 am to 5 pm. Admission is US$1.50, but Thursdays are free.

Festivals
Tilcara celebrates several festivals throughout the year, the most notable of which are the February **Carnaval** (equally important in other Quebrada villages), **Holy Week** in April, and the indigenous **Pachamama** (Mother Earth) in August.

Places to Stay & Eat
Residencial El Edén, on Rivadavia 1½ blocks from the central Plaza Prado, charges US$4/6 a single/double for rooms with sagging beds and shared bath (cold showers only), but it's clean and friendly. Juan Brambati and family offer lodging for up to four people at US$7 per person, with breakfast for US$2.50 and dinner for US$3.70. In addition, Juan can arrange trekking and vehicle tours. Write to Juan Brambati, 4624 Tilcara, Provincia de Jujuy, for more information or booking.

Residencial El Antigal, also on Rivadavia half a block from the plaza, is probably the best choice in town at US$10/16 with private bath, hot water, and an outstanding restaurant – try the locro, a spicy stew of maize, beans, beef, pork and sausage. *Restaurant Pucará*, on the plaza, is also popular.

Autocamping Tilcara, on Belgrano near the river, is a very congenial place with hot showers and attractive vegetable and flower gardens, all for US$2 per person. There is an adequate free site, with picnic tables, near the

YPF petrol station along the highway, but it has no potable water or sanitary facilities.

Getting There & Away
There are nine buses daily to Jujuy, four of which continue to Salta. Northward services to Humahuaca and La Quiaca also stop in Tilcara. There is a large marker where the road to Humahuaca crosses the Tropic of Capricorn.

HUMAHUACA
Picturesque Humahuaca, the largest settlement between Jujuy and the Bolivian border, is a village of narrow, cobbled streets lined with adobe houses, with a large Quechua Indian population. Nearly 3000 metres above sea level, it is the most popular destination for budget travellers exploring the Quebrada. It can be aggressively touristy; many people will offer unsolicited guide services.

Orientation
Humahuaca straddles the Río Grande, east of national Ruta 9. The city centre is between the highway and the river, but there are important archaeological sites across the bridge. The town is very compact and everything is within easy walking distance.

Information
Tourist Office The tourist office is in the Cabildo, at Tucumán and Jujuy, open weekdays only.

Post & Telecommunications The post office is across from the plaza. The long-distance telephone office, on the main floor of the Hotel de Turismo on Buenos Aires, is open from 7 am to 8 pm.

Medical Services The Hospital Belgrano (☎ 09) is at Santa Fe 34. It's open from 8 am to 1 pm and 2 to 6 pm, but there is always someone on duty for emergencies.

Cabildo
Municipal offices occupy the cabildo, famous for its clock tower, from which the life-size figure of San Francisco Solano emerges daily at noon and midnight to deliver a benediction. Both tourists and locals gather in the plaza to watch the spectacle, but arrive early, since the clock is erratic and the figure appears only very briefly.

Iglesia de la Candelaria
Humahuaca's church, built in 1641, contains an image of the town's patron saint and 18th-century oils by Marcos Sapaca, a painter of the Cuzco school.

Monumento a la Independencia
This monstrosity dominates the hill overlooking Humahuaca, but is not the best work of Tilcara sculptor Ernesto Soto Avendaño. The Indian statue is a textbook example of *indigenismo*, a distorted nationalist tendency in Latin American art and literature which romantically extols the virtues of native cultures which European society obliterated.

Museo Folklórico Regional
Sixto Vázquez Zuleta, a local writer and Indian activist who prefers his Quechua name of Toqo, is a mine of information on local history and culture. He offers guided tours only of the museum, housed in the Humahuaca youth hostel, Buenos Aires 435/447. It's open from 8 am to 8 pm daily, but only when there's a group of three or four to justify the effort. Price for admission and tour is US$2 per person. Toqo speaks little English but passable German.

Festivals
Besides the **Carnaval Norteño**, celebrated throughout the Quebrada in February, Humahuaca observes February 2 as the day of its patron saint, the **Virgin of Candelaria**.

Places to Stay
Camping The municipal site across the bridge was closed recently, but it's still possible to park or pitch a tent there for free. Toqo, who also runs the youth hostel, was planning to open a private campground with

sanitary facilities, so ask there for more information.

Hostels, Hospedajes, Residenciales & Hotels

For budget travellers, the most popular accommodation is the youth hostel at Buenos Aires 435, which does not require an international youth hostel card. For US$5 per person, it offers hot showers, cooking facilities and the opportunity to encounter both Argentine and international travellers. Unlike many Argentine hostels, it's open all year. About the same price is *Hospedaje Río Grande* at Corrientes 480.

There are two other simple and inexpensive hotels. *Residencial Humahuaca*, at Córdoba 401 near Corrientes half a block from the bus terminal, charges US$10/12 a single/double for rooms with shared bath, slightly more with private bath. *Residencial Colonial*, Entre Ríos 110, is comparable in price and quality.

The three-star *Hotel de Turismo*, Buenos Aires 650, is the town's top-end accommodation, although the interior is very run-down, at US$20/30 with private bath.

Places to Eat

It doesn't look like much, but *Restaurant El Rancho*, near the bus terminal, has outstanding spicy empanadas and humitas (corn tamales). There is an acceptable confitería at the bus terminal, and a few other funky restaurants.

Things to Buy

Visit the handicrafts market, near the train station, for woollen goods, other souvenirs, and atmosphere. The quality of the materials is excellent, but those heading north will probably find similar items at lower prices in Bolivia.

Getting There & Away

Bus The bus terminal is very central at Belgrano and Entre Ríos. Panamericano has four buses daily to Jujuy, five to Tres Cruces and La Quiaca. Atahualpa has six daily to Jujuy, three to Salta, and five to La Quiaca, plus weekend service to the mining settlement of Mina El Aguilar. Cota Norte has seven buses daily to Jujuy.

Transportes Mendoza offers a Saturday service to the scenic Andean village of Iruya; ask at the convenience store Almacén Mendoza from where the buses leave. There are also buses to the remote altiplano settlement of Susques, which has an interesting Andean church and is near an important wildlife reserve.

Train The Belgrano station is opposite the bus terminal. The train is crowded and uncomfortable, but its arrival in town is a major event, well worth seeing. For details of services, see section on Jujuy.

AROUND HUMAHUACA

Coctaca

Ten km from Humahuaca by a dirt road which leads north from the east side of the bridge across the Río Grande, these are the most extensive pre-Columbian ruins in north-western Argentina, covering about 40 hectares. Although they have not yet been excavated, many of the ruins appear to be broad agricultural terraces on an alluvial fan, but there are also obvious outlines of clusters of buildings.

In the rainy season the road may be impassable. It is possible to walk to the ruins, but leave before the heat of the day and take water. After crossing the bridge across the Río Grande in Humahuaca, follow the road north and bear left except when in sight of the village of Coctaca.

LA QUIACA

North of Humahuaca, Ruta 9 becomes an unpaved road which climbs steeply to the high steppe (altiplano) typical of western Bolivia. Except during the summer rainy season, frosts occur almost nightly, making agriculture a precarious activity and concentrating subsistence efforts on livestock which can survive on the sparse *ichu* grass – llamas, sheep, goats and a few cattle. Off the main highway, you may see flocks of the endangered vicuña, a wild relative of the llama and alpaca. At the end of the highway

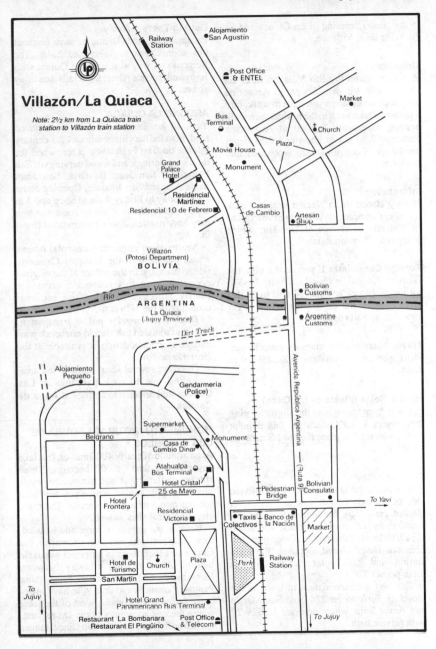

Villazón/La Quiaca

Note: 2½ km from La Quiaca train station to Villazón train station

Railway Station

Alojamiento San Agustín

Post Office & ENTEL

Market

Bus Terminal

Church

Plaza

Movie House

Monument

Grand Palace Hotel

Residencial Martínez

Residencial 10 de Febrero

Casas de Cambio

Artesan Shop

Villazón (Potosí Department)
BOLIVIA

Bolivian Customs

Rio — Villazón

ARGENTINA

La Quiaca (Jujuy Province)

Argentine Customs

Dirt Track

Alojamiento Pequeño

Gendarmería (Police)

Supermarket

Belgrano

Casa de Cambio Dinar

Monument

Atahualpa Bus Terminal

Hotel Cristal

25 de Mayo

Hotel Frontera

Residencial Victoria

Hotel de Turismo

Church

San Martín

Plaza

Park

Pedestrian Bridge

Bolivian Consulate

To Yavi

Avenida República Argentina — (Ruta 9)

Taxis Colectivos

Banco de la Nación

Market

Railway Station

To Jujuy

Hotel Grand Panamericano Bus Terminal

Restaurant La Bombanara
Restaurant El Pingüino

Post Office & Telecom

To Jujuy

is the border crossing of La Quiaca and its Bolivian twin, Villazón.

Orientation

A bridge across the Río Villazón links La Quiaca with Villazón. To get to Argentine and Bolivian customs you have to walk, hire a porter, or take a cab to the bridge, then walk across. Hours are limited at Argentine customs: 7.30 am to noon and 3 to 6 pm weekdays, 9 am to 11 am weekends and holidays.

Information

Money Banco de la Nación will not cash travellers' cheques, so you may have to cross to Villazón to change at Uni-Tur, which charges a 7% commission.

Foreign Consulates If you need a visa, the Bolivian Consulate charges a hefty US$15 for the privilege. You may be able to do this more cheaply and expeditiously in a larger city such as Salta or Jujuy.

Travel Agencies For maps or motorist services, visit the ACA station on Ruta 9 at 9 de Julio.

Manca Fiesta (Fiesta de las Ollas)

Artisans from throughout the altiplano bring their wares to La Quiaca for this popular event, which takes place the third Sunday in October.

Places to Stay

Accommodation is cheaper on the Bolivian side of the border, but you can try *Hotel Cristal* (☎ 2255), Sarmiento 519, recommended by LP correspondents, for about US$7/10 for singles/doubles. Other possibilities are *Hotel Grand*, opposite the train station, and *Residencial Victoria*, on the main plaza.

The best accommodation in town is the *Hotel de Turismo* (☎ 2243), at San Martín and Arabe Siria, where rates are US$20/27 with private bath.

Getting There & Away

Panamericano and Atahualpa have frequent bus connections to Jujuy and Salta. The Belgrano railway also links La Quiaca with Jujuy and Buenos Aires; for details, see Jujuy above.

AROUND LA QUIACA

Yavi, 16 km from La Quiaca via a paved road, is an Indian village whose 17th-century **Iglesia de San Francisco** is renowned for its altar, paintings, and wood carvings of San Francisco, San Juan Bautista, San José, Santa Ana and San Joaquín. Opening hours are Tuesday to Friday 9 am to noon and 3 to 6 pm, and Saturday 9 am to noon, but you may have to track down the caretaker to get in.

Nearby is an interesting **colonial house** which belonged to the Marqués Campero, whose marriage to the holder of the original encomienda in this reducción created a family which dominated the regional economy in the 18th century.

There is no regular public transport to Yavi, but a shared cab should not break your budget. Accommodation is available at the *Hostería de Yavi*.

There are several short hikes in the area, including one to rock paintings at **Las Cuevas** and another to springs at **Agua de Castilla.**

MONUMENTO NATURAL LAGUNA DE LOS POZUELOS

At an altitude of nearly 4000 metres, this lake covers more than 16,000 hectares. Three species of flamingos and many other birds breed along its shores, where you may also see the rare, endangered vicuña. There are archaeological sites as well.

Because the park is so large and isolated, a car is the best transportation alternative, but carry extra fuel; there is no petrol available beyond Abra Pampa, midway between Humahuaca and La Quiaca. From Abra Pampa, Panamericano and Vilte have infrequent buses to Rinconada, west of the lake, where there is accommodation. On request, the bus will drop you at the Río Cincel ranger station, where it is possible to camp. With luck, you can accompany the rangers on their rounds. For more information, ask at tourist offices in Jujuy or La Quiaca, or at the Centro Cultural in Abra Pampa.

PARQUE NACIONAL CALILEGUA

On the eastern borders of Jujuy province, the high and dry altiplano gives way to the dense subtropical cloud forest of the Serranía de Calilegua, whose preservation is the goal of this accessible, 75,000-hectare park. At the park's highest elevations, about 3600 metres, verdant Cerro Hermoso reaches above the forest and offer limitless views of the Gran Chaco to the east. Bird life is abundant and colourful, but the tracks of rare mammals, such as the puma and jaguar, are more common than the animals themselves.

Information

Park headquarters (☎ 22046) is in the village of Calilegua, just north of Libertador General San Martín. The building, donated by the Ledesma sugar mill, will soon be a visitor centre with exhibits on the region's national parks, including Calilegua, Baritú, El Rey and Laguna Pozuelos. They can also give you the latest information on road conditions, since many areas are inaccessible during the summer rainy season. Buses Veloz del Norte, between Salta and Orán, stop at the excellent restaurant belonging to the Club Social San Lorenzo, next door to park headquarters.

Flora

Receiving 2000 mm of precipitation a year, but with a defined winter dry season, Calilegua comprises a variety of ecosystems correlated with altitude. The 'transitional selva', at elevations between 350 and 500 metres, consists of tree species common in the Gran Chaco, such as lapacho and *palo amarillo*, which drop their leaves in the winter. Between 550 and 1600 metres, the 'cloud forest' forms a dark, dense canopy of trees more than 30 metres tall, punctuated by ferns, epiphytes and lianas, covered by a thick fog in summer and autumn. Above

1200 metres is the 'montane forest' comprised of 'pines' (a general term for almost any conifer, such as cedar), *aliso*, and *queñoa*. Above 2600 metres this grades into moist puna grasslands, which become drier as one goes west toward the Quebrada de Humahuaca.

Things to Do

Nature-oriented activities will be the focus of any visit to Calilegua. The 230 species of birds include the condor, brown eagle, torrent duck and the colourful toucan. Important mammals, rarely seen in the dense forest, include tapir, puma, jaguar, collared peccary and otter. The best places to view birds and mammals are near the streamcourses in the early morning or very late afternoon, just before dark. From the ranger station at Mesada de las Colmenas, there is a steep, rugged, badly overgrown trail down to a beautiful creek where animal tracks are numerous, including those of large cats. The descent takes perhaps an hour, the ascent twice that.

There are excellent views from 3600-metre Cerro Hermoso; although there are no detailed maps, ask the rangers for directions. From Valle Grande, beyond the park boundaries to the west, it is possible to hike to Humahuaca along the Sierra de Zenta. For details, see Hilary Bradt and John Pilkington's *Backpacking in Chile and Argentina*. Ordinary vehicles cannot go far past the Mesada de las Colmenas, but the road itself offers outstanding views of Cerro Hermoso and the nearly impenetrable forests of its steep ravines.

Places to Stay

There are several residenciales in nearby Libertador General San Martín, but camping is the only alternative in the park itself. There is a developed site at Aguas Negras, on a short lateral road near the ranger station at the entrance, but from late 1990 the bathrooms were closed and there was no running water except that from the river. Beware of mosquitos, which are much less a problem at higher elevations.

Although there are no other developed campsites, there is a level area where you can camp at the ranger station at Mesada de las Colmenas, which has great open views to the east.

Getting There & Away

From the bus terminal at Libertador General San Martín, a 4WD Dodge pickup does the climb to Parque Calilegua and the village of Valle Grande twice-weekly throughout the year. Departure times are Tuesday and Saturday at 7.30 am, while return trips are on Sunday and Thursday at 9 am. The fare is US$10 one way.

It should be possible to hitch to the park and Valle Grande with the logging trucks which pass through the park. Start from the bridge at the north end of the town of Libertador General San Martín, where there is a good dirt road through mostly shady terrain to Aguas Negras, eight km away.

Salta Province

In the Andean North-West, Salta is the province with everything. The best preserved colonial city in Argentina is the centre for excursions to the montane subtropical forests of Parque Nacional El Rey, the polychrome desert canyons of El Toro and Cafayate, along with their vineyards, and the sterile but scenic salt lakes and volcanos of the high puna. Hundreds of archaeological sites and colonial buildings testify to Salta's importance in pre-Hispanic and colonial periods, even though it declined with Argentine independence.

During colonial times, Salta's marshy but fertile Lerma Valley pastured thousands of mules that were bred on the Pampas of Buenos Aires and sold at an annual fair – in the 17th and 18th centuries as many as 70,000 animals per year found their way to Bolivia and Peru, where they performed a wide variety of tasks in the mining industry. Independence and political fragmentation reduced this trade, a blow from which Salta has never completely recovered. Today, it is primarily an agricultural province, dependent on sugar cane, tobacco, and increasingly on tourism, with minor contributions from mining and petroleum.

SALTA

Founded in 1582 by Hernando de Lerma, Salta lies at 1200 metres in a basin surrounded by verdant peaks. This valley's perpetual spring attracted the Spaniards, who could pasture animals in the surrounding countryside and produce crops which could not grow in the frigid Bolivian highlands, where the mining industry created enormous demand for hides, mules and food. When extension of the Belgrano railroad made it feasible to market sugar to the immigrant cities of the Pampas, the city recovered to some degree from its 19th-century economic decline.

Orientation

At the town of General Güemes, national Ruta 9 veers sharply west to climb gradually through endless canefields before dropping steeply into the Lerma Valley and the city of Salta. From the central Plaza 9 de Julio, the conventional grid pattern extends in all directions until it ascends the eastern overlooks of Cerro 20 de Febrero and Cerro San Bernardo, whose streets hug their contours.

Although Salta has sprawled considerably over the past several years, most points of interest to the visitor are within a few blocks of the plaza. The commercial centre is southwest of the plaza, where both Alberdi and Florida are pedestrian malls between Caseros and Avenida San Martín. North-south streets change their name on either side of the plaza, but the names of east-west streets are continuous.

Information

Tourist Office The tourist office (☎ 21-5927) is at Buenos Aires 93, near Alvarado. They have some brochures and maps, but are most helpful in locating accommodation in private houses. Hours are 8 am to 9 pm. The smaller office at the bus terminal closes for siesta.

Money Cambio Dinar, Mitre 101 on the Plaza 9 de Julio, will change cash and travellers' cheques, the latter at a very unfavourable rate with high commission. Try also Banco de la Nación at Mitre and Avenida Belgrano.

As in Jujuy, there is a black (parallel) market for bonos, which operates in the arcade near the Café del Consejo on the Plaza. Remember that bonos have no value outside the province of issue, have an expiration date, and are not accepted for some purchases, most notably transportation.

Post & Telecommunications The post office is at Dean Funes 140, between España and Avenida Belgrano. For long-distance telephone service, go to Telecom at Vicente López 146 or at Belgrano 824 near 20 de Febrero.

Foreign Consulates Bolivia has a consulate (☎ 21-1927) at Santiago del Estero 179. The Chilean Consulate (☎ 21-0827) is at Ejército del Norte 312, behind the monument to General Güemes.

Travel Agencies ACA (☎ 21-0002) is at Rivadavia and Mitre. Among the dozens of travel agencies in Salta, it is difficult to recommend one over the others. Try Saltur (☎ 21-2012) at Caseros 525 or, if you're interested in 'adventure tourism', try Turismo Mallorca (☎ 22-2075) at Caseros 527 (see also Organised Tours below). For student bargains, check out ATESA (Asociación Turismo Estudiantil Argentino) at Zuviría 522.

Bookshops The English-language bookshop Iei-Inglés, at Zuviría 518, has a modest selection of reading material.

Walking Tour
Salta's historic centre features a number of colonial buildings which have become important museums. Even if you arrive on a Monday, when most are closed, you should have a look around just to absorb the colonial atmosphere. You can see most of them on a walk starting from Florida and Alvarado, up Caseros past the Plaza to Avenida Hipólito Yrigoyen to Belgrano and up to the Güemes monument, returning down Belgrano to Buenos Aires and back to Alvarado. Ask at the tourist office for its brochure on the *Circuito Peatonal*.

Museo Histórico del Norte
The 18th-century Cabildo which houses this museum, at Caseros 549 on the main plaza, is worthwhile in its own right, but also holds collections of religious and modern art, period furniture, and historic coins and paper money, plus horse-drawn and ox-drawn vehicles, including an old postal wagon and a hearse. Admission is US$1. Hours are Tuesday to Saturday from 10 am to 2 pm and 3.30 to 7.30 pm, Sunday 10 am to 2 pm.

Museo de Bellas Artes
Lodged in the two-storey colonial mansion of the Arias Rengel family at Florida 18, the fine arts museum displays both modern painting and sculpture. Its adobe walls are two metres thick. In the interior patio, a wooden staircase leads to a hanging balcony. The building and museum are open daily except Monday, 9 am to 1 pm and 3 to 9 pm. Admission is US$0.60.

Casa Uriburu
The family of José Evaristo Uriburu, twice briefly President of the Republic, lived in this 18th-century house at Caseros 417. It has a well-preserved collection of period furniture, and is open Tuesday to Saturday 10 am to 2 pm and 3.30 to 7.30 pm.

Iglesia Catedral
This 19th-century church, at España 596, contains the ashes of General Martín Miguel de Güemes, a native Salteño and hero of the wars of independence, as well as other important historical figures; even today, the gauchos of Salta province proudly flaunt their red-striped *ponchos de Güemes*.

Salta

0 100 200 m

Iglesia San Francisco

Ornate almost to the point of gaudiness, with a highly visible bell tower, this brightly painted church at Caseros and Córdoba is an unmistakeable Salta landmark. It's open daily from 7 am to noon and 5.30 to 9 pm.

Convento de San Bernardo

Only Carmelite nuns can enter this 16th-century convent at Caseros and Santa Fe, but you can approach the blindingly white-washed adobe building to admire the algarrobo door, which was carved in the 18th

century. It was originally a hermitage, later a hospital, and only later still a convent proper.

Museo de Arte Popular

This private institution at Caseros 476 exhibits representative artisanal crafts from throughout the Americas, focusing on Mexico, Peru, Argentina, Chile, Brazil and Paraguay. Some items are for sale in a shop on the main floor. Admission is US$1; opening hours are Monday to Saturday from 9.30 am to 12.30 pm and 5.30 to 9.30 pm, except for Wednesday mornings.

■ PLACES TO STAY

2	Residencial Güemes
3	Residencial Astur
6	Residencial Balcarce
13	Residencial Centra
19	Residencial España
25	Hotel California
28	Residencial Sandra
34	Residencial Royal
35	Residencial Florida
37	Hotel Italia
38	Residencial Elena
39	Hotel Petit
40	Hotel Continental

▼ PLACES TO EAT

7	Sociedad Italiana
11	Snack Bar Whympy
16	Heladería Gianni
17	La Posta
22	Cafe del Consejo
27	La Casona

OTHER

1	Train Station
4	ACA
5	Plaza Güemes
8	Bolivian Consulate
9	Museo Antropológico Juan M Leguizamón
10	Telecom (International)
12	Telecom
14	Cambio Dinar
15	Iglesia Catedral
18	Post Office
20	Museo de Arte Popular
21	Plaza 9 de Julio
23	Casa de Gobierno
24	Museo de Bellas Artes (Casa Arias Rengel)
26	Cabildo/Museo Histórico del Norte
29	Aerolíneas Argentinas/ Hotel Salta
30	Tourist Office
31	Casa Uriburu
32	Iglesia San Francisco
33	Convento de San Bernado
36	Central Market
41	Bus Station

Cerro San Bernardo

For outstanding views of Salta and its surroundings, take the *teleférico* (gondola) from Parque San Martín to the top and back (US$6 return). There is also a trail up the hill which begins at the Güemes monument at the top of Avenida General Güemes.

Museo Antropológico Juan M Leguizamón

On the lower slopes of Cerro San Bernardo, at Ejército del Norte and Polo Sur, this modern museum has good exhibits of local ceramics, especially from the Tastil site in the Quebrada de Toro, but also contains some outdated and even bizarre material on the peopling of the Americas, including one panel which suggests that humans might have reached the Americas originally via Antarctica.

Admission is US$0.60. Opening hours are Tuesday to Friday 8.30 am to 12.30 pm and 2.30 to 6.30 pm, Saturday 3 to 6.30 pm, Sunday 4 to 6.30 pm.

Organised Tours

Visitors with little time but with a real interest in sights off the beaten track may want to contact Turismo Mallorca (☎ 22-2075) at Caseros 527, which operates treks, horseback and fishing trips, ornithological and archaeological tours, and visits to aboriginal reserves. Among the possibilities are visits to Parque Nacional Baritú and Parque Nacional El Rey, both difficult to reach by public transport. They can arrange bilingual guides in English, German, French and Italian.

Places to Stay – bottom end

Camping Although a bit outside the centre, *Camping Municipal Carlos Xamena* is one of the best campgrounds in Argentina. It is alongside one of the world's largest swimming pools (it takes a week to fill in the spring). Fees are US$1.50 per car, US$2 per tent, US$1 per adult and US$0.50 per child. Its only drawback is that in summer, when Salteños flock here to catch some rays, they play unpleasantly loud music for the swimmers and sunbathers. Mercifully, they switch off the sound system by early evening. You can purchase food and drink at the nearby supermarket.

From the centre, take bus No 13 ('Balneario'), which also connects with the train station.

Private Houses, Residenciales & Hotels

Private houses are an excellent alternative to bottom-end hotels; the tourist office maintains a list of such accommodation. One of the most popular and central is the house at 915 Mendoza, run by one of three sisters (the other two occupy and let rooms in their own houses at 917 and 919 Mendoza). All have pleasant patios, cooking facilities, and spotless bathrooms, for about US$6 per person.

The dingy *Residencial Sandra* (☎ 21-1241) is at Alvarado 630. One traveller reports that it is great value at US$4.50 a single with private bath, but the manager is unfriendly. Between the bus terminal and downtown you will find *Residencial Royal*, Alvarado 107, which is reasonably quiet and has singles/doubles with shared bath for US$7/10. Another possibility is *Residencial España* (☎ 21-7898), at España 319.

Most inexpensive accommodation is near the train station rather than the bus terminal. Directly across from the station, on Ameghino, you will find *Residencial Colón*, *Residencial Splendid*, *Residencial Tito* and *Residencial Roma*, any of which is worthwhile if you're catching an early train. *Residencial Güemes*, on Nechochea between Balcarce and Mitre, is similar. Prices are comparable to Residencial Royal or a bit cheaper. *Residencial Balcarce* (☎ 21-8023), Balcarce 460, is also near the train station, with rates of about US$10/16. *Residencial Astur* (☎ 21-2107), which is slightly costlier, is a few blocks away.

Hotel Italia (☎ 21-4050), at Alberdi 231 on Urquiza, charges about US$12/20. For the same price, another central place is the architecturally undistinguished *Residencial Florida* (☎ 21-2133), at Urquiza 722 on Florida.

There are enthusiastic reports on *Residencial Elena* (☎ 21-1529), at Buenos Aires 256, a colonial building with an attractive interior patio, which costs US$15 a single.

Places to Stay – middle

Midrange hotels start at about US$20/30. *Hotel Petit* (☎ 21-3012) at Hipólito Yrigoyen 225, *Hotel Continental* (☎ 21-3040) at Hipólito Yrigoyen 295, and *Hotel Las Tinajas* at Lerma 288 are all close to the bus terminal. Downtown, try *Hotel Cabildo* (☎ 22-4589) on the plaza at Caseros 527, *Hotel California* (☎ 21-6266) at Alvarado 646, or the costlier *Hotel Colonial* (☎ 21-3057) at Zuviría 6.

Places to Stay – top end

Another step up is the *Victoria Plaza Hotel* (☎ 21-1222), at Zuviría 16, which charges about US$26/35. At the attractive, centrally located *Hotel Salta* (☎ 21-1011), Buenos Aires 1 at Caseros, rates start at US$30/45. Try also *Hotel Provincial* (☎ 21-8400) at Caseros 786.

Places to Eat

One of the best and cheapest places to eat is Salta's large and lively but tidy market, Florida and San Martín, where you can supplement inexpensive pizza, empanadas and humitas with fresh fruit and vegetables. Even if you're not a bottom-end budget traveller, you should pay the market a visit.

There are many cheap restaurants, pizzerías and confiterías around Belgrano and Zuviría. Despite its unappealing moniker, *Snack Bar Whympy* at Zuviría 223 is good, inexpensive and filling. The *Sociedad Italiana*, Zuviría and Santiago del Estero, has quality four-course meals for about US$2. *Restaurant Alvarez*, Avenida San Martín and Buenos Aires, also has large portions of good, cheap food. *Café del*

Consejo, on Mitre opposite the Plaza, is a confitería with the cheapest lager beer in town. Don't miss *Heladería Gianni*, España 486, one of the best ice cream shops in Argentina despite its very modest decor.

La Casona, Caseros 511 at the end of a corridor off the colonnade, is an outstanding choice, with a wide-ranging menu, attractive decor, friendly and attentive service, and reasonable prices. Do not miss the humitas (corn tamales) or other regional specialities. *La Posta*, at España 476, is a highly recommended but pricey parrilla.

Entertainment
In the same building as La Casona restaurant, you will find the Club Amigos del Tango, which promotes the traditional Argentine dance.

Things to Buy
For useful souvenirs, the most noteworthy place is the provincially sponsored Mercado Artesanal, in a colonial building at Avenida San Martín, where you can find native hand icrafts such as hammocks, string bags, ceramics and basketry, leatherwork, and the region's distinctive ponchos. Tiwanaku, Caseros 424, also has good quality pottery, ceramics, copperware and woollens. There is another good shop at Catamarca 82.

Getting There & Away
Air Aerolíneas Argentinas (☎ 21-4757) is at Caseros 475. It has flights to Buenos Aires daily except Sunday, a Monday flight to Córdoba, and a Monday flight to Santa Cruz de la Sierra, Bolivia. Austral (☎ 22-4590), at Buenos Aires 46, has flights daily to Buenos Aires. Lloyd Aéreo Boliviano (LAB) (☎ 21-7753) has offices at Caseros 376.

Bus Salta has frequent bus services to all parts of the country. Most are located in the terminal, but a few companies have their offices elsewhere in town.

Chevallier has daily buses to Buenos Aires (US$75). Veloz del Norte serves Mar del Plata (US$90, 29 hours), Buenos Aires, Santa Fe (US$60), Mendoza (US$45), San

Juan (US$40), Córdoba (US$45), Resistencia (US$40), La Rioja (US$35), Catamarca (US$26) and Santiago del Estero (US$20).

Panamericano has frequent service to Tucumán (US$17), Santiago del Estero and Córdoba, plus Mar del Plata.

Atalhualpa goes to Jujuy and up the Quebrada de Humahuaca, across the northern Argentine Chaco to Formosa (US$20), and to Antofagasta, Chile (Wednesdays, summer only). Empresa Geminis also has summer crossings on Saturdays to Antofagasta (US$40) in Chile, and also serves Calama, Iquique (US$50) and Arica (US$55). Buses to Chile are few and always very full, so buy your ticket well in advance if possible at its office at Dionísio Puch 117, opposite the terminal.

El Indio goes three times daily to Cafayate for US$10. There are daily buses up the Quebrada de Toro to San Antonio de los Cobres for US$9. Empresa Marco Ruedas (☎ 21-4447), Islas Malvinas 393, serves the altiplano village of Cachi.

Train The Belgrano railway (☎ 21-3161) is at Ameghino 690. There is service to Retiro Station, Buenos Aires, on Wednesdays, Fridays and Sundays at 7.05 am. Fares are US$40 primera, US$35 in hard-backed turista class. There is also a train from Salta to Pocitos, on the Bolivian border, on Mondays at 7.45 pm, for US$12 primera, US$10 turista.

One of Salta's popular attractions used to be the scenic ride to the mining town of San Antonio de los Cobres on the famous Tren a las Nubes (Train to the Clouds) – see the section on San Antonio de los Cobres for details. Formerly it left on Saturdays at 7.05 am between April and November. At present, however, this service has been suspended.

Wednesdays at 7.27 am, the local freight train is a cheaper alternative to the Tren a las Nubes. Fares to San Antonio de los Cobres are US$6 primera, US$5 turista; for the 29-hour marathon to the Chilean border at Socompa, the price is US$15 primera,

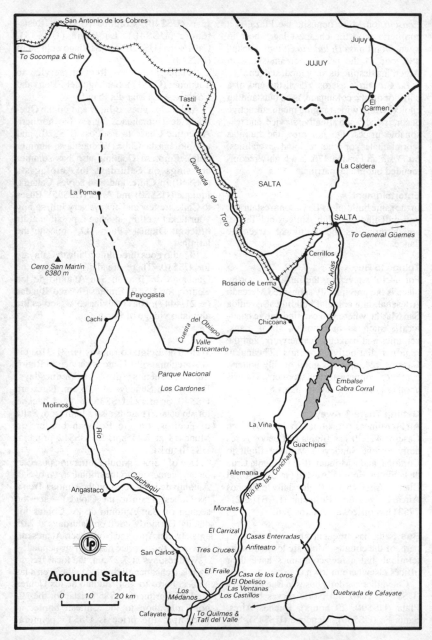

Around Salta

0   10   20 km

US$12 turista. From San Antonio de los Cobres you can catch a return bus to Salta.

Car Rental Renting a car is a good way to see Salta and its countryside, but it is not cheap. Agencies include López Fleming (☎ 21-1381), at Güemes 92, and Ruiz Moreno (☎ 21-2069), Buenos Aires 1. Daily rates start at US$20 plus US$8 insurance plus US$0.20 per km. Weekly rates start at about US$400 plus US$100 insurance, with 1500 free km included.

Getting Around
Local bus No 5 connects the train station and downtown with the bus terminal on Avenida Hipólito Yrigoyen, which is south-east of downtown. Bus No 13 connects the station with the municipal campground.

QUEBRADA DE CAFAYATE
Salta sits in a valley which receives abundant rainfall from summer storms which drop their load on the slopes which surround the city. To the south and west, though, higher ranges of peaks inhibit the penetration of subtropical storms. In several areas, the rivers which descend from the Andes have carved deep *quebradas* (canyons) through these arid zones, exposing the multicoloured sedimentary strata which underlay the surface soils.

Many of these layers have eroded to strange, sometimes unearthly formations which travellers up the Quebrada from Salta can appreciate from the highway, but which are even more intriguing when explored up close. For its extraordinary scenery, the canyon deserves national or provincial park status.

Properly speaking, the Quebrada de Cafayate is the Quebrada del Río de las Conchas, after the river which eroded the canyon. After the tiny village of Alemania, about 100 km south of Salta, the scenery changes suddenly and dramatically from verdant hillsides to barren reddish sandstones. To the east, the Sierra de Carahuasl is the backdrop for distinctive landforms which bear evocative names, like Garganta

del Diablo (Devil's Throat), El Anfiteatro (The Amphitheatre), El Sapo (The Toad), El Fraile (The Friar), El Obelisco (The Obelisk), and Los Castillos (The Castles). Before arriving in Cafayate, you'll see an extensive field of sand dunes at Los Médanos.

Getting There & Away
Other than renting a car (possible in Salta but not in Cafayate), the only ways to see the Quebrada are to take the bus, hitch or walk. Tours available from Salta are brief and regimented. You can disembark from any of El Indio's buses anywhere in the canyon and a succeeding bus will pick you up, but you should be aware of the schedules between Salta and Cafayate, since you probably don't want to get stuck in the canyon after dark (although there are worse places to camp if you have your tent along). The same holds if you hitch between the most interesting sites – you may want to catch one of the buses if it gets late.

Walking will allow you to see the canyon at your own pace, but you do need to carry food and water in this hot, dry environment. A good place to start is the impressive box canyon of Garganta del Diablo. Remember that the most interesting portion is much too far to walk in a single day, so see as much as you can before continuing to Cafayate – you can always double back the next day.

CAFAYATE
Cafayate, the most important town in the extreme south-western part of Salta province, has a warm, dry and sunny climate which makes it makes it ideal for the cultivation of wine grapes. Several major Argentine winemakers have vineyards here, including Etchart and Michel Torino. It is a popular tourist destination, but not overrun with visitors.

Orientation
Cafayate sits at 1660 metres at the foot of the Calchaquí valley, near the junction between national Ruta 40, which goes north-west to Molinos and Cachi, and provincial Ruta 68,

1 Comfort Hotel
2 Post Office
3 Residencial Colonial
4 Hotel Melchor
5 Residencial Arroyo
6 Church
7 Plaza
8 Hotel Emperador
9 Buses El Indio
10 Hotel Gran Real
11 Hotel Asturias
12 Hotel Briones
13 Banco de la Nación
14 Museo Arqueológico
15 Museo de Vitivinicultura
16 Bodega la Rosa
17 Camping Lorahuasi

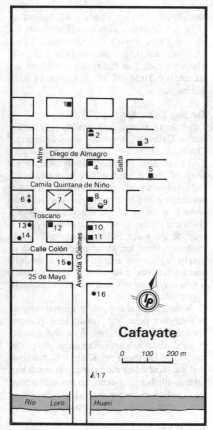

Cafayate

0   100   200 m

which goes to Salta. Through town, Ruta 40 is Avenida Güemes. As in many small provincial towns, few people even know the street names.

Information
Tourist Office There is a tourist information kiosk on Güemes, opposite the plaza, but its opening hours are erratic.

Money It is better to change in Salta, but try Banco de la Nación on the plaza, or the larger shops or hotels.

Post & Telecommunications The post office is on Güemes, toward the west end of town. Long-distance phone calls can be an agonisingly time-consuming experience at the small office on the west side of the plaza.

Museo Arqueológico
Señor Rodolfo Bravo, a dedicated aficionado and expert on the region, gives guided tours of his astounding personal collection of Calchaquí (Diaguita) Indian ceramics, in his house on Calle Colón, for US$1 per person. There are also colonial and more recent artefacts, such as elaborate horse gear and wine casks. Drop in at any reasonable hour.

Museo de Vitivinicultura
On Güemes near Colón, this museum details the history of local wine production. Ask at the bodegas for tours and tasting; the Etchart tour has been recommended. A local speciality is the sweet white *torrontés*.

Places to Stay
Camping Although it can be dusty in the wind, the municipal *Camping Lorahuasi* charges US$1 per car, per person and per tent, for excellent facilities, which include hot showers and a swimming pool. There is a small grocery, but you can also buy food in town, which is only a 10-minute walk away.

Residenciales & Hotels Cafayate has a good selection of hotels in all categories except luxury. The best budget choice is probably *Residencial Colonial* (☎ 21223), which charges US$6 per person with shared bath, but may lack hot water at times. *Residencial Arroyo* is comparable. *Hotel Briones* (☎ 21270), on the plaza at Toscano 80, is great value at US$20 double, and has a decent confitería.

At US$15/25 per single/double, *Hostería ACA* (☎ 21296) is a bargain for ACA members. Slightly costlier are *Hotel Emperador* (☎ 21023) at Güemes 42, and *Hotel Gran Real* (☎ 21016) at Güemes 128. The latter has a dingy downstairs confitería and may be closed except in summer.

Several others are rather higher priced at about US$30/40, including *Hotel Melchor* (☎ 21065), at Güemes and Almagro, and *Hotel Asturias* (☎ 21040) at Güemes 158.

Places to Eat

Local cuisine concentrates on parrillada, and sometimes puts decor before food, as at *La López Pereyra*. You can also try *La Carreta de Don Olegario*, on Güemes at the plaza, but there are several cheaper places.

Things to Buy

Check the Mercado Artesanal, on the plaza near the tourist office, for local handicrafts. There are many young artists and craftspeople in Cafayate.

Getting There & Away

El Indio has three buses daily to Salta, except on Thursday when there are four. The four-hour trip costs US$10. There are also four daily to San Carlos, up the Valle Calchaquí, and one to Angastaco (US$5).

Use the daily buses to Santa María to visit the important ruins at Quilmes (see below), in Tucumán province. Three buses weekly connect Cafayate with the city of Tucumán via a very scenic and worthwhile route through Tafí del Valle.

VALLES CALCHAQUÍES

In this valley north and south of Cafayate,

which was one of the principal routes across the Andes to Chile and Peru, the Calchaquí Indians put up some of the stiffest resistance to Spanish colonial rule. In the 17th century, plagued with labour shortages, the Spaniards twice tried to impose forced labour obligations on the Calchaquíes, but found themselves having to maintain armed forces to prevent the Indians from sowing crops and attacking pack trains.

Military domination did not solve Spanish labour problems, since their only solution was to relocate the Indians as far away as Buenos Aires, whose suburb of Quilmes bears the name of one group of these displaced people. The last of the descendants of the 270 families transported to the capital had died or dispersed by the time of Argentine independence.

When their resistance failed, the Calchaquíes lost a productive land which had sustained them for centuries and would have done so much longer. According to the American geographer Isaiah Bowman, visiting the area in the 1920s, 'So fertile is the soil of the Calchaquí valley...that alfalfa lasts for twenty five years without resowing...'. Those riches found their way into the hands of Spaniards who formed large rural estates, the haciendas of the Andes.

QUILMES

Although it is in the province of Tucumán, the pre-Hispanic fortress of Quilmes is only 50 km south of Cafayate and most travellers will approach it from this direction. Probably the best preserved ruins in all of Argentina, this pucará deserves a visit despite its location five km off the main highway. See the Tucumán chapter for details.

ANGASTACO

Angastaco resembles the other oasis settlements, which are placed at regular intervals in the Valles Calchaquíes, with vineyards, fields of peppers, and ruins of an ancient pucará. There is also an archaeological museum.

The ASEMBAL hostería has rooms for US$10/16 a single/double, but there is also

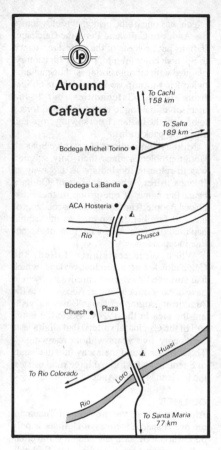

Around Cafayate

To Cachi
158 km

To Salta
189 km

Bodega Michel Torino ●

Bodega La Banda ●

ACA Hosteria ●

Rio   Chusca

Church ●   Plaza

Huasi

To Rio Colorado

Loro

Rio

To Santa Maria
77 km

a cheaper residencial. Very early on Thursday morning, Expreso Marcos Rueda has a bus to Salta, which returns to Angastaco on Sunday afternoon. There is a daily bus to Cafayate.

MOLINOS

Like Angastaco, Molinos was a way station on the trans-Andean route to Chile and Peru. Well into this century, pack trains passed here with skins, wool, blankets and wood for sale in Salta and subsequent shipment to Buenos Aires. Molinos takes its name from the still operative grain mill on the Río

Calchaquí, and also features an important 18th-century church. In the surrounding villages you can find the traditional 'ponchos de Güemes' for sale. There is lodging at the *Hostal Provincial de Molinos* (☎ 21-4871) for US$28/45 a single/double.

CACHI

With its scenic surroundings, 18th-century church and archaeological museum, Cachi is probably the most worthwhile stopover among the accessible settlements in the valley. There are several possibilities for lodging: the municipal campground and hostel, the *Hotel Nevado de Cachi*, and the *Hostería ACA*, which has singles/doubles for US$15/25 for members. Nonmembers pay higher rates. There are several restaurants.

You can reach Cachi either from Cafayate or, more easily and frequently, by the Marcos Rueda bus from Salta. This route passes across the scenic Cuesta de Obispo past the new Parque Nacional Los Cardones (see below).

From Cachi, buses continue to La Poma, an old hacienda town which, for all practical purposes, is the end of the line. The road beyond, to San Antonio de los Cobres, is impassable except for vehicles with 4WD. It is much easier to approach San Antonio from Salta via the Quebrada del Toro.

SAN ANTONIO DE LOS COBRES

In the colonial period, transportation from north-western Argentina depended on pack trains, most of which passed through the Quebrada de Humahuaca on the way to Potosí, but an alternative route crossed the rugged elevations of the Puna de Atacama to the Pacific and thence to Lima. A member of Diego de Almagro's party, the first Spaniards to cross the puna, left an indelible account of the miserable 800-km crossing, which took twenty days in the best of times:

Many men and many horses froze to death, for neither their clothes nor their armour could protect them from the freezing wind...Many of those who had died remained, frozen solid, still on foot and propped against the rocks, and the horses they had been

Guanaco

loading also frozen, not decomposed, but as fresh as if they had just died; and later expeditions...short of food, came upon these horses and were glad to eat them.

For travellers across the Andes, the area around the bleak mining town of San Antonio de los Cobres (altitude 3700 metres) must have seemed an oasis, though even in 1914 it had a population below 1000. Until well into this century, it continued to be an important way station for drovers moving their stock across the mountains to arid Chile, whose narrow alluvial valleys could not produce the food needed for the nitrate miners of the Atacama Desert. Later, railroads and motor roads supplanted mules for shipping food and supplies to Argentine mining settlements and across the Andes.

San Antonio de los Cobres is a largely Indian town, but the posters and political graffiti scribbled on its adobe walls tell you that it's still part of Argentina. Formerly, it offered one of the most interesting border crossings in all of Argentina, paralleling the routes of the mule drivers across the Puna de Atacama to the Pacific coast of Chile via the famous Train to the Clouds.

Places to Stay
There is no luxury accommodation or upscale food in San Antonio. What you see is what you get. What you get is basic lodging at *Hospedaje Belgrano* or *Hospedaje Los Andes* for about US$4 per night per person with shared bath. There are plenty of blankets, since nights are cold at this altitude. Hospedaje Los Andes has a restaurant, otherwise you can buy food and drink in the few shops.

Getting There & Away
There are five weekly buses from Salta to San Antonio de los Cobres with El Quebradeño, at US$10 for the four-hour trip. See the section below on El Tren a las Nubes for details on the picturesque train trip from Salta to San Antonio de los Cobres and beyond.

EL TREN A LAS NUBES & THE CHILEAN CROSSING
At present, the Train to the Clouds service is closed, and is undergoing privatisation. In the hope that the service will resume in the near future, a description of what you can expect is offered here.

From Salta, the Train to the Clouds leaves the Lerma valley to ascend the multicoloured Quebrada del Toro past the important ruins of Tastil, paralleling national Ruta 51, which goes to the Huaytiquina pass and across the Andes to the Chilean oasis of San Pedro de Atacama. The track makes countless switchbacks and even spirals to reach the heights of the puna. The highlight of the trip is the stunning viaduct at La Polvorilla, spanning an enormous desert canyon, a magnificent engineering achievement unjustified on any reasonable economic grounds.

The freight trains, which you may be able to catch in San Antonio de los Cobres, are a cheaper alternative to the Train to the Clouds and will take you past the gigantic salt lakes of the puna to the Chilean border station at Socompa. From there it is possible to catch the Chilean freight train to the Atacama station of Baquedano on the Pan American Highway, about 100 km from the port of Antofagasta. On the Chilean side, this is a rugged, uncomfortable trip, not for the squeamish – the Chilean crew is unfriendly and the train truly filthy.

At Socompa, 3900 metres above sea level, you must clear Argentine and Chilean immigration and customs before seeking permission to ride the infrequent freights – it is not unusual to wait several days for a train. The Chilean station agent will radio for permission to carry passengers in the train's caboose; while permission is fairly routine, it is not guaranteed. Purchase a quantity of Chilean pesos before leaving Salta, since the agent may offer *very* unfavourable rates for US dollars.

From Socompa, the train descends with impressive views of 6051-metre Volcán Socompa to the east and 6739-metre Llullaillaco to the south, through vast monochrome deserts which few visitors to the continent ever see. At the abandoned mining station of Augusta Victoria, the crew may ask you to disembark while the train backtracks to another isolated mining outpost, but it will return. You may, however, wish to try your luck at hitching to Antofagasta – in this isolated area, mining trucks are informal public transportation and are almost certain to stop. Otherwise, you can sleep in the abandoned station, which is far more comfortable than the caboose, until the train returns.

While the Tren a las Nubes service is suspended, freight trains are your only alternative. It is possible to take a freight train to the Chilean border, but it's difficult to organise.

Getting There & Away

Do not waste time trying to hitch across the Andes because there are no vehicles except for the summer buses operated by Geminis and Atahualpa from Salta. These are invariably full, so you cannot catch them in San Antonio de los Cobres.

The Train to the Clouds (if it resumes running) goes only as far as the spectacular La Polvorilla viaduct, but it is possible to continue to the Chilean border at Socompa and, with patience, to Chile. For details, see the description above and the Getting There & Away section of Salta.

NATIONAL PARKS OF SALTA PROVINCE

Salta has three important national parks but only one, Los Cardones, enjoys easy access. Baritú must be approached through Bolivia, while Finca El Rey is only inaccessible during the rainy summer.

Parque Nacional Los Cardones

There is some confusion as to whether Parque Nacional Los Cardones yet constitutes a park or ever will, but it theoretically occupies some 70,000 hectares on both sides of the winding highway from Salta to Cachi across the Cuesta del Obispo. Only 100 km from Salta, the park takes its name from the candelabra cactus known as the cardón *(Trichocereus pasacana)*, the most striking plant species within the park boundaries.

In the absence of forest in the Andean foothills and the puna, the cardón has long been an important source of timber for rafters, doors, window frames and other uses. As such, it is commonly found in native construction and in the colonial churches of the region. According to the Argentine writer Federico Kirbus, clusters of cardones can be a good indicator of archaeological sites: the Indians of the puna ate its sweet black seed which, after passing through the intestinal tract, readily seeded itself around their latrines.

Pending finalisation of park status, there are no visitor services in Los Cardones, but this should not deter prospective visitors. Buses between Salta and Cachi will drop you off or pick you up. If you visit Buenos Aires before going to Salta, visit the national parks office there for the latest information. Otherwise try the tourist office in Salta.

Parque Nacional Baritú

Along the Bolivian border in Salta province, Baritú is the most northerly of the three Argentine parks which conserve subtropical montane forest. Like Calilegua (see the entry under Jujuy province) and Finca El Rey (see below), it protects diverse flora and harbours a large number of endangered or threatened mammals, including black howler and capuchin monkeys, the southern river otter, Geoffroy's cat, the jaguar and the Brazilian tapir. The symbol of the park is the *ardilla roja* (yungas forest squirrel), which inhabits the moist montane forest above 1300 metres.

At present, the only access to Baritú is through Bolivia, where southbound travellers from Tarija may want to inquire about entry via a lateral off the highway which goes to the border station at Bermejo/Aguas Blancas. For information in Argentina, contact the visitor centre at Parque Nacional Calilegua (☎ 22046) in the village of Calilegua, Jujuy.

Parque Nacional Finca el Rey

Argentina's subtropical humid forests are confined to a narrow strip, not wider than about 50 km, extending from the Bolivian frontier south of Tarija almost to the border between Tucumán and Catamarca provinces. Parque Nacional El Rey, comprising 44,000 hectares almost directly east of Salta, is the most southerly of the Argentine parks which protect this unusual habitat, the most biologically diverse in the country. It takes its name from the estancia which formerly occupied the area, whose expropriation created the park.

The park's emblem is the giant toucan, appropriate because of the abundant bird life, but there are also most of the same mammals as found in Baritú and Calilegua. The staff maintain a vehicular nature trail along the Río Popayán and and plan to make a foot trail. There is a comfortable hostería at park headquarters, but it was closed recently because of a change in concessionaires. For up-to-date information and reservations, contact the visitor centre at Calilegua (☎ 22046).

As the crow flies, Parque Nacional El Rey is only about 100 km from Salta, but via national Ruta 9, provincial Ruta 5 and provincial Ruta 20, it is more than 200 km from the provincial capital. There is public transport as far as the junction of Ruta 9 and Ruta 5, but even if you can hitch to the second junction, there is almost no traffic for the last 46 km to park headquarters. In the summer rainy season, only 4WD vehicles will be able to pass. In Salta, Turismo Mallorca is a good bet for arranging excursions to the park.

Tucumán & Santiago del Estero Provinces

Tucumán is the smallest province in Argentina, but its size belies its importance. From the colonial period, when it was an important way station en route to Potosí, through the early independence period, and into the present, Tucumán has played a critical role in the country's political and economic history.

In modern Argentina, Tucumán means sugar. Unlike areas to the north, Tucumán benefits from both its proximity to the high Sierra de Aconquija to the west and the absence of a front range to the east. This permits warm easterly winds to drop their moisture on the Sierra and moderate winter temperatures – the area within 60 km of its slopes is frost-free. The humid slopes and dense subtropical forests give birth to permanent streams for irrigation. While the sugar monoculture has enabled the province to develop secondary industry, it has also created tremendous inequities in wealth and land distribution, as well as ecological problems.

The extreme west of the province is a high, arid extension of the Valles Calchaquíes, but the scenic area around Tafí del Valle is a climatic anomaly, a cool, damp valley between subtropical mountains and arid puna. The precipitous mountain road from

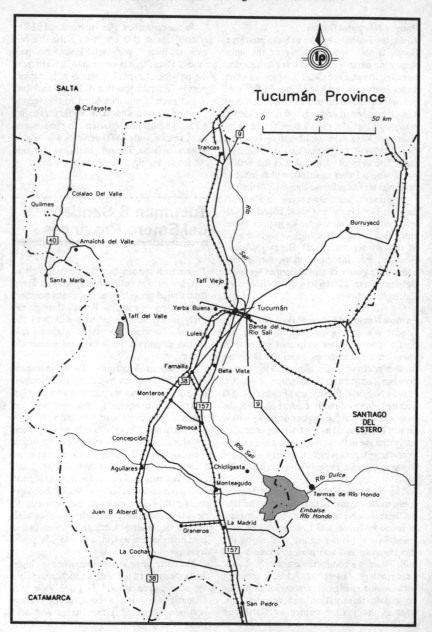

SALTA

Cafayate

Colalao Del Valle

Quilmes

Amaichá del Valle

Santa María

Taff del Valle

Trancas

Burruyacú

Río Salí

Taff Viejo

Yerba Buena

Tucumán

Banda del Río Salí

Lules

Famailla

Bella Vista

Monteros

SANTIAGO DEL ESTERO

Simoca

Concepción

Río Salí

Aguilares

Chicligasta

Río Dulce

Monteagudo

Termas de Río Hondo

Juan B Alberdi

Embalse Río Hondo

Graneros

La Madrid

La Cocha

CATAMARCA

San Pedro

Tucumán Province

0   25   50 km

Top: Canyon of Río Santa Cruz, Santa Cruz Province
Bottom: The Old Patagonian Express? El Maitén, Chubut Province

Top: Moreno Glacier, Parque Nacional Los Glaciares, Santa Cruz Province
Left: Cuernos del Paine, Parque Nacional Torres del Paine, Chile
Right: Parque Nacional Tierra del Fuego

Tucumán to Tafí de Valle is a spectacular trip which no visitor to the area should miss.

The province of Santiago del Estero is a hot subtropical lowland which is a transitional area between the Gran Chaco and the Andes. Its capital, Santiago del Estero, is the oldest city in Argentina, from which the region's other cities were founded. Cotton is the province's dominant crop. Termas de Río Hondo, the province's second city, is an important winter resort for its thermal mineral waters.

TUCUMÁN

Only during and after Argentine independence did Tucumán distinguish itself from the rest of the region. Founded in 1565 as San Miguel de Tucumán, the city and its hinterland were oriented toward Salta and Bolivia during most of the colonial period, as roads from Rosario, Córdoba and Santa Fe converged here.

During the ferment of the early 19th century, Tucumán hosted the congress which declared Argentine independence in 1816. Dominated by Unitarists and composed of merchants, lawyers, soldiers and clergy, and despite a virtual boycott by Federalist factions, the Congress accomplished little else as it failed to agree on a constitution which would have institutionalised a constitutional monarchy in hope of attracting European assistance.

Unlike other colonial cities of the North-West, Tucumán successfully reoriented its economy in the postindependence period. Modern Tucumán dates from the late 19th century and owes its importance to location – at the southern end of the frost-free zone of sugar cane production, it was just close enough to Buenos Aires to take advantage of access to the growing market of the federal capital. By 1874, a railroad connected Tucumán with Córdoba, permitting easy transport of this commodity. Local and British capital contributed to the industry's growth.

Sugar continues to dominate the provincial economy, occupying more than 60% of the total agricultural land and causing social,

economic and ecological problems. Large farms and factories characterise the industry, whose seasonal labour requirements during the winter *zafra* (harvest) contribute to high unemployment the rest of the year. Attempts to diversify the agricultural economy have had little success.

Orientation

Tucumán sits on the west bank of the Río Salí, only a few km east of the precipitous Sierra de Aconquija. National Ruta 9 passes the city's outskirts en route from Santiago del Estero to Salta. The Mitre and Belgrano railways connect Tucumán with Buenos Aires, while the Belgrano serves Jujuy and the Bolivian border at La Quiaca.

One of the first cities founded in Argentina, Tucumán's centre is the rectangular Plaza de la Independencia. Although it is the commercial and administrative centre for the sugar industry, Tucumán preserves important remnants of its colonial past. Less than a kilometre east of the plaza, the 100-hectare Parque 9 de Julio is an accessible recreational resource. Street names change on each side of Avenida 24 de Setiembre and on each side of Avenidas Avellaneda and Sáenz Peña.

The slopes of the Sierra, a short bus ride from Tucumán to the suburb of Yerba Buena, offer good hiking on gaucho stock trails. There is still a yearly rodeo of semiwild cattle from the Sierra.

Information

Tourist Office Tucumán's tourist office (☎ 21-8591) is at 24 de Setiembre 484, on the main plaza. It's conveniently open daily, including weekends, from 7 am to 11 pm, but the provincial financial crisis has left it short on maps and brochures. There is also a very helpful information service at the bus terminal.

Money There are several cambios along San Martín, including Maguitur at San Martín 765, which cashes travellers' cheques for a 2% commission with a US$5 minimum exchange.

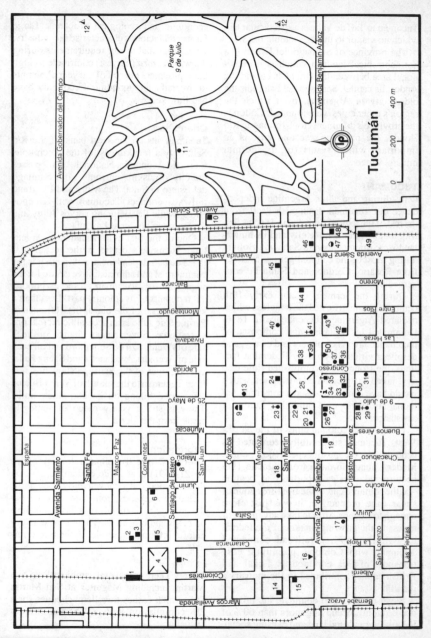

Tucumán

■ PLACES TO STAY

2   Hotel Norte
3   Hotel California
5   Hotel Tucumán
6   Hotel Miami
7   Residencial Viena
10   Gran Hotel de
     Tucumán
14   Residencial Roni
15   Residencial Royal
19   Residencial Florida
24   Hotel Plaza
27   Hotel Metropol
28   Hotel Premier
32   Hotel Francia
36   Hotel Congreso/
     Hotel Astoria
38   Hotel del Sol
42   Hotel Impala
44   Residencial
     Independencia
45   Hotel Colonial
46   Hospedaje la Estrella
48   Residencial El Pargue

▼ PLACES TO EAT

16   Sociedad Italiana
39   Feria de Artesanos
     Tucumanos
50   Adela

OTHER

1   Mitre Station
4   Plaza Alberdi
8   Telecom
9   Post Office
11   Casa de Obispo
     Colombres
12   Municipal Campsites
13   Centro Cultural de la
     Universidad Nacional
     de Tucumán
17   ACA
18   Maguitur (Casa de Cambio)
20   Museo Folklórico Manuel
     Belgrano
21   Casa Padilla
22   Casa de Gobierno
23   Iglesia San Francisco
25   Plaza Independencia
26   Austral
29   Iglesia Santo Domingo
30   Aerolíneas Argentinas
31   Casa Histórica
33   Museo de Bellas Artes
34   Tourist Office
35   Cathedral
37   Museo Histrico de
     la Provincia
40   Casa de la Cultura
     Lola Mora
41   Iglesia la Merced
43   Museo Iramain
47   Bus Terminal
49   Belgrano Station

Post & Telecommunications The post office is at 25 de Mayo and Córdoba. Long-distance telephones are at Maipú 480.

Cultural Centres For information on what's happening in Tucumán, go to the Centro Cultural de la Universidad Nacional de Tucumán, 25 de Mayo 265.

Travel Agencies ACA (☎ 21-6049) is at Crisóstomo Alvarez and Jujuy.

Museums
Tucumán is an historic city with a wealth of museums and other attractions too numerous to detail completely. The **Museo Iramain**, at

Entre Ríos 27, has collections of sculpture and art on Argentine themes. It's open weekdays from 9 am to 1 pm. Other art museums include the **Museo de Bellas Artes**, 9 de Julio 44, open 9 am to noon and 5.30 to 8.30 pm daily, except Monday; and the **Museo de Arte Sacro**, a religious collection at the Cathedral, open Monday to Saturday from 10 am to noon.

Other significant museums include the **Museo Histórico de la Provincia** at Congreso 56, once the home of President Nicolás Avellaneda, open weekdays only from 9 am to 12.30 pm and daily from 5 to 8 pm; the **Museo Arqueológico**, with collections on the prehistory of north-western Argentina, at

25 de Mayo 265, open weekdays from 8 am to noon and 4 to 8 pm; and the **Museo Policial**, at Salta and Santa Fe, open 8 am to noon and 4 to 8 pm.

Casa de la Independencia
Wear sunglasses when you approach this dazzlingly whitewashed colonial house at Congreso 151, 1½ blocks from Plaza Independencia, where the mostly Unitarist lawyers and clerics declared Argentina's independence from Spain on 9 July 1816. Portraits of these men line the walls of the room in which the declaration was signed. Federalists boycotted the meeting.

Continue to the interior patio, a pleasant refuge from Tucumán's commercial bustle. Provincial financial crises have caused limited opening hours, so you can go only on Tuesday to Friday between 8.30 am and 1.30 pm, or weekends from 9 am to 1 pm. Admission is US$1.

Museo Folklórico Manuel Belgrano
Occupying a colonial house which belonged to the family of Bishop Colombres, at 24 de Setiembre 565, this pleasant and interesting museum features a good collection of River Plate horsegear, indigenous musical instruments and weavings, plus samples of *randa*, an intricate lace resembling Paraguayan *ñandutí*, from the village of Monteros, 53 km south of Tucumán. It's open Tuesday to Friday from 9 am to 12 noon, otherwise 5.30 to 8.30 pm. There is no admission charge.

Casa de Obispo Colombres
In the centre of Parque 9 de Julio, this 18th-century house contains the first primitive *trapiche* (sugar mill) of Tucumán's postindependence industry. There are guided tours in Spanish explaining the operation of the mill, and some of its equipment is still in working order. Hours are weekdays 9 am to 12.30 pm and 3 to 6.30 pm, weekends 9 am to 6 pm. Admission is US$0.50.

Instituto Miguel Lillo
The garden of this natural history museum, at Miguel Lillo 205 near the Mercado de Abasto, has life-size replicas of dinosaurs and other fossils from Parque Provincial Ischigualasto in San Juan province. It's open weekdays from 9 am to noon and 3 to 6 pm.

Mercado de Abasto
Photographers especially should not miss this colourful wholesale/retail market, one of the finest in all of South America, where brightly painted horsecarts from the countryside haul their goods to town. Unlike most markets, it is liveliest in mid to late afternoon, when the city's restauranteurs go to purchase their produce. It's about one km from the centre, at San Lorenzo and Miguel Lillo. You can eat cheaply in the market cafés.

Festivals
Celebrations on **Independence Day** are especially vigorous in Tucumán, the cradle of the country's independence. Tucumanos also celebrate the **Battle of Tucumán** on September 24.

Places to Stay – bottom end
Camping There are two campgrounds in Parque 9 de Julio, the better of which is *Las Lomitas*. Take bus No 1 from Crisóstomo Alvarez down Avenida Benjamín Aráoz past the university. Unusually for Argentina, the campground is unenthusiastic about backpackers – stress that you are a foreigner.

Camping fees are computed by a remarkably complex formula decreed by municipal bureaucracy, but should cost roughly US$1.50 per person plus US$1 per tent. The unfenced site is less secure than most Argentine campgrounds – although theft is unlikely, let the attendant know when you leave.

Hospedajes, Residenciales & Hotels
Hotels in Tucumán are generally modern and lack character. The cheaper ones are concentrated around the Mitre train station and the bus terminal.

Near the train station, try *Hotel Tucumán* at Catamarca 563, which is shabby but passable. Singles/doubles with shared bath cost

US$6/9, slightly more with private bath. *Hotel Norte*, Catamarca 639, is cheaper but seamier. About five blocks south is *Residencial Royal*, San Martín 1196 near Colombres, which charges US$6/9 with shared bath, US$10/13 with private bath. *Hotel Castelar* (☎ 21-8311), Maipú 342 between Córdoba and San Juan, is closer to the centre and has a good restaurant downstairs.

Near the bus terminal, check out friendly *Hospedaje La Estrella*, Avenida Benjamín Aráoz 36, where doubles are US$10. Nearby and only slightly cheaper is the dingy and noisy *Residencial El Parque*, Sargento Gómez 22, which has an indifferent staff. *Residencial Independencia*, 1½ blocks away at Balcarce 50, charges US$12/15 with private bath.

More central is the modern, boxy *Hotel Astoria*, just off Plaza Independencia at Congreso 92, where rates are US$8/12 with shared bath, slightly more with private bath. Next door, at Congreso 74, *Hotel Congreso* is slightly more expensive. The street itself is very noisy.

Places to Stay – middle

Residencial Florida (☎ 22-1785), just off the plaza at 24 de Setiembre 610, is friendly, quiet and central, but very small. Upstairs rooms have more light. Rooms with fans and shared bath are US$14/16, with private bath only very slightly more. Rates are comparable at *Hotel Colonial*, San Martín 35 between Avenida Avellaneda and Balcarce, which comes very highly recommended. *Hotel Impala*, Cristóstomo Alvarez 274, is clean and modern for US$15/20 with private bath. *Hotel Petit*, Cristóstomo Alvarez 675, is comparable but has slightly cheaper rooms with shared bath.

Residencial Viena, Santiago del Estero 1054 opposite the train station, has rooms for US$15/22. *Residencial Roni*, San Martín 1177, is a bit farther away. The central *Hotel Plaza*, San Martín 435, charges similar rates.

Other midrange places are slightly costlier at about US$20/30, including *Hotel California* (☎ 22-9259) at Corrientes 985 and *Hotel Miami* at Junín 580, both near the Mitre station. Downtown, try *Hotel Francia* (☎ 22-9780) at Cristóstomo Alvarez 467, and *Hotel Premier* at Cristóstomo Alvarez 510.

Places to Stay – top end

Near Parque 9 de Julio, a bit away from the centre, is *Gran Hotel de Tucumán*, where rooms cost US$50/65. More expensive but perhaps lesser value are the modern, high-rise central places such as *Hotel Metropol*, 24 de Setiembre 524, and *Hotel del Sol*, Laprida 32, where rates are about US$55/70.

Places to Eat

One of the best places to explore for inexpensive food is the Mercado de Abasto (see above). The Mercado del Norte, at Mendoza and Maipú, is another possibility. Closer to downtown, try the outstanding Feria de Artesanos Tucumanos, on 24 de Setiembre half a block from Plaza Independencia. Behind its crafts shops, a variety of small stands prepare tasty regional specialties. Other regional foods are available at *Restaurant de Tino*, Maipú 344, next to Hotel Castelar.

For Italian food, try the *Sociedad Italiana* at 24 de Setiembre 1021. Middle Eastern food is the speciality at *Adela*, on 24 de Setiembre near Plaza Independencia. One LP reader has highly recommended *El Duque* at San Lorenzo 440.

Getting There & Away

Air Aerolíneas Argentinas (☎ 31-1747) is at 9 de Julio 112. It has flights to Buenos Aires daily, except Saturday. Austral (☎ 22-4920) is at 24 de Setiembre 546, next to Hotel Metropol. It has daily flights to Buenos Aires; on weekends, these stop over in Córdoba. Austral flights have a direct bus connection to Termas de Río Hondo.

Bus The bus terminal is at Avenidas Sáenz Peña and Benjamín Aráoz, only a few blocks from Plaza Independencia.

Panamericano heads north to Salta and Jujuy, south to Córdoba. La Estrella goes daily to Mendoza via Catamarca and La Rioja.

El Rayo crosses the Chaco to Roque Sáenz Peña, Resistencia and Corrientes. Empresa Itatí goes to Posadas, Puerto Iguazú, and Buenos Aires (US$60, 20 hours). Atahualpa goes to Pocitos, on the Bolivian border, for US$30. Chevallier serves Rosario, Córdoba and Buenos Aires, more cheaply than Itatí.

Aconquija has two morning and two afternoon buses to Tafí del Valle. The fare is US$6. La Unión and El Ranchilleño have several buses daily to Termas de Río Hondo (US$4) and Santiago del Estero (US$7).

Train The Mitre railway station is at Catamarca and Corrientes, opposite Plaza Alberdi. It has a daily service to Retiro Station, Buenos Aires, at 5 pm. Pullman class costs US$40, primera US$30, and turista class US$25. On Wednesday and Sunday there is a sleeper car service for US$90. Passengers from Retiro continuing to Salta are met immediately by the Veloz del Norte bus.

The Belgrano railway station, which is on Avenida Sáenz Peña opposite the bus terminal, goes north to Jujuy and La Quiaca on Tuesdays and Fridays at 3.40 pm. Fares are US$16 primera, US$13 turista.

Car Rental Try Móvil Renta (☎ 21-8635) at San Lorenzo 370.

Getting Around

The airport bus leaves from the Austral office. Tucumán city buses do not accept cash, so you must buy cospeles at downtown kiosks. Two cospeles, roughly US$0.25 each, are needed for each ride. They are less easily available outside the centre.

AROUND TUCUMÁN
Ruins of San José de Lules

Until 1767, this mission 20 km south of Tucumán was a Jesuit reducción among the Lule Indians of the region. After the expulsion of the Jesuits, Dominicans assumed control of the complex, which later served as a school. There are numerous ghost stories about the place, and legends of buried Jesuit treasure.

TAFÍ DEL VALLE

From Tucumán, national Ruta 38 heads south-west through sprawling canefields, punctuated by the ingenios (industrial mills) of the large sugar companies, before intersecting provincial Ruta 307 at Acheral. From Acheral, the road snakes up the narrow gorge of the Río de los Sosas where, in places, the rising river has so eroded the highway that even a single vehicle can barely pass. On all sides dense, verdant subtropical forest covers the hills – this is the refuge where the Argentine army wiped out the People's Revolutionary Army (ERP), ending their dreams of emulating Fidel Castro's success in the Sierra Maestra of Cuba, another sugar-producing zone.

About 100 km from Tucumán, the gorge opens onto a misty valley below the snowy peaks of the Nevado del Aconquija. When the summer heat drives Tucumanos out of the city, they seek relief in the cool heights around Tafí del Valle. Beyond Tafí, the road zigzags over the 3050-metre pass known as Abra del Infiernillo (Little Hell), an alternative route to Cafayate and Salta. It is possible to visit the impressive Diaguita Indians ruins at Quilmes.

Prior to the arrival of the Spaniards, Calchaquí Indians inhabited the Tafí valley, raising potatoes and herding llamas in dispersed settlements. After the Spanish conquest and decline of the encomienda, the Jesuits acquired the valley, which enjoyed a new prosperity until their expulsion in 1767. With Argentine independence, the isolated valley declined economically for more than a century until a new highway made it possible to get crops to market and tourists to the valley.

A temperate island in a subtropical sea, Tafí del Valle produces seed potatoes and fruits (apples, pears and peaches) for Tucumán. It also pastures cattle, sheep and, at higher altitudes, llamas. Typical products include sweets and dairy products – in February, the town celebrates the Fiesta

Nacional del Queso (National Cheese Festival). There is good fishing in La Angostura, the artificial lake formed by El Mollar dam.

Orientation
Tafí del Valle (population 6000) sits at 2000 metres above sea level, at the north end of the lake formed by the dam.

Information
Tourist Office There is a helpful tourist office (☎ 21023) in the Centro Cívico, which features an unusual circular plaza. There is an excellent small café in the same building.

Money You can exchange cash at Banco de la Provincia, at the Centro Cívico.

Capilla La Banda
This 18th-century chapel, built by the Jesuits and acquired by the Frías Silva family of Tucumán on the Jesuits' expulsion, was restored to its original configuration in the 1970s. A short distance out of town, it now contains a museum and an artisans' market.

Parque Los Menhires
More than eighty aboriginal granite monuments, resembling the standing stones of the Scottish Hebrides, cover the hillside at the southern end of La Angostura reservoir. Collected from various sites throughout the valley, these sculptures of human and animal forms had a ritual significance, which has not been completely deciphered by archaeologists.

Places to Stay
Residencial El Cumbre, Diego de Roca 120, charges US$7 per person for rooms with shared bath. ACA has an hostería, open to members only, for US$18/30 with shared bath.

Recently, the municipal campground was closed while in the process of privatisation, but the facilities appear to be excellent. There is a free site, with picnic tables, just outside the regular campground.

Getting There & Away
Aconquija has two buses daily between Tucumán and Tafí del Valle. It is difficult to hitch through this area.

QUILMES
More than just a fortress, Quilmes was a highly complex urban settlement dating from about 1000 AD. Spread over about 30 hectares, it housed as many as 5000 people. The Quilmes Indians abided contact with the Incas from about 1480 AD, but could not outlast the siege of the Spanish who, in 1667, deported the last 2000 Quilmes to Buenos Aires.

The thick walls of Quilmes' buildings underscore the city's defensive functions, but evidence of dense human occupation sprawls both north and south from the central nucleus, the outlines of whose buildings, in a variety of shapes, are obvious even to the casual observer. For revealing views of the form, density and extent of the ruins, climb the trails up either flank of the nucleus, which offer vistas of the valley once only glimpsed by the defenders of the city. Give yourself at least half a day and preferably more to explore the nucleus and the surrounding area.

There is a small museum at the entrance, whose US$1 admission charge also entitles you to explore the ruins. It is possible to camp on the site. Buses from Cafayate to Santa María will drop you at the junction, but from there you'll have to walk or hitch (there is little traffic) the five km to the ruins. It will probably be easier to get a lift back to the highway, since you can approach any vehicle which visits the ruins.

SANTIAGO DEL ESTERO
Founded in 1553 by Francisco de Aguirre, Santiago del Estero is the oldest city in Argentina. Like other cities in the colonial era, it was an important stopover between the Pampas and the mines of Bolivia. The city and province rely on agriculture, cotton being the most important crop, but irrigation supplements rainfall which is not always dependable. Often, crops are

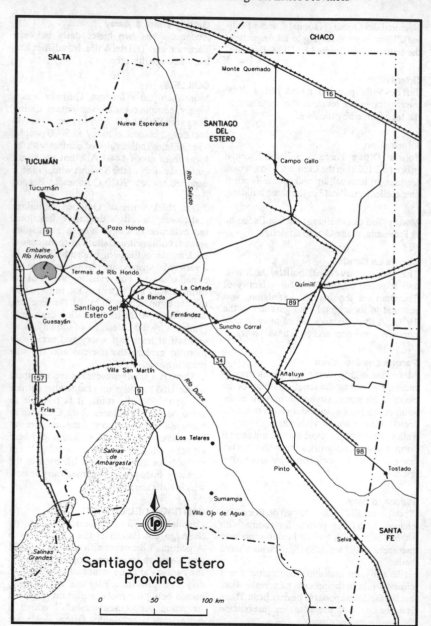

SALTA

CHACO

Monte Quemado

16

Nueva Esperanza

SANTIAGO
DEL
ESTERO

Campo Gallo

TUCUMÁN

Río Salado

Tucumán

9

Pozo Hondo

Embalse
Río Hondo

Termas de Río Hondo

La Cañada

Quimilí

La Banda

89

Santiago del
Estero

Fernández

Guasayán

Suncho Corral

Villa San Martín

34

Añatuya

157

9

Río Dulce

Frías

Los Telares

98

Tostado

Pinto

Salinas
de
Ambargasta

Sumampa

Villa Ojo de Agua

SANTA
FE

Selva

Salinas
Grandes

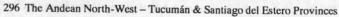

Santiago del Estero
Province

0   50   100 km

grown on seasonally inundated bañados as flood waters recede. These areas shift with the annual movements of the Río Dulce.

Orientation

Santiago del Estero, with a population of about 150,000, sits on the right bank of the Río Dulce, 1045 km north-west of Buenos Aires. It is about 350 km north of Córdoba by national Ruta 9 and 170 km south-east from Tucumán by the same road.

Reflecting its early settlement, Santiago's urban plan is more irregular than most Argentine cities. The town centre is Plaza Libertad. From the plaza Avenida Libertad, trending south-west to north-east, bisects the city. At its northern end, woodsy Parque Aguirre offers relief from summer heat. On either side of the plaza, the peatonal Avenida Tucumán and Avenida Independencia are important commercial areas, but Avenida Belgrano, crossing Avenida Libertad and roughly parallel to Tucumán and Independencia, is the main thoroughfare.

Information

Tourist Office The Dirección Provincial de Turismo (☎ 21-4243) is at Avenida Libertad 417, opposite Plaza Libertad. Besides tourist information, it displays work by local artists. Opening hours are weekdays 7 am to 1 pm and 4 to 9 pm.

Money Noroeste Cambio, on 24 de Setiembre between 9 de Julio and Urquiza, will change cash but not travellers' cheques. You can also try Banco de la Nación at 9 de Julio and 24 de Setiembre, or Banco de la Provincia on Avenida Belgrano between Sarmiento and San Martín.

Post & Telecommunications ENCOTEL is at Buenos Aires and Urquiza. Telecom is on Mendoza between Independencia and Buenos Aires, with additional long-distance telephone facilities at the bus terminal.

Travel Agencies ACA is at Avenidas Sáenz Peña and Belgrano.

Museums & Historic Buildings

Santiago has many interesting colonial buildings and museums. Besides those described below, you should see the **Convento de San Francisco** on Avellaneda between Avenida General Roca and Olaechea, which also contains the **Museo de Arte Sacro** (religious art museum); the **Iglesia de Santo Domingo** at 25 de Mayo and Urquiza; and the **Casa de los Taboada** at Buenos Aires 136. The **Museo Provincial de Bellas Artes** at Independencia 222 also deserves a visit.

Museo Wagner

This archaeological museum, at Avellaneda 355, has a superb, chronologically arranged and splendidly displayed collection of fossils, funerary urns (owls and snakes are recurring motifs), and the ethnography of the Chaco region. The friendly staff offer free guided tours weekdays from 7 am to 1 pm.

Museo Histórico Provincial

Exhibits at the late colonial house of Pedro Díaz Gallo, with its beautiful patios and colonnades, emphasise postcolonial history. It is rather disorganised because of restoration work, but contains religious and civil art, materials on important local families, and informative displays of coins and paper money. At Urquiza 354, it's open weekdays from 8 am to noon.

Parque Aguirre

Named for the city's founder, this enormous park is readily accessible from the city centre. It has a small zoo, camping areas, a swimming pool (when there is sufficient water from the Río Dulce) and (watch your step!) a drivers' training centre operated by ACA.

Festivals

Santiago's chaotic **Carnaval**, in February, resembles celebrations in the Quebrada de Humahuaca. During the entire last week of July, Santiagueños observe the founding of the city.

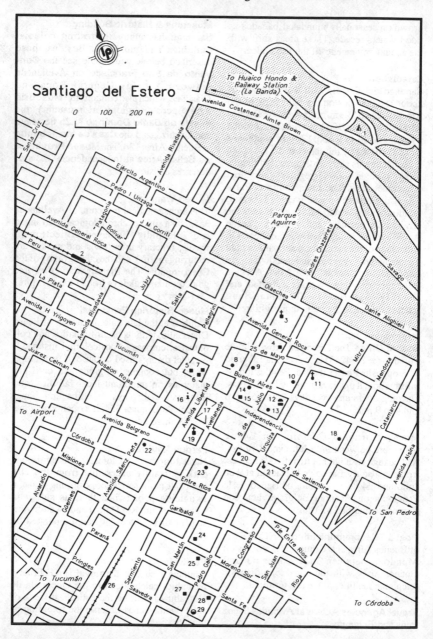

Santiago del Estero

0   100   200 m

■ PLACES TO STAY

1   Campamento Las Casuarinas
     (Municipal Campground)
4   Hotel Centro
5   Hotel Savoy
6   Hotel Palace
7   Hotel Florida
15 Hotel Grand
24 Residencial Iovino
25 Residencial Emaus/
     Hotel Bristol
27 Hotel Rodas
28 Residencial Santa Rita

OTHER

2   Old Mitre Station
3   Convento San Francisco
8   Aerolíneas Argentinas
9   Museo Wagner
10 Museo Histórico Provincial
11 Iglesia de Santo Domingo
12 Post Office
13 Museo Provincial
     de Bellas Artes
14 Casa de los Taboada
16 Tourist Office
17 Plaza Libertad
18 Telecom
19 Iglesia Catedral
20 Banco de la Nación
21 Iglesia de la Merced
22 ACA
23 Banco de la Provincial
26 Old Belgrano Station
29 Bus Terminal

Places to Stay – bottom end

Camping The municipal *Campamento Las Casuarinas* is a pleasant, shady, secure area in Parque Aguirre, less than a kilometre from Plaza Libertad. Fees are about US$1.50 per vehicle, plus $1 per person and per tent.

Residenciales & Hotels Except around the bus terminal, there is not much really cheap lodging in Santiago del Estero. At *Residencial Santa Rita*, Santa Fe 273, has singles/doubles with shared bath for US$6/10, with private bath for US$8/15. Tiny *Residencial Emaus*, Moreno Sur 673

between Pedro Gallo and San Martín, has only five rooms, but is friendly and spotlessly clean for US$10/16. Almost next door to the terminal is *Hotel Rodas* (☎ 21-8484), at Pedro Gallo 430 between Santa Fe and Saavedra.

Places to Stay – middle

Midrange hotels start at about US$20/25 with shared bath, US$25/35 with private bath. *Residencial Iovino*, Moreno Sur 602 at San Martín, is near the bus terminal. *Hotel Savoy*, Tucumán 39 near Plaza Libertad, has more character than the more expensive *Hotel Palace*, Tucumán 19. Try also *Hotel Florida*, at Avenida Libertad 355.

Places to Stay – top end

Hotel Centro, 9 de Julio 131, and *Hotel Bristol*, at Moreno Sur 677 next to Residencial Emaus, charge about US$40/50 with private bath. *Hotel Grand*, at Avellaneda and Independencia, is the best in town at US$50/65.

Places to Eat

The *Comedor Universitario* at Avellaneda 364, with cheap if uninspiring food, offers opportunities to meet local students. You'll find better food, but also reasonably priced, at the *Comedor Centro de Viajantes*, Buenos Aires 37. Other inexpensive eating places are near the bus terminal.

There are several better restaurants and confiterías around Plaza Libertad.

Getting There & Away

Air Aerolíneas Argentinas (☎ 21-9242) is at Buenos Aires 60. It has flights to Buenos Aires on Mondays, Wednesday, Fridays, Saturdays and Sundays. The one-hour flight costs about US$160.

Bus The bus terminal is at Pedro Gallo and Saavedra, eight blocks south of Plaza Libertad. Santiago del Estero is a junction for important highways in several directions.

To Termas de Río Hondo, an hour to the north-west, La Unión has 14 buses daily (US$3), continuing to Tucumán (US$7).

Termas de
Río Hondo

0   100   200 m

1	Bus Terminal
2	Post Office
3	Centro Cultural
4	Telecom
5	Casino Center Hotel
6	Tourist Office
7	Atlantic Hotel
8	Hotel Termal Los Felipe
9	Nuevo Banco
10	Municipalidad
11	Banco de la Nación
12	Banco Provincial
13	Banco Commercial
14	Hospital
15	Mercado Municipal

Panamericano goes north to Salta (US$25) and Jujuy (US$28, seven hours); their express services are faster and more comfortable, but only slightly costlier, than their locals.

Cacorba has five buses daily to Córdoba (US$18, five hours) and one daily to Buenos Aires (US$45, 16 hours). Chevallier, slightly cheaper to the capital, also has two daily buses to Rosario (US$25). La Estrella serves Santa Fe (US$30), Paraná (US$32), and Mar del Plata (US$52). El Rayo crosses the Chaco to Roque Sáenz Peña (US$20), Resistencia (US$25), and Corrientes (US$27, nine hours), with connections to Puerto Iguazú.

Libertador goes three times weekly to La Rioja (US$16), San Juan (US$32), and Mendoza (US$36). Bosio has daily buses to Catamarca for US$14.

Train The Ferrocarril Mitre's station is in the suburb of La Banda.

Its Estrella del Norte train leaves daily for Buenos Aires at 7.47 pm, but the Wednesday and Sunday Expreso Independencia is more comfortable and more expensive. Tariffs on the Estrella·are US$22 turista, US$26 primera, and US$35 pullman. On the Independencia, fares are US$50 pullman, US$80 for a sleeper berth.

Getting Around
The central part of Santiago del Estero is compact and walking suffices for almost everything except connections to the train station. It is reached by the No 17 or No 21 bus from Moreno and Libertad. Bus No 19 takes you to the airport.

TERMAS DE RÍO HONDO
On national Ruta 9 midway between Santiago del Estero and Tucumán, Termas de Río Hondo lives and dies by tourism, with 12,000 hotel beds, plus rental apartments, houses and chalets, plus three campgrounds in a town of 22,000 people. The competition keeps prices reasonable. Outside the winter season, May to October, most accommodation and businesses shut down.

The primary attraction of Termas de Río Hondo is its thermal springs – even the most basic accommodation has hot mineral baths. Outside town, the Dique Frontal forms an enormous artificial lake which is used for water sports such as swimming, boating, fishing and windsurfing.

The town itself has two unusual features – a rather interesting triangular plaza, and one of few monuments in the country with busts of both Juan and Evita Perón.

Information
Tourist Office For such a tourist-oriented town, the tourist office on Caseros, between Rivadavia and Sarmiento, is remarkably short on staff and information.

Money There are several banks, including Banco de la Nación on Caseros, but don't expect to change travellers' cheques.

Places to Stay
Most of Río Hondo's hotels close in summer, but a few remain open. Try the exceptionally

friendly *Atlantic Hotel* (☎ 21708), Absalón Rojas 32, at US$6 per person out of season, U$8 per person in season. *Hotel Termal Los Felipe* (☎ 21484) at San Francisco Solano 230, is comparable.

The *Casino Center Hotel* (☎ 21346), at Caseros 126, is the most extravagant lodging in town.

Getting There & Away
The bus terminal is on Las Heras between España and 12 de Octubre, half a dozen blocks west of the plaza and two blocks north of Ruta 9 (Avenida Alberdi). La Unión has 14 daily buses between Santiago del Estero and Tucumán, via Termas de Río Hondo.

La Rioja & Catamarca Provinces

Isolated Catamarca and La Rioja, Argentina's most obscure Andean provinces, have much worth seeing. In the mid-19th century Domingo Faustino Sarmiento compared the Riojano landscape to that of the Middle East:

...in the reddish or ochreous tints of the soil, the dryness of some regions and their cisterns; also the orange-trees, vines and fig-trees bearing exquisite and enormous fruits, which are raised along the course of some turbid and confined Jordan. There is a strange combination of mountain and plain, fruitfulness and aridity, parched and bristling heights, and hills covered with dark green forests as lofty as the cedars of Lebanon.

Among the modern provinces of Argentina, La Rioja and Catamarca are poor relations, but they are rich in scenery, folklore and tradition. Both were home to several important pre-Columbian cultures, mostly maize cultivators, who developed unique pottery techniques and styles – the region has many important archaeological sites. Inca influence did not touch the Diaguitas until the late 15th century, just before the arrival of the Spaniards.

This region has produced some of

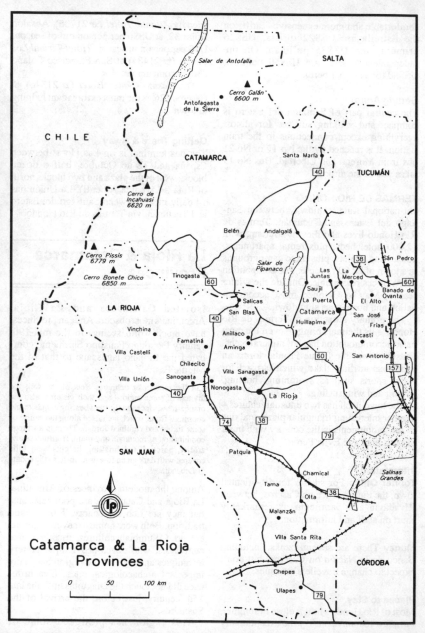

Catamarca & La Rioja Provinces

0   50   100 km

Argentina's most memorable historical figures, such as caudillos Facundo Quiroga, Chacho Peñaloza and Felipe Varela – objects of Sarmiento's scorn in his famous diatribe against the rise of provincial strongmen. To balance the books, La Rioja also gave the country intellectuals like Joaquín V González, a writer, politician and founder of La Plata university, and Arturo Marasso, also a writer and educator.

Presently, both provinces are economic backwaters with a low standard of living, especially in Catamarca. The area is politically influential, though – President Carlos Menem and his mercurial family are Riojanos, while the prominent Saadis have run Catamarca almost as a family fiefdom. Both, to some degree, are modern counterparts of Facundo and his contemporaries, relying on personal connections rather than political principle for their support.

Corruption and nepotism are widespread and often get out of hand – in 1990, when Governor Ramón Saadi of Catamarca was thought to have obstructed the rape/murder investigation of the son of one of his political protegés, a Catholic nun led repeated local protests which finally forced Buenos Aires to intervene in the provincial court system. According to a local priest, cited in the Porteño daily *Página 12*, 'Beneath the cloak of the Virgin of the Valley, Catamarca is a sewer'.

LA RIOJA

Juan Ramírez de Velasco founded the city of Todos los Santos de la Nueva Rioja in 1591. Dominican, Jesuit and Franciscan missionaries helped pacify the Diaguita Indians and paved the way for Spanish colonisation. The city's appearance reflects the interaction between coloniser and colonised, combining European designs with native techniques and local materials. Many buildings were destroyed in the 1894 earthquake, but the city has been entirely rebuilt. The recently restored commercial centre, by the Plaza 25 de Mayo, is a good replica of colonial architecture, as are several churches and private homes.

Orientation

Situated at the base of the picturesque Sierra de Velasco, La Rioja is 154 km south of Catamarca, 515 km north of San Juan, 460 km west of Córdoba, and 1167 km north and west of Buenos Aires. With a population of 100,000, it is relatively small, with all points of interest and most hotels located within easy walking distance of each other. The commercial centre surrounds Plaza 25 de Mayo and continues along Pelagio Luna and 25 de Mayo. North-south streets change their names at Rivadavia, but east-west streets are continuous.

Information

Tourist Office The Dirección General de Turismo (☎ 28834, 28839) is at Avenida Perón and Urquiza. The friendly, eager staff have a good city map and brochures of other destinations in the province. Hotel information includes only registered hotels, which excludes many possibilities, but there is a list of casas de familia. Opening hours are 6.30 am to 9.30 pm.

Money There are no cambios in La Rioja. Banco de la Nación is at Belgrano and Pelagio Luna, while Banco de La Rioja is at Rivadavia and San Martín. Bank hours are limited, but most travel agencies will change money (see below).

Post & Telecommunications ENCOTEL is at Avenida Perón 764. Telecom is at Pelagio Luna and Joaquín V González.

Travel Agencies ACA (☎ 25381) is at Dalmacio Vélez and Copiapó. Tur Rioja (☎ 26997) is at Rivadavia 578, Velasco Tur (☎ 27272) at Buenos Aires 252, Marco Polo (☎ 22005) at Avenida Perón and Avenida Quiroga, Yafar Turismo (☎ 23053) at Lamadrid 170, Anillaco Turismo (☎ 24484) at Buenos Aires 124, and Parme Tur (☎ 25369) is at 25 de Mayo 156.

Medical Services The Hospital Presidente Plaza (☎ 27814) is at San Nicolás de Bari Este 97.

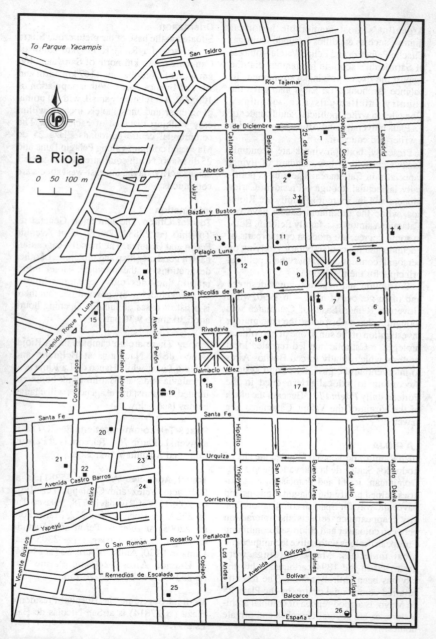

La Rioja

0   50 100 m

■ PLACES TO STAY

1	Residencial Florida
7	Hotel Plaza
14	Residencial Margarita
15	Hotel Savoy
17	Hotel El Libertador
20	Hotel Imperial
21	Residencial Petit
22	Residencial Sumaj Kanki
24	Hotel Talampaya
25	Hotel de Turismo

OTHER

2	Museo Inca Huasi
3	Convento de San Francisco
4	Convento de Santo Domingo
5	Telecom
6	Museo Histórico de La Rioja
8	Iglesia Catedral
9	Casa de Gobierno
10	Aerolíneas Argentinas
11	Banco de la Nacion
12	Mercado Artesanal de La Rioja
13	Museo Folklórico
16	Banco de la Rioja
18	ACA
19	ENCOTEL
23	Tourist Office
26	Bus Terminal

Museo Folklórico

This very interesting museum recreates an authentic 19th-century house, with all the furnishings and objects necessary for everyday life. The shady patio, with comfortable benches, is a good place to take refuge from the heat. One room has ceramic reproductions representing mythological beings from local folklore. At Pelagio Luna 811, it's open Tuesday to Sunday from 8 am to noon, and 4 to 8 pm.

Museo Inca Huasi

More than 12,000 pieces, including tools and artefacts of stone, wood, metal and bone, plus Diaguita ceramics and weavings, fill this paleontological and archaeological museum at Alberdi 650.

Museo Histórico de La Rioja

La Rioja was the land of the caudillos so deplored by Sarmiento, including the famous Facundo Quiroga, Felipe Varela and Angel (Chacho) Peñaloza. Some Argentines say that President Carlos Menem models himself on Facundo, down to his muttonchop sideburns. This museum, which contains Quiroga's stagecoach, military paraphernalia, and the die of the first coin used by his army, offers some insight on the province's political development. It's at Adolfo Dávila 79.

Religious Buildings

La Rioja is an important religious centre. The **Convento de Santo Domingo** at Pelagio Luna and Lamadrid, built in 1623 by Diaguita Indians under the direction of Dominican friars, is the oldest convent in the country. The date appears in the elaborately carved algarrobo door frame, also the work of Indian artists.

See also the **Convento de San Francisco**, at 25 de Mayo and Bazán y Bustos, which houses the image of the Niño Alcalde, an important religious icon featuring the Baby Jesus as the city's mayor. This convent also contains the cell occupied in 1592 by San Francisco Solano, a priest known for educating the native people and defending their rights.

The **Iglesia Catedral**, at San Nicolás and 25 de Mayo, contains the image of patron saint Nicolás de Bari, an object of devotion for both Riojanos and the peoples of neighbouring provinces.

Parque Yacampis

On the outskirts of town at the foot of the Sierra de Velasco, this well-landscaped park has panoramic views, an artificial lake, a small zoo where some local fauna such as rheas run free, and a swimming pool.

Festivals

El Tinkunako This religious ritual, which

takes place at midday December 31, re-enacts the original ceremony of San Francisco Solano's mediation between the Diaguitas and their Spanish conquerors in 1593. For accepting peace, the Diaguitas imposed two conditions: the resignation of the Spanish mayor and his replacement by the Christ Child. Some Riojanos wear indigenous clothing and sing traditional songs in a procession in which they carry the image of their patron saint, San Nicolás de Bari, to meet the Niño Alcalde in front of the government palace. In deference to the mayor, the saint bows three times.

La Chaya This folkloric festival, the local variant of Carnaval, attracts people from throughout the country. Its name, which derives from a Quechua word meaning 'to get someone wet', should give you an idea what to expect. The festival takes place around the figure of Pujllay, the indigenous deity responsible for the happiness of the poor. He is born at Carnaval, lives for three days and dies on Sunday.

Festival del Viñador This festival, honouring wine makers, takes place at the beginning of the March grape harvest in Villa Unión. During the festival there is music, dancing, and tasting of the famous regional wines, in particular the artisanal *vino patero*, made by traditional foot stomping of the grapes.

Places to Stay – bottom end
Camping The very pleasant Parque Yacampis, at Avenida Ramírez de Velasco km 3, has a shady, well-kept campground with clean bathrooms and showers. There are several campgrounds along provincial Ruta 1, including *Country Las Vegas* at km 7, *Sociedad Siriolibanesa* at km 10, and *Balneario Los Sauces* at km 12.

Residenciales La Rioja does not have a large tourist infrastructure, especially in budget hotels. Many residenciales closed in the early 1990s, but the remainder are perfectly acceptable.
Residencial Sumaj Kanki, at Avenida Castro Barros and Coronel Lagos, which provides modest but clean accommodation, can get a bit noisy. Rooms with shared bath cost US$4 per person. Around the corner is *Residencial Petit*, Lagos 427, whose triples with bath for US$17 are a great value. The friendly, flexible owner allows some cooking and clothes' washing. Once a grand place, the building still conserves some of its past splendour.

Residencial Margarita, at Avenida Perón 407 behind a kiosk, has small, dark but clean rooms at US$5 per person with bath. Another fairly central place is *Residencial Florida*, 8 de Diciembre 524, with small but comfortable singles/doubles for US$9/16. Since the elderly owner lives way out the back, you should walk in if nobody answers the bell.

Places to Stay – middle
The few hotels in this category vary widely in their prices for single rooms. *Hotel Savoy* (☎ 26894), Avenida Roque A Luna 14, has comfortable rooms with bath, air-conditioning and telephone for US$17/21. There is a bar and confitería for breakfast. A bit away from the centre at Avenida Perón 951, *Hotel Talampaya* (☎ 24010) offers similar accommodation for US$12/20. The nearby *Hotel Imperial* (☎ 22478), Mariano Moreno 345, has doubles/triples for US$21/26.

Places to Stay – top end
Hotel El Libertador (☎ 26052), Buenos Aires 253, has rooms for US$35/48 and offers a 10% cash discount for ACA members. At *Hotel Plaza* (☎ 25215), 9 de Julio and San Nicolás de Bari, rates are US$46/57. There is room service, a swimming pool and bar.

Other hotels in this group are quite distant from the centre. The cheapest is ACA's *Motel Yacampis* (☎ 25216), located in the beautiful Parque Yacampis, north-west of the city. Singles/doubles are US$17/28 for members and US$26/41 for nonmembers. It has a good restaurant and confitería. At the southern entrance of town, *Hotel de Turismo* (☎ 25240), Avenida Perón and Avenida Quiroga, is a bit more luxurious than the others, with a swimming pool and solarium. Rooms cost US\$56/76. The nearby *Hotel King's* (☎ 25272) at Avenida Quiroga and Copiapó, also has a swimming pool but is cheaper at US\$36/52.

Places to Eat

Regional cuisine, which is readily available at festivals and special events, can also be found at local restaurants. Some dishes to look for include: locro (stew), juicy and spicy empanadas which differ from the drier ones of the Pampas, chivito asado (barbecued goat), humita (stuffed corn dough), quesillo (a cheese speciality), and olives. Don't miss the irresistible bread, baked in hornos de barro (adobe ovens). There is also a good selection of dried fruits, preserves and jams from apples, figs, peaches and pears.

Places that serve regional food include: *Restaurant Cavadini*, Avenida Quiroga 1135; *La Cantina de Juan*, Hipólito Yrigoyen 190; *La Vieja Casona*, Rivadavia 427; *El Milagro*, Avenida Perón and Remedios de Escalada; and *La Lala*, Avenida Quiroga and Güemes. All serve standard Argentine dishes like parrilladas. Don't hesitate to order house wines, which are invariably excellent.

La Fragata, Copiapó 235, serves basic dishes at reasonable prices. A good-value place is the *Comedor de la Sociedad Española*, 9 de Julio 237, with tasty Spanish food. *La Taberna de Don Carlos*, Rivadavia 459, serves good Arab dishes.

Things to Buy

La Rioja has unique weavings that combine indigenous techniques and skill with Spanish designs and colour combinations. The typical mantas (bedspreads) feature floral patterns over a solid background. Spanish influence is also visible in silverwork, including tableware, ornaments, religious objects and horse gear. La Rioja's famous pottery is entirely indigenous – artists utilise local clay to make distinctive pots, plates, and flower pots. Vino Riojano has a national reputation.

The Mercado Artesanal de La Rioja, Pelagio Luna 790, exhibits and sells these items and other popular artworks at prices lower than souvenir shops.

Getting There & Away

Air Aerolíneas Argentinas (☎ 27353, 26307) is at Belgrano 63. It flies to Catamarca and Buenos Aires daily, except Sunday, at 1.05 pm. Aeropuerto Vicente Almonacíd is east of La Rioja, on provincial Ruta 5, km 7.

Bus The bus terminal (☎ 25453) is at Artigas and España.

Empresa El Cóndor (☎ 26436) travels daily to destinations within the province (Sanagasta, Castro Barros, Arauco, San Blas de los Sauces and Chilecito), as well as to Córdoba, Catamarca and San Luis, daily except Saturday.

COTIL (☎ 26312) services Córdoba three times daily, with student discounts. It also has buses to local destinations: San Martín, Chilecito (three daily), Julapes (three weekly), Chepes (on Fridays), Olta (two daily), Chamical (four daily), Vinchina (one daily) and Villa Unión (one daily).

Expreso Nacate serves San Juan three times weekly. Transportes Libertador has daily buses to Mendoza, San Juan, Catamarca and Tucumán, and to Santiago del Estero three times weekly.

Empresa ABLO (☎ 26444) has buses to Córdoba, Santa Fe, San Luis, Buenos Aires and Mar del Plata. La Estrella (☎ 26306) goes to San Juan, Mendoza and Tucumán. Empresa General Urquiza (☎ 26306) has buses to Santa Fe and Buenos Aires.

Typical fares are: Córdoba US\$16, San Luis US\$18, Santiago del Estero US\$22, Catamarca US\$6 and Tucumán US\$15.

Train There is no direct passenger train to La Rioja, but there is a bus-train combination, the Ferro Automotor. It links the bus terminals at Catamarca and La Rioja with the Ferrocarril Belgrano at Córdoba, which travels to Retiro Station in Buenos Aires. The bus departs La Rioja at 10 pm daily.

Car Rental There are two car rental agencies, Auto Tur (☎ 21687) at Santiago del Estero 32, and Planas (☎ 24065) at Buenos Aires 244.

AROUND LA RIOJA
Monumento Histórico Las Padercitas
Franciscan missionaries built this adobe chapel, protected by a later stone structure, seven km west of town on provincial Ruta 1. According to legend, San Francisco Solano converted many Diaguita Indians here in the 16th century. On the second Sunday of August, pilgrims convene to pay homage to the saint.

Dique Los Sauces
Beyond Las Padercitas, Ruta 1 climbs and winds past attractive summer homes and bright red sandstone cliffs, lush vegetation and dark purple peaks. Cacti remind you that the area is semidesert. Balneario Los Sauces, 15 km from La Rioja at the dam, is a pleasant place for a leisurely picnic or outing.

From Balneario Los Sauces it is possible to hike or drive up the dirt road to Cerro de la Cruz (1680 metres), which has fantastic views of the Yacampis valley and the village of Sanagasta. The top also has a ramp for hang-gliding, a popular activity in La Rioja.

SANAGASTA
At the end of the pavement through the captivating valley of the Río Huaco, Ruta 1 leaves you at the village of Sanagasta, 30 km from La Rioja. Poplars line its narrow streets, where you will see summer homes and vineyards. There is a small, well-restored chapel, and an intriguing museum. The *Hostería Municipal* is very attractive, with reasonable prices.

CHILECITO
Originally called Santa Rita, Chilecito (population 20,000) is the second-largest city in the province. Its name testifies to the presence of Chileans who worked the gold mines of Famatina in the 19th century; at one time, the provincial government briefly relocated here to escape the intimidation of Facundo Quiroga. Because of the importance of the mines, in 1892 Chilecito became the site of the second branch of the Banco de la Nación in the country. In 1903 it built one of the world's largest aerial engineering projects, the 34-km cable car to La Mejicana mine, which reaches an altitude of 4500 metres.

Although in the early 1900s there where 10 foundries in the area, agriculture has replaced mining as the main economic activity. Chilecito is famous for its wines, olives and walnuts.

Orientation
Chilecito lies 192 km north-west of La Rioja, in a picturesque valley at the foot of the massive Nevado de Famatina and Cerro Velazco.

Information
Tourist Office The tourist office (☎ 2688), at Libertad and Independencia, has enthusiastic staff and good material. Alberto Decaro, its director, has written an excellent work on Parque Provincial Talampaya.

Post & Telecommunications The post office is at Joaquín V González and B Mitre. Telecom is at Castro y Bazán 27.

Money Banco de la Nación and Banco Provincia are on opposite corners of Plaza Sarmiento.

Museo Molino de San Francisco
This colonial flour mill, at J Ocampo 63, belonged to Don Domingo de Castro y Bazán, the city's founder. Today its museum houses an eclectic collection of antique arms, early colonial documents, archaeological tools, minerals, traditional wood and leather crafts, plus weavings and paintings. The building itself merits a visit, but the artefacts are a big plus. Opening hours are Tuesday to Sunday, 8 am to noon and 3 to 7 pm.

Samay Huasi
This building was the country retreat of Dr Joaquín V González, the founder of the Universidad de La Plata, one of the most prestigious in the country. Now belonging to

Chilecito

0   100   200 m

Map Legend

1   Museo Molino
    San Francisco
2   Municipalidad
3   ENCOTEL
4   Bus Terminal
5   Banco de la Nación
6   Residencial Wamatinac
7   Residencial Riviera
8   Plaza Sarmiento
9   Banco Provincia
10 Hotel Bel-Sa-Vac
11 Tourist Office
12 Residencial Americano
13 Hotel Chilecito

the university, the building houses a natural sciences, archaeology and mineralogy museum, and a valuable collection of paintings by Argentine artists. Located 3 km from Chilecito past La Puntilla, it's open Tuesday to Sunday from 8 am to noon and 3 to 7 pm.

Wine Tasting
The Cooperativa La Riojana, La Plata 246, is the largest winery in the province. It's open to visitors on weekdays for tours and tasting.

Organised Tours
For information about guided tours of the

Estación No 1 del Cable Carril, an historical monument where you can see some of the machinery used for gold extraction, ask at the tourist office. The tourist office also has descriptions of nearby villages to visit and places to hike, as well as information on organised treks to Los Nevados del Famatina.

Places to Stay
The tourist office keeps a list of casas de familia, which are the cheapest accommodation in town, charging about US$5 per person. Residencial Americano (☎ 8104), at

Libertad 68, has singles/doubles for US$6/12, with shared bath. The very central *Residencial Wamatinac*, at 25 de Mayo 19, has rooms for US$8/12. Rates at *Residencial Riviera*, Castro Barros 133, and *Hotel Bel-Sa-Vac* (☎ 2277), 9 de Julio and Dávila, are US$12/19.

The best accommodation is ACA's *Hotel Chilecito* (☎ 2801), at Poeta Ocampo and T Gordillo, which has a good restaurant. Rooms with bath are US$17/27 for members and US$26/41 for nonmembers.

Places to Eat

The hospitable owners of *Restaurant Club Arabe*, 25 de Mayo and Santa Rosa, offer great food despite a small menu. During summer, ask for fresh grapes from the garden. There is an automatic 10% tourist discount off the already reasonable prices.

Listo El Pollo, at Pelagio Luna 30, and *El Quincho*, Joaquín V González 50, serve parrilladas. *El Gallo*, at Libertad and Illia, and *Toscanini*, at San Martín and Santa Rosa, offer standard menus.

Getting There & Away

COTIL (☎ 2726) has daily buses to Villa Unión and La Rioja. Expreso Santa Rita (☎ 2522) services nearby locations such as Miranda, Famatina and Tinogasta. ABLO (☎ 2224) travels to Villa María (Córdoba province), Rosario and Buenos Aires.

NONOGASTA

This small town, in a prosperous agricultural valley 16 km south of Chilecito, features charming adobe architecture, polite and friendly people, and the good wines from Bodegas Nicarí. Only the roaring water of the acequias disrupts the peaceful dirt streets. The birthplace of Joaquín V González, founder of the Universidad de La Plata, still stands. There is also a 17th-century Jesuit church.

CUESTA DE MIRANDA

With 800 turns, this mountain road through the Sierra de Sañogasta, about 56 km west of Chilecito, is one of the most spectacular in

the northern Andes and one of the major scenic attractions in the province. Although not paved, the surface is very smooth and wide enough for vehicle safety, but sounding the horn before the innumerable blind turns is a good idea.

At the highest point, 2020 metres, there is a vista point from which the Río Miranda looks like a frozen silver ribbon below. COTIL buses between Chilecito and Villa Unión usually take this highway.

VILLA UNIÓN

Villa Unión sits in a valley between the Nevado de Famatina and the precordillera, at an altitude of 1140 metres. Near the banks of the Río Bermejo (also called Vinchina), this inviting village is at the intersection of national Ruta 40 and provincial Ruta 26. On the outskirts of town, a mirador provides a panoramic view of valley, village and surrounding mountains. Don't let the 130 steps up the hill discourage you. The austere modern church has very striking carvings made from cardón cactus.

Places to Stay & Eat

The highly recommended *Hostería Villa Unión* (☎ 7271), on the main street, is the de facto tourist office. It provides good accommodation, excellent information, and even changes money. Rooms without food cost US$7 per person with shared bath, US$9 with private bath. Group rates include room, breakfast and dinner for about US$23 per person with bath. The friendly and helpful owner has maps of the area drawn in the 1970s and 1980s by her now frail and elderly father, Ingeniero Bernard Lorenz. There are also detailed descriptions of the area.

Hospedaje Paola is basic and friendly, with rooms for US$5 with shared bath. There is also a pensión, owned by Señora de Rodríguez, which is cheap but only so-so. *Comedor Hospedaje El Changuito*, owned by a hospitable family, has good, cheap food (mostly minutas) and excellent regional wine. It also has a few beds.

Getting There & Away

COTIL has a daily bus to Chilecito and La Rioja, via the Cuesta de Miranda, departing at 3.45 pm. TAC has two weekly buses from San Juan.

PARQUE PROVINCIAL TALAMPAYA

In Quechua, Talampaya means Dry River of the Tala, which accurately describes the area's landscape and climate: a desert with hot days and chill nights, torrential summer rains, and strong winds in spring. Local people like to compare it to Arizona's Grand Canyon.

Talampaya is an extensive (270,000 hectares) fauna and flora reserve, as well as an important paleontological and archaeological site. Only professional guides with 4WD vehicles are authorised to offer two-hour tours through the colourful canyon, with its aboriginal petroglyphs and nesting condors, who scatter from their cliffside nests when vehicles invade their otherwise undisturbed territory.

From the visitor centre, the vehicle passes the vast dunes of **El Playón**, leading to the **Puerta de Talampaya** (Gate of Talampaya), the entrance to the canyon. During a brief stop, passengers walk along a sandy trail to the petroglyphs and mortars.

Back on the road, the truck enters the breathtaking canyon, whose eastern wall reveals an enormous geological fault. Travelling on the river bed, you'll also see the debris transported by summer flash floods. The next major stops are at **El Balcón**, an extraordinary echo chamber where your voice seems to come back louder than your original call, and a nature trail to the **Bosquecillo** (Little Forest), a representative sample of native vegetation. On the return the major point is **El Cañón de los Farallones** (Canyon of Cliffs) where, besides condors and turkey vultures, you may see eagles and other birds of prey.

By making prior arrangements at the tourist office in Chilecito, it is possible to take a longer excursion that traverses the entire canyon, and also to trek and hike. The two-hour excursion costs US$16 for up to six people; proceeds go directly to the guide. If you can, sit in front with the guide one way, and in the back of the truck the other way. Besides in-depth knowledge of the canyon, you'll hear some local folklore.

CATAMARCA

Londres, the first city in present-day Catamarca province, was founded as early as 1559, but hostile Indians delayed the permanent establishment of any city until 1683, when Don Fernando Mendoza de Mate de Luna founded San Fernando del Valle de Catamarca, or Catamarca for short. Economically, it has remained a provincial backwater, although major holidays attract large numbers of visitors.

Orientation

Located in the valley of the Río del Valle, flanked by the Sierra del Colorado in the west and the Sierra Graciana in the east, Catamarca is 156 km north-east of La Rioja, 238 km from Tucumán and 218 km from Santiago del Estero. Dense clouds often disrupt the view.

Four wide avenues, enclosing an area 12 blocks square, form the city centre, with nearly everything within walking distance. These are Avenidas Belgrano in the north, Alem in the east, Güemes to the south and Urquiza/Mitre in the west. The centre proper is the beautifully designed Plaza 25 de Mayo (the work of Carlos Thays, who also designed Parque San Martín in Mendoza and Parque 9 de Julio in Tucumán), a shady refuge from the summer heat. On Avenida Belgrano is Parque Adán Quiroga, another green space in this relatively treeless city.

Information

Tourist Office The municipal tourist office (☎ 24721), at Urquiza 951, is in the Manzana del Turismo (Tourism Block), a short distance from the city centre. It has a basic map of the city, but the friendly staff will make up for lack of brochures. It opens from 7 am to 1 pm, and 2 to 8 pm. Around the corner on General Roca is the Dirección Provincial de

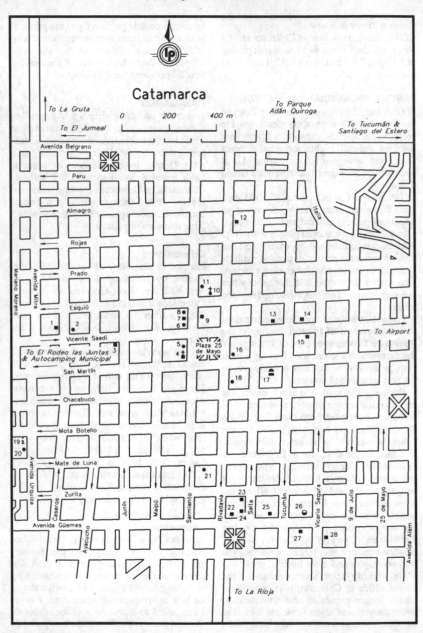

Catamarca

Turismo, whose director, Señora de Agüero, is also very helpful.

Money There are no cambios in Catamarca, but you can exchange cash only at Banco de la Nación, San Martín 626, and Banco Provincia, Vicente Saadi 480. Also try travel agencies and some hotels.

Post & Telecommunications The post office is at San Martín 753, and Telecom is at Rivadavia 758. They are painfully slow at arranging international calls.

Travel Agencies Turi-Cat (☎ 25499) is at Vicente Saadi (ex-República) 832. Yokavil (☎ 28717) is in the Galería Paseo del Centro,

at Rivadavia 922. Bosio (☎ 24339) is at Sarmiento 555, and Tula Norri (☎ 29422) at Mate de Luna 744.

Medical Services The Hospital de Emergencias is on Ayacucho between Chacabuco and Mota Botello.

Museo Arqueológico Adán Quiroga
The three different collections in this museum do not always fit well together. The first room contains a fine assortment of tools, pottery, funerary pots, and mummies from 3000 BC to the 18th century, but is arranged in a tedious, traditional style of glass cabinets with sequences of tools or objects, with descriptive data on date, place, and use. The second room, on colonial history, mixes rifles and musical instruments with fossils. The third room, also historical, presents religious material and the personal effects of the priest Fray Mamerto Esquiú.

Opening hours are weekdays 8 am to 1 pm and 2.30 to 8 pm, and weekends 8 am to noon. Guides for large groups are available on request.

Museo de Bellas Artes Laureano Brizuela
The fine arts museum, in the Paseo General Navarro (also known as La Alameda), is named after this prominent Catamarqueño painter. His works are exhibited together with others by Varela Lezama, Roberto Gray, Antonio Berni, Benito Quinquela Martín, Vicente Forte and others.

Iglesia y Convento de San Francisco
This impressive neocolonial church, at Esquiú and Rivadavia, holds the cell of Fray Mamerto Esquiú, a 19th-century priest famous for speeches in defence of the constitution. A crystal box, containing the priest's heart, is now kept in a locked room after it was stolen and left on the church's roof some years ago.

Catedral
In front of the Plaza 25 de Mayo, the Cathedral contains the image of the Virgen del

Valle, Patron of Catamarca, one of the most venerated images in northern Argentina since the 17th century. Both in early April and on 8 December, multitudes of pilgrims convene here to pay homage to her. The church also has an exhibition of paintings of the virgin, an elaborate altar to Saint Joseph carved in wood, and an ornate baroque pulpit. Her crown, with more than a hundred diamonds, can be seen during the holidays.

Festivals
Fiesta de Nuestra Señora del Valle The Sunday after Easter, in an impressive manifestation of popular religion, large numbers of pilgrims come from the interior and from other Andean provinces to honor the Virgen del Valle. At the end of the *novena* (nine days of prayer), she is taken in procession around the plaza.

Fiesta Nacional del Poncho In July, a crafts and industrial fair accompanies this festival of folkloric music and dance which celebrates the importance of the poncho in the province. The shows, which attract well-known musicians, and exhibitions take place in the Manzana del Turismo on Urquiza. There are also scattered *peñas*, informal gatherings with music, dance and typical food – ask the tourist office for suggestions, and don't miss them.

Places to Stay – bottom end
Camping The *Autocamping Municipal*, on provincial Ruta 4 towards El Rodeo las Juntas, is a pleasant spot about four km from the centre by the Río El Tala, in the foothills of the Sierra de Ambato. It presents two inconveniences: as a balneario, it is the major recreation spot for people from the city, with loud and heavy use on weekends and holidays, and it also has ferocious mosquitos.

The bathrooms and showers are clean, and there is electricity. In summer, two swimming pools, one for adults and another for children, are also open. There is a confitería with very friendly staff and basic food, but it is cheaper to buy your own in town.

Charges are US$5 per tent per day. Take

bus No 10 from Convento de San Francisco, on Esquiú, or from the bus terminal on Vicario Segura. Climb to the top of the hill for a great view.

Casas de Familia, Residenciales & Hotels
The tourist office has a list of casas de familia, which supplement their income by offering inexpensive lodging. Also modest is *Pensión Molina*, (☎ 22706), Vicente Saadi 721, with rooms for US$7 per person. An anonymous hospedaje at San Martín 776 offers singles/doubles at US$15/18.

There are a number of basic hotels near the bus terminal. A nameless pensión on Tucumán 1294 has clean rooms with shared bath (no hot water) at US$4 per person. *Residencial Menem* (!) (☎ 22139), Avenida Güemes 793, has rooms with shared bath at US$8/13 and others with private bath at US$12/15.

Similar in price and standard is *Residencial Avenida* (☎ 22139), Avenida Güemes 754. A block away at Avenida Güemes 841, *Residencial Familiar* (☎ 22142) has rooms with bath at US$10/16. *Residencial Yunka Suma*, Vicario Segura 1255 is a good deal at US$5/10 with bath.

Places to Stay – middle
Prices vary greatly within the middle range. *Sol Hotel* (☎ 24134), Salta 1142, is good value at US$21/28. For a pleasant place with friendly staff, try *Hotel Colonial* (☎ 23502), Vicente Saadi 802, for US$28/38. Similar in price is *Hotel Comodoro* (☎ 23490) on Vicente Saadi 855.

Not far from the bus terminal, *Cerros Hotel* (☎ 20715), Avenida Güemes 630, has rooms with bath and breakfast for US$31/38. The very central *Hotel Suma Huasi* (☎ 22301), Sarmiento 547, with rates of US$39/48, offers discounts to ACA members.

Places to Stay – top end
All hotels in this category charge about US$49/61. Services are similar except at *Hotel Sussex* (☎ 22368), on the road to the airport, which has a swimming pool, and the

more central *Hotel Ancasti* (☎ 25001), Sarmiento 520. Both include breakfast. The modern *Hotel Inti Huasi* (☎ 24664), on Vicente Saadi 297, gives discounts to ACA members. *Hotel Pucará* (☎ 23898), Caseros 501, has pleasant rooms with television.

Places to Eat

The most inexpensive places cater to pilgrims. In the gallery behind the Cathedral is *Comedor El Peregrino*, with two dishes (empanadas and pasta) for about US$2, or a larger option including meat for US$4. *Restaurante y Parrilla La Abuela*, on Sarmiento close to Hotel Ancasti, also has an inexpensive fixed menu with several choices. Other parrillas include *Rancho Chirot*, on Vicente Saadi 750, where a plentiful parrillada for two with salad and wine costs US$9; at night it has folk music. *La Tinaja* on Sarmiento 533 also has music and low prices.

Two other good parrillas are a bit away from the centre. *La Churrasquita*, Avenida Castillo and Avenida Belgrano, serves large portions of good beef. *El Aljibe* is on Avenida Belgrano and José Luna (across the street from the police club).

The *Círculo Policial*, open to the general public at Avenida Belgrano 1172, has very reasonable prices. *Sociedad Española*, close to the tourist office at Urquiza 725, has good seafood and traditional dishes. For good pasta the place to go is the *Sociedad Italiana*, Moreno 152.

For a more elegant place with a varied menu, try *Restaurant Maxims* at the Hotel Sussex, on national Ruta 33.

Things to Buy

For Catamarca's well-known hand-tied rugs, visit the Mercado Artesanal Permanente y Fábrica de Alfombras at Urquiza 945, next to the tourist office. It is possible to see the rugmakers at work on weekday mornings, from 7 am to noon. Besides rugs the market sells traditional ponchos, blankets, jewellery, red onyx sculptures, musical instruments, hand-spun sheep and llama wool, and basketry.

Regional speciality shops are concentrated on Sarmiento, between the plaza and the Convento de San Francisco. Catamarca is the place to buy inexpensive, delicious walnuts, including *nueces confitadas* (sugared walnuts), which are very rich but tasty. Other delicacies are olives, raisins and wines.

Getting There & Away

Air Aeropuerto Felipe Varela is on provincial Ruta 33, 22 km east of the city. Aerolíneas Argentinas (☎ 24450), at Sarmiento and Esquiú, has flights to La Rioja and Buenos Aires daily, except Sunday, at 3.10 pm.

Bus The bus terminal, a really depressing place, is at Avenida Güemes 856. Chevallier has two buses each evening to Buenos Aires, via Córdoba and Rosario. Cacorba serves the same route.

COTIL has buses to the Sierras de Córdoba via La Rioja, Chilecito and Villa Unión. Bosio services Tucumán (six daily), Salta, La Rioja, San Juan, Mendoza and Santiago del Estero.

Typical fares are: Buenos Aires US$60, Córdoba US$19, Salta US$24, La Rioja US$6 and Santiago del Estero US$12.

Train There is no train service to Catamarca, but twice-weekly there is a direct bus connection to the Ferrocarril Mitre in Córdoba for Retiro Station in Buenos Aires.

AROUND CATAMARCA

Parque Zoológico y Botánico de San Antonio

Although locals will recommend this park, located 13 km from Catamarca on provincial Ruta 41, you should be aware of the crowded conditions under which its 350 animals (mostly Argentine species) are kept. Bus No 6 ('Cementerio') and No 7 (on weekends only to the entrance) go there.

Gruta de la Virgen del Valle

According to local legend, in 1619 or 1620 the image of the Virgen del Valle was found in this grotto seven km from the city centre, on provincial Ruta 32. The cave is protected by a structure, and the present image is a replica of the original in the Cathedral.

Empresa COTCA's bus No 22 goes there every 40 minutes.

Cuesta de El Portezuelo

In 20 km this hairpin road climbs more than 1000 metres to the top of the Sierras de Ancasti, for ever more distant views of the city of Catamarca. There are several turnouts for panoramic vistas and photography. Unfortunately, since passenger buses no longer take this route, private car or an organised tour are the only alternatives. Yokavil Turismo has a daily tour, which stops short of the summit, for US$8.

Villa Las Pirquitas

The Sierra de Famatina, the highest mountain range in the province, is visible from the road to this picturesque village near the dam of the same name, 29 km from Catamarca. The foothills en route shelter small villages with hospitable people and interesting architecture. At the entrance to Villa Las Pirquitas, the house with the humble sign *Hay Pan* sells the best home-baked bread in Catamarca.

Camping is allowed in the basic balneario, where the shallows are too muddy for swimming. The very attractive *Hostería Municipal* offers a great deal at US$12 per person with meals.

Empresa COTCA's bus No 1 goes there hourly from Catamarca.

Patagonia

A popular destination for independent travellers, Patagonia is that enormous region south of the Río Colorado, just beyond the province of Buenos Aires, all the way to the Straits of Magellan. Beyond the Straits is the archipelago of Tierra del Fuego, shared by Argentina and Chile.

History

Despite its often monotonous landscape, Patagonia has always held a place in the geography of European imagination. Of the many exotic places Charles Darwin saw in his five years on the *Beagle*, Patagonia remained longest and most vividly in his memory:

In calling up images of the past, I find that the plains of Patagonia frequently cross before my eyes; yet these plains are pronounced by all wretched and useless. They can be described only by negative characters; without habitations, without water, without trees, without mountains, they support merely a few dwarf plants. Why then, and the case is not peculiar to myself, have these arid wastes taken so firm a hold on my memory? Why have not the still more level, the greener and more fertile Pampas, which are serviceable to mankind, produced an equal impression? I can scarcely analyze these feelings: but it must be partly owing to the free scope given to the imagination. The plains of Patagonia are boundless, for they are scarcely passable, and hence unknown; they bear the stamp of having lasted, as they are now, for ages, and there appears to be no limit to their duration during future time. If, as the ancients supposed, the flat earth was surrounded by an impassable breadth of water, or by deserts heated to an intolerable excess, who would not look at these last boundaries to man's knowledge with deep but ill-defined sensations?

The origin of Patagonia's name is obscure, but one theory asserts that it derives from the region's native inhabitants, encountered by Magellan's crew as they wintered in 1520 at Bahía San Julián, in the province of Santa Cruz. According to this explanation, the Tehuelche Indians, tall of stature and wearing moccasins which made their feet appear exceptionally large, may have led Magellan to adopt the name after the Spanish word *pata*, meaning paw or foot. On first encountering one of Tehuelches, an Italian nobleman on Magellan's crew noted with considerable exaggeration that

He was so tall we reached only to his waist, and he was well proportioned...He was dressed in the skins of animals skilfully sewn together...His feet were shod with the same kind of skins, which covered his feet in the manner of shoes...The captain-general (Magellan) called these people Patagoni.

Bruce Chatwin, however, speculates that Magellan may have adopted the term 'Patagon', describing a fictional monster from a Spanish romance of the period, and applied it to the aboriginal inhabitants of the area. In another parallel to the romance itself,

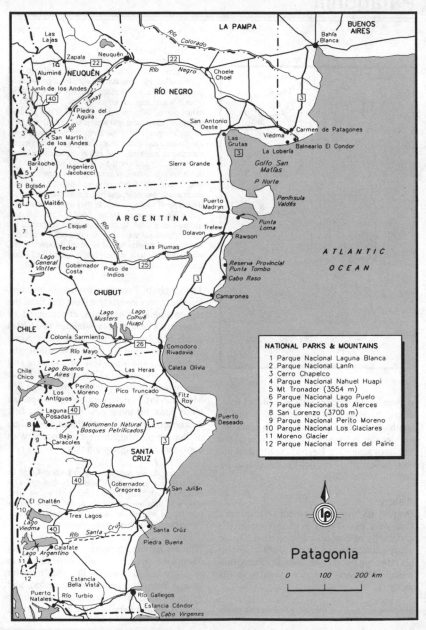

Patagonia

0   100   200 km

NATIONAL PARKS & MOUNTAINS

1 Parque Nacional Laguna Blanca
2 Parque Nacional Lanín
3 Cerro Chapelco
4 Parque Nacional Nahuel Huapi
5 Mt Tronador (3554 m)
6 Parque Nacional Lago Puelo
7 Parque Nacional Los Alerces
8 San Lorenzo (3700 m)
9 Parque Nacional Perito Moreno
10 Parque Nacional Los Glaciares
11 Moreno Glacier
12 Parque Nacional Torres del Paine

Magellan abducted and attempted to take back two of these natives to Spain, but one escaped and the other died en route. This story found its way into English literature in *The Tempest*, in which Shakespeare's savage Caliban is abducted for the pleasure of a European monarch.

This was not the only fanciful account of the region. Since the early 16th century, the gold-hungry Spanish had spread tales of Trapalanda, an austral El Dorado somewhere in the southern Andes, but no early expedition had ever found it or even ventured very deeply into the region. Marvels such as the Moreno Glacier remained unseen by Europeans until the 19th century.

It would be unfair to ignore less fanciful but more meaningful efforts, for Spain contributed scientists as well as fortune-seekers and plunderers to the region. The late 18th-century expedition of Alejandro Malaspina, for example, returned with a wealth of systematic information about Spain's American possessions, but Malaspina's unfortunate fall from political favour at court meant that he and his crew never received the recognition due them and their research. Iris Engstrad's *Spanish Scientists in the New World* (Seattle, 1981) contains a good account of Malaspina's and other Spanish scientific endeavours in the Americas.

Even after independence opened much of South America to visitors from countries other than Spain, Patagonia was among the last areas to be fully explored. Undoubtedly the most memorable early visit was that of Darwin, who dispelled some of the mystery and romance surrounding the Tehuelches:

We had an interview at Cape Gregory with the famous so-called gigantic Patagonians, who gave us cordial reception. Their height appears greater than it really is, from their large guanaco mantles, their long flowing hair, and general figure; on an average their height is about six feet, with some men taller and only a few shorter; and the women are also tall; altogether they are certainly the tallest race which we anywhere saw...

Darwin recognised, though, that the arrival of the white man meant the disappearance or subjugation of the Indian. Recording a massacre of Indians by Argentine soldiers, he ruefully observed that:

Every one here is fully convinced that this is the justest war, because it is against barbarians. Who would believe that in this age in a Christian civilised country that such atrocities were committed...Great as it is, in another half century I think there will not be a wild Indian in the Pampas north of Río Negro.

Darwin's predictions were remarkably precise. Although Patagonia remained a frontier area for some decades, the inevitable occupation was bloody and brutal. In 1865 Welsh nationalists settled peaceably in eastern Chubut province and eventually spread westward, but from 1879 General Julio Argentino Roca carried out a ruthless war of extermination, known euphemistically as the Conquista del Desierto (Conquest of the Desert), against the inhabitants of the region. This war effectively doubled the area under state control and opened up Patagonia to settlement.

Within a few years after Roca's campaign, more than half a million cattle and sheep grazed Indian lands in northern Patagonia. Eager to occupy the area before the Chileans could, the Argentine government made enormous land grants which became the large sheep estancias which still occupy most of the area today. In a few favoured zones, such as the valley of the Río Negro near Neuquén, irrigated agriculture and the arrival of the railway encouraged colonisation and brought eventual prosperity.

Geography & Climate

All of Argentine Patagonia lies in the rain shadow of the Chilean Andes, which block most of the precipitation from Pacific storms. Consequently, except in a few favoured locations along the Andean divide, the region is semi-arid to arid. Chilean Patagonia is more vulnerable to these westerly storms and thus supports a denser forest cover. The southern continental icefield extends from Chile into parts of Argentina.

Although they drop their moisture in

Chile, powerful westerly winds blow almost incessantly across the Patagonian plains. Because of oceanic influence as the South American continent narrows toward the south, the climate throughout the region is generally temperate, but winter temperatures can drop well below freezing.

Economy

The most visible aspect of the economy is the sprawling sheep estancias which occupy almost every part of the region south of the Río Negro all the way to Tierra del Fuego. Cattle are fewer and much less important. The irrigated Río Negro valley, east of the city of Neuquén, has an ideal climate for fresh temperate fruits such as apples, which are sold throughout Argentina and also pro-cessed into products like cider. Since extensive land uses like ranching employ relatively few people, the area south of the Río Negro is only thinly populated.

More importantly, Patagonia is Argentina's energy storehouse. Major oil fields near Comodoro Rivadavia in Chubut province, Plaza Huincúl in Neuquén, and San Sebastían in Tierra del Fuego help make Argentina self-sufficient in petroleum and it even exports small amounts to neighbouring countries. At Río Turbio, Santa Cruz province, there are coal reserves, among the very few on the South American continent.

Tourism is a significant and growing part of the Patagonian economy. The region contains most of the country's national park lands, including three heavily visited units in

The Patagonian Landscape

Visually, Patagonia has little in common with urbane Buenos Aires and the verdant Pampas provinces which surround the capital. On the sparsely vegetated plains of eastern Patagonia, visitors see a few straggling sheep and the occasional guanaco or rhea, but the few cities and towns are often hundreds of kilometres apart. Only a few sheltered and well-watered river valleys support any cultivation.

Traditionally, the Patagonian sheep estancia is the most important economic institution. Like the cattle estancia of the Pampas, it represents the concentration of large amounts of land in the hands of relatively few people, who employ a dependent, resident labour force. Like the cattle estancia, it also concentrated political power in the hands of an regional elite which, when threatened, has not been reluctant to use force to suppress discontent, although pay and working conditions have improved in recent decades.

Estancia names can be quietly eloquent. Many are optimistic, contrasting with the bleak steppes which surround them: *La Esperanza* (Hope), *Bella Vista* (Beautiful View), *La Armonía* (Harmony), *La Confianza* (Trust). Frequently they bear women's names: *La Julia, La Margarita, La Sarita*. A few commemorate an important date: *Primero de Abril, Tres de Enero*. Others bear indirect tribute to the aboriginal Tehuelches or Mapuches they dispossessed: *PaliAike* (Place of Hunger), *OtotelAike* (Place of Springs), *Choike Aike* (Place of the Rhea).

The central nucleus of an estancia usually consists of a settlement cluster, including the owner's or manager's casco, family housing for foremen and other married employees, and a bunkhouse for single men. There are also garages, workshops, a *pulpería* or company store, corrals, and a woolshed for shearing the sheep and storing the clip. Outside the settlement, sheep graze in the *campos*, fenced paddocks often thousands of hectares in size. In the more remote parts of the estancia, there will be an isolated puesto, where a resident shepherd will tend the sheep. Only during the spring shearing season will the sheep be gathered and brought into the settlement.

Most of the few cities in Patagonia, like Comodoro Rivadavia and Río Gallegos, are service centres for the estancias and the oil industry. Others, like Bariloche and Ushuaia, are tourist destinations in their own right. Wages are often much higher in Patagonia than elsewhere in the country, but few Argentines willingly relocate in what most perceive as an Argentine Siberia. When the recent Radical government of President Raúl Alfonsín proposed moving the seat of federal government from Buenos Aires to the northern Patagonian city of Viedma, shocked legislators and civil servants, accustomed to the amenities of the capital, forced him to reconsider and abandon the project. Much of Patagonia is still gaucho country, although the modern gaucho is now a dependent labourer whose past is idealised by Argentines in urban folklore festivals. ∎

Top: Ross Road, Stanley
Left: Shearing at Port Louis, East Falkland
Right: King Penguins, Volunteer Point, East Falkland

Top: Loading wool on jetty, Weddell Island, West Falkland
Bottom: Sunset, Arch Islands, West Falkland

the Andean Lake District, where many Argentines spend their summer holidays: Nahuel Huapi and Los Arrayanes, near Bariloche; Lanín, near San Martín de los Andes; and Los Alerces, near Esquel. These are also popular winter sports centres.

Farther south Los Glaciares, near Calafate, is also a major attraction. Access is difficult to several lesser known parks, like Perito Moreno and Bosques Petrificados, but anyone who makes the effort to reach them will be well rewarded.

Río Negro & Neuquén Provinces

Like the rest of the Patagonia, Río Negro and Neuquén provinces together stretch from the Atlantic to the Andes. Most places of interest are near or along the Andes, but southbound visitors along the coast should at least stop over at Carmen de Patagones, a colonial relic.

The interior of northern Patagonia is mountainous, with alpine glaciers at the highest elevations. Near the Andean divide, diverse Valdivian forests cover the slopes, comprising extensive stands of southern beech, gigantic alerce, and the distinctive pehuén, known to English speakers as the monkey puzzle tree.

During the colonial era, expeditions into the region sought but never found the 'City of the Cacsars', a southern El Dorado, but did see Lago Nahuel Huapi, still the centrepiece of the country's best known national park. Jesuit and Franciscan missionaries penetrated the region as early as the 17th century, but few survived their incursions into the area because of organised resistance by native peoples.

The native peoples of Río Negro and Neuquén were Puelches and Pehuenches, later dominated by Mapuches who crossed the low Andean passes from Chile. Like the Plains Indians of North America, the Indians of Patagonia quickly learned to tame and ride

the feral horses which had multiplied on the Pampas, and used their new mobility to make life hard on anyone who presumed to invade their territory. Like the Plains Indians, they suffered when the state decided their presence was intolerable.

Only in the late 19th century did Argentina establish a permanent presence. Government placed such a high priority on settling the region that the Roca railway actually reached Neuquén before the turn of the century, but did not connect to Bahía Blanca in southern Buenos Aires province until the 1930s.

Today the centre of attraction is Bariloche in Río Negro province, from which you can explore Nahuel Huapi National Park and others within a few hours north or south. Both winter and summer sports are popular. The city itself has rapidly overdeveloped, losing much of its former charm, but the surrounding countryside is still quiet and pleasant.

CARMEN DE PATAGONES

In fact the southernmost city in Buenos Aires province, this small town along Ruta 3 is the gateway to Patagonia. Founded in 1779, it conserves much of its late colonial heritage; its name derives from its patron Virgen del Carmen and from the local peoples who inhabited the region. Since many colonists came from the county of Maragatería in León, Spain, the townspeople are called Maragatos. In 1827, during the war with Brazil, they repelled invaders superior in numbers and weapons.

Orientation

Located on the north bank of the Río Negro, Carmen de Patagones depends economically on the larger city of Viedma, the capital of Río Negro province. People regularly cross the river by launch for work, school, shopping and entertainment, although you should note that, during the summer, Carmen is an hour ahead of Viedma. The civic centre and most historical landmarks are within a few blocks of the passenger pier. Both sides of the river have recreational balnearios, widely used for picnics and swimming in summer.

Information

Tourist Office The municipal tourist office, at Comodoro Rivadavia and 7 de Marzo across the street from the main plaza, provides a good town map and an excellent guide for a walking tour.

Money Try Banco de la Nación, Bynon 142; Banco de la Provincia de Buenos Aires, Comodoro Rivadavia and Alsina; and Banco del Sud at Avellaneda 16. All have morning hours only.

Post & Telecommunications ENCOTEL, the post and telegraph office, is at Paraguay and Villegas. Telefónica has an office at 7 de Marzo 81.

Travel Agencies Sudel Turismo (☎ 61594) is at Perito Moreno 6.

Walking Tour

The tourist office distributes a brochure (in Spanish only) which describes the historic sites of Carmen de Patagones. Begin at **Plaza 7 de Marzo**, whose original name, Plaza del Carmen, was changed after the 1827 victory over the Brazilians. The **Iglesia Parroquial**,

Carmen de Patagones

■ PLACES TO STAY

3 Residencial Reggiani

OTHER

1 Bus Terminal
2 Banco del Sud
4 Banco de la Provincia
de Buenos Aires
5 Cuevas Maragatas
6 Telefónica
7 Torre Del Fuerte
8 Municipality, Tourist Office
& Cathedral
9 Casa De La Cultura
10 Banco de la Nación
11 Post Office
12 La Carlota House
13 Casa Histórica del
Banco de Provincia
14 Passenger Jetty

Viedma

■ PLACES TO STAY

18 Hotel Austral
20 Hotel Nuevo Roma
23 Hotel Peumayén
24 Hotel Comahue
30 Camping Municipal
31 Hotel Roca

OTHER

15 Passenger Jetty
16 Museo del Rió Negro
17 Civic Centre
19 Banco Provincia
de Río Negro
21 Provincial Tourist Office
22 Municipality
25 Municipal Tourist Office
26 Governor's House
27 Museo Gobernador
Eugenio Tello
28 Aerolíneas Argentinas
29 Cathedral & Museo
Cardenal Cagliero
32 Post Office
33 Telefónica
34 Bus Terminal

or parish church, was built by the Salesians in the late 19th century; its image of the Virgin, dating from 1780, is the oldest in southern Argentina. Two of the original seven Brazilian flags captured in 1827 are on the altar. The **Torre del Fuerte** is the last vestige of the fort that occupied the entire block when built in 1780.

The recently constructed (1960s) **Escalinata** (steps) exhibit two cannons from the forts that guarded the Patagonian frontier. **Rancho de Rial**, an adobe house built in 1820, belonged to Juan J Rial, the town's first elected mayor and later justice of the peace. The **Casa de la Cultura**, built in the early 19th century and restored in 1981, belonged to Bernardo Bartruille and was the site of a *tahona*, or flour mill. **La Carlota**, named after its last owner, is a house with typical 19th-century furnishings.

Mazzini & Giraudini was the home of

prosperous merchants who owned the shop across the street from the pier. Its facade was restored in 1985. The house is part of the **Zona del Puerto** (port), which connected the town with the rest of the viceroyalty. At the **Solar Natal de Piedra Buena**, there is a bust of naval officer and Patagonian hero Luis Piedra Buena. It once included the general store, bar, and naval stores supply of his father.

The **Casa Histórica del Banco de la Provincia de Buenos Aires** originally housed naval stores, but became in succession a girls' school, a branch of the Banco de la Provincia, and of the Banco de la Nación. Destroyed by a flood that ravaged Viedma and the coastal neighborhood of Carmen de Patagones in 1899, it was rebuilt and occupied by several shops until 1984, when the Banco de la Provincia restored it.

Since 1988, it has become a museum,

open daily from 10 to 12 am. Nearby is **El Puerto**, a former waterfront bar.

Things to See

La Maragata, the first locomotive to arrive at Carmen de Patagones in 1921, is across from the train station at Juan de la Piedra and Italia. The **Cuevas Maragatas** (Maragatas Caves), excavated in the river bank, sheltered the first Spanish families who arrived in the 18th century. They are on Rivadavia, west of the central plaza. **Cerro de la Caballada**, where the battle with the Brazilians took place, offers a panoramic view.

Places to Stay & Eat

Viedma offers more choice in accommodation, but there are three hotels in town. *Residencial Patagones* (☎ 61495), at Comodoro Rivadavia and Irigoyen, has singles/doubles for US$14/22, as well as multi-bed rooms at a slightly lower price per person. It has tourist discounts at the beginning of summer, and also offers a reasonable breakfast. *Residencial Reggiani* (☎ 61389) at Bynon 422 has doubles with shared bath for US$14 and with private bath for US$17. The tiny *Residencial Strauss* (☎ 62461) at Italia 393 has doubles for US$19.

Restaurant *El Entrerriano* at Dr Barajas 368 is the most central place to eat. Others are *Leonardo I* at M Crespo and San Juan, *La Terminal* at Barbieri and Bertorello, *Club Deportivo Patagones* at España and Rivadavia and *Koki's Pizzería* at Comodoro Rivadavia 367. *La Confitería* at Comodoro Rivadavia 218 is a pleasant café.

Getting There & Away

The bus terminal (☎ 62666) is at Barbieri and Méjico and the train station is on Juan de la Piedra. Two bridges connect Carmen de Patagones with Viedma, and the balsa (launch) crosses the river on demand. Connections with the rest of the country by bus, train or plane are more frequent in Viedma.

VIEDMA

In 1779, with his men dying of fever and lack of water at Península Valdés, Francisco de Viedma put ashore to found the city that would later take his name, on the bank of the Río Curru Leuvu (now the Río Negro). In 1879 it became the residence of the governor of Patagonia and the political and administrative center of the country's enormous southern territory. Even after territorial division, Viedma remained an important administrative site.

During the 1980s the Alfonsín administration proposed moving the national capital from Buenos Aires. Although these plans never materialised, some migrants who had anticipated the move have remained. In addition to numerous secondary schools, Viedma houses a campus of the Universidad del Comahue, and a physical education centre. Population is about 40,000.

Orientation

Located on the south bank of the Río Negro, 30 km from the Atlantic Ocean, Viedma is a compact town, suitable for walking.

Information

Tourist Office In summer the municipal tourist office, on Plaza Alsina, is open 7 am to 1 pm and 5 pm to midnight. They have some crafts and regional products for sale. The provincial tourist office (☎ 22150), on the Costanera Avenida Francisco de Viedma 57 overlooking the river, has brochures and information for the whole province.

Money Banks are open from 8 am to 12.30 pm. Banco Hipotecario is on Sarmiento at 25 de Mayo, Banco Provincia de Río Negro at the Civic Centre. Also try travel agents.

Post & Telecommunications The post office is on Rivadavia 151, between Alvaro Barros and Mitre. Telefónica (☎ 22286) is at Mitre 531.

Walking Tour

Every Tuesday at 8 pm (or thereabouts), if there is sufficient demand, the municipal tourist office provides a worthwhile guided tour for US$1.50. It includes the principal buildings, the cathedral, government offices, museums, and sometimes the governor's residence.

Museums

The historical and ecclesiastical **Museo Cardenal Cagliero**, at Rivadavia 34, tells the story of the important Salesian Order, which catechised and educated Patagonian Indians.

At the **Museo del Río Negro**, on the Costanera Avenida Villarino at Saavedra, the Fundación Ameghino has organised an interesting display on the river's natural history.

Museo Gobernador Eugenio Tello

This anthropological and historical museum, at San Martín 263, also functions as a provincial research centre in architecture, archaeology, physical and cultural anthropology, and geography. It has an impressive collection of tools, artefacts and human remains of the Tehuelche culture of northern Patagonia, as well as exhibits on European settlement.

Organised Tours

The catamaran *Curru Leuvu II* leaves from the pier Tuesdays to Sundays at 4 pm. The fare is US$1.50 per adult and US$.80 for children up to 12 years old. On Sundays their longer tour around the river islands takes about two hours and costs US$2.50.

Festivals

The **Regata del Río Negro**, in the second half of January, includes a kayak race which begins in Neuquén and ends in Viedma, a distance of about 500 km. There is also the **Fiesta Nacional del Golfo Azul** in Balneario Las Grutas/San Antonio Oeste, in the first week of February.

Places to Stay – bottom end

Camping The riverside *Camping Municipal*, easily reached by bus from the town centre, charges US$1 per person and US$2 per tent. For noncampers, showers cost US$0.80. The grounds are very clean, although the plots are not clearly marked. Beware of mosquitos in summer.

Hotels Except for camping, truly inexpensive accommodation is scarce in Viedma. *Hotel Nuevo Roma* (☎ 24510), at 25 de Mayo 174 is clean and friendly. It has singles/doubles for US$12/15, and good, inexpensive food. *Hotel Buenos Aires* (☎ 24351), at Buenos Aires 153, is basic. *Hotel Roca* (☎ 23071) at Roca 347 is worth trying, with rooms at US$15/23. There are other inexpensive hotels along 25 de Mayo.

Places to Stay – middle

Hotel Comahue (☎ 24291), at Colón 385, has pleasant, quiet single/double rooms for US$19/29. *Hotel Viedma* (☎ 25481) at Urquiza and Zatti is also good value, with rooms at US$17/26.

Places to Stay – top end

The most expensive is the *Hotel Austral* (☎ 22615, 22619), at Costanera Avenida Villarino 292, which has nice views of the river. Singles/doubles are US$34/49. *Hotel Peumayén* (☎ 25222) on Buenos Aires 334 (across the street from the tourist office) overlooks Plaza Alsina. Rooms are US$23/35.

Things to Buy

Mapuche Indian weavings are available at the tourist office. The best place to visit and to buy wines is La Bodega de Marzio, San Martín 319, which offers *vinos de la zona fría*, or wines from cool climate grapes. Also try the pottery shop next to the post office.

Getting There & Away

Air Aerolíneas Argentinas (☎ 22018), on San Martín between Saavedra and Colón, has direct flights from Buenos Aires on Monday, Wednesday and Friday. The Wednesday flight continues to Comodoro Rivadavia. LADE (☎ 24420) is at Saavedra 403.

Bus The bus terminal (☎ 22748) is at Zatti 350. La Puntual has buses to Buenos Aires daily and south along Ruta 3. La Estrella/El Cóndor has buses to Buenos Aires and to Bariloche, via the Río Negro valley. Fares to Buenos Aires are about US$46.

Train Ferrocarril Roca (☎ 22130) has passenger trains to Buenos Aires (US$ 18) and Bariloche (US$15).

COASTAL RÍO NEGRO

Río Negro's 400 km of coastline offers many beaches, wildlife reserves and summer resorts to attract tourists.

Balneario El Cóndor

This small resort, 32 km from Viedma, features a century-old lighthouse, the oldest in Patagonia. It has little accommodation, but there is a free campsite, plus excellent fishing for the tasty corvina. After the departure of the last tourists in late March, it shuts down for the winter.

La Lobería

This permanent colony of about 2000 Southern sea lions *(Otaria flavescens)* is some 60 km from Viedma, near the mouth of the Río Negro on the north coast of the Gulf of San Matías. At one time, indiscriminate commercial slaughter threatened the colony's survival, but the reserve has encouraged conservation, education and research. The area's scenery, featuring high bluffs with distinct strata and sandy beaches with occasional rock outcrops and tidal pools, is striking. The mostly paved road runs along dunes covered by low grasses and native shrubs.

Activity at the colony is highly seasonal. The largest numbers are in the spring mating season, when males come ashore to establish harems of up to 10 females each. Fights are common. From December on, females give birth. The balcony from which visitors can watch, directly above the mating beaches, is safe and unobtrusive.

Numerous coastal birds frequent the area, both seasonally and permanently. The most common migrants are snowy sheathbills, gulls, cormorants, sandpipers, and oystercatchers. Black eagles, peregrine falcons, turkey vultures and chimangos prey on the parakeets and swallows that nest in the cliffs. Dunes provide habitat for guanacos, rheas, maras (Patagonian hares), wildcats, vizcachas, skunks, foxes, armadillos, small reptiles and rodents. The visitor centre has both photographic and taxidermic displays of stuffed local fauna. The rangers, local biology students, are knowledgeable, enthusiastic and sincerely committed to conservation.

It is possible to camp at a nearby beach, where there are sanitary facilities and a store.

Las Grutas

Rionegrinos congregate here, 179 km south of Viedma along Ruta 3, in summer. Because of an extraordinary tidal range, the beaches can expand for hundreds of metres or shrink to just a few. Five formal *bajadas* (paths) provide access from town to the beaches. The town owes its name, The Grottos, to the caves which the sea has eroded in the cliffs.

Dunes, white sand beaches, and cliffs create a pleasant environment for walking, jogging, or simply resting. Swimming, surfing, windsurfing, and diving are very popular. The abundance of hotels and campgrounds and (since 1988) a casino, will discourage those in search of quiet and solitude. Las Grutas gets crowded!

The tourist office at Galería Antares, Primera Bajada, has good information about accommodation, plus restaurant menus with prices. In general, hotels are rather costly. Tritón Turismo at Galería Casablanca, Local 15, Tercera Bajada, organises ecologically oriented tours. There are hourly buses to San Antonio Oeste, 15 km away.

BARILOCHE

San Carlos de Bariloche, 460 km south-east of Neuquén, is the urban centre of the Argentine Lake District and the base for exploring Parque Nacional Nahuel Huapi. In many ways, not all of them positive, it resembles European alpine resorts. The surrounding scenery is always pleasant and often spectacular, but crowds and traffic can be intolerable in the winter ski season and in summer. Uncontrolled growth has cost the city much of its former character as quaint neighbourhoods have lost their views to multistorey apartment buildings. Recent commercial development has impacted the city's lakefront like a wisdom tooth.

Until the late 19th century, Mapuche Indians successfully resisted Argentine occupation, but General Roca's Conquista del Desierto made the area safe for white settlers. The city itself was officially founded in 1902, but only after the southern branch of the Roca railway arrived in 1934 did real expansion begin. Architect Ezequiel Bustillo adapted Middle European styles into an attractive urban plan which the last decade's construction has unfortunately overwhelmed.

Orientation

At an altitude of 770 metres, Bariloche sits at the eastern end of the south shore of Lago Nahuel Huapi, source of the Río Negro. Entering town from the east, national Ruta 237 becomes the Costanera Avenida 12 de Octubre, continuing westward to the lakeside resort of Llao Llao.

The city has a fairly conventional grid pattern west of the Río Nireco and east of Bustillo's famous Centro Cívico (civic centre), but the north-south streets rise steeply from the lake. The principal commercial area is along Avenida Bartolomé Mitre. Do not confuse the similarly named Eduardo O'Connor and John O'Connor, which cross each other near the lakefront, nor Perito Moreno and Ruiz Moreno, which intersect near Diagonal Capraro, at the south end of the downtown area.

Information

Tourist Office The municipal tourist office (☎ 23022) is at the Centro Cívico, at the east end of Avenida Bartolomé Mitre, across from the equestrian statue of General Roca. It opens from 8.30 am to 8 pm weekdays and Saturdays. It has many giveaways, including the blatantly commercial but still useful *Guia Busch*, which is loaded with basic tourist information about Bariloche and its surroundings, and is updated annually. *Guia Pulmari* is another free commercial brochure.

There is a smaller provincial tourist office at the Paseo de los Artesanos, Perito Moreno and Villegas.

Money You can change foreign cash and travellers' cheques at Casa Piano, Avenida Bartolomé Mitre 131. Bariloche is one of few places outside Buenos Aires where currencies other than the US dollar will find a market.

Post & Telecommunications The post office is next door to the tourist office, at the Centro Cívico. There are several phone offices, but the best is at Bariloche Center, San Martín and Pagano, where there is a direct line to North America for collect and credit card calls. There are also direct lines to Japan, Italy, Chile and Brazil.

Foreign Consulates The Chilean Consulate (☎ 23050) has recently moved to Rolando 310, on the 7th floor, near Elflein. It's open weekdays from 9 am to 2 pm. There are several European consulates, including Germany (☎ 22205) at Perito Moreno 19, and Spain (☎ 22179) at 1st floor, Rolando 268. France has a consul (☎ 48094) at the outlying resort of Llao Llao.

National Parks Office The Parques Nacionales office is at San Martín 24. Another good source for parks information is the Club Andino Bariloche (☎ 22266) at 20 de Febrero 30. It is easy to find rental equipment for outdoor activities in Bariloche. For further information, see the separate section on Parque Nacional Nahuel Huapi below.

Cultural Centres The Centro Atómico Bariloche (☎ 61002), at km 10 on the road to Llao Llao but easily reached by bus or thumb, offers free or inexpensive films and other activities. Watch for posters or flyers in town. There are occasional exhibitions at the Salón Cultural de Usos Múltiples, Perito Moreno and Villegas, which goes by the unfortunate acronym of SCUM.

Travel Agencies Bariloche may sink below

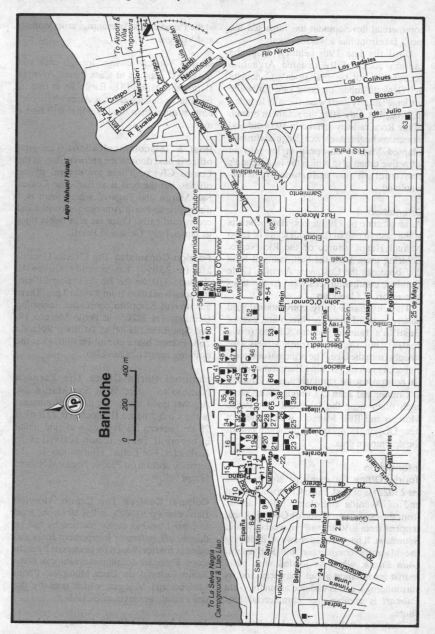

■ PLACES TO STAY

1 Youth Hostel
2 Casa Familiar Arko
3 Residencial Wickter
4 Residencial Martín
5 Residencial Campana
6 Residencial Elisabeth
7 Hotel Aconcagua
9 Hotel Ebelweiss
21 Residencial Nogaré
23 Hotel Carlos V
24 Residencial Nikola
25 El Cieruo Rojo
32 Hotel Internacional
39 La Casa Nogueira
    (Residencial)
41 Hotel Interlaken
40 Rosidencial Sur
51 Hostería Piuke
52 Hospedaje El Mirador
55 Hosteria Ivalú/El Viejo Aljibe
56 Casa Familiar (Lodgias)
57 Residencial Torres
58 Hotel Pilmayquén
60 Hostería El Niro
61 Residencial Tito
63 Hospedaje Monte Grand

▼ PLACES TO EAT

10 Helados Bari
11 Restaurant Oriente Jabalí
17 Confitería Cocodrilo's
18 Pizzería La Andinita
26 Parrilla 1810
27 Restaurant Villegas
34 Confitería El Viejo Munich
36 Caffe Status37
    Restaurant Jauja

38 Restaurant La Vizsacha
40 Pizzería Pin 9
42 Restaurant Familia Weiss
43 Confitería Copos
47 El Mundo de la Pizza
48 Restaurant Mangiare
62 Restaurant Chile

OTHER

8 Buses Cooperativa El Valle,
   Don Otto, TAC & Bus Norte
12 National Parks Office
13 Post Office
14 Municipal Tourist Office
15 Museo de la Patagonia
16 TAN
19 Buses TIRSA
20 German Consulate
22 Club Andino Bariloche
28 Buses Chevallier & Ko-Ko
29 Buses Charter
30 Paseo de los Artesands,
   Provincial Tourist Office &
   Spanish Consulate
31 Casa Piano
33 Aerolíneas Argentinas
   & LADE
35 Austral
44 Airport Mini Buses/
   Turismo Catedral
45 Local Bus Station
46 Buses la Estrella
50 Cathedral
53 Telefónica
54 Hospital Zonal
59 ACA
64 Train Station
65 SCUM
66 Chilean Consulate

lake level from the weight of its travel agencies, most of which are along Avenida Bartolomé Mitre and its immediate cross streets. ACA (☎ 23001) is at 12 de Octubre 785.

Medical Services The Hospital Zonal (☎ 26100) is at Perito Moreno 601.

Centro Cívico
The last decade's orgy of construction has eliminated most of Bariloche's European charm, but Bustillo's log and stone buildings housing the post office, tourist office, and museum still deserve a visit, if you can fend off the plaza photographers soliciting your portrait with their St Bernards or Siberian huskies. Come in the morning or at midday, before the shadows of the tawdry high-rise casino block the sun.

Just to the north, builders are dumping fill into Lago Nahuel Huapi for the massive new Puerto de San Carlos de Bariloche, described as a 'recreational and shopping centre', which will harbour yachts and cruise ships. When completed, the facility will eliminate lake views from there.

Museo de la Patagonia

On the Centro Cívico, this is one of the most worthwhile museums in the country. The stuffed animals in the natural history exhibit are lifelike, and the archaeological and ethnographic materials are well-prepared. Historical exhibits acknowledge Mapuche resistance to the Conquista del Desierto, and in summer 1991 also included a valuable photographic display on Bariloche's urban development. There is a bookshop at the entrance.

Admission is US$1. Opening hours are Tuesday to Saturday from 10 am to 12.30 pm and 2 to 7 pm, Sundays from 2 to 7 pm only.

Skiing

In winter at least, most people come to Bariloche for skiing. Two formerly separate areas, Cerro Catedral and Lado Bueno, have been amalgamated so you can buy one ticket for lifts in both areas. The runs around Bariloche are probably the trendiest and best known in South America. For more information, see the section on Cerro Catedral in Parque Nacional Nahuel Huapi below.

Organised Tours

Bariloche itself offers little beyond the opportunity to eat and drink well, see and be seen, but Parque Nacional Nahuel Huapi has many more possibilities. This section lists organised excursions, but consult the separate entry for Parque Nacional Nahuel Huapi for more detailed information.

City Tour Pochi's gaudy motorised *trencito* (little train) makes regular trips within town, starting at the Centro Cívico, but is hardly worthwhile unless you're too tired to walk.

Half-day trips from Bariloche include Cerro Otto, Cerro Catedral, the Circuito Chico west of town, Cascada de los Césares, and Isla Victoria and Parque Nacional Los Arrayanes (for more detailed information on the latter, see Villa La Angostura, Neuquén

province). The latter can also be done as a full-day trip. Other full-day trips include Puerto Blest and Laguna Frías, Cerro Tronador and Cascada Los Alerces via Lago Mascardi, El Bolsón, and the Circuito Grande to San Martín de los Andes via Siete Lagos. Catedral Turismo (☎ 25443) at Avenida Bartolomé Mitre 399 covers all these destinations.

After Villa Mascardi, 30 km from Bariloche, the scenic highway to El Bolsón is a washboard surface covered with large stones, making day trips tiring and inadvisable.

If you belong to ACA (☎ 23001), their agency at Costanera 12 de Octubre 785 can arrange all these excursions at discounts of at least 10%.

Festivals

In both January and February, there are important music festivals. In March, the **Muestra Floral de Otoño** allows the city's horticulturalists to show off their green thumbs, while in April there are displays of plastic arts at the **Salón Cultural de Usos Múltiples**.

During the ski season, Bariloche holds its **Fiesta Nacional de la Nieve**, or snow festival, while in October horticulturalists again display their results at the **Fiesta del Tulipán** (tulip festival) and the **Muestra Floral de Primavera** (spring flower show). November features the **Salón Nacional de Fotografía**, while December has the **Navidad Coral** (Christmas Chorus).

Places to Stay

Bariloche has an abundance of high quality accommodation, from camping and private houses to five-star hotels. The municipal tourist office maintains a computer data base with current prices. Even in high season, it is possible to find reasonable lodging, but you may wish to look outside town, where the ambience is more pleasant. The list below does not exhaust the possibilities.

Places to Stay – bottom end

Camping For the time being, those with

vehicles can camp free at the parking lot across from the ACA service station at Goedecke and the Costanera 12 de Octubre. Signs prohibit tent camping, but this rule is rarely enforced. If discreet, you can use the toilets and washrooms at the station.

The nearest organised camping area to Bariloche is *La Selva Negra*, three km west of town on the road to Llao Llao. There are some recent negative reports on the site, but it has good facilities and you can step outside your tent to pick apples in the fall. Fees are US$3 per person. There are three other sites between Bariloche and Llao Llao.

Hostels & Casas de Familia Probably the cheapest lodging in town is the homey private house (casa de familia) at Emilio Frey 635, between Tiscornia and Albarracin, at US$4 per person. It has hot showers and cooking facilities. Similar possibilities include Señora Carlotta Baumann (☎ 25402) at Los Pioneros 860, Señora Arko at Güemes 671, and Señora Heydée (☎ 24590) at Martín Fierro 1525. There is a recommended youth hostel at Belgrano 660, and another on the Llao Llao road five km from town. Hostels will only be open during summer and winter holidays.

Residenciales, Hosterías & Hotels Try also *Residencial Tito* (☎ 24039), an unimpressive building but a friendly place at Eduardo O'Connor 745, which is often full. *Hospedaje El Mirador* (☎ 22221), a converted private house at Perito Moreno 658, charges US$4 per person with shared bath and US$5 with private bath. At *Hospedaje Monte Grande* (☎ 22159), 25 de Mayo 1544, rates are US$6 per person.

Others in this category include quiet, comfortable *Residencial Nogaré* (☎ 22438) at Elflein 56; *Residencial Elisabeth* (☎ 24853) at Juan J Paso 117; *Residencial Nikola* (☎ 22500) at Elflein 49; *Residencial Martín* at 20 de Febrero 555; *Residencial Torres* (☎ 23355) at Tiscornia 747; and the appealing *Residencial Wickler* (☎ 23248) at Güemes 566. Slightly more expensive, at about US$7 per person, are *La Casa Nogueira* at Elflein 205; *El Ciervo Rojo* (☎ 23810); at Elflein 115 and *Residencial Campana* (☎ 22162), Belgrano 165.

Residencial Sur (☎ 22677), Beschtedt 101 at Eduardo O'Connor, has very large beds in some very small rooms, with private bath, for US$9 per person. This includes a generous breakfast; there is a 10% discount for ACA members. Across the street, at Beschtedt 136, is the unfortunately named *Hostería Piuké* (☎ 23044). *Hostería Ivalú* (☎ 23237), Frey 535, and *El Viejo Aljibe* (☎ 23316), nearby at Emilio Frey 571, are both attractive hillside hotels with rooms at US$11/20 a single/double with breakfast.

Hostería El Ñire (☎ 23041), Eduardo O'Connor 702, is equally attractive and more central, one block from the Cathedral. The comparably priced *Hotel Pilmayquén* (☎ 26175), Costanera 12 de Octubre 705 at John O'Connor, has lake views from the front rooms.

Places to Stay – middle
There are numerous possibilities in this category from about US$18/30 to US$30/50. From the bottom of the scale, try *Hotel Internacional* (☎ 25938), Avenida Bartolomé Mitre 171; *Hotel Carlos V* (☎ 25474), Morales 420; or *Hotel Aconcagua* (☎ 24718), San Martín 289.

Places to Stay – top end
Hotel Interlaken (☎ 26156), a four-star, lakefront view-blocker at Eduardo O'Connor 383, charges US$52/87 a single/double. The five-star *Hotel Edelweiss* (☎ 26165), San Martín 202, extorts US$67/100, while the budget-breakers at *Hotel Panamericano* (☎ 25846), San Martín 536, charge US$92/144.

Places to Eat
For all its faults, Bariloche has some of the best food in Argentina. It is unlikely you will have time or money enough to sample all the worthwhile restaurants. There is a sample below, but you may wish to leaf through the *Guía Gastronómico Datos*, published twice yearly and available free from the municipal

tourist office, with discount coupons. The guide also contains information on areas outside Bariloche proper, and may eventually encompass the Chilean side of the border.

Some regional specialities deserve mention. These include jabalí (wild boar), ciervo (venison), and trucha (trout). Some places, such as *Familia Weiss* at Palacios 167, specialise in smoked game and fish. *Restaurant Villegas* at Villegas 363 emphasises trout. *Restaurant Oriente Jabalí*, San Martín 130, serves all of the above, as well as a Chinese buffet.

Restaurant Mangiare, Palacios 150, is an Italian restaurant rather than a parrilla which also serves pasta. Although not really cheap, it is superb value for money. Pizzas, ñoquis (gnocchi) and ravioli are excellent, along with the unusual orange and onion salad with cream. If you linger after its 2 pm afternoon closing, the waiters can get surly.

La Vizcacha, at Rolando 279, is one of the best and cheapest parrillas in Argentina, with a pleasant atmosphere and outstanding service. Its standard parrillada for two includes not only the usual beef but also chicken breast, with garnishes such as red peppers and parsley. In addition to butter, you get deer paté and roquefort cheese for your bread. With a litre of house wine, the total bill comes to about US$12.

Another parrilla is *1810* at Elflein 167, although some LP readers have complained of high prices, unfriendly service and the staff's unwillingness to allow diners to share a portion. However, *Restaurant La Andina*, on the corner of Morelos and Quaglia, has been recommended for good food, large portions and moderate prices – and they don't object to portion-sharing. *Restaurant Jauja*, Perito Moreno 220, has a good European-style menu but with erratic service, smaller portions and high prices. If you can't cross the border, there is Chilean food at *Restaurant Chile*, a bit away from the centre at Ruiz Moreno 329.

There are innumerable confiterías. *Copos*, at Avenida Bartolomé Mitre 392, is open 24 hours. It has good coffee and hot chocolate,

and fresh croissants at reasonable prices. *Cocodrilo's*, Avenida Bartolomé Mitre 5, is fashionable and much more expensive. Befitting its name, *El Viejo Munich*, at Avenida Bartolomé Mitre 102, has excellent draught beer served with complimentary peanuts. Try also *Caffe Status* at Avenida Bartolomé Mitre 298.

There are many pizzerías. *Pin 9*, at Rolando 118, has good pizza and beer, but portions are small. Also try *La Andinita* at Avenida Bartolomé Mitre 56, *El Mundo de la Pizza* at Avenida Bartolomé Mitre 370, or *Pizzaiola* at Pagano 275.

You can get outstanding ice cream at *Helados Bari*, España 7, a block from the Centro Cívico.

Entertainment
Cinemas Besides the club at the Centro Atómico outside town, there are two cinemas: Cine Arrayanes at Perito Moreno 39, and Coliseo at Avenida Bartolomé Mitre 281.

Discos There is a disco Wednesday and Friday nights at the rotating confitería on Cerro Otto, starting at 11 pm. There are several others on the downtown cross-streets along Avenida Bartolomé Mitre.

Things to Buy
Bariloche is renowned for its sweets and confections. Del Turista and Fenoglio, across the street from each other on Avenida Bartolomé Mitre, are virtual supermarkets of chocolate. They are also good places for a cheap stand-up cup of coffee, hot chocolate, or dessert.

Local craftspeople display their wares in wool, wood, leather and other media at the Paseo de los Artesanos, Villegas and Perito Moreno. Hours are 10 am to 1 pm and 4 to 9 pm daily.

Getting There & Away
Air Aerolíneas Argentinas (☎ 22425) and LADE (☎ 22355) are both at Avenida Bartolomé Mitre 199. Aerolíneas Argentinas has 10 flights weekly to Buenos Aires and

two to Mendoza, one of which continues to Buenos Aires. One of these connects to Puerto Iguazú and São Paulo, Brazil. Austral (☎ 23123), Rolando 157, has daily flights to Buenos Aires. One-way fares to Buenos Aires cost about US$240.

TAN (☎ 24869), Neuquén's provincial carrier, is at Avenida Bartolomé Mitre 26. It has flights to Patagonian destinations such as San Martín de los Andes and Esquel, and across the Andes to Puerto Montt, Chile.

Turismo Catedral, Avenida Bartolomé Mitre 399, runs a minibus service to Bariloche airport.

Bus Bariloche is a hub for regional bus services, but there is no central terminal. Most companies have downtown offices, some of them shared, from which their buses leave.

Chevallier (☎ 23090), Perito Moreno 107, has daily departures at 2 pm for Buenos Aires via Santa Rosa, La Pampa province. The trip costs US$84 and takes 22 hours. La Estrella (☎ 22140), Palacios 246, leaves daily at 3 pm and costs US$82. With Cooperativa El Valle (☎ 20188), San Martín 283, the trip via Neuquén, Viedma and Bahía Blanca leaves daily at 3.45 pm and costs US$74. El Valle also serves General Roca via Neuquén, daily at 11 am. Friday service to Mar del Plata, taking 24 hours, costs US$51.

TUS (☎ 24565), Elflein and Rolando, serves Córdoba twice weekly, a 24-hour trip. Don Otto, sharing offices with Cooperativa El Valle (see above), goes twice weekly to Río Gallegos via Esquel and Comodoro Rivadavia for US$68. One correspondent calls the 28-hour plus trip 'agonising'.

Charter (☎ 21689), Perito Moreno 126, has two buses daily to El Bolsón. The 3½-hour trip costs US$9. Mercedes (☎ 26000), Avenida Bartolomé Mitre 161, does the same route daily, twice on Tuesday, and continues to Esquel via El Maitén. The trip takes nine hours and costs US$25. Mercedes also runs buses four times weekly which connect with the narrow gauge railway from Ingeniero Jacobacci (US$6) to Esquel, and two daily to Neuquén (US$25). To Mar del Plata, three

times weekly via Necochea and Miramar, costs US$52.

TAC, sharing offices with El Valle, runs three buses weekly to Mendoza via Zapala, Chos Malal, San Rafael, and Malargüe. The 22-hour trip costs US$55.

Chevallier's twice-weekly service to Rosario via Santa Rosa is US$60. TIRSA (☎ 26076), Quaglia 197, also goes twice weekly for the same fare. The trip last 24 hours.

La Puntual (☎ 22231), San Martín 283, connects Bariloche with Viedma, the provincial capital. Monday and Friday services take 16 hours and cost US$22.

Turismo Algarrobal (☎ 22774), San Martín 459, and Mercedes both serve Villa La Angostura, on the north side of Lago Nahuel Huapi. There are at least two trips daily, lasting two hours and costing US$5. They are also the agents for TICSA, which has three buses a week to San Luis and San Juan (US$50, 27 hours).

Ko-Ko (☎ 23090), Perito Moreno 107, and El Valle both have buses to San Martín de los Andes, some via La Rinconada rather than the more scenic Siete Lagos route. Fares are US$15.

Several companies cover the route between Bariloche and Chile. Mercedes and Bus Norte (☎ 20188), at San Martín 283, TAS Choapa (☎ 22774), at San Martín 459, and Cruz del Sur (☎ 24163) at San Martín 453, all charge about US$25 to Puerto Montt, with connections to northern destinations. Catedral Turismo (see above) arranges the bus-boat combination over the Andes to Puerto Montt for US$36.

Train The train station is across the Río Ñireco along Ruta 237. Four times weekly, the Roca line does the 36-hour trip to Constitución Station in Buenos Aires. It costs about US$35 in hard-backed turista, $45 in primera, $53 pullman and $65 for a sleeper. Trains can be very crowded in summer and, if there is a strike, you may have to return by bus.

Car Rental Bariloche is loaded with car

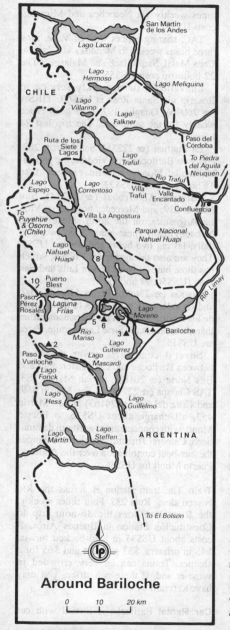

Around Bariloche

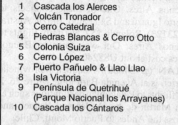

```
1   Cascada los Alerces
2   Volcán Tronador
3   Cerro Catedral
4   Piedras Blancas & Cerro Otto
5   Colonia Suiza
6   Cerro López
7   Puerto Pañuelo & Llao Llao
8   Isla Victoria
9   Península de Quetrihué
    (Parque Nacional los Arrayanes)
10  Cascada los Cántaros
```

rental agencies. At Carro's (☎ 24869), Avenida Bartolomé Mitre 26, rates start at US$33 per day plus US$0.33 per km, plus US$11 per day insurance. For every six days, you get one day free.

All the other standard agencies are here, including A1 (☎ 22582) at San Martín 235, Avis (☎ 25371) at Libertad 124 and Budget (☎ 22482) at Perito Moreno 46.

Getting Around

Bus Transporte Mercedes runs six buses daily to Cerro Catedral, starting at 11 am, for US$2 one-way, and slightly cheaper for a return.

Bus No 20 leaves every 20 minutes to the attractive lakeside town of Llao Llao. No 50 goes to Lago Gutiérrez on the same schedule. No 10 also goes to Llao Llao via Colonia Suiza, seven times daily, allowing you to do the Circuito Chico (see the section on Parque Nacional Nahuel Huapi below) on inexpensive public transport. You can walk any section and flag down the buses en route.

Bicycle Bicycles are ideal for the Circuito Chico and other trips near Bariloche, where most roads are paved, even the gravel roads are good, and Argentine drivers are less ruthless, slowing and even stopping for the scenery. Try Baratta e Hijos (☎ 22930) at Belgrano 50, Pochi (☎ 26693) at Moreno 1035, or Ramírez (☎ 25229) at 9 de Julio 961. The Spanish term for mountain bike is *bicicleta todo terreno*.

PARQUE NACIONAL NAHUEL HUAPI

Nahuel Huapi National Park occupies 750,000 hectares in mountainous southwestern Neuquén and western Río Negro provinces. Its centrepiece is Lago Nahuel Huapi, a glacial relic over 100 km in length and covering more than 500 square km. To the west a ridge of high peaks separates Argentina from Chile. The tallest is 3554-metre Tronador, an extinct volcano which still lives up to its name of Thunderer when blocks of ice tumble from its glaciers. During the summer, wildflowers cover alpine meadows.

Besides its scenery, Nahuel Huapi was created to preserve local flora and fauna, including its Andean-Patagonian forests and rare animals. Tree species are much the same as those found in Parque Nacional Los Alerces (see below), while the important animal species include the *huemul* or Andean deer *(Hippocamelus bisulcus)* and the miniature deer known as *pudú (Pudu pudu)*. Most visitors are not likely to see either of these, but several species of introduced deer are common, along with native birds. Both native and introduced fish species offer excellent sport.

As the oldest and one of the most heavily visited units in the Argentine system, Nahuel Huapi plays the same role as Yosemite in the United States, attracting so many people that the very values it intends to preserve are at risk. Bariloche, like Yosemite Valley, has grown from a modest village to an urban enclave which threatens its surrounding environment with noise, pollution and sprawl. Part of Nahuel Huapi's problems stem from the fact that nearly half the park is a 'national reserve', in which certain commercial activities are permitted or even encouraged, as opposed to having a strictly protected status.

For trekking maps and information about hiking in the region, see Clem Lindenmayer's LP guide *Trekking in the Patagonian Andes*.

Circuito Chico

One of the most popular trips in the area,

Huemul

with excellent views, this excursion begins on Avenida Bustillo, on the outskirts of Bariloche and continues to the tranquil resort of Llao Llao, named after the so-called 'Indian bread' fungus. At Cerro Campanario, you can take the chairlift for a panoramic view of Lago Nahuel Huapi.

Llao Llao's Puerto Pañuelo is the point of departure for the boat-bus excursion across the Andes to Chile. Have a look at the grounds of the state-owned Hotel Llao Llao, a national treasure which became a topic of political controversy when, in the summer of 1990-91, two Italian businessmen who had given Argentine President Carlos Menem an expensive sportscar a few months earlier sought government permission to take it over.

From Llao Llao you can continue to Colonia Suiza, named for its early colonists, where there is a modest confitería with excellent pastries. Camping is possible. The road passes the trailhead to 2075-metre Cerro López, a four-hour climb, before returning to Bariloche. At the top, the Club Andino Bariloche has a refugio where you can spend the night.

Although travel agencies operate this as a tour, you can do it easily on public transportation. For details, see the Getting Around section in Bariloche.

Cerro Otto

Cerro Otto, 1405 metres, is an eight-km walk on a gravel road west from Bariloche. There is also a gondola to the summit.

Cerro Catedral

This 2400-metre peak, 20 km west of Bariloche, is an important ski centre. Chairlifts and a large cable car, which also operate during the summer, take you to the 2000-metre elevation, where there is a restaurant/confitería, with excellent panoramas. Several trekking trails begin here; one relatively easy walk goes to Club Andino's Refugio Frey. This refugio is exposed, but there are sheltered tent sites.

There is a good mix of easy, intermediate and advanced skiing runs, with some very steep advanced runs at the top and some tree runs near the base. As it's such a popular resort, lift lines can develop, but lift capacity is fairly impressive so you shouldn't have to wait too long.

One reader has complained that much of the lift equipment is outmoded, the loading process badly organised and 'a number of Argentines have very poor skiing manners anyhow'. The authors' impression is that Argentines probably ski like they drive and tend to ignore queues and behave in a slightly unruly fashion. So what may seem like unacceptable crowding and pushing to eg an American may be perfectly acceptable to an Argentine.

Access from Bariloche is excellent, consisting of regular buses which leave every 15 minutes or so. There is also a good road to the large carpark at the base of the skiing area.

Volcán Tronador

This full-day trip up a one-way dirt road from Lago Mascardi visits the Black Glacier and the base of Tronador. Traffic goes up in the morning and down in the afternoon. Some have found the trip itself dusty and unpleasant. You can approach the Club Andino's snowline Refugio Meiling on foot from Laguna Frías, or camp at Pampa Linda.

Isla Victoria

In Lago Nahuel Huapi, Isla Victoria is the large island on which the Argentine park service's training school for park rangers attracts students from throughout Latin America. Boats to Isla Victoria and to Parque Nacional Los Arrayanes on the Quetrihué peninsula leave from Puerto Pañuelo at Llao Llao, but you can visit Los Arrayanes more easily and cheaply from Villa La Angostura (see the Neuquén section below).

Some of the better hiking country in Nahuel Huapi can be reached only by a boat-bus-boat combination from Llao Llao. Options include Mt Vichadero, a return to Puerto Blest via Laguna Los Clavos, the Frías Glacier, and Paso de las Nubes to Pampa Linda, near Tronador, from where you can return to Bariloche.

Siete Lagos

For details of this excursion, see Villa La Angostura, in the Neuquén section.

El Bolsón

Though day trips are possible to this picturesque town, most visitors will find an extended visit far preferable. See the separate section below for details.

Fishing

Fishing in Argentina's more accessible Andean-Patagonian parks, from Lago Puelo and Los Alerces in the south to Lanín in the north, brings visitors from around the world. There are both native and introduced species. On the larger lakes, such as Nahuel Huapi, trolling is the preferred method, while fly fishing is the rule on most rivers. Licences are available at the parks administration in

Bariloche, where it is also possible to rent equipment. The season runs from November 15 to April 15.

The most popular introduced species are European brown trout, rainbow trout, brook trout and landlocked Atlantic salmon, which reach impressive sizes. Native species, which should be thrown back, are generally smaller. These include *perca* (perch), catfish, *puyen*, Patagonian pejerrey and the rare *peladilla*. For more information, contact the Club de Caza y Pesca in Bariloche at Costanera 12 de Octubre and Onelli (☎ 22403).

Water Sports

Sailboating, windsurfing, canoeing and kayaking are all popular on Lago Nahuel Huapi and other lakes and streams. For equipment, try Baruzzi (☎ 24922) at Urquiza 250 or other sporting goods dealers.

Places to Stay

There are numerous campgrounds in the Bariloche area. Besides those in the immediate Bariloche area, there are sites at Lago Mascardi, Lago Los Moscos, Lago Roca, Lago Guillelmo and Pampa Linda. With permission from park rangers, free camping is possible in certain areas.

Within the park there are a number of hotels which tend to the luxurious. One of the best is *Hotel Tronador* on Lago Mascardi, where singles/doubles are US$50/96 with all meals included.

Refugios charge US$7 per night, US$2 for day use, and US$2 extra for kitchen privileges.

EL BOLSÓN

According to its reputation throughout Argentina and South America, El Bolsón is a tolerant mecca for ponytailed hippies who live on woodsy communes, drive VW Kombis, eat macrobiotic food, and make a living selling handmade jewellery and pottery on the streets. In part, this image is accurate, making this 1960s anachronism and its surroundings a pleasant relief from Bariloche's crass commercialism. The utterly dismal highway between Bariloche

and El Bolsón holds back the deluge of Porteños who overrun the Nahuel Huapi area throughout the year. Instead, El Bolsón invites backpackers.

Near the south-eastern border of Río Negro province, 130 km from Bariloche, El Bolsón lies in a basin surrounded by high mountains, dominated by the longitudinal ridges of Cerro Piltriquitrón to the east and the Cordón Nevado along the Chilean border to the west. Uniquely in Argentina, the 3500 townspeople and their government have declared the area a 'nonnuclear zone' and 'ecological municipality'. This broadly supported policy is in part a response to the Menem administration's attempt, since abandoned, to locate a nuclear dump in nearby Chubut province. Communications are in fact better with northern Chubut than with Río Negro.

The local economy relies on tourism, agriculture, and forestry. Rows of poplar trees give a Mediterranean appearance to the chacras, most of which are devoted to hops (nearly three-quarters of the country's production), soft fruits such as raspberries and strawberries, and orchard crops such as cherries and apples. Beer and sweets made from the local harvest are excellent.

Orientation

At an elevation of 300 metres on the east bank of the Río Quemquemtreu, El Bolsón is about equidistant between Bariloche and Esquel on national Ruta 258. South of Bolsón, in Chubut, the road is either paved or in the process, but for about 90 km north of Bolsón toward Bariloche it is one of the worst roads in all of Argentina.

From the south, Ruta 258 enters town as a diagonal, the Avenida Belgrano, but briefly becomes Avenida Bolívar and north-south Avenida San Martín through the town centre, whose principal landmark is the semi-oval Plaza Pagano, which has a small artificial lake. Most services are nearby, but the area's attractions are mostly outside town.

Information

Tourist Office The tourist office (☎ 92204)

To Cascada
Escondida

To Bariloche

Avenida Pueytredón

To Camping
La Alegria

1

Angel del Agua

2

Balcarce

Castello

3

5 4

José Hernández

9

6 7

8

Plaza
España

To Río Azul &
Cabeza del Indio

O'Connor

Larrea

P Mascardi

S Azcona

Larrea

Islas Malvinas

Azcuenaga

10

11

13 16

Coronel Dorrego

12 14

19

El Bolsón

Avenida Sarmiento

0   200   400 m

15

17 18

Roca

Plaza
Pagano

Perito Moreno

P Feliciano

20

21

22 23

Pellegrini

25

24

27

Pablo Hube

30

26

28 29

32

French

Rivadavia

34

31

36

37

Avenida Castelli

33

Berutti

Avenida Bolívar

35

38

Güemes

Avenida San Martín

39

Lavalle

Granollers

41

Cac Linares

Paso

Nuevo

Rivadavia

40

O'Higgins

Avenida Belgrano

9 de Julio

Viamonte

Perito Moreno

Pagano

Anden

Liniers

Pastorino

(Ruta 258)

Alberti

de Mayo

25

Alberti

Gral las Heras

P Guillelmo

42

To Lago Puelo
(20 km)

To El Hoyo

■ PLACES TO STAY	OTHER
1 Residencial Edelwiss	2 Regionales Lida
3 Hospedaje Los Amigos	4 LADE
6 Hotel Cordillera	11 Pulmari Turismo
8 Hotel Amancay	12 Post Office
9 Residencial Lostra	14 Banco de la Provincia
35 Camping del Sol	del Río Negro
39 La Posada de Hamelin	15 Tourist Office
41 Camping La Chacra	16 La Soja
42 Youth Hostel	18 Municipalidad de
	El Bolsón
▼ PLACES TO EAT	19 Cooperativa de
	Ceramistas
5 Restaurant Luigi	22 Feria Artesanal
7 Restaurant Don Diego	23 Hospital
10 Heladería Moni	24 Banco de la Nación
13 Holadería Jauja	25 Buses Charter SRL
17 Confitería Ricar-Dos	27 Cooperativa Telefónica
20 Restaurant Viejo Maitén	(Telephones)
21 Confitería Rivendel	29 Patagonia Adventure
26 Pizzería Cerro Lindo	32 ACA
28 Café Plaza	34 Taller del Arte Sano
30 Restaurant El Candil	36 Buses Mercedes/
31 Restaurant Achachay	Don Otto
33 Restaurant Portal del Río	37 Cabaña Micó
38 Restaurant El Rancho	40 Centro Artesanal
de Fernando	Cumey Antu

is at the north end of the Plaza Pagano, at Avenida San Martín and Roca. It will provide a good town map and brochures, along with complete, well-organised information on accommodation, food, tours and services.

Money Banco de la Nación is at Avenida San Martín and Pellegrini, across from the south end of the Plaza Pagano. Banco de la Provincia del Río Negro is just north of the tourist office.

Post & Telecommunications The post office is at Avenida San Martín 2608, near Coronel Dorrego. The telephone cooperative is at Juez Fernández 429, at the south end of Plaza Pagano.

Travel Agencies There are several, including Pulmari Turismo (☎ 92670) at Avenida San Martín 2995 and Patagonia Adventure

(☎ 92513) at Pablo Hube 418. For motorists, ACA is at Avenidas Bolívar and San Martín.

Medical Services The hospital is on Perito Moreno, behind Plaza Pagano.

Feria Artesanal
On Thursdays and Saturdays in summer, and Saturdays only the rest of the year, local craftspeople sell their wares at the south end of the Plaza Pagano. Hours are 10 am to 2 pm.

Festival Nacional del Lúpulo
Local beer gets headlines during the national hops festival, over four days in late February.

Places to Stay – bottom end
Camping There are many campgrounds, the most central of which is the dusty but shady *Camping del Sol*, at the west end of Avenida Castelli. There are hot showers, a small

confitería, and swimming in the river, at US$2 per person per day. Others in the immediate area are comparable in price and services: *Camping La Chacra*, off Avenida Belgrano, one km from the centre; *Camping La Alegría*, on Camino de los Nogales north of town; and *Camping Río Azul*, to the west.

Hostels & Hospedajes Budget travellers are more than welcome in El Bolsón, where reasonable prices are the rule rather than the exception. In town, the cheapest will be the youth hostel (☎ 92523) at Avenida San Martín 1360. *Hospedaje Los Amigos*, on Islas Malvinas at the west end of Balcárce, charges about US$4 per person, but with a tent you can camp in the garden for a bit less. The tourist office maintains a long list of private houses which offer lodging.

Residenciales, Hosterías & Motels At *Residencial Edelweiss* (☎ 92594), Angel del Agua 360 near Avenida San Martín, rates are US$4.50/8 per single/double with shared bath. At *Residencial Lostra* (☎ 92252), Avenida Sarmiento 3212 at José Hernández, and *Villa Turismo*, on Ruta 258 at the southern outskirts of town, rooms are US$6/10 with private bath.

Slightly more expensive are *Motel La Posta* (☎ 92297), on Ruta 258 at the northern entrance to town, and *Hostería Steiner* (☎ 92224), Avenida San Martín 600.

Places to Stay – middle
La Posada de Hamelin (☎ 92030), Granollers 2179, and *Hotel Amancay* (☎ 92222), Avenida San Martín 3217, have rooms with bath at about US$12/20.

Places to Stay – top end
Even the best accommodation in town is reasonable at the three-star *Hotel Cordillera* (☎ 92235), Avenida San Martín 3210, at US$21/32.

Places to Eat
Food in El Bolsón is not the gourmet experience of dining in Bariloche, but it is more than passable. *Achachay* is a reasonable

parrilla at Avenidas San Martín and Bolívar, while *Cerro Lindo*, Avenida San Martín 2526, has large, tasty pizzas, good music, and excellent, friendly service. *Café Plaza*, at Avenida San Martín 2557, is a first-class confitería. You can also gorge yourself on astoundingly good home-made, fruit-flavoured ice cream at *Heladería Jauja*, one of the best in all of Argentina. It's at Avenida San Martín 2867, with a smaller outlet on Avenida San Martín near Bolívar.

Things to Buy
There are plenty of goodies in El Bolsón. For fresh fruit and homemade jams and preserves, visit the berry plantations at Cabaña Micó, just a few blocks from the east end of General Roca. The owners have a modern, water-saving drip and micro-spray irrigation system for their raspberries and strawberries.Other good places for regional sweets are Dulces del Dr Miklos, on Balcárce near Avenida Sarmiento, and La Soja, the health-food store on Dorrego just off Avenida San Martín. Heladería Jauja (see Places to Eat above) and Regionales Lida, Avenida San Martín 3440, sell outstanding chocolate products.

Besides the twice-weekly Feria Artesanal (see above), there are several other outlets for local arts and crafts. Taller del Arte Sano, Avenida Sarmiento 2350, exhibits paintings, sculptures and wood sculptures, and unique furniture, from 3 to 8 pm daily. Centro Artesanal Cumey Antu, Avenida San Martín 2020, sells Mapuche clothing and weavings; hours are 9 am to 1 pm. At the Cooperativa de Ceramistas, upstairs at General Roca and Saavedra, you can buy local ceramics and chat with the potters at work from 2 to 9 pm.

Taller Artesanal Sukal, two km outside town on the road to Cerro Piltriquitrón, sells dried flower arrangements and products of painted wood, such as jewellery boxes.

Getting There & Away
Air LADE (☎ 92206) is at Castello 3259. El Bolsón is a twice-weekly stop on flights between Bariloche and Comodoro

Rivadavia, which also stop at El Maitén and Esquel.

Bus There is no central bus terminal. Several companies go to Bariloche, including Charter SRL (☎ 92333) Avenida San Martín 2536 near Pablo Hube, and Mercedes (☎ 92727) and Don Otto at Perito Moreno 2377. Both Mercedes and Don Otto go to Esquel, with some trips via Parque Nacional Los Alerces. Mercedes also serves El Maitén, Neuquén, Mar del Plata and Buenos Aires.

Locally, La Golondrina goes to El Hoyo, Mallín Ahogado and Cholila. Quimey Quipan goes to Lago Puelo and back.

AROUND EL BOLSÓN
Cabeza del Indio
On a ridgetop eight km west of town, this metamorphic rock formation truly resembles a stereotypical profile of the 'noble savage'. Part of the trail traverses a narrow ledge which offers the best views of the formation itself, but by climbing from an earlier junction you can obtain better views of the Río Azul and, in the distance to the south, Parque Nacional Lago Puelo.

Cascada Mallín Ahogado
This waterfall on the Arroyo del Medio, a tributary of the Río Quemquemtreu, is 10 km north of town, west of Ruta 258. Beyond the falls there is a trail to **Cerro Perito Moreno**, where the Club Andino Piltriquitrón's refugio (☎ 92763) offers lodging for US$3 per night. Meals are additional. In winter, there is skiing here.

Cascada Escondida
Downstream from the Cascada Mallín Ahogado, this waterfall is eight km from El Bolsón. There is a footpath beyond the bridge across the river at the west end of Avenida Pueyrredón.

Cerro Piltriquitrón
This granitic ridge dominates the landscape east of Bolsón. After driving to the 1000-metre level, an hour's walk takes you to the Club Andino's refugio (☎ 92024) where you can stay for US$3 per person – outstanding value. Meals are available, but bring your own sleeping bag.

Cerro Lindo
Southwest of Bolsón, a trail from the Río Azul campground goes to a refugio here (☎ 92763), where you can get a bed for US$4, with meals extra.

El Hoyo
Across the provincial border in Chubut, this town's microclimate makes it the local 'fresh fruit capital'. Nearby is Lago Epuyén, where there is good camping and hiking.

Parque Nacional Lago Puelo
In Chubut province, but only 15 km south of El Bolsón, this windy azure lake is suitable for swimming, fishing, boating, hiking and camping. There are regular buses from El Bolsón, but reduced service on Sunday, when you may have to hitch. Both free and paying campsites are at the park entrance.

Translago's launch takes passengers across the lake to its Pacific Ocean outlet at the Chilean border. With the hubris of military bureaucracy, the Argentine navy maintains a mobile prefecture in a caravan near the dock.

NEUQUÉN
Neuquén is the capital of its province, and also an important service centre for the agricultural towns of the Río Negro valley. As the road and rail gateway to the Andean Lake District, it has good connections to Bariloche, where you can also continue to Chile.

Orientation
At the confluence of the Río Limay and the Río Neuquén, 265 metres above sea level, Neuquén (population 300,000) is the easternmost city in its province. Excellent paved roads go east to the Río Negro valley, west toward Zapala, and south-west toward Bariloche and the lake district.

East-west national Ruta 22, a few blocks

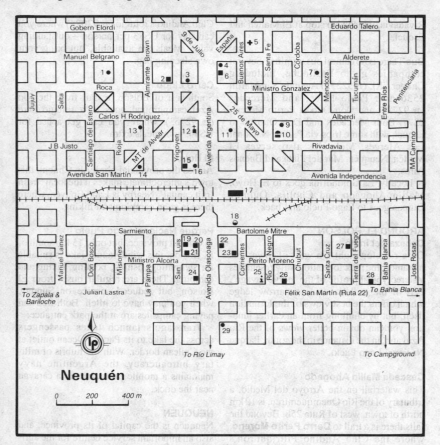

Neuquén

0   200   400 m

south of the city centre, is the main highway through town. The principal north-south thoroughfare is Avenida Argentina (Avenida Olascoaga south of the train station). Street names change on each side of Avenida Argentina and the train station. Several diagonals bisect the conventional grid. Do not confuse Avenida San Martín, the obligatory tribute to Argentina's national hero, with Félix San Martín, a few blocks to the south and a major national highway.

Information
Tourist Office The tourist office is at Félix

San Martín 182, corner of Río Negro, three blocks south of the train station. It opens weekdays from 7 am to 9 pm, weekends 7.30 am to 9.30 pm. For tourist information, the province of Neuquén is one of the best organised in the entire country, with free, up-to-date maps and brochures which contain truly useful material rather than glossy photos.

Money Besides the usual banks there are two cambios: Olano at J B Justo 45, near Avenida Argentina, and Pullman at Ministro Alcorta 163, between San Luis and La Pampa.

■ PLACES TO STAY

2 Residencial Neuquén
15 Hotel Imperio
19 Hotel Charbel
20 Hotel Ideal
21 Residencial El Rey
22 Hotel Crystal/
    Hotel Iberia
23 Hotel Premier
24 Hotel Apolo
26 Hotel Buffet
27 Residencial Musters
28 Residencial Inglés

▼ PLACES TO EAT

8 Restaurant las
   Tres Marías

OTHER

1 Casa de Gobierno
3 Artesanías Mapuches
4 Municipalidad
5 Hospital
6 Austral/TAN
7 Jefatura de Policía
9 Telefónica
10 Post Office
11 Municipalidad
12 Cathedral
13 LADE
14 Artesanías Neuquinas
16 Aerolíneas Argentinas
17 Train Station
18 Bus Terminal
25 Tourist Office
29 Police

Post & Telecommunications The post office is at Rivadavia and Santa Fe, at the intersection with the 25 de Mayo diagonal. Telefónica is nearby on Alberdi, between Santa Fe and Córdoba.

Travel Agencies Neuquén has literally dozens of travel agencies, including those mentioned under Money above. Almost all are near the centre.

Medical Services Neuquén is known throughout Argentina for the quality of its medical services which, in some circumstances, are free. You should not hesitate to consult the regional hospital (☎ 31474) at Buenos Aires 421.

Regata del Río Negro
This annual January kayak race starts in Neuquén and ends in Viedma, at the Atlantic mouth of the Río Negro.

Places to Stay – bottom end
Camping There is a campground at the Balneario Municipal, along the river, reached by bus No 103 from the centre.

Residenciales & Hotels Neuquén's hotels are numerous but not really cheap. The best bargain is *Residencial Ruca Puel* (☎ 30757), Coronel Suárez 1518, at US$8/11 a single/double, but it is some distance from the centre. Comparably priced but more central is the dingy *Hotel Imperio* (☎ 22488), Yrigoyen 65. *Hotel Premier*, at the corner of Perito Moreno and Corrientes, has rooms with bath for US$11/17. *Hotel Buffet*, on Félix San Martín near the tourist office, charges US$13/18 with shared bath, slightly more with private bath. The numerous single men who loiter in the lobby may discourage single women. *Hotel Charbel* (☎ 24143), San Luis 268, is comparably priced.

Places to Stay – middle
There are many hotels in the range of US$16/22. Try *Residencial Inglés* (☎ 22252) at Félix San Martín 534; *Residencial Musters* (☎ 30237), Tierra del Fuego 255; *Residencial Neuquén* (☎ 22403), Roca 109; *Residencial El Rey* (☎ 22652), Ministro Alcorta 84; and *Residencial Pani*, Félix San Martín 236, near Hotel Buffet.

Slightly higher, at about US$23/33, are *Hotel Iberia* (☎ 22372), Avenida Olascoaga 294; *Hotel Crystal* (☎ 22414), Olascoaga 268, and *Hotel Ideal* (☎ 22431), Avenida Olascoaga 243. Only a block further away, at Avenida Olascoaga 361, is *Hotel Apolo* (☎ 22334).

Places to Stay – top end

Top of the line in Neuquén is the five-star *Hotel del Comahue* (☎ 22439, 22440), Avenida Argentina 387. Rooms are US$52/62, but there is a 20% discount for payment in cash.

Places to Eat

There are numerous restaurants, parrillas and confiterías in Neuquén. *Las Tres Marías*, a parrilla at Alberdi 126, deserves special mention for its exceptionally varied menu at reasonable prices, in addition to cheap daily specials, in a pleasant environment with attentive service. *El Plato*, at Alberdi 158, also has a good reputation. The many confiterías along Avenida Argentina are pleasant places for morning coffee.

Things to Buy

Neuquén offers a good selection of regional handicrafts. Try Artesanías Neuquinas at Avenida San Martín 291, on the Alvear diagonal. For Mapuche Indian crafts, visit Artesanías Mapuches, Roca 62.

Getting There & Away

Air Aerolíneas Argentinas (☎ 25087) is at Avenida Argentina 16, with daily service to and from Buenos Aires. Austral (☎ 22409), at Avenida Argentina 363, flies to Buenos Aires twice daily, in the afternoon and evening, except Sunday when there is no afternoon flight. Fares to Buenos Aires are about US$170.

LADE (☎ 22453), at Almirante Brown 163, and TAN (☎ 23076), Avenida Argentina 383, serve Patagonian destinations such as Bariloche, Esquel, and Comodoro Rivadavia, with additional routes northward to Mendoza.

Bus The bus terminal (☎ 24903) is at Bartolomé Mitre 147, conveniently adjacent to the train station. El Petróleo is the major provincial carrier, with regular services to Zapala (three hours), Junín de los Andes (six hours), and San Martín de los Andes (seven hours). El Valle runs the same routes, as well as to Bariloche, Mar del Plata and Buenos

Aires. Andesmar connects Mendoza with Río Gallegos in Patagonia, while Don Otto also goes to the far south. Alto Valle's service to Mendoza costs about US$25. TUS goes to Córdoba.

Empresa Pehuenche goes to Buenos Aires via Santa Rosa, La Pampa province. La Estrella also serves the federal capital. La Unión del Sud and Empresa San Martín cross the border to Villarica and Temuco, Chile, via the scenic Tromen Pass.

Train The Roca railway, from Constitución Station in Buenos Aires, takes about 21 hours to Neuquén. The station is at Avenida Argentina and Avenida Independencia.

Car Rental There are several car rental agencies, including A1 (☎ 30362) at Avenida San Martín 1269; Avis (☎ 30216) at Avenida Argentina 363; Hertz (☎ 28872) at Leloir 639; and Rent Movil (☎ 20875) at La Pampa 462. Neuquén is a good province to explore by automobile, but foreigners should know that Ruta 22, both east along the valley of the Río Negro and west towards Zapala, has some of the most dangerous drivers in Argentina.

PIEDRA DEL AGUILA

Piedra del Aguila, 225 km south-west of Neuquén on national Ruta 237, is a possible stopover en route to Bariloche, with several residenciales and a municipal campground. At Baja Colorada, 47 km farther south, the Auca Cuyin zoo of the Fundación Dehais displays fauna typical of the region.

ZAPALA

Windy, dusty Zapala is the end of the line for the northern branch of the Roca railway. Although it is a fairly ordinary desert mining town, there are several worthwhile destinations nearby.

Orientation

Zapala is a junction for several important highways, including Ruta 22 east to Neuquén and north to Las Lajas, Ruta 40 south-west to Junín de los Andes and San

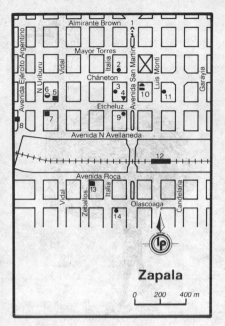

Zapala

0   200   400 m

1   Tourist Office
2   Banco de la Provincia
    del Neuquén
3   Telefónica
4   El Chancho Rengo
5   Nuevo Pehuén Hotel
6   Bus Terminal
7   Residencial Coliqueo
8   Residencial Odetto
9   Banco de la Nación
10 Post Office
11 Escuela de Cerámica
12 Train Station
13 Residencial Huincúl
14 Museo Olsacher

exhibits, including numerous fossils, from 80 different countries. The owner, Señor Garatte, lives on site at Olascoaga 421, south of the train station. It is open from 4 pm weekdays.

Places to Stay & Eat

There is limited but decent accommodation in Zapala. The cheapest is *Residencial Odetto* (☎ 21328), Ejército Argentino 455, at about US$6 per person. *Residencial Coliqueo* (☎ 21308), Etcheluz 165, and *Residencial Huincúl* (☎ 21300), Avenida Roca 311, both charge about US$11/17 a single/double, while *Nuevo Pehuén Hotel* (☎ 21360), a block from the bus station at Etcheluz and Vidal, is slightly more expensive but highly recommended. The best in town is the three-star *Hotel Hue Melen* (☎ 22391), Almirante Brown 929, where rooms are US$25/40.

Residencial Huincul, Residencial Odetto, and Hotel Hue Melen all have restaurants. *El Chancho Rengo*, at Avenida San Martín and Etcheluz, is a good confitería for a light lunch.

Things to Buy

The Escuela de Cerámica (ceramics school) at Luis Monti 240 sells pottery made by students from local materials. Artesanías Neuquinas, at Avenida San Martín and Cháneton, sells regional crafts.

Martín de los Andes and north to Chos Malal, and Ruta 13 west to Primeros Pinos. The main street is Avenida San Martín, a exit off the roundabout at which Ruta 22 and Ruta 40 meet.

Information

Tourist Office The tourist office is a kiosk on the grassy median of Avenida San Martín, at Almirante Brown.

Money Banco de la Provincia del Neuquén, Cháneton 460, is open from 7 am to 1.30 pm. Banco de la Nación is at Avenida San Martín and Etcheluz.

Post & Telecommunications The post office is at Avenida San Martín and Cháneton. Telefónica is at Italia 248.

Museo Olsacher

This small but significant private mineralogical museum contains more than 3500

Getting There & Away

Air LADE (☎ 21967), Uriburu and Etcheluz, and TAN (☎ 21281), Avenida San Martín and Cháneton, have infrequent flights. Zapala airport is south of town, at the junction of Ruta 40 and Ruta 46.

Bus The terminal (☎ 21370) is at Etcheluz and Uriburu.

El Petróleo goes direct to Buenos Aires on Sunday; otherwise, it is necessary to change at Neuquén. Fares are about US$65. It also has two buses daily to San Martín de los Andes and daily service to the resort of Copahue, on the Chilean border.

In summer, Mutisia Viajes runs buses to the Atlantic beach resorts of Necochea, Miramar and Mar del Plata. Fares are about US$45. TICSA serves San Juan and San Luis three times weekly, while TAC connects Mendoza and Bariloche via Zapala, also three times weekly in each direction. The fare to Mendoza is about US$40, to Bariloche US$16. Chevallier goes daily to Buenos Aires in the late afternoon.

Four times weekly La Unión del Sud crosses the Andes to Temuco, Chile, for US$40.

Train The terminal (☎ 21210) is at Avenida San Martín and Roca. Trains go via Neuquén to Constitución Station in Buenos Aires.

AROUND ZAPALA
Parque Nacional Laguna Blanca

Surrounded by striking volcanic deserts, Laguna Blanca is the centrepiece of 11,250-hectare Parque Nacional Laguna Blanca, one of Argentina's least known reserves. Only 30 km from Zapala, the park was created to protect the black-necked swan *Cygnus melancoryphus*, which spends the entire year here; its breeding colonies, on a peninsula in the lake, have been fenced off to prevent their disturbance by livestock.

Laguna Blanca is a shallow, interior drainage lake formed when lava flows dammed two small streams. It is too alkaline for fish, but there are many species of birds, including

Ñandú

coots, grebes, upland geese, gulls and even a few flamingos.

Ten km south of Zapala, the paved and well-marked Ruta 46 leads directly through the park toward the Andean town of Aluminé. On Mondays, Wednesdays and Fridays at midnight a bus leaves Zapala for Aluminé, and will drop you at the ranger station, where there is a very basic and unsheltered campground which you may not even see if there is no moon. The return bus leaves Aluminé at 7 am. If this schedule does not serve you, there is sufficient traffic on the route to make hitching feasible.

Ask the ranger, who also has a small exhibit of artefacts and natural history, for information on hiking in the area. Bring all your own food – the intended visitor centre and confitería is a white elephant, in ruins, never having found a concessionaire. It stands as a monument to unrealistic commercial expectations, but the unspoiled park itself will be enough for most visitors.

ALUMINÉ
Aluminé, 103 km north of Junín de los Andes on provincial Ruta 23, offers access to the northern sector of Parque Nacional Lanín. For information, consult the tourist office at the Plazoleta at the entrance to town. The Río Aluminé, which parallels the highway for most of its length, is one of the most highly regarded trout streams in the country. There are several Mapuche Indian reservations nearby, where traditional weavings can be purchased. In early April, Aluminé celebrates the **Fiesta del Pehuén** in honour of the unique trees which forest the slopes of the Andes.

JUNÍN DE LOS ANDES
Junín is a modest livestock centre of 8000 people on the Río Chimehuín, 41 km north of San Martín de los Andes. Founded as a military outpost in 1883 during the Conquest of the Desert, it is less attractive, but much less expensive, than fashionable San Martín, and has better access to many parts of Parque Nacional Lanín. It calls itself the 'trout capital' of Neuquén.

Orientation
Junín de los Andes is just south of the confluence of the Río Curruhue and the larger Río Chimehuín, which forms the city's eastern limit. Paved Ruta 234 (named in town as Boulevard Juan Manuel de Rosas) is the main thoroughfare, leading south to San Martín de los Andes and 116 km north-west to Zapala via Ruta 40. North of town, gravelled provincial Ruta 23 heads to the fishing resort of Aluminé, while several other roads branch westward to Parque Nacional Lanín.

The city centre is between the highway and the river. Do not confuse Avenida San Martín, which runs along the plaza, with Félix San Martín, two blocks west.

Information
Tourist Office The tourist office is on the main plaza, at the corner of Padre Milanesio

and Coronel Suárez. Opening hours are 8 am to 9 pm.

Money Banco de la Provincia del Neuquén is on Avenida San Martín, opposite the plaza, between Coronel Suárez and Lamadrid. Outside its limited hours, you can change cash at reasonable rates in the shop on the opposite side of the plaza.

Post & Telecommunications The post office is at Coronel Suárez and Don Bosco. Telefónica is on the opposite corner, but it is easier to make local or long-distance calls from the shop on Padre Milanesio, opposite the plaza.

Things to See & Do
Junín's surroundings are more appealing than Junín itself. Parque Nacional Lanín (see below) justifies an extended stay for campers, hikers, climbers and fishing enthusiasts. Many North Americans return for annual fishing holidays. The Río Aluminé, north of Junín, is an especially popular area, but fishing is possible even within the city limits. Hunting for red deer (raised on game farms) and waterfowl is possible in season.

For detailed information on fishing and hunting, contact the Club de Caza y Pesca Chimehuín, Avenida San Martín 555.

Festivals
Every year, Junín celebrates its own lively **Carnaval del Pehuén**, with parades, disguises, live music and the usual water balloons. No one will mistake it for Río de Janeiro or Bahía, but if you're in the area it can be entertaining.

In January, the **Feria y Exposición Ganadera** displays the best of local livestock – cattle, horses and sheep, along with poultry and rabbits. There are also exhibitions of gaucho horsemanship, and local crafts shows.

Places to Stay
Camping The municipal campground, only three blocks from the plaza on the banks of the Río Chimehuín, has all facilities. Fees are

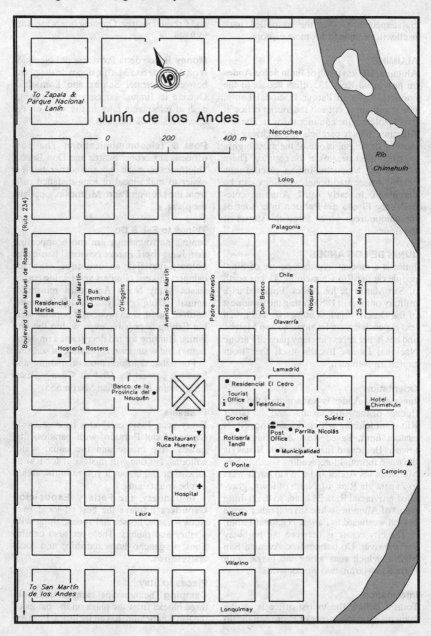

Junín de los Andes

0   200   400 m

To Zapala &
Parque Nacional
Lanín

(Ruta 234)

Boulevard Juan Manuel de Rosas

Félix San Martín

Avenida San Martín

Padre Milanesio

Necochea

Río
Chimehuín

Lolog

Patagonia

Chile

Don Bosco

Noquería

25 de Mayo

Olavarría

Lamadrid

Residencial
Marisa

Bus
Terminal

O'Higgins

Hostería Rosters

Banco de la
Provincia del Neuquén

Residencial El Cedro

Tourist
Office

Telefónica

Hotel
Chimehuín

Coronel

Suárez

Restaurant
Ruca Hueney

Rotisería
Tandil

Post
Office

Parrilla Nicolás

Municipalidad

G Ponte

Camping

Hospital

Laura

Vicuña

Cementerio

Villarino

To San Martín
de los Andes

Lonquimay

US$2 per person per day, plus an additional one-time charge of US$2 per tent.

Residenciales, Hosterías & Hotels
Junín's accommodation is modest in price and quality. *Residencial El Cedro* (☎ 91182), Lamadrid 409, and *Residencial Marisa* (☎ 91175), Blvd Rosas 360, both charge about US$8/13 for a single/double, breakfast extra. *Hostería Rosters* (☎ 91114), Lamadrid 66, is slightly more expensive.

Hotel Chimehuín (☎ 91132), Coronel Suárez and 25 de Mayo, has rooms at US$13/22, while at *Hotel Alejandro Primo*, on Blvd Rosas at the northern outskirts of town, prices are US$18/28.

Places to Eat
Junín has fairly standard restaurants, although some local specialities such as trout, wild boar or venison may be available. Try *Restaurant Ruca Hueney*, Padre Milanesio 641, or *Parrilla Nicolás*, Coronel Suárez 559. There is a good rotisería, with excellent takeaway empanadas, at Coronel Suárez 431, just east of the plaza.

Getting There & Away
Air Chapelco Airport is midway between Junín and San Martín de los Andes. For further information, see the entry under San Martín de los Andes below.

Bus The bus terminal is at Olavarría and Félix San Martín. Services are nearly the same as those to and from San Martín de los Andes.

AROUND JUNÍN DE LOS ANDES
Estancia Huechahue
This Anglo-Argentine estancia, in a sheltered valley on the Río Chimehuín about 30 km east of Junín on the road to Zapala, offers all-inclusive fishing, riding and trekking holidays in pleasant surroundings both there and in Parque Nacional Lanín. Accommodation is very comfortable, amidst apple orchards and the tranquil forest plantations of estancia owners Jim and Ann Wood.

The basic price of $150 per day includes transportation between the estancia and Bariloche or San Martín de los Andes, lodging, plus all meals and beverages (with minor exceptions). For further information contact Jane Williams, Estancia Huechahue (☎ 28276), 8371 Junín de los Andes, Provincia Neuquén.

SAN MARTÍN DE LOS ANDES
Despite some problems, San Martín de los Andes still has much of the charm which once attracted people to Bariloche. Founded as an army post in 1898, it has grown so rapidly in recent years that an inadequate sewage system has contaminated Lake Lolog's attractive beaches. You will see disconcerting graffiti exalting Colonel Mohammed Ali Seineldín, a leader of the Argentine army's ultranationalist carapintada movement, who has been under arrest here.

Orientation
At 642 metres above sea level at the east end of Lake Lolog, San Martín is surrounded by attractive mountain scenery. National Ruta 234 from Zapala via Junín de los Andes passes through town on the way to Villa La Angostura, which is on the north shore of Lake Nahuel Huapi.

Avenida San Martín, from the lakefront to the Junín highway, is the main commercial street, bounding the civic centre plaza along with Avenida Roca, Mariano Moreno and Capitán Drury. Almost everything in San Martín de los Andes is walking distance from the civic centre. The shady lakefront park and pier are a delightful place to spend the afternoon.

Information
Tourist Office The tourist office (☎ 27347) is a airy modern building in the civic centre, at Avenidas San Martín and Rosas. The staff will provide surprisingly candid information, warning you for example against swimming in Lake Lolog. It has details about hotels and restaurants, plus excellent brochures and maps, including an updated road

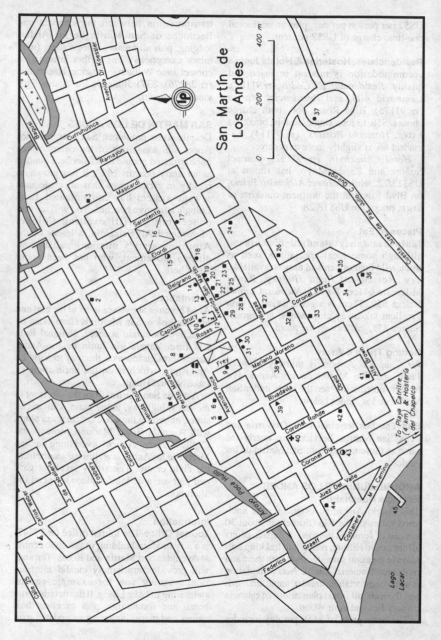

San Martín de
Los Andes

■ PLACES TO STAY	▼ PLACES TO EAT
1 Camping Los Andes	30 Café de la Plaza
2 Hotel Crismalu	38 Restaurant Piscis
3 Residencial Laura	39 Restaurant Sayhueque
4 Hostería Nevada	
5 Hotel Curruhuinca	OTHER
6 Hostería La Cheminee	
8 Hostería Las Lucarnas	7 Post Office
21 Hostería Peumayén	9 National Parks Office
22 Hotel Nevegal	10 Artesanías Mapuches
23 Hotel Chapelco Ski	11 Telephone Co-op
24 Hostería Cumelén	12 Tourist Office/Artesanías
26 Hostería La Masia	Neuquinas
27 Residencial Villalago	13 Fenoglio (chocolates)
28 Hostería Anay	14 Cambio Andina
29 Hostería Tisú	Internacional
32 Residencial Italia	15 Astete Viajes
33 Residencial Casa Alta	(Airport Bus)
34 Hotel Berna	16 Plaza Sarmiento
35 Hostería La Raclette	17 La Oveja Negra
36 Hostería Las Lengas	18 LADE/TAN
41 Residencial Los Pinos	19 Aerolíneas Argentinas
42 Hostal del Esquiador	20 Banco de La Provincia
44 Hostería La Posta	25 Kosem Artesanías
del Cazador	31 Banco de la Nación
	37 Casino
	40 Hospital
	43 Bus Terminal
	45 Pier

map of the province produced but not sold by the automobile club, for US$2.

Money Weekdays, try Banco de la Nación at Avenida San Martín 687 or Banco de la Provincia at Avenida San Martín 899. The only official exchange house is Andina Internacional, 1st floor, Avenida San Martín 876, but the many travel agencies will often buy cash dollars.

Post & Telecommunications The post office is at the civic centre, Roca and Coronel Pérez. There is a telephone cooperative at Capitán Drury 761, between Avenida San Martín and Roca.

National Parks Office Open weekdays only, the Intendencia of Parque Nacional Lanín is located at the civic centre, at Emilio Frey

749. Limited maps and brochures are available here.

Travel Agencies San Martín has many interchangeable travel agencies. Almost all are near the civic centre, along Avenida San Martín, Belgrano and Elordi. Astete Viajes (☎ 27398), Elordi 729, operates buses to Chapelco Airport.

Medical Services The Hospital Rural Ramón Castillo (☎ 27211) is at Coronel Rohde and Avenida San Martín.

Museo Regional Municipal
Next door to the tourist office, this museum displays indigenous artefacts, including arrowheads, spearpoints, pottery and musical instruments from the region. There are also mineral and fossil exhibits.

Festivals
February 4 is the anniversary of the founding of San Martín de los Andes, celebrated with speeches, parades and other festivities. In December, the Christmas **Fiesta Nacional de la Navidad Cordillerana** lasts nearly two weeks but is most notable between Christmas Eve and New Year's Day.

Places to Stay – bottom end
Camping *Camping Los Andes* is fairly central on Juez del Valle, across the bridge over Arroyo Poca Hullo, but can be very crowded in summer. Fees are US$3 per person; there are also *cabañas* (cabins), but these are often occupied by groups. On the eastern outskirts of town, ACA has a more attractive campground at Avenida Koessler 2176, but charges US$10 per site, which is more expensive unless four people share the cost.

Residenciales & Hotels As a tourist centre, San Martín is loaded with accommodation, but it is relatively expensive in all categories. The least costly is *Residencial Villalago* (☎ 27454), Villegas 717, at US$6 per person without breakfast. Prices may rise after its current remodelling. Others in this category, charging about US$9/16 a single/double, include *Residencial Casa Alta* (☎ 27456) at Obeid 659, *Residencial Italia* (☎ 27590) at Coronel Pérez 977, *Residencial Laura* (☎ 27271) at Mascardi 632, *Residencial Los Pinos* at Almirante Brown 420, *Hotel Berna* (☎ 27217) at Coronel Pérez 1127, *Hotel Curruhuinca* (☎ 27224) at Rivadavia 686, and *Hotel Crismalu* (☎ 27283), Rudecindo Roca 975.

Places to Stay – middle
Midrange hotels start at about US$13/22. Typical in this category are *Hostería Tisu* (☎ 27231) at Avenida San Martín 771, *Hotel Nevegal* (☎ 27484) at Avenida San Martín 817, *Hostería Anay* (☎ 27514) at Capitán Drury 841, *Hostería Peumayen* (☎ 27232) at Avenida San Martín 851, *Hostería Las Lucarnas* (☎ 27085) at Coronel Pérez 632, *Hostería Nevada* (☎ 27301) at Mariano

Moreno 590, *Hostal del Esquiador* at Coronel Rohde 975, and *Hostería Cumelén* (☎ 27304) at Elordi 931.

Places to Stay – top end
Hostería del Chapelco, Brown 297, is the lowest in this category at US$20 per person. *Hotel Chapelco Ski* (☎ 27480), Belgrano 869, is slightly dearer. At *Hostería La Raclette* (☎ 27664), Coronel Pérez 1170, and *Hostería La Posta del Cazador* (☎ 27501), Avenida San Martín 175, rates are about US$30/40 for singles/doubles.

Others charge about US$38/50, such as *Hostería La Masia* (☎ 27688) at Obeid 811, and *Hostería Las Lengas* (☎ 27659) at Coronel Pérez 1175. There is more luxurious accommodation at *Hostería La Cheminee* at Avenida Roca and Mariano Moreno, where doubles are US$85, and the five-star *Hotel Sol de Los Andes*, on a hill overlooking the southern approach to town, at US$50 per person including breakfast, US$65 with half-pension.

Places to Eat
There is a wide selection of excellent restaurants and confiterías in San Martín. Try *Piscis*, at Villegas and Mariano Moreno, an outstanding midprice parrilla which is mobbed in the evenings. *Sayhueque*, a parrilla at Rivadavia 825, also draws big crowds.

Café de la Plaza, at Avenida San Martín and Coronel Pérez, is a pleasant sidewalk confitería, although it is not really cheap.

Things to Buy
There are many shops which sell regional products and handicrafts. Artesanías Mapuches, Rosas 770, has local Indian weavings. La Oveja Negra, Avenida San Martín 1045, and Kosem, Capitán Drury 846, also sell artisanal textiles. Chocolates are available at Fenoglio, Avenida San Martín 836.

Getting There & Away
Air Aerolíneas Argentinas (☎ 27003) is at Avenida San Martín and Belgrano. It has

three flights weekly between Buenos Aires and Chapelco Airport (US$154 on banda negativa). LADE (☎ 27672) and TAN (☎ 27872) have adjacent offices at Avenida San Martín 915. LADE has two flights weekly from the capital, and a Friday flight to Comodoro Rivadavia (US$90) via El Bolsón, El Maitén, and Esquel.

TAN flights from Neuquén continue to Bariloche (US$20) and either Esquel (US$50) or Puerto Montt, Chile (US$56). There are connections via Neuquén to Mendoza (US$110) and Temuco, Chile (US$73). Inquire for student standby (50% discount) and 'punto a punto' (30% discount) fares.

Bus The bus terminal (☎ 27044) is at Villegas and Coronel Díaz. Regional carrier El Petróleo serves northern destinations (Aluminé, Junín de los Andes, Zapala), the Río Negro valley to the east, and Pirehueico, Chile. El Valle has four weekly buses to Buenos Aires for US$60, while La Estrella's Sunday service costs US$70. Chevallier goes daily to Buenos Aires.

TUS goes to Córdoba on Mondays for US$70; on other days make connections in Bariloche. Buses JAC has four weekly departures for Pucón, Villarica, Temuco and Santiago, Chile. Igi-Llaima goes daily except Sunday to Temuco (US$30).

Car Rental There are several car rental agencies, including A1 (By Mich) (☎ 27997) at Avenida San Martín 1142, Avis (☎ 27704) at Avenida San Martín 998, and National (☎ 27218) at Avenida San Martín 943. Daily rates start at about US$35 per day for a Renault 12, plus US$0.35 per km, plus US$11 for insurance. Weekly rates for the same car are about $200 per week, plus mileage charge, plus insurance.

AROUND SAN MARTÍN DE LOS ANDES
Skiing
Cerro Chapelco, 20 km south-east of San Martín, is the principal winter sports centre, with runs for beginners and experts, at a maximum elevation of 1920 metres. Rental equipment is available on site.

There are provincial skiing championships every August, depending on conditions. Also in the first half of August is the **Fiesta Nacional del Montañes**, the annual ski festival.

PARQUE NACIONAL LANÍN
Parque Nacional Lanín, created in 1937 to protect the native Patagonian forest, extends from Parque Nacional Nahuel Huapi in the south to Lago Ñorquinco in the north, a distance of about 150 km. Hugging the Chilean border in the west, its centerpiece is 3776-metre Volcán Lanín, a snow-capped symmetrical cone which dominates its surroundings. Tranquil Lanín has so far escaped the frantic commercial development which has blemished Nahuel Huapi and Bariloche.

Parque Lanín has many of the same species which characterise more southerly Patagonian forests, such as the southern beeches *lenga*, *ñire*, and *coihue*. More importantly, it also contains extensive stands of the broadleaf deciduous southern beech known as *raulí (Nothofagus nervosa)* and the curious pehuén or monkey puzzle tree *(Araucaria araucana)*, a member of the pine family.

Besides the views of Volcán Lanín and these unusual forests, the park has further recreational attractions in the numerous finger-shaped lakes left behind by Pleistocene glaciers. There are many excellent campsites, although some of the less developed but more accessible ones are unfortunately dirty and polluted.

Things to See & Do
From south to north, the towns of San Martín de los Andes, Junín de los Andes, and Aluminé are the best starting points for exploring Lanín, its lakes, and the backcountry. This section begins at San Martín and works northwards.

Lago Lacar From San Martín, at the east end of the lake, you can sail its length to Paso Hua Hum and cross by road to Pirihueico,

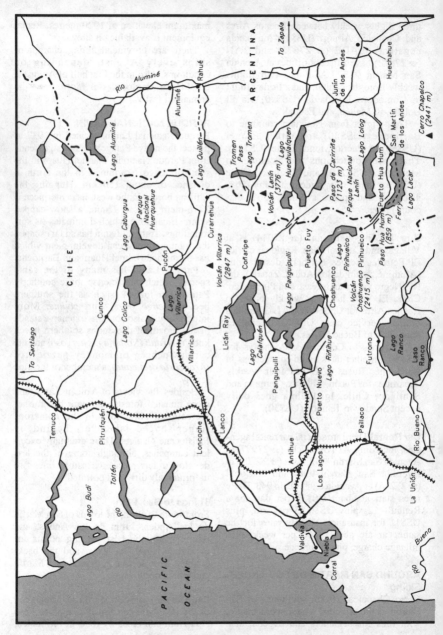

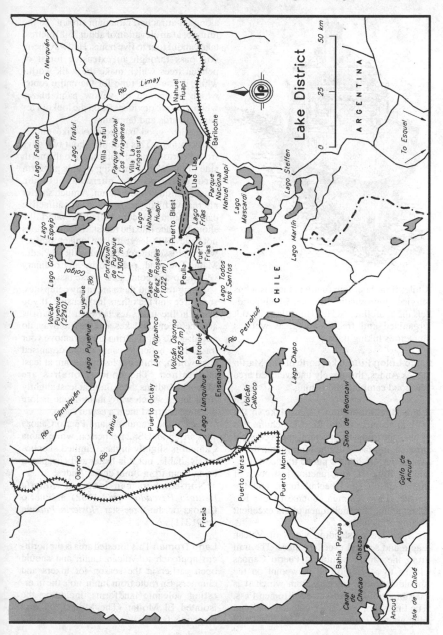

Chile. If no boats are running, there is a bus service on provincial Ruta 48, which parallels the shoreline. At Hua Hum, there is both organised and free camping, as well as numerous hiking trails.

Lago Lolog Fifteen km north of San Martín de los Andes, this largely undeveloped area has good camping and fishing.

Lago Huechulafquen Largest lake in the park and source of the Río Chimehuín, this is also one of the most central and accessible areas, being easily reached from Junín de los Andes despite limited public transport. Provincial Ruta 61, at a junction just north of Junín, climbs to Huechulafquen and the smaller Lago Paimún. Source of the Río Chimehuín, Huechulafquen offers excellent fishing at its outlet.

There are outstanding views of Volcán Lanín and several excellent hikes. The trail from the ranger station at Puerto Canoas climbs to a refugio and viewpoint on the shoulder of the volcano, from which it is possible to hike across to the Tromen Pass. The first segment is an abandoned road, but after about 40 minutes it becomes a real trail

along an attractive mountain stream. To the refugio, at an elevation of about 2500 metres, takes about four to five hours. Halfway there, you pass through an extensive forest of pehuén trees which make the walk worthwhile if you lack time for the entire route, which is marked by yellow paint blazes where it is not obvious. Be on the lookout for hares, lizards and tarantulas.

Another good backcountry hike circles Lago Paimún. This requires about two days from Puerto Canoas; you return to the north side of the lake by crossing a cable platform strung across the narrows between Huechulafquen and Paimún. A much shorter alternative hike goes from the very attractive campground at Piedra Mala to a waterfall a short distance into the forest. If your car does not have 4WD, leave it at the logjam 'bridge' which crosses the creek and walk to Piedra Mala. The road, passable by any ordinary vehicle to this point, gets worse fast.

Along the road there are many campsites, some free and the others inexpensive. If you camp in the free sites between the narrow area between the lakes and the highway, do not forget to dig a latrine and to remove your trash. It is better to camp at the organised sites which, while not luxurious, are at least maintained. The concessionaires are Mapuche Indians, benefiting at least slightly from lands which were theirs alone before the state usurped them a century ago.

Fees at the Raquithue and Puerto Canoas sites are about US$2 per person, while Bahía Cañicul is slightly higher. Limited supplies are available, but it is better and cheaper to bring them from Junín de los Andes.

Non-campers can lodge at *Hostería Refugio Pescador* (☎ 91132) at Puerto Canoas or the three-star *Hostería Paimún* (☎ 91211).

Lago Tromen This forested area is the northern approach to Volcán Lanín and should open earlier in the season for hikers and climbers. En route from Junín, note the interesting volcanic landforms, including the isolated El Mollar (The Molar), an oral surgeon's fantasy.

To climb Volcán Lanín, which straddles the Argentine-Chilean border, ask permission at the national parks office in San Martín or, if necessary, of military authorities in Junín. The trailhead is at the Argentine border station. There is a refugio at about 2500 metres, but you will need snow climbing equipment above that point. It is possible to hike south across the Sierra Mamuil Malal to Lago Huechulafquen.

Lago Quillén This isolated lake is accessible by dirt road from Rahué, 17 km south of Aluminé, and has many good campsites. Other nearby lakes include Lago Rucachoroi, directly west of Aluminé, and Lago Ñorquinco on the park's northern border. This area contains the densest pehuén forests in the area. At Rucachoroi and Quillén, there are Mapuche Indian reservations.

Getting There & Away
Although the park is close to San Martín and Junín, public transport is minimal, but with some patience hitching is feasible in high season. The buses over the Hua Hum and Tromen passes from San Martín and Junín to Chile will take passengers to intermediate destinations.

In the summer, according to park rangers, lorries meet arriving trains at Zapala station and take backpackers to Huechulafquen. Although officially they are not allowed to carry passengers into the park, such traffic is unofficially tolerated. Pickup trucks from Junín will carry six or seven backpackers for about US$4 per person.

VILLA LA ANGOSTURA
About 100 km south of San Martín de los Andes, surrounded by Parque Nacional Nahuel Huapi, the quiet lakeside resort of Villa La Angostura is well worth a visit.

Orientation
On the north shore of Lago Nahuel Huapi, placid Villa La Angostura (altitude 850 metres) is near the junction of national Ruta 231 from Bariloche, which crosses the Andes

to Puyehue and Osorno, Chile, and national Ruta 234, which leads northward to San Martín de los Andes and Parque Nacional Lanín. Through town, Ruta 231 is known as Avenida Los Arrayanes and Avenida Los Lagos.

Villa La Angostura takes its name from the 91-metre isthmus which connects it with the Quetrihué peninsula, which protrudes southward into the lake. In fact, the village consists of two distinct areas: El Cruce is the commercial centre along the highway, while La Villa, three km south, is more residential but still has hotels, shops, services and lake access. Unlike Bariloche, densely forested Villa La Angostura does not dominate its surroundings, so that, except along the highway, you are hardly aware of being in a town. The population is about 2000.

Information
Tourist Office The tourist office (☎ 94124) is at the junction of Avenida Los Arrayanes and Avenida Los Lagos. It has a good selection of maps and brochures.

Money Banco de la Provincia is on Los Arrayanes between Las Mutisias and Los Notros, but it should be possible to exchange cash dollars in almost any shop.

Post & Telecommunications The post office is in La Villa, on Nahuel Huapi. The telephone office is at El Cruce, near the tourist office.

National Parks Office The office is on Nahuel Huapi, in La Villa.

Things to See & Do
Both town and surrounding area are best seen on foot. Local buses and taxis will get you to most of the trailheads if necessary.

Parque Nacional Los Arrayanes This overlooked park, occupying the entire Quetrihué peninsula, protects remaining stands of the cinnamon-barked arrayán *(Myrceugenella apiculata)*, a member of the myrtle family. The peninsula's Mapuche name means Place of the Arrayanes.

Park headquarters, near the largest concentration of arrayanes, is 12 km away at the southern end of the peninsula, but you can walk there easily from La Villa in three hours on an excellent interpretive nature trail (brochures are available in the tourist office at El Cruce). Since regulations require hikers to leave the park by 4 pm, you should start early in the morning. Another alternative is to rent mountain bikes at El Cruce for US$2 per hour. There are two small lakes along the trail

From the park's northern entrance at La Villa, there is also a very steep, 20-minute hike to two panoramic overlooks of Lago Nahuel Huapi.

Cerro Belvedere This four-km walk to an overlook offers good views of Lago Correntoso, Nahuel Huapi and surrounding mountains. Another three km will take you to the summit. After visiting the overlook, retrace your steps to a nearby junction which will take you to Cascada Inayacal, a 50-metre waterfall.

Cerro Bayo Lifts take skiers as high as 1600 metres at this winter resort, nine km from El Cruce. The season lasts from June to September.

Siete Lagos From Villa La Angostura, provincial Ruta 234 follows an especially scenic route past numerous alpine lakes to San Martín de los Andes. For transportation details see Getting There & Away below.

Festivals

For four days during Holy Week, the **Campeonato de Pesca Semana Santa** attracts fishing enthusiasts to the area. The **Fiestas Mayas** in the second half of May celebrate local and national patriotic holidays.

Places to Stay

Camping *Camping El Cruce*, on Los Lagos 500 metres beyond the tourist office, charges US$1.50 per person plus an extra US$1 for electrical hookups, with small discounts for students and ACA members. There are hot showers, but the toilets are sometimes dirty. At *Camping Correntoso*, on Lago Correntoso north of town, sites are US$3 per person plus US$1.50 per vehicle. There are also free sites along Lago Nahuel Huapi.

Residenciales, Hosterías & Hotels Except for camping, accommodation is not cheap. *Residencial La Granja* (☎ 94193), on Nahuel Huapi in La Villa, is the most reasonable at US$13/25 for singles/doubles. *Residencial Don Pedro* (☎ 94269), on Belvedere in El Cruce, charges US$15/20. In La Villa, at *Residencial Río Bonito* (☎ 94110), on Topa Topa, and *Hotel Angostura* (☎ 94224), on Nahuel Huapi, rates are around US$22/32.

Hotel Correntoso, north of El Cruce on Ruta 231, charges US$60 double. At the three-star *Hostería Las Balsas*, a few km south of El Cruce, rooms are US$60 per person with breakfast.

Places to Eat

There are several restaurants and confiterías along Los Arrayanes and its cross streets in El Cruce.

Things to Buy

On weekends, artisans sell their own handicrafts from kiosks on the newly landscaped plaza, Blvd Nahuel Huapi between Las Frambuesas and Los Maquis, a block from El Cruce.

Getting There & Away

There is no formal bus terminal, but all buses in all directions must pass El Cruce.

Transporte Algarrobal has two buses daily in each direction between Villa La Angostura and Bariloche. Fares are US$5, and tickets are available through Village SA (☎ 94292) on Los Arrayanes. Transporte Unión del Sud connects Villa La Angostura with Neuquén via San Martín de los Andes and Junín de los Andes three times weekly in each direction. Fares are US$8 to San Martín, US$9 to Junín, and US$23 to Neuquén. For information and tickets, go to Cantina Los Amigos (☎ 94322) on Los Taiques.

International services between Bariloche and Osorno and Puerto Montt (Chile) stop in Villa La Angostura, but are often very crowded. For Transporte Mercedes, TAS Choapa and Bus Norte, inquire at Cantina Los Amigos.

VILLA TRAFUL

Villa Traful sits on the south shore of Lago Traful, about 80 km north of Bariloche on provincial Ruta 65 in Parque Nacional Nahuel Huapi. Opportunities for camping, hiking and fishing are excellent. There are bus services on Fridays at 8 am from the village to national Ruta 237 at Confluencia, where the Río Traful meets the Río Negro between Bariloche and Neuquén.

Other than camping, the cheapest lodging is *Hostería Villa Traful* at US$11 per person with breakfast. The most extravagant is the *Rincon del Pescador* (☎ 22181 or fax 0944-26215), whose glossy brochure offers 'wall to wall wrags' and 'scrumbled eggs for your breakfast' for US$80 per person.

Chubut Province

The third-largest Argentine province after Buenos Aires and Santa Cruz, Chubut stretches from the Atlantic to the Andes. Its eastern plains, with numerous sheep estancias, surround the prosperous, irrigated Río Chubut valley. Road and air communications with Buenos Aires are excellent.

To the west, on the eastern slope of the Andes, is Chubut's portion of the scenic Argentine Lake District. An excellent paved highway connects the area with the Atlantic coast, but it is also accessible from the popular resort of Bariloche, in Río Negro province to the north.

History

Although Magellan's expedition entered Golfo Nuevo, site of present-day Puerto Madryn, Europeans generally avoided Chubut until the mid-19th century. At that time Welsh nationalists, frustrated with English domination, sought a land where they could exercise sufficient political autonomy to retain their language, religion, and identity. Deciding on desolate Patagonia, they appealed to the government of Argentina which, after initial misgivings due at least in part to the British presence in the Falkland Islands, offered them a land grant in the lower Río Chubut valley in 1863.

Disillusion and misfortune plagued the 153 first arrivals from the brig *Mimosa* in the winter of 1865. The Patagonian desert bore no resemblance to their verdant homeland, and several children did not survive a storm which turned a two-day coastal voyage into a 17-day ordeal. Only a handful were farmers in well-watered Wales, yet their livelihood was to be agriculture in arid Chubut. After near starvation in the early years, the colonists engineered suitable irrigation systems and increased their harvests, permitting the gradual absorption of more immigrants from Wales.

Eventually, the Welsh occupied the entire lower Chubut valley and founded towns at Rawson (named in honour of the Argentine minister who arranged their land grant), Trelew (after Lewis Jones, a founding member of the colony), Puerto Madryn (after the colonist Parry Madryn), and Gaiman (a Tehuelche word meaning Stony Point). Even so, by 1895 the European population of the province was fewer than 4000. Only after the turn of the century did immigration from Europe – Italian, Scottish, English and other – and from central Argentina transform the territory.

All this immigration had been made possible by General Roca's Conquest of the Desert. To their credit, the Welsh did not participate in this slaughter of the Indians, but their settlement in the region constituted a foothold for the Argentine state in an area previously outside its authority.

With the outbreak of WW I, Welsh immigration ceased and there began a slow process of assimilation into Argentine society. Welsh surnames are still common, and Welsh cultural traditions such as tea houses and the *Eisteddfod* (folk festival) in Gaiman endure, but younger people speak Spanish by preference. The province's cultural landscape still reflects the Welsh presence, with its stone buildings and monuments in typical villages such as Dolavon, near Gaiman, and Trevelin, near Esquel.

The most accessible book on the area is Anglo-Argentine journalist Andrew Graham-Yooll's *The Forgotten Colony* (Hutchinson, London, 1981), a comprehensive account of British immigration into Argentina, which contains a chapter on the Welsh settlements. More complete is Glyn Williams' historical geography *The Desert and the Dream: A History of the Welsh Colonisation of Patagonia, 1865-1915* (University of Wales Press, Cardiff, 1975). More recently he has produced *The Welsh in Patagonia: the State and the Ethnic Community* (University of Wales Press, 1991).

PUERTO MADRYN

This isolated desert port, founded by Welsh settlers in 1886, took its name from Love Parry, Baron of Madryn, but only the street names reflect its Welsh past. Today, immigrants greatly outnumber self-identified NICs *(nacido y criado*, or 'born and raised'). After 1974, with construction of the Storni pier and Argentina's first aluminum plant (ALUAR), the town's population multiplied near tenfold, to 50,000 by 1988. Inadequate planning encouraged spontaneous housing and has caused serious water and sewage problems.

The only other important local industries are seafood processing and tourism. As the closest urban centre to Península Valdés, it is usually the starting point for visits to the famous wildlife reserves of the area. There is also a campus of the Universidad de la Patagonia, with departments of marine biology, computer science and engineering.

Orientation

Puerto Madryn lies on a protected site on the Golfo Nuevo, 1371 km south of Buenos Aires, 439 km north of Comodoro Riva-

davia, and only 65 km from Trelew. Its broad beach and the costanera Avenida Roca are the principal areas of interest to visitors.

Information

Tourist Office The tourist office (☎ 73029) is at Avenida Roca 444 near the corner with 9 de Julio. It is open 7 days a week, but hours vary. During summer, they offer a series of videos and lectures at 9 pm daily – ask for the weekly program. For more in-depth history and natural history, or for a guided tour, contact Peter Seibt (German speaker) or Chris Fillmore (English) at 25 de Mayo 1016.

Money There are several exchange houses and banks in Puerto Madryn. Banco de la Nación, 9 de Julio 117, changes American Express travellers' cheques. Also try Banco del Sud at Roque Sáenz Peña and 25 de Mayo, and Banco de la Provincia del Chubut at 25 de Mayo 154. The cambios are La Moneda at 28 de Julio 21 (Local 4), Golfo Nuevo at 28 de Julio 21, Coyun-Co (☎ 71772) at Avenida Roca 161, and Turismo Pu-ma (☎ 73063) at 28 de Julio 48.

Post & Telecommunications ENCOTEL is at the corner of Belgrano and Gobernador Maíz. Telefónica has two offices, the main one on Avenida Roca near Belgrano and the other at 28 de Julio 334.

Travel Agencies Sur Turismo (☎ 73585) at Avenida Roca 612 organises tours of the area and Península Valdés to match visitors' interests, including photographic safaris, both overland and submarine, educational tours and whale watching; nearly all its guides speak English.

Acuatours Pinino (☎ 73800), at Mitre 80, has daily videos on diving and whales. For small groups, Turismo Pu-ma (☎ 73063), at 28 de Julio 42, organises nature walks, lasting about four hours, along the coast as well as in the countryside.

Monuments & Industrial Plants

On the Costanera, the unique **Monumento a**

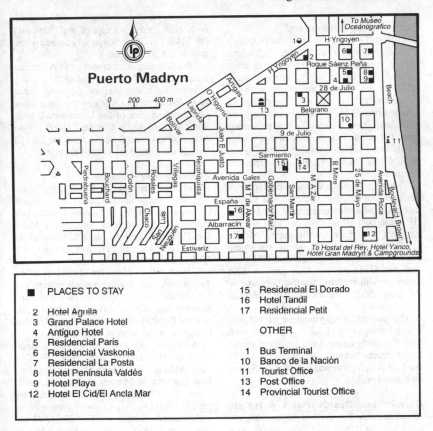

Puerto Madryn

0   200   400 m

To Museo Oceánografico

	PLACES TO STAY
2	Hotel Aguila
3	Grand Palace Hotel
4	Antíguo Hotel
5	Residencial París
6	Residencial Vaskonia
7	Residencial La Posta
8	Hotel Península Valdés
9	Hotel Playa
12	Hotel El Cid/El Ancla Mar
15	Residencial El Dorado
16	Hotel Tandil
17	Residencial Petit

OTHER

1	Bus Terminal
10	Banco de la Nación
11	Tourist Office
13	Post Office
14	Provincial Tourist Office

La Mujer Galesa acknowledges the contribution of Welsh women to regional history.

You can visit the seafood processing plants, **Harengus** and **Conarpesa**, by arrangement with the tourist office. In summer, the tourist office also arranges organised tours of **ALUAR**, the aluminium plant, but the rest of the year, visitors should contact the plant's public relations office directly.

Museo Oceanográfico y de Ciencias Naturales

Since 1972, this museum has been housed in the historic Chalet Pujol, at Domec García and Menéndez. It has good displays of Patagonian flora and fauna, both marine and terrestrial, and a library. There are panoramic views from the loft, which often has lectures and shows. It's open weekdays from 9 to 11.30 am and from 6 to 9 pm.

Beaches

Playa Acuario is the most central, developed and crowded beach, but it is still a pleasant place for cold beer, snacks and opportunities to mix with locals. More southerly beaches are less protected from the constant wind, but more suitable for windsurfing or diving.

Places to Stay – bottom end

Camping There are several campgrounds toward Punta Cuevas and the Tehuelche Indian monument. The oldest and most pleasant belongs to ACA, which charges US$9 per day for up to four people with car, trailer, and tent, but adds a 10% surcharge for nonmembers. This is the only campground with large trees offering some protection from the wind. Reservations are advisable for the busy summer, through *Camping del ACA*, Punta Cuevas, Casilla de Correo 68, Puerto Madryn.

Camping Municipal Sud, which is well designed but less well sheltered, has several categories of accommodation. Their 'A' and 'B' areas cost US$8 daily for four people, tent, car and trailer, while their perfectly acceptable 'C' and 'D' areas are much cheaper at U$1 a day per person, US$1 per tent, and US$1 per car. They provide 20% discount with student identification, and to ACA members. Children under six years old stay without charge.

The newest campground is *El Golfito*, which belongs to the Club Náutico Atlántico Sud. It is partly forested and has direct access to the beach. Nonmember prices are US$7 for four people, tent and car, plus US$3 per additional person.

Dormitories, Residenciales & Hotels

Residencial Jo's at Bolívar 75 has singles/doubles for US$10/15. The clean and friendly *Hotel Tandil* (☎ 71017), at Juan B Justo 770, has rooms without bath at US$12/18. *Hotel París*, at the corner of Roque Sáenz Peña and 25 de Mayo, has very basic rooms at US$13/14. The manager is friendly but not always available.

Despite its dark, narrow entrance, *Antiguo Hotel* (☎ 73742) at 28 de Julio 148 is very friendly and pleasant, but it has 'considerable night activity', according to one reader. Rooms are US$12/21 with bath. *Residencial Petit* (☎ 71460) at M T de Alvear 845 has rooms with bath at US$14/21. Similarly priced are residenciales *El Dorado* (71026) at San Martín 545, *La Posta* (☎ 72422) at Avenida Roca 33 (rooms are rather small,

with bunk beds, but clean), and *Vaskonia* (☎ 74427) at 25 de Mayo 43 (probably the best of the cheap hotels).

Hotel Aguila, at the corner of M A Zar and Roque Sáenz Peña, is cheap but some women have complained of harassment here. Another reasonable summer alternative is the dormitories of the Universidad de la Patagonia, *El Ancla Mar* (☎ 71809), 25 de Mayo 880, whose double rooms are US$10 with student card and US$14 without.

Places to Stay – middle

Hotel Azul (☎ 74429), Gobernador Maíz 545, has rooms at US$14/25, while *Hotel Atalaya* (☎ 73006) at Domec García 149 charges US$15/26 with bath. *Hotel Mora* (☎ 71424) at Juan B Justo 654, which is slightly less central, has rooms for US$15/26.

Grand Palace Hotel (☎ 71009), at 28 de Julio 390, has good rooms upstairs for US$18/29, but the downstairs rooms are poorer value. The *Hostal del Rey* (☎ 71156) at Blvd Brown 681, is perhaps the best in this category, with rooms at US$20/30.

A bit more expensive, but of similar standard to the above, are *Hotel El Cid* (☎ 71416) at 25 de Mayo 850 and *Residencial Carrera* at Marcos A Zar 852, with rooms for US$26/34. *Hotel Gran Madryn* (☎72141) at Lugones 40 is very pleasant and well-located. Rooms are US$27/36. *Hotel Yanco* (☎ 71581) at Avenida Roca 626 has good views and a pleasant atmosphere, but its disco makes sleep problematical. Rooms are US$22/29.

Places to Stay – top end

The costliest hotel in Puerto Madryn is the *Península Valdés* (☎ 71292) at Avenida Roca 163, with rooms at US$50/60. A bit outside the centre is the *Southern Cross Inn*, also known by its Spanish homonym *Posada Estrella del Sur*, at Abraham Mathews 2951. At US$27/36, the rooms are very spacious. Their restaurant offers a wide range of international dishes, and the hotel has its own transportation to town and the airport.

Other hotels in this category include the

Hotel Costanera (☎ 72234), at Blvd Brown 759, with rooms at US$30/44; and the *Hotel Playa* (☎ 71446), Avenida Roca 181, where rates are US$29/40.

The tourist office will provide information and photos of apartments and houses for rent on a daily, weekly or monthly basis. Prices vary from US$36 per day for six people to US$100 a day for a entire house for four people.

Places to Eat

Puerto Madryn has good food at reasonable prices. Although beef is rather more expensive than in the Pampas, there are several good parrillas, including the highly recommended *Estela* at Roque Sáenz Peña 28, *Parrilla de Matías* at Roque Sáenz Peña 214, and *Baldomero* at Roque Sáenz Peña 390. Also try the beautifully decorated *La Tablita* on the Ribera Norte.

Also along Ribera Norte are the *Restaurant del ACA* and *Club Náutico*, both good but a bit pricey. Club Náutico also has a cheaper, popular *Cantina El Náutico* at Avenida Roca and Lugones. The family-run *La Cheminée*, Moreno 60, has upscale prices but the food, particularly the fondue, is good value for money.

Cheaper alternatives include the restaurant at *Hotel París*, just around the corner from the hotel entrance (some have complained of poor service and mediocre food, but it has a good local reputation), and *El Aguila* at M A Zar 75. For superb lasagna and other Italian food, try *La Tua Pasta* at Belgrano 138.

There are a number of good pizza places, including *Almacén del 900* at 9 de Julio 245 and *Halloween II* at 28 de Julio 322. Perhaps the best are the large and tasty pizzas at *Cabil-Dos*, H Yrigoyen and Avenida Roca, which also serves great baked empanadas. Takeaway service is available.

Getting There & Away

Air Although Puerto Madryn has had its own airport since 1989, most flights still arrive at Trelew, 65 km south (see the section under Trelew). If you need to catch a ride to

Madryn walk to the Trelew airport entrance on Ruta 3 and wait for the intercity bus, which runs every half-hour but does not stop within the airport.

Bus The bus terminal is at H Yrigoyen between M A Zar and San Martín.

Empresa Andesmar (☎ 73764) has daily buses to Mendoza (with connections to Salta), and Caleta Olivia. On Tuesday evenings there is a bus to Río Gallegos.

Empresa Don Otto (☎ 71575) has one daily direct bus to Buenos Aires, one to Comodoro Rivadavia, and one to Río Gallegos and intermediate stops. It also goes to Neuquén five times weekly, and to Esquel four times weekly. El Condor/La Puntual (☎ 71125) also has daily buses to Buenos Aires, four weekly to Bahía Blanca via Viedma and Carmen de Patagones, and four to Comodoro Rivadavia.

Transportadora Patagónica has two buses a week to Mar del Plata. TUP travels three times weekly to Córdoba, and to Camarones and Comodoro Rivadavia. Mar y Valle has three buses weekly to Esquel.

Typical fares are: Trelew US$2, Buenos Aires US$59, Río Gallegos US$44, Neuquén US$27, Comodoro Rivadavia US$22, and Esquel US$29.

Car Rental Renting a car is a good way to see Puerto Madryn and its surroundings, especially Península Valdés. Rent-A-Car (☎ 71797), at Avenida Roca 117, charges US$22 a day for a small car, plus US$0.22 per km, plus a daily insurance fee of US$9. They are open seven days a week. Fiorasi (☎ 71660) is at Belgrano 196, and VIP Car (☎ 71772) at Avenida Roca 171.

AROUND PUERTO MADRYN
Monumento al Indio Tehuelche

Six km south of downtown, along the waterfront road to Punta Cuevas, are the beaches of Golfo Nuevo and the Tehuelche Indian monument. This massive sculpture by Luis Perlotti, unveiled on the centenary of the arrival of the Welsh colonists in 1965, acknowledges their debt to the native peoples of the province.

Reserva Faunística Punta Loma

This sea lion rookery is 17 km south-west of Puerto Madryn, along a good but winding gravel road. There is a visitor centre and an overlook about 15 metres from the animals. Some travel agencies will organise tours; otherwise you can hire a car or taxi.

PENÍNSULA VALDÉS

About 18 km north of Puerto Madryn, paved provincial Ruta 2 branches off Ruta 3 across the Istmo Carlos Ameghino to Península Valdés, one of the finest wildlife reserves in South America. Sea lions, elephant seals, guanacos, rheas, Magellanic penguins and many other seabirds are present in large numbers on the beaches and headlands. Sheep estancias occupy most of the peninsula's interior, which includes one of

---

FAUNA OF PENÍNSULA VALDÉS & PATAGONIA

The animal life of Península Valdés is generally typical of the entire Patagonian coast as far as Tierra del Fuego, with a few exceptions. This is especially true with respect to shorebirds, including penguins, and marine mammals, including whales and seals.

Penguins

Until the era of European exploration in the 16th century, penguins were unknown outside the Southern Hemisphere, and these large flightless birds are still a novelty outside their range. The most northerly penguins are found in the Galápagos Islands of Ecuador, but they are most numerous in the higher latitudes of Patagonia and Antarctica. The only species which regularly visits Península Valdés is the Magellanic or jackass penguin, *Spheniscus magellanicus*.

The first Europeans to see penguins were the Portuguese navigators who rounded the Cape of Good Hope in the late 15th century, but the first European to publicise them was the Italian nobleman Antonio Pigafetta, the diarist on Magellan's expedition which circumnavigated the globe in the early 16th century. The late naturalist George Gaylord Simpson believes that Magellan's crew saw them at Punta Tombo, today another large reserve south of Puerto Madryn.

There are four species of the genus *Spheniscus*. In the South Atlantic, *S magellanicus* has a breeding range from Península Valdés, at about 42° south latitude, around the tip of South America to near Valparaíso, Chile, about 33° south in the colder Pacific. It spends winter at sea, but comes ashore to breed in September and hatch its eggs in shoreline burrows. Unable to feed themselves until they mature enough to swim, chicks depend on their parents to feed them with regurgitated squid and other food ingested on daily trips to the ocean.

Penguins are awkward on land, tobogganing on their wings for speed when threatened. In the water they are swift and graceful, their webbed feet serving as rudders. In fact, it is not quite correct to call them flightless when, according to Simpson:

They fly in the water...They are propelled in the water by their wings, which move in unison as in usual flight and are as heavily muscled as those of aerial fliers.

Despite their enormous numbers, penguins have many predators. In the water, southern sea lions, leopard seals, and killer whales take adult birds. On land, eggs and chicks are vulnerable to gulls, skuas, and other large birds. Both aboriginal peoples, such as the Maori of New Zealand, and Europeans have consumed them for food; French naturalist Antoine Pernety, visiting the Falklands in the late 18th century, wrote that French colonists there ate penguins 'several times in ragouts, which we found to be as good as those made of hares'. Even today, Falkland Islanders collect penguin eggs in the spring, but no longer are penguins killed and boiled down to top off casks of whale and seal oil.

Magellanic penguins sometimes frequent the beach at Puerto Pirámides on Península Valdés. Otherwise you can see them along Caleta Valdés, although there are much larger numbers farther south at Punta Tombo and Cabo Dos Bahías. For information on other penguin species, see the chapter on the Falkland Islands, below. A readable account of the history and natural history of penguins is Simpson's *Penguins: Past and Present, Here and There* (Yale, 1976).

the lowest continental depressions in the world, the salt flats of Salina Grande and Salina Chica, 42 metres below sea level. The province of Chubut oversees visitor activities.

At the entrance to the reserve, provincial officials collect a fee of US$3 per person. The visitor centre has a small exhibit of local fauna and flora, plus an observation tower from which one can see across the desert landscape to Golfo San José to the north and Golfo Nuevo in the south. In the Golfo San José, just off the isthmus, is the Isla de los Pájaros, a bird sanctuary off limits to humans but visible through a powerful telescope. Common species include gulls, cormorants, flamingos, oystercatchers and egrets.

Puerto Pirámide, the peninsula's only village, was the port of exit for salt from Salina Grande at the turn of the century, but now depends exclusively on tourism. Its sandy white beaches, visited by right whales

Whales

Whales, as everyone knows, are the world's largest living animals. There are two orders: the toothed whales (including dolphins, porpoises and the killer whale *Orcinus orca)* feed mainly on fish and squid, while the baleen whales (including the southern right whale *Eubalaena australis)* trap plankton and krill (small crustaceans) as sea water filters through plates in their jaws. A layer of blubber beneath their skin insulates them from the cold ocean waters.

Their bodies black with white underbellies, pods of killer whales frequent the waters around Península Valdés. Males can reach more than nine metres in length and weigh as much as 950 kg, although most specimens and females are considerably smaller. Their ominous dorsal fin is up to two metres high. Near the top of the food chain, they prey on fish, penguins, dolphins, seals and on rare occasion larger whales.

Averaging nearly twelve metres in length and weighing more than thirty tonnes, right whales enter the shallow waters of the Golfo Nuevo and the Golfo San José in spring to breed and bear their young. September and October are the best months to see them. At Puerto Pirámide, launches take visitors out into the harbour for closer views. After more than half a century of legal protection, right whale populations are slowly recovering in the South Atlantic from virtual extinction after exploitation for meat and oil.

Elephant Seals & Sea Lions

The southern elephant seal *(Mirounga leonina)* and the southern sea lion *(Otaria flavescens)* belong to the order of pinnipeds or eared seals, which are widely distributed throughout Patagonia and other southern midlatitude and sub-Antarctic areas and islands.

Elephant seals take their common name from the male's enormous proboscis, which does indeed resemble an elephant's trunk. These ponderous animals reach nearly seven metres in length and weigh up to 4500 kg, but the females are so much smaller that it would be possible to mistake them for a different species. They spend most of the year at sea, diving several hundred metres up to half an hour per dive, in search of squid and other fish.

Península Valdés has the only breeding colony of southern elephant seals on the South American continent. The bull elephant seal comes ashore in late winter or early spring, breeding shortly after the already pregnant females arrive and give birth. Dominant males, known as 'beachmasters', control harems of up to 100 females, but must constantly fight off challenges from bachelor males. Fights are frequent and spectacular, leaving many adult males disfigured.

In the course of these fights, bulls accidentally crush many seal pups. Those which survive gain weight rapidly for about three weeks before being abandoned by their mothers, and head to sea by the end of the year. There are substantial numbers of elephant seals at the Punta Norte reserve, but access to them is better on the gravel spit at Caleta Valdés.

Aggressive southern sea lions will occasionally drag away a helpless elephant seal pup, but they too feed largely on squid and the occasional penguin. The male is an imposing specimen, whose mane truly resembles that of an African lion. Like the African lion, it is very quick and aggressive on land. Do not approach too closely for photographs. ∎

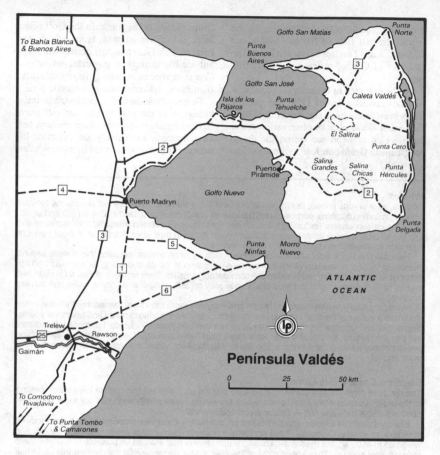

Península Valdés

0   25   50 km

between July and December, and the warm clear waters of the Golfo Nuevo attract fishers and water sports enthusiasts. During the season, launches can approach right whales in the harbour.

Puerto Pirámide is an excellent base for exploring the peninsula and its numerous wildlife colonies. For visitors without cars, there is a sea lion colony only four km from town, with good views (and sunsets) across the Golfo Nuevo toward Puerto Madryn.

To visit remaining wildlife sites, it is essential to have a car or take an organised tour; beyond Puerto Pirámide, the roads are

gravelled, with occasional soft sand, but present no obstacle to prudent drivers. Just north of Punta Delgada, in the south-east corner of the peninsula, there is a large colony of sea lions visible from the cliffs, but the better sites are farther north. At most sites, it is foolish to attempt to descend the precipitous, unconsolidated cliffs to get close to the animals. Male sea lions, in addition, are quick, aggressive and dangerous.

Caleta Valdés, on the eastern shore, is a sheltered bay with a long gravel spit onto which elephant seals haul up in the spring. They are easily photographed, but should not be approached too closely. Guanaco sometimes stroll across the beach. Between Caleta Valdés and Punta Norte, there is a substantial colony of burrowing Magellanic penguins. At Punta Norte itself is an enormous mixed colony of sea lions and elephant seals, with clearly marked trails and fences to discourage either side from too close an encounter.

Places to Stay & Eat

Accommodation in Puerto Pirámide is limited but good, and people are very friendly. Since the only street parallels the beach, all hotels have good beach access. Change money in Puerto Madryn or Trelew.

There is basic but acceptable lodging at *Hospedaje Paraíso*; for US$6 per person, you get clean rooms and toilets, with hot showers. Another good-value place is *Hospedaje Torino* (☎ 71001) with doubles for US$12. It has a video-bar, and a shop with film and regional handicrafts. *El Libanés* (☎ 72041) has modest rooms for US$23 double with bath, and a small confitería that serves a reasonable breakfast. *The Paradise*, a very casual, friendly place whose owner speaks fluent English, serves sandwiches and a broad selection of pizzas. The most expensive accommodation is the *Hostería ACA* (☎ 72057), with doubles for US$30 and a costly restaurant.

Sites at Puerto Pirámide's municipal campground, though not well marked, are protected from the wind by dunes and trees. In summer, the place gets very crowded and somewhat noisy, but a persistent search will reward you with a quiet site. It has clean toilets, hot showers and a store with groceries and cold beer, mineral water and soft drinks. Prices are US$5 for a tent and car, US$2.50 for tent only, and US$0.80 for showers. Because of extreme water shortages, showers are carefully timed.

Outside Puerto Pirámide, camping is actively discouraged on the peninsula, although controls are irregular. It is nearly impossible at Punta Norte and Punta Delgada.

Getting There & Away

There is a bus that goes Tuesday to Sunday from Puerto Madryn to Puerto Pirámide at 8.55 am and returns at 7 pm. The fare is about US$5. Taking one of the tours from Puerto Madryn, you can be dropped off there and return at your leisure on another day for no additional charge.

Getting Around

Hitchhiking in Península Valdés is nearly impossible, so to visit sites any distance from Puerto Pirámide, the alternatives are renting a car or taking an organised tour. Since the latter tend to stay only briefly at each point, it is best to drive on your own. Most travel agencies in Puerto Madryn organise day trips for about US$20.

TRELEW

Founded in 1886 as a railway junction to unite the Chubut valley and the beaches of the Golfo Nuevo, Trelew takes its Welsh name from Lewis Jones, who promoted expansion of the railway – *tre* means Town, while 'Lew' was short for Lewis. Its first Eisteddfod (a poetry and music competition still held the third Saturday of October) took place in 1890, when the population did not exceed 80.

During the next 25 years, though, important changes occurred as the railway reached Gaiman, the Welsh built the Salón San David, and Italian immigrants constructed the Teatro Verdi. By 1915 the population reached 4400, but it stabilised at this level until 1956, when government customs preferences in Patagonia promoted industrial development. Trelew became very attractive to immigrants from all over the country and, by 1970, its population had risen to 24,000.

In the early 1970s, Trelew became notorious for the massacre of political prisoners who escaped the local prison and held the airport for some hours. The 1980s witnessed another wave of immigration for which city planners were unprepared – towards the end of the decade, Trelew's population had reached 90,000, but after 1989 the abandon-

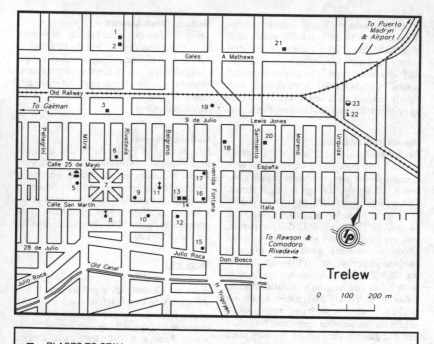

ment of industrial promotion policies caused many people to leave the area.

Orientation
Trelew is 65 km south of Puerto Madryn along Ruta 3, in the valley of the Río Chubut. The centre of town is Plaza Independencia.

Most of the main sights are on Calles 25 de Mayo and San Martín, at the north and south ends of the Plaza, and along Avenida Fontana, two blocks east.

Information
Tourist Office The main tourist office

(☎ 33112), at the bus terminal, has a good map, brochures with recommended short tours, and two very good publications in Spanish on Chubut province. There are also information booths at the airport, and at Salón San David, Calle San Martín at Belgrano.

Money Banks in Trelew are open from 7.30 am to 12.30 pm. Banco de la Nación is at Avenida Fontana and Calle 25 de Mayo, Banco de la Provincia del Chubut at Rivadavia and Calle 25 de Mayo, and Banco del Sud at 9 de Julio 320. It is more efficient to change money at the travel agencies like Sur Turismo (☎ 34550), Belgrano 326, which also changes travellers' cheques, or at Supermercado La Anónima, Calle 25 de Mayo and Belgrano, or H Yrigoyen 1650.

Post & Telecommunications ENCOTEL is at Calle 25 de Mayo and Mitre, while Telefónica is at the corner of Julio Roca and Avenida Fontana.

Travel Agencies Local agencies organise tours to Península Valdés and penguin reserves at Punta Tombo. These include Sur Turismo, Belgrano 326; Península Valdés Turismo (☎ 33898), Belgrano 291; Punta Tombo Turismo (☎ 30658), Calle San Martín 150; Turismo Trelew (☎ 30598), Pasaje Santa Cruz 439; and Estrella del Sur Turismo (☎ 31282), Calle San Martín 129.

Walking Tour
Museum guides lead an organised walking historical tour of the city. You can register for it at the tourist office or directly at the museum, where the tour starts. There is a nominal fee.

The visit includes the **Regional Historical Museum** at the ex-railway station; the **Banco de la Nación**, the town's first bank; the **Salón San David**, a community centre where the Eisteddfod often takes place; the 1889 **Capilla Tabernacl**, the oldest building in town, which has Welsh mass on alternate Sundays; the **Teatro Verdi**, inaugurated by the Italian community in 1914; the **Munici-**

palidad; Plaza Independencia, with its Victorian kiosk; the **Distrito Militar**, which housed Trelew's first school; and the **Teatro Español**, built by turn-of-the-century Spanish immigrants.

Museo Regional
Located in the former railway station at Avenida Fontana and 9 de Julio, this museum is open from 8.30 am to 12.30 pm and from 4 to 8 pm. Displays include Welsh and indigenous history, as well as Patagonian flora and fauna.

Museo Paleontológico
The display of fossils and geologic samples is superb at this new museum at 9 de Julio 631, open daily from 4 to 11 pm. Entrance fee is US$2 for adults and US$0.80 for children under 12 years old.

Places to Stay – bottom end
Camping The only campground, with basic facilities, belongs to Club Huracán and is on Ruta 25 between the bridge and the traffic circle towards Comodoro Rivadavia.

Residenciales & Hotels *Hostal Avenida* (☎ 34172), Lewis Jones 49, is friendly, quiet, and very close to the bus terminal. It has singles/doubles for US$10/12 without bath, with an inexpensive breakfast. *Residencial San Carlos* (☎ 31538), Sarmiento 758, has small but clean rooms at US$12/14 with bath. Residencial Rivadavia (☎ 34472), at Rivadavia 55, is good value and has modest rooms with bath for US$10/14. Others in this range include *Residencial Sarmiento* (☎ 31228) at Sarmiento 264, *Hotel Esquel* (☎ 33619) at Rondeau and Belgrano, and *Hotel El Provinciano* (☎ 35544) at H Yrigoyen 625, which also has a small restaurant.

Hotel Touring Club (☎ 33998) at Avenida Fontana 240 has the atmosphere of a classic hotel from the silent film era, with rooms at US$11/18 and a confitería which is a must for coffee or midmorning aperitif.

Places to Stay – middle

Hotel Cheltum (☎ 31384) at H Yrigoyen 1485 has rooms with bath for US$21/32. *Hotel Galicia* (☎ 33803), 9 de Julio 214, has nice rooms for US$17/26 without bath. At *Hotel Amancay* (☎ 31662), Paraguay 953, some distance from the centre, rooms are US$16/22. *City Hotel* (☎ 35050), Rivadavia 254, and *Parque Hotel* (☎ 30098), at H Yrigoyen and Cangallo on the outskirts of town, have similar prices.

Places to Stay – top end

There are very few hotels in this category. The most expensive, and no doubt most luxurious hotel in town, is *Hotel Rayentray* (☎ 34702) at Calle San Martín and Belgrano; it has a good restaurant, swimming pools, gym, and sauna. Rooms are US$64/75. Nearby, the much cheaper *Hotel Centenario* (☎ 36241) at San Martín 150, which costs about US$31/40, also has a good restaurant. Try also *Hotel Libertador* (☎ 35132), at Rivadavia 73, which has a restaurant and a bar/confitería.

Places to Eat

Trelew has a good selection of restaurants. *Eulogia Fuentes*, at Don Bosco 23, has good food at moderate prices. *La Cantina*, at Calle 25 de Mayo and A P Bell, has good pasta and parrillada. *Capítulo II*, at Julio Roca 393, is inexpensive and has a good salad bar. *Restaurant Valentino*, at A P Bell 434, offers wild game and other unusual foods as well as Italian cuisine. The most inexpensive restaurants are *El Reloj* at Calle San Martín 60, and *La Ley* at Calle 25 de Mayo 128. The *Comedor Universitario*, at Fontana and 9 de Julio, offers cheap, wholesome meals.

One of the special attractions of the area are the *casas de té*, or Welsh tea houses. Trelew's only tea house, which is highly recommended, is *Roger's Shop*, Moreno 463. They serve Welsh tea with great cakes from 5 to 7 pm, and also sell whole cakes. English, Welsh and Spanish are spoken.

Things to Buy

The area's most famous product is the Welsh fruitcake. Some of the stores that sell them are Torta Típica Galesa at A P Bell 315, La Tienda del Sol at Pasaje La Rioja, and Ñuque Mapu at the bus terminal. For beautiful leather goods, horse gear and woollens, try Jagüel at Belgrano and Estados Unidos.

Getting There & Away

Air Trelew's modern airport (☎ 33746) is on Ruta 3, five km from town. Aerolíneas Argentinas (☎ 35297, or 30016 at the airport) has an office at Calle 25 de Mayo 33. It flies daily from Buenos Aires to Ushuaia with stops at Trelew and Comodoro Rivadavia.

Austral (☎ 35603, or 32257 at the airport), at 25 de Mayo 259, flies to Buenos Aires daily and to Comodoro Rivadavia daily except Sunday. LADE (☎ 35244), at Avenida Fontana 227, flies daily to Río Gallegos, and twice weekly to Esquel and Bariloche. Fares to Buenos Aires are about US$150.

Bus The bus terminal (☎ 31765) is at Urquiza and Lewis Jones. Empresa 28 de Julio has hourly buses to Puerto Madryn, Monday to Saturday, and eleven buses per day on Sundays and holidays. It also has frequent service to Gaiman and Dolavon.

Empresa Mar y Valle has buses to Puerto Pirámide on Tuesday, Thursday, Saturday and Sunday. Buses leave Trelew at 7.45 am and return from Puerto Pirámide at 6.30 pm. Empresas Rawson and 28 de Julio have buses to Rawson every 15 minutes, starting at 5.30 am.

Empresa Andesmar (☎ 33535) goes daily to Mendoza and to Caleta Olivia, and to Río Gallegos on Tuesday evenings.

Empresa TUP (☎ 31343) travels to Córdoba three afternoons a week, and to Camarones and Comodoro Rivadavia three mornings a week.

Empresa El Cóndor/La Puntual (☎ 33748) has two daily buses to Buenos Aires, and four weekly to Bahía Blanca via Viedma and Carmen de Patagones.·

Transportadora Patagónica (☎ 32428) has two buses a week to Mar del Plata.

Empresa Don Otto (☎ 32434) has a daily direct bus to Buenos Aires, two to Comodoro Rivadavia (four hours, US$22), and one to Rio Gallegos (nine hours, US$34). There are also three buses weekly to Puerto Deseado, two to Esquel, and five to Neuquén.

Fares to Buenos Aires are US$60.

Car Rental There are several car rental agencies in Trelew: National Car Rental (☎ 35238) at Calle San Martín 125; Alquilauto Fiorasi (☎ 35344) at España 344; VIP Car (☎ 35251), at A P Bell 250, which is about 20% cheaper than the others but still no bargain at about US$60 plus US$0.55 per km; and Rent a Car (☎ 30098) at Calle San Martín 90.

GAIMAN

Gaiman, 17 km west of Trelew, is one of the few demonstrably Welsh towns remaining in Patagonia, although its owes its name (Stony Point) to the Tehuelche Indians who used to winter in the area. The oldest municipality of Chubut province, its population is about 5000.

Welsh presence here dates from 1874. Later immigrants, including Creoles, Germans and Anglos, also cultivated fruit, vegetables and fodder in the lower Chubut valley. Industry followed later, including Argentina's only seaweed processing plant, a nylon stockings factory, and a polyethylene packaging factory.

Things to See & Do

Welsh culture is still evident in the stone architecture along Avenida Eugenio Tello, as well as in local customs. There are numerous tea houses, offering a variety of home-made cakes and sweets, and the **Eisteddfod**, with choir singing and poetry competitions, which still takes place regularly.

Churches and chapels of many denominations persist. The secondary school, **Camwy**, dates from 1899; while the **cemetery**, at the entrance of town, has many gravestones with Welsh inscriptions. The old train station, at the corner of Sarmiento and 28 de Julio, houses the **Museo Histórico Regional de Gaiman**, an excellent small museum attended by Welsh and English-speaking volunteers, with an interesting collection of photographs and household items from the pioneers. Entrance costs US$0.50.

Nearby, at the town's entrance is the **Túnel del Ferrocarril** (railway tunnel), through which the first trains passed; from its top there is a good view of the valley and town.

One of the most interesting sights in Patagonia, or anywhere in conformist Argentina, is **Parque El Desafío**. Lonely Planet reader Paul Bruthiaux describes it as:

Gaiman's answer to Disneyland. It's a wonderful, wild, wacky miniature theme park built by local political protestor and conservationist Joaquín Alonso, exclusively from bits of string, bottles, cans, and other junk long before the rest of the world knew the meaning of recycling. Admission is $4 for 'functionaries of the state, lawmakers, and politicians', $0.40 for you and me.

Places to Stay

There is one small residencial which is only rarely open. Otherwise the only alternative is camping. The small riverside municipal campground, on H Yrigoyen between Libertad and Independencia, is inaccessible when it rains.

Places to Eat

One cannot leave Gaiman without visiting one of the local Welsh tea houses, with their abundant home-baked sweets. Most open by 3 pm, so make sure you have only a light lunch. Try *Ty Gwyn* at 9 de Julio 147; *Casa de Té Gaiman,* at H Yrigoyen between Sarmiento and San Martín; or *Elma* at Avenida Eugenio Tello 571. Tourist buses stop at *Ty Nain*, H Yrigoyen 283, a beautiful house.

The oldest is *Plas y Coed*, at Miguel D Jones 123, run by Marta Rees, the original owner's daughter-in-law and a charming and wonderful cook, who speaks English. She personally makes sure that every client is satisfied, even offering a doggy bag to those who can't finish the spread.

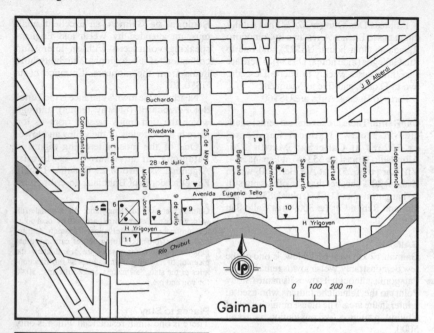

Gaiman

Getting There & Away

Empresa 28 de Julio has several buses a day from Trelew via Gaiman to Dolavon. The return fare to Gaiman is US$2.50.

DOLAVON

Provincial Ruta 7, a good gravel road, leads 35 km west from Trelew to this historic Welsh agricultural town, whose name means River Meadow. The 1920s flour mill, today a museum, still has a functioning water wheel. It has a good campsite. There is one hotel, the *Hotel Pierse* (☎ 92013), at 28 de Julio 45, and a tea house. Empresa 28 de Julio runs 10 buses daily to Dolavon, via Gaiman, from the Trelew bus terminal.

RAWSON

Named for the Argentine minister who granted the Welsh refuge, Rawson (population 30,000), has always been a politically important town, with many influential residents. Territorial capital since 1884, Rawson became provincial capital three years after Chubut attained provincial status in 1955.

Since 1923 its beach, Playa Unión, has been a favourite holiday destination. The modern civic centre contains all government offices, but Trelew is far more important commercially.

Orientation

Rawson is 20 km east of Trelew, on the Río Chubut. Fishers return every afternoon to nearby Puerto Rawson, at the mouth of the river, where you can taste the catch at the cantinas near the pier, or at Playa Unión. Playa Unión has no hotels, but can be crowded with local tourists (mostly from the valleys) who keep summer houses at the beach. Camping is permitted.

Information

Tourist office The tourist office (☎ 81113) is at the corner of Avenida San Martín and Don Bosco. The staff are friendly but have no brochures or maps.

Money Banco de la Nación is at the corner of Avenida San Martín and 25 de Mayo; Banco de la Provincia del Chubut is at Rivadavia 615. Travel agencies Turismo Rawson, Moreno 810, and Gallatts Turismo, at Moreno 719, also change money.

Things to See

The chapel of **Capilla María Auxiliadora**, with interesting architecture and fine murals, has very limited opening hours. So does the **Museo Regional Salesiano**, located in the Colegio Don Bosco. It has an important collection of weapons used in the Conquista del Desierto, as well as fossils, minerals, and artefacts from the province. It opens Tuesday and Friday from 10 am to noon, and Monday, Wednesday and Thursday from 5 to 8 pm.

Places to Stay & Eat

There are two hospedajes, both modest in price and appearance. The cheaper one, *Hospedaje San Pedro,* at Belgrano 744, has singles/doubles for US$10/18 with shared bath. *Hospedaje Papaiani*, at A Maíz 377, has rooms for US$12/16 with shared bath.

Hotel Provincial (☎ (81300), frequented by visiting politicians, is at Mitre 551. It has rooms for US$15/21 with bath, and also

some triples. Its restaurant and confitería are also very good.

At Playa Unión, the cantinas *El Marinero* and *Gallisky* offer a variety of fish and shellfish.

Getting There & Away

Rawson has no central bus terminal. Empresas Rawson and 28 de Julio run buses from Trelew every 15 minutes Monday to Friday, every half-hour on Saturdays and hourly on Sundays and holidays. Buses run from 6 am to 1 am. Empresa Bahía connects downtown Rawson, Puerto Rawson and Playa Unión.

RESERVA PROVINCIAL PUNTA TOMBO

Punta Tombo is on the Atlantic coast, 110 km south of Trelew. Half a million Magellanic penguins breed here, the largest penguin nesting ground in continental South America. There are many other species of seabirds and shorebirds, most notably king and rock cormorants, giant petrels, kelp gulls, flightless steamer ducks, and black oystercatchers.

There is a US$3 entry fee per person. Early morning visits beat the numerous tourist buses from Trelew, but camping is forbidden. Most of the nesting area is fenced off; this does not prevent your approaching the birds for photography, but remember that penguins can inflict a bite serious enough to require stitches. They remain on land from September to April.

There are three ways of getting there: by arranging a tour with a travel agency in Trelew (about US$15), hiring a taxi, or renting a car, which permits you to remain as long as you wish. The gravel road from Trelew to the reserve, via Rawson, is in very good condition. Alternative routes are poorly marked and hard on vehicles. If you have a car, you can proceed south to Camarones (see below) via the scenic but desolate Cabo Raso.

CAMARONES

From Ruta 3, about 180 km south of Trelew, newly paved provincial Ruta 30 leads 72 km to this small, dilapidated but somehow charming fishing port. A weekend here is certain to be a quiet one. Motorists should know that the town's only petrol station rarely has fuel. Juan Perón's father operated an sheep estancia in this area, and the town figures, perhaps apocryphally, in Tomás Eloy Martínez's *The Perón Novel.* There is a **Fiesta Nacional del Salmón** (National Salmon Festival) every year.

Places to Stay & Eat
The municipal campground near the naval prefecture, open all year, charges US$0.60 per person and per tent.

Hotel Kau-i-keukenk is acceptable lodging at US$6 per person, but its restaurant deserves special mention. The friendly owner serves outstanding grilled salmon, cooked to order, exquisite escabeche de mariscos (marinated shellfish), and home-made flan at reasonable prices.

Getting There & Away
Mondays and Fridays, Empresa Don Otto leaves Trelew for Camarones at 8 am, returning the same day at 4 pm. The trip lasts 3½ hours and costs US$9 single. At 10 pm, a Don Otto bus stops at the service station on the junction with Ruta 3, where you can make connections south.

AROUND CAMARONES
Cabo Dos Bahías
This nature reserve, 30 km from town, offers a wide selection of Patagonian maritime and terrestrial wildlife, including penguins, other seabirds, sea lions, fur seals, rheas and foxes. Camping is possible at beaches en route and at the reserve itself. If you have no car, you may be able to hire a taxi in Camarones.

Cabo Raso
Just a few families eke out a bleak existence at this virtual ghost town, about 85 km north of Camarones, on the road to Punta Tombo. Camping is possible in the ruins near the shingle beach, where elephant seals sometimes haul ashore.

COMODORO RIVADAVIA
The southernmost city in Chubut, Comodoro Rivadavia is the centre of the Argentine oil industry. Storage tanks and pipelines are everywhere, while seismic survey lines crisscross the desert landscape. However, the Atlantic beaches and headlands are starkly scenic. Ruta 3 connects the city with Buenos Aires to the north and Río Gallegos to the south.

Founded in 1901, Comodoro (as it is commonly known) boomed a few years later when workers drilling for water made the first major petroleum strike in the country. Although foreign companies played a significant minority role in early Argentine oil development, the state soon dominated the sector through Yacimientos Petrolíferos Fiscales (YPF), 'the first vertically integrated state petroleum industry outside the Soviet Union', according to historian David Rock. Argentina is self-sufficient in petroleum, about a third of its production coming from this area.

While not a major tourist destination in its own right, Comodoro is a frequent stopover for southbound travellers. YPF has spared no expense on the new petroleum museum, one of the best of its kind in the world, which no visitor passing through town should miss.

Orientation
Most of central Comodoro sits on a narrow wave-cut platform, behind which hills rise steeply. Cerro Chenque, just north of the city centre, is a stiff climb which rewards the effort with outstanding views.

Unlike most Argentine cities, Comodoro Rivadavia has no central plaza around which major public buildings cluster. The principal commercial street is Avenida San Martín, which trends east-west below Cerro Chenque. With the north-south Avenida Alsina and the Atlantic shoreline, San Martín forms a triangle which defines the city centre.

Information
Tourist Office In 1991, the tourist office lost its office space at the bus terminal. Inquire

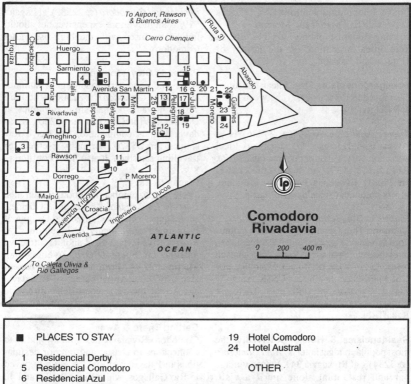

To Airport, Rawson & Buenos Aires

(Ruta 3)

Cerro Chenque

Comodoro
Rivadavia

ATLANTIC
OCEAN

0   200   400 m

To Caleta Olivia &
Río Gallegos

■	PLACES TO STAY	19	Hotel Comodoro
		24	Hotel Austral
1	Residencial Derby		
5	Residencial Comodoro		OTHER
6	Residencial Azul		
8	Residencial Chubut	2	Museo Regional
9	Hotel Sevilla/	3	Telefónica
	Residencial Paena	4	Banco de la Provincia
10	Hospedaje Belgrano		del Chubut
11	Residencial Venus	7	Chilean Consulate
12	Bus Terminal	18	LADE
13	Hotel Italiano	20	Austral
14	Aerolíneas Argentinas	21	Post Office
15	Hotel Español	22	Banco de la
16	Hotel Colón		Nación
17	Hotel Comercio	23	Municipalidad

instead at the Municipalidad, at Moreno and Rivadavia. Large hotels, such as Hotel Austral at Rivadavia 190, have maps and brochures. ACA (☎ 24036) has excellent maps and information at its office, on Dorrego at Alvear.

Money The principal banks are Banco de la Nación, at Avenida San Martín 102, and Banco de la Provincia del Chubut, at Avenida San Martín and España. Travel agencies along Avenida San Martín will also change cash.

Post & Telecommunications ENCOTEL is at Avenida San Martín and Moreno.

Long-distance phone services are at Telefónica Argentina, on the corner of Urquiza and Rawson.

Foreign Consulates The Chilean consulate has moved to Rivadavia 671, between Mitre and Belgrano.

Travel Agencies ACA (☎ 24036) is at Alvear and Dorrego. For visits to local attractions, try Turismo Puelche (☎ 23012), Rivadavia 439, or Roqueta Travel (☎ 26081), Rivadavia 396. There are many others on or near Avenida San Martín.

Places to Stay – bottom end
Camping There is no campground in Comodoro Rivadavia proper, but ACA has taken over the municipal site at Rada Tilly, a beach resort 15 km south on Ruta 3. Members pay US$4 per site, nonmembers US$8. After the first day, charges are US$1 less. There are frequent local buses between Comodoro and Rada Tilly.

Residenciales & Hotels Deservedly, the most popular budget hotel is *Hotel Comercio* (☎ 32341), at Rivadavia 341, whose vintage bar and restaurant alone merit a visit. Singles/doubles with shared bath are US$6/9, rooms with private bath slightly higher. At *Hotel Italiano*, across from the bus terminal at Rivadavia 481, singles with shared bath are US$7.

Other hotels in this category include *Residencial Chubut* (☎ 28777), Belgrano 738 between Rivadavia and Ameghino; *Hotel Sevilla* and *Residencial Paena*, both around the corner on Ameghino; *Residencial Venus*, on Rawson near Belgrano; *Hotel Colón* (☎ 22283), Avenida San Martín 341 at 9 de Julio; the quiet *Hospedaje Belgrano*, Belgrano 546 at Dorrego; and *Hotel Español*, 9 de Julio near Sarmiento.

Places to Stay – middle
Residencial Azul (☎ 24874), Sarmiento 724 near España, charges US$15/20 with bath.

Residencial Comodoro (☎ 22582), at España 919, is slightly more expensive, but should not be confused with the high-rise Hotel Comodoro.

Places to Stay – top end
After undergoing remodelling in summer 1991, *Hotel Comodoro* (☎ 32300), 9 de Julio 770 at Rivadavia, has singles/doubles at US$32/45. *Hotel Austral* (☎ 32200), Rivadavia 190, is comparable, but has a few singles for US$20, normally reserved for travelling salesmen. It also has a confitería.

Places to Eat
There are a number of good restaurants. *Parrilla La Cabaña*, Rivadavia at Güemes, serves superb bife de chorizo and lasagna. It is jammed with locals at lunchtime. *La Rastra*, Rivadavia 348, is another attractive parrilla. *La Fonte D'Oro*, Avenida San Martín at 25 de Mayo, is a good but expensive confitería. At the corner of Rivadavia and Alvear, there is a superb deli with a wide variety of exquisite empanadas for takeaway.

Getting There & Away
Comodoro Rivadavia has both air and road connections to coastal and interior destinations in Patagonia. Ruta 3 is entirely paved to Río Gallegos, while Rutas 26, 20 and 40 are paved to Esquel, the Andean foothill gateway to Parque Nacional Los Alerces.

Air Aerolíneas Argentinas (☎ 22294) is at Avenida San Martín 421. Daily except Sunday, it has morning nonstops to Buenos Aires, while Thursday, Friday and Sunday it has evening nonstops to the capital. Austral (☎ 22191) is at Avenida San Martín 291. It has two daily flights to Buenos Aires except Sunday, when there is only one. All stop in Trelew, Bahía Blanca or Mar del Plata. Southbound Austral flights continue to Río Gallegos, Río Grande and Ushuaia.

LADE, on Rivadavia between Pellegrini and 9 de Julio, has Monday flights to and from Río Gallegos (US$40) via Perito Moreno and Gobernador Gregores. There are also Monday flights to Gallegos via

Puerto Deseado, San Julián and Puerto Santa Cruz. On Wednesdays, it serves Bariloche (US$55) via Esquel (US$30) and El Maitén, and continues to Chapelco (San Martín de los Andes), Zapala and Cutralcó. Friday services to Bariloche stop at Trelew, Viedma and Neuquén.

Bus La Puntual has daily buses to Buenos Aires (US$60) via Viedma (US$30) and Bahía Blanca (US$35). The trip to Buenos Aires takes 24 hours.

Empresa Don Otto has almost identical service to Buenos Aires, but also goes daily to Río Gallegos (US$20), and Tuesday and Sunday evenings to Bariloche (US$35) via Gobernador Costa and Esquel.

Angel Giobbi SA departs at 1 am Monday, Wednesday and Friday for Río Mayo (US$13), with connections to Coyhaique, Chile. These buses are often very full.

If hitching south, take a local bus to the Astra service station on the outskirts of Comodoro. It is worth asking long-distance truckers for a lift.

Car Rental Rental cars are available at National (☎ 32300), 9 de Julio 770.

Getting Around
The bus terminal is at Pellegrini and 25 de Mayo. Comodoro Rivadavia airport is north of the city, but the No 9 bus goes there directly from the centre. LADE flights are frequently overbooked, but you stand a good chance of getting on at the airport itself.

AROUND COMODORO RIVADAVIA
Museo del Petróleo
Perhaps the best museum in all of Argentina, and one of the best of its kind in the world, this alone justifies a stopover in Comodoro. YPF, the state oil agency, has organised exceptionally vivid exhibits on the region's natural and cultural history, early and modern oil technology, and social and historical aspects of petroleum development. Historical photographs are especially outstanding, but there are also fascinating,

detailed models of tankers, refineries, and the entire zone of exploitation.

The grounds include the site of the original gusher and an excellent display of restored antique drilling equipment and vehicles. The adjacent video salon offers an impressive slide show, marred only slightly by its bombastic taped narration.

Actually located in the smaller town of General Mosconi (named for the first administrator of YPF), a few kilometres north of Comodoro, the museum is on Lavalle between Viedma and Carlos Calvo. From downtown Comodoro, either the No 7 or 8 bus will take you there.

Admission is free. Between April and November, it is open Tuesday to Friday, 9 am to noon and 2 to 6 pm, weekends 3 to 9 pm. Between December and March, hours are Tuesday to Sunday, 5 to 9 pm.

Astra Museum
About 15 km north of Comodoro on Ruta 3, this is an open-air display of early oil-drilling equipment, with a small but impressive semisubterranean exhibit on Patagonian paleontology and minerals. Admission is free, but the mineral exhibit has very limited opening hours: Wednesday from 2 to 4 pm, and weekends from 2 to 5 pm.

Petrified Forests
South of Colonia Sarmiento, an agricultural town 148 km west of Comodoro, are two petrified forests more accessible than Monumento Natural Bosques Petrificados (see Santa Cruz province below). From Sarmiento, which is easily reached by bus, it is possible to arrange a car and driver to the Ormachea (30 km) and Szlapelis (20 km farther) reserves. Travel agencies in Comodoro may offer occasional tours or suggestions.

RÍO MAYO
At this dusty western crossroads, 274 paved km from Comodoro Rivadavia, highways head south to Perito Moreno and Los Antíguos, north to Esquel, El Bolsón and Bariloche, and west to Coyhaique, Chile. At

the entrance to the army base, an enormous signboard declares the Argentine military's determination to retake the Falkland/Malvinas Islands by force. Only gauchos and conscripts are likely to spend more than a night here.

If necessary, you should be able to change cash dollars at Banco de la Provincia del Chubut.

Things to See & Do
The small **Museo Regional**, Yrigoyen 552 at Belgrano, has exhibits on local ethnology (including a full Tehuelche Indian skeleton) and history. It's open Tuesday to Saturday, 10 am to noon and 3 to 7 pm. In the spring, the **Festival Nacional de la Esquila** features sheep-shearing competitions.

Places to Stay & Eat
Río Mayo has plenty of reasonable accommodation. *Hotel San Martín*, 693 Perito Moreno at San Martín, charges US$4 per person with shared bath, and also has a restaurant/bar with takeaway food. *Hotel El Pingüino*, San Martín 640, charges US$6 for a single with private bath. At *Hotel Covadonga*, San Martín 573, singles with bath are US$7. It also has a restaurant, and a classic Old West bar.

Getting There & Away
There are three buses weekly to and from Comodoro Rivadavia (see the section above); these continue to Coyhaique, Chile, but are often very full. Mondays and Thursdays at 6 am, Angel Giobbi SA covers the 350 km to Esquel via Gobernador Costa for US$23. There is no public transportation southwards toward Perito Moreno and Los Antíguos, but patience may get you a lift.

GOBERNADOR COSTA
This cattle town, midway between Río Mayo and Esquel, and also on the route between Esquel and Comodoro Rivadavia, has good travellers' services. Both *Hotel Jair* and *Hotel Vega* have singles for US$7 with bath, as well as restaurants. There is also a free municipal campground. Banco de la Pro-

vincia del Chubut will change cash dollars. On February 28, the town celebrates its annual festival, the **Día del Pueblo**.

Twenty km west of town, a provincial highway leads to Lago General Vintter, in a less frequented part of the Argentine Lake District, and several smaller lakes near the Chilean border. There is good trout and salmon fishing.

Getting There & Away
Provincial bus services are frequent. Empresa Don Otto has five weekly in each direction between Trelew and Esquel, and two in each direction between Comodoro Rivadavia and Bariloche. Angel Giobbi serves Río Mayo (see above) via Río Senguer.

ESQUEL
Of Welsh origins, sunny Esquel (population 20,000) is the commercial and livestock centre of the Andean foothills of western Chubut. It is also the terminus for the picturesque narrow-gauge railway from Ingeniero Jacobacci in Río Negro province, and the gateway to Parque Nacional Los Alerces and other mountain recreation areas.

Orientation
Situated on the north shore of Arroyo Esquel, the town has a fairly standard grid pattern. Provincial Ruta 259 zigzags through town to a junction with Ruta 40, which heads north to El Bolsón and Bariloche, and south-east towards Comodoro Rivadavia. South of town, Ruta 259 leads to the Welsh settlement of Trevelin, with junctions to Parque Nacional Los Alerces and other Andean attractions.

Information
Tourist Office Esquel's well-organised tourist office (☎ 2369) is at the bus terminal, on the corner of Fontana and Alvear. It has a complete list of local hotels (with current prices), campgrounds, private houses, camping and lodging in Parque Nacional Los Alerces, travel agencies and tours, transportation and recreation.

Money There are no cambios, but it is easy to change money at Banco de la Nación, Alvear and Roca; Banco de la Provincia del Chubut, at Alvear 1131 or Banco del Sud, 25 de Mayo 758 between Alvear and 9 de Julio. Banco de la Nación changes Amex travellers' cheques only; other banks change only US dollars cash.

Outside banking hours, travel agencies or many shops, such as the ice-creamery on Alvear near Sarmiento, will help out at reasonable rates.

Post & Telecommunications The post office across the street from the tourist office, at Alvear 1192. Telefónica is at San Martín 850, between Belgrano and Roca.

Foreign Consulates There is a Chilean consulate at 25 de Mayo 726, just off Alvear.

Travel Agencies ACA is at 25 de Mayo and Ameghino.

There are several agencies, including Esquel Tours, Fontana 754, and Carlos Paz, at the bus terminal. If you plan to take the Circuito Lacustre boat excursion in Parque Nacional Los Alerces, buying a ticket in Esquel will assure you a place on this often crowded trip.

Medical Services The local hospital (☎ 2414) is at 25 de Mayo 150.

Things to See

Most of the area's attractions, most notably Parque Nacional Los Alerces are outside rather than in Esquel. The **Museo Indigenista y de Ciencias Naturales** is at Belgrano 330, between Ameghino and Chacabuco. If you come by air or bus, you should still not miss the arrival of **El Trencito**, the narrow-gauge steam train, although the town of El Maitén, on the border of Río Negro province, will be more interesting to railroad fanatics.

Organised Tours

Travel agencies run many excursions. The full-day trip to Parque Nacional Los Alerces includes the lake cruise described in the section on the park, below. There are also full-day trips to Futaleufú in Chile, Cholila and Lago Rivadavia, and El Bolsón and Lago Puelo.

Half-day trips include the La Hoya winter sports complex, Trevelin and the Futaleufú hydroelectric complex, a city tour, and Corcovado and Lago Rosario.

Fishing

The fishing season in local lakes and rivers runs from early November to mid-April. Seasonal licences, valid throughout the Patagonian provinces of Chubut, Santa Cruz, Río Negro and Neuquén, and in national parks, cost US$55. Weekly and monthly licences are cheaper. All are available at the Esquel tourist office and at neighbouring municipalities.

Places to Stay – bottom end

Camping Camping is popular and inexpensive in this part of the country. Esquel's *Quimei Mapu* municipal site, five km south of town on the highway to Trevelin, has hot showers, picnic tables, firepits, and electricity. Charges are US$2 per person, plus a one-time charge of US$1 per vehicle. It also contains a hostel, where quadruple rooms with shared bath are US$4 per person.

Casas de Familia The most reasonable places to stay are the casas de familia (family homes), for about US$4 to US$5 per person, some which have private baths. Try Juana Gingins (☎ 2452), Rivadavia 1243; Raquel Alemán de Abraham (☎ 2696), Alberdi 529; *Al Sol* (☎ 3447), Chacabuco 762. Isabel Barutta (who speaks some English) runs the highly recommended *Alojamento Familiar Lago Verde* (☎ 2251), at Volta 1081 near the train station.

Hospedajes, Hosterías & Hotels
Hospedaje Argentino (☎ 2237), 25 de Mayo 862, is the cheapest of the hotels at US$5 per person. *Hospedaje Zacarías* (☎ 2270), General Roca 634, is slightly more expensive. There are many others in this category,

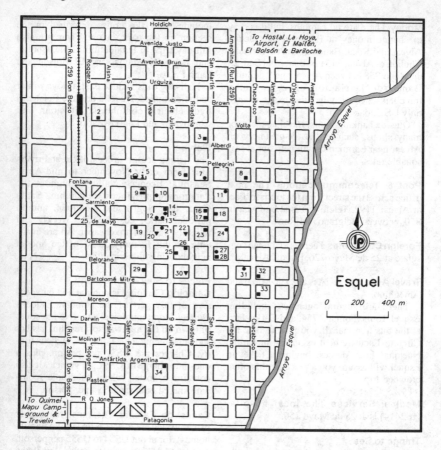

Esquel

0   200   400 m

such as *Hostería Huentru-Niyeu* (☎ 2576) at Chacabuco 606; *Hotel Ski* (☎ 2254), San Martín 96-1967; *Hostería Angelina* (☎ 2763), Alvear 758; *Hotel Los Tulipanes* (☎ 2748), Fontana 365; *Hostería Arrayan* (☎ 2082), Antártida Argentina 767; and *Hotel Huenu* (☎ 2589), San Martín 822.

Places to Stay – middle

The friendly but undistinguished *Hotel Esquel* (☎ 2534), San Martín 1044, charges US$9 per person with private bath. You will find similar quality and prices at *Hotel Maika* (☎ 2457), 25 de Mayo and San Martín, *Hotel*

Huemul (☎ 2149), Alvear and 25 de Mayo, and *Hostal La Hoya* (☎ 2473), on the edge of town at Ameghino 2296.

Places to Stay – top end

At *Hostería La Tour D'Argent* (☎ 2530), San Martín 1063, and at *Hotel Sol del Sur* (☎ 2189, 2427), 9 de Julio 1086, rooms are about US$22 per person. At *Hotel Tehuelche* (☎ 2420/1), at 9 de Julio 825, rates start at US$32 per person.

Places to Eat

Food in Esquel is good but not exceptional.

■ PLACES TO STAY

2	Casa de Familia Barutta
3	Casa de Familia Alemánde Abraham
6	Casa de Familia Gingins
8	Hotel Los Tulipanes
14	Hotel Sol del Sur
16	Hotel Esquel
17	Hotel Maika
18	Hostería La Tour D'Argent
19	Hospedaje Argentino
23	Hotel Ski
25	Hotel Tehuelche
26	Hospedaje Zacarías
28	Hotel Huenú
29	Hostería Angelina
32	Casa de Familia Al Sol
33	Hostería Huentru-Niyeu
34	Hostería Arrayan

▼ PLACES TO EAT

20	Restaurant Jockey Club
22	Restaurant Don Pipo
30	Parrilla Yauqueñ

OTHER

1	Train Station
4	Bus Terminal
5	Tourist Office
7	Mercado Comunitario
9	Post Office
10	Banco de la Provincia del Chubut
11	Aerolíneas Argentinas
12	LADE
13	Chilean Consulate
15	TAN
21	Banco del Sud
24	ACA
27	Telefónica
31	Museo Indigenista y de Ciencias Naturales

Parrilla Yauquén, Rivadavia 740, is a reasonable parrilla, friendly and pleasant, but with erratic service. *Restaurant Jockey Club*, at Alvear 949, is comparable. *Hotel Sol del Sur* (see above) serves a good fixed-price dinner for less than US$5, without drinks. *Restaurant La Vascongada*, 9 de Julio and Mitre, has good food in generous portions and friendly and attentive service.

Don Pipo, at Rivadavia 924, has decent pizza. *Confitería Atelier*, 25 de Mayo and San Martín, has excellent coffee and chocolate, and is open 24 hours. There is a good ice cream shop on Rivadavia, near Fontana.

Things to Buy
La Casona de Olgbrun, San Martín 1137, has attractive but expensive copperwork and other artisanal crafts. The Mercado Comunitario at San Martín and Fontana has an excellent variety of local crafts at more reasonable prices.

Getting There & Away
Air Aerolíneas Argentinas (☎ 3749), at Fontana and Ameghino, flies Mondays, Thursdays, and Saturdays to Buenos Aires (US$214) via Bariloche (US$33), and Tuesdays to Trelew (US$80), with connections to the capital.

LADE (☎ 2227), 25 de Mayo 777, has many flights throughout Patagonia. Its Wednesday Twin Otter flight from Comodoro Rivadavia continues via Esquel to El Maitén (US$12), El Bolsón, Bariloche (US$21), Chapelco/San Martín de los Andes (US$24), and Zapala (US$27). Its Friday flight from Bariloche continues to Comodoro Rivadavia (US$40).

LADE's Monday Fokker F-27 flight from Trelew and Comodoro goes via Esquel to Bariloche (US$12), Neuquén (US$16), and Viedma (US$43). From Bariloche there are connections to Bahía Blanca (US$62), Mar del Plata (US$90), and Buenos Aires (US$100). On Fridays, there is a service to Trelew (US$30) and Comodoro (US$35).

TAN, Transportes Aéreos Neuquén (☎ 2427), 9 de Julio 1086, flies twice weekly to Comodoro Rivadavia and three times weekly to Bariloche and Neuquén, with connections to Mendoza. Fares are rather higher than LADE's.

The airport is 20 km east of town, on Ruta 40. Esquel Tours runs an minibus according to flight schedules.

Bus To Bariloche, Transportes Automotores Mercedes (TAM) runs four buses weekly via El Maitén, two via Cholila, and seven via Parque Nacional Los Alerces. Fares to Bariloche are US$19. Empresa Don Otto's twice-weekly service to Bariloche via Epuyén is rather cheaper. Transportes Esquel has daily return services to Los Alerces.

Don Otto also goes twice weekly to Comodoro Rivadavia for US$20, with connections to Río Gallegos (US$40), and four times weekly to Buenos Aires (US$50) via Trelew and Bahía Blanca. They also serve nearby provincial destinations such as Trevelin, La Balsa, Corcovado and Carrenleufú.

Empresa Chubut has five express buses weekly via Tecka to Trelew; fares are US$16. Empresa Mar y Valle has three weekly via Paso de Indios, with fares slightly higher.

For those unable to get a train ticket, Transportes Jacobsen connects Esquel with Ingeniero Jacobacci via El Maitén Mondays and Wednesdays.

Train The narrow-gauge steam train *El Trencito* of the Ferrocarril General Roca connects Esquel with Buenos Aires, via Ingeniero Jacobacci, on the main line between Bariloche and Constitución. It leaves Esquel Wednesdays and Saturdays at 9.30 am. Primera fares are US$6 to El Maitén, US$10 to Jacobacci, US$28 to Bahía Blanca, and US$40 to Constitución. Turista class is only slightly cheaper, and much less comfortable for long trips. Between Jacobacci and Constitución, there are reclining pullman seats and sleepers.

AROUND ESQUEL
La Hoya
Just 15 km north from Esquel, at an altitude of 1350 metres, this winter sports area is cheaper and less crowded than Bariloche. The ski season is June to October; equipment can be rented on site or in Esquel. There is a regular bus service from town, and several different lifts and runs.

Cholila
Butch Cassidy and the Sundance Kid once ranched near this small town, north of Esquel via Parque Nacional Los Alerces. Bruce Chatwin's *In Patagonia* recounts the story.

TREVELIN
Just 24 km south of Esquel by paved road, historic Trevelin (population 5500) is the only community in the interior of Chubut which retains something of its Welsh character. Its name derives from the Welsh words for town *(tre)* and mill *(velin)*, after its first grain mill, which is now a museum. It is suitable for either an overnight stay or a day-trip from Esquel.

Orientation
For an Argentine city, Trevelin's urban plan is very irregular. Entering on Ruta 259 from Esquel, you arrive at the Plaza Coronel Fontana, off which eight streets radiate like the spokes of a wheel. The principal of these, Avenida San Martín, is the southward extension of Ruta 259, toward Corcovado.

Information
Tourist Office The tourist office (☎ 8120) is directly on the plaza. It's open daily from 8.30 am to 10.30 pm, and is exceptionally helpful. Mapuche Indian weavings are on sale here. Occasionally it will have discount coupons for Welsh tea houses.

Money You can change money at Banco de la Provincia, on the corner of Avenida San Martín and Brown, but do so before noon.

Post Office The post office is on Avenida San Martín, just off the plaza.

Medical Services The hospital is on the corner of San Martín and John Evans.

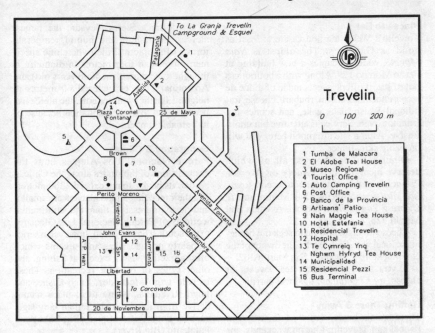

To La Granja Trevelin
Campground & Esquel

Trevelin

0   100   200 m

1 Tumba de Malacara
2 El Adobe Tea House
3 Museo Regional
4 Tourist Office
5 Auto Camping Trevelin
6 Post Office
7 Banco de la Provincia
8 Artisans' Patio
9 Nain Maggie Tea House
10 Hotel Estefania
11 Residencial Trevelin
12 Hospital
13 Te Cymreig Ynq
   Nghwm Hyfryd Tea House
14 Municipalidad
15 Residencial Pezzi
16 Bus Terminal

To Corcovado

Things to See

The **Museo Regional**, in the restored remains of the old grain mill (which was destroyed by fire), is open Tuesday to Sunday, 3 to 7 pm. The **Capilla Bethel** is a Welsh chapel, built in 1910. The monument **Tumba de Malacara** holds the remains of a horse whose bravery enabled its rider, John Evans, to escape a retaliatory raid by Indians who had been attacked by the Argentine army during the Conquista del Desierto.

Places to Stay

Camping The most central is *Auto Camping Trevelin*, the former municipal site, only a block from the plaza. It is not so attractive as some Argentine campgrounds, but the new owners appear committed to improvement. It has hot showers, running water at every site, and the toilet facilities are spotless. Fees are US$2 per person, plus a one-time charge of US$1 per tent.

Three km north, on the road to Esquel, *La Granja Trevelin* has similar camping prices, but also has rooms with all (macrobiotic) meals for US$28 per person. Cabins with six beds rent for US$65 per night. There are also activities such as horseback riding and yoga.

Residenciales & Hotels Trevelin has modest but pleasant accommodation. *Residencial Trevelin* (☎ 8102), Avenida San Martín 327, has singles/doubles with shared bath for US$7/10, slightly higher for rooms with private bath. *Hotel Estefania* (☎ 8148), at Perito Moreno and 13 de Diciembre, has similar prices.

Residencial Pezzi (☎ 8146), Sarmiento 353, is a pleasant, family-run hotel with a large garden, which charges US$12 per person, with dinner for US$5. It is often heavily booked in summer; for reservations, contact Señora Pezzi at the above address or at Beschtedt 666, 8400 Bariloche (☎ 20636), or in Buenos Aires (☎ 432-5542).

Places to Eat

Trevelin's Welsh tea houses are at least as good as Gaiman's. The oldest is *Nain Maggie*, which occupies a new building at Perito Moreno 179. Along with a bottomless pot of tea, it offers sweets made of dulce de leche, chocolate, cream, rhubarb, cheese, traditional Welsh black cake, and scones hot from the oven. Service is attentive but unobtrusive. After a late afternoon here, you will probably skip dinner.

Other local tea houses, all of which deserve mention, are *El Adobe* on Avenida Patagonia at the northern entrance to town, *Las Mutisias* on Avenida San Martín, and *Te Cymreig Yng Nghwm Hyfryd*, Avenida San Martín 328.

Cheese lovers will want to seek out homemade local varieties. Ask for the owner of the clothing store at Avenida San Martín 302.

If you need more than tea, sweets or cheese, try *El Quincho*, the local parrilla.

Getting There & Away

There are six buses each weekday between Esquel and Trevelin, four on weekends, for US$1. There are three weekly to Río Grande, on the Chilean border, and another three to Carrenleufú, another Chilean border crossing. To travel north, you must go to Esquel.

AROUND TREVELIN

On Ruta 259, 17 km from Trevelin, a trail leads to a series of waterfalls known by their Welsh name of **Nant-y-Fall**. There is camping at the **Futaleufú** hydroelectric project, 18 km away, which submerged a chain of lakes in the southern part of Parque Nacional Los Alerces. **Lago Rosario**, 24 km away, has a Mapuche Indian reservation. At Arroyo Baguilt there is an **Estación de Piscicultura** (salmon hatchery), open for visits on weekdays from 7 am to 1 pm.

PARQUE NACIONAL LOS ALERCES

West of Esquel, this 263,000-hectare reserve protects some of the largest remaining forests of the Patagonian cypress *(Fitzroya cupressoides)*, commonly known in Spanish as the *alerce*. Resembling the giant sequoias

of California's Sierra Nevada, the largest alerces flourish in the humid temperate forests of southern Chile (where one specimen more than four metres in diametre is thought to be more than 4000 years old) and Argentina. They can exceed 60 metres in height. Like the giant sequoia, the alerce has been subject to overexploitation because of its valuable timber.

Geography & Climate

Parque Nacional Los Alerces hugs the eastern slope of the Andes along the Chilean border. Its peaks do not exceed 2300 metres, and their receding alpine glaciers are smaller and less impressive than the continental icefields of Parque Nacional Los Glaciares to the south. They have left, however, a series of nearly pristine lakes and streams which offer attractive vistas, excellent fishing, and other types of outdoor recreation. These include Lago Menéndez, Lago Cisne, and Lago Rivadavia. Many local place names derive from the Mapuche Indian language, such as Lago Futalaufquen (Big Lake) and Futaleufú (Big River).

Because the Andes are relatively low here, westerly storms drop nearly three metres of rain annually to support the humid Valdivian forest. The eastern part of the park, though, is much drier. Winter temperatures average 2°C, but can be much colder. The summer mean high reaches 24°C, with cool evenings.

Flora

Although its wild backcountry supports wildlife, Los Alerces exists primarily because of its botanical significance. Besides the alerce, other important coniferous and broadleaf trees, both evergreen and deciduous, characterise the dense, humid Valdivian forest, with its almost impenetrable undergrowth of *chusquea*, a solid rather than hollow bamboo. Conifers include another species of cypress *(Pilgerodendron uviferum)* and the aromatic Chilean incense cedar *(Austrocedrus chilensis)*.

Broadleaf trees include the southern beeches ñire *(Nothofagus antarctica)*, coihue *(Nothofagus dombeyi)* and lenga

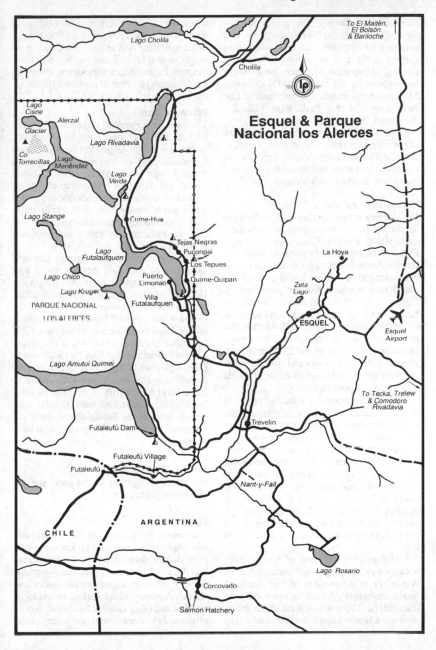

**Esquel & Parque
Nacional los Alerces**

(*Nothofagus pumilio*). The genus *Nothofagus* (false beech) exists only in the southern hemisphere. Another interesting species is the arrayán, whose foliage and peeling, cinnamon-coloured bark bears resemblance to the madrone of California. More extensive stands can be found at Los Arrayanes National Park, near Villa La Angostura, Neuquén province.

For a good display on the natural history of the park, stop at the visitor centre museum at Villa Futalaufquen. It also includes an aquarium, and historical displays and documentation about the park's creation in 1937.

Things to See & Do

Los Alerces is best seen by boat or on foot. Traditionally, the most popular excursion sails from Puerto Limonao up Lago Futalaufquen through the narrow channel of the Río Arrayanes to Lago Verde, but recent dry years and low water levels have eliminated this segment for the time being. Currently, launches from Puerto Chucao, on Lago Menéndez, handle the second segment of the trip to the nature trail to **El Alerzal**, the most accessible stand of alerces. The voyage between Puerto Chucao and El Alerzal lasts about two hours each way and costs US$18; purchase tickets in Esquel to assure yourself a place on this popular trip.

The launch remains there for more than an hour, sufficient time for a deliberate hike around the loop trail which also passes Lago Cisne and an attractive waterfall to end up at **El Abuelo** (The Grandfather), the finest specimen of alerce in the immediate area. Local guides are knowledgeable on forest ecology and conservation, but even if you are fluent in Spanish you may find the group uncomfortably large. If so, you may go ahead or lag behind the group, so long as you get back to the launch in time for the return trip.

Unfortunately, because of fire hazard, backcountry camping is not permitted at El Alerzal or in other parts of Los Alerces' 'zona intangible', which is open only to researchers. There are several more interpretive trails near Lago Futalaufquen for day

hikes, but the only alternative for trekkers is the trail from Lago Krüger up the Río Stange to Lago Chico. Ask at the visitor centre or ranger station for information. You will need to cross Estrecho Los Mónstruos (Strait of the Monsters) by boat to get to the trailhead.

Places to Stay

There are five organised campgrounds in the park, at Los Maitenes, Lago Futalaufquen, Bahía Rosales, Lago Verde and Lago Rivadavia, and an inexpensive refugio at Lago Krüger. Charges are about $2 per person per day, plus a one-time charge of US$1 for car or tent. There are free campsites near some of these paying sites. Park regulations unfortunately permit livestock, so you may be awakened by moos and cowbells rather than bird calls.

Small to medium-sized groups can rent cabins. *Cabañas Los Tepues*, on Lago Futalaufquen, rents three-person cabins for US$30 per day. Nearby *Cabañas Tejas Negras* has five-person cabins for US$105.

There are several hosterías and hotels around Lago Futalaufquen. *Motel Pucón Pai* (☎ 2828) has singles/doubles with private bath and breakfast for US$25/35. *Hostería Quime Quipan* charges US$45 per person, for half-pension, with private bath. *Hostería Cume Hue* (☎ 2858) offers complete pension for US$40 with shared bath, US$50 with private bath. *Hotel Futalaufquen*, the most luxurious, costs US$70 per person with half-pension.

Getting There & Away

For details of getting to the park, see the section on Esquel above.

EL MAITÉN

This small, dusty town, on the border with Río Negro province about 70 km south-east of El Bolsón, deserves a visit if only because it is the service centre for the narrow-gauge railway between Ingeniero Jacobacci and Esquel. A graveyard for antique steam locomotives and other railroad hardware, it is an aficionado's dream and an exceptional subject for photography. The surrounding area is cattle and sheep country.

Every February, the **Fiesta Provincial del Trencito** honours the railroad which put El Maitén on the map and keeps it there. It draws people from all over the province (bring ear plugs should the provincial police band of Rawson do its usual annual performance) and the country. There are excellent local pastries and produce, including homemade jams and jellies, and riding and horse-taming competitions.

The municipal campground, on the river, charges US$2 per person but can get crowded and noisy during the festival. *Hostería La Vasconia*, on the plaza across from the train station, has rooms for US$8 per person, but vacancies are unlikely during the festival.

Getting There & Away

There are regular bus services to El Maitén from Esquel and from El Bolsón.

Santa Cruz Province

Santa Cruz province consists of three distinct zones: the Atlantic coast, the Patagonian *meseta* (steppe) extending several hundred km inland, and the Andean Lake District, famous for its rugged glacial terrain. Río Santa Cruz, born in the Fitzroy range and the glacial troughs of lakes Viedma and Argentina, cuts through the steppe to form a deep, broad and scenic canyon, eventually reaching the sea at Puerto Santa Cruz. Several lesser rivers also originate in the glaciers and lakes of the Andes.

The aboriginal inhabitants of Santa Cruz were the nomadic Tehuelche Indians, hunters of guanaco, rhea and lesser wildlife. The first Europeans to set foot in the province probably came from Magellan's 1520 expedition, which wintered at San Julián and eventually circumnavigated the globe. The arid, windy meseta had little to attract Euro peans, although missionaries began to penetrate the region in the 18th century,

when Spain established a series of outposts, including a whaling station at Puerto Deseado.

Even after Argentine independence, settlement lagged until opportunities in wool attracted British pioneers. Many settlers came from the Falkland Islands, where large grazing units had already occupied all available pastoral land. Many surnames are still common in both the Falklands and Santa Cruz.

Although vast Santa Cruz offered almost unlimited grazing over nearly 250,000 sq km, the human population grew very slowly. In 1895, it barely surpassed a thousand, and in 1914 was still less than 10,000. The earliest towns were small ports such as San Julián, Santa Cruz and Río Gallegos, which transferred the wool clip to ocean-going vessels.

Nowadays, the 7 million-plus sheep in Santa Cruz are still the most conspicuous sector of the economy, but the province has also diversified with coal, oil and tourism. National Ruta 3, the principal north-south highway in Argentina, connects the fast-growing provincial capital of Río Gallegos with Buenos Aires and intermediate destinations. South of the provincial capital, to the Chilean border and Tierra del Fuego, it is unpaved.

For both Argentines and foreigners, Santa Cruz is a popular summertime destination because of Parque Nacional Los Glaciares, which features both the famous Moreno Glacier, one of few in the world which is actually advancing, and the spectacular pinnacles of the Fitzroy range. The coast and steppe, though much less popular, are not uninteresting; it is possible to see both maritime and terrestrial wildlife, and to visit the sheep estancias which made European settlement possible.

RÍO GALLEGOS

On the south bank of its namesake river, near the southern tip of continental Argentina, the provincial capital and port of 100,000 is the country's largest city south of Comodoro Rivadavia. Founded in 1885, it continues its

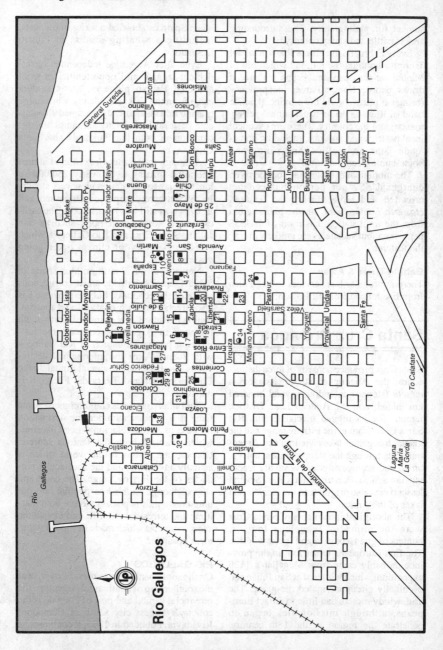

Río Gallegos

Punta Arenas or Tierra del Fuego, but a day spent here need not be a wasted one.

Orientation

Central Río Gallegos has a fairly standard Argentine grid pattern, centered on two major avenues, Avenida Julio Roca and Avenida San Martín, which run at right angles to each other. Most areas frequented by tourists will be found in the south-west quadrant formed by these streets, although the attractive, newly developed riverfront park at the north end of Avenida San Martín deserves a visit. In this area, and along the side streets off Avenida Julio Roca, the sheep estancias and the companies which service them have their business offices.

Information

Tourist Office The energetic tourist office, at Avenida Julio Roca 1551, is open Monday to Friday from 8 am to 7 pm. It has maps and a helpful list of accommodation (omitting the very cheapest and most unsavoury alternatives), transport and excursions. There is also a branch, open on weekends as well, at the bus terminal.

Money Cambio El Pingüino, Zapiola 469, will change cash dollars, travellers' cheques (for a modest commission), and Chilean pesos; but Cambio Sur, near Aerolíneas Argentinas on Avenida San Martín near Avenida Julio Roca, may have significantly better rates, especially when the Argentine currency is unstable. There are several banks nearby.

Post & Telecommunications ENCOTEL occupies an interesting building at the corner of Avenidas Julio Roca and San Martín. Telefónica is at the intersection of Avenida Julio Roca and Chile.

Foreign Consulates The Chilean consulate, at Mariano Moreno 136 between Fagnano and Rivadavia, is open Monday to Friday, 9 am to 2 pm.

Books & Films Bruce Chatwin's literary

tradition of service to the wool industry, but is also an important centre for energy development. The narrow-gauge railway from the coal deposits at Río Turbio, 230 km west near the Chilean border, discharges its cargo to ocean-going vessels here, while the Argentine state oil company operates a refinery with the output from its nearby oilfields. For most travellers, it will only be a stopover en route to Calafate and the Moreno Glacier, travelogue *In Patagonia* vividly retells the story of the Anarchist rebellion of 1921 and subsequent massacre of labourers at Estancia La Anita by the Argentine army. *La Patagonia Rebelde*, a film based on Argentine historian Osvaldo Bayer's account of the period, depicts the Anglo-Argentine wool-growers of Río Gallegos in a very unfavourable light. It sometimes shows at universities in Europe and the United States, and may be available on video.

Museo Provincial Mario Echeverría Baleta

At Perito Moreno 45 near Avenida Julio Roca, this museum has good exhibits on geology, the ethnology of the Tehuelches (with excellent photographs), and local history. One of the grislier exhibits is the skull of a striker shot at Estancia San José, near the Fitzroy section of Parque Nacional Los Glaciares, in 1921. It's open weekdays from 8 am to 7 pm, weekends 3 to 8 pm.

Museo de los Pioneros

In a metal-clad house typical of southern Patagonia, this museum at Elcano and Alberdi has displays of early immigrant life. It's open daily from 3 to 8 pm.

Places to Stay – bottom end

Inexpensive accommodation exists in Río Gallegos, but it is hard to recommend. Several truly seedy places in and around the 600 block of Zapiola, between Ameghino and Corrientes, have singles at US$5 or less. *Pensión Esmeralda*, *Hotel Amanecer Argentino*, *Hotel Libertad* and *Hotel Bar El Gaucho* have more than their share of serious drunks; women especially should avoid them.

Hotel Viejo La Fuente (☎ 20304), Vélez Sarsfield 64, appears the best of the cheapest, with warm, clean and spacious but basic singles for about US$6, with shared bath. Other acceptable places include *Hotel Colonial*, Rivadavia and Urquiza, where singles/doubles with shared bath are US$6/11, and *Hotel Puerto Santa Cruz* (☎ 20099), at Zapiola 238, with prices at

US$7/11 with private bath (do not confuse it with Hotel Santa Cruz).

Rates are similar at *Hotel Central*, Avenida Julio Roca 1127, which is reputed to be a 'local drinking hangout'; the boxy *Hotel Ampuero* (☎ 21189), Federico Sphur 38, and the nearby *Hotel Punta Arenas* (☎ 22743); *Hotel Cabo Virgenes* (☎ 22141), Rivadavia 259; *Hotel Laguna Azul* (☎ 22165), Estrada 298 at Urquiza; and *Hotel Mariano* (☎ 22110), Pellegrini 454.

Places to Stay – middle

In this category the best value is the spotless, quiet, comfortable and central *Hotel Covadonga* (☎ 20190), Avenida Julio Roca 1244, where rooms with private bath are US$13/20, but rooms with washbasin and mirror (shared bath) cost only US$8/14. *Hotel Río Turbio* (☎ 22155), Zapiola 486, *Hotel Piscis* (☎ 25064), Avellaneda 485, and *Hotel París* (☎ 20111), Avenida Julio Roca 1040 are comparable.

Places to Stay – top end

Several central hotels have rooms with private bath for about US$22/33, such as *Hotel Santa Cruz* (☎ 20601), Avenida Julio Roca and Rivadavia, and the modern *Hotel Comercio* (☎ 22172), Avenida Julio Roca 1302. *Hotel Alonso* (☎ 22414), which is less central at Corrientes 33, is slightly cheaper. *Hotel Costa Río*, Avenida San Martín 673, is the newest and costliest in town at US$32/45, with discounts for cash and for ACA members.

Places to Eat

For a town of its size, Río Gallegos has few outstanding eating places. *Restaurant Montecarlo*, Zapiola 558, has informal decor and good seafood. *Restaurant Díaz*, Avenida Julio Roca 1143, has adequate but expensive food and surly waiters.

Snack Bar Jardín, Avenida Julio Roca 1311, has cheap, filling minutas. *Le Croissant*, at Zapiola and Estrada, has a wide variety of attractive baked goods, prepared on the premises. Nearby *Heladería Tito* has very good and imaginative ice cream flavours, even by Argentine standards – try orange in white chocolate.

Things to Buy

Local woollen goods, leatherwork, fruit preserves, sweets and other items are available at Artesanías Keokén, Avenida San Martín 336, an offshoot business of Estancia Cóndor. Also worth a visit is Artesanías Santacruceñas at Avenida Julio Roca 658.

Getting There & Away

From Río Gallegos, there are several Patagonian options: to Chile's Puerto Natales and Parque Nacional Torres del Paine via Calafate and Parque Nacional Los Glaciares, or via the Argentine coal mining town of Río Turbio; or south to Punta Arenas and across the Strait of Magellan to Tierra del Fuego. It is also possible to visit the Fitzroy section of Los Glaciares without passing through dull, expensive Calafate.

Air Aerolíneas Argentinas (☎ 22342), Avenida San Martín 545, has daily flights between Buenos Aires and Ushuaia, which also stop at intermediate destinations like Bahía Blanca, Río Gallegos and Trelew, as well as Río Grande. Its twice-weekly transpolar flights from Buenos Aires to Auckland and Sydney stop here for refuelling.

Austral (☎ 20038), Avenida Julio Roca 917 near Avenida San Martín, has daily flights to Río Grande, Ushuaia, Comodoro Rivadavia and Buenos Aires.

LADE's offices (☎ 22249) are at Fagnano 53. Generally cheaper (and slower) than Aerolíneas and Austral on the same routes, it also reaches lesser or more remote Patagonian destinations like Puerto Deseado (US$50), San Julián, Santa Cruz, Perito Moreno (US$55), Gobernador Gregores (US$40), Río Turbio (US$27) and Calafate (US$31). Its flights to Comodoro Rivadavia have connections to Bariloche (US$140).

Aeroposta, a small private airline, flies daily to Ushuaia (US$37) and Calafate (US$31).

Bus Río Gallegos is a major hub for provincial bus travel. El Pingüino (☎ 22388), Zapiola 445, goes twice daily to Río Turbio (US$13), and daily to Punta Arenas (US$13) and Calafate (US$16). Buenos Aires, a 32-hour marathon starting nightly at 10 pm, costs US$100. There are also daily services north to the oil town of Caleta Olivia (US$17) and intermediate destinations, with connections to the delightful Andean oasis of Los Antiguos (US$30). Empresa Don Otto (☎ 21215) also goes to Buenos Aires, with connections via Comodoro Rivadavia to Bariloche (US$46), Neuquén (US$48), and Mar del Plata (US$ 69).

Transporte Ruta 3 (☎ 24999), Entre Ríos 354, covers the northern routes for roughly the same prices as El Pingüino, with additional services to Córdoba (US$103) on Tuesday and Thursday and connections to northern Argentina and Chile.

Interlagos Turismo (☎ 22614), Fagnano 35 near LADE's offices, goes to Calafate and the Moreno Glacier. Midway on the five-hour trip to Calafate, most buses stop at the roadside confitería at La Esperanza, whose truly extortionate prices for everything on its menu will shock you – bring a snack. Interlagos buses to and from Calafate will stop at the airport.

As of February 1991, Transporte Trevisan began a new service between Río Gallegos and Chaltén (Fitzroy section of Parque Nacional Los Glaciares) via Piedra Buena and Tres Lagos. This avoids overpriced Calafate, which is of little interest for those who have already visited the Moreno Glacier. Departures for the nine-hour journey are Tuesdays at 8 am and Fridays at 2 pm.

Transporte Mansilla and Transporte Vera (☎ 22701), occupying the same office at Avenida San Martín 565 near Aerolíneas Argentinas, both do the six-hour trip to Punta Arenas.

Car Rental A1 (☎ 22453), Entre Ríos 350, rents cars for excursions to outlying places like Cabo Vírgenes or Bella Vista.

Getting Around

There is no regular public transport to or from Río Gallegos airport except for cabs, which cost about US$6 to the city centre. To save money, share a cab with other arrivals.

Most long-distance companies have offices near the centre, but the new terminal is on the southern outskirts, at Avenida Evita Perón and Ruta 3, reached by bus Nos 1 or 12 (the placard must say 'terminal') from Avenida Julio Roca. Local buses in Río Gallegos are the most expensive in Argentina, at about US$0.50 per trip.

CABO VIRGENES

This colony of some 30,000 Magellanic penguins is about 120 km south-east of Río Gallegos. There is no public transportation, but it may be possible to catch a lift with sheep farmers or oil workers at the clearly marked junction about 15 km south of town. Camping is possible near the attractive but very exposed beach, but there are no facilities or even running water, although the small, isolated naval detachment may help. The estancias along provincial Ruta 1 will often provide a bed for the night, but you should arrange this in Río Gallegos. Estancia Cóndor, a beautiful settlement midway to Cabo Virgenes, has a store from which it may be possible to purchase supplies. In season, you can also watch sheep shearing here.

ESTANCIA BELLA VISTA

This estancia's hotel, 80 km west of Río Gallegos on the highway to Río Turbio, offers summer fishing holidays (October to March) at the hefty price of US$150 per day per person, with full room and board. Even at this price, it is often full.

RÍO TURBIO

Coal deposits, rare in South America, are the sole reason for the existence of this desolate border town. Many, if not most, employees of the Argentine state mining company are Chileans who commute from Puerto Natales, 30 km south. A narrow-gauge railway hauls the coal to the port of Río Gallegos, but there are no passenger services.

Things to See & Do

With permission, it is possible to visit the mines. There is also a ski area outside town during the winter.

Places to Stay

The cheapest place in town, usually occupied by miners, is the *Albergue Municipal* at Paraje Mina 1, where four-to-a-room dormitory beds cost the equivalent of six litres of super petrol per night – about US$5 at 1991 prices. Alternatives include the recommended *Hotel Gato Negro* (☎ 91226) on Roque Sáenz Peña, with singles/doubles at US$8/13 with shared bath and US$13/20 with private bath, and the slightly cheaper *Hotel Azteca* (☎ 91285) at Jorge Newbery 98.

Getting There & Away

Air LADE's flights to Río Gallegos, three times weekly, are the only alternative here. Their office is at Mineros 375.

Bus Buses to Puerto Natales take about 1½ hours, and leave from the west end of Jorge Newbery. At the border, you change to a Chilean bus for the remainder of the trip.

El Pingüino, on Jorge Newbery near Mineros, has daily service to Río Gallegos. Three times weekly, Buses San Ceferino, whose office is on Castillo, does the same six-hour journey across the monochrome Patagonian steppe.

CALAFATE

On the south shore of Lago Argentino, Calafate is an almost unavoidable stopover en route to some of the most visited tourist sights in Argentina. There is little worthwhile in the town itself, which is an oversized encampment of rapacious merchants intent on earning a year's income in just a few months.

During the season, Calafate swarms with Porteño tourists, most of whom come to spend a few hours at the Moreno Glacier. January and February are the most popular months so, if possible, plan your visit just before or just after peak season. Between

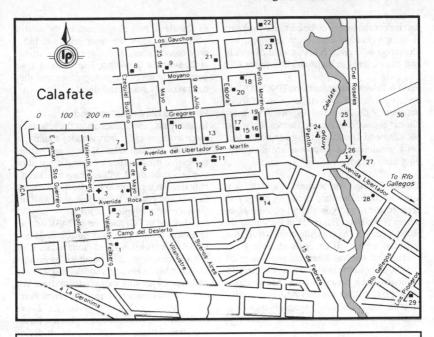

Calafate

0   100   200 m

PLACES TO STAY

1   Hospedaje Familiar
    Las Cabañitas
2   Hostería Kalkén
5   Hostería Lago Argentino
8   Hotel Los Alamos
9   Hospedaje Los Lagos
10 Hotel El Quijote
12 Hostería La Aldea
13 Hotel Amado
14 Hotel La Loma
15 Hospedaje Echeverría
16 Hotel Avenida
17 Hospedaje Alejandra
18 Hospedaje Jorgito
19 Hospedaje Lago Azul
21 Hotel Michelangelo
22 Hospedaje Belén
23 Hospedaje Del Norte

24 Campground
25 Campground
29 Albergue del Glaciar

▼ **PLACES TO EAT**

27 Parrilla La Tablita

    OTHER

3   Hospital
4   ACA
6   Banco de la Provincia
    de Santa Cruz
7   National Parks Office
11 Post Office
20 Telephone Cooperative
26 Tourist Office
28 Museo Regional El Calafate
30 Airport

May and September, tourist activity is much
reduced and prices may be more reasonable,
but the main attractions are less accessible.

Information

Tourist Office The overstaffed and
underworked tourist office, a pseudo-chalet

just before the bridge at the entrance to town, is open weekdays from 8 am to 8 pm, but closed on weekends. It keeps a list of hotels and prices, and has maps and brochures.

Post & Telecommunications ENCOTEL is on Avenida del Libertador San Martín, between 9 de Julio and Espora. The telephone cooperative is on Espora between Moyano and Gregores; there are no collect calls possible, and discounts are available only after 10 pm.

Money Though (or because) Calafate is a key tourist destination, changing money is problematical and you should change elsewhere if possible. Banco de la Provincia de Santa Cruz, on the opposite corner from the national parks office, will change cash dollars (but not travellers' cheques) at rates only slightly worse than Buenos Aires or Río Gallegos, but it closes by 1 pm. Many shops readily buy dollars, but the rate drops rapidly after the bank closes and especially on weekends.

National Parks Office The attractively landscaped national parks office, at Avenida del Libertador San Martín and Ezequiel Bustillo, is open weekday mornings and has brochures which include a decent map (though not adequate for trekking) of Parque Nacional Los Glaciares.

Things to See
West and north of Calafate, **Parque Nacional Los Glaciares** offers several of the most spectacular natural attractions in South America: the **Moreno Glacier**, the **Upsala Glacier**, and the **Fitzroy Range** of the southern Andes. For details, see the separate section on the park below.

Beware the video presentation on the breakup of the Moreno Glacier and the ascent of Cerro Torre at Audiovisual Tío Cacho, on 9 de Julio. An irritating soundtrack, at maximum distortion, makes this amateur production utterly intolerable, especially at US$5 per person.

As of summer 1991, the **Museo Regional**

El Calafate, two blocks east of the tourist office, was closed for reorganisation, but it may reopen soon. There are rock paintings at **Cuevas de Gualicho**, 7 km east of town near the shores of Lago Argentino, but they have recently been vandalised.

Places to Stay – bottom end
In the past, unquestionably the cheapest place to stay was the free, woodsy municipal campsite, on both sides of the creek behind the tourist office. After its recent renovation and privatisation, it will no longer be such a bargain, but it has good toilets, hot showers, firepits and potable water. It is easy walking distance from anyplace in town.

Albergue del Glaciar (☎ 91243), on Los Pioneros, is the local youth hostel. Beds cost US$7.50, with kitchen and laundry facilities, but it is sometimes fully occupied by groups. Director Mario Feldman speaks English and will happily provide visitor information. You can also make reservations in Buenos Aires (☎ 71-9344, 312-8486). *Hotel La Loma* (☎ 91016), on Avenida Roca, also has hostel accommodation, in addition to midprice rooms.

Although prices can vary considerably with the season, the cheapest places are family inns such as *Hospedaje Alejandra* (☎ 91328), Espora 60, where singles/doubles with shared bath are US$5/10. About the same price are the recommended *Hospedaje Echeverría*, Avenida del Libertador San Martín 959; *Hospedaje Belén* (☎ 91028) at Perito Moreno and Los Gauchos; *Hospedaje Lago Azul* (☎ 91419) at Perito Moreno 83; and (Hospedaje Jorgito (☎ 91323) at Moyano 943.

Places to Stay – middle
Slightly more expensive are *Hospedaje Del Norte* (☎ 91117), Los Gauchos 813 at Pantín, and *Hospedaje Los Lagos* (☎ 91170), 25 de Mayo 220 at Moyano, and *Hospedaje Familiar Las Cabañitas* (☎ 91118) at Valentín Feilberg 218. At all three, rooms with private bath are about US$11/19.

At *Hostería La Aldea* (ex-Hotel Glanesa,

☎ 91009), Avenida del Libertador San Martín 1108, *Hotel Amado* (☎ 91023), Avenida del Libertador San Martín 1072, and *Hotel Avenida* (☎ 91083), Avenida del Libertador San Martín 83, rates are around US$17/26. Several readers have recommended *Hostería Lago Argentino* (☎ 91384), at Avenida Roca and Primero de Mayo, which charges about the same in low season but 20% more in high season. The *Hostería ACA* (☎ 91004) at Primero de Mayo and Roca is higher yet, but there are discounts for members.

Places to Stay – top end

There is no shortage of costly accommodation in Calafate. Several charge upwards of US$40/60 per night, including the stiflingly hot but otherwise pleasant *Hostería Kalkén* (☎ 91073) at Valentín Feilberg and Avenida Roca, which serves an excellent breakfast. Others in this category include *Hotel Michelangelo* (☎ 91045), at Moyano and Espora, *Hotel La Loma* (☎ 91016) at Avenida Roca, and *Hotel El Quijote* (☎ 91017), Gregores and 25 de Mayo.

In a class by itself is *Hotel Los Alamos* (☎ 91144), Moyano and Ezequiel Bustillo, where rates are US$65/85.

Places to Eat

In general, Calafate restaurants are poor value for money. The most dependable is *Confitería Casa Blanca* at Avenida del Libertador San Martín and 25 de Mayo, which has good pizza and reasonable beer; *Pizzería Onelli* across the street also has its adherents. Many hotels have restaurants, but avoid the rubber chicken at *Hotel Amado*.

The kitchen at *Hotel Michelangelo* offers decent food but (unusually for Argentina) in microscopic portions, and it's not cheap. *Parrilla La Tablita*, across from the tourist office, and *Restaurante Macías*, on Los Gauchos opposite Hospedaje del Norte, are more reasonable. The best ice cream is at *Heladería Tito*, next door to LADE, just before the bridge crosses into town from the airport.

Things to Buy

Woollen clothing and other artisanal goods are available at Keokén, a branch of the Río Gallegos shop, at 25 de Mayo 50, and at El Puesto, at Gregores and Espora.

Getting There & Away

Air LADE, just east of the bridge at the entrance to town, is open from 9 am to 5 weekdays. Their twice-weekly flights to Río Gallegos and Ushuaia are heavily booked. They can also book and confirm reservations on Aerolíneas Argentinas and Austral. Calafate airport is walking distance from their office.

Aeroposta, a new private airline, covers the same route daily in summer. Inquire at travel agencies.

Bus Buses Pingüino and Interlagos both cover the 306 km of provincial route 5, now almost completely paved between Calafate and Río Gallegos. Both are on Avenida del Libertador San Martín within a short distance of each other. On request, they will drop you at Río Gallegos airport, saving you a cab fare.

It is possible to hitch between Río Gallegos and Calafate, but competition for rides is considerable and most Argentine vehicles are jammed with families. A possible alternative is provincial Ruta 9, a gravelled surface which leaves Ruta 3 about 45 km south of Piedra Buena. There are many estancias, and outstanding views of the canyon of the Río Santa Cruz.

During the summer Chaltén Patagonia (☎ 91055), Roca 1269, makes the 10-hour trip to Torres del Paine National Park in Chile on Tuesday, Thursday and Saturday at 8 am. The fare is US$45.

Daily at 6 am during summer, Buses Los Glaciares (☎ 91159) leaves Calafate for Chaltén and the Fitzroy Range. The fare is normally US$45 return, but $10 higher on Mondays, Wednesdays and Fridays. The return service leaves Chaltén at 6 pm. Auto traffic between Calafate and Chaltén is almost non-existent, so hitching is not advisable. Winter schedules may differ.

On national Ruta 40, north of Calafate to the small agricultural town of Perito Moreno and the junction to Los Antíguos, there is no public transportation and very little traffic of any kind. Returning to Río Gallegos is almost unavoidable.

PARQUE NACIONAL LOS GLACIARES

Nourished by several huge glaciers which descend from the Andean crest, Lago Argentino and Lago Viedma in turn feed southern Patagonia's largest river, the Río Santa Cruz. Along with the Iguazú Falls, this conjunction of ice, rock and water is one of the greatest attractions in Argentina and all of South America.

Its centrepiece is the breathtaking **Moreno Glacier** which, because of unusually favourable local conditions, is one of the planet's few advancing glaciers. A gap in the Andes allows moisture-laden Pacific storms to drop their loads west of the continental divide, where they accumulate as snow. Over the millennia, under tremendous weight, this snow has recrystallised into ice and flowed eastward. The trough of Lago Argentino is itself evidence that the glaciers were once far more extensive than today.

As the 60-metre high glacier advances, it periodically dams the **Brazo Rico** (Rico Arm) of Lago Argentino, causing the water to rise. Eventually, the melting ice below can no longer support the weight of the water behind it and the dam collapses in an explosion of ice and water. To be present when this spectacular cataclysm occurs, approximately every four years, is unforgettable.

Even in ordinary years, the Moreno Glacier merits a visit. It is no less an auditory than visual experience, when huge icebergs on the glacier's face calve and collapse into the **Canal de los Témpanos** (Channel of Icebergs). From a series of catwalks and vantage points on the Península de Magallanes, you can see, hear and photograph the glacier safely as these enormous chunks crash into the water. Because of the danger of falling icebergs and their backwash, it is no longer possible to descend to the shores of the canal.

The massive but less spectacular **Upsala Glacier**, to the north, can be visited by launch from Puerto Bandera, which is 45 km west of Calafate. Many visitors recommend the trip for the hike to iceberg-choked Lago Onelli. It is possible to camp at a refugio and return to Puerto Bandera another day.

Places to Stay

There are two organised campsites, with facilities, on Península Magallanes en route to the glacier. The nearer one is eight km away. There is another at La Jerónima, on Brazo Sur, where Cerro Cristal, a rugged but rewarding hike beginning at the concrete bunker near the campground entrance, offers views from Torres del Paine in the south to Cerro Fitzroy in the north. Fishing and horseback riding are also possible. Prices are about US$4 per person; there is a confitería, and hot showers from 7 to 11 pm.

Getting There & Away

The Moreno Glacier is about 80 km from Calafate over a rough gravelled road. Bus tours are frequent and numerous in summer, but off-season transportation can still be arranged. Calafate's numerous tour operators offer trips to all major tourist sites, but concentrate on the Moreno and Upsala glaciers. Interlagos, Lake Travel, Gador Viajes, Receptivo Calafate, Ice Master and others line both sides of Avenida del Libertador San Martín. There is little to choose between them but inquire at Interlagos if you prefer an English-speaking guide. The return fare to Moreno Glacier is about US$15.

Albergue del Glaciar, the youth hostel, has its own minivan excursions to the glacier; these leave about 9 am and return about 5 pm. They also arrange bus/motorboat trips to the Upsala Glacier for about $45. Hotel La Loma does similar minivan trips. Many people feel that daytrips leave insufficient time to appreciate the glacier, especially if the frequent inclemency limits visibility. The changeable weather is almost sure to provide a window on the glacier at some time during your trip, but it is also worth exploring the possibilities for camping nearby.

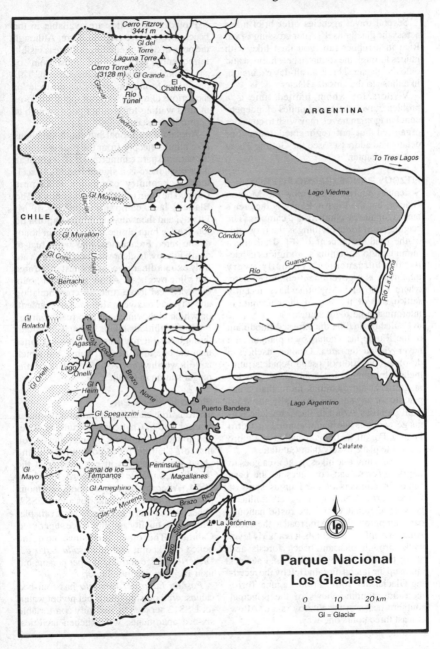

**Parque Nacional
Los Glaciares**

0   10   20 km

Gl = Glaciar

Several travel agencies offer brief hikes across the glacier itself. After crossing Brazo Rico in a rubber raft, you then hike with guides through the southern beech forest and onto the glacier. This is an all-day excursion, like those to the Upsala Glacier.

Visitors for whom limited time is a problem, given the uncertainties of independent Patagonian travel, may wish to consider organised but not regimented tours. For details and addresses, see the Getting There & Away chapter.

FITZROY RANGE (CERRO FITZROY)

Sedentary tourists can enjoy the Moreno Glacier, but the Fitzroy Range is the area's mecca for hikers, climbers and campers. The staging point for everything is the tiny, end-of-the-road settlement of El Chaltén, a monument to Argentina's prodigious capacity for bureaucracy. Virtually every inhabitant is a government employee here, where Chile and Argentina have recently settled one of the last of their seemingly interminable border disputes.

Foolishly sited on the exposed floodplain of the Río de las Vueltas by a planner who never visited the area, Chaltén itself is a desolate collection of pseudo-chalets pummelled by almost incessant wind, but the magnificent surroundings more than compensate for any squalor. Ironically, the word itself signifies Azure in the Tehuelche language and was the name applied to Cerro Fitzroy. For all its faults, Chaltén is a more agreeable place to stay than Calafate.

One of many fine hikes in the area goes to **Laguna Torre**, and continues to the base camp for climbers of the famous spire of **Cerro Torre**. There is a signed trailhead between the chalets and the rustic national park campground along the road to the north. After an gentle initial climb, it is a fairly level walk through pleasant beech forests and along the Río Fitzroy until a final steeper climb up the lateral moraine left by the receding Glaciar del Torre. From Laguna Torre, there are stunning views of the principal southern peaks of the Fitzroy range. Allow at least three hours one-way.

Protected campsites are available in the beech forest above Laguna Torre. Although the peak of 3128-metre Cerro Torre is visible infrequently, look for the 'mushroom' of snow and ice which caps the summit. This precarious formation is the final obstacle for the serious climbers who can spend weeks or months waiting for weather good enough to permit their ascent.

Another exceptional but more strenuous hike climbs steeply from the pack station at the national park campground; after about an hour plus, there is a signed lateral to excellent backcountry campsites at **Laguna Capri**. The main trail continues gently to **Río Blanco**, base camp for climbers of Mt Fitzroy, and then very steeply to **Laguna de los Tres**, a high alpine tarn named in honor of the three Frenchmen who were first to climb Fitzroy. In clear weather, the views are truly extraordinary – condors nest in the area and glide overhead. Allow about four hours one-way, and leave time for contemplation and physical recovery after the last segment, on which high winds can be a real hazard.

More ambitious hikers can make a circuit through the Fitzroy Range which is shorter than the one in Torres del Paine, but which is still worthwhile. Ask for details at the ranger station in Chaltén.

Places to Stay & Eat

There is free camping at the national parks Madsen site in Chaltén, with running water and abundant firewood, but no toilets – you must dig a latrine. If you don't mind walking about ten minutes, you can shower at the friendly *Confitería La Senyera* for about US$1. After drying off, try their enormous portions of chocolate cake for about US$2. Other snacks and light meals are available, with prices, quality and ambience superior to Calafate. The other campsites, near the police checkpoint and at *Posada Lago del Desierto*, charge about US$8 per person, but their facilities are little better.

Posada Lago del Desierto has four-bed cabins, with outside toilets but no hot water, for US$12 per person, and very comfortable six-bed apartments, with kitchen facilities, private bath and hot water, for US$18 per person. Meals are expensive. At the new *Fitzroy Inn*, rooms with half-pension cost US$35 per person. *Estancia La Quinta*, on the outskirts of Chaltén, offers lodging as well; make arrangements at agencies in Calafate.

For cheap eats, try the kitchen in Juan Borrego's converted bus. It is also a hangout for climbers, and Juan's humour helps pass the time on those days when weather does not permit outdoor activities. There is one grocery, but prices are higher than in Calafate.

Getting There & Away
See the section on Calafate for details on daily buses to and from Chaltén. It is now possible to travel directly between Chaltén and Río Gallegos via Tres Lagos and Piedra Buena, avoiding Calafate. Transporte Trevisan, a pickup truck, leaves Chaltén on Wednesdays at 8 am and Sundays at 2 pm, taking nine hours. Gallegos departures are Tuesdays at 8 am and Fridays at 2 pm.

Motorists should know that petrol is not available at Chaltén except in very serious emergencies; carry a spare fuel can. The nearest station is at Tres Lagos, 123 km east.

CALETA OLIVIA
Less publicised than the Andean Lake District, the eastern part of Santa Cruz province, along the Atlantic coast and longitudinal Ruta 3, is still interesting. The starting point is the oil port of Caleta Olivia, from which there is also access to several petrified forests and the Andean oasis of Los Antíguos, from which it is possible to cross into Chile.

For southbound travellers on Ruta 3, Caleta Olivia (population 35,000) is the first stop in Santa Cruz province. Founded in 1901 as a port to discharge cargo for the Buenos Aires-Cabo Vírgenes telegraph line, its most visible landmark is the massive, 10-metre monument of El Gorosito, the oil worker, which dominates the traffic circle in the town centre. Other industries include seafood processing and wool. If driving or hitching south, or heading east toward the Andes, you may spend a night here.

Information & Orientation
Entering Caleta Olivia from the north, Ruta 3 becomes part of Avenida Jorge Newbery and then Avenida San Martín (the main street in town), before taking a dogleg at the monument, where it becomes Avenida Güemes. The friendly and enthusiastic tourist office (☎ 61085) is a cubbyhole on Avenida San Martín, also near the monument. Three nearby banks will change cash but not travellers' cheques. On Avenida Independencia is the **Museo del Hombre** (Museum of Man).

Places to Stay & Eat
The municipal campground is the most economical alternative, at US$1 per car, per tent and per person. There is 24-hour hot water and other services.

Otherwise, the cheapest lodging in town is *Hotel Alvear*, Avenida Güemes 1676, where singles/doubles are US$9/13 with shared bath. *Hotel Grand* (☎ 61393), at Avenida Jorge Newbery and Moscone, is slightly more expensive. At the comfortable *Residencial Las Vegas* (☎ 61177), Hipólito Yrigoyen 2094, one block from El Gorosito, rates are US$11/16 with private bath. *Hotel Capri* (☎ 61132), José Hernández 1145, and *Hotel Robert* (☎ 61452), Avenida San Martín 2151, are comparable.

Italo-Argentine food is available at *Pizzería Romanela*, José Hernández 1300. *El Hueso Perdido*, a parrilla, is downstairs at Hotel Grand. *Restaurante Royal* and *El Abuelo*, the best and most expensive in town, are both on Avenida Independencia, near El Gorosito. YPF, the state oil company on Avenida Güemes (Ruta 3), has a restaurant which serves seafood specialities, with discounts for backpackers.

Getting There & Away
Caleta Olivia is a hub for travel in northern Santa Cruz province. There are no air or rail

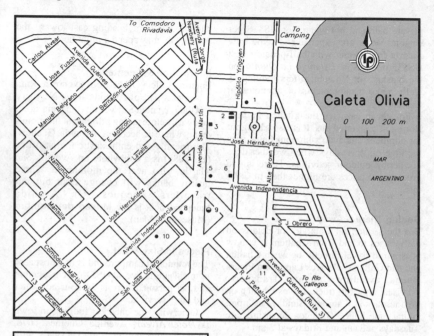

1	Telefónica
2	Post Office
3	Hotel Robert
4	Tourist Office
5	Banco de la Nación
6	Residencial Las Vegas
7	El Gorosito Monument
8	Banco de la Provincia del Santa Cruz
9	Bus Terminal
10	Museo del Hombre
11	Hotel Alvear

services, but excellent paved roads lead north to Comodoro Rivadavia, south to Río Gallegos, and west to Los Antíguos. The bus terminal is at Avenida San Martín and Independencia, across from the monument. On the southern outskirts of town, there is a police checkpoint which is the best place to hitch.

Transporte La Unión departs hourly for Comodoro Rivadavia between 7 am and 10 pm. The one-hour trip costs US$3. Twice daily, morning and evening, it goes to isolated but picturesque Puerto Deseado for US$9.

Transport El Pingüino covers the 722 km to Río Gallegos for US$17, with connections to Punta Arenas and Puerto Natales in Chile. There is a direct service from Caleta Olivia to Buenos Aires twice weekly with Empresa Don Otto, but through buses from Río Gallegos will also take northbound passengers.

Twice weekly, Transporte Co-mi goes to and from the town of Perito Moreno (do not confuse it with Moreno Glacier or with Parque Nacional Perito Moreno) and Los Antíguos, on Lago Buenos Aires. Because there is an excellent paved road, passing through the oil towns of Pico Truncado and Las Heras, it may be possible to hitch to Los Antíguos, where many residents of Comodoro Rivadavia and Caleta Olivia take their holidays.

MONUMENTO NATURAL BOSQUES PETRIFICADOS

In the Argentine national park system, natural monuments are the only units invulnerable to commercial exploitation. The 15,000 hectares of Monumento Natural Bosques Petrificados (Petrified Forest Natural Monument) contain no hotels, restaurants, confiterías and other concessions as in Nahuel Huapi, Los Glaciares and other overdeveloped parks. Bosques Petrificados has only its volcanic, polychrome desert landscape, fossilised forests, and solitude to recommend it. Just off Ruta 3, 157 km south of Caleta Olivia, an excellent gravel road leads 50 km west to the park, one of the finest in the country. Guanaco are a common sight along the road.

During the Jurassic era, 150 million years ago, this area had a humid, temperate climate, but intense volcanic activity levelled the forests which flourished here. Buried in volcanic ash and slowly mineralised, specimens up to three metres in diameter and 35 metres in length were later exposed to view by erosion. A short interpretive trail leads from park headquarters to the largest concentration of petrified *Proaraucaria* trees, ancestors of modern *Araucaria*, a member of the pine family unique to the southern hemisphere. Until its legal protection in 1954, the area was consistently plundered for some of its finest specimens; do not perpetuate this unfortunate tradition by taking even the tiniest souvenir.

Other parts of the scenic desert park also merit exploration, but consult with park ranger Carlos Balestra before continuing far on the road toward the peak of Madre e Hijo (Mother and Son). You can pitch a tent free of charge near the dry creek, within sight of headquarters, where there is a small display of local artefacts and fauna. Since there is no water at the site, bring your own if you have a vehicle. Otherwise, you *may* be able to obtain some from headquarters. Like the rest of Patagonia, it is extremely windy, but the clear southern sky offers a spectacular display of stars at night.

Patagonian Hares

There is no public transportation directly to the park, although you can rent a car in Comodoro Rivadavia or try hitching. Buses from Caleta Olivia will drop you at the junction, but you may wait several hours for any vehicle to continue. Do not attempt hitching in winter, when the area is bitterly cold.

SAN JULIÁN

The modest port of San Julián (population 4500) is 341 km south of Caleta Olivia and a few km east of Ruta 3. In the winter of 1520, Magellan's crew wintered in its sheltered harbour, while in 1780 Antonio de Viedma established a colony which lasted only a few years. Only the wool boom of the late 19th century brought permanent settlement, although seafood processing has become a secondary industry. If driving or hitching, you can break the long trip between Caleta Olivia and Río Gallegos here.

Information & Orientation

San Julián occupies a small peninsula in the protected bay of the same name. Avenida San Martín, the main drag, is an eastward extension of the junction at Ruta 3. The small tourist kiosk here is rarely open, but the nearby municipalidad has plentiful information, including maps and brochures.

Almost all public services are near the east end of Avenida San Martín, close to the tip of the peninsula. The post office and telephone office are both at Avenida San Martín and Belgrano. Banco de la Nación occupies an attractive Victorian building at Mitre and Belgrano.

Things to See
The **Museo Regional y de Arte Marino**, at the east end of town between Mitre and Colón, features archaeological artefacts and historical exhibits on local estancias, as well as painting and sculpture. Ten km out of town are the ruins of **Floridablanca**, Viedma's short-lived colony of 1780. The Swift **Frigorífico** (mutton freezer), which operated between 1912 and 1967, is north of town.

Launches can be hired to visit rookeries of penguins, cormorants, and other seabirds at Banco Cormorán and Banco Justicia, in the harbour.

Places to Stay & Eat
San Julian's municipal campground (☎ 2160), on the waterfront, has first-rate facilities, including hot showers, a laundry and playground, for less than US$1 per person, plus US$1.50 per car. There are other beachfront sites at Cabo Curioso (20 km north of town) and Playa La Mina, farther north, where there is a sea lion rookery.

Hotel Colón, Avenida San Martín 301, is the cheapest. *Hotel Sada* (☎ 2013), Avenida San Martín 1112 at Piedrabuena, has singles/doubles with bath for US$13/20. *Hotel Municipal de Turismo* (☎ 2300), 25 de Mayo 917, is slightly more expensive.

Restaurant Sportsman, Mitre 301 at 25 de Mayo, has excellent parrillada and pasta (especially ñoquis) at reasonable prices. There are several other restaurants, including *Dos Anclas*, Berutti 1080, for seafood.

Getting There & Away
Air LADE's Monday flights from Comodoro Rivadavia to Río Gallegos via Puerto Deseado stop here. The airport is at the Ruta 3 junction.

Bus Transportadora Patagónica's Río Gallegos-Buenos Aires services pick up passengers here, but any bus on Ruta 3 will take passengers from the junction. Transportes Staller and El Cordillerano have weekly services to Laguna Posadas, near the Chilean border, via Gobernador Gregores and Bajo Caracoles. This is the only feasible public transport to the junction to the otherwise inaccessible Parque Nacional Perito Moreno (see the section on the park below).

GOBERNADOR GREGORES
Gobernador Gregores is the nearest town to Parque Nacional Perito Moreno. Although it is still more than 200 km east of the park, you should arrange a car and driver here rather than at the town of Perito Moreno. LADE's weekly return flights between Comodoro Rivadavia and Río Gallegos via Perito Moreno stop here. There is a twice-weekly bus service from San Julián.

Hostería Adelino, Avenida San Martín 1043, charges US$30 a single. *Residencial Alvarez* (☎ 7053), Pueyrredón 367, may be cheaper.

COMANDANTE LUIS PIEDRA BUENA
On the north bank of the Río Santa Cruz, Piedra Buena is just off Ruta 3, 127 km south of San Julián and 235 km north of Río Gallegos. Although it has no major attractions, it is a common stopover. Hitchhikers, who must often wait in line at the junction near the ACA service station, confitería and motel, can at least get food and drink here. There is a large army camp north of town.

Orientation & Information
From Ruta 3, Avenida Belgrano goes directly into town, where it intersects the riverfront Avenida Gregorio Ibáñez, which becomes Avenida San Martín to the south. There is tourist information available at the munici-

pal offices at Ibáñez and Gobernador Lista. You can try changing money at Banco de la Provincia de Santa Cruz on Avenida San Martín.

Things to See & Do

At **Isla Pavon**, in the river three km south of the highway junction, a museum honors Piedra Buena, who first raised the Argentine flag here in 1859. Fishing, water-skiing and other aquatic sports are popular. There are several campsites.

Places to Stay & Eat

Hotel Iris (☎ 7134), Avenida Gregorio Ibáñez 13, is reasonable at US$7/10 with bath, and even cheaper with shared bath. Avoid the nearby slummy *Petit Hotel. Hotel Internacional* (☎ 7197), Avenida Gregorio Ibáñez 99, charges US$10 per person with shared bath.

The *ACA Motel* (☎ 7245) is good value at US$10/14 for members, but nonmembers pay half as much again. Its restaurant is dependable and reasonable. *Hotel Huayen* (☎ 7265, Belgrano 321, is comparable in price.

Getting There & Away

Hitching is difficult because of competition, but passing buses will pick up passengers on Ruta 3. Forty-five km south of Piedra Buena, it may be possible to hitch to Calafate along a decent gravel road which passes numerous estancias, with panoramic views of the canyon of the Río Santa Cruz.

Transporte Trevisan passes through Piedra Buena twice weekly in each direction between Río Gallegos and El Chaltén, in the Fitzroy section of Parque Nacional Los Glaciares. For details, see the Río Gallegos section.

PERITO MORENO

Visitors should avoid confusing this small agricultural settlement, a brief stopover en route to Los Antíguos, with either the Moreno Glacier in Parque Nacional Los Glaciares, or with Parque Nacional Perito Moreno.

Orientation & Information

Perito Moreno's main street, Avenida San Martín, leads north to Provincial Ruta 43, an excellent paved road which forks west to Los Antíguos and east toward Caleta Olivia. At the south end of town it becomes Ruta 40, a *very* rough highway to the bleak oasis of Bajo Caracoles and to Perito Moreno National Park.

Near the south end of town is the pretty **Laguna de los Cisnes**, at whose tiny campground the tourist office is located. The post office is on Buenos Aires, near Belgrano. Banco de la Provincia de Santa Cruz, Banco de la Nación and Hotel Belgrano will change cash dollars.

Places to Stay & Eat

The municipal campsite at Laguna de los Cisnes is the cheapest place in town, where you can pitch a tent for US$1 or rent one of the few small cabins at $5 per person.

Hotel Argentino, at Buenos Aires and Belgrano, charges US$5 per person. *Hotel Santa Cruz*, around the corner on Belgrano, is comparably priced. The best in town, *Hotel Belgrano* (☎ 2019) at Avenida San Martín 1001, costs US$12/15 with bath, and also has a restaurant.

Getting There & Away

Air LADE is at the corner of Mariano Moreno and Avenida San Martín. On Thursdays, flights from Comodoro Rivadavia (US$23) stop here en route to Gobernador Gregores and Río Gallegos (US$38) in the morning and return by the same route in the afternoon.

Bus From Perito Moreno, you can proceed west to Los Antíguos, on Lago Buenos Aires, and cross into Chile, or else head east to Caleta Olivia and then north of Comodoro Rivadavia or south to Río Gallegos. The Co-mi bus offices are near Hotel Argentino.

There is no public transportation southwards toward Parque Nacional Perito Moreno, and very little traffic of any sort, but a group may find a taxi and driver to take you there. Ruta 40 is very rough but scenic along

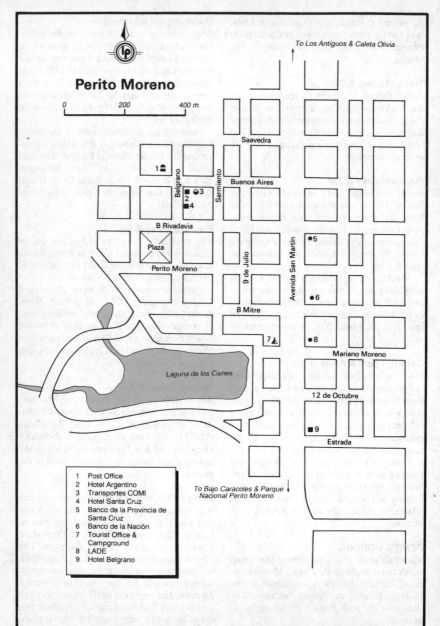

Perito Moreno

0   200   400 m

To Los Antíguos & Caleta Olivia

Saavedra

Belgrano

Sarmiento

Buenos Aires

1

2 ●3
  4

B Rivadavia

Plaza

Perito Moreno

9 de Julio

B Mitre

Avenida San Martín

●5

●6

7

●8

Mariano Moreno

12 de Octubre

■9

Estrada

Laguna de los Cisnes

To Bajo Caracoles & Parque
Nacional Perito Moreno

1   Post Office
2   Hotel Argentino
3   Transportes COMI
4   Hotel Santa Cruz
5   Banco de la Provincia de
    Santa Cruz
6   Banco de la Nación
7   Tourist Office &
    Campground
8   LADE
9   Hotel Belgrano

the Río Pinturas, where there are several archaeological sites, including the famous Cueva de las Manos (Cave of Hands).

BAJO CARACOLES

For motorists on rugged Ruta 40, this tiny oasis has the only petrol between Tres Lagos and Perito Moreno, a distance of nearly 500 km. The arrival of any vehicle is such an event that if you wait at the pump, the attendant will soon come to you. Only regular grade is available.

Surprisingly, for such a bleak, remote place, there is good accommodation at *Hotel Bajo Caracoles* for US$7 per person. Its restaurant is also good, but not really cheap.

PARQUE NACIONAL PERITO FRANCISCO P MORENO

Seldom visited by anyone but the friendly estancieros who live nearby, this gem of the Argentine park system honours the system's founder. Its 115,000 hectares abut the Chilean border, 310 km by road from the town of Perito Moreno. As of early 1991, it lacked even rangers, but it was still possible to visit and camp.

In the park, glacier-covered summits as high as the 3700-metre San Lorenzo tower over aquamarine lakes such as Lago Belgrano, alongside which herds of guanacos graze peacefully. The Sierra Colorada, in the north-east corner of the park, is a painter's pallette of sedimentary peaks. There are also pumas, foxes, wildcats, perhaps *huemuls* (Chilean deer), and many birds, including condors, rheas, flamingos, black-necked swans, upland geese, and crested caracaras (caranchos). The Tehuelche Indians left evidence of their presence with rock paintings of guanaco and human hands in caves at Lago Burmeister.

As precipitation increases toward the west, the Patagonian steppe grasslands of the park's eastern border become sub-Antarctic forests of southern beech, lenga and coihue. Because the altitude exceeds 900 metres, which is considerably higher than the more accessible southerly parks such as Los Glaciares, the weather can be severe.

Summer visits are usually comfortable, but warm clothing and equipment are imperative. Perito Moreno's quiet and solitude are a blessing, but visitors should be especially careful with fire in the frequent high winds. You must bring all food and supplies, although water is pure and plentiful, and dead wood may be collected for fuel.

Places to Stay

Camping is the only choice. One good site is just beyond the isthmus which separates the two arms of Lago Belgrano, about 10 km from Estancia Belgrano. In the interior of this peninsula, there are several smallish lakes which harbour abundant waterfowl and offer sheltered backcountry campsites. Ask at Estancia Belgrano for directions to the pictographs at Lago Burmeister.

You can also camp near Estancia La Oriental, on the north shore of Lago Belgrano, from which it is possible to hike up nearby Cerro Léon.

As of early 1991, the Argentine park service intended to install a ranger at the park entrance, near Estancia Belgrano.

LOS ANTÍGUOS

Los Antíguos, on the southern shore of Lago Buenos Aires near the Chilean border, is a pleasant retreat for a tranquil holiday. Picturesque rows of Lombardy poplars are windbreaks for its irrigated chacras, which yield an abundant harvest of fresh fruit which, for lack of large nearby markets, is absurdly cheap. In the surrounding countryside, there is good fishing and hiking. Tourist facilities are good, but the area has not yet been overrun by outsiders.

Before the arrival of Europeans, Tehuelche Indians and their forerunners frequented this 'banana belt' in their old age – the town's name is a near-literal translation of a Tehuelche word meaning Place of the Elders. In August of 1991, the eruption of Volcán Hudson on the Chilean side of the border covered both Los Antíguos and Chile Chico in volcanic ash and forced their evacuation, so inquire in Buenos Aires,

Comodoro Rivadavia or Caleta Olivia before visiting the area.

Orientation & Information

Los Antíguos occupies the delta formed by the Río Jeinemeni, which constitutes the border with Chile, and the Río Los Antíguos. As in many smaller Argentine towns, there are few street signs and even fewer street numbers, but the main Avenida 11 de Julio runs the length of town. The municipal tourist office is here, along with the Banco de la Provincia. To the west, the avenue reaches and crosses the border to Chile Chico.

Things to See & Do

In summer, **Lago Buenos Aires** is warm enough for swimming from the beaches at the municipal campground at the east end of Avenida 11 de Julio. Juan Carlos Pellón, owner of Hotel Argentino, will guide fishermen to pejerrey and rainbow trout on Lago Buenos Aires. **Monte Zeballos**, 50 km south, offers good hiking in southern beech forests. The road to Monte Zeballos may be extended southward to Paso Roballos, permitting a scenic circuit around the volcanic Meseta del Lago Buenos Aires via Lago Posadas, Bajo Caracoles and Perito Moreno.

Since 1989, Los Antíguos has held an annual **cherry festival**, lasting three days, in the second week of January. Other local fruits, including raspberries, strawberries, apples, apricots, pears, peaches, plums and prunes, are equally delectable. You can purchase these, and home-made fruit preserves,

directly from the farms. Señora Regina de Jomñuk's Chacra El Porvenir is easy walking distance from the main avenue, but there are many others.

Other local celebrations are **Día del Lago Buenos Aires** on 29 October, and **Día de los Antíguos** on 5 February.

Places to Stay & Eat

The municipal campground, on the lakeshore at the east end of the avenue, is one of the best and cheapest in Argentina. Forest plantings shelter the sites, each of which has tables and firepits, from the wind. Hot showers are available from 5.30 to 10 pm. Fees are absurdly low at US$0.60 per person, plus US$0.15 per tent and per vehicle. There are also a limited number of cabins, which can hold up to six persons.

Restaurant-Confitería Pablo also offers lodging at US$6 per person, with shared bath. The only other possibility is *Hotel Argentino*, US$10/18 with private bath, whose restaurant has excellent fixed-price dinners, with desserts of local produce, and an outstanding breakfast. *Restaurant El Triunfo* is also inviting.

Getting There & Away

LADE serves the nearest airport, at Perito Moreno 64 km east. Buses El Pingüino and Transportes Co-mi run between Caleta Olivia and Los Antíguos (US$11). Transportes VH crosses the border to Chile Chico (US$3 return) three times daily from Monday to Thursday, once on Friday and Saturday, but never on Sunday.

Tierra del Fuego & Chilean Patagonia

Since the 16th-century voyages of Magellan, to the 19th-century explorations of Fitzroy and Darwin on the *Beagle* and even to the present, this 'uttermost part of the earth' has held an ambivalent fascination for travellers of many nationalities. For more than three centuries, its climate and terrain discouraged European settlement, yet indigenous people considered it a 'land of plenty'. Its scenery, with glaciers descending nearly to the ocean in many places, is truly enthralling.

The Yahgan Indians, now nearly extinct, built the fires which inspired Europeans to give this region its name, now famous throughout the world. It consists of one large island, Isla Grande de Tierra del Fuego, and many smaller ones, only a few of which are inhabited. The Strait of Magellan separates the archipelago from the South American mainland.

History

While Magellan passed through the Strait which bears his name in 1520, neither he nor anyone else had any immediate interest in the land and its people. In search of a passage to the spice islands of Asia, early navigators feared and detested the stiff westerlies, hazardous currents, and violent seas which impeded their progress. Consequently the Ona, Haush, Yahgan and Alacaluf Indians who populated the area faced no immediate competition for their lands.

All these groups were mobile hunters and gatherers. The Ona, also known as Selknam, and Haush subsisted primarily on terrestrial resources, hunting the guanaco and dressing in its skins, while the Yahgans and Alacalufes, known collectively as 'Canoe Indians', lived primarily on fish, shellfish, and marine mammals. The Yahgans, also known as the Yamana, consumed the 'Indian bread' fungus *(Cytarria* spp.) which parasitises the ñire, a species of southern beech. Despite the usually inclement weather, they used little or no clothing, but constant fires, even in their bark canoes, kept them warm.

After the demise of Spain's American empire, the area slowly opened to European settlement and the rapid demise of the indigenous Fuegians, whom Europeans struggled to understand, began. Charles Darwin, visiting the area in 1834, wrote that the difference between the Fuegians, 'among the most abject and miserable creatures I ever saw', and Europeans was greater than that between wild and domestic animals. On a previous voyage, however, Captain Robert Fitzroy of the *Beagle* had abducted several Yahgans who, after several years of missionary education in England, he returned to their distant home.

From the 1850s, there were attempts to

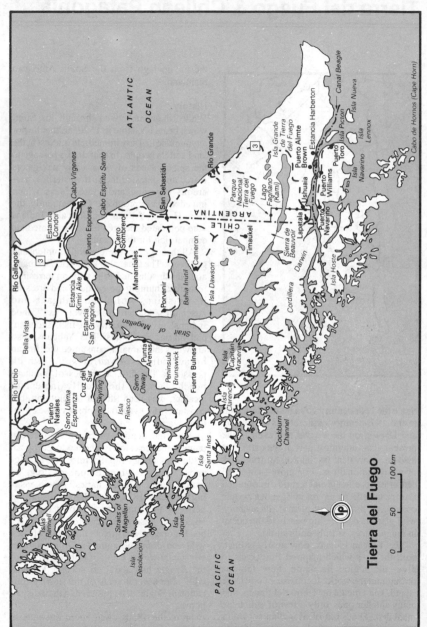

Tierra del Fuego

catechise the Fuegians, the earliest of which ended in failure with the death by starvation of British missionary Allen Gardiner. Gardiner's successors, working from a base at Keppel Island in the Falklands, were more successful despite the massacre of one party by Fuegians at Navarino Island. Thomas Bridges, a young man at Keppel, learned to speak the Yahgan language and became one of the first settlers at Ushuaia, in what is now Argentine Tierra del Fuego. His son Lucas Bridges, born at Ushuaia in 1874, left a fascinating memoir of his experiences among the Yahgans and Onas entitled *The Uttermost Part of the Earth*.

Although the Bridges family and many of those who followed had the best motives, the increasing European presence exposed the Fuegians to diseases, such as typhoid and measles, to which they had no exposure and little resistance. One measles epidemic wiped out half the native population in the district, and recurrent contagion nearly extinguished them over the next half-century. Some early sheep ranchers made things worse with their violent persecution of the Indians, who had resorted to preying on domestic flocks as guanaco populations declined.

Since no European power had any interest in settling the region until Britain occupied the Falklands in the 1770s, Spain too paid little attention to Tierra del Fuego. The successor governments of Argentina and Chile felt differently. The Chilean presence on the Strait of Magellan from 1843 and the increasing British mission activity spurred Argentina to formalise its authority at Ushuaia in 1884, with the installation of a territorial governor the following year. International border issues in the area were only finally resolved in 1984, when an Argentine plebiscite ratified a diplomatic settlement of a dispute over three small islands in the Beagle Channel which had lingered for decades and nearly brought the two countries to open warfare in 1979.

Despite minor gold and lumbering booms, for many years Ushuaia was primarily a penal settlement for both political prisoners and common criminals. Sheep farming brought great wealth and is still the island's economic backbone, although the northeastern section near San Sebastián has substantial petroleum and natural gas reserves. Since the 1960s, the tourist industry has become so important that flights and hotels are often heavily booked during the summer. The spectacular mountain and coastal scenery in the immediate countryside of Ushuaia, including Parque Nacional Tierra del Fuego, attracts both Argentines and foreigners.

Geography & Climate

Surrounded by the South Atlantic Ocean, the Strait of Magellan and the easternmost part of the Pacific Ocean, the archipelago of Tierra del Fuego has a land area of roughly 76,000 sq km, about the size of Ireland or South Carolina. The Chilean-Argentine border runs directly south from Cape Espíritu Santo, at the eastern entrance of the Straits of Magellan, to the Beagle Channel (Canal Beagle), where it trends eastward to the Channel's mouth at Nueva Island. Most of Isla Grande belongs to Chile, but the Argentine side is more densely populated, with the substantial towns of Ushuaia and Río Grande. Porvenir (see the section on Chilean Patagonia) is the only significant town on the Chilean side.

The plains of northern Isla Grande are a landscape of almost unrelenting wind, enormous flocks of Corriedales, and oil derricks, while the mountainous southern part of the island offers scenic glaciers, lakes, rivers and seacoasts. The mostly maritime climate is surprisingly mild, even in winter, but its changeability makes warm, dry clothing important, especially when hiking or at higher elevations. The mountains of the Cordillera Darwin and the Sierra de Beauvoir, reaching as high as 2500 metres in the west, intercept Antarctic storms, leaving the plains around Río Grande much drier than areas nearer the Beagle Channel.

The higher southern rainfall supports dense forests of southern beech *(Notho-fagus)*, both deciduous and evergreen, while the drier north consists of extensive native pasture grasses and low-growing shrubs. Storms batter the bogs and truncated beeches of the remote southern and western zones of the archipelago. Guanaco, rhea and condor can still be seen in the north, but marine mammals and shorebirds are the most common wildlife in the tourist destinations along the Beagle Channel.

Getting There & Around
Overland, the simplest route to Argentine Tierra del Fuego is via Porvenir, across the Strait of Magellan from Punta Arenas; for details, see the section on Chilean Patagonia. There is also a ferry across the narrows at Punta Delgada, but no public transportation to it. The principal border crossing is San Sebastián, a truly desolate place about midway between Porvenir and Río Grande. Except in the towns themselves, all roads are gravelled, and some are very bad.

Tierra del Fuego

RÍO GRANDE
Founded in 1894, Río Grande is a bleak, windswept petroleum and agricultural service centre on the estuary of its namesake river. Most visitors will pass through quickly en route to Ushuaia, but it is not completely without interest.

Orientation & Information
Most important services are close to the main plaza. For tourist information, visit the office (☎ 21701) at Rosales and Fagnano. For money exchange, try Banco de la Nación, San Martín at 9 de Julio (do not confuse the similarly named streets 9 de Julio and 11 de Julio, which are parallel but two blocks apart). The post office is at Ameghino 712, between Piedrabuena and Estrada, while telephone services are at Piedrabuena 787, corner of Perito Moreno.

Places to Stay
Because of its large number of single labourers, Río Grande is notorious for lack of hotel space, especially at the bottom end of the scale. Patience and perseverance are necessary to find acceptable accommodation, which may be a dormitory bed. Single women will probably prefer midrange hotels.

Places to Stay – bottom end
Hospedaje Argentina (☎ 22365), at San Martín 64 between 11 de Julio and Libertad, is probably the best bargain in town, but its dormitory beds are often full. *Hospedaje Irmary*, Estrada 743 between San Martín and Perito Moreno, has singles at US$8, as does *Hotel Anexo Villa*, Piedrabuena 641 between San Martín and Rosales.

Places to Stay – middle
Hospedaje Miramar (☎ 22462), Mackinlay 595 at Belgrano, one of the best hotels in town, has clean, well-heated singles/doubles at US$8/11 with shared bath and US$11/15 with private bath. *Gran Hotel Villa* (☎ 22312), San Martín 277 between 9 de Julio and Espora, is comparable and has a restaurant/confitería downstairs. *Residencial Rawson*, Estrada 750 across from Hospedaje Irmary, is slightly more expensive.

Places to Stay – top end
All top-end hotels charge about the same, US$44/58. *Posada de los Sauces* (☎ 22895), Elcano 839, has had an enthusiastic recommendation. *Hotel Isla del Mar* (☎ 21518), Güemes 963, also has a good reputation. *Los Yaganes*, Belgrano 319 (☎ 22372), belongs to the ACA and offers a 30% discount to club members. Also in this category are *Hotel Federico Ibarra* (☎ 21071), on Rosales near Fagnano, and *Hotel Atlántida* (☎ 22592) at Belgrano 582.

Places to Eat
Gran Hotel Villa, *Hotel Ibarra* and *Hotel Los Yaganes* all have restaurants. You can also try *El Porteñito*, Lasserre 566 near Belgrano. For short orders and sandwiches, there are

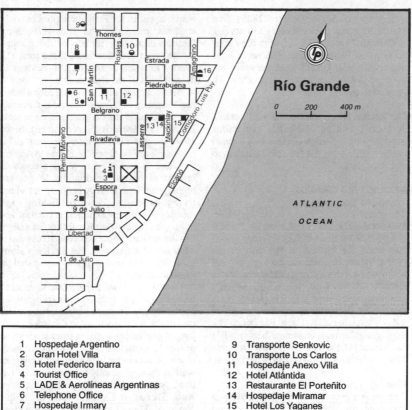

Río Grande

0   200   400 m

ATLANTIC
OCEAN

1	Hospedaje Argentino	9	Transporte Senkovic
2	Gran Hotel Villa	10	Transporte Los Carlos
3	Hotel Federico Ibarra	11	Hospedaje Anexo Villa
4	Tourist Office	12	Hotel Atlántida
5	LADE & Aerolíneas Argentinas	13	Restaurante El Porteñito
6	Telephone Office	14	Hospedaje Miramar
7	Hospedaje Irmary	15	Hotel Los Yaganes
8	Residencial Rawson	16	Post Office

many confiterías in and around the centre, including the one at Residencial Rawson.

Getting There & Away

Air Aerolíneas Argentinas (☎ 22410) and LADE (☎ 21151) are both at San Martín 607, at the corner of Belgrano. Aerolíneas has daily flights to Buenos Aires.

Austral (☎ 21388) is at Perito Moreno 352. Its daily flights from Ushuaia continue to Río Gallegos, Comodoro Rivadavia, Bahía Blanca and Buenos Aires. Connections from the north are similar.

LADE flies daily to Calafate, Ushuaia (US$39), and Río Gallegos, with connections to Buenos Aires and northern Patagonian destinations such as Comodoro Rivadavia and Trelew. Líneas Aéreas Kaikén, a private airline, serves the same destinations as LADE.

Bus Transportes Los Carlos (☎ 21188), Estrada 568, has daily buses to Ushuaia during summer, less frequently during winter, when snow can close the Garibaldi Pass. The four-hour trip costs about US$19.

Transporte Senkovic (☎ 22345), San Martín 959, goes twice weekly to Porvenir in Chilean Tierra del Fuego, with ferry connections to Punta Arenas. The seven-hour trip costs about US$11 from Porvenir, but may be more expensive to purchase in Argentina than in Chile.

Car Rental Given the limited public transportation, fishing and other excursions outside town are much simpler with a rental car, available from A-1 (☎ 22657), Belgrano and Ameghino.

AROUND RÍO GRANDE
Things to See
The most historic place is the **Salesian Museum**, 11 km north of town on Ruta 3, established by the missionary order which converted the Indians in this part of the island. It has exhibits on geology, natural history and ethnography. **Estancia María Behety**, 20 km west, features the world's largest shearing shed. The Río Grande meat freezer, or **Frigorífico**, can process up to 2400 sheep per day. **Lago Fagnano**, the huge glacial trough on Ruta 3 between Río Grande and Ushuaia, merits a visit. *Hostería Kaikén* offers lodging for US$14 per person.

Fishing
Fishing is a popular recreational activity in many nearby rivers. For information on guided trips on the Fuego, Menéndez, Candelaria, Ewan and MacLennan rivers, contact the Club de Pesca John Goodall in Río Grande. One highly recommended place is the *Hostería San Pablo*, 120 km south-east of Río Grande, where there is good fly fishing for trout and salmon on the Río Irigoyen.

USHUAIA
Argentines and Chileans dispute which is the world's southernmost city, but fast-growing Ushuaia clearly overshadows modest Puerto Williams (see the Chilean Patagonia section). In 1870, the South American Missionary Society, a British-based organisation, made Ushuaia its first permanent outpost in the Fuegian region, but only artefacts, memories and Thomas Bridges' famous dictionary remain of the Yahgan Indians who once flourished in the area. The nearby Estancia Harberton still belongs to descendents of the Bridges family.

Between 1884 and 1947, Argentina incarcerated many of its most notorious criminals and political prisoners here and on remote Isla de Los Estados (Staten Island). Since 1950, the town has been an important naval base, supporting Argentine claims to Antarctica, and in recent years it has become an important tourist destination. Wages are higher than in central Argentina, but so are living expenses. Forestry, fishing, and tourism are the most important industries, although efforts to attract electronics assembly have had some success. Ushuaia is supposedly a free port, but foreign visitors will find few real bargains compared to Punta Arenas.

Over the past two decades, the town itself has sprawled and spread from its original site on the Beagle Channel, but the setting is still one of the most dramatic in the world, with jagged glacial peaks rising from sea level to nearly 1500 metres. This surrounding landscape offers trekking, fishing, and skiing, as well as the opportunity to go as far south as roads go, and is Ushuaia's greatest attraction; Ruta 3 ends at Lapataia Bay, in Parque Nacional Tierra del Fuego, 3242 km from Buenos Aires.

Orientation
Ushuaia is on the north shore of the Beagle Channel, its harbour protected by the nearby peninsula on which the airport has been constructed. The shoreline Avenida Maipú, which becomes Avenida Islas Malvinas west of the cemetery, is also Ruta 3 and leads west to Parque Nacional Tierra del Fuego. The waterfront is a good place to observe shorebirds.

The principal commercial street is Avenida San Martín, one block north of Avenida Maipú. Most hotels and tourist services are located within a few blocks of here. Unlike most Argentine cities, Ushuaia has no central plaza, but Avenida San Martín is a pedestrian mall between 9 de Julio and 25 de Mayo, with benches and a playground for children. North of Avenida San Martín, the streets rise very steeply, giving good views of the Beagle Channel.

Information

Tourist Office The tourist office (☎ 21423) has moved to the lobby of the Hotel Albatros, at the corner of Avenida Maipú and Lasserre. The friendly, patient and helpful staff speak some English. They have a complete list of hotel accommodation and current prices, and will assist in finding a room with private families. There is a small branch office at the airport.

Post & Telecommunications ENCOTEL is on Avenida San Martín, at the corner with Godoy. Telefónica Argentina, the long-distance phone office, is at Roca 154, just north of Avenida San Martín.

Money Banco de la Nación is on Avenida San Martín near Rivadavia, while Banco del Sud is at Avenida Maipú 761. Try to change money in the morning, when the banks are open, rather than in the afternoon when they are closed and informal rates are extortionate. The cambio at the tourist office, open from 4 pm to 7.30 pm daily, collects a hefty 10% commission on travellers' cheques.

Foreign Consulates Chile has a consulate at Avenida Islas Malvinas 236, corner of Jainén. If crossing into Chile via Parque Nacional Tierra del Fuego, you must obtain authorisation here first.

Books Rae Natalie Prosser Goodall's detailed, bilingual guidebook *Tierra del Fuego* is essential for anyone spending more than a few days on the island. A new edition was due out in late 1991, and should be available both in Buenos Aires and local bookshops (try the museum). Hilary Bradt and John Pilkington's *Backpacking in Chile & Argentina* (Bradt Enterprises) describes treks in the area. William Leitch's *South*

America's National Parks (The Mountaineers, Seattle) has a useful chapter on the park, with special emphasis on natural history.

Museo Territorial Fin del Mundo

On the waterfront at Avenida Maipú and Rivadavia, this museum has an informed, enthusiastic staff who oversee exhibits on natural history, Indian life, the early penal colonies (complete with a photographic rogues' gallery), and replicas of an early general store and bank. There is also a bookstore and a good specialised library.

Well worth the admission charge of US$1.50, the museum is open weekdays from 3 to 6 pm, and weekends from 4 to 8 pm. At 5 pm daily, museum personnel also lead tours of the former prison, now part of the naval base at the east end of Avenida San Martín.

Organised Tours

For public transport to Parque Nacional Tierra del Fuego, see the Getting There & Away section of the park below.

Local operators offer tours to the principal tourist attractions in and around Ushuaia, including Parque Nacional Tierra del Fuego. Among them are Onas Turismo (☎ 23429), 25 de Mayo 50 at Avenida Maipú, Rumbo Sur (☎ 21139) at Avenida San Martín 342, and Turismo Alternativo Caminante (☎ 22723), Gobernador Deloquí 368, which specialises in trekking to destinations like Lago Fagnano.

Boat trips, with destinations like the sea lion colony at Isla de los Lobos, are also popular during summer. These leave from the Muelle Comercial (commercial jetty) opposite the Hotel Albatros, and cost about US$20 for a 6-hour excursion. The most common species is the southern sea lion *Otaria flavescens*, whose thick mane will make you wonder why Spanish speakers call it *lobo marino* (sea wolf). Fur seals, nearly extinct because of commercial overexploitation during the past century, may be seen in much smaller numbers. Isla de Pájaros, also in the Beagle Channel, has many species of

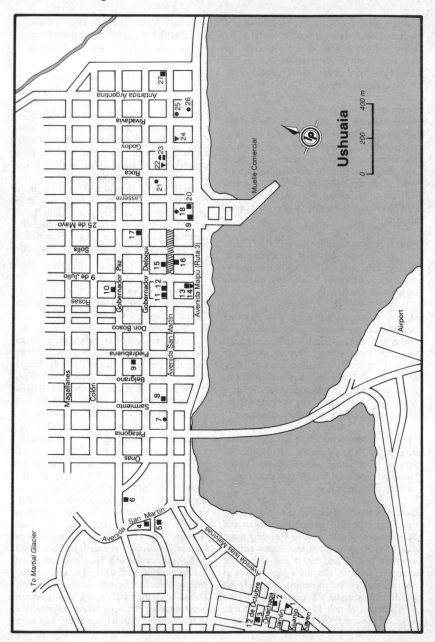

Ushuaia

■ PLACES TO STAY

2 Residencial Fernández
3 Hotel Maitén
4 Hotel Antártida
5 Hotel Las Lengas
6 Hospedaje América
8 Hostería Monte Cervantes
9 Hostería Mustapic
10 Pensión Rosita
11 Hotel Cabo de Hornos
12 Hospedaje No. 845
13 Hospedaje Ona
15 Hospedaje César
16 Residencial Capri
17 Hospedaje Malvinas
19 Hotel Canal Beagle
20 Hotel Albatros/Aerolíneas
      Argentinas & Tourist Office
27 Hotel Mafalda

▼ PLACES TO EAT

14 Restaurante Los Canelos
22 Cafetería Ideal
24 Restaurante Moustacchio

OTHER

1 Chilean Consulate
7 Administration del Parque
      Nacional Tierra del Fuego
18 LADE & AUSTRAL
21 Telefónica
23 Post Office
25 Banco de la Nación
26 Museo Territorial
      Fin del Munde

birds, including extensive cormorant colonies.

Trips to historic Estancia Harberton, east of Ushuaia, can be arranged with sufficient notice, but no one should arrive unannounced. There are also city tours, excursions over Garibaldi Pass to Lago Fagnano and Río Grande, and various other cruises. The tourist office provides a useful descriptive brochure.

Places to Stay – bottom end
Camping There is a free municipal campsite at Río Pipo, 5 km west of town, but facilities are minimal. Other campsites, both free and paying, are found at Tierra del Fuego National Park.

Casas de Familia The tourist office may be able to arrange rooms in private homes, which are much cheaper than hotels. One which has been highly recommended is at Primer Argentino 176, outside the centre. Try also Ernesto Campos at Juana Fadul Solís 368, where bed and breakfast cost US$10. Near the airport and the trail to Martial Glacier, Elvira's house (☎ 23123) at Fuegia Basket 419 is slightly cheaper but also warmly recommended.

Hospedajes, Pensions & Residenciales
Since the apparent closure of the truly squalid *Las Goletas*, Avenida Maipú 857, there is little real budget accommodation in Ushuaia; if desperate, check to see if it has reopened. The next cheapest choice is *Hospedaje Ona*, 9 de Julio 27 at Avenida Maipú, where dormitory-style beds cost US$5. Weekly rates are slightly lower.

Pensión Rosita, on Gobernador Paz between Rosas (ex-Triunvirato) and 9 de Julio, charges US$12 per person in a more family-oriented environment. *Hospedaje América* (☎ 23858), Gobernador Paz 1600, has singles/doubles at US$12/16. Recommendations for *Residencial Capri* (☎ 21833), Avenida San Martín 720, which has beds at $15, are as tepid as their showers.

Places to Stay – middle
Midrange hotels are easier to find, but still may be very crowded in summer. The enthusiastically recommended *Hospedaje Fernández* (☎ 21453), Onachaga 68, has doubles at US$19. Other possibilities in this price range are *Hospedaje Cesar* (☎ 21460) at Avenida San Martín 753 for US$17/27, *Hospedaje Malvinas* (☎ 22626) at Gobernador Deloquí 609 for US$25/35, *Hostería Mustapic* (☎ 21718) at Piedrabuena 230 for US$25/30, and *Hotel Maitén* (☎ 22745) at 12 de Octubre 140 for US$18/22.

Places to Stay – top end

Waterfront hotels have the best views and highest prices. Among them are *Hotel Albatros* (☎ 22504), Avenida Maipú 505 at Lasserre, at US$31/60 with breakfast, and ACA's *Hotel Canal Beagle* (☎ 21117), Avenida Maipú 599 at 25 de Mayo, which is costlier at US$44/58. Also central are *Hotel Cabo de Hornos* (☎ 22187), Avenida San Martín at Rosas for US$38/45, and the new and pleasant *Hotel Mafalda* (☎ 22373) at Avenida San Martín 15 for US$38/50, breakfast not included.

Outside the centre, but still within reasonable walking distance, are the Tudor-style *Hostería Monte Cervantes* (☎ 22153), Avenida San Martín at Sarmiento, and the highly recommended *Hotel Antártida* (☎ 21807) at Avenida San Martín 1600 for US$38/47.

At *Estancia Río Pipo* (☎ 23411), 5 km west of town, cabañas rent for US$78/88.

Places to Eat

Food which is both cheap and good is not easily available in Ushuaia. For seafood, which is good but not up to the best Chilean standards, try *Los Canelos*, Avenida Maipú at 9 de Julio. The lively *Cafetería Ideal*, Avenida San Martín 393 at Roca, is good and reasonable.

Costlier, but good value with excellent food and service, is *Moustacchio* (☎ 23308), Avenida San Martín 298. *Tante Elvira* (☎ 21982, 21249), Avenida San Martín 234, also has a good reputation. One LP reader enthusiastically endorsed *Parrilla Tío Carlos*, Colón 758, for high quality and abundant portions. Beware the expensive but erratic *Casita Azul*, Avenida San Martín at 9 de Julio. At the more expensive restaurants, reservations are essential for groups of any size.

Getting There & Away

Air Ushuaia has frequent air connections to Buenos Aires and to other parts of Patagonia. LADE (☎ 21123), Avenida San Martín 564, has daily departures to Calafate via Río Grande (US$35) and Río Gallegos (US$60).

Austral's local agent (☎ 23235) is at Avenida San Martín 638.

Aerolíneas Argentinas (☎ 21218), downstairs at the Hotel Albatros, has daily flights to Buenos Aires, with stopovers at various intermediate destinations such as Río Gallegos, Trelew and Bahía Blanca. Austral has similar services. One-way fares cost about US$250.

Líneas Aéreas Kaikén, Antártida Argentina 75 near Avenida San Martín, serves the same destinations as LADE plus Punta Arenas (US$120), and also operates charter overflights of Cape Horn.

The airport is on the peninsula across from the waterfront, linked to town by a causeway. Cabs are reasonable, but there is also a bus service along Avenida Maipú. The short runway, steep approach and frequent high winds make landing at Ushuaia an adventure which timid flyers may wish to avoid.

Bus Transporte Los Carlos (☎ 22337), Rosas 57, crosses the Garibaldi Pass via Lago Fagnano to Río Grande, where connections can be made to Porvenir and Punta Arenas. The four-hour trip costs about US$19. For transportation to Parque Nacional Tierra del Fuego, see the Getting There & Away section of the park, below.

Car Rental Although rural public transport is better than at Río Grande, it is still limited. There are, however, several rental car agencies. U-Rent-a-Car operates from the same offices as Líneas Aéreas Kaikén (see above). Other agencies include Rent Austral (☎ 22422), Gobernador Paz 1022, and Autograd (☎ 22723), Gobernador Deloquí 368.

Boat At 8 am Saturdays, there is a ferry from Ushuaia to Puerto Williams, Chile, for US$50. The crossing takes 1½ hours. From Puerto Williams, there are weekly sea and air connections to Punta Arenas.

AROUND USHUAIA
Martial Glacier

Just within the borders of Parque Nacional

Top Left: Communications Tower, Montevideo (RS)
Top Right: Conventillo, Ciudad Vieja, Montevideo
Bottom Left: Colonial Estancia El Talar, Uruguay
Bottom Right: Old car, Colonia, Uruguay (DS)

Top: Paysandú, Uruguay
Left: Punta del Este, Uruguay
Right: Sculpture in Casa Pueblo, Punta Ballena, Uruguay

Tierra del Fuego, Martial Glacier is a magnificent walk which begins from the west end of Avenida San Martín, past the national parks office, and climbs the zigzag road (there are many hiker shortcuts) to the ski run seven km north-west of town. It is possible to hitch or take a taxi to the chairlift which, as of summer 1991, was not operating due to a contract dispute (the lift fare is about US$5 and saves an hour's walk). From the base of the lift, the glacier is about a two-hour walk, with awesome views of Ushuaia and the Beagle Channel. Weather is very changeable, so take warm, dry clothing and sturdy footwear.

Fishing

Fishing is a popular pastime for both Argentines and foreigners; the required licence is available from the Gobernación (government house) in Ushuaia; inquire there for other regulations. Spinning and fly casting are the most common means of getting brown trout, rainbow trait, Atlantic salmon, and others. The nearest site is Río Pipo, 5 km west of town. It is possible to visit the fish hatchery at Río Olivia, 2 km beyond. The tourist office has a good informational brochure with other recommendations.

PARQUE NACIONAL TIERRA DEL FUEGO

This 63,000-hectare unit, extending from the Beagle Channel in the south along the Chilean border to beyond Lago Fagnano in the north, is the only coastal national park in Argentina. Just 18 km west of Ushuaia, its forests, bays, lakes, rivers, peaks and glaciers attract many visitors and hikers, both Argentine and foreign, although the park lacks the integrated network of hiking trails of Chile's Torres del Paine park. There are, however, many shorter hiking trails and one major trek which deserve mention.

Three species of southern beech (*Nothofagus*) dominate the dense native forests; these are known by their common names coihue, lenga, and ñire. The evergreen coihue and the deciduous lenga thrive on the heavy coastal rainfall at lower elevations, but

Cauquén

the deciduous ñire tints the Fuegian hillsides during the fall months. Other tree species are much less significant and conspicuous.

The *Sphagnum* peat bogs in some parts of the park support ferns, colourful wildflowers, and some insectivorous plants; these may be seen on the self-guided Laguna Negra nature trail. To avoid damage to the bog and danger to yourself, stay on the trail, part of which consists of a catwalk for easier passage across the swampy terrain.

Park mammals are few, although guanacos and foxes exist. Visitors are most likely to see two unfortunate introductions, the European rabbit and the North American beaver, both of which have caused ecological havoc and proved impossible to eradicate. The former numbers up to 70 per hectare in some areas, while the latter's handiwork is visible in the ponds and by the dead beeches along the Sendero de los Castores (Trail of the Beavers) to Bahía Lapataia. Originally introduced at Lake Fagnano in the 1940s, beavers quickly spread throughout the island.

Bird life is much more abundant, especially along the coastal section, including Lapataia and Bahía Ensenada. The Andean condor and the maritime black-browed albatross overlap ranges here, although neither is common. Numerous species of shorebirds such as cormorants, gulls, terns, oystercatchers, grebes, steamer ducks and kelp geese are common. The large, striking upland goose *(cauquén)* is widely distributed farther inland. Space prohibits a detailed description here, but an outstanding guide is Claudio Venegas Canelo's *Aves de Patagonia y Tierra del Fuego Chileno-Argentina* (Punta Arenas, 1986).

Marine mammals are most commonly seen on offshore islands.

Trekking

Most park trails are relatively short, but at least two merit longer trips. With permission from the Chilean Consulate and Argentine authorities in Ushuaia, it is possible to hike from Lapataia into Chile, along the north shore of Lago Roca. There is also an extended trek up the Río Pipo, across the Martial Mountains to Lake Fagnano. This rugged trip, 30 km each way, begins at the Río Pipo campsite. It should be simple for experienced, independent hikers, but travel agencies in Ushuaia can also assist (see Organised Tours in the Ushuaia section above). Take warm, dry clothing, good footwear, a sleeping bag, a tent, and plenty of food.

Unfortunately, because of Argentina's perpetual fiscal crisis and the military's proprietary attitude toward border zones, there are no official, detailed, easily available maps, but the route is fairly straightforward. Probably the best map you'll find is the detailed walking map contained in LP's *Trekking in the Patagonian Andes* by Clem Lindenmayer.

Places to Stay

Since the *Hostería Alakush* at Lago Roca burned to the ground, camping is the only alternative for those wishing to stay here. The only organised campsite within the park, also at Lago Roca, has hot showers, a confitería, and groceries. At US$6 per person, it is not really cheap, but there are free campsites without facilities at Lapataia, Ensenada, and Río Pipo.

Getting There & Away

During summer, Línea Parque Nacional leaves daily from Avenida Maipú 329 in Ushuaia at 10 am, 3.30 pm, and 7.30 pm, returning from the Lago Roca camping area at 11 am, 4.30 pm, and 8.30 pm. The round-trip fare is US$10, and you need not return the same day.

Hitching to the park is possible, although most Argentine families will have little room in their vehicles. Park admission, payable at the ranger station on Ruta 3, is US$3 per person. There are also ranger stations at Lago Roca and Lapataia.

Chilean Patagonia

Chilean Patagonia, south of the mainland Lake District, consists of the provinces of Aysén and Magallanes. It is a rugged, mountainous area, battered by westerly winds and storms which drop enormous amounts of snow and rain on the seaward slopes of the Andes. The southern continental icefield separates the two provinces; Magallanes and its capital of Punta Arenas are more easily accessible from Argentine Patagonia and Tierra del Fuego than from Aysén or the Chilean mainland, from which the principal transportation connections are by air, sea, or overland through Argentina.

Ona, Yahgan, Haush, Alacaluf and Tehuelche Indians, subsisting through fishing, hunting and gathering, were the region's original inhabitants. There remain very few individuals of identifiable Ona, Haush or Yahgan descent, while the Alacalufes and Tehuelches survive in much reduced numbers. Magellan, in 1520, was the first European to visit the area, but early Spanish colonisation attempts failed; tiny Puerto Hambre (Port Famine) on the Straits is a reminder of these efforts. Nearby, the restored wooden bulwarks of Fort Bulnes recall Chile's first colonisation of 1843, when President Manuel Bulnes ordered the army south to the area, then only sparsely populated by indigenous peoples.

Punta Arenas itself owes its origins to the California Gold Rush, but its enduring prosperity derived from the wool and mutton industry which transformed both Argentine and Chilean Patagonia in the late 19th century, and on the maritime traffic which passed the Straits between Europe, on the one hand, and California and Australia on the other. With the opening of the Panama Canal and the reduction of traffic around Cape Horn, the port's international importance diminished.

Besides wool, its modern economy depends on commerce, provincial petroleum development, and fisheries, which have made the province the most prosperous in Chile, with the highest levels of employment, housing quality, school attendance and public services in the country. The region's impressive natural assets, particularly Parque Nacional Torres del Paine, have made it an increasingly popular tourist destination.

VISITING CHILEAN PATAGONIA

Many people who visit Argentine Patagonia's popular natural attractions also visit Chilean Patagonia. Basic information on Chilean travel is provided here, but those spending an extended period in other parts of Chile should obtain Lonely Planet's *Chile & Easter Island – a travel survival kit.*

Visas

Nationals of countries with whom Chile has diplomatic relations, including the USA, Canada, Western Europe, Japan, Australia and many others, need passports but not visas to enter the country. All visitors do need a tourist card, which is issued at the port of entry. Like the Argentine tourist card, it is valid for 90 days and renewable for another 90. Unlike the Argentine card, it is taken very seriously, so keep close tabs and avoid the hassle of replacement. Chilean border offi-

cials are generally reasonable and friendly, however.

Customs

Chilean customs permits the importation of personal belongings, 500 cigarettes, 100 cigars, and two litres of alcoholic beverages, plus gifts and souvenirs. Normally customs officials are not difficult to deal with, although returning to Puerto Montt or Santiago from Punta Arenas (a free zone where electronics items are very cheap), you may encounter a thorough internal customs check. Unless you are carrying, say, half a dozen cameras of the same brand and model, you are not likely to be seriously inconvenienced.

Money & Costs

The peso (Ch$) is the unit of currency. It is much more stable than Argentine currency, and has maintained its rate of exchange of around Ch$330 per US dollar for quite some time. Banknote denominations are 500, 1000 and 5000 pesos, although breaking a 5000-peso note can be a great nuisance for small purchases. There are also coins of five, 10, 50 and 100 pesos.

For basic costs such as accommodation, food and transport, foreign visitors will find Chile more expensive than the central Andean countries but cheaper than Argentina. Chilean Patagonia, however, generally has a higher cost of living than the rest of the country because of its distance and relative isolation.

Health

Conditions are much the same as in Argentina; see the section on health in Facts for the Visitor. Chile does not demand any unusual health precautions – although the 1991 Peruvian cholera outbreak had more impact here than in Argentina, it was still a relatively minor matter. No vaccinations are required as a condition of entry.

Getting There & Away

For travel to Chilean Patagonia, your options are air or boat unless you go overland through Argentina. Chile's two major airlines, LAN-Chile and Ladeco, are both comfortable and efficient. A new airline, SABA, has begun to offer discount fares throughout the country; but they have recently run into financial and legal problems and the airline may soon be sold. Travellers have reported that purchased tickets have not been honoured by SABA, so it would be wise to inquire before buying one of their tickets.

There are regular ferry services between Puerto Montt, on the Chilean mainland, and Puerto Natales, in Magallanes.

Within Chilean Patagonia, Aerovías DAP serves Chilean Tierra del Fuego, also flying to Antarctica and the Falkland Islands. There are ferries between Punta Arenas and Porvenir, in Tierra del Fuego.

Good, comfortable buses connect Punta Arenas, Puerto Natales and Parque Nacional Torres del Paine, the main centres of tourist interest in Chilean Patagonia.

PUNTA ARENAS

At the foot of the Andes on the western side of the Strait of Magellan, Punta Arenas has nearly 100,000 inhabitants. Its free port facilities have promoted local commerce and encouraged immigration from central Chile; many luxury items, such as automobiles, are much less expensive here, although the basic cost of living is higher. As the best and largest port for thousands of kilometres, it attracts ships from the burgeoning South Atlantic fishery as well as Antarctic research and tourist vessels. The city centre features many mansions and other impressive buildings dating from the wool boom of the late 19th and early 20th centuries.

History

Founded in 1848, Punta Arenas was originally a military garrison and penal settlement which proved to be conveniently situated for shipping en route to California during the Gold Rush. Compared to the initial Chilean settlement at Fuerte Bulnes, 60 km south, it had superior supplies of wood and water, and a better port in a more protected site. For

many years, this site had been known on English maritime charts as Sandy Point, and this became its rough Spanish equivalent.

In Punta Arenas' early years, its economy depended on wild animal products, including sealskins, guanaco hides and feathers; mineral products, including coal, gold and guano; and firewood and timber. None of these was a truly major industry, and the economy did not take off until the last quarter of the 19th century, after the territorial governor authorised the purchase of 300 purebred sheep from the Falkland Islands. The success of this experiment encouraged others to invest in sheep and, by the turn of the century, there were nearly two million animals in the territory.

In 1875, the population of Magallanes province was barely 1000, but European immigration accelerated as the wool market boomed. Among the most significant immigrants were Portuguese businessman José Nogueira, Irish doctor Thomas Fenton, who founded one of the island's largest sheep stations, and José Menéndez, an Asturian entrepreneur who would become one of the wealthiest and most influential individuals not just in Patagonia, but in all of South America.

First engaged solely in commerce, Menéndez soon began to acquire pastoral property, founding the famous Sociedad Explotadora de Tierra del Fuego, which controlled nearly a million hectares in Magallanes alone and other properties across the border – one of the greatest estancias in Argentina, near Río Grande, still bears the name of his wife, María Behety. With another important family, the Brauns, the descendents of Menéndez comprised one of the wealthiest and most powerful regional elites in all of Latin America. Although few remain in Punta Arenas (having relocated to Santiago and Buenos Aires), their downtown mansions remain as symbols of Punta Arenas' golden age.

Menéndez and his colleagues could not have built their commercial and pastoral empires without the labour of immigrants from many lands: English, Irish, Scots,

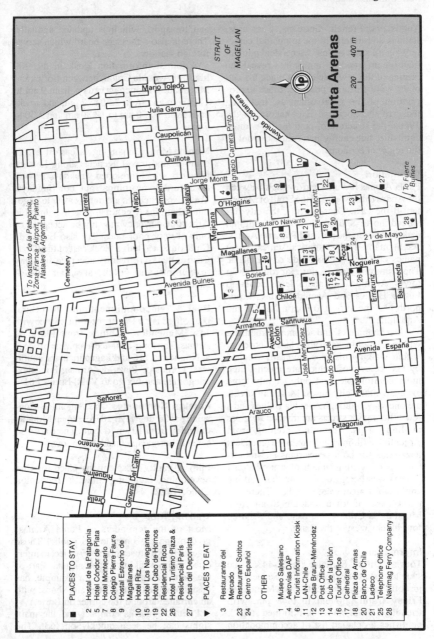

STRAIT OF MAGELLAN

Punta Arenas

0   200   400 m

To Fuerte Bulnes

To Instituto de la Patagonia, Zona Franca Airport, Puerto Natales & Argentina

Mario Toledo
Julia Garay
Caupolicán
Quillota
Jorge Montt
O'Higgins
Lautaro Navarro
Magallanes
Avenida Bulnes
Bories
Chiloé
Armando
Sanhueza
Arauco
Patagonia
Avenida España
Avenida Colón
José Menéndez
Waldo Seguel
Fagnano
Nogueira
Errázuriz
Balmaceda
21 de Mayo
Roca
Pedro Montt
Mejicana
Yugoslavia
Sarmiento
Maipú
Carrera
Cemetery
Señoret
Zenteno
General Del Canto
Riquelme
Orella
Angamos
Ignacio Carrera Pinto
Avenida Costanera

PLACES TO STAY

2   Hostal de la Patagonia
5   Hotel Cóndor de Plata
7   Hotel Montecarlo
8   Colegio Pierre Faure
9   Hostal Estrecho de Magallanes
10   Hotel Ritz
15   Hotel Los Navegantes
19   Hotel Cabo de Hornos
22   Residencial Roca
26   Hotel Turismo Plaza & Residencial París
27   Casa del Deportista

PLACES TO EAT

3   Restaurante del Mercado
23   Restaurant Sotitos
24   Centro Español

OTHER

1   Museo Salesiano
4   Aerovías DAP
6   Tourist Information Kiosk
11   LAN-Chile
12   Casa Braun-Menéndez
13   Post Office
14   Club de la Unión
16   Tourist Office
17   Cathedral
18   Plaza de Armas
20   Banco de Chile
21   Ladeco
25   Telephone Office
28   Navimag Ferry Company

Yugoslavs, French, Germans, Spaniards, Italians and others. In the municipal cemetery, on all sides of José Menéndez' opulent mausoleum, modest tombstones reveal the origins of those whose efforts made his and other wool fortunes possible. Since expropriation of the great estancias, including those of the Sociedad Explotadora, in the 1960s, the structure of land tenure is more equitable, but energy has eclipsed wool in the regional economy.

Orientation

Punta Arenas lies on a narrow shelf between the Andes to the west and the Strait of Magellan to the east. Consequently, the city has spread north and south from its original centre between the port and Plaza de Armas. As in many Latin American cities, street names change on either side of the plaza. There are only two major exit routes from town: Avenida Costanera leads south to Fuerte Bulnes and Avenida Bulnes heads north past the airport to Puerto Natales and Argentina.

Most landmarks, and accommodation, are within a few blocks of the plaza. Those not within walking distance are easily reached by taxi colectivos, which are much faster, more comfortable, and only slightly more expensive than city buses. Most city streets are one-way, although Avenida Bulnes and a few other major streets are divided by grass median strips. Travellers coming from Argentina will find Chilean traffic much less hazardous for both pedestrians and motorists. As of writing, much of central Punta Arenas was being repaved, so that parking and motor transit were irregular. There is a good view of town and the Strait from Mirador La Cruz, at Fagnano and Señoret, four blocks west of the Plaza.

Information

Tourist Office Sernatur (☎ 22-4435), the state tourist agency, is at Waldo Seguel 689, just off Plaza de Armas. It's open Monday to Friday from 8.30 am to 6.45 pm, with friendly, helpful, and well-informed staff. It publishes a detailed list of accommodation and transport, which is updated annually. There is also a message board which serves foreign visitors.

A tourist information kiosk in the 700 block of Avenida Colón, between Bories and Magallanes, is open weekdays from 9 am to 12.30 pm and from 2.30 to 7 pm, and weekends from 10.30 am to 12.30 am and 2.30 to 7 pm.

Money Money changing is easiest at the cambios and travel agencies along Lautaro Navarro, which are open weekdays as well as Saturday mornings, but not Sundays. Travellers' cheques are much easier to negotiate than in Argentina, but the unstable Argentine currency may not be accepted, or only at very poor rates. Try also Banco de Chile on Roca, half a block east of the Plaza. Cash dollars are readily accepted in many restaurants and hotels, at a fair rate of exchange.

Post & Telecommunications The central post office is on Bories, near the corner with José Menéndez, a block from Plaza de Armas. The long-distance telephone office is at Nogueira 1116 and Fagnano, at the southwest corner of Plaza de Armas. For telex, telegrams, and fax go to VTR, Bories 801.

Foreign Consulates The Argentine Consulate, at 21 de Mayo 1878, is open Monday to Friday from 10 am to 2 pm. There are also several European consulates in town.

Film A good, conscientious place for film developing, including slides, is Todocolor, Chiloé 1422.

Walking Tour

Most of the reminders of Punta Arenas' golden age are open to the public. Those which are not museums rarely object to interested visitors taking a look around. Part of the Sara Braun mansion, for example, has been converted into offices and shops, with an entrance around the corner on Bories.

Punta Arenas is compact and the main sights can be seen quickly on foot. The logical starting place is the lovingly maintained **Plaza de Armas**, landscaped with a variety of exotic conifers. There is an artisans' shop in the Victorian kiosk. Around the Plaza are the **Club de la Unión** (formerly the Sara Braun mansion, built by a French architect), the **Catedral**, and other monuments to the city's turn-of-the-century splendour.

Half a block north, at Magallanes 949, is the spectacular **Casa Braun-Menéndez**, the famous family's mansion which is now a cultural centre and regional history museum. Three blocks west of the Plaza, the house at **Avenida España 959**, was the house of Charly Milward, whose eccentric exploits inspired his distant relation Bruce Chatwin to write the extraordinary travelogue *In Patagonia*.

Four blocks south of the Plaza, at the foot of Avenida Independencia, is the entrance to the **port**, which is open to the public. At the end of the pier, you may see ships and sailors from Spain, Poland, Japan, France, the USA and many other countries, as well as local fishers, the Chilean navy, and countless seabirds. Photographic opportunities are excellent.

Six blocks north of the Plaza, at Bories and Sarmiento, is the **Museo Salesiano** (Salesian Museum). Another four blocks north is the entrance to the **Cementerio Municipal** (Municipal Cemetery), an open-air historical museum in its own right.

Casa Braun-Menéndez

Also known as the Palacio Mauricio Braun, this impressive mansion is a testament to the opulence of pioneer sheep farmers in the late 19th century. The last remaining daughter of the marriage between Mauricio Braun (brother of Sara Braun) and Josefina Menéndez Behety (daughter of José Menéndez and María Behety) is alive at age 91 in Buenos Aires, but the family has donated the house to the state. Much remains as it did when still occupied by the family, with original furnishings. At present, only the main floor is open to the public, but restoration may permit access to the upper floors.

The museum also has excellent historical photographs and artefacts of early European settlement. Admission charges are modest, but there is an extra charge for photographing the interior. Hours are Tuesday to Saturday, 11 am to 4 pm and Sunday from 11 am to 1 pm. Access to the grounds is easiest from Magallanes, but you must go to the back of the house to enter the museum.

Museo Regional Salesiano Mayorino Borgatello

The Salesian College Museum, at Avenida Bulnes 374 near Sarmiento, features anthropological, historical and natural history exhibits from materials collected by a missionary order which was especially important in European settlement of the region. In summer, it is open Tuesday to Sunday from 10 am to 1 pm and from 3 to 6 pm; in winter, weekday hours are from 3 to 6 pm only, while weekend hours are identical to summer.

Cementerio Municipal

The walled municipal cemetery, at Avenida Bulnes 949, tells a great deal about the history and social structure of the region. The first families of Punta Arenas flaunted their wealth in death as in life – wool baron José Menéndez has one of the most extravagant tombs – but the headstones among the topiary cypresses also tell the stories of Anglo, German, Scandinavian and Yugoslav immigrants who supported them with their labour. There is also a monument to the now nearly extinct Onas. Open daily, the cemetery is about a 15-minute walk from the plaza, although you can also take any taxi colectivo from the entrance of the Centro Cultural Braun-Menéndez on Magallanes.

Instituto de la Patagonia

Part of the Universidad de Magallanes, the Patagonian Institute features an interesting collection of early farm and industrial machinery imported from Europe, a typical pioneer house and shearing shed (both reconstructed), and a wooden-wheeled trailer which served as shelter for outside shepherds. Visitors can wander among the outdoor exhibits at will, but ask the caretaker at the library for admission to the buildings.

The library also has a display of historical maps, and a series of historical and scientific publications for sale to the public. A rather overgrown botanical garden, a small zoo, and experimental garden plots and greenhouses are also open to the public.

Opening hours are Monday to Friday, 8.30 am to 12.30 pm and 2.30 to 6.30 pm. Weekend visits may be possible by prior arrangement. Any taxi colectivo to the Zona Franca (the Free Zone, see below) will drop you across the street.

Organised Tours

Several agencies run trips to the important tourist sites near Punta Arenas, as well as to more distant destinations like Torres del Paine. Karú-Kinká (☎ 22-7868), Arauco 1792, offers guided excursions to the Club Andino (Andean Club, which offers winter skiing) for US$9, a city tour for US$15, and trips to the Otway penguin colony and Fuerte Bulnes for US$45 each. Guides speak German, French and Dutch. Torres del Paine excursions start at US$270, and include overnight camping or hotels; up to four people per vehicle may split the cost.

Turismo Pali Aike (☎ 22-3301), José Menéndez 556, has slightly cheaper trips to the Otway penguin colony and Fuerte Bulnes, which include sandwiches and soft drinks. There is an additional itinerary to Río Verde, on Seno Skyring (Skyring Sound), for US$12. Regular departures are limited. Arka Patagonia (☎ 22-6370), Roca 886, Local 7, also runs trips for similar prices.

Traveltur (☎ 22-8159), Roca 886, Local 25, arranges sailings to Parque Nacional Los Pingüinos between November and March, on request and weather permitting, and also visits Otway Sound, Fuerte Bulnes, and Torres del Paine. Inquire for prices.

Places to Stay – bottom end

Prices for accommodation have risen recently, but there are still good-value places. One of the best is the *Colegio Pierre Faure*, Lautaro Navarro 842, a private school which operates as a hostel during the summer months of January and February, although the staff may be able to accommodate visitors at other times of the year. Singles are US$4.50, with breakfast, but you can also pitch a tent in the rear garden for US$2.50 per person. All baths are shared, but there is plenty of hot water, and it is a good place to meet other travellers.

Residencial Roca (☎ 22-3654), at Roca 1058 near O'Higgins, welcomes backpackers but is often full. Situated in a well-heated but leaky building, a single bed in a six-bed room costs US$4.50 without breakfast, while a private single costs US$9 when available. The *Casa del Deportista*, near the port at O'Higgins 1205, also charges US$4.50 per person for a shared room. At the same price *Residencial Internacional*, Arauco 154, is popular but not especially clean, while *Residencial Rubio*, Avenida España 640, is good value at US$6.50 a single with breakfast.

Residencial París (☎ 22-3112), 3rd floor, Nogueira 1116, half a block from Plaza de Armas, costs US$9 per person. *Hotel Montecarlo* (☎ 22-3448), an old but spacious building at Avenida Colón 605 and Chiloé, has singles/doubles with shared bath at US$10.50/18. Rooms with private bath are more expensive.

Places to Stay – middle

Hostal Estrecho de Magallanes (☎ 22-6011), José Menéndez 1048, and the highly recommended *Hotel Ritz* (☎ 22-4422), Pedro Montt 1102, both have rooms for about US$15/22. At the *Hostal de la Patagonia* (☎ 22-3521), O'Higgins 472, rates are US$22/29.

Hotel Turismo Plaza (☎ 22-1300), one floor below Residencial Paris, charges US$32/39, while *Hotel Cóndor de Plata* (☎ 22-7987), Avenida Colón 556, is a comfortable modern place for US$36/40.

Places to Stay – top end

Perhaps the best in town, *Hotel Los Navegantes* (☎ 22-4677), José Menéndez 647, has rooms for US$65/75, while the slightly more central *Hotel Cabo de Hornos* (☎ 22-2134), on Plaza de Armas, charges US$89/105. The latter has a good but costly bar, and its solarium features a number of stuffed birds, including rockhopper and macaroni penguins, which visitors to local penguin colonies are unlikely to see.

Places to Eat

If Argentine food, with its heavy reliance on beef, has become tiresome, Punta Arenas offers the chance to feast on the excellent seafood which characterises Chilean cuisine. Both finfish and shellfish are superb. The traditional Chilean salad, consisting of tomato and onion, is simple but tasty.

Sotitos, at O'Higgins 1138, has an outstanding reputation for dishes such as centolla (king crab), but is not cheap. The same holds for the nearby *Bar Grill Beagle*. Prices are moderate at *Restaurant Taverna*, also on O'Higgins, but its fish is often deep-fried.

The *Centro Español*, above the Teatro Cervantes on Plaza de Armas, serves delicious cóngrio (conger eel) and ostiones (scallops), among other specialities. An extravagant meal, with wine, will cost about US$10, but you can eat well for half that. The *Restaurante del Mercado*, upstairs at Mejicana and Chiloé, prepares a spicy ostiones al pil pil and a delicate but filling chupe de locos (an abalone dish). Due to overexploitation of abalone, the latter dish has become costly.

Other popular regional dishes include cholgas (mussels) and erizos (sea urchins), the latter definitely an acquired taste. If you are with a group, you may wish to order curanto, a tasty, filling stew made of shellfish, chicken, potatoes and vegetables.

As of summer 1991, the *Club de la Unión*, located in the former Sara Braun mansion on the Plaza, was closed for a change of management. When it reopens, it should be worth a visit, if only for its turn-of-the-century atmosphere.

Many restaurants, including all the above, serve more conventional parrilla dishes. *La Carioca*, Chiloé and José Menéndez, has good sandwiches and lager beer, although its pizzas are small and expensive. A good place for breakfast and *onces* ('elevenses', Chilean afternoon tea) is *Café Garogha*, Bories 817, which has CNN on television.

Entertainment

Since the end of the military dictatorship, which regularly enforced a curfew, Chilean nightlife is more exuberant. Café Garogha has a lively crowd late into the evening, and sometimes has live entertainment. As in any port, there are numerous bars: try the Ñandú Café Grill, at Waldo Seguel 670, which also serves meals. Peña El Trovador, Pedro Montt 919, was closed in the summer of 1991, but may reopen.

There are two cinemas, including the Teatro Cervantes on Plaza de Armas, which often show American and European films.

On the outskirts of the centre is the municipal racetrack. There is also a stadium where the local representative of the Chilean soccer league plays.

Things to Buy

The Zona Franca (duty-free zone) in Punta Arenas is a good place to replace a lost or stolen camera, and to buy film and other luxury items. Fujichrome slide film, 36 exposures, costs about US$5 per roll without developing; print film is correspondingly cheap. Taxi colectivos from the centre to the Zona Franca, which is open daily except Sunday, are frequent.

Chile Típico, Carrera Pinto 1015, offers artisanal items in copper, bronze, and other materials.

Getting There & Away

The tourist office distributes a useful brochure with complete information on all forms of transportation and their schedules to and from Punta Arenas, Puerto Natales, and Tierra del Fuego, including those which go to or through Argentina.

Air LAN-Chile (☎ 22-3338), Lautaro Navarro 999 at the corner of Pedro Montt, flies to Puerto Montt (US$144) and Santiago (US$234) daily except Thursday. Children's fares (ages two to 12) are slightly more than half adult price.

Ladeco (☎ 22-6100), at Roca 924 near O'Higgins, flies the same routes daily except Wednesday. Fares are identical to LAN. SABA (☎ 22-2831), a new Chilean airline at Pedro Montt 957, has been offering promotional fares between Santiago and Punta Arenas for about US$240 return; however, see our warning in the introductory part of the Chilean Patagonia section.

Aerovías DAP (☎ 22-3958), Ignacio Carrera Pinto 1022 near Jorge Montt, flies to Porvenir and back twice daily, Monday to Saturday, for US$13.50 one way. On Tuesday, it goes to and from Puerto Williams, on Isla Navarino, for US$62 one way, slightly cheaper return. Children below the age of six travel for half-price. During the summer, it has weekly flights to the Falkland Islands for US$365 single; during winter, these flights are every other week. It also has monthly flights to Teniente Marsh air base in Antarctica for US$1000 single. The schedule permits one or two nights in Antarctica before returning to Punta Arenas.

The Chilean Air Force (FACh) has irregular flights to Puerto Montt which are cheaper than commercial flights. Inquire at the tourist office or airport.

Aeropuerto Presidente Carlos Ibáñez del Campo is 20 km north of town. DAP runs its own bus service to the airport, while LAN and Ladeco use local bus companies.

Bus Punta Arenas has no central bus terminal; each company has its own office from which its buses depart, although most of these are fairly close together, on or near Lautaro Navarro. There are direct buses to Puerto Natales, Río Grande and Río Gallegos in Argentina, and mainland Chilean destinations via Argentina.

Buses Fernández (☎ 22-2313), Chiloé 930, and Bus Sur (☎ 22-4864), José Menéndez 556, each have two buses daily to Puerto Natales for US$6. Buses Victoria Sur (☎ 22-6213), Avenida Colón 793, also twice daily except Sunday, is slightly more expensive.

Buses Pacheco (☎ 22-5641), at Lautaro Navarro 601, goes twice weekly to Río Grande, in Argentine Tierra del Fuego, from where it is possible to make a connection to Ushuaia. The fare, including the ferry crossing from Punta Arenas to Porvenir, is US$25.

There are numerous services to Río Gallegos, Argentina, all for about US$15. The most frequent is Buses Pingüino (☎ 22-2396), at Roca 915. Buses Ghisoni (☎ 22-2078), Navarro 975, and Agencia Taurus (☎ 22-2223), 21 de Mayo 1502, also have several departures. Buses Mansilla (☎ 22-1516), José Menéndez 556, is less frequent.

Fares to central Chile, via Argentina, are more variable. Ghisoni, Bus Sur, Fernández, Bus Norte (☎ 22-2599) on the Plaza de Armas, Turibus (☎ 22-3795), at José Menéndez 647, and Ettabus (☎ 22-6370), at Roca 886, Local 7, all go to Osorno and Puerto Montt in the Chilean Lake District. Fares to Santiago range from US$66 (Bus Norte) to US$100 (Bus Sur). These trips take as long as two days, but the buses are very comfortable, with frequent stops for meals.

Car Rental There are several car rental agencies in Punta Arenas. Avis (☎ 22-7050) is at the airport as well as downtown at Lautaro Navarro 1065, while Hertz (☎ 22-2013) is across the street at Lautaro Navarro 1064. Budget (☎ 22-5696) and the Automóvil Club de Chile (☎ 22-1888) are at O'Higgins 964 and O'Higgins 931, respectively.

Boat The Navimag ferry company (☎ 22-2593), which offers passage from Puerto Natales to Puerto Montt via the spectacular Chilean fjords, has an office at Avenida Independencia 830. For further information, see the Puerto Natales section below.

Transbordador Austral Broom (☎ 22-

8204) charges US$6 per single between Punta Arenas and Porvenir (US$35 for an automobile). Their ferry departs from Tres Puentes, readily accessible by taxi colectivo from the Braun-Menéndez house. On Sundays and holidays, when the ferry returns at 5 pm, it is possible to do this as a day trip without rushing.

The *Beaulieu*, a small cargo vessel, can take two or three passengers on its monthly trip to Puerto Williams, for US$300 per person return. Those with patience can sometimes obtain passage to Puerto Williams on board Chilean naval vessels. Inquire at Tercera Zona Naval, a beautiful Victorian building at Lautaro Navarro 1150.

Getting Around
Bus & Colectivo Although most places of interest are within easy walking distance of the centre, public transportation is excellent to outlying sights like the Instituto de la Patagonia and the Zona Franca. Taxi colectivos, with numbered routes, are only slightly more expensive than buses (about US$0.30, a bit more late at night and on Sundays), much more comfortable, and much quicker.

AROUND PUNTA ARENAS
Penguin Colonies
There are two substantial Magellanic penguin colonies near Punta Arenas. Easier to reach is the one on Seno Otway (Otway Sound), north-west of the city, while the larger and more interesting one is Monumento Natural Los Pingüinos, accessible only by boat. Several species of gulls and cormorants are also common, along with southern sea lions. Since there is no scheduled public transport to either, it is necessary to rent a car or take a tour to visit them. For details, see the Organised Tours and Getting There & Away sections of Punta Arenas.

Also known as the jackass penguin for its characteristic braying sound, *Spheniscus magellanicus* comes ashore in the southern spring to breed and lay its eggs in sandy burrows or under shrubs a short distance inland. Magellanic penguins are naturally

curious and tame, although if approached too quickly they will scamper into their burrows or toboggan awkwardly across the sand back into the water. If approached too closely, they will bite, and their bills can open a cut large enough to require stitches – never stick your hand or face into a burrow. The least disruptive way to observe them is to seat yourself among the burrows and wait for their curiosity to get the better of them. With reasonable patience, good photographs are easy.

Fuerte Bulnes
Named for the Chilean president who ordered the occupation of the territory in 1843, Fort Bulnes is 55 km south of Punta Arenas. Only a few years after its founding, it was abandoned because of its poor, rocky soil and inferior pasture, lack of potable water, and exposed site. A gravel road runs from Punta Arenas to the restored wooden fort, which is surrounded by a fence of sharp stakes, but there is no public transport. Several travel agencies make half-day excursions to Fuerte Bulnes and the nearby fishing village of Puerto Hambre; for details, see the Organised Tours section of Punta Arenas above.

Estancia San Gregorio
Some 125 km north-east of Punta Arenas, on the highway to Río Gallegos in Argentina, this once enormous (90,000 hectares) estancia is now a cooperative. Since most of the numerous buildings (employee residences, warehouses, chapel and pulpería) have been abandoned, it has the aspect of an enormous ghost town. The casco still belongs to a descendent of the famous and influential Menéndez family, but the cooperative uses the large shearing shed.

The nearest accommodation is the *Hostería Tehuelche*, 29 km north-east, where buses to and from Río Gallegos stop for lunch or dinner; this is also the junction for the road to the ferry which crosses the Strait of Magellan from Punta Delgada to Chilean Tierra del Fuego. Until 1968, the hostería was the casco for Estancia Kimiri Aike, pioneered by the Woods, a British immigrant family. It has clean, comfortable rooms for US$11/21 single/double, and a good restaurant and bar. Hotel staff will change American dollars at fair rates, but Argentine currency is better changed before leaving Río Gallegos.

PUERTO NATALES

Puerto Natales, a port town of 18,000 about 250 km north-west of Punta Arenas via a good paved road, lies on the eastern shore of Seno Ultima Esperanza (Last Hope Sound). Traditionally dependent on wool, mutton, and fishing, it has become an essential stopover for hikers and other visitors en route to Torres del Paine National Park. It offers the best access to Parque Nacional Balmaceda and the famous Milodon Cave, and is also the terminus for the ferry from Puerto Montt via the Chilean fjords. From here, you can also cross the Argentine border to the coalmining town of Río Turbio, where many Chileans work, and to Parque Nacional Los Glaciares.

History

The first Europeans to visit the area of Last Hope Sound were the 16th-century Spaniards Juan Ladrillero and Pedro Sarmiento de Gamboa, in search of a route to the Pacific, but their expeditions left no permanent legacy. In part because of Indian resistance, there were no European settlers until the late 19th century, when the German explorer Hermann Eberhard established a sheep estancia near Puerto Prat, the initial settlement in the area, later superseded by Puerto Natales.

The dominant economic enterprise was the slaughterhouse and meat packing plant at Bories, operated by the Sociedad Explotadora de Tierra del Fuego, which drew livestock from throughout south-western Argentina as well. This factory still operates, although it has declined in importance.

Orientation

Puerto Natales itself is compact enough that walking suffices for most purposes. Although its grid is more irregular than many Chilean cities, most destinations are easily visible from the waterfront, where the Costanera Pedro Montt runs roughly north-south. Near the shore, notice the black-necked swans, which are easily photographed with a medium telephoto lens, while gulls and cormorants blanket the old jetty pilings near the tourist office. The Milodon Cave and Bories are on the Torres del Paine highway north of town.

Information

Tourist Office The tourist office, which has maps and information about hotels, restaurants and transportation, is a chalet on the Costanera Pedro Montt at the intersection with the Phillippi diagonal. Its hours are 9.30 am to 1 pm and 3 to 7 pm, Monday to Saturday.

Money There are several cambios on Blanco Encalada near Eberhard, one block east of the plaza. Relojería Omega, the jewellery repair shop, will change travellers' cheques. All will exchange Argentine currency, unless the rates are too volatile.

Post & Telecommunications The post office is directly on Plaza de Armas, Eberhard 423 near Tomás Rogers; it also contains the offices of Telex Chile. The long-distance telephone office, Blanco Encalada 23 at Phillippi, opens at 8 am and closes at 10 pm.

Organised Tours

There are many travel agencies in Puerto Natales which offer visits to the main local attractions. Eduardo Scott at the Hotel Austral (see below) speaks English and can take eight to 10 passengers to Torres del Paine and other destinations in his minibus. Andes Patagónicos (☎ 41-1594), Blanco Encalada 226, and Stop Cambios (☎ 41-1393), Baquedano 380, have similar services. Three-day excursions to Torres del Paine cost about US$120 per person with Buses Fernández.

Puerto Natales

```
0        200       400 m
```

To Bories, Cueva del
Milodon, Punta Arenas
& Torres del Paine

■ PLACES TO STAY

3 Residencial Grey
4 Hotel Palace
6 Hotel Eberhard
7 Hotel Juan Ladrilleros
9 Residencial Dickson
10 Hotel Natalino
12 Residencial Carahué
13 Residencial Bulnes
17 Residencial La Florida
24 Residencial Temuco
25 Hotel Austral

▼ PLACES TO EAT

11 Restaurant Midas
18 Café Tranquera

OTHER

1 Harbour Master
2 Navimag Ferry Company
5 Cutter to Parque Nacional
  Balmaceda
8 Tourist Office
14 Post Office
15 Municipalidad
16 Parish Church
19 Ladeco
20 Buses Fernández
21 Telephone Office
22 LAN–Chile
23 Buses to Río Turbio
  (Argentina)
26 Cemetery

Places to Stay – bottom end

Puerto Natales is popular with low-budget travellers. When your bus arrives, you will likely be greeted with a card or slip of paper offering directions to such accommodation. *Residencial La Florida* (☎ 41-1361), O'Higgins 431, costs US$3 a single, while *Residencial Grey*, in a typical regional house at Bulnes 90, is a similar bargain. One LP reader highly recommends *Elsa's* private house at Phillippi 427, with bed, breakfast and hot showers for US$5.

Residencial Dickson (☎ 41-1218) at Bulnes 307, costs US$4.50 per single. Virtu-

ally the same price are *Residencial Temuco* (☎ 41-1120) at Ramirez 202, *La Bahía* (☎ 41-1297) at Serrano 434, and *Residencial Carahué* (☎ 41-1339) at Bulnes 370. *Residencial Bulnes* (☎ 41-1307), Bulnes 407, is slightly costlier at US$6/12 for a single/double with bath.

Places to Stay – middle

A favorite midrange place is Eduardo Scott's *Hotel Austral* (☎ 41-1593), at Valdivia 955, where rooms with shared bath are US$7.50/10, while those with private bath are US$9/16. Also recommended is *Hotel*

Natalino (☎ 41-1968) at Eberhard 371 near Tomás Rogers, where rooms with shared bath are US$9/13; those with private bath are US$11/17.

Places to Stay – top end
Probably the best in town is the waterfront *Hotel Eberhard* (☎ 41-1208), Costanera Pedro Montt 25 at Señoret, where rooms with bath are US$52/56, although the showers are tiny. There is an excellent dining room with a panoramic view of Last Hope Sound, and an attractive 2nd-floor lounge with cable TV.

Slightly cheaper, but comparable, are the *Hotel Palace* (☎ 41-1134) at Ladrilleros 209, and *Hotel Juan Ladrilleros* (☎ 41-1652) at Pedro Montt 161.

Places to Eat
For a small provincial town, Puerto Natales has excellent restaurants, which specialise in good and reasonably priced seafood. *Hotel Austral* has a good restaurant, while the unpretentious *La Bahía* has a huge dining room which can accommodate large groups for a superb curanto, with sufficient notice. It is a bit outside the centre, but still reasonable walking distance. One waiter has an uncanny resemblance to Manuel on *Fawlty Towers*.

Another good, popular and lively place is *Restaurant Midas*, on the plaza at Tomás Rogers 169. *Café Tranquera* at Bulnes 579 has been recommended for snacks and sandwiches.

Getting There & Away
Air There are no air services to Puerto Natales; the nearest commercial airport is in Punta Arenas. Ladeco's office at Bulnes 530 can make reservations for flights to mainland Chile; for LAN-Chile or Aerovías DAP, try them or one of the other travel agencies. Buses to Punta Arenas will drop you at the airport.

Bus Puerto Natales has no central bus terminal. Buses Fernández (☎ 41-1111) is at Eberhard 555, while Bus Sur (☎ 41-1325) is at Baquedano 534. For details of their services between Punta Arenas and Puerto Natales, see the Punta Arenas section above. In summer, Bus Sur also goes daily to Parque Nacional Torres del Paine for US$7 single, slightly cheaper return, and twice weekly to Río Gallegos, Argentina, for US$15. Some buses continue from Torres del Paine to Calafate for US$45 single.

Turisur and Cotra have many buses daily from the corner of Phillippi and Baquedano to the Argentine coal mining town of Río Turbio for US$1. From there it is possible to make connections to Río Gallegos and to Calafate.

Car Rental Rental cars are available in Puerto Natales, and can be a reasonable alternative to buses if the expenses are shared. Andes Patagónicos offers intermediate size cars for US$20 per day, plus US$8 insurance and US$0.20 per km. For US$60 plus insurance you are allowed 350 km per day. Larger cars cost about 15% more.

Boat Services to Puerto Montt via the awesome Chilean fjords appear to be in flux. By one report, Navimag (☎ 41-1287), on the Costanera Pedro Montt, has sold the ferry *Tierra del Fuego* to Italian interests, but continues to operate the *Evangelista*, on a monthly basis during the winter. This service is heavily booked during the summer, when three trips monthly are the rule, so try to reserve as far ahead as possible. Passages include meals, and range from US$100 with a reclining (pullman) seat to US$150 with bunk.

AROUND PUERTO NATALES
Bories
The **Frigorífico**, built in 1913 with British capital, is 4 km north of town. At one time, it processed huge amounts of meats, tallow, hides and wool from estancias in both Chile and Argentina for export to Europe, but its operations are now much reduced. There remain several interesting metal-clad buildings and houses, classic examples of hybrid Victorian/Magellanic architecture.

Parque Nacional Balmaceda

This otherwise inaccessible park is the final destination of a spectacular boat ride from Puerto Natales through Seno Ultima Esperanza (Last Hope Sound). En route, you will glimpse the meat packing plant at Bories, several small estancias whose only access to Puerto Natales is via water, numerous glaciers and waterfalls, a large cormorant rookery, a smaller sea lion rookery, and possibly Andean condors. It is four hours to Puerto Toro, where a footpath leads from the jetty to the base of the Serrano Glacier. On a clear day, the Torres del Paine are visible in the distance. The return trip takes the same route.

The Chilean cutter *21 de Mayo* makes the trip daily during summer, weather permitting, and will go at other times if demand is sufficient. The cost is US$24 per person. Decent meals are available on board for about US$6, as are hot and cold drinks. For reservations, contact the owners (☎ 41-1176) at Ladrilleros 171. They can also arrange hiking and rafting excursions to Torres del Paine via Paso de los Toros and Río Serrano.

Cueva del Milodón

This national monument, administered by the Chilean forest service CONAF, is 24 km north-west of Puerto Natales. The cave itself is the site where, in the 1890s, Captain Hermann Eberhard discovered the well-preserved remains of the enormous ground sloth called the milodon.

The milodon was an herbivorous mammal which, like the mammoth and many other American megafauna, became extinct near the end of the Pleistocene era. More than twice the height of a human, it pulled down small trees and branches for their succulent leaves. A full-size replica of the animal stands in the cave, which is 30 metres high, 80 metres wide, and 200 metres deep. Indians later occupied it as a shelter, well after the animal's extinction. There are smaller caves nearby which can be explored with a torch.

Many fanciful stories, including legends that Indians kept it penned as a domestic animal and that some specimens remained alive into the last century, have grown up about the milodon. Bruce Chatwin's literary travelogue *In Patagonia* amusingly recounts these tales.

Although there is no hotel accommodation closer than Puerto Natales, camping and picnicking are possible near the site. CONAF charges US$1.50 for admission, less for Chilean nationals and children. Buses to Torres del Paine will drop you at the entrance, which is several km walk from the cave proper. Alternatively, you can take a taxi or hitch from Puerto Natales.

PARQUE NACIONAL TORRES DEL PAINE

The Torres del Paine (Towers of Paine) are spectacular granite pillars which soar almost vertically more than 2000 metres above the Patagonian steppe. The Torres and other high peaks, though, are only one feature of what may be the finest national park in all of South America, a miniature Alaska of shimmering turquoise lakes, roaring creeks, rivers and waterfalls, sprawling glaciers, dense forests and abundant wildlife. The issue is not whether to come here, but how much time to spend.

For hikers and backpackers, the 2000-sq-km park is an unequalled destination, with a well-developed trail network as well as opportunities for cross-country travel. The weather is changeable, with the strong westerlies which typify Patagonia, but very long summer days make outdoor activities possible late into the evening. Good foul-weather gear is essential, and a warm sleeping bag and good tent are imperative for those undertaking the popular Paine circuit.

Before its creation in 1959, the park was part of a large sheep estancia, but it is recovering from nearly a century of over-exploitation of its pastures, forests and wildlife. Now it shelters large and growing herds of guanacos (relatives of the domesticated llama of the central Andes), flocks of the flightless ostrich-like rhea (known locally as the ñandú), Andean condors, fla-

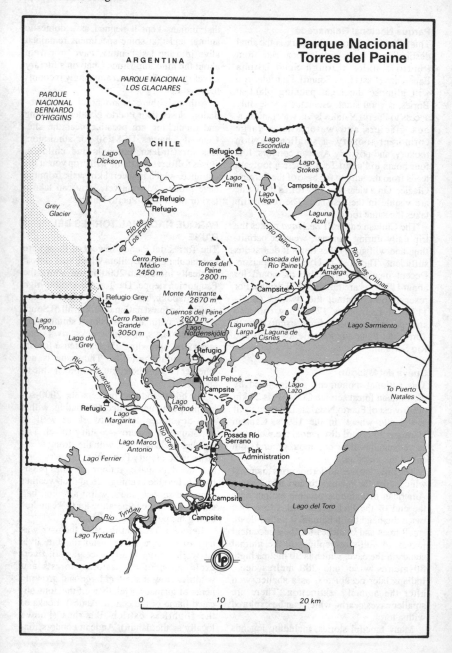

Parque Nacional Torres del Paine

ARGENTINA

PARQUE NACIONAL
LOS GLACIARES

PARQUE
NACIONAL
BERNARDO
O'HIGGINS

CHILE

Lago
Dickson

Lago
Escondida

Refugio

Lago
Stokes

Lago
Paine

Campsite

Lago
Vega

Grey
Glacier

Refugio
Refugio

Laguna
Azul

Rio de
Los Perros

Rio Paine

Cerro Paine
Médio
2450 m

Torres del
Paine
2800 m

Cascada del
Rio Paine

Lago
Amarga

Rio de las Chinas

Refugio Grey

Monte Almirante
2670 m

Campsite

Cerro Paine
Grande
3050 m

Cuernos del Paine
2600 m

Lago
Nordenskjöld

Laguna
Larga

Lago Sarmiento

Lago
Pingo

Laguna de
Cisnes

Lago de
Grey

Refugio

Rio
Avutardas

Hotel Pehoé

Campsite

Lago
Lazo

To Puerto
Natales

Refugio

Lago
Margarita

Lago
Pehoé

Lago Marco
Antonio

Rio Grey

Posada Río
Serrano

Lago Ferrier

Park
Administration

Campsite

Rio Tyndall

Campsite

Lago del Toro

Lago Tyndall

0   10   20 km

Cerro Torre, Torre Egger & Cerro Stanhardt

mingos and many other species. Since 1978, it has been part of the United Nations' Biosphere Reserve system. For visitors from the Northern Hemisphere, almost everything will be new.

The park's outstanding wildlife conservation success has undoubtedly been the guanaco *(Lama guanicoe)*, which grazes the open steppes where its main natural enemy, the puma, cannot approach undetected. After more than a decade of effective protection

from hunters and poachers, the guanaco barely flinches when humans or vehicles approach. The elusive huemul, or Chilean deer, is much more difficult to spot.

Guided daytrips from Puerto Natales are possible, but permit only a superficial reconnaissance. It is better to explore the several options for staying at the park, including camping at both backcountry and improved sites, and staying at the guest houses near the park headquarters and at Lago Pehoé.

Entry

There is an entry charge of US$4.50 per person (less for Chilean nationals), collected at the park entrance on the north side of Lago Sarmiento, on the Puerto Natales road. If you intend to hike the Paine circuit (see below), it is necessary to register with the ranger here or at the park administration at Río Serrano. Maps and informational brochures are available here.

Maps & Trekking Information

For hikers and trekkers, there is an excellent topographic map at a scale of 1:100,000, published by the Sociedad Turística Kaoniken in Puerto Natales, and readily available there, in Punta Arenas, and in the park itself, for about US$2. It also includes detailed maps of the Paine and Grey Glacier circuits.

Do not, however, assume that everything on these maps is correct. Careless campers have burned several of the backcountry refugios, once 'outside houses' on the estancia, to the ground. Nothing remains, for instance, of Refugio Grey (ironically known to hikers as the 'Grey Hilton'), at the foot of the Grey Glacier. For this reason, a tent is an absolute necessity.

Ask rangers and other hikers about trail conditions. In late summer, the abandoned garden at Refugio Dickson still produces an abundant harvest of gooseberries. Be sure to bring food, since prices at the small grocery at the Posada Río Serrano near park headquarters are at least 50% higher than in Punta Arenas or Puerto Natales, and the selection is minimal.

Floods in the early 1980s destroyed several bridges and required CONAF to relocate the Paine circuit trail, for which you should allot at least five days, preferably more for bad weather. At least one layover day is desirable, since the route is strenuous, especially the rough segments on the east side of Lago Grey and over the 1241-metre pass to or from the Río de los Perros.

Since a hiker disappeared in the summer of 1990-91, CONAF no longer permits solo treks, but it is not difficult to link up with others. There is at least one potentially hazardous stream ford across the Río de los Perros, as well as a rickety log bridge. If you follow the circuit counter-clockwise, beginning at the Lago Sarmiento entrance, you will exit at park headquarters, where you can get hot food and a shower, but it is possible to do it in either direction.

The Paine circuit is not the only possibility for backcountry exploration. From the outlet of Lago Grey, 18 km from park headquarters by a passable road, there is a good trail to Lago Pingo, on the eastern edge of the southern continental ice field.

For more information on trekking and camping, including detailed contour maps, consult the LP guide *Trekking in the Patagonian Andes* by Clem Lindenmayer. Other sources include Hilary Bradt & John Pilkington's *Backpacking in Chile & Argentina* and William Leitch's *South America's National Parks*, both of which have chapters on Torres del Paine.

Places to Stay & Eat

There are two hotels in the park, both often crowded in summer. The *Hotel Pehoé*, on a small island in the lake of the same name and linked to the mainland by a footbridge, charges US$56/66 a single/double for its views of the peaks called Cuernos del Paine (Horns of Paine) and 3050-metre Paine Grande, the highest point in the park. It has a restaurant and bar, both open to the public. Bookings can be arranged in Punta Arenas (☎ 22-4223) or Puerto Natales (☎ 41-1442). Its boat trip to the Grey Glacier costs US$25 per person, weather permitting.

More economical is the *Posada Río Serrano*, a remodelled estancia building near park headquarters, where rooms cost US$20/25. It has a reasonably priced restaurant and bar, with occasional informal, live entertainment. Arrange bookings in advance in Puerto Natales (☎ 41-1355).

Other low cost and even free accommodation exists. A short distance from Posada Río Serrano is a CONAF refugio with beds and hot showers for US$3, but your own sleeping bag is necessary. Other refugios, such as that at Pudeto on Lago Pehoé are free but *very* rustic. There are several organised campsites, including those on Lago Pehoé and at Río Serrano, which charge US$7 for up to six people. These charges include firewood and hot showers, available in the morning but evenings only by request. At the more remote and rustic Laguna Azul site, which has no showers, site charges are US$5 per night.

At Río Serrano, see Brigitte Buhoffer about riding horses, which costs US$18 per day. Pack horses cost US$32 per day.

Getting There & Away

For details of transportation to the park, see the Puerto Natales section above. Bus services drop you at the administration at Río Serrano, although you can disembark at Lago Sarmiento, to begin the Paine Circuit, or elsewhere upon request. Hitching from Puerto Natales is possible, but competition is considerable.

There are now summer bus services between Torres del Paine and Calafate, Argentina, via the Río Don Guillermo border crossing and La Esperanza. Inquire at park headquarters. If Calafate merchants drop their opposition, the much more convenient route via the Sierra Baguales, north of Laguna Azul, will permit direct travel to Parque Nacional Los Glaciares and its famous Moreno Glacier in only a few hours. At present, the trip requires a full day to Calafate alone.

PORVENIR

Porvenir, founded less than a century ago to service the new sheep estancias across the Straits of Magellan from Punta Arenas, is the largest settlement on Chilean Tierra del Fuego. Its 6400 inhabitants include many of Yugoslav descent, to whom there are monuments commemorating the brief gold rush of the 1880s and their continuing presence in the area.

Porvenir only becomes visible as the ferry approaches its sheltered, nearly hidden harbour. The waterfront road, or costanera, leads from the ferry terminal to a cluster of rusting, metal-clad Victorians which belie the town's optimistic name (The Future). Although it does have a beautifully manicured central plaza with a worthwhile museum, as well as a pleasant waterfront park, for most travellers Porvenir is only a stopover en route to or from Ushuaia, on the Argentine side of Tierra del Fuego.

Information

Tourist Office Tourist information is available from the kiosk on the costanera between Mardones and Muñoz Gamero. Ferry tickets to Punta Arenas are also available, and the bus to the ferry terminal arrives and departs here.

Museo Provincial

The museum, on the main plaza, has natural history, archaeological, and historical exhibits, including one on early Chilean cinematography. Its hours are Monday to Friday from 8.30 am to 12.30 pm and 2.30 to 6 pm.

Places to Stay & Eat

For its size, Porvenir has good accommodation and food. The cheapest rooms are at the *Residencial Colón* (☎ 58-0108), Damián Riobó 108, where doubles with shared bath cost US$4.50. Other reasonable choices are the *Hotel Rosas* (☎ 58-0088), Phillippi 296, which charges US$10.50/16.50 for singles/doubles, and the nearby *Hotel Central* (☎ 58-0077), at Phillippi 298. For upscale comfort, try *Hostería Los Flamencos* (☎ 58-0049), on Teniente Merino, where prices are US$48/56.

Hotel Rosas has a good, inexpensive restaurant specialising in seafood. The *Yugoslav Club*, on the costanera, has also been recommended, along with the *Restaurant Puerto Montt*, on the costanera at Teniente Merino.

Getting There & Away

Air Aerovías DAP (☎ 58-0089), on Manuel Señoret, flies across the Straits to Punta Arenas in 10 minutes for US$13.50, twice daily Monday to Saturday.

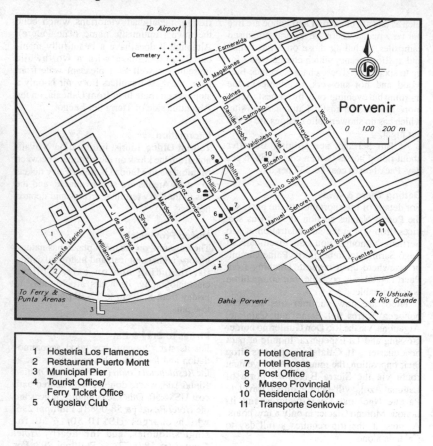

1	Hostería Los Flamencos
2	Restaurant Puerto Montt
3	Municipal Pier
4	Tourist Office/
	Ferry Ticket Office
5	Yugoslav Club
6	Hotel Central
7	Hotel Rosas
8	Post Office
9	Museo Provincial
10	Residencial Colón
11	Transporte Senkovic

Bus Transporte Senkovic, Carlos Bories 295, departs Tuesday and Saturday for Río Grande, in Argentine Tierra del Fuego, for US$11. From there it is possible to make connections to Ushuaia.

Boat Transbordadora Broom operates a car/passenger ferry to Punta Arenas; for details see the Punta Arenas section above. The crossing takes about 2½ hours. The bus to the ferry terminal, leaving from the tourist kiosk about an hour before the ferry's departure, provides a good excursion through

Porvenir for US$0.75. Taxis cost at least four times as much.

PUERTO WILLIAMS
On Isla Navarino on the south side of the Beagle Channel, directly opposite Argentine Tierra del Fuego, Puerto Williams is a Chilean naval base and settlement with a population of about 1000. It was nearby that Fitzroy encountered the Yahgan Indians who accompanied the *Beagle* back to England for several years. Missionaries in the mid-19th century and fortune-seekers during the local

gold rush of the 1890s established a permanent European presence.

A few people of Yahgan descent still reside near Puerto Williams, which is named for the founder of Fuerte Bulnes. A territorial dispute over the three small islands of Lennox, Nueva and Picton, east of Navarino, nearly brought Argentina and Chile to war in 1978, but papal intervention defused the situation and the islands remain in Chilean possession.

Information
There is a cluster of public services, including telephone, post office, supermarket, and tourist office, on President Ibáñez. Money exchange is possible at the only travel agency.

Things to See & Do
The **Museo Martín Gusinde**, honouring the German priest and ethnographer who worked among the Yahgans, has exhibits on natural history and anthropology of the area. It's open Monday to Friday from 9 am to 1 pm, and daily from 3 to 6 pm.

East of town, at **Ukika**, live the few remaining Yahgan people. There is good hiking in the surrounding countryside, but the changeable weather demands warm, water-resistant clothing.

Places to Stay & Eat
Residencial Onashaga, in the centre, is basic but clean and comfortable for US$7.50 a single. Camping is possible near the upscale, highly recommended *Hostería Patagonia* (☎ 22-6100 in Punta Arenas), which has singles/doubles at US$70/87. Winter prices may be negotiable. Both hotels serve meals.

Getting There & Away
Air Aerovías DAP flies to and from Punta Arenas on Tuesdays for US$62 one way, slightly cheaper return. Seats are limited and advance reservations essential. DAP flights to Antarctica make a brief stopover here.

Boat Chilean naval supply vessels, which sail irregularly between Punta Arenas and Puerto Williams, sometimes take passengers. On Saturdays, at least during summer, it is possible to cross from Ushuaia to Puerto Williams, or vice-versa, for US$50. Inquire at the tourist office in either place.

Falkland Islands
Islas Malvinas

Falkland Islands (Islas Malvinas)

Surrounded by the South Atlantic Ocean and centuries of controversy, the Falkland Islands lie some 300 miles east of the Patagonian mainland. Consisting of two main islands, East and West Falkland, and several hundred smaller ones, they support a permanent population of fewer than 2000, most of whom live in the capital of Stanley. The remainder live on widely dispersed sheep stations.

HISTORY

Although there is some evidence that Patagonian Indians may have reached the Falklands in rudimentary canoes, the Islands were uninhabited when Europeans began to frequent the area in the late 17th century. Their Spanish name, Islas Malvinas, derives from the early French navigators from the Channel port of St Malo.

No European power saw fit to remain until 1764, when the French established a garrison at Port Louis on East Falkland, despite Spanish claims under the papal Treaty of Tordesillas which divided the New World between Spain and Portugal. Unknown to either France or Spain, Britain soon planted a West Falkland outpost at Port Egmont, on Saunders Island. Spain, meanwhile, discovered and then supplanted the French colony after an amicable diplomatic settlement between the two European states, after which Spanish forces detected and expelled the British in 1767. Under threat of war, Spain restored Port Egmont to the British, who only a few years later abandoned the area without, however, renouncing their territorial claims.

For the rest of the 18th century, Spain maintained the Islands as one of the most secure penal colonies in the world. After she abandoned them in the early 1800s, only maverick whalers and sealers visited until, in the early 1820s, the United Provinces of the River Plate sent a military governor to assert its claim as successor to Spain. Later, a naturalised Buenos Aires entrepreneur named Louis Vernet initiated a project to monitor uncontrolled sealers and exploit local fur seal populations in a sustainable manner, as well as tame the numerous wild cattle and horses which had multiplied on the abundant pastures since the departure of the Spaniards.

Vernet's seizure of three American sealers triggered reprisals from a hot-headed American naval officer, who vandalised the Port Louis settlement beyond recovery in 1831. After Vernet's departure, Buenos Aires kept a token force there until early 1833, when it was expelled by British forces. Since then, Argentina has pursued its claim to the islands both by diplomacy and, in 1982, by force. Vernet pursued his claims for damages and lost property in British courts for nearly 30 years, with little success.

Under the British, the Falklands languished until the mid-19th century, when sheep began to replace cattle, and wool became an important export commodity. The Falkland Islands Company, founded by an Englishman from Montevideo, became the Islands' largest landholder, but other immigrant entrepreneurs occupied all available pastoral lands, many in holdings exceeding 100,000 acres, by the 1870s.

The population, at first a mix of stranded mariners and holdover gauchos from the Vernet era, was augmented by the steady arrival of English and Scottish immigrants. Roughly half resided in the new capital and port of Stanley, founded in 1844, while the remainder became resident labourers on large sheep stations resembling those in Australia. The population has never exceeded its 1931 maximum of 2400. Although most of the original landowners lived and worked in the Falklands, in time they or their descendents returned to Britain and ran their businesses as absentees. For nearly a century, the Falkland Islands Company, owner of nearly half the land and livestock, dominated the local economy.

Until the late 1970s, at which time the

The Warrah, the Yahgans & the Discovery of the Falklands

Who discovered the Falklands? Opinions depend, it seems, on who's speaking and what that person's native language is. Spanish speakers argue forcefully, almost without exception, that a ship from Magellan's 1520 expedition wintered at the Islands, while English speakers strongly assert that privateer John Davis discovered them in 1592. Unfortunately, no Yahgan speakers remain to tell us whether the 'Canoe Indians' of Tierra del Fuego might have been the first to set foot on the Islands.

The evidence, admittedly, is slim and the idea seems at first glance unconventional and unlikely. The Yahgans navigated the waters of the Beagle Channel and the Strait of Magellan in simple beech bark canoes held together with whalebone and shredded saplings. By all accounts, these leaky vessels required constant bailing, but the Yahgans did use sealskin sails in favourable winds. In these canoes they certainly arrived at Staten Island at the eastern tip of Tierra del Fuego and, some speculate, more than 500 miles north-east in the Falklands. Early settlers found canoes washed up on the shores of West Falkland, but the most concrete evidence for at least a temporary Indian presence was the Islands' only native land mammal, the warrah or Falklands fox, Dusicyon australis.

When Europeans first landed, the Falklands were unpeopled but the warrah (its name probably derived from the Australian Aboriginal word warrigal used to describe the dingo) aroused the interest of visitors like Darwin, who wrote that:

...there is no other instance in any part of the world of so small a mass of broken land, distant from a continent, possessing so large an aboriginal quadruped peculiar to itself...Within a very few years after these islands shall have become regularly settled, in all probability this fox will be classed with the dodo, as an animal which has perished from the face of the earth.

Darwin and others remarked on the animal's extraordinary tameness, a characteristic which would support British biologist Juliet Clutton-Brock's conclusion that the warrah was a feral dog or a cross of feral dog and South American fox. Analysing the animal's physical characteristics from specimens in the British Museum, she concluded that, like the Australian dingo, the warrah had been domesticated and likely brought across several hundred miles of open ocean in Yahgan canoes.

Was this possible? No one can be absolutely positive, but indigenous peoples navigated thousands of miles of the open Pacific, although their watercraft were more sophisticated than the Yahgans'. The Yahgans were a hardy people, though, and chances are that a canoe or two might have ridden the prevailing winds and currents from the Strait of Lemaire to the Falklands. If, as was usual, they carried a dog or two, perhaps a pregnant bitch, it is reasonable to believe those animals might have bred on the Islands. Whether these presumed discoverers of the Falklands were able to return to Tierra del Fuego is even more speculative, but just considering the idea makes us rethink, once again, the myth of European 'discovery'. As Darwin predicted, the warrah itself did not survive European settlement – perceived as a threat to sheep, the last individual was shot on West Falkland in the 1870s. ∎

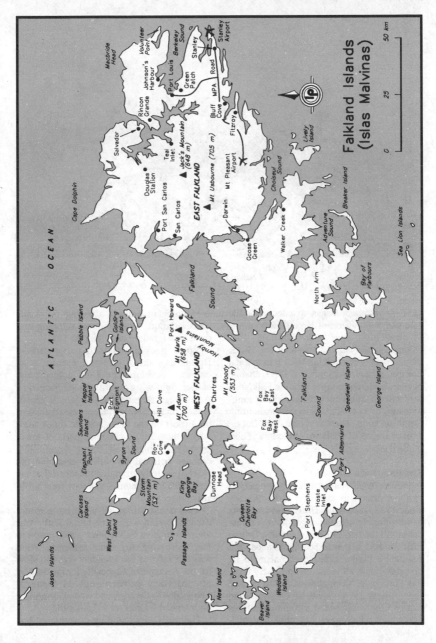

Falkland Islands
(Islas Malvinas)

Whaling in the 1800's

local government began to encourage the sale and subdivision of large land holdings to slow high rates of emigration, little changed in the Islands' only industry. Since then, nearly every unit has been sold to local family farmers. Beginning in 1982, change became even more rapid with the Falklands war and the subsequent expansion of long-distance, deep-sea fishing in the surrounding South Atlantic. There is speculation, but no firm evidence, of offshore petroleum in Falklands waters.

The Falklands War

Although Argentina has regularly and persistently affirmed its claim for the Falklands since 1833, successive British governments never publicly acknowledged their seriousness until the late 1960s. Apparently, British officials had begun to see the Islands as a politically burdensome anachronism to be discarded with all judicious speed. By then, the Foreign & Commonwealth Office and the military government of General Juan Carlos Onganía reached a communications agreement which gave Argentina a signifi-

cant voice in matters affecting Falklands transportation, fuel supplies, shipping and even immigration, beginning in 1971.

Local people and their supporters in Britain saw the Argentine presence as an ominous development. Only a few years earlier, right-wing guerrillas had hijacked an Aerolíneas Argentinas jet, which crash-landed on the Stanley racecourse (there was no airport on the Islands at the time), after which they briefly occupied parts of town. Islanders, concerned about Argentina's chronic political instability, suspected the FCO of secretly arranging the transfer of the Falklands to Argentina, and they were probably correct.

This process dragged on for more than a decade, during which the brutal Dirty War after 1976 gave Falklanders good reason to fear increasing Argentine presence. What was too fast for the Islanders was too slow for the Argentines, especially for the desperate military government of General Leopoldo Galtieri, which invaded the almost undefended Islands on 2 April 1982.

Galtieri's disintegrating government had

come under increasing pressure from Argentines fed up with the corruption, economic chaos and totalitarian ruthlessness of the Proceso, but his seizure of the Malvinas briefly united a divided country and made him an ephemeral hero. Galtieri and his advisers did not anticipate that British Prime Minister Margaret Thatcher, herself in precarious political circumstances, would respond so decisively. In a struggle whose loser would not survive politically, the Argentine sought diplomatic approval of his *fait accompli*, while the Briton organised an enormous naval task force to recover the lost territory.

The military outcome was one-sided, despite substantial British naval losses, as experienced British troops landed at San Carlos Bay and routed the ill-trained and poorly supplied Argentine conscripts. The most serious fighting took place at Goose Green, on East Falkland, but the Argentine army's surrender at Stanley averted the destruction of the capital. Near Stanley and a few other sites around the Islands there remain unexploded mines, but minefields are clearly marked and pose no danger to anyone exercising reasonable caution.

GEOGRAPHY & CLIMATE

The Falklands' total land area is 4700 square miles, about the same as that of Northern Ireland or the American state of Connecticut. There are two main islands, East and West Falkland, separated by the Falkland Sound. Of the many smaller islands, only a handful are large enough for human habitation. Despite a reputation for dismal weather, the Islands' oceanic climate is temperate despite frequent high winds. Maximum temperatures rarely reach 75°F (25°C), while even on the coldest winter days the temperature usually rises above freezing at some time during the day. The average annual rainfall at Stanley, one of the wettest places in the Islands, is only about 24 inches (600 mm).

Except for the low-lying southern half of East Falkland, known as Lafonia, the terrain is generally hilly to mountainous, although the highest peaks do not exceed 2300 feet

(690 metres). Among the most interesting geological features are the 'stone runs' of quartzite boulders which descend from many of the ridges and peaks on East and West Falkland. The numerous bays, inlets, estuaries and beaches present an often spectacular coastline, with abundant, accessible and remarkably tame wildlife.

Because the settlements are so far apart, often separated by water, and the Islands' road network is so limited, light aircraft is the easiest way of visiting areas beyond the immediate Stanley area. In some areas, riding is still a common means of travel, but the Land Rover and the motorcycle have for the most part supplanted the horse. For adventurous travellers, walking is feasible, but walkers must be prepared for changeable, sometimes inclement weather.

FLORA & FAUNA

Grasslands and prostrate shrubs dominate the flora of the Falklands; there are no native trees. At the time of their discovery by Europeans, the coastline was dominated by extensive stands of the native tussock grass *Parodiochloa flabellata*, which proved to be nutritious fodder for livestock but highly susceptible to overgrazing and fire. Today very little tussock remains on East and West Falkland, although well-managed farms on offshore islands have preserved significant areas of it. Most of the native pasture is rank white grass *(Cortaderia pilosa)* which supports only about one sheep per four or five acres.

Most visitors will find the Falklands' fauna more varied and interesting, and remarkably tame and accessible – only the Galápagos or the Everglades are comparable. The Islands' beaches, headlands and offshore waters support the largest and finest concentrations of South Atlantic wildlife north of South Georgia Island and Antarctica. The Magellanic penguin, the only species which visits the South American continent, is common, but four other species breed regularly in the Falklands: the rockhopper, the closely related macaroni, the gentoo and the king. Four other species have been recorded, but do not breed there.

Many other birds, equally interesting and uncommon, breed in the Falklands; for visitors from the Northern Hemisphere, almost all of them will be new. Undoubtedly the most beautiful is the black-browed albatross, but there are also caracaras, coots, cormorants, gulls, hawks, peregrine falcons, oystercatchers, snowy sheathbills, sheldgeese, steamer ducks and swans – among others. Most of them are present in very large and impressive breeding colonies, and are easy to photograph.

Also present, in locally large numbers, are marine mammals. Elephant seals, southern sea lions and southern fur seals breed on the beaches, while six species of dolphins have been observed offshore. Killer whales are common, but the larger species of South Atlantic whales are rarely seen.

While the Falklands have no formal national parks, there are many outstanding wildlife sites. Over the past decade, local government has encouraged nature-oriented tourism, constructing small lodges near some of the best areas, but there are also less-structured opportunities away from these places. Hiking and trekking possibilities are excellent.

GOVERNMENT

In international politics the Falklands remain a colonial anachronism, administered by a Governor appointed by the Foreign & Commonwealth Office (FCO) in London, but in local affairs the nine-member, elected Legislative Council (Legco) exercises considerable power. Traditionally, five of the nine members come from Stanley, while the remainder represent the countryside, or The Camp. Selected members of the Legislative Council advise the Governor as part of his Executive Council (Exco), which also includes other FCO appointees.

ECONOMY

From the mid-19th century, the Falklands' economy has depended almost exclusively on the export of wool. Since 1986, however, fishing has eclipsed agriculture as a revenue producer under a licensing regime established by the local government with the approval of the British FCO. Asian and European fleets seeking both squid and fin fish have brought an unprecedented infusion of cash into the Islands, most of which has gone to fund overdue improvements in public services, such as roads, telephones and medical care. Tourism is not yet economically significant, but facilities in Stanley and at some wildlife sites are more than adequate and often excellent.

Most of the population of Stanley works for local government (FIG) or for the Falkland Islands Company (FIC), which has been the major landowner and economic power in the Islands for more than a century. The Company has recently sold all of its pastoral property to the government for subdivision and sale to local people, but continues to provide shipping and other commercial services for ranchers and other residents of the Islands. In The Camp, nearly everyone is involved in ranching on relatively small, widely dispersed family-owned units.

POPULATION & PEOPLE

According to the 1986 census, the population of the Falklands is 1916, of whom about two-thirds live in Stanley and the remainder in The Camp. Two-thirds of the population is native-born, some tracing their ancestry back six or more generations, while the great majority of the remainder are immigrants or temporary residents from the United Kingdom. Islanders' surnames indicate that their origins can be traced to a variety of European backgrounds, but English is both the official language and the language of preference, even though a few people speak and understand Spanish. There is a handful of immigrants from South America, nearly all of them Chilean.

Because of the Islands' isolation and small population, Falkland Islanders are very versatile and adaptable. Almost every male, for example, is an expert mechanic, while lack of spare parts has encouraged many to become improvisational machinists. This adaptability is also a virtue for individuals who rely on seasonal labour such as sheep shearing and peat cutting, both of which are well paid. In The Camp, many women also perform a variety of tasks, including shearing.

The Islands' history of colonial rule and the paternalistic social system of the large sheep stations and other workplaces has left an unfortunate legacy of public timidity in the face of authority, even when private opinions are very strong. At the same time, Falkland Islanders are extraordinarily hospitable, often welcoming visitors into their homes for 'smoko', the traditional midmorning tea or coffee break, or for a drink. This is especially true in The Camp, where visitors of any kind can be infrequent. When visiting people in The Camp, it is customary to bring a small gift – rum is a special favourite. Stanley's several pubs are popular meeting places.

No visitor should miss the annual summer sports meetings, which consist of horse racing, bull riding and similar competitions. These take place in Stanley between Christmas and New Year's, and on West Falkland at the end of the shearing season, usually in late February. The West Falkland sports rotate yearly among the settlements.

Approximately 2000 British military personnel, commonly referred to as 'squaddies', reside at the Mt Pleasant Airport complex, about 35 miles south-west of Stanley, and at a few other scattered sites around the Islands. Civilian-military relations are generally cordial but now rather distant.

Facts for the Visitor

Although the Falklands are small and Falkland Islanders are few, in many ways the Islands are a small country, with their own immigration regulations, customs requirements, currency and other unique features. Bureaucracy is generally not odious or cumbersome, but expatriate colonial officials sometimes play things 'by the book'.

VISAS & CUSTOMS

All nationalities, including British citizens, must carry valid passports. For non-Britons, visa requirements are generally the same as those for foreigners visiting the UK, except that Argentines must obtain a visa in advance, which is not easily done. For more detailed information, inquire at the Islands' UK representative at Falkland House (☎ 222-2542), 14 Broadway, Westminster, London SW1H 0BH. In Punta Arenas, Chile, contact Aerovías DAP (☎ 22-3958), Ignacio Carrera Pinto 1022 near Jorge Montt, which operates flights to the Islands, or the British vice-consul, Roderick Mathewson, Casilla 327 (a post office box).

Customs regulations are few except for limits on importation of alcohol and tobacco, which are heavily taxed but readily available in the Islands.

MONEY & COSTS

The legal currency is the Falkland Islands pound (£), on a par with sterling. There are banknotes for £5, £10 and £20, and coins for 1p, 5p, 10p, 20p and 50p. Sterling notes and coins circulate alongside local currency, but visitors should be aware that Falklands currency is not legal tender in the UK, nor on Ascension Island, where flights to and from the UK make a brief refuelling stop. Ascension/St Helena banknotes and coins are not legal tender in the Falklands.

Credit cards are not used in the Islands, but travellers' cheques are readily accepted with a minimum of bureaucracy. Britons with guarantee cards can easily cash personal cheques up to £50 at the Standard Chartered Bank in Stanley.

Recent tourist development in the Falklands has encouraged short-stay, top-end accommodation and services at prices up to £50 per day (all meals included), but there are cheaper alternatives, such as bed and breakfast in Stanley from about £18.50. In The Camp, there are lower-cost, self-catering cabins and opportunities for trekking and camping at virtually no cost. Many Camp families in isolated areas still welcome visitors without charge.

Transportation outside the Stanley/Mount Pleasant area is not cheap, since almost everywhere must be reached via the Falkland Islands Government Air Service, which charges about £1 per minute flying time for non-Islanders. This would make the fare to Port Stephens, a distant settlement on West Falkland, about £60 one-way.

Food prices are roughly equivalent to the UK, but fresh meat (chiefly mutton) is extremely cheap. Restaurant meals are fairly expensive, but there are inexpensive short orders and snacks available in Stanley.

WHEN TO GO & WHAT TO BRING

Since the primary attraction of the Islands is wildlife, the best time to go is from October to March, when migratory birds, including penguins, and marine mammals return to the beaches and headlands. December and January are the best months, since the very long days permit outdoor activities even if inclement weather spoils part of the day.

Since the weather is changeable, visitors should bring good waterproof clothing suitable for spring in the northern British Isles. A pair of Wellingtons is often useful in in wet weather. While summer never gets truly hot and the wind can lower the ambient temperature considerably, the climate does not justify Antarctic preparations. For trekkers, a sturdy tent with rainfly and a warm sleeping bag are essential.

TOURIST OFFICES

For information in the UK, contact the Islands' representative at Falkland House (☎ 222-2542), 14 Broadway, Westminster, London SW1H 0BH. You can also write to Falkland Islands Tourism at 56 John St, Stanley, via GPO London.

USEFUL ORGANISATIONS

Based in both the UK and Stanley, Falklands Conservation is a non-profit organisation promoting wildlife conservation research as well as the preservation of wrecks and historic sites in the Islands. Membership, which costs £15 per year and includes its annual newsletter, is available from Falklands Con-

servation (☎ 556-6226), 21 Regent Terrace, Edinburgh EH7 5BT, Scotland.

The Falkland Islands Association (☎ 222-0028), 2 Greycoat Place, Westminster, London SW1P 1SD, is a political lobbying group which publishes a quarterly newsletter on the Falklands which includes much interesting information.

BUSINESS HOURS & HOLIDAYS

Falkland Islands government offices are open weekdays from 8.30 am to noon and from 1.15 to 4.30 pm. Most large businesses in Stanley, such as the FIC's West Store, keep similar hours, but small shops are often open only a few hours a day. On weekends, business hours are much reduced. The few stores in The Camp, such as those at Fox Bay East and Port Howard, have a very limited regular schedule but will often open on request.

January 1
    New Year's Day
March/April (date varies)
    Good Friday
April 21
    Queen's Birthday
June 14
    Liberation Day
1st Monday in October
    Bank Holiday
December 8
    Battle of the Falklands (1914)
December 25
    Christmas Day
December 26
    Boxing Day (Stanley Sports day)
December 27
    Stanley Sports (2nd day)

CULTURAL EVENTS

On both East and West Falkland, the annual sports meetings have been a tradition since the advent of sheep farming in the 19th century. In a land where most people lived a very isolated existence, they provided a regular opportunity to get together and share news, meet new people, and participate in friendly competitions such as horse racing, bull riding and sheep dog trials. The rotating camp sports meeting on West Falkland carries on this tradition best, hosting 'two-

Top Left: Ñandutí lace, Itauguá, Paraguay
Top Right: Canecutter, Piribebuy, Paraguay
Bottom Left: Alfredo Stroessner, champion of peace, democracy and freedom
Bottom Right: Parque Nacional Ybycuí, Paraguay

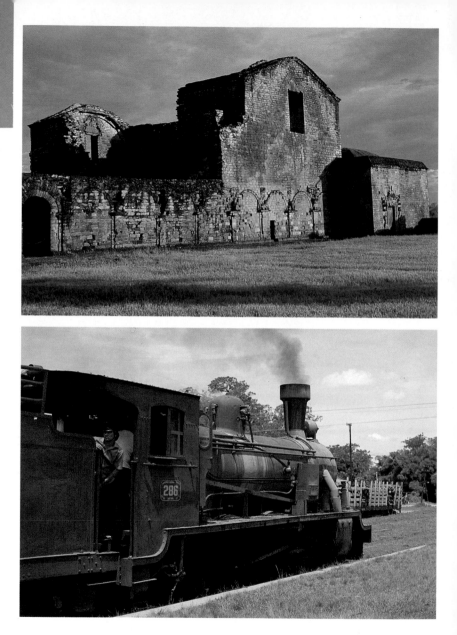

Top: Trinidad mission, Paraguay
Bottom: Steam train, Asunción to Areguá, Paraguay

nighters' during which Islanders party till they drop, go to sleep for a few hours, and get up and start all over again.

Since large sheep stations hosted these gatherings, their subdivision in recent years may undermine the custom, although conveniently located Port Howard, a cooperative, may carry it on. Independent visitors to the Falklands should not feel shy about showing up at one of these events, although it is best to arrange for accommodation in advance – this will usually mean floor space for your sleeping bag.

POST & TELECOMMUNICATIONS

Postal services are very dependable. There are two airmail services weekly to and from the UK, but parcels larger than about one lb (0.45 kg) arrive or depart by sea four to five times yearly. The Government Air Service delivers the post to outer settlements and islands. If expecting mail in the Islands, instruct correspondents to address their letters to the 'Post Office, Stanley, Falkland Islands, via London, England'.

Cable and Wireless PLC operates both local and long-distance telephone services; the system has recently been modernised, replacing the old manual exchange and radio-telephone system. Local calls cost 5p per minute, calls to the UK 15p for six seconds, and calls to the rest of the world 18p per minute. Operator-assisted calls are more expensive.

TIME

The Falklands are four hours behind GMT. In summer, Stanley goes on daylight savings time, but The Camp remains on standard time.

WEIGHTS & MEASURES

The metric system is now official, but in everyday matters people more commonly use English measurements. Since elevations on the Directorate of Overseas Survey's maps are in feet and most of the tourist literature uses English units, this chapter uses the English system, with the metric equivalent in brackets.

BOOKS & MAPS

Many books have been written since the 1982 war, but the most readily available general account is the third edition of Ian Strange's *The Falkland Islands* (London, David & Charles, 1983), which deals with the geography, history and natural history of the Islands. An interesting historical work on pioneer sheep farming in the South Atlantic, based on private correspondence, is Michael Mainwaring's *From the Falklands to Patagonia* (London, Allison & Busby, 1983).

For a good contemporary account of the Falklands, see Robert Fox's *Antarctica and the South Atlantic: Discovery, Development and Dispute* (London, BBC Books, 1985). Of the numerous books on the war, one of the best is Max Hastings' and Simon Jenkins' *Battle for the Falklands* (London, Pan, 1983).

Those interested in wildlife should acquire Robin Woods' *Falkland Islands Birds* (Oswestry, Shropshire, Anthony Nelson, 1982), which is a suitable field guide with excellent photographs. More detailed, but unsuitable for field use, is his *The Birds of the Falkland Islands* (Nelson, 1975).

Excellent topographic maps, prepared by the Directorate of Overseas Surveys, are available from the Secretariat in Stanley for about £2 each. There is a two-sheet, 1:250,000 map of the entire Islands which is suitable for most purposes, but for more detail obtain the 1:50,000 sheets.

MEDIA

Radio is the most important communications medium. The Falkland Islands Broadcasting Service (FIBS) produces local programming and also carries news from the BBC and programs from the British Forces Broadcasting Service (BFBS). Do not miss the nightly announcements, to which local people listen religiously – the Falklands may be the only place in the world the purchase of air time is within anybody's reach.

Television is available a few hours a day from the BFBS station at Mt Pleasant Airport; programs are taped and flown in from the UK on a regular basis. The only print medium is the fortnightly newspaper *Penguin News* of Stanley.

FILM & PHOTOGRAPHY

Colour and B&W print film are readily available at reasonable prices, although they're cheaper in the UK and the United States. Colour slide film is less dependably available, so you may want to bring all you need. If you are coming from Punta Arenas, Chile, slide film is available there at very reasonable prices.

HEALTH

No special health precautions need be taken in the Falklands, although you should be sure to have adequate insurance. There are excellent medical and dental facilities at the new King Edward VII Memorial Hospital, a joint civilian-military facility in Stanley.

Despite relatively cool temperatures, the deceptive combination of wind and sun can severely sunburn unsuspecting visitors. In the event of inclement weather, the wind can contribute to the danger of hypothermia.

DANGERS & ANNOYANCES

Near Stanley and in a few locations in The Camp on both East and West Falkland, there remain unexploded plastic land mines, but minefields are clearly marked and, in the 10 years since the Falklands war, no civilian has been injured. *Never* even consider entering one of these fields – the mines will bear the weight of a penguin or even a sheep, but not of a human. Report any suspicious object to the Explosive Ordnance Disposal (EOD) office (☎ 22229) near the town hall, which has free minefield maps (which, incidentally, are handy for walks in the Stanley area).

Walkers in The Camp should be aware that the so-called 'soft camp', covered by white grass, is boggy despite its firm appearance. Step carefully or risk sinking.

WORK

There is a chronic labour shortage in Stanley and it is not difficult to obtain a work permit. There is also, however, a chronic housing shortage which makes it nearly impossible to find lodging. In the past, it was possible to obtain seasonal work on the large sheep stations belonging to the Falkland Islands Company and other companies, but agrarian reform has nearly eliminated this option. You should not come to the Falklands in search of employment, but neither should you hesitate to inquire about opportunities – the major employers are the FIC and FIG.

ACTIVITIES

Wildlife will be the major attraction for most visitors. Penguins, other shorebirds and marine mammals are tame and easily approached even at developed tourist sites like Sea Lion Island and Pebble Island, but there are other equally interesting, undeveloped sites. At Port Howard, a large and picturesque sheep station on West Falkland, fishing is excellent and walking and riding are possible. Trekking and camping are possible in many parts of the Islands, although most visitors will prefer to stay near the coast, where the scenery and wildlife are most appealing. It is possible to visit the 1982 battlefields on both East and West Falkland.

Windsurfing is possible in sheltered waters like Stanley Harbour, but probably only the truly experienced can avoid going to South Africa on the prevailing winds. Experienced divers may find it interesting to explore some of the Falklands' numerous wrecks.

ACCOMMODATION

Accommodation is limited. In Stanley, there are several bed-and-breakfast houses and two hotels. In The Camp, several farms have converted surplus buildings into lodges, some of them very comfortable, to accommodate tourists, but there are also some self-catering cottages. A few have caravans or surplus Portakabin shelters obtained from the British military.

In areas not frequented by tourists, Falkland Islanders often welcome house guests; in addition, many farms have 'outside houses' or shanties which visitors may use with permission. Except for Stanley, camping is possible almost everywhere, again with permission.

FOOD & DRINKS

Wool has long been the staple of the Falklands economy and mutton the staple of the Falklander's diet. While it is not true that Islanders eat mutton 365 days a year, it is nearly true – on Christmas Day they eat lamb, or at least the story goes. Vegetarians will have a hard time of it, but meat is at least cheap. The very few vegetables and fruits grown in the Islands rarely appear on the market, since people grow their own in kitchen gardens, although a hydroponic market garden has begun to produce aubergines (eggplant), tomatoes, lettuce and other salad greens throughout the year.

Snack bars in Stanley offer fast food such as fish and chips, mutton-burgers (not as bad as it sounds), sausage rolls and pasties. There are respectable restaurants, but obviously nothing of international stature. Stanley has several well-patronised pubs, where beer and hard liquor (whiskey, rum) are the favourites, although wine has become more popular over the past few years. All drinks are imported.

Getting There & Away

Getting to the Falklands is dear, although cheaper than it has been. Unless you have your own boat, your options are limited but increasing, since there are now communications both with the UK and with South America. Since 1986, with the completion of the Mount Pleasant International Airport 35 miles south-west of Stanley, there have been twice-weekly flights from RAF Brize Norton, in Oxfordshire, via the tiny South Atlantic island of Ascension. Southbound, these flights leave Brize Norton on Mondays and Thursdays, arriving Tuesdays and Fridays; northbound, they leave Mt Pleasant on Wednesdays and Saturdays, arriving Thursdays and Sundays.

The flight takes 16 hours, plus an hour's stopover for refuelling on Ascension. The economy return fare is £1900, but there is a reduced APEX return fare of £1180 with 30-day advance purchase. One-way tickets can be purchased if you wish to continue to Chile. For reservations in the UK, contact Carol Stewart, Travel Coordinator, at FIG's London offices (☎ 222-5852), Falkland House, 14 Broadway, Westminster, London SW1H 0BH. In Stanley, contact the FIC (☎ 27633) on Crozier Place.

For travellers visiting South America, the new air connection with Punta Arenas, Chile, will be more attractive. There are now weekly summer flights with Aerovías DAP (☎ 22-3958), Ignacio Carrera Pinto 1022, Punta Arenas. One-way fares are US$400. In winter, the flights are fortnightly.

Stanley

Stanley, the Falklands' capital, is in reality little more than a village which, by historical accident, acquired a political status totally out of proportion to its size. Because many of its houses were built from available materials, often locally quarried stone and timber from shipwrecks, it has a certain ramshackle charm, as the houses' metal cladding and brightly painted corrugated iron roofs contrast dramatically with the surrounding moorland. Nearly all the houses have large kitchen gardens, where residents grow much of their own food and enough ornamentals to give the townscape a spot of colour. Almost every household depends on peat fuel, whose sweetish fragrance permeates the town on calm evenings.

Stanley was founded in 1845, when the Colonial Office ordered the removal of the seat of government from Port Louis, on Berkeley Sound, to the more sheltered harbour of Port Jackson, since renamed Stanley Harbour. Originally a tiny outpost of colonial officials, vagabond sailors and British military pensioners, the town grew slowly as a supply and repair port for ships rounding Cape Horn en route to the California gold rush. Some vessels were damaged and limped back into port, their cargos legitimately being condemned and sold, but shipping began to avoid the port when others were scuttled under such questionable circumstances that the town acquired an unsavoury reputation which undoubtedly discouraged growth. Only as sheep replaced cattle in the last third of the 19th century did Stanley begin to grow more rapidly, as it became the transshipment point for wool between The Camp and the UK.

As the wool trade grew, so did the influence of the Falkland Islands Company, already the Islands' largest landowner. The FIC soon became the town's largest employer, especially after acquiring the property of J M Dean, its only commercial rival, in the late 19th century. Over the next century, the FIC's political and economic dominance was uncontested, as it ruled the town no less absolutely than the owners of the large sheep stations ruled The Camp. At the same time, the Company's relatively high wages and good housing provided a paternalistic security, although these 'tied houses' were available only so long as the employee remained with the Company.

During the 1982 war, despite its occupation by thousands of Argentine troops, the capital escaped almost unscathed. The two major exceptions were both ironic: a British mortar hit a house on the outskirts of Stanley, killing three local women, while Argentine conscripts rioted against their officers after the surrender and burned the historic Globe Store, a business owned by an Anglo-Argentine who had died only a few years earlier.

Stanley remains the service centre for the wool industry, but since the declaration of a 150-mile fisheries protection zone around the Islands it has become an important port for the deep-water fishing industry, and many Asian and European fishing companies have offices in town.

Orientation

On a steep hillside on the south shore of Stanley Harbour, Port William's sheltered inner harbour on East Falkland, Stanley is surrounded by water and low hills. For protection from the prevailing south-west winds, the town has sprawled east and west along the harbour rather than onto the exposed ridge of Stanley Common, to the south. Ross Rd, which runs the length of the harbour, is the main street, but the town centre is still fairly compact, with most government offices, businesses and houses within a few blocks of each other. Most Stanley roads are paved, but outside town limits they are invariably gravelled. The only good road outside Stanley is the one to Mount Pleasant Airport.

Information

Tourist Office The Falkland Islands Tourist Board (☎ 22215) is at 56 John St. It distributes an excellent guide to Stanley and small brochures on Sea Lion Island, Pebble Island and Port Howard, and has a list of accommodation in the Islands. Hours are weekdays, from 8.30 am to noon and 1.15 to 4.30 pm.

Money Standard Chartered Bank is on Ross Rd at Barrack St, opposite the post office. It will change foreign currency and travellers' cheques, and cash personal cheques drawn on several UK banks with the appropriate guarantee card. Opening hours are weekdays from 8.30 am to noon and 1.15 to 3 pm. Remember that Falklands currency has no value outside the Islands – change your local notes for sterling or dollars before leaving.

Most businesses in Stanley will readily accept travellers' cheques.

Post & Telecommunications The post office (☎ 27180), in the town hall on Ross Rd at Barrack St, is open weekdays from 8 am to noon and from 1.15 pm to 4.30 pm. Stamp collectors should visit the Philatelic Bureau, in the same building, which sells stamps from the Falklands themselves, the Falkland Islands Dependencies (including South Georgia), and the British Antarctic Territories. Hours are weekdays from 9 am to noon and 1.15 to 4 pm.

Easily identified by its satellite dish, Cable and Wireless PLC (☎ 20804) operates the

Falklands' phone, telegram, telex and fax services from its offices on Ross Rd near Government House. To make an overseas call from the booths in the office, purchase a magnetic card over the counter – this is cheaper than an operator-assisted call. Counter hours are 8.30 am to 5 pm, but public booths are open 24 hours.

Travel Agencies For special itineraries or assistance for groups or individuals within the Islands, contact Debbie Johnson at Stanley Services (☎ 22624) on St Mary's Walk, Stanley.

Medical Services The King Edward VII Memorial Hospital (☎ 27328 for appointments; (☎ 27410 for emergencies), a joint military-civilian facility, is probably the best in the world for a community of Stanley's size. Dental services are also excellent. Since care is on a fee-for-service basis, you should be certain to have insurance.

Film Proooooing Falkland Printz (☎ 32185), at Mount Pleasant Airport, stocks and develops both colour print and slide film. In Stanley, leave your film at Pastimes, on Dean St near Ross Rd behind the FIC's West Store, for 24-hour service.

Government House
Probably Stanley's most photographed landmark, rambling Government House has been the residence of London-appointed governors since the mid-19th century. It is traditional for all visitors to the Falklands to sign the register of visitors, although this custom has declined with the increased passenger traffic of the postwar period. The governorship was once a very minor post within the FCO, but it is much more significant now.

Christ Church Cathedral
Completed in 1892 and undoubtedly the most distinguished building in town, the Cathedral is a massive brick and stone construction with a brightly painted corrugated iron roof. It has attractive stained glass windows, while several plaques honour the memory of local men who served in the British Forces in WW I and WW II. On the small plaza next to the Cathedral, the Whalebone Arch commemorates the 1933 centenary of British rule in the Falklands.

Battle of the Falklands Memorial (1914)
On Ross Rd West, just past Government House, this memorial commemorates the naval engagement between British and German forces in WW I. Nine British ships, in port for refuelling, quickly responded to sink four of five German cruisers which had earlier surprised them in southern Chile.

1982 War Memorial
Just west of the Secretariat, on Ross Rd, is the memorial to the victims of the 1982 Falklands conflict. Designed by a Falkland Islander living overseas, it was paid for by public subscription and built with volunteer labour. Every 14 June there are sombre ceremonies here.

Cemetery
At the east end of Ross Rd, the Stanley Cemetery is a testament to local history, where both the Islands' tiny elite and working class can be found. Note the tombstones of three young Whitingtons, children of an unsuccessful 19th-century pioneer whose departure must have been a sad one. Other surnames, such as Felton and Biggs, are as common in the Islands as Smith and Jones are in the UK.

Britannia House Museum
Ironically, the building which houses the Falklands museum was built for the Argentine Air Force officer who was the local representative of LADE, which until 1982 operated air services between Comodoro Rivadavia and Stanley. For several years after the war, it was the residence of the Commander of British Forces Falkland Islands (BFFI), but after the garrison moved to Mount Pleasant it became the new home of the local museum.

On Ross Rd West, just beyond the 1914

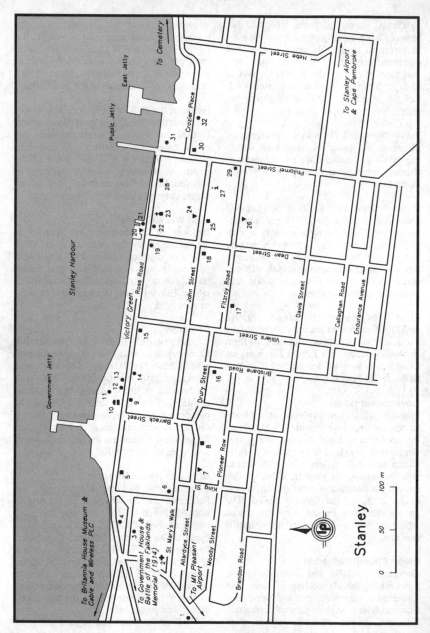

Stanley

■ PLACES TO STAY

5 Malvina House Hotel
8 Sparrowhawk Guest House
15 Upland Goose Hotel
16 Rose Hotel
17 Fenton Guest House
18 Monty's Restaurant
    and Hotel
25 Beauchene Guest House
28 Emma's Guest House
30 Globe Hotel

▼ PLACES TO EAT

7 Home Cookin'
20 Boathouse Café
24 Penguin Snacks
26 Woodbine Café

OTHER

1 Swimming Pool
2 King Edward VII
   Memorial Hospital
3 Secretariat
4 1982 War Memorial
6 Stanley Services
9 Standard Chartered Bank
10 Town Hall/Post Office
11 EOD (Bomb Disposal)
12 Home Industries
    Cooperative
13 Gymnasium
14 Police Station
19 FIC West Store
21 South Atlantic
    Marine Services
22 Whalebone Arch
23 Christ Church Cathedral
27 Tourist Office
29 Victory Bar
31 FIGAS/Customs House/
    British Antarctic Survey
32 Falkland Islands
    Company (FIC)

hours are Tuesday to Friday from 10 am to noon and 2 to 4 pm, Wednesday evenings from 6 to 8 pm, and Sunday from 10 am to noon. There is no charge for admission.

Activities

Stanley's new public swimming pool, on the Reservoir Rd near the Mount Pleasant Rd, has become a very popular recreational resource. Opening hours vary – check at the pool or with the tourist office.

Fishing for sea trout, mullet and smelt is also a popular pastime; the nearest site is the Murrell River, which is walking distance from Stanley. There are many other suitable places in The Camp, some easy accessible from the Mount Pleasant highway. Sea trout require a licence, available without charge from the police. The season runs from 1 September to 30 April.

Festivals

Stanley's most noteworthy public event is the annual **sports meeting** between Christmas and New Year's, which features horse racing (bets are legal), bull riding, and other competitions.

Every March, the Falkland Islands Horticultural Society presents a competitive **Horticultural Show** in the town gymnasium, displaying the produce of kitchen gardens in Stanley and The Camp, plus a wide variety of baked goods. At the end of the day, the produce is sold in a spirited auction.

In July, the annual **Crafts Fair** in the gymnasium displays the work of local weavers, leatherworkers, photographers, and artists (there are many talented illustrators and painters). Particularly interesting is the horse gear, whose origins can be traced to 19th-century gaucho traditions.

Battle Memorial, the museum is a recent project and the exhibits are subject to change. John Smith, the curator, is especially conversant with the Islands' maritime history; his booklet *Condemned at Stanley* relates the stories of the numerous shipwrecks which dot the harbour. Opening

Places to Stay

Accommodation in Stanley is good but limited and not cheap – reservations are a good idea. There are several bed-and-breakfast places, most of which offer the option of full board. The most economical is the *Sparrowhawk Guest House* (☎ 21568), at 7

Drury St, which charges £18.50 per person with breakfast only and £34 for full board.

Emma's Guest House (☎ 21056), a popular place on Ross Rd, charges £25 with bed and breakfast, with other meals available, and £32 with full board. Ask for cheaper rooms in the annex next door. At *Beauchene Guest House* (☎ 21252), a 19th-century stone building on John St, rates are £30 with breakfast. Rose Stewart's *Fenton Guest House* (☎ 21282), 7 Fitzroy Rd, has singles for £30, with breakfast and evening meal.

Malvina House Hotel (☎ 21355), 3 Ross Rd, has the most congenial ambience in town, with beautiful grounds and conservatory. Rates are £27.70 a single with breakfast, £32.65 a single in a twin room, and £21.70 per person in a shared twin. Group bookings pay £45 per person for full board. The *Upland Goose Hotel* (☎ 21455), Stanley's oldest at 20/22 Ross Rd, charges £32.50 with breakfast, £45 with full board (per person per day) for tour groups. *Monty's Restaurant and Hotel* (☎ 21292) on John St, which may reopen soon, is at the top end of the scale.

Places to Eat
There are several eating places in Stanley, most of which are very modest and inexpensive snack bars which keep limited hours. *Penguin Snacks* on John St, opposite Goodwin's Guest House, has fresh sausage rolls and pasties, plus sweets and homemade ice cream. It's open weekdays from 10.30 am to 5 pm. *Home Cookin'*, in an old Stanley cottage at 3 Drury St, has similar fare daily, except Wednesday and Friday, from 6.30 to 9.30 pm.

The *Boathouse Café*, on Ross Rd near the cathedral, is open for lunch Monday to Thursday from 10 am to 3 pm, and on Sunday from 11 am to 2.30 pm. The *Woodbine Café*, at 29 Fitzroy Rd, serves fish and chips, pizza, sausage rolls and similar items. It's open Tuesday to Friday from 10 am to 2 pm, Wednesday from 7 to 9 pm, Friday from 8 to 10.30 pm, and Saturday from 10 am to 3 pm.

For more elaborate meals, try the restaurants at *Emma's Guest House*, *Malvina House Hotel* and the *Upland Goose Hotel*. The latter two have three-course meals and bar snacks. *Monty's Restaurant and Hotel* on John St is also worth a try.

Entertainment
Stanley is no centre for nightlife, but there are several pubs which are heavily patronised. The most popular is the Globe Hotel at Crozier Place and Philomel St, but try also the Rose Hotel on Brisbane Rd and the Victory Bar on Philomel St at Fitzroy Rd. The Upland Goose Hotel has a public bar and Monty's also has a bar, called Deano's.

In the winter the three main pubs sponsor a darts league which is very popular. Darts tournaments take place in the Town Hall auditorium, where there are also many dances, with live music, in the course of the year.

There are no cinemas, but most of the hotels and guest houses have video lounges.

Things to Buy
There are a few Falklands souvenirs, but most of them are produced in the UK. The exception is locally spun and knitted woollen goods, some of which are outstanding. Try the Home Industries Cooperative on Ross Rd, open weekdays from 9.30 am to noon and 1.30 to 4.30 pm.

Getting There & Away
Air For information on international flights, see the Getting There & Away section above.

The Falkland Islands Government Air Service (FIGAS) (☎ 27219), on Ross Rd near the Philomel Store, serves all outlying destinations in 10-passenger Norman-Britten Islander aircraft. Instead of regular schedules, the service sets up itineraries according to demand; as soon as you know when and where you wish to go, contact them and listen to the FIBS announcements at 6.30 pm the night before your departure to learn your departure time. On rare occasions, usually around holidays, flights are heavily booked and you may not get on. Because some grass airstrips can only accept a limited payload, luggage is restricted to 30 lb (13.5 kg) per person.

Passages may also be arranged through the Falkland Islands Tourist Board at 56 John St.

Bus There are few places accessible by road in the Falklands, but Bob Stewart's Stanley Bus Service (☎ 21191) serves Stanley and Mount Pleasant airports, and will also make day trips to Goose Green during the summer months.

Getting Around
To/From the Airport The Falklands have two airports. Mount Pleasant International Airport is 35 miles (56 km) south-west of Stanley via a good gravelled road, while Stanley Airport, for local flights only, is about three miles (five km) east of town. Bob Stewart's Stanley Bus Service (☎ 21191) takes passengers to Mount Pleasant Airport for £10 single; call for reservations the day before your flight. He will also take groups to Stanley Airport or meet them there.

Taxi Jane McEachern (☎ 21105) has a Land Rover taxi which is on call weekdays between 8 am and 8 pm, for trips around Stanley and to Stanley and Mount Pleasant airports.

Car Rental Since there are few roads in the Falklands, it is hard to justify renting a car, but the Falkland Islands Company (☎ 27633) rents Fiat Stradas for road use only for £125 per week. By asking around it may be possible to rent a Land Rover for Camp travel, but inexperienced drivers often find themselves stuck in the boggy camp.

AROUND STANLEY
Stanley Harbour Maritime History Trail
See the tourist office on John St for an information brochure on the various wrecks and condemned ships in Stanley Harbour. There are now information panels erected near the remains of vessels such as the *Jhelum*, a sinking East Indiaman deserted by her crew

in 1871, the *Charles Cooper*, an American packet ship from 1866 which the FIC still uses for storage, and the *Lady Elizabeth*, a striking three-masted freighter which limped into Stanley after striking a rock in 1913.

Penguin Walk & Gypsy Cove
To visit the most convenient penguin colonies, about 1½ hours' walk north-east of Stanley, go to the east end of Ross Rd beyond the cemetery and cross the bridge over the inlet known as The Canache, past the wreck of the *Lady Elizabeth* and Stanley Airport. Gentoo penguins crowd the large sand beach at Yorke Bay, on the north side of the airport where, unfortunately, the Argentines anticipated a British frontal assault and buried countless plastic mines. While you cannot go onto the beach itself, you can get a good view of the penguins by walking along the minefield fence.

Farther on, at Gypsy Cove, there are Magellanic penguins, upland geese, kelp geese and many other shorebirds. There are no known mines in this area, but it is possible that some may have been washed up on shore.

Cape Pembroke Lighthouse
Built in 1855 and rebuilt in 1906, this now abandoned lighthouse is a full day's walk from Stanley Airport. In the late 19th century, the entire Cape Pembroke peninsula constituted one of the few small farms on the Islands, and was leased by the government to Stanley resident James Smith. He was a vocal advocate of agrarian reform, which finally came about a century later.

Kidney Island
Kidney Island is a small nature reserve, covered with tussock grass, which is habitat for a wide variety of wildlife, including rockhopper penguins, sea lions and other species. There is a shanty in which it is possible to camp, but a tent may be a better choice. The only way to reach Kidney Island is to charter a vessel – contact Dave or Carol Eynon at South Atlantic Marine Services

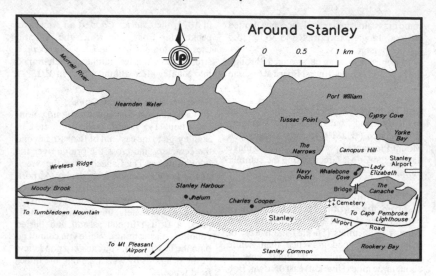

(☎ 21145), in the Boathouse Café on Ross Rd.

The Camp

Every part of the Falklands outside Stanley is The Camp. This includes both those parts of East Falkland accessible by road from Stanley, all of West Falkland, and the numerous smaller offshore islands, only a few of which are inhabited. Nearly everyone in The Camp is engaged in sheep ranching, although a few work in tourism and minor cottage industries.

Since the advent of the large sheep stations in the late 19th century, rural settlement in the Falklands has consisted of tiny hamlets, really company towns, near sheltered harbours where coastal shipping could collect the wool clip. In fact, these settlements were the models for the sheep estancias of Patagonia, many of which were founded by Falklands emigrants. On nearly all of them, shepherds lived at 'outside houses' which still dot the countryside. Since the agrarian reform of the late 1970s and

1980s, this pattern of residence has not changed greatly despite the creation of many new farms.

Many but not all of the Islands' best wildlife sites are on smaller offshore islands such as Sea Lion Island and Pebble Island, where there are comfortable but fairly costly tourist lodges. These are described in detail below, but there are also alternatives for budget travellers. Some of the most interesting islands have few or no visitor facilities and very difficult access, but it is worthwhile asking about them when you arrive in the Falkland Islands.

EAST FALKLAND
East Falkland has the Islands' most extensive road network, consisting of a good highway to Mount Pleasant International Airport and a serviceable track to the FIC's settlement at Goose Green (recently sold to the FIG). From the Mt Pleasant highway, there is also a good track north to the Estancia, a farm west of Stanley, which has recently been extended to Port Louis. Most other tracks are usable for Land Rovers only and, consequently, FIGAS is still the quickest and most reliable means of transport.

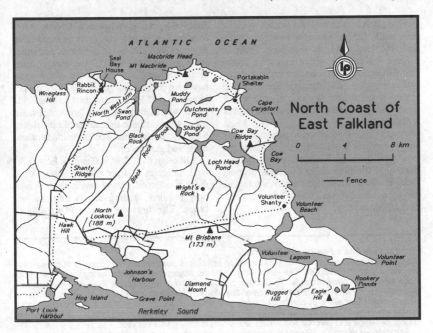

North Coast of East Falkland

Salvador

Salvador is one of the oldest owner-occupied sheep farms on East Falkland, originally founded by Andrés Pitaluga, a Gibraltarian who arrived in the Islands via South America in the 1830s. On the station's north coast, there are colonies of five different species of penguins and many other shorebirds and waterfowl, while Centre Island in Salvador Water has breeding populations of elephant seals and sea lions. Trekking along the north coast is possible with permission.

Owner Rob Pitaluga of *Salvador Lodge* (☎ 31150) offers full-board for £26.50 per day.

Trekking the North-East Coast

If you can do only one trek in the Islands, this is the one. From Seal Bay to Volunteer Point on the north coast of East Falkland, a mixture of broad, sandy beaches and rugged headlands, a trekker is literally never out of sight of a penguin.

Port Louis to Seal Bay Port Louis is the starting point, reached by FIGAS from Stanley, although with luck you may find a vehicle, especially on weekends – ask around town. It is also possible to hike from Stanley in one very long day. You will need permission from station manager Michael Morrison at Port Louis (☎ 31004) and owner Osmond Smith of Johnson's Harbour (☎ 31399).

Port Louis is the Falklands' oldest settlement, dating from the French foundation of the colony by Louis de Bougainville in 1764. One of the oldest buildings in the colony is the ivy-covered 19th-century farmhouse, still occupied by farm employees, but there are also ruins of the French governor's house and fortress and Louis Vernet's settlement scattered nearby. Visit the grave of Matthew Brisbane, Vernet's lieutenant, who was murdered by gauchos after the British naval officer J J Onslow left him in charge of the settlement in early 1833.

From Port Louis, Seal Bay is a six to eight hour walk, depending on the weather – with luck, the wind will be at your back. There is a Land Rover track which follows a fence line almost all the way; be sure to close gates whenever you pass through them. Since much of the hiking is through soft white grass camp, choose your route to avoid sinking in.

Ask Michael Morrison's permission to stay or camp at Seal Bay House, where there is a peat-burning Rayburn stove, before beginning the hike along the coast proper. Here, in the solitude of the north coast, you can get an idea of what it was to be a shepherd in the 19th century.

Seal Bay to Dutchman's Brook After leaving Seal Bay House, carry as much fresh water as you can, since penguins and other birds have fouled most of the watercourses along the way. Follow the arc of the coast eastward past several colonies of rockhopper penguins and king cormorants to Macbride Head, where there is a sea lion colony. En route, there are also thousands of burrows of Magellanic penguins and occasional macaronis and gentoos.

Although the 1:250,000 map of East Falkland indicates a large inlet at Swan Pond, there is a broad, sandy beach there which only requires wading across one shallow creek. The best campsite is Dutchman's

---

Penguins & Their Feathered Friends

On the Patagonian mainland, the only breeding species of penguin is the burrowing Magellanic. In the cooler waters around the Falklands, large schools of squid are food for many more species of these fascinating birds of the family *Spheniscidae* – rockhoppers, gentoos, kings and macaronis – plus other seabirds which are rarely seen on the mainland. In some cases, their numbers are almost incomprehensible, while in others there are just a few, at the limits of their sub-Antarctic range. Rockhoppers and Magellanics spend most of the year at sea, coming ashore to breed in the southern spring, but kings and gentoos remain in the Falklands throughout the year.

Rockhopper penguins *(Eudyptes crestatus)*, affectionately called 'rockies', are the most common species in the Falklands. Although resembling the macaroni penguin *(Eudyptes chrysolophus)*, rockies are easily distinguished by their floppy yellow crests, while the macaroni's crest is orange and more erect, resembling the foppish 18th-century male hairstyle which gave the bird its common English name. The rockhopper is also smaller, weighing only 5.5 pounds (2.5 kg), while the macaroni reaches 10 pounds (4.5 kg).

Falklands rockhopper colonies are the largest in the world – in the spring, perhaps as many as five million birds climb rugged, wave-battered headlands to breed in stony amphitheatres like the one on Sea Lion Island. Scaling these nearly vertical cliffs is no easy task – more often than not, as soon as the rocky leaves the water a breaker thrashes it against a rock and it falls back into the sea. Persistence triumphs, as the bird reaches the top after many false starts. Once reaching the top, male and female mate and produce two eggs of unequal size, only the larger of which hatches and reaches maturity. Daily, the birds must return to the sea in search of squid which they digest and regurgitate to their young.

While rockhoppers can be pugnacious, careful visitors able to tolerate the overpowering odor of ammonia from penguin excreta can walk among them without even disturbing a nesting mother. Rarely do these colonies, which can cover many acres, consist of rockies alone. In their eastern breeding sites, rockies mix with king cormorants *(Phalacrocorax albiventer)*, while in the west they share their space with the strikingly beautiful black-browed albatross *(Diomedea melanophris)*. On rare occasions you will see a solitary pair of macaronis among the breeding rockhoppers or even a single macaroni who, unable to find a mate of its own species, has nested with a rocky. More common on sub-Antarctic islands like South Georgia, the macaroni is at the limits of its range in the Falklands.

The gentoo *(Pygoscelis papua)* is much more common than the macaroni but not so common as the rocky. Its distinguishing features are its size (although smaller than the king, it weighs up to 13.5 pounds or six kg), its bright orange bill, and the white band which connects the eyes, across the crown. For nesting, it favours open, level sites some distance from the ocean. Gentoo routes to and from the sea are like ant trails, often long and indirect. Traditionally, Falkland Islanders have collected gentoo eggs in the spring but, unlike the rockhopper, the gentoo will lay a second egg if the first is removed.

Brook, where there is a Portakabin shelter, but no dependable source of fresh water.

Dutchman's Brook to Volunteer Shanty
About 1½ hours south of Dutchman's Brook, in a patch of white grass along a fence line near a colony of gentoo penguins, there is a tiny spring which is the only likely source of fresh water until Volunteer Shanty, another four hours south. On the way, you will see many more penguins, elephant seals, nesting turkey vultures, upland and kelp geese and many other birds. Volunteer Shanty is in fact a well-maintained outside house, but Osmond Smith no longer permits non-farm personnel to use it. You can,

however, camp nearby, collect fresh water from the tap, and use its very tidy outhouse.

Volunteer Shanty to Johnson's Harbour
Volunteer Beach has the largest concentration of the photogenic king penguins in the Falklands, where the species is at the northern limit of its range. This colony has grown steadily over the past two decades and now contains about 150 breeding pairs. At Volunteer Point, several hours' walk from the shanty, there is an offshore breeding colony of southern fur seals which can be seen with binoculars. Return along Volunteer Lagoon to see more birds and elephant seals.

From Volunteer Beach, the settlement at

Gentoos are popular with Falklands farmers, since they uproot the common *diddle-dee* shrub (*Empetrum rubrum*), which has no pasture value, while fine pasture grasses quickly colonise abandoned gentoo nesting sites. The application of the popular name gentoo to the species is obscure, since the word describes a non-Moslem inhabitant of India – one explanation is that the band across the gentoo's head resembles a turban.

Still, the undisputed monarch of Falklands penguins is, appropriately, the king (*Aptenodytes patagonicus*). This enormous, regal bird is unmistakable, standing more than three feet (almost a metre) in height and weighing more than 35 pounds (16 kg), with a bright orangeish ear patch which connects to a golden patch on the breast. It resembles the much larger emperor penguin (*Aptenodytes forsteri*) of Antarctica. Once nearly extinct in the Falklands, the king has reappeared at several different sites throughout the Islands, most notably at Volunteer Point, where a breeding colony of more than 150 pairs exists.

King penguins breed on flat, open areas among gentoos, but they do not nest, instead incubating their single egg on their feet and protecting it among loose folds of skin. The most extraordinary thing about the bird is its erratic breeding cycle, which is not synchronised with the seasons or the year – no scientist has successfully explained why 14 to 16 months pass between eggs. Because of the kings' beauty and rarity, Falklands farms which have breeding populations take great pride in their presence.

Many other birds are worth seeing, but one deserves special mention: the black-browed albatross, which nests on precipitous, west-facing headlands on New Island, West Point, Saunders Island and a few other places. Tiny but inaccessible Beauchene Island, an isolated southern outlier of East Falkland, has an astonishing two million birds. In total, the Falklands have more than three-quarters of the world's population of the species.

With an eight-foot (nearly three-metre) wingspan and flat webbed feet, this enormous bird is ungainly on land, getting airborne only by leaping off cliffs into the prevailing westerlies. It spends most of the winter at sea, and some individuals migrate across the entire South Atlantic in a circular pattern. Like the penguins among which it nests, the black-browed albatross has little fear of humans. By sitting near the colony, you will arouse enough interest that this curious bird will come to you instead of your having to go to it.

Unfortunately, all is not idyllic in this wildlife paradise. Since 1986, revenue from fishing licences has brought the Islands unprecedented prosperity, but Asian and European fleets may have over-exploited the stocks of squid and finfish upon which penguins, black-browed albatrosses and many other birds feed. Falklands Conservation, a pro-wildlife organisation with branches in both Stanley and the UK, is currently conducting seabird monitoring and research projects to determine the threat which commercial fishing poses to local wildlife. For more information, see the listing under Useful Organisations in this chapter. ∎

Johnson's Harbour is an easy four to five hour walk along Mt Brisbane. If possible, make advance arrangements to have FIGAS pick you up for the return to Stanley. If you are trekking back to Stanley, there is a small store at Johnson's Harbour where you can obtain some supplies.

San Carlos

On San Carlos Water on the Falkland Sound side of East Falkland, San Carlos settlement was the landing point for British forces during the 1982 conflict. Until 1983, when it was subdivided and sold to half a dozen local families, it was a traditional large sheep station. There is fishing on the San Carlos River, to the north of the settlement, while the comfortable *Blue Beach Lodge*, operated by William and Lynda Anderson, charges £45 for full board. The isolated 'big house', with its lengthy approach, will give you some idea how farm owners and managers distanced themselves from the labourers on large sheep stations.

There is a small military cemetery near the settlement. Across San Carlos Water, on Ajax Bay, are the fascinating ruins of the Ajax Bay Refrigeration Plant, a Colonial Development Corporation boondoggle of the 1950s which failed when farmers could not provide it with sufficient high-quality mutton from flocks which were raised primarily for wool. After its abandonment, pre-fab houses which were imported for labourers were dismantled and moved to Stanley, where they can be seen on Ross Rd West. Gentoo penguins occasionally wander through the ruins, which served as a military field hospital during the 1982 conflict. Take a flashlight if you plan to explore the ruins, which are about a four-hour walk around the south end of San Carlos Water.

Sea Lion Island

The most southerly inhabited island in the Falklands, tiny Sea Lion Island is less than a mile across at its widest point. Still, it has more wildlife in a smaller area than almost anyplace else in the Islands, including all five species of Falklands penguins, enor-

mous colonies of cormorants, giant petrels, and the remarkably tame and charming predator known locally as the 'Johnny Rook', more properly the striated caracara *(Phalcoboenus australis)*. On its sandy beaches, hundreds of elephant seals haul up every spring to breed, while sea lions line the narrow gravel beaches below the southern bluffs and lurk among the towering tussock grass.

For most of its history, Sea Lion's isolation and difficult access has undoubtedly contributed to the continuing abundance of wildlife, but much of the credit has to go to Terry and Doreen Clifton, who farmed Sea Lion Island since the mid-1970s before selling it recently. The Cliftons developed their 2300-acre farm with the idea that wildlife, habitat and livestock were compatible uses. Sea Lion Island is one of few working farms in the Falklands with any substantial cover of native tussock, which once covered the coastal fringe of both East and West Falkland and many offshore islands before careless fires and overgrazing nearly eliminated it.

Through improved fencing and other conscientious management decisions, the Cliftons made the island both a successful sheep station and a popular tourist site, mostly for day trips from Stanley and the military base at Mount Pleasant. Since 1986 the modern *Sea Lion Lodge* (☎ 32004), operated by Dave and Pat Grey, has offered twin-bedded rooms with full board for £47 per person, including access to a County Land Rover for visiting wildlife sites, although almost anyone can walk the length of the island in a few hours.

Since the quasi-governmental Falkland Islands Development Corporation (FIDC), which built the lodge, has recently bought Sea Lion Island, it is uncertain whether they will continue the Cliftons' policy of encouraging budget travellers by allowing camping and renting a small caravan for self-catering parties. At least two full days would be desirable for seeing the island in its entirety. There is a grass airstrip on which FIGAS Islanders can land.

WEST FALKLAND

Nearly as large as East Falkland, West Falkland has no roads, but rather a system of rough tracks suitable only for Land Rovers and motorcycles. Although offshore Saunders Island was the site of the first British garrison in 1765, it was settled permanently only in the late 1860s, when pioneer sheep farmer J L Waldron founded Port Howard station, on Falkland Sound. In short order, British entrepreneurs established sheep stations at Hill Cove, Fox Bay, Port Stephens, Roy Cove, Chartres and many smaller offshore islands. One of the most interesting experiments was the founding of a mission for Indians from Tierra del Fuego on Keppel Island.

There are outstanding wildlife sites on West Falkland and adjacent offshore islands, and good trekking in its interior, which is generally more mountainous than East Falkland. Only a few of these sites have formal tourist infrastructure, but independent travellers should look into visiting all parts of the island.

Port Howard

The oldest farm on West Falkland, Port Howard is one of very few large sheep stations remaining since the agrarian reform of recent years. For more than a century it belonged to J L Waldron Ltd, but in 1987 it was sold to local managers Robin and Rodney Lee, who have kept the farm and settlement intact rather than subdivide it. About 50 people live on the station, which has its own dairy, grocery, abattoir, social club and other amenities. Unusually for the Falklands, employees have been given the opportunity to purchase their houses and at least one has chosen to retire here rather than move to Stanley. Port Howard will be the West Falkland terminus of the anticipated ferry across Falkland Sound.

Port Howard is a very scenic settlement at the foot of 2158-ft Mt Maria, at the north end of the Hornby range. Although there is wildlife, most of it is distant from the settlement, whose immediate surroundings offer opportunities for hiking, horseback riding and fishing. It is also possible to view the summer shearing and other camp activities, and there is a small museum of artefacts from the 1982 war, when Argentine forces occupied the settlement.

Port Howard Lodge (☎ 42150) is the former manager's house, a classic of its era with a beautiful conservatory which feels like the tropics when the sun comes out – see also the antique West Falkland telephone exchange, which no longer functions. Accommodation costs £47 per person with full board, but make arrangements in advance to lodge at the farm's cookhouse for a fraction of the cost.

From Port Howard it is possible to hike up the valley of the Warrah River, a good trout stream, and past the Turkey Rocks to the Blackburn River and Hill Cove settlement, another pioneer 19th-century farm. Where the track is unclear, look for the remains of the old telephone lines. Ask permission to cross property boundaries, and remember to close gates. There are other, longer hikes southwards toward Chartres, Fox Bay and Port Stephens.

Pebble Island

Pebble is an elongated island off the north coast of West Falkland, with varied topography and a good sampling of wildlife. *Pebble Island Hotel* (☎ 41097) charges £47 per person for room with full board, but there should be self-catering cottages and a shanty available at the west end of the island.

Keppel Island

While it has no formal tourist facilities, Keppel Island has one of the most interesting histories of any island in the Falklands. In 1853, the South American Missionary Society established an outpost here to catechise Yahgan Indians from Tierra del Fuego and teach them to become potato growers instead of hunters and gatherers. The mission was controversial because the government suspected that Indians had been brought against their will, but it lasted until 1898, despite the Indians' susceptibility to disease even when Europeans remained healthy –

contrast the unmarked Yahgan graves with those of the mission personnel. One Falklands governor attributed numerous Yahgan deaths from tuberculosis to their:

...delicacy of constitution...developed owing to the warm clothing which they are for the sake of decency required to adopt after having been for 15 or 20 years roaming about in their canoes in a very cold climate without clothing of any kind.

Probably hard physical labour, change of diet, European contagion and living conditions in their small, damp stone houses played a greater role in the demise of the Yahgans than any inherent delicacy of constitution. The mission was undoubtedly prosperous, however, bringing in nearly £1000 annual income from its herds of cattle, flocks of sheep and gardens by 1877.

Although Keppel is now exclusively a sheep farm, there remain several interesting ruins. The former chapel is now a wool shed, while the stone walls of the Yahgan dwellings remain in fairly good condition. The mission bailiff's house is standing intact, although in poor repair. Keppel is also a good place to see penguins. If interested in visiting the island, contact Mr L R Fell (☎ 41001).

Saunders Island

Only a few miles west of Keppel, Port Egmont on Saunders Island was the site of the first British garrison on the Falklands in 1765. In 1767, after France ceded its colony to Spain, Spanish forces dislodged the British from Saunders Island and nearly precipitated a general war between the two countries. After the British left voluntarily in 1774, the Spaniards razed the settlement, including its impressive blockhouse, nearly to the ground, but the extensive foundations and some of the buildings' walls, plus the garden terraces built by the British marines still remain. One British sailor left a memoir indicating how well developed the settlement was:

The glory of our colony was the gardens, which we cultivated with the greatest care, as being fully convinced how much the comforts of our situation depended on our being supplied with vegetables...We were plentifully supplied with potatoes, cabbages, broccoli, carrots, borecole, spinach, parsley, lettuce, English celery, mustard, cresses, and some few, but very fine cauliflowers.

Saunders Island continued to be controversial into the late 1980s because the property passed by inheritance into the hands of Argentine descendents of the Scottish pioneer sheep farmer John Hamilton, who had extensive properties near Río Gallegos in Santa Cruz province. For years, Islanders agitated for the farm's expropriation, but the owners finally consented to sell the Island to its local managers in 1987.

In addition to its historical resources, Saunders Island has an excellent sample of Falklands wildlife and offers good trekking, especially out the north side of Brett Harbour to The Neck. This sandspit beach connects Saunders Island to the Elephant Point peninsula, once a separate island, about four hours' walk from the settlement. There is a Portakabin shelter near a large colony of black-browed albatrosses and rockhopper penguins here, as well as a few king penguins. Farther on, toward Elephant Point proper, there are thousands of Magellanic penguins, breeding kelp gulls, skuas, and a colony of elephant seals in a very scenic area. From The Neck, Elephant Point is about a four hours' walk one way.

Although Saunders Island has no formal tourist facilities, intending visitors should contact Tony or Biffo Pole-Evans on Saunders (☎ 41299).

Carcass Island

Carcass Island is a small, scenic island west of Saunders Island which has a good sample of wildlife and is a popular weekend and holiday vacation spot for people from Stanley. There are a couple of self-catering cottages in the settlement; for information, contact Rob McGill on Carcass Island (☎ 41106).

Chartres

Chartres is a medium-sized West Falkland

farm which offers good trout fishing on the Chartres River. For information, contact Bill Luxton at the *Chartres Lodge* (☎ 42250), where room and full board are available for £34 per person.

Port Stephens

Unquestionably the most scenic part of the Falklands, Port Stephens' rugged headlands are open to the blustery South Atlantic and battered by storms out of the Antarctic. Thousands upon thousands of rockhopper penguins, cormorants and other seabirds breed on the exposed coast, only a short distance from the settlement's sheltered harbour, until recently the centre of one of the FIC's largest stations. Like many other settlements, Port Stephens has no formal tourist facilities, but it is well worth a visit.

Less than an hour's walk from the settlement, Wood Cove and Stephens Peak are excellent places to see gentoo and rockhopper penguins and other local birds. The peak of Calm Head, about two hours' walk, has excellent views of the jagged shoreline and the powerful open South Atlantic.

One interesting longer trek goes from the settlement to the abandoned sealing station at Port Albemarle and huge gentoo penguin colonies near the Arch Islands. Hoste Inlet, where there is a habitable outside house, is about five hours' walk in good weather, while the sealing station, another post-WW II Colonial Development Corporation blunder, is four hours farther. Like the Ajax Bay freezer, the sealing station is a monument to bureaucratic ineptitude, but photographers and aficionados of industrial archaeology will find its derelict power station, boilers, rail track, water tanks, jetty and Nissen huts surrealistically intriguing. There is a habitable shanty with a functional Rayburn stove nearby, but unfortunately squaddies from the radar station on Mt Alice have vandalised the larger outside house.

The massive penguin colonies are an hour's walk beyond the sealing station. The Arch Islands, unfortunately inaccessible except by boat, take their name from the opening which the ocean has eroded in the largest of the group – and it is large enough to allow a good-sized vessel to pass through it.

If interested in visiting Port Stephens and trekking in the vicinity, contact Peter or Anne Robertson (☎ 42007) at the settlement.

New Island

The most westerly inhabited island in the Falklands, New Island is almost inaccessible unless the new grass airstrip has been finished, but it has great historic interest, having been a refuge for whalers from Britain and North America from the late 18th century well into the 19th, despite the objections of Spanish and British authorities. In the early 20th century, a Norwegian concern opened a shore-based whaling factory, but it failed because there simply were not enough whales. Ruins of the factory can be visited.

There are gigantic colonies of rockhopper penguins and black-browed albatrosses and a large rookery of southern fur seals on the precipitous west coast. Facilities are few, but potential visitors should contact Tony or Annie Chater (☎ 21399) or Ian or María Strange (☎ 21185) in Stanley.

Uruguay

Facts about the Country

About the size of Buenos Aires province, Uruguay is a classic political buffer between the South American megastates of Argentina and Brazil. While relatively few independent travellers visit the country, from Buenos Aires it is only a short hop across the Rió de la Plata to the fascinating colonial contraband centre of Colonia and a few hours more to Montevideo, one of South America's most interesting capitals. East of Montevideo, the Atlantic beaches attract many Uruguayans and Argentines for summer holidays, but the towns up the Río Uruguay, opposite Argentine Mesopotamia, are also clean and attractive. Uruguay's hilly interior is agreeable but rarely visited gaucho country.

Known officially as the República Oriental del Uruguay (Eastern Republic of Uruguay), the area was long called the Banda Oriental or 'Eastern Shore' of the River Plate. For most of this century, foreigners knew Uruguay as the 'Switzerland of South America', but political and economic events of the past 20 years have undermined this favourable image.

HISTORY

Uruguay's aboriginal inhabitants were the Charrúa Indians, a hunting and gathering people who also fished extensively. Hostile to outsiders, they discouraged settlement for more than a century by killing Spanish explorer Juan de Solís and most of his party in 1516. In any event, there was little to attract the Spanish who, according to William Henry Hudson, 'loved gold and adventure above everything, and finding neither in the Banda, they little esteemed it'.

In the 17th century, the Charrúas acquired the horse and prospered on wild cattle, eventually trading with the Spanish. Never numerous, they no longer exist as a definable tribal entity, although there remain some mestizo people in the interior along the Brazilian border. As on the Argentine Pampas, the gauchos subsisted on wild cattle, but in time the establishment of *estancias* pushed them back into the interior.

European Colonisation

The first Europeans on the Banda Oriental were Jesuit missionaries who settled near present-day Soriano, on the Río Uruguay. In 1680 the Portuguese established a beachhead at Nova Colônia do Sacramento, opposite Buenos Aires on the estuary of the Rió de la Plata. As a fortress and contraband centre, Colonia was a direct challenge to Spanish authority, forcing the Spanish to build their own citadel at the sheltered port of Montevideo.

This rivalry between Spain and Portugal led eventually to Uruguayan independence. José Gervasio Artigas, Uruguay's greatest

national hero, allied with the United Provinces of the River Plate against Spain, but was unable to prevent Uruguay's takeover by Brazil. Exiled to Paraguay, he inspired the famous '33 Orientales', Uruguayan patriots under General Juan Lavalleja who, with Argentine support, launched a campaign to liberate the Banda Oriental from Brazilian control. In 1828, after three years' struggle, a British-mediated treaty between Argentina and Brazil established Uruguay as a small independent buffer between the emerging continental powers.

Independence & Development

For most of the 19th century, Uruguay's independence was a fragile one, pressured politically and militarily by Argentina and Brazil and economically by Britain. Federalist forces, with the support of the Argentine dictator Rosas, besieged Montevideo from 1838-51. From this period, Uruguay's two major political parties, the Blancos and the Colorados, can trace their origins as armed gaucho sympathisers of the Federalist and Unitarist causes. As Hudson wrote in *The Purple Land*, 'Endless struggles for mastery ensued, in which the Argentines and Brazilians, forgetting their solemn compact, were for ever taking sides'.

British interest in the Banda Oriental, aroused by their occupation of the city in 1807, grew after independence. The UK had long been a market for hides, and in 1840 this market was expanded when the British introduced Merino sheep for wool, while the Liebig Meat Extract Company of London (producers of the well-known product Oxo) opened a plant at Fray Bentos in 1864. In 1868 a British company started the first railway to connect Montevideo with The Camp (the countryside), and later in the century Hereford and Shorthorn cattle began to replace rangy criollo breeds.

At the turn of the century, Fray Bentos was also the site of the country's first *frigorífico*, the massive Anglo plant which is now an industrial museum. This increasing commercialisation of one of the country's few abundant resources brought about the demise of the independent gaucho who, as in Argentina, became attached to estancias whose boundaries were now fixed by the introduction of barbed wire. As elsewhere in Latin America, large landholdings (*latifundios*) became a way of life in Uruguay, and these made a major, if reluctant, contribution to the general welfare.

Batlle & the Modernisation of Uruguay

One of the most visionary politicians in Latin American history was Uruguay's José Batlle y Ordóñez, who devised the region's first comprehensive social welfare state. During his two terms as president, from 1903-07 and 1911-15, he accomplished such innovations as modern pensions, farm credits, unemployment compensation and eight-hour workdays. Despite his own strong presidency and interventionist approach to government, he also sought to overcome the legacy of *caudillismo* (the strong-arm rule of the *caudillo*) by constitutional reform. He created a collegial executive on the Swiss model, but this reform was never completely successful. State intervention in the economy resulted in the nationalisation of

many industries, the creation of others, and an unparalleled general prosperity.

To implement and finance his reforms, Batlle depended on the wealth provided by the rural livestock sector, so that by taxing exports he obtained the revenue to build the state sector. This worked well so long as there seemed to be no limits to Uruguay's commodity exports, but as this sector failed to grow, the welfare state became unsustainable.

Conservative economists have blamed the state for 'killing the goose that laid the golden egg' by exploiting the pastoral sector to the limit for Montevideo's benefit and for political patronage. But it appears that even before the welfare state became a fact, landowners were slow to reinvest their earnings to increase productivity, mainly preferring to squander their wealth in conspicuous consumption. Redistributive policies worked only as long as there was something to redistribute.

Economic Decline & Political Breakdown

From the mid-20th century, economic stagnation affected the entire country, but particularly the city of Montevideo, which had become accustomed to middle-class prosperity. State-supported enterprise became riddled with patronage and corruption, and the economy was unable to support a pensioner class which numbered more than 25% of the total workforce. By the mid-1960s this had reached crisis proportions, with serious political unrest, but the 1966 election to the presidency of Colorado candidate Oscar Gestido, a highly regarded retired general, appeared to give some cause for optimism and recovery. Shortly after taking office, however, Gestido died, and was replaced by Vice-President Jorge Pacheco Areco, a virtual unknown who proved to have disturbing authoritarian tendencies.

Under Pacheco, the country slid into dictatorship. He outlawed leftist parties, closed newspapers, and invoked state of siege measures because of guerrilla threats. The major guerrilla force was the Movimiento de Liberación Nacional (National Liberation Movement), more commonly known as the Tupamaros, a socialist faction who had organised secretly as early as 1963 but did not reveal their existence publicly until 1967. Although almost exclusively an urban, middle-class movement in a country populated almost exclusively by descendants of Europeans, the Tupamaros took their name from a Peruvian Indian who led an 18th-century rebellion against the Spanish crown.

At first, public support for the Tupamaros was considerable, but this eroded quickly as Uruguayans began to blame them for the ever more repressive measures of the Pacheco government, which went so far as to dismiss a police official who openly disapproved of torture. After the Tupamaros kidnapped and executed suspected CIA agent Dan Mitrione (an incident dramatised in Costa-Gavras' film *State of Siege*), and then engineered the escape of more than one hundred of their comrades from prison, Pacheco put the military rather than the police in charge of counter-insurgency.

Presidential elections went on as scheduled in November 1971, but Pacheco's hand-picked successor, Juan M Bordaberry, invited the military to participate in government, ruling with a National Security Council and finally dissolving the General Assembly.

The Military Dictatorship & Its Aftermath

While the Uruguayan military takeover did not exhibit either the shocking suddenness of the Chilean coup or the sustained brutality of the Argentine Dirty War, it was perhaps even more insidious in the context of Uruguayan history. Virtually eliminating free expression, the armed forces occupied almost every position of importance in the entire country, and increased the military budget dramatically in the interests of a 'national security state'.

Torture or the threat of torture became routine, with the detention of more than 60,000 citizens. The military established a political classification system which deter-mined eligibility for public employment, subjected all political offences to military courts, actively censored public libraries, and even subjected large family gatherings to prior police approval.

Attempting to institutionalise their role in the political process, the armed forces drafted a constitution. However, the electorate rejected it in a plebiscite in 1980 despite warnings that such rejection would delay any return to civilian rule. Indeed, four more years passed before voters could elect Colorado presidential candidate Julio María Sanguinetti under the Constitution of 1967. Sanguinetti, though not a tool of the military, won only because they prohibited the candidacy of popular Blanco leader Wilson Ferreira Aldunate, a vocal opponent of the dictatorship.

Sanguinetti's presidency, while not spectacular, seemed to indicate a return to Uruguay's democratic traditions. He did, however, support a controversial amnesty bill for military human rights violations which was submitted to a referendum of all Uruguayans in April 1989. Despite serious misgivings on the part of many, a majority of voters approved the amnesty. Later that year, Blanco presidential candidate Luis Lacalle succeeded Sanguinetti in a peaceful transition of power.

GEOGRAPHY & CLIMATE

Although one of South America's smallest countries, Uruguay is large by European standards. Its area of 187,000 sq km is slightly larger than England and Wales combined, or about the size of North Dakota. Lacking energy resources (except for a few hydroelectric sites), minerals and commercial forests, its principal natural asset is agricultural land, which is abundant but not so fertile as the Argentine Pampas. For the most part, the country's rolling topography is an extension of southern Brazil, with two main ranges of interior hills, the Cuchilla de Haedo, west of Tacuarembó, and the Cuchilla Grande, south of Melo, neither of which exceed 500 metres in height. West of Montevideo, the terrain is more level, resembling the Pampas, while east of the capital the coastal area has impressive beaches, dunes and headlands. There are some large lagoons near the Atlantic border with Brazil, including the huge Laguna Merín.

The climate is mild, even in winter, and frosts are almost unknown. Along the coast, daytime temperatures average 28°C in January and 15°C in June, while nighttime temperatures average 17°C in January and 7°C in June. Rainfall, evenly distributed throughout the year, averages about 1000 mm per year over the whole country.

FLORA & FAUNA

Consisting mostly of grasslands and gallery forests, Uruguay's native vegetation does not differ greatly from that of the Argentine Pampas or southern Brazil. In the south-east, along the Brazilian border, there remain some areas of palm savanna, but only a very small percentage of the land is forested.

Wild animals of any size are uncommon, although rhea can still be found in areas close to the Río Uruguay. Uruguay's nature reserves are few and offer little out of the ordinary, although the seal colonies near

Political Departments of Uruguay

Punta del Este and at Cabo Polonio make worthwhile visits.

GOVERNMENT

Uruguay is a republic whose 1967 constitution establishes three separate branches of government. The president heads the executive branch, while the legislative General Assembly consists of a 99-seat Chamber of Deputies and a 30-member Senate, all of whom are elected every five years. The Supreme Court is the highest judicial power. Administratively, the country consists of 19 departments whose organisation resembles that of the national government.

The electoral system is very complex. While the legislature is chosen by proportional representation, each party may offer several presidential candidates, and the winner is the one who gets the most votes for the party with the most votes. This means that the winning candidate almost certainly will not win a majority (even within his own party) and may not even be the candidate with the most votes overall. In eight elections between 1946 and 1984, no winning candidate obtained more than 31% of the vote.

The major political parties are the Colorados, the inheritors of the legacy of *Batllismo*, and the generally more conservative Blancos. Julio María Sanguinetti, of the Colorado party, was the first post-military president between 1984 and 1989, while current President Luis Lacalle belongs to the Blancos. A third force which has been growing in power is the Frente Amplio, a coalition of leftist groups which controls the mayorship of Montevideo. Ironically, their most prominent figure is a retired general, Liber Seregni.

ECONOMY

Uruguay is resource-poor and underpopulated. Historically, the dominant and most productive part of the Uruguayan economy has been the pastoral sector. Cattle and sheep estancias occupy more than three-quarters of the land, grazing over nine million cattle and 23 million sheep, but as the pastoral economy has stagnated from the *estancieros'* unwillingness to invest in improvements, the country has been unable to sustain the progressive social programs established by José Batlle. Low international prices for wool, the country's primary export, have been a major factor in recent years. Only along the south-west littoral does the country support intensive agriculture, although wet-rice cultivation has recently increased around Laguna Merín near the Brazilian border. Cropland is relatively small in area, but makes a disproportionately high contribution to the economy.

Uruguay's manufacturing is restricted mostly to the area around Montevideo. In part because of Batlle's legacy of encouraging self-sufficiency despite a tiny internal market, many inefficient state-supported industries produce inferior products at very high cost, surviving only because of protective tariffs. Among the economic activities traditionally controlled by the government are railroads, banking, insurance, telephones, electricity, water supply, oil refining, fisheries and Montevideo's meat supply, giving the country the most state-dominated economy in Latin America. Social security pensions consume 60% of public expenditure.

Tourism plays an increasingly important role in the economy, as the beaches east of Montevideo attract wealthy Argentines. In many ways, Uruguay is an economic satellite of both Brazil and Argentina as well as a political buffer between the two major South American powers. Along with these two countries and Paraguay, Uruguay is to be a partner in the new Mercosur common market which goes into effect in 1995. Conceivably, by encouraging investment, this opening could reduce the emigration which has deprived Uruguay of many of its most youthful and capable people, who have sought employment in neighbouring countries.

Hyperinflation required the introduction in 1975 of a new currency, the *peso nuevo*. Inflation is currently running at similar levels to Argentina – at the time of writing, it was about 129%, but gradual devaluation of the peso is keeping prices relatively stable in dollar terms. Foreign debt is a major concern, as Uruguay has one of the largest per capita burdens in all of Latin America. Historically, the country's liberal banking laws have made Uruguay a destination for capital from neighbouring countries, but usually only as a way station en route to Switzerland or the United States.

POPULATION & PEOPLE

With a population of just over 3.1 million, Uruguay is the smallest Spanish-speaking country in South America. Its population is highly urbanised, more than 85% of Uruguayans residing in cities. Nearly half live in Montevideo, leading one political scientist to call Uruguay a 'city-state' even though, historically, the rural sector has produced most of its wealth. The next largest city, Salto, has fewer than 100,000 inhabitants.

By world standards, the welfare of Uruguayans ranks high. Infant mortality rates are low, and the life expectancy of 71 years is the highest in South America and only slightly below that of many Western European countries. Yet limited economic opportunity has forced half a million Uruguayans to live outside the country, mostly in Brazil and Argentina.

Most Uruguayans are White, and are predominantly of Spanish and Italian origin. European immigration has overwhelmed the small but still visible Black population of perhaps 60,000, descendents of slaves imported into the country in the 19th century, who once comprised nearly 20% of the population of Montevideo.

EDUCATION

For more than a century, primary education has been free, secular and compulsory, with per capita government expenditures among the highest in Latin America. Literacy is among the foremost in the region, and secondary enrolment is also very high.

Montevideo's Universidad de la República is the only public university. Since a disproportionate number of university students read law or medicine, professions which are oversupplied, the country lacks trained people in more technically oriented professions.

ARTS

For such a small country, Uruguay has an impressive literary and artistic tradition: for details on literature, see the Books & Maps section in the Facts for the Visitor chapter.

Theatre is a popular medium and playwrights are very prominent. One is Mauricio Rosencof, a Tupamaros founder whose plays have been produced since his release from prison, where he was tortured by the military government in the 1970s.

Uruguayan artists such as Pedro Figari, who paints rural scenes, have earned recognition well beyond the country's borders. Punta Ballena, near Punta del Este, is well known as an artists' colony.

RELIGION

Uruguayans are almost exclusively Roman Catholic, but church and state are officially separate. There is a small Jewish minority, probably numbering only about 25,000, who live almost exclusively in Montevideo. Evangelical Protestantism has made some inroads, and Sun Myung Moon's Unification Church owns the afternoon daily *Ultimas Noticias.*

LANGUAGE

Spanish is the official language and is universally understood. Uruguayans fluctuate between use of the *voseo* and *tuteo* (see the Glossary) in their everyday speech, but either will be readily understood. In the north, along the Brazilian border, many people are bilingual in Spanish and Portuguese. See the Language section in Argentina – Facts about the Country for more information on Latin American Spanish.

Facts for the Visitor

Although Uruguay is a very distinct country, travelling there very much resembles travelling in Argentina. Only those facts for the visitor which differ significantly from Argentina are mentioned below.

VISAS & EMBASSIES

Uruguay requires visas of all foreigners, except those from neighbouring countries (who need only national identification cards) and nationals of Western Europe, Canada, Israel, Japan and the USA. All visitors need a tourist card, which is valid for 90 days and is renewable for another 90. To extend your visa or tourist card, visit the Dirección Nacional de Migración (☎ 96-0471) at Misiones 1513 in Montevideo. Summer hours are 7.15 am to 1 pm.

Uruguayan Embassies & Consulates

Uruguay has diplomatic representation in neighbouring countries and overseas, although its network is not so extensive as Argentina's.

Argentina
    Las Heras 1907, Buenos Aires (☎ 803-6030)
    Rivadavia 510 Gualeguaychú (☎ 6168)
Australia
    1st floor, Embassy Tower, Suite 107 (GPO Box 318), Woden, ACT, 2606 (☎ (06) 282-4800)
Brazil
    Rua Arthur Bernardes 30, Catete, Río de Janeiro, (☎ 225-0089)
Canada
    Suite 1905, 130 Albert St, Ottawa, Ontario (☎ 234-2937)
Chile
    Pedro de Valdivia 711, Santiago (☎ 223-8398)
Paraguay
    Avenida Brasil at Siria, Asunción (☎ 44242)
UK
    48 Lennox Gardens, London SW1X 0DL (☎ (71) 584-8192)
USA
    1918 F St NW, Washington, DC (☎ 331-4219)

Foreign Embassies & Consulates in Uruguay

South American countries, the USA and most Western European countries have diplomatic representation in Montevideo, but Australians and New Zealanders must depend on their consulates in Buenos Aires. In a pinch, they should be able to contact the UK Embassy.

Both Argentina and Brazil have consulates in border towns, which are mentioned in the appropriate chapters of the text.

Argentina
    Río Branco 1281 (☎ 90-0897)
Bolivia
    4th floor, Río Branco 1320 (☎ 91-2394)
Brazil
    Blvd Artigas 1257 (☎ 49-4110)
Canada
    1st floor, Juan Carlos Gómez 1348 (☎ 95-8583)
Chile
    1st floor, Andes 1365 (☎ 98-2223)
Denmark
    5th floor, Colonia 981 (☎ 91-5238)
France
    Uruguay 853 (☎ 92-0078)
Israel
    Blvd Artigas 1585 (☎ 40-4164)
Japan
    5th floor, Rincón 487 (☎ 96-1238)
Netherlands
    Ap 202, Leyenda Patria 2880 (☎ 70-1631)
Paraguay
    Blvd Artigas 1191 (☎ 45810)
Peru
    Soriano 1124 (☎ 92-1046)
Spain
    Libertad 2738 (☎ 78-6763)
Sweden
    6th floor, Avenida Brasil 3079 (☎ 78-1504)
Switzerland
    11th floor, Federico Abadie 2936 (☎ 70-4315)
UK
    Marco Bruto 1073 (☎ 62-3630)
USA
    Lauro Muller 1776 (☎ 40-9051)

DOCUMENTS

Passports are necessary for many everyday transactions, such as cashing travellers' cheques and checking into hotels. Theoretically, Uruguay does not recognise the International Driving Permit, requiring instead the Inter-American Driving Permit, but this appeared to make no difference in the one instance in which police asked us for identification.

At border crossings, the Ministerio de Turismo sells a 'Tarjeta Turística' (not to be mistaken for the required immigration tourist card) which provides a number of tourist services, such as automobile insurance and medical and legal assistance in case of sickness or accident. It also provides discounts at many tourist sites throughout the country and can be worthwhile if you are spending some time in Uruguay. For non-motorists, the 'Tarjeta Azul' costs US$20 per month, while the 'Tarjeta Roja' for motorists costs US$26 per month.

CUSTOMS
Uruguayan customs regulations permit the entry of used personal effects and other articles in 'reasonable quantities'.

MONEY
The unit of currency is the *peso nuevo* (N$), which replaced an older peso in 1975 after several years' hyperinflation. Banknote values are 50, 100, 200, 500, 1000, 5000 and 10,000 pesos.

Inflation, at a current rate of 129%, is running at even higher levels than Argentina, although for foreign travellers, devaluations keep prices from rising substantially in dollar terms. Travel costs in Uruguay are slightly lower than in Argentina, especially with respect to accommodation and transportation. Prices in this book are given in US dollars.

Money is readily exchanged at casas de cambio in Montevideo, Colonia and the Atlantic beach resorts, but banks are the rule in the interior. Casas de cambio accept travellers' cheques at slightly lower rates than cash dollars and sometimes charge commissions, although these are not as high as those levied in Argentina. There is no black market for dollars or other foreign currency,

which can be purchased without difficulty. Most better hotels, restaurants and shops accept credit cards.

Exchange Rates
Because the peso is steadily declining against the dollar, exchange rates are likely to work in your favour. At the time of writing the rate of exchange had climbed gradually against the US dollar in recent times.

A$1	=	N$1813
US$1	=	N$2392
UK£1	=	N$4111
FFr1	=	N$423.60
It£1	=	N$1.92
DM1	=	N$1435
BraCr1	=	N$1.36
Arg$1	=	N$2420
Par₲1	=	N$1.87
Bol$1	=	N$636

WHEN TO GO & WHAT TO BRING
Since Uruguay's major tourist attraction is its beaches, most visitors come in summer and dress accordingly, but the year-round temperate climate requires no special preparations. In ritzy resorts like Punta del Este, people often dress their best when out for the evening.

Montevideo's urban attractions are independent of the seasons. Along the Río Uruguay in summer, temperatures can be smotheringly hot, but the interior hill country is slightly cooler, especially at night.

TOURIST OFFICES
As in Argentina, almost every department and municipality has a tourist office, usually on the main plaza or at the bus terminal. Uruguayan maps are not quite as good as those in most Argentine tourist offices, but many of the brochures have excellent historical information.

Foreign Representatives
The larger Uruguayan consulates, such as those in New York and Los Angeles, usually

have a tourist representative in their delegation, but they are not especially helpful.

Australia
There is no specific tourist information office in Australia. Tourist inquiries should be directed to the Uruguayan Consulate-General, GPO Box 717, Sydney, NSW, 2001 (☎ (02) 232-8029)
Canada
Suite 1905, 130 Albert St, Ottawa, Ontario (☎ 234-2937)
UK
Tourist information can be obtained from the Uruguayan Embassy, 48 Lennox Gardens, London SW1X 0DL (☎ (71) 584-8192)
USA
541 Lexington Ave, New York, NY (☎ 755-1200, ext 346)
429 Santa Monica Blvd, No 400, Santa Monica, California (☎ 394-5777)
1918 F St NW, Washington DC (☎ 331-1313)

USEFUL ORGANISATIONS
Uruguay's youth hostel network, while limited, is a good alternative to standard accommodation, and a youth hostel card may prove worthwhile. For more information, contact the Asociación de Alberguistas del Uruguay (☎ 98-1234), Calle Pablo de María 1583, Montevideo.

BUSINESS HOURS & HOLIDAYS
Business Hours
Most shops are open weekdays and Saturdays from 8.30 am to 12.30 or 1 pm, then close until midafternoon and reopen until 7 or 8 pm. Food shops also open on Sunday mornings.

Government office hours vary with the season – in summer, from mid-November to mid-March, they open from 7.30 am to 1.30 pm, while the rest of the year they open from noon to 7 pm. Banks open weekday afternoons in Montevideo, but outside the capital they are usually open only in the mornings. Exceptions are noted in the text.

Public Holidays
January 1
Año Nuevo (New Year's Day)
January 6
Epifanía (Epiphany)

March/April (dates vary)
Viernes Santo/Pascua (Good Friday/Easter)
April 19
Desembarco de los 33 (Return of the 33 Exiles)
May 1
Día del Trabajador (Labour Day)
May 18
Batalla de Las Piedras (Battle of Las Piedras)
June 19
Natalicio de Artigas (Artigas' Birthday)
July 18
Jura de la Constitución (Constitution Day)
August 25
Dia de la Independencia (Independence Day)
October 12
Día de la Raza (Columbus Day)
November 2
Día de los Muertos (All Souls' Day)
December 25
Navidad (Christmas Day)

CULTURAL EVENTS
Uruguay's **Carnaval**, which takes place the Monday and Tuesday before Ash Wednesday, is livelier than its Argentine counterparts but not so lively as in Brazil. Visit Montevideo's Barrio Sur, where the city's Black population celebrates traditional *candomblé* ceremonies.

Holy Week (Easter) is also **La Semana Criolla**, which offers traditional gaucho activities like *asados* (barbeques) and folk music. Most businesses close for the duration.

POST & TELECOMMUNICATIONS
Rates are reasonable, but postal and telecommunications services are no better in Uruguay than in Argentina. As in Argentina, letters and parcels are likely to be opened if they appear to contain anything of value. If something is truly important, send it by registered mail.

For poste restante, address mail to the main post office in Montevideo. It will hold mail for up to a month, or up to two months with authorisation.

Telephone
ANTEL is the state telephone monopoly, with central long-distance offices which resemble those of ENTel in Argentina. As in Argentina, public telephones take *fichas*

(tokens) rather than coins. Each ficha is good for about three minutes. Between 10 pm and 7 am there are discount rates for long-distance calls.

Credit card or collect calls to the United States and other overseas destinations are cheaper than paying locally. ANTEL honours AT&T credit cards – 000410 is the direct access code for the USA.

BOOKS & MAPS

Uruguay's best known contemporary writers are Juan Carlos Onetti, whose novels *No Man's Land*, *The Shipyard*, and *A Brief Life* (New York, Grossman, 1976) are available in English, and poet, essayist and novelist Mario Benedetti. Historian Eduardo Galeano, whose *Open Veins of Latin America* is discussed in the section on Argentine history, is also a Uruguayan.

Probably Uruguay's most famous writer is José Enrique Rodó, whose turn-of-the-century essay *Ariel*, contrasting North American and Latin American civilisation, is a classic of the country's literature. While none of 19th-century writer Javier de Viana's work has been translated into English, he and his 'gauchesco' novels are the subject of John F Garganigo's biography *Javier de Viana* (New York, Twayne, 1972).

History

Compared with neighbouring countries, there is surprisingly little material available on Uruguay in English. For a discussion of the rise of Uruguay's unusual social welfare policies, see George Pendle's *Uruguay, South America's First Welfare State*, 3rd ed. (London, 1963), and Milton Vanger's *The Model Country: Jose Batlle y Ordóñez of Uruguay, 1907-1915* (Brandeis University Press, 1980).

The country's agrarian history is covered in R H Brannon's *The Agricultural Development of Uruguay* (London, 1968). Even those with great patience and a command of Spanish will find José Pedro Barrán and Benjamin Nahum's seven-volume *Historia Rural del Uruguay Moderno* imposing, but they summarise their conclusions in 'Uruguayan Rural History', an article in *Hispanic American Historical Review* (November, 1984). A 19th-century classic is William Henry Hudson's *The Purple Land* (Berkeley, Creative Arts Book Company, 1979).

For a sympathetic explanation of the rise of the 1960s guerrilla movements, see María Esther Gilio's *The Tupamaro Guerrillas* (New York, Ballantine, 1973). Costa-Gavras's famous and engrossing film *State of Siege*, filmed in Allende's Chile, deals with the Tupamaros' kidnapping and execution of suspected American CIA officer Dan Mitrione.

Contemporary Government & Politics

A good starting point for looking at modern Uruguay is Henry Finch's edited collection *Contemporary Uruguay: Problems and Prospects* (Liverpool, Institute for Latin American Studies, 1980). See also Luis González's *Political Parties and Redemocratization in Uruguay* (Washington, DC,

The Wilson Center, 1985), and Martin Weinstein's *Uruguay, Democracy at the Crossroads* (Boulder, Colorado, Westview Press, 1987). For an account of Uruguay's own Dirty War, see Lawrence Weschler's *A Miracle, A Universe: Settling Accounts with Torturers* (New York, Pantheon, 1990).

Maps

Uruguayan road maps are only a partial guide to the country's highways, but see the Automóvil Club Uruguayo, Shell and Ancap for the best available. For more detailed maps, try the Instituto Geográfico Militar (☎ 81-6868), on the corner of 12 de Octubre and Abreu, Montevideo.

MEDIA

Newspapers are very important in Uruguay, which ranks second on the continent (after Argentina) in total circulation per 1000 inhabitants. Montevideo has a variety of newspapers, including the morning dailies *El Día* (founded by José Batlle), *La República*, *La Mañana* and *El País*.

Gaceta Comercial is the voice of the business community. Afternoon papers are *El Diario*, *Mundocolor* and *Ultimas Noticias*, a recent arrival operated by followers of Reverend Sun Myung Moon. For the most part, newspapers are identified with specific political parties, but a relatively new weekly, *Búsqueda*, takes a more independent stance with respect to political and economic matters.

The *Buenos Aires Herald* and other Porteño newspapers are readily available in Montevideo, Punta del Este and Colonia.

Radio and television are popular, with 20 television stations (four in Montevideo) and 100 radio stations (about 40 in the capital) for Uruguay's three million people.

HIGHLIGHTS

For most visitors, Montevideo and the Atlantic beach resorts will be Uruguay's main attractions. The narrow streets and port zone of Montevideo's Ciudad Vieja (Old City),

currently being redeveloped, have immense colonial charm, while its hilly topography adds a dimension which even Buenos Aires' more picturesque neighbourhoods lack. Besides its sophisticated resorts and broad sandy beaches, the Atlantic coast also has scenic headlands.

Up the estuary of the Rió de la Plata, the colonial contraband port of Colonia is one of the continent's least known treasures – every visitor to Buenos Aires should plan at least a day trip and preferably a weekend here. Further up, on the Río Uruguay, there is first-rate river fishing. Uruguay's undulating interior literally offers relief from the monotony of the Argentine Pampas.

FOOD & DRINKS

Per capita, Uruguayans consume even more beef than Argentines, and the *parrillada* (beef platter) is a standard here. Likewise, the kinds of eating places are very similar – *confiterías* (cafés), pizzerías and restaurants closely resemble their Argentine counterparts. There are good international restaurants in Montevideo, Punta del Este and some other beach resorts, but elsewhere the food is fairly uniform. Uruguayan seafood is almost always a good choice.

The standard of Uruguayan short orders is *chivito*, which is not goat but rather a tasty and filling steak sandwich with a variety of additions – cheese, lettuce, tomato, bacon or other odds and ends. Even more filling is the *chivito al plato*, in which the steak is served topped with a fried egg, plus potato salad, green salad and chips. Other typically Uruguayan short orders include *olímpicos*, which are club sandwiches, and *húngaros*, which are spicy sausages on a hot dog roll (probably too spicy for young children, who will prefer the blander *panchos*).

Uruguayans consume even more *mate* (Paraguayan tea) than Argentines and Paraguayans, many lugging a thermos wherever they go. Uruguayan wines are very decent, especially in the form of *clericó*, a mixture of white wine and fruit juice. Another popular alcoholic drink is the *medio y medio,* a mixture of sparkling wine and white wine. Beers are equally good.

ENTERTAINMENT

Cinema is extremely popular in Montevideo and throughout the country, although there is no domestic film industry. Live theatre is also very well patronised, especially in Montevideo.

Soccer is the most popular spectator and participant sport; the most popular teams are Nacional and Peñarol. Tango is nearly as popular as in Argentina, while Afro-Uru-guayan *candombe* music and dance adds a unique dimension not present in Uruguay's dominating neighbour.

THINGS TO BUY

Most shoppers in Uruguay will be interested in leather clothing and accessories, woollen clothing and fabrics, agates and gems, ceramics, wood crafts and decorated gourds.

One of the most popular places is the artisans' cooperative Manos del Uruguay, with several locations in Montevideo. For more details, see listings under Montevideo.

Getting There & Away

For getting there and away, Uruguay is almost a satellite of Argentina. Most international flights to and from the country go to Buenos Aires' Ezeiza Airport before continuing to Montevideo, while all river transport and the great majority of land transport also passes through Argentina. There are several direct land crossings from Brazil.

AIR
To/From the USA
United has three direct flights weekly from Miami to Montevideo, with a stopover in Río de Janeiro. Otherwise, all flights pass through Ezeiza.

To/From Europe
Uruguay's national carrier PLUNA has Thursday and Sunday flights from Madrid, stopping in Recife and and Río de Janeiro. Iberia, KLM and Lufthansa have direct flights, but all other carriers servicing Uruguay stop over in Ezeiza.

To/From Neighbouring Countries
There are frequent flights between Montevideo's Carrasco Airport and Buenos Aires' Aeroparque Jorge Newbery, as well as from Punta del Este and Colonia to Aeroparque. Although it is possible to fly between Carrasco and Ezeiza, it is more expensive and much less convenient unless your ticket is valid for an ongoing flight.

PLUNA flies to Brazilian destinations, including Porto Alegre (once per week), Río de Janeiro (six) and São Paulo (nine). Varig and Cruzeiro fly similar routes, as do other major European airlines which serve Brazil.

To/From Other South American Countries
PLUNA also flies to Asunción, Paraguay (weekly), and Santiago, Chile (twice weekly). These flights originate in Punta del Este. Líneas Aéreas Paraguayas (LAP) and LAN-Chile serve their respective countries. Avianca and KLM also go to Santiago.

LAND
Uruguay shares borders with the Argentine province of Entre Ríos and the southern Brazilian state of Río Grande do Sul. Highway and bus services are generally good, but there are no rail services.

To/From Argentina
There are direct buses from Montevideo to Buenos Aires via Gualeguaychú, but these are slower and less convenient than the land/river combinations across the Rió de la Plata. For more details on the bridge crossings of the Río Uruguay see the Getting There & Away chapter in Argentina.

To/From Brazil
Chuy to Chui & Pelotas Reached by an excellent paved highway from Montevideo, this is the most frequently used border crossing from Uruguay into Brazil. Chuy and Chui are twin cities whose parallel main streets are separated only by a median strip, but Uruguayan immigration is about one km before the actual border and Brazilian immigration two km beyond it. If continuing any distance into Brazil, you will have to complete border formalities on both sides.

Río Branco to Jaguarão Less frequently used than Chuy, this is an alternative route to Pelotas and Porto Alegre via the town of Treinta y Tres, in the department of the same name, or Melo, in the department of Cerro Largo. There are buses from Jaguarão to Pelotas.

Rivera to Livramento In the department of the same name, this offers an alternative route to Livramento, Brazil, from Paysandú, on the Argentine border, via the interior city of Tacuarembó. There are regular buses from Livramento to Porto Alegre.

Artigas to Quaraí This route crosses the Puente de la Concordia over the Río Quareim, but the principal highway goes south-east to Livramento.

Bella Unión to Barra do Quaraí In the extreme north-west corner of Uruguay, this crossing leads to the Brazilian city of Uruguaiana, where you can cross into the Argentine province of Corrientes and north to Paraguay or to Iguazú Falls. Overland travel to Iguazú Falls through southern Brazil is slow and difficult.

RIVER
From Montevideo, the most common means of crossing to Argentina involves ferry or hydrofoil, usually requiring bus combinations to Colonia. The main companies are Ferrytur (☎ 90-4668) at Río Branco 1368, Montevideo; ONDA at San José 1145, Montevideo; and Buquebus (☎ 92-0670) at Río Negro 1400, also in Montevideo.

Colonia to Buenos Aires Ferrytur and ONDA have morning and evening sailings between Colonia and Buenos Aires. The trip costs US$20 and takes 2½ hours. From Colonia, you can make direct bus connections to Montevideo, a three-hour trip. Alíscafos Belt, the hydrofoil, takes only an hour to Colonia.

Carmelo to Tigre There are launches across the estuary of the Río de la Plata to the Buenos Aires suburb of Tigre. Arrangements can be made in Montevideo at Lanchas (☎ 91-7637), Plaza Cagancha 1340, Montevideo.

LEAVING URUGUAY
Departure Tax
International passengers from Carrasco Airport pay a departure tax of US$2.50 to Argentina, US$4.50 to other South American countries, and US$7 for other destinations.

Getting Around

AIR

Domestic air services in Uruguay are very limited. The national airline PLUNA has flights to and from Punta del Este, while the military airline TAMU serves the interior cities of Artigas, Salto, Rivera, Paysandú, Melo and Tacuarembó. TAMU fares are absurdly cheap: Artigas, for example, is 601 km from Montevideo by road, yet the fare is only US$20 single, US$36 return. TAMU, however, only flies Fokker F27s.

Both PLUNA and TAMU publish timetables which can easily be obtained at their offices. There are four flights weekly to Salto, two to Artigas and Tacuarembó, four to Paysandú, four to Rivera and four to Melo.

BUS

Buses in Uruguay are not quite so comfortable as those in Argentina, but the rides are shorter and they are perfectly acceptable. Most Uruguayan cities do not have central bus terminals, but the companies are always within easy walking distance of each other, usually around the central plaza. Many companies publish their timetables.

Buses are very frequent to destinations all around the country, so reservations should only be necessary on or near holidays. Fares are very reasonable – for example, Montevideo to Fray Bentos, a distance of about 300 km, costs only about US$8.

TRAIN

Passenger services on Uruguayan trains ceased completely in 1988.

CAR

Uruguayans are somewhat less ruthless on the road than Argentines, although it has been said that dividing lines are there for decoration only. There are in any event plenty of Argentines on the road, so watch out for Argentine number plates. Outside Montevideo and the coastal areas, traffic is minimal and poses few problems, although some interior roads are very rough. For visitors lulled to sleep by the endlessly flat Pampas, Uruguay's winding roads and hilly terrain require close attention.

Uruguay ostensibly requires the Inter-American Driving Permit, rather than the International Driving Permit, in addition to a state or national driver's licence, but we found the police paid no attention so long as we had something that looked official. Arbitrary police stops and searches are less common than in Argentina, but the police are not above soliciting a bribe for traffic violations.

Driving can be even more expensive in Uruguay than in Argentina, since Uruguay imports all its oil and its cars – there is no domestic automobile industry. Consequently, you will see so many lovingly maintained, truly antique vehicles *(cachilas)* on the streets of Montevideo that you may think you've stumbled onto the set of a gangster movie. If you plan to purchase a car, Argentina is a better bet. Car rental is just as costly as in Argentina.

The Automóvil Club del Uruguay (☎ 91-1251), on the corner of Colonia and Yi in Montevideo, is the equivalent of Argentina's ACA, although it is not so widespread. It does have good maps and information.

LOCAL TRANSPORT
To/From the Airport

Due to the shorter distances involved, air travel is less important in Uruguay than in Argentina. There is a regular city bus service to Montevideo's Carrasco Airport. For details, see the chapter on Montevideo. Special taxis serve the airport and cost more than regular ones, but any cab can take you there. Since the airport is beyond the city limits, fares will exceed the metre reading (see the Taxi section below).

Bus

Montevideo has an extensive but chaotic

public transport system. To make sense of it, ask a local or buy the *Guia de Montevideo Eureka*, available at bookshops or kiosks, which lists routes and schedules. As in Argentina, the driver or conductor will ask your destination. Retain your ticket, as an inspector may check it. The standard fare is about US$0.25.

Taxi

Taxis have metres and, as in Buenos Aires, drivers correlate the metre reading with a photocopied fare chart. Between midnight and 6 am fares are higher. There is a small additional charge for luggage, and passengers generally round off the fare to the next hundred pesos.

Montevideo

Montevideo dominates the political, economic and cultural life of Uruguay even more than Buenos Aires does that of Argentina. Nearly half Uruguay's 3.1 million citizens live here, while no other city has even 100,000 residents. There is a certain logic to this, though, as Montevideo's port links the country to overseas commerce, and such a small country with an almost exclusively rural economy hardly requires a competing metropolis for trade and administration. The country's tax burden, however, has fallen unevenly on the rural export sector and has unquestionably contributed to the capital's dominance. The rural sector subsidises not only Uruguay's inefficient domestic industries but also the country's progressive social welfare policies.

History

Spain's founding of Montevideo in 1726 was a response to concern over Portugal's growing influence in the River Plate area; since 1680, the fortress and contraband port of Colonia had been a thorn in Spain's side. Montevideo was in turn a fortress against the Portuguese as well as British, French and Danish privateers who came in search of hides on the Banda Oriental. Even more isolated than Buenos Aires, it was modest and unimpressive despite its official status as port of call for ships en route to the Pacific. A British visitor to the present-day Plaza Zabala observed in 1797 that

The fort seems to be the only object on which any attention has been bestowed; it is large, handsomely built, and consists of four bastions, on which are apparently very good brass cannon...

The church is the next principal building; it is large and clean, but has nothing remarkable about it: the houses, many of which lie scattered about in a very irregular manner, with very pleasing gardens and little plantations attached to them, are all low and meanly built, very few being higher than the ground floor; but their tiled tops, with the green trees waving over them, have, taken altogether, rather a pretty effect.

Many of Montevideo's early residents were Canary Islanders. Its port, superior to Buenos Aires in every respect except its access to the Humid Pampa, soon made it a focal point for overseas shipping. In the early 19th century, a construction boom resulted in a new Iglesia Matriz, the Cabildo and other neoclassical late colonial monuments, but after independence Uruguayan authorities demolished many of these buildings and planned a new centre east of the peninsula, which is now known as the Ciudad Vieja (Old City). No wonder, when it could be an unsalubrious place – one British visitor in 1807 described the hazards of walking in the city at night:

...through long narrow streets so infested with voracious rats as to make it perilous sometimes to face them...Around the offals of carrion, vegetables and stale fruit accumulated there, the rats absolutely mustered in legions. If I attempted to pass near those formidable banditti, or to interrupt their meals or orgies, they gnashed their teeth upon me like so many evening wolves. So far they were from running in affright to their numerous burrows, that they turned round, set up a raven cry, and rushed at my legs in a way to make my blood run chill.

Montevideños had other worries, though. During the mid-19th century, the city endured an almost constant state of siege by the Argentine dictator Rosas, who was determined to create a small client state to Buenos Aires. After Rosas' fall in 1851, normal commerce resumed and, between 1860 and 1911, the British-built railroad network assisted the capital's growth. Like Buenos Aires, Montevideo absorbed numerous European immigrants in the early 20th century, mostly from Spain and Italy; by 1908, 30% of Montevideo's population was foreign-born.

Around this time, construction of the city's first locally financed frigorífico was followed by two similar foreign-backed enterprises, as the country became ever more closely linked to the export trade. Growth has continued to stimulate agricultural intensification near Montevideo to feed the rapidly increasing urban population. Much of this population, refugees from rural poverty, lives in *conventillos*, large older houses which have been converted into multi-family slum dwellings. Many of these are in the Ciudad Vieja, but even this population is being displaced as urban redevelopment usurps this picturesque but valuable central area.

Orientation

Montevideo lies on the east bank of the Río de la Plata, almost directly east of Buenos Aires on the west bank. For most visitors, the most intriguing area will be the Ciudad Vieja, a grid on a small peninsula near the port and harbour, but the city's functional centre is Plaza Independencia to the east, with many historic public buildings of the republican era. Here begins Avenida 18 de Julio, the city's most important commercial and entertainment area. Plaza Cagancha, through which Avenida 18 de Julio runs, is the main staging area for national and international public transportation, while most of the inexpensive accommodation is on its side streets.

From Plaza del Entrevero, on 18 de Julio, the diagonal Avenida Libertador General Lavalleja leads to the imposing Palacio Legislativo, site of the General Assembly. From the 11th-floor terrace of the Palacio Municipal, at Avenida 18 de Julio and Ejido, there are spectacular views of the city. At the north-eastern end of Avenida 18 de Julio is Parque José Batlle y Ordóñez, a large public park which contains the Estadio Centenario, the 75,000-seat stadium built to commemorate the country's centenary in 1930. Running perpendicular to its terminus is Bulevar Artigas, another major artery, while the nearby Avenida Italia is the main highway east to Punta del Este and the rest of the Uruguayan Riviera.

Many points of interest are beyond downtown, as Montevideo has sprawled both east and west along the river. Across the harbour to the west, the 132-metre Cerro de Montevideo was a landmark for early navigators, 'a conical mountain of a stupendous height' according to an 18th-century English visitor, which now offers outstanding views of the city. To the east, the Rambla or riverfront road leads past attractive residential suburbs with numerous public parks, including Parque Rodó at the south end of Bulevar Artigas. Farther on, but well within the city limits, are numerous sandy beaches which the capital's residents frequent in the summer and on weekends throughout the year.

Information

Tourist Office The most convenient tourist office (☎ 90-5216) is in Plaza Cagancha, near most of the major bus companies. The Ministerio de Turismo (☎ 90-4148), 4th floor, Avenida Lavalleja 1409, is extremely bureaucratic, but persistence will yield a good city map if the Plaza Cagancha office doesn't have one. There is also an office at the airport (☎ 50-3812), which is reputed to be next to useless.

There is much useful information in the weekly *Guía del Ocio*, which lists cultural events and has two-for-one coupons for many cinemas, theatres and restaurants. If your Spanish is good, dial 124 for general information on virtually anything in Montevideo.

Money There are many exchange houses around Plaza Cagancha and on Avenida 18 de Julio. Indamex, at the entrance to the Balmoral Plaza Hotel on Plaza Cagancha, is open 24 hours.

Post & Telecommunications The Correo Central (main post office) is at Buenos Aires 451 in the Ciudad Vieja. ANTEL has several convenient offices: at D Fernández Crespo 1534, San José 1108 (open 24 hours), and Rincón 501 in the Ciudad Vieja. For telegrams, go to Treinta y Tres 1418.

Foreign Embassies For diplomatic representatives from overseas and neighbouring

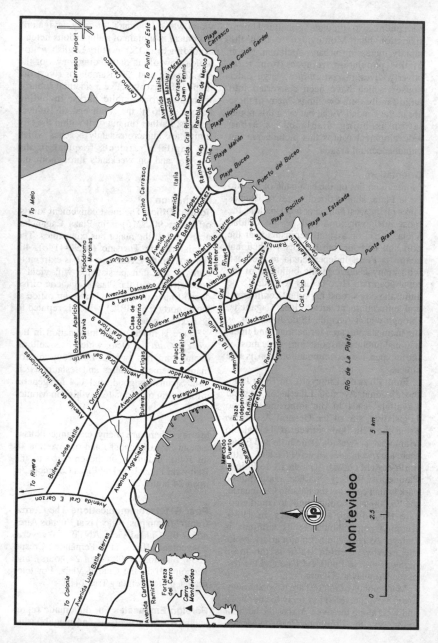

Montevideo

countries, see the Facts for the Visitor chapter for Uruguay.

Cultural Centres Run by the United States Information Service, the Biblioteca Artigas-Washington (☎ 91-5232), Paraguay 1217, is a very substantial library with books and newspapers in English, plus special programs and lectures. Hours are Monday from noon to 7 pm and Tuesday to Friday from 11.15 am to 7 pm.

The Anglo-Uruguayan Cultural Institute (☎ 90-3708), San José 1426, also has an English-language library. Montevideo also has branches of the Goethe Institute, at Canelones 1524, and the Alliance Française, at Soriano 1180.

Travel Agencies Viajes Cynsa (☎ 98-2042), Paraguay 1311, VP Turismo (☎ 90-3730), San José 1073, and Viajes COT (☎ 96-3197), on Plaza Cagancha, will arrange travel in and out of Montevideo and to neighbouring countries.

Bookshops Montevideo has several excellent bookshops. Linardi y Risso, at Juan Carlos Gómez 1435 in the Ciudad Vieja, is the equivalent of Platero in Buenos Aires, with outstanding selections in history and literature, including many out of print items. Another good shop, the largest in the city, is Barreiro y Ramos at 25 de Mayo and Juan Carlos Gómez in the Ciudad Vieja, with branches at 18 de Julio 941 and in the suburbs of Pocitos and Carrasco. The Librería Inglesa-Británica, Sarandí 580 in the Ciudad Vieja, has English-language books, including Penguin paperbacks.

Medical Services The most convenient hospital is the Hospital Maciel at 25 de Mayo and Maciel, in the Ciudad Vieja.

Film Kilómetro Cero, 18 de Julio 1180 on Plaza Cagancha, and Kodak Uruguaya, Yí 1532, offer dependable developing. Tech-nifilm, 18 de Julio 1202, is the place to go for camera repairs.

Walking Tour
To orient yourself in downtown Montevideo, take a walk from **Plaza Independencia** through the Ciudad Vieja to the port. On the plaza, an honour guard keeps 24-hour vigil over the **Mausoleo de Artigas**, which is topped by a 17-metre, 30-tonne statue of the country's greatest hero. The 18th-century **Palacio Estévez**, on the south side, was Government House until 1985, while the ornate, 26-storey **Palacio Salvo**, on the east side, was the tallest building in South America when built in 1927 and is still the tallest in the city. Just off the Plaza is the **Teatro Solís** (see below).

At the west end of the Plaza is **La Puerta de la Ciudadela**, a modified remnant of the colonial citadel which dominated the area before its demolition in 1833. Calle Sarandí takes you to the **Plaza Constitución**, also known as Plaza Matriz, whose centrepiece is a sculpture by the Italian Juan Ferrari which commemorates the establishment of Montevideo's first waterworks. There is a museum in the **Cabildo** (see below), a neo-classical stone structure designed by the Spanish architect Tomás Toribio and finished in 1812. Begun in 1784 and completed in 1799, the **Iglesia Matriz** (Cathedral), on the corner of Sarandí and Ituzaingó, is the oldest public building in Montevideo, the work of Portuguese architect José de Sáa y Faria.

Continue to the **Casa Rivera**, Rincón and Misiones, the **Museo Romántico**, 25 de Mayo 428, and the **Casa Lavalleja**, Zabala and 25 de Mayo, all part of the Museo Histórico Nacional (see below). See also the **Palacio Taranco**, built in an 18th-century European style by French architects commissioned by a wealthy merchant. Half a block west is the **Casa Garibaldi**, where the Italian hero once lived. From there, visit the **Plaza Zabala**, site of the colonial governor's house until its demolition in 1878. There is a statue to Bruno Mauricio de Zabala, founder of the city, by the Spanish sculptor

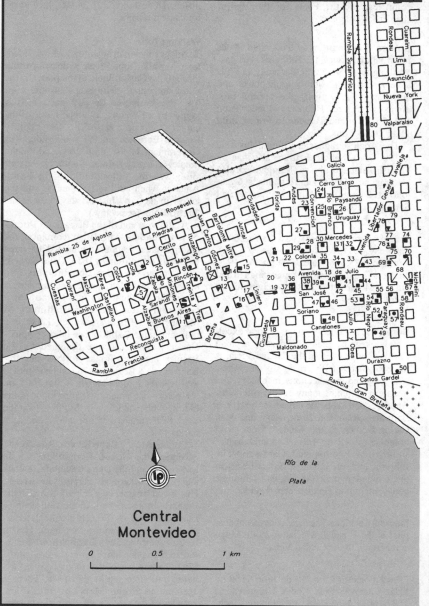

Central
Montevideo

0   0.5   1 km

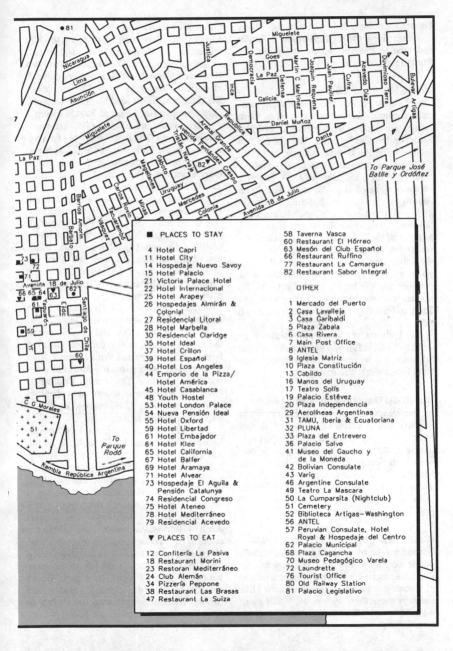

■ PLACES TO STAY

4 Hotel Capri
11 Hotel City
14 Hospedaje Nuevo Savoy
15 Hotel Palacio
21 Victoria Palace Hotel
22 Hotel Internacional
25 Hotel Arapey
26 Hospedajes Almirán & Colonial
27 Residencial Litoral
28 Hotel Marbella
30 Residencial Claridge
35 Hotel Ideal
37 Hotel Crillon
39 Hotel Español
40 Hotel Los Angeles
44 Emporio de la Pizza/ Hotel América
45 Hotel Casablanca
48 Youth Hostel
53 Hotel London Palace
54 Nueva Pensión Ideal
55 Hotel Oxford
59 Hotel Libertad
61 Hotel Embajador
64 Hotel Klee
65 Hotel California
67 Hotel Balfer
69 Hotel Aramaya
71 Hotel Alvear
73 Hospedaje El Aguila & Pensión Catalunya
74 Residencial Congreso
75 Hotel Ateneo
78 Hotel Mediterráneo
79 Residencial Acevedo

▼ PLACES TO EAT

12 Confitería La Pasiva
18 Restaurant Morini
23 Restoran Mediterráneo
24 Club Alemán
34 Pizzería Peppone
38 Restaurant Las Brasas
47 Restaurant La Suiza
58 Taverna Vasca
60 Restaurant El Hórreo
63 Mesón del Club Español
66 Restaurant Ruffino
77 Restaurant La Camargue
82 Restaurant Sabor Integral

OTHER

1 Mercado del Puerto
2 Casa Lavalleja
3 Casa Garibaldi
5 Plaza Zabala
6 Casa Rivera
7 Main Post Office
8 ANTEL
9 Iglesia Matriz
10 Plaza Constitución
13 Cabildo
16 Manos del Uruguay
17 Teatro Solís
19 Palacio Estévez
20 Plaza Independencia
29 Aerolíneas Argentinas
31 TAMU, Iberia & Ecuatoriana
32 PLUNA
33 Plaza del Entrevero
36 Palacio Salvo
41 Museo del Gaucho y de la Moneda
42 Bolivian Consulate
43 Varig
46 Argentine Consulate
49 Teatro La Mascara
50 La Cumparsita (Nightclub)
51 Cemetery
52 Biblioteca Artigas–Washington
56 ANTEL
57 Peruvian Consulate, Hotel Royal & Hospedaje del Centro
62 Palacio Municipal
68 Plaza Cagancha
70 Museo Pedagógico Varela
72 Laundrette
76 Tourist Office
80 Old Railway Station
81 Palacio Legislativo

Lorenzo Coullant Valera. From the Plaza, continue along Calle Washington to Colón and then to Piedras and the **Mercado del Puerto** (see below).

Museo Histórico Nacional

The National History Museum actually consists of four different houses, most of them former residences of Uruguayan national heroes in the Ciudad Vieja. Built in the late 18th century, the **Casa Lavalleja**, at Zabala 1469, was the home of General Lavalleja from 1830 until his death in 1853; in 1940, his heirs donated it to the state. The **Casa Rivera**, a 19th-century building at Rincón 437, was the house of General Fructuoso Rivera, Uruguay's first president and founder of the Colorado party. The **Casa de Garibaldi**, at 25 de Mayo 314, belonged to the Italian patriot who commanded the Uruguayan Navy from 1843-51, and now contains many of his personal effects. All the houses are open Tuesday to Friday from 1 to 7 pm and Sundays and holidays from 2 to 6 pm.

The 18th-century **Museo Romántico**, 25 de Mayo 428, is full of paintings and antique furniture, but its exterior has been modified from the original colonial style.

Museo del Gaucho y de la Moneda

In the headquarters of the Banco de la República at Avenida 18 de Julio 998, this museum displays the artefacts of Uruguay's gaucho history, including horse gear, silverwork and weapons, plus a collection of banknotes and coins. Opening hours are Tuesday to Friday from 9.30 am to 12.30 pm, and daily except Monday from 3.30 to 7.30 pm.

Museo Pedagógico José Pedro Varela

Named for the man who devised Uruguay's public education system, this museum on Plaza Cagancha has an interesting collection of teaching materials, suggesting how Uruguayans view their own country. It's open weekdays from 10 am to 8 pm, and Saturdays from 8 am to noon.

Other Museums

Montevideo has many other worthwhile museums, mostly downtown and almost all closed on Mondays. The **Museo y Archivo Histórico Municipal** (Municipal Archive & Historical Museum) is in the Cabildo, opposite the Cathedral at Juan Carlos Gómez and Sarandí, open daily except Monday from 2 to 6 pm. There are English-speaking tours. The **Museo de Arte Decorativo** is a fine arts museum in the Palacio Taranco, 25 de Mayo 376, while the **Museo Municipal de la Construcción**, Piedras 528, is open Tuesday to Friday from 2 to 6 pm.

The **Museo de Historia Natural** (Natural History Museum) is in the Teatro Solís building, at Buenos Aires 652. The Automóvil Club del Uruguay's **Museo del Automóvil**, 6th floor, Colonia 1251, has a superb collection of antique cars, although you'll see just as many or more on city streets. It's open Tuesday to Friday from 5 to 9 pm and weekends from 3 to 9 pm.

Outside the centre, the **Museo del Cerro** in Parque Carlos Vaz Ferreira has an excellent weapons collection and good views of the city from across the harbour. Opening hours are Thursday and Friday from 1.30 to 5.45 pm and Sunday from 9.30 am to noon and 2 to 5.45 pm. The **Jardín Zoológico** (zoo) and **Planetario Municipal** (planetarium) are at Rivera 3245, reached by No 60 tram from Avenida 18 de Julio.

The **Museo Zoológico Larrañaga**, Rambla República de Chile 4215 in the suburb of Buceo, has exhibits of stuffed animals, birds and other fauna from Uruguay and neighbouring countries. The building, with its gilded tower and tiles, deserves a visit in its own right – it's open from 3 to 7 pm daily, except Mondays. The **Museo Juan M Blanes**, Avenida Millán 4016 in the suburb of Prado, displays the work of Uruguay's most famous painter, including many historical scenes not just of Uruguay but of the whole River Plate region. Hours are from 4 to 8 pm daily, except Monday. The Estadio Centenario's **Museo del Fútbol** is open Thursday, weekends and holidays from noon to 5 pm.

Teatro Solís

Named for the first Spaniard to set foot in what is now Uruguayan territory, this is Montevideo's leading theatre; artists who have performed here include Caruso, Toscanini, Pavlova, Nijinski, Sarah Bernhardt, Rostropovich and Twyla Tharpe. Located on Plaza Independencia at Buenos Aires 678, it has superb acoustics and now offers concerts, ballet, opera and plays throughout the year. The Teatro is also home to the Comedia Nacional, the municipal theatre company. You can usually get tickets a few days before events, but the earlier the better.

Mercado del Puerto

At its opening in 1868, Montevideo's port was the finest in South America, but its market now survives on personality and atmosphere. No visitor should miss the old port market building at the foot of Calle Pérez Castellano, whose impressive wrought-iron superstructure shelters a gaggle of reasonably priced parrillas (choose your cut off the grill) and some more upmarket restaurants with outstanding seafood. About 40 years ago, local entrepreneurs began to add more sophisticated restaurants to the grills which already fed the people who brought their produce to the market, and the market gradually became a local phenomenon.

Especially on Saturdays, it is a lively, colourful place where the city's artists and street musicians, including candombe drummers, hang out. Cafe Roldos, which has been at the same site since 1886, serves the popular medio y medio, a mixture of white and sparkling wines.

Feria de Tristán Narvaja

A 60-year tradition begun by Italian immigrants, this Sunday morning outdoor market sprawls from 18 de Julio along Calle Tristán Narvaja to Galicia, spilling over onto side streets. Besides groceries, you can find many interesting trinkets, antiques and souvenirs in its many dozens of makeshift stalls.

Organised Tours

Viajes Cynsa (see Travel Agencies above) offers city tours which leave daily at 9 am from major hotels and their own offices. It also runs 'Montevideo by Night' tours on Fridays and Saturdays.

Festivals

Montevideo's late summer **Carnaval** is well worth the trip for those who can't make it to Río de Janeiro. **Semana Criolla** festivities, during Holy Week, take place at Parque Prado, north of downtown.

Places to Stay – bottom end

For budget travellers, the most reasonable and central lodging is the *Albergue* (☎ 98-1324), the official youth hostel at Canelones 935, which costs about US$3 per night with hostel card and has kitchen facilities, a lounge, and information. Its 11 pm curfew could restrict your night life. In the Ciudad Vieja, near the Mercado del Puerto, there are two very cheap places on the margins of acceptability: *Alojamiento Piedras*, at Piedras 270, and *Hotel Universal*, at Piedras 272, both of which charge about US$3 per person. The former is in slightly better condition. *Hospedaje del Este*, Soriano 1137, costs about US$6 a single with shared bath but is not recommended.

Nueva Pensión Ideal (☎ 98-2193), Soriano 1073, is good value for budget travellers, with singles/doubles with private bath for US$6.50/9. *Hospedaje del Centro*, at Soriano 1126 next door to the Peruvian Consulate, charges US$6/9 with shared bath, US$8/11 with private bath; it's clean, but clearly declining, and some rooms are very dark. *Hospedaje El Aguila*, an old and funky but friendly place at Colonia 1235, has rooms with shared bath for US$5.50/8. *Pensión Catalunya*, nearby at Colonia 1223, is very clean and slightly cheaper, although the size of rooms varies greatly. The friendly, attractive *Hotel Libertad*, Yí 1223, charges US$8.50 a double with shared bath, and US$10 with private bath. *Hotel Capri* (☎ 95-5970), in the red-light district of the Ciudad Vieja at Colón 1460, has doubles with bath and colour TV for US$10. *Hotel City* (☎ 98-2913), Buenos Aires 462, is recommended and comparably priced.

Without a doubt, the best budget accommodation in Montevideo is *Hotel Palacio* (☎ 96-3612) at Bartolomé Mitre 1364. Rooms with brass beds, antique furniture, and balconies cost US$10 per double with private bath – ask for the 6th-floor rooms, whose balconies are nearly as large as the rooms themselves and have exceptional views of the Ciudad Vieja. Its exceptionally *simpática* owner is eager to please her clientele. Across the street at Bartolomé Mitre 1371, *Hospedaje Nuevo Savoy* has bright, freshly painted doubles with shared bath for US$8, with private bath for US$11.

Hotel Casablanca (☎ 91-0918), which is central at San José 1039, charges US$13 per double with private bath. *Hotel Ideal* (☎ 91-6389), Colonia 914, is clean and friendly with good bathrooms; singles/doubles with shared bath are US$9/11, with private bath US$11/13. *Residencial Congreso* (☎ 90-6593), Rondeau 1446, has seen better days – it has a classic elevator but sagging beds and peeling paint. Rooms are US$8/12 with shared bath, US$12/14 with private bath. There are also recommendations for *Residencial Claridge* (☎ 91-5746) at Mercedes 924, and *Residencial Litoral* (☎ 90-5812) at Mercedes 887.

At *Hotel Ateneo* (☎ 91-2630), Colonia 1147, rates are US$12/14 with private bath and television, but some rooms are a bit dark. *Residencial Acevedo*, Uruguay 1127, has rooms for US$12 with shared bath or US$14 with private bath, single or double. *Hotel Aramaya* (☎ 98-6192), at 18 de Julio 1103 conveniently close to the Plaza Cagancha bus terminals, has rooms for US$10/13 with shared bath, US$15/19 with private bath. *Hotel Royal* (☎ 98-3115), at Soriano 1120, costs US$9/13 with shared bath and US$15/20 with private bath. Another good place is *Hotel Arapey* (☎ 90-7032) at Uruguay 925.

In Parque Rodó there is an authorised campground exclusively for vehicles, with a 24-hour limit on stays. There are also sites at Parque Lecocq, west of Montevideo on Avenida Luis Batlle Berres, and at Parque Nacional Franklin D Roosevelt, east of the city toward Carrasco Airport.

Places to Stay – middle

Midrange hotels cost from about US$22/30 to about US$27/35. Typical places in this category would be *Hotel Crillon* (☎ 92-0195) at Andes 1318; *Hotel Mediterráneo* (☎ 90-5090) at Paraguay 1486; *Hotel Balfer* (☎ 91-2647) at Michelini 1328; *Hotel Español* (☎ 90-3816) at Convención 1317; *Hotel Oxford* (☎ 92-0046) at Paraguay 1286; *Hotel Lancaster* (☎ 92-0154) at Plaza Cagancha 1334; and *Hotel California* (☎ 92-0408) at San José 1237.

Places to Stay – top end

Top-end hotels start around the US$30/40 range, but there is none of Buenos Aires' five-star luxury. Try *Hotel Los Angeles* (☎ 92-1072), 18 de Julio 974; *Hotel Alvear* (☎ 92-0274), Yí 1372; or *Hotel Klee* (☎ 91-0671), Yaguarón 1306. *Hotel Internacional* (☎ 90-5794), Colonia 823, *Hotel America* (☎ 92-0392), Río Negro 1330, and *Hotel London Palace* (☎ 92-0024), Río Negro 1278, all charge about US$38/52. *Hotel Embajador* (☎ 92-0009), San José 1212, is comparable. Closest to a true luxury hotel is the *Victoria Palace* (☎ 98-9565), Plaza Independencia 759.

Places to Eat

Montevideo falls short of Buenos Aires' sophistication and variety, but its numerous restaurants are unpretentious and offer excellent value for money. Reasonably priced, worthwhile downtown restaurants include *Restaurant Morini*, Ciudadela 1229; *Mesón Viejo Sancho*, San José 1229; and *Restaurant del Ferrocarril*, in the old train station at Río Negro 1746.

Uruguayans eat even more meat than Argentines, so parrillada is always a reliable choice. Central parrillas include *El Fogón* at San José 1080, *Las Brasas* at San José 909, and the many stalls at the Mercado del Puerto. The *Victoria Plaza Hotel* has a pricey rooftop parrilla during the summer months. A bit less central, but still accessible, is *Entrevero*, 21 de Setiembre 2774. One of the most highly regarded parrillas in Montevideo is *Forte di Makale*, Requena García and Rambla Wilson, in Parque Rodó.

If you've OD'd on meat, there are several vegetarian restaurants: *La Vegetariana* at Yí 1334 and San José 1056, *Natura* at Rincón 414, *Sabor Integral* at Avenida Fernández Crespo 1531, and *Vida Natural* at San José 1184.

Seafood is another possibility. *La Posada del Puerto* has two stalls in the Mercado del Puerto, while *La Tasca del Puerto* is outside on the peatonal Pérez Castellano. We would most highly recommend *La Proa*, a sidewalk café on the peatonal Pérez Castellano, whose seafood plate (pretentiously named 'Sinfonia de Mariscos') is a delight. With entrees at about US$5/6, it is not cheap, but it is good value; with drinks, dinner for two should cost about US$20. It serves as many as 800 people per day, but the service is still friendly and personal. Another popular place in the Mercado is *El Palenque*.

Italian immigration into Uruguay has left its mark on the country's cuisine. For pizza, try *Pizzería Peppone*, Río Branco 1364, or *Emporio de la Pizza*, Río Negro 1311; while for more elaborate dishes visit *Ruffino*, San José 1166, *Gatto Rosso* at J B Blanco 913, or the rather pricier *Bellini* at San Salvador 1644.

For French cuisine, *La Camargue* at Mercedes 1133 has an outstanding reputation but is not cheap. Ditto for *Dona Flor*, Bulevar Artigas 1034, and *Le Gavroche*, Rivera 1989. Spanish food is available at *La Genovesa*, San José 1242, *Meson del Club Español*, 18 de Julio 1332, and *El Hórreo*, Santiago de Chile 1137, which has flamenco shows on Fridays. For Basque food, visit *Taberna Vasca*, at San José 1168.

Other European places include the *Club Alemán* at Paysandú 935 for German food, while Swiss specialities including fondue can be found at *La Suiza*, Soriano 939, and *Bungalow Suizo*, some distance outside the centre at Camino Carrasco 150.

Mexican restaurants are uncommon in the Southern Cone – Buenos Aires has none – but Montevideo has two: *Chac-Mool* at Mercedes and Carlos Roxlo and *Pancho Villa* at Ellauri 938. For something a bit more exotic, try *Ponte Vecchio*, which despite its name is an Armenian restaurant at Rivera 2638. There are also two Arab restaurants: *Aide Polo* at Ellauri 1308 and *Restoran Mediterráneo* in the Club Libanés at Paysandú 896.

Confitería La Pasiva, at Juan Carlos Gómez and Sarandí in the Ciudad Vieja, has excellent, reasonably priced minutas and superb flan casero in a very traditional atmosphere (except for the digital readout menu on one wall). There are other branches at Rinconada de la Plaza Independencia, and at 18 de Julio and Ejido. Other decent confiterías include *Oro del Rhin*, the oldest in the city at Convención 1403, and *Hamburgo*, with excellent baked goods, at Rivera 2081.

Montevideo's Chinese food outshines that of Buenos Aires. Try *Gran Canton Chino* at Andes 1311, or *Nan King* at Pablo de María 1445. A bit outside the centre but easily reached by public transport is *Taiwan*, 21 de Setiembre 2996, three blocks above the Rambla Mahatma Gandhi.

Entertainment

Cinemas Montevideo's commercial cinemas offer films from around the world and Latin America, lagging only a little behind Buenos Aires. The Cinemateca Uruguaya (☎ 48-2460), a film club at Lorenzo Carnelli 1311, has a very modest membership fee which allows unlimited viewing at the five cinemas it runs.

Theatre Montevideo has a lively theatre community. Besides the Teatro Solís, there are the Casa del Teatro at Mercedes 1878, Teatro Circular at Rondeau 1388, La Mascara at Río Negro 1180, Teatro del Anglo at San José 1426, and Teatro Stella at Mercedes and Tristán Narvaja. Prices are very reasonable, from about US$3.

Tango Gardel spent time in Montevideo,

where the tango is no less popular than in Buenos Aires. La Cumparsita (☎ 91-6245), appropriately located at Carlos Gardel 1181, is crowded, so make reservations. It also features candombe dancing.

Spectator Sports Soccer, a Uruguayan passion, is one of the main popular entertainments. The main stadium, the amazing Estadio Centenerio, opened in 1930 for the first World Cup. It was later declared a Historic Monument.

Things to Buy

Montevideo's main shopping area is the Avenida 18 de Julio, although the Ciudad Vieja is becoming more attractive as it is redeveloped.

For attractive artisanal items, at reasonable prices in an informal atmosphere, visit Mercado de los Artesanos, which has branches on the Plaza Cagancha and at Bartolomé Mitre 1367 in the Ciudad Vieja. Hours are 10 am to 8 pm weekdays and 10 am to 2 pm Saturdays. Manos del Uruguay, at San José 1111 and Reconquista 602, is famous for the quality of its goods.

Other crafts centres include Artesanía Rinconada, Bulevar Artigas 2315, Centro Artesanal at Río Negro 1183, and Artesanía Candil, Montecaseros 3435. There is a daily crafts market in the Plaza Cagancha which is a hangout for many younger Uruguayans.

As in Argentina, leather is a popular item. Places worth checking out include Casa Mario at Piedras 641 in the Ciudad Vieja, its branch called the Leather Corner at San José and Río Branco, and the Montevideo Leather Factory at Plaza Independencia 832, on the 2nd floor. Sheepskin clothing is good at Peletería Holandesa, Colonia 890 or 18 de Julio 1020. For footwear, try Arbiter-Pasqualini at 18 de Julio 943, or Impel at Luis B Cavia 2898, both of which make shoes to order.

Uruguayan woollens are excellent. Besides Manos del Uruguay, try La Calesa, on Río Negro between 18 de Julio and San José, or Uruwool, Tacuarembó 1531. Gaucho clothing can be bought at Casa Puzzi

at Río Negro 1615 or Casa Schiavo at Uruguay 1050.

Uruguay's very limited mining industry produces some worthwhile gemstones, particularly amethysts and agates. Good jewellers include Cabildo Piedras at Sarandí 610, Cuarzos del Uruguay at Sarandí 604, and Carlos Andersen at Julio Herrera y Obes 1284.

Getting There & Away

Air Fewer international airlines serve Montevideo than Buenos Aires, but many still have offices in the capital. Commuter airlines also provide international services between the two countries. The most frequently used airlines are PLUNA, Aerolíneas Argentinas and Varig-Cruzeiro, all of which fly to neighbouring countries.

Aerolíneas Argentinas
    Colonia 851 (☎ 91-9466)
Aerolíneas Uruguayas
    Plaza Cagancha 1343 (☎ 90-1868)
Ecuatoriana
    Colonia 981 (☎ 91-3570)
Iberia
    Colonia 975 (☎ 98-1032)
LAN-Chile
    11th floor, Plaza Cagancha 1335 (☎ 98-2727)
Líneas Aéreas Paraguayas (LAP)
    Colonia 1001 (☎ 90-7946)
Líneas Aéreas Privadas Argentinas (LAPA)
    Plaza Cagancha 1339 (☎ 90-8765)
Lufthansa
    Plaza Independencia 749 (☎ 98-9265)
PLUNA
    Colonia 1021 (☎ 98-0606, 92-1414)
Varig/Cruzeiro
    Río Negro 1362 (☎ 98-2321)

LAPA (☎ 90-8765), Plaza Cagancha 1339, has 18 flights weekly to Buenos Aires' Aeroparque Jorge Newberry. The fare is US$38. Aerolíneas Uruguayas (☎ 90-1868), Plaza Cagancha 1343, flies to Aeroparque for US$74 return.

The military airline TAMU (☎ 90-0904; 60-8383 at Carrasco Airport), Colonia 959, flies Monday, Thursday, Friday and Saturday to Salto (US$17); Monday and Friday to Tacuarembó (US$13) and Artigas (US$20); Monday, Thursday, Friday and Saturday to

Salto (US$17); Monday, Thursday, Friday and Saturday to Rivera (US$17); and Monday, Thursday, Friday and Saturday to Melo (US$13). You can also make TAMU reservations at PLUNA offices.

Bus Montevideo has no central bus terminal, but most bus companies are on or very near Plaza Cagancha. COT (☎ 91-1200), Plaza Cagancha 1124, has more than 20 buses per day to Punta del Este via Piriápolis, Pan de Azúcar, San Carlos and Maldonado. The trip takes about 2½ hours. COT also has 10 buses daily to Colonia, also 2½ hours, for US$4.

ONDA (☎ 91-2333), Plaza Cagancha 1142, has buses to the Brazilian border crossings at Chuy (six daily, US$8), Río Branco (two, US$10), Melo (five, US$10), and Rivera (six, US$12). It also goes hourly to Punta del Este (US$4), and has eight buses daily to Durazno (US$4), three to La Paloma (US$6), seven to Treinta y Tres (US$7), ten to Piriápolis (US$2.50), and four to Paysandú (US$10). Nuñez (☎ 90-0483), Plaza Cagancha 1174, serves interior destinations like Minas, Varela, Treinta y Tres, Melo, Río Branco and Rivera. Buses Nassar, Colonia 1197, has five daily buses to Durazno for US$4, one of which continues to Paso de los Toros. CYNSA (☎ 90-5321), Paraguay 1311, has four daily to Chuy and six to La Paloma. CORMI (☎ 90-4989), Avenida Uruguay 1053, has three buses daily to Río Branco (US$10).

Several companies go to Argentina, including CITA (☎ 91-0100), Plaza Cagancha 1149; General Urquiza (☎ 91-2333), Plaza Cagancha 1142; ENCON (☎ 90-8733), Avenida Lavalleja 1440; and CORA (☎ 91-7954), which goes to Córdoba. Nuñez has one bus daily to Santa Fe, Rosario, Córdoba (US$47) and Villa Carlos Paz. COT/Bus de la Carrera has four direct buses daily to Buenos Aires (US$20, eight hours). It has one bus daily to Porto Alegre, Brazil (US$20, 12 hours).

Other companies which serve Brazil are ONDA, CYNSA and TTL (☎ 91-5482), Plaza Cagancha 1345, which goes nightly to Pelotas (US$15) and Porto Alegre (US$20),

and to Florianópolis (US$27), Camboriú (US$29), Curitibá (US$33), and São Paulo (US$40). To Chile, check out COT/Tas-Choapa, or Empresa General Artigas (☎ 94-0389), Avenida Lavalleja 1945, which goes on Saturdays to Mendoza in Argentina, near the Chilean border (US$90, 21 hours), and Mondays and Thursdays to Santiago, Chile (US$148, 29 hours).

Car Rental Budget (☎ 91-6363), at Mercedes 935, has Volkswagen 1600s from US$20 per day, but there are three-day (US$120) and one-week (US$240) rates with unlimited kilometres. Insurance (about US$13 per day) and IVA (22%) are extra. Multicar (☎ 90-5079), Yaguarón 1344, is about a third cheaper. Punta Car (☎ 90-2772), Yaguarón 1523, gives a 10% discount with the 'Tarjeta Turística'. Try also Autocar (☎ 98-5153) at Mercedes 863 or Auto Rental International (☎ 92-0573) at Yaguarón 1683.

River The bus-boat combination Buquebus (☎ 92-0670) is at Río Negro 1400. It leaves Montevideo for Buenos Aires via Colonia del Sacramento daily, except Sunday, at 12.45 am, 8.30 am and 4 pm. Sunday departure times are 12.30 am, 8 am and 4 pm. One-way fares are US$23 for adults, US$14 for children up to 10 years old, and US$18 for retirees. Return fares are about 10% cheaper.

Alíscafos Belt (☎ 90-2951) is at Plaza Cagancha 1325.

Getting Around

To/From the Airport For US$2, there is a special airport bus from PLUNA's downtown offices; see the schedule posted there. TAMU passengers can take advantage of free bus services to Carrasco Airport. The D-1 Express bus from the Ciudad Vieja also goes to Carrasco. COT's buses to Punta del Este stop at the airport.

Bus Montevideo's buses will leave you gasping for breath with their noxious diesel exhaust, but they go everywhere for about US$0.25. The *Guia de Montevideo Eureka*, available at bookshops or kiosks, lists routes and schedules. As in Argentina, the driver or conductor will ask your destination. Retain your ticket, which may be inspected at any time.

Taxi Taxis have metres and, as in Buenos Aires, drivers correlate the metre reading with a photocopied fare chart. Between midnight and 6 am fares are higher. There is a small additional charge for luggage, and riders generally round off the fare to the next hundred pesos.

The Uruguayan Littoral

West of Montevideo, the littoral is that portion of Uruguay which fronts the Río de la Plata and the Río Uruguay, opposite Argentine Mesopotamia. Originally, it was Indian and gaucho country, but with the developments of the past century it has become the country's most important agricultural area, with wheatfields and gardens feeding the growing population of the capital.

It has one can't-miss attraction, the 17th-century Portuguese contraband port and fortress of Colonia, opposite Buenos Aires, and several lesser sights which make worthwhile day trips from either Colonia or Montevideo. If coming overland from Argentine Mesopotamia, you'll find the towns along the Río Uruguay – like Salto, Paysandú, Fray Bentos and Mercedes – pleasant enough to justify a stopover en route to Colonia and Montevideo.

COLONIA

Only an hour or two from Buenos Aires, Colonia (full name Colonia del Sacramento) is one of the unappreciated gems of South America, attracting many thousands of Argentines but only a handful of the many foreign tourists who visit the Argentine capital.

Founded in 1680 by the Portuguese Manoel de Lobo, it occupied a strategic position almost exactly opposite Buenos Aires across the Río de la Plata, but its major importance was as a source of contraband, undercutting Spain's jealously defended mercantile trade policy. British goods made their way into Buenos Aires and the interior through surreptitious exchange with the Portuguese in the Paraná delta. For this reason Spanish forces intermittently besieged Portugal's riverside outpost for decades. The Jesuit father Martin Dobrizhoffer vividly described the Colonia of the mid-18th century:

The houses are few and low, forming a village, rather than city, yet it is far from despicable; opulent merchants, wares of every kind, gold, silver, and diamonds are concealed beneath its miserable roofs. Surrounded with a single and very slender wall...the land under Portuguese authority is of such small circumference that the most inactive person might walk round it in half an hour. Portuguese ships, laden with English and Dutch wares, and Negro slaves...crowd to this port, and the Spanish sentinels, either bribed or deceived, convey the goods to Paraguay, Peru, or Chili. It is incredible how many millions are lost to the Spaniards in this forbidden traffic.

Although the two powers agreed over the cession of Colonia to Spain around 1750, the agreement failed when Jesuit missionaries on the upper Paraná refused to comply with the proposed exchange of territory in their area. Spain finally captured the city in 1762, but could not hold it until 1777, when the Viceroyalty of the River Plate was formed. From this time, the city's commercial importance declined as foreign goods could proceed directly to Buenos Aires.

The capital of its department, Colonia is a pleasant town of about 20,000, the streets of its historic colonial core shaded by sycamores in the summer heat. In the course of the day, the town discloses its many aspects as sunlight strikes whitewashed colonial buildings and the river; the latter, living up to its name, is silvery in the morning but turns brownish by midday. The townspeople are extremely polite, motorists even stopping for pedestrians.

Orientation

Colonia del Sacramento sits on the east bank of the Río de la Plata, 180 km west of Montevideo but only 50 km from Buenos Aires by ferry or hydrofoil. Like Montevideo, it features an irregular colonial nucleus of narrow cobbled streets, now known as the Barrio Histórico, located on a small peninsula jutting into the river, which is a must-see for visitors to the area. The town's commercial centre, around Plaza 25 de Agosto, and

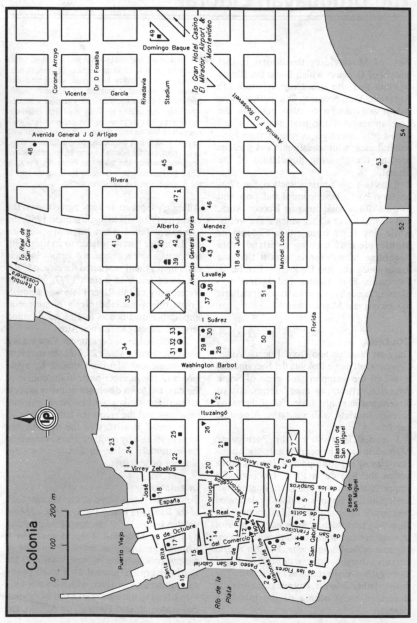

Colonia

■ PLACES TO STAY

21	La Posada del Gobernador
25	Hotel Esperanza
28	Hospedaje Ciudadela
29	Hotel Royal
31	Hotel Beltrán
34	Hospedaje Rincón del Río
37	Hotel Natal John
45	Hotel Leoncia
49	Hotel Los Angeles
50	Hotel Italiano
51	Hotel Español

▼ PLACES TO EAT

11	Pulpería de los Faroles
13	La Casona del Sur
26	Parrilla El Suizo
27	Parrilla (unnamed)
33	Parrilla El Portón
44	Confitería El Colonial

OTHER

1	Bastión de San Pedro
2	Museo de los Azulejos
3	Convento de San Francisco
4	Casa de Lavalleja
5	Museo Portugués
6	Puerta de Campo
7	Plazoleta 1811
8	Plaza Mayor 25 de Mayo
9	Museo Municipal
10	Casa del Virrey
12	Archivo Regional
14	Capilla Jesuítica
15	Plazoleta San Martín
16	Bastión de Santa Rita
17	Motorcycle Rental
18	Museo Español
19	Plaza de Armas (Plaza Manuel Lobo)
20	Iglesia Matriz
22	Argentine Consulate
23	Bastión del Carmen
24	Teatro del Bastión
30	Cambio Viaggio
32	Omnibus Colonia
35	LAPA
36	Plaza 25 de Agosto
38	Buses ONDA
39	Post Office
40	ANTEL
41	Buses Chadre & Buses Berutti
42	Cambio Colonia
43	Buses COT & Tourino
46	Budget Rent-a-car
47	Tourist Office
48	Museo Indígena
52	Ferry Dock
53	Hydrofoil
54	Buquebus Dock

the river port are a few blocks east, where the Rambla Costanera leads north along the river to the Real de San Carlos, another area of interest to visitors. The diagonal Avenida F D Roosevelt is the main highway to Montevideo.

Information

Tourist Office The tourist office (☎ 2182) is at General Flores 499. While not especially well informed, the staff have numerous brochures which are difficult to obtain elsewhere. Hours are weekdays from 7 am to 8 pm, weekends from 10 am to 7 pm. The ferry port branch is much more efficient and helpful.

Money Arriving at the port from Buenos Aires, you can change money at Cambio Libertad or Banco República, which pays slightly lower rates and charges US$1 commission for travellers' cheques. Downtown, try Cambio Viaggio at Avenida General Flores 350. It's open Sundays from 10 am to 6 pm and will change travellers' cheques for 2½% commission.

Post & Telecommunications The post office is at Lavalleja 226. ANTEL, at Rivadavia 420, has direct optic lines to the USA (AT&T and MCI) and the UK.

Foreign Consulates The Argentine Consulate (☎ 2091) is at Avenida General Flores and Virrey Zeballos. It is not especially helpful in renewing visas which have been obtained in other Argentine consulates, so try to do that in Montevideo unless you have no alternative. It's open weekdays from 8 am to 1 pm.

Walking Tour

Also known as La Colonia Portuguesa, the Portuguese colony, Colonia's Barrio Histórico begins at the **Puerta de Campo**, the restored entrance to the old city on Calle Manoel Lobo, which dates from the governorship of Vasconcellos in 1745. A thick fortified wall runs south along the Paseo de San Miguel to the river. A short distance west is the **Plaza Mayor 25 de Mayo**, off which leads the narrow, cobbled **Calle de los Suspiros** (Street of Whispers), with tile-and-stucco colonial houses on all sides. Just beyond is the **Museo Portugués**, which has good exhibits on the Portuguese period, including Lusitanian and colonial dress. Colonia's museums are generally open from 11.30 am to 6 pm.

At the south-west end of the Plaza Mayor are the **Casa de Lavalleja**, once the residence of General Lavalleja, and the ruins of the 17th-century **Convento de San Francisco** and the 19th-century **Faro** (lighthouse). At its west end, on Calle del Comercio, is the **Museo Municipal**, which was closed for repairs recently. Next door is the so-called **Casa del Virrey**, the Viceroy's House, although there was never a viceroy in Colonia. At the north-west corner of the Plaza, on Calle de las Misiones de los Tapes, is the **Archivo Regional**, with a small museum and bookshop.

At the west end of Misiones de los Tapes is the **Museo de los Azulejos** (Museum of Tiles), a 17th-century house with a sampling of colonial tilework; but it has erratic opening hours. From there, the riverfront **Paseo de San Gabriel** leads to Calle del Colegio, where a right to Calle del Comercio takes you to the **Capilla Jesuítica**, the ruined Jesuit chapel. Going east along Avenida General Flores and then turning south on Calle Vasconcellos, you reach the landmark **Iglesia Matriz** (see below) on the

Plaza de Armas, also known as Plaza Manoel Lobo.

Across Avenida General Flores, at España and San José, visit the **Museo Español**, which has exhibitions of replica pottery, clothing, and maps of the colonial period. It's closed Tuesday and Wednesday. At the north end of the street is the **Puerto Viejo**, the old port. One block east, at Calle del Virrey Cevallos and Rivadavia, is the **Teatro Bastión del Carmen**, a theatre building which incorporates the part of the city's ancient fortifications.

Iglesia Matriz

Begun in 1680, Colonia's church is the oldest in Uruguay. Although it has undergone many changes over three centuries, it came to occupy its present perimeter between 1722 and 1749, under Portuguese Governor Pedro Vasconcellos. Nearly destroyed by fire in 1799, it was rebuilt by Spanish architect Tomás Toribio, who also designed the Cabildo of Montevideo.

The church suffered further misfortune when, during the Brazilian occupation of 1823, lightning struck a powder magazine in the sacristy, producing an explosion which destroyed part of the lateral walls, two-thirds of the vault, the altar, the posterior wall, and produced cracks in many other parts of the building. Between 1836 and 1842, under the direction of Padre Domingo Rama and the sponsorship of General Fructuoso Rivera, it was again rebuilt; since then, changes have been primarily cosmetic. It's located on Calle Vasconcellos, between Avenida General Flores and the Plaza de Armas.

Festivals

In early March, Colonia hosts the **Fiesta Nacional de La Leche** (National Dairy Festival), which attracts many Uruguayans and has excellent local food and music.

Places to Stay – bottom end

Camping The *Camping Municipal de Colonia* (☎ 4444) is in a grove of eucalyptus trees at the Real de San Carlos, 5 km from the Barrio Histórico. It has excellent facilities, is close to the Balneario Municipal, and is easily reached by public transport. Fees are about US$1 per person.

Hospedajes & Hotels Except for camping, there is not much really cheap accommodation in Colonia. Cheapest in town is the *Hotel Español*, Manoel Lobo (ex-Henríquez de la Peña) 377, with large but dark rooms for US$5 a single (if available), US$10 a double with shared bath. *Hotel Italiano* (☎ 2103), Manoel Lobo 341, has small rooms with shared bath for US$6/10 per single/double.

One of the best value places is the very central but quiet *Hospedaje Rincón del Río* (☎ 3002), on tree-lined Washington Barbot 258 near a pleasant sand beach, which charges US$7 per person with shared bath, US$8 with private bath. *Hotel Beltrán* (☎ 2955), Avenida General Flores 311, is one of the oldest hotels in town, and is friendly, quiet and very clean, with all rooms facing onto a central patio. Rates are US$8 per person with shared bath, but it has few singles. Another good choice is *Hospedaje Ciudadela* (☎ 2683), Washington Barbot 164, where rates are US$9 per person.

Places to Stay – middle
Hotel Esperanza (☎ 2922), near the entrance to the Barrio Histórico at Avenida General Flores 237, charges US$34 a double. *Hotel Natal John* (☎ 2081), Avenida General Flores 394, costs US$36 a double. *Hotel Los Angeles* (☎ 2335), Avenida F D Roosevelt 203, is a modern, rather impersonal hotel on a busy street some distance from the Barrio Histórico. Rates are US$21/32. Rates are comparable at *Hotel Leoncia* (☎ 2369), Rivera 214.

Places to Stay – top end
Probably your best choice is *La Posada del Gobernador* (☎ 3018), on 18 de Julio in the Barrio Histórico, where rooms are US$34 per person. Somewhat cheaper, but still central, is *Hotel Royal* (☎ 3139), Avenida General Flores 340, at US$28 per person. The *Gran Hotel Casino El Mirador*

(☎ 2004), distant from the Barrio on Avenida F D Roosevelt, is a high-rise hotel with every modern luxury and nothing of Colonia's unique personality. Rates are US$62 per person with half-pension, US$70 with full pension.

Places to Eat
One of the best value places in town is a nameless parrilla at Ituzaingó 186, which is jammed with locals. *El Portón*, Avenida General Flores 333, is a more upscale but appealing parrilla. *El Suizo*, another parrilla at Avenida General Flores and Ituzaingó, appears to charge more because of its attractive colonial setting than its food. *Pulpería de los Faroles*, on del Comercio and Misiones de los Tapes in the Barrio Histórico, has an upscale ambience but is not outrageously expensive for a good meal. *La Casona del Sur*, two doors away, is a good confitería which doubles as a handicrafts market. At night, it has live music.

Confitería El Colonial, Avenida General Flores 432, is an excellent and reasonably priced breakfast spot, with enormous hot croissants. At the tip of the Barrio Histórico there is a good pizzería in a remodelled tower.

Things to Buy
For handicrafts, check out the Sunday market in the Barrio Histórico's Plaza Mayor. La Casona del Sur, a confitería on Misiones de los Tapes, also has a good selection. El Musguito, nearby on Calle de La Playa, is an artisans' cooperative with ceramics, leatherwork, and wood carvings.

Getting There & Away
Air Recently, LAPA (☎ 2006), Rivadavia 383, had suspended its 25 weekly flights to Aeroparque in Buenos Aires because of repairs to Colonia airport. The 15-minute crossings, which should resume soon, cost US$24 a single. Those from Aeroparque continue to Montevideo.

Bus Like Montevideo, Colonia has no central bus terminal. COT (☎ 3121),

Avenida General Flores 430, has 11 buses daily to Montevideo; the 2½-hour trip costs US$4. It also has nine daily to Colonia Suiza, Rosario, and Juan Lacaze, except on Sundays when there are only eight.

ONDA, Avenida General Flores 396, has six buses daily to Colonia Suiza (US$1.50) and eight to Montevideo. Touriño, Avenida General Flores 432, has six daily to Carmelo except Sundays, when there are only two. Omnibus Colonia, on Avenida General Flores near Hotel Beltrán, goes to Rosario, Colonia Suiza and Riachuelo.

Car & Motorbike Rental Budget (☎ 4712) is at Avenida General Flores 472. In the Barrio Histórico, there is a small motorbike rental agency on Plaza Santa Rita, between 8 de Octubre and del Comercio.

River The ferry from the port to Buenos Aires takes 2½ hours and costs US$22 one way, US$39 return. Children pay US$14/23. Cars weighing up to 800 kg pay US$35 exclusive of passenger fares, while those over 800 kg pay US$57. Boats leave daily at 5 am and 12.30, 7.30 and 9 pm in summer, but the 5 am service is suspended at the end of summer.

Alíscafos Belt has four hydrofoils daily to Buenos Aires for US$21 one way. This is faster, taking only an hour, but is more crowded and has a luggage limitation. Departures are at 8.30 am and 12.30, 4.30 and 7.30 pm.

Getting Around

COTUC, the city bus company, goes to the Camping Municipal and the Real de San Carlos. Otherwise, Colonia is extremely compact and encourages walking.

AROUND COLONIA
Real de San Carlos

At the turn of the century, the naturalised Argentine enterpreneur Nicolás Mihanovich invested US$1.5 million to build an enormous tourist complex at the Real de San Carlos, five km west of Colonia, where Spanish troops once camped before attack-

ing the Portuguese outpost. Among the attractions erected by Mihanovich, a Dalmatian immigrant, were a bull ring seating 10,000 spectators (bullfights were prohibited in Uruguay in 1912), a jai alai fronton seating 3000, a hotel-casino with its own power plant (the casino failed in 1917 when the Argentine government placed a tax on every boat across the river), and a racecourse.

Only the racecourse functions today, but the ruins make an interesting excursion. There is also the **Museo Municipal Real de San Carlos**, focusing on paleontology, which is open daily except Monday from 2 to 7 pm.

COLONIA SUIZA

In the department of Colonia, Colonia Suiza (also known as Nueva Helvecia) is 120 km from Montevideo and 60 km from the city of Colonia del Sacramento. Settled by Swiss immigrants in 1862, it was the country's first interior agricultural colony, providing wheat for the mills of Montevideo. A quiet, pleasant destination with a demonstrably European ambience, its dairy products are known throughout the country – 60% of Uruguay's cheese comes from here.

Information

Tourist Office There is no formal tourist office, but there is a woman in the police station opposite the plaza who will help out with information and even provide a guided tour of the town.

Money To change cash, try the Banco de Crédito at Berna 1314 or the Banco La Caja Obrera on 18 de Julio.

Telecommunications ANTEL is at Artigas and Dreyer, across from the OSE water tower.

Medical Services The hospital (☎ 4057) is at 18 de Julio and C Cunier.

Things to See

The centre of the town is the Plaza de los

Fundadores, with an impressive sculpture, **El Surco**, commemorating the original Swiss pioneers. There are several interesting buildings, including the ruins of the first flour mill, the **Molino Quemado**, and the historic **Hotel del Prado**, which also functions as a youth hostel.

Places to Stay & Eat

The most reasonable accommodation is the friendly *Hotel Comercio* at 18 de Julio 1209 – but its entrance near Colón is completely unmarked. Singles with private bath are about US$6. The 80-room *Hotel del Prado* (☎ 4052), in the Barrio Hoteles on the outskirts of town, is a magnificent if declining building with huge balconies, dating from 1884. Rooms are US$11 per person, but it is also the youth hostel, offering beds with shared bath for US$3. It requires a youth hostel card, which you must obtain in Montevideo.

Dating from 1872, the *Hotel Suizo* (☎ 4002), Avenida Federico Fischer, is the oldest tourist hotel in the country, and has renowned restaurant. Without a doubt, though, the top of the line is the luxurious *Hotel Nirvana* (☎ 4081; 90-3823 in Montevideo), Avenida Batlle y Ordóñez, where singles/doubles are US$85/100 with breakfast in the high season (15 December to 1 April) and US$75/90 in low season. It offers a swimming pool, tennis courts, horseback riding, facilities for children and 25 hectares of beautifully landscaped grounds.

Colonia Suiza has several excellent restaurants. Besides the Hotel Suizo, try *La Gondola*, Luis Dreyer and 25 de Agosto, *L'Arbalete* on Avenida Batlle y Ordóñez, and *Don José*, 18 de Julio 1214.

Getting There & Away

ONDA, Treinta y Tres 1142, has buses to Montevideo. Omnibus Colonia, 25 de Agosto and Berna, has nine buses daily to Colonia. ONDA and COT (☎ 5231), next to Bar Meny at 18 de Julio and Treinta y Tres, have services to Montevideo, Colonia, Fray Bentos (three daily) and Paysandú (one daily).

CARMELO

Where the Río Uruguay broadens and becomes the Río de la Plata, Carmelo sits opposite the Paraná delta, 75 km north-west of Colonia del Sacramento and 235 km from Montevideo. Launches connect it to the Buenos Aires suburb of Tigre. Part of the department of Colonia, it is a centre for yachting and boating on the Río Uruguay and the Río de la Plata, and for exploring the delta.

Carmelo dates from 1816, when residents of the village of Las Víboras petitioned to move to the more hospitable Arroyo de las Vacas. Permission was granted by Artigas, for whom the town's original central plaza is named. The local economy depends on tourism, livestock and agriculture – local wines have an excellent reputation.

Orientation

Carmelo straddles the Arroyo de las Vacas, a protected harbour on the Río de la Plata. North of the Arroyo, shady Plaza Independencia is now the commercial centre. Most of the town's businesses are located along 19 de Abril, which leads to the bridge across the Arroyo, where a large park offers open space, camping, swimming and a monstrous casino.

Information

Tourist Office The tourist office (☎ 2001) is at 19 de Abril 250, on the corner of Barrios, four blocks from the bridge over the Arroyo de las Vacas.

Money There are two exchange houses: Lerga at 19 de Abril and Rodríguez, and Viaggio on 19 de Abril and Roosevelt, which is open 10 am to 6 pm weekdays but will not cash travellers' cheques.

Post The post office is at Uruguay 368.

Foreign Consulates The Argentine Consulate (☎ 2266) is at Roosevelt 442.

Travel Agencies When the tourist office is not open, ask for information at West Tour

(☎ 2719), 19 de Abril 267, whose staff are extremely helpful and well informed.

Medical Services The hospital (☎ 2107) is at Uruguay and Avenida Artigas.

Things to See

The **Santuario del Carmen**, at Lavalleja and El Carmen, dates from 1830. Next door is the **Archivo y Museo Parroquial**, which features documents and objects of local historical importance. Dating from 1860, the **Casa de Ignacio Barrios**, at Barrios and 19 de Abril, once belonged to one of San Martín's lieutenants, who was also a signer of the Uruguayan declaration of independence.

Places to Stay

Camping At the *Camping Náutico Las Higueritas* (☎ 2058), on the south side of the Arroyo de las Vacas, charges are US$1 per person. *Camping Don Mauro* is at Ignacio Barros and Arroyo de las Vacas, six blocks from the centre of town. Charges are also US$1 per person.

Hotels Cheapest in town is the very basic and run-down *Hotel Carmelo*, 19 de Abril 561 at 25 de Mayo, where rooms with shared bath are US$2.50 per person. *Hotel Oriental*, 19 de Abril 286 near Rodríguez, is also basic, with several beds to a room. Adults pay US$4.50 a single, children US$3.

Hotel Paraná (☎ 2480), 19 de Abril 585, has singles for US$6 with private bath. *Hotel La Unión*, next to the post office at Uruguay 368, is very nice and clean, with singles with shared bath for US$6. Singles/doubles with private bath cost US$10/16. The friendly *Hotel San Fernando* (☎ 2503), 19 de Abril 161 near Barrios, has clean rooms with private bath for US$9/14. At the *Palace Hotel* (☎ 2622), Sarandí 308, doubles are US$16.

The modern and clean but ugly *Hotel Bertoletti* (☎ 2030), Uruguay 171, has doubles for US$21. At *Hotel Rambla* (☎ 2390), conveniently close to the launch docks at Uruguay 55, doubles are US$27

with breakfast included. Top of the line is the *Hotel Casino* (☎ 2314), on Avenida Rodó across the Arroyo de las Vacas, where rates are US$40 per person with half-pension, US$50 with full pension, plus IVA (VAT).

Places to Eat

El Vesubio, 19 de Abril 451, serves an enormous and tasty chivito al plato, plus a variety of other dishes. Other restaurants include *Perrini* at 19 de Abril 440, and the *Yacht Club*, *Morales*, and *El Refugio*, all across the bridge in the park.

Getting There & Away

Bus All the bus companies are on or near Plaza Independencia. Sabelín has three buses a day to Montevideo, Chadre two, and ONDA six. The fare is US$5. Berutti and Touriño both go to Colonia (US$1.50).

River Deltanave, Constituyentes 263, has two crossings daily to Tigre, at 4 am and noon. Cacciola, Constituyentes 219, goes at 11 am and 6.30 pm. The fare is US$10 one way for adults, US$6 one way for children.

AROUND CARMELO
La Estancia de Narbona

Despite the deteriorating condition of its buildings, this 18th-century estancia on the Arroyo Víboras, about 20 km west of Carmelo on the road to Nueva Palmira, is deservedly a national historical monument. Its casco and its chapel, with a three-storey bell tower, sit on the summit of a small hill about two km from the main road. At the junction, the **Puente Castells**, the first bridge of its kind in the country, has stood for more than 130 years, near a hydraulic mill erected to process local wheat.

Estancia de las Vacas

Just east of Carmelo, Estancia de las Vacas was an 18th-century Jesuit enterprise, probably the most advanced of its kind in the Banda Oriental, with its chapel, patios, lodging, blacksmiths' and carpenters' workshops, looms, bakery, dairy, and brick and tile factories, as well as the first vincyards in

Uruguay, and 30,000 head of cattle. More than 200 people, including Indian peons and black slaves, lived here.

After the expulsion of the Jesuits in 1767, Juan de San Martín, father of the Argentine hero, was the estancia's administrator until 1774. After his departure, it passed into the hands of another monastic order, much less able administrators, under whom it fell into disrepair. It is now a national historical monument, also known as the Calera de las Huérfanas.

FRAY BENTOS

Capital of the department of Río Negro, about 300 km west of Montevideo, Fray Bentos is the southernmost overland crossing point from Argentina, reached by a bridge over the Río Uruguay. It lies on the east bank of the Río Uruguay, opposite the Argentine city of Gualeguaychú.

In 1864, Fray Bentos was the site of the country's first meat extract plant, while in 1902 British interests located Uruguay's first frigorífico here. The enormous Anglo plant, once a company town, has closed but the Uruguayan government is preserving it as a museum.

Orientation

Fray Bentos has a very regular grid pattern centred on the surprisingly open Plaza Constitución, which has only a few palm trees and a Victorian bandshell, a replica of London's Crystal Palace donated by Liebig Meats in 1902. The main commercial street is 18 de Julio, leading east to Ruta 2 to Mercedes and Montevideo, while 25 de Mayo heads north, passing the shadier Plaza Hargain, toward the Libertador General San Martín bridge toward Argentina.

Information

Tourist Office The tourist office (☎ 2737) is on Treinta y Tres, opposite Plaza Constitución. With a friendly, helpful and knowledgeable staff, it's open weekdays from 8 am to noon and 5 to 9 pm.

Money Cambio Fagalde, on 18 de Julio near

the Plaza Hotel, is open weekdays and Saturdays from 8 am to noon and 3.30 to 7.30 pm. There is a street changer outside the Confitería Mafalda who gives slightly better rates and keeps longer hours.

Post & Telecommunications The post office is at Treinta y Tres 3271, between 18 de Julio and Zorrilla. ANTEL is at Zorrilla 1127 near Treinta y Tres.

Foreign Consulates The Argentine Consulate (☎ 2638), Sarandí 3193 near Rincón, is open weekdays from 8 am to 1 pm.

Medical Services The Hospital Salúd Pública (☎ 2533) is at Echeverría and Lavalleja.

Teatro Young

Probably Fray Bentos' most architecturally distinguished landmark, the 400-seat Teatro Young bears the name of the wealthy Anglo-Uruguayan estanciero who sponsored its construction between 1909 and 1912. Now municipal property, it hosts cultural events throughout the year, but can be visited upon request. It's a block from the plaza, on the corner of 25 de Mayo and Zorrilla.

Teatro Municipal de Verano

In Parque Roosevelt, at the west end of town, this open-air amphitheatre on the banks of the river seats 4000 and has excellent acoustics.

Barrio Histórico del Anglo

South-west of the town centre, most of the installations of the now defunct Frigorífico Anglo del Uruguay are being restored as the **Museo de la Revolución Industrial**, at the same time that local authorities are trying to attract light industry to the area. Here, also, the Liebig Extract of Meat Company located its pioneer South American plant in 1865, soon giving Fray Bentos the most important industrial complex in Uruguay.

Although the plant no longer operates, it is the dominant landmark in a still lively neighbourhood whose landscape and street

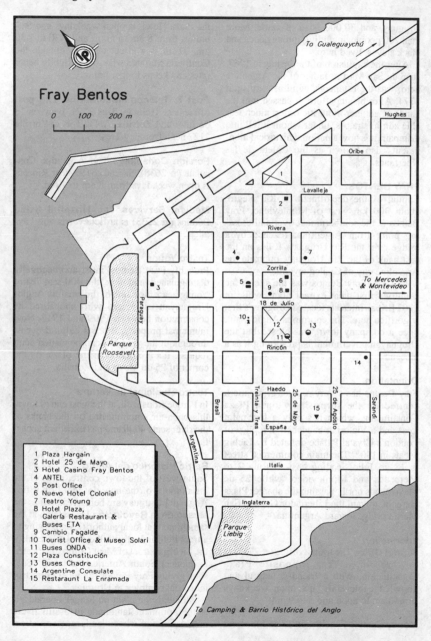

Fray Bentos

0   100   200 m

To Gualeguaychú

Hughes

Oribe

Lavalleja

Rivera

Zorrilla

To Mercedes
& Montevideo

18 de Julio

Rincón

Paraguay

Parque
Roosevelt

Haedo

Brasil

Argentina

Treinta y Tres

25 de Mayo

25 de Agosto

Sarandí

España

Italia

Inglaterra

Parque
Liebig

To Camping & Barrio Histórico del Anglo

1 Plaza Hargain
2 Hotel 25 de Mayo
3 Hotel Casino Fray Bentos
4 ANTEL
5 Post Office
6 Nuevo Hotel Colonial
7 Teatro Young
8 Hotel Plaza,
   Galería Restaurant &
   Buses ETA
9 Cambio Fagalde
10 Tourist Office & Museo Solari
11 Buses ONDA
12 Plaza Constitución
13 Buses Chadre
14 Argentine Consulate
15 Restaraunt La Enramada

life offer great photographic opportunities. Note especially the manager's residence and the former British Consulate. At the time of writing, it was not yet open formally to the public, but the tourist office can put you in touch with the museum curator.

Places to Stay

For accommodation in private houses, ask at the tourist office.

Camping There is a campground at the *Club Atlético Anglo*, 10 blocks from the Plaza. Eight km south of town is the municipal *Balneario Las Cañas* (☎ 1611), where fees are US$1 per person and US$1 per tent, plus US$1.50 per vehicle.

Hotels & Motels *Nuevo Hotel Colonial* (☎ 2260), 25 de Mayo 3293 near Zorrilla, is very clean and friendly, with rooms arranged around an interior patio. Rates are US$4 per person per single with shared bath, US$5 with private bath. *Hotel 25 de Mayo* (☎ 2586), on the corner of 25 de Mayo and Lavalleja, is a modernised 19th-century building with singles/doubles with shared bath for US$6/10, US$8/12 with private bath.

Hotel Plaza, exactly where it says on the corner of 18 de Julio and 25 de Mayo, charges US$11/20 for rooms with private bath. *Balneario Las Cañas* (☎ 1611), eight km from town, has motel accommodation with private bath and kitchenette for US$15/20. *Hotel Casino Fray Bentos* (☎ 2358), on the waterfront Calle Paraguay between 18 de Julio and Zorrilla, charges US$30/40 plus IVA.

Places to Eat

Food in Fray Bentos is nothing to write home about. *Galería Restaurant*, downstairs in the same building as the Hotel Plaza, has good salads and large portions but entrees are mediocre and not especially cheap. Try also *La Enramada*, on España between 25 de Mayo and 25 de Agosto. The best in town may be the *Club de Remeros*, where the yacht crowd hangs out, near Parque Roosevelt.

Getting There & Away

ONDA, at Rincón and 25 de Mayo, has three buses daily to Montevideo (US$7) and one to Paysandú. ETA, with offices at the Plaza Hotel, has three buses daily to Gualeguaychú (US$3), as does CUT, which has four daily to Mercedes (US$1) and four to Montevideo.

Buses Chadre, on the plaza at 25 de Mayo, has two buses daily in each direction between Bella Unión and Montevideo, stopping at Salto, Paysandú, Fray Bentos, Mercedes, Dolores, Nueva Palmira, Carmelo and Colonia. Southbound buses stop at Fray Bentos at 9.45 am and 7.45 pm, northbound buses at 10 am and 6.30 pm.

MERCEDES

Capital of the department of Soriano, only 30 km from Fray Bentos and 270 km from Montevideo, Mercedes is a livestock centre and minor resort on the south bank of the Río Negro, a tributary of the Río Uruguay. The principal activities are boating, fishing, and swimming along its sandy beaches. It has more frequent connections to Montevideo and other points throughout the country than Fray Bentos.

Orientation

Mercedes has a standard grid pattern, centred on Plaza Independencia. The main commercial streets are the parallel north-south Calles Colón and Artigas, on each side of the plaza. To the north, both intersect the very pleasant, shady riverside which is the town's main attraction.

Information

Tourist Office The tourist office, whose staff are friendly and enthusiastic, is on Colón between Giménez and Castro y Careaga, opposite Plaza Independencia. They have a good city map, and the office is open weekdays from 7.30 am to 1.30 pm and 3.30 to 9.30 pm.

Money Cambio Fagalde, next to Buses Klüver, or Cambio España, Colón 262, will change cash but not travellers' cheques.

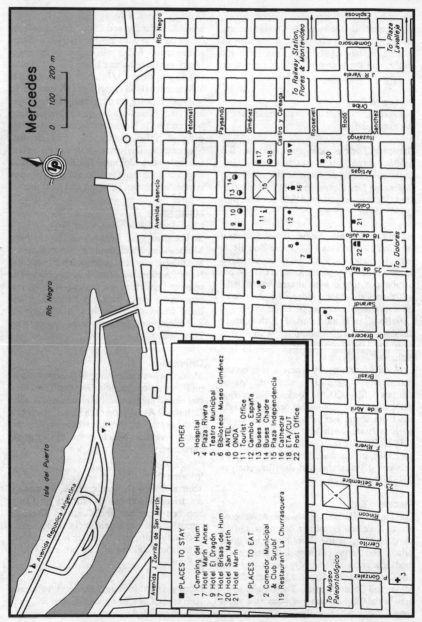

Mercedes

0   100   200 m

PLACES TO STAY

1 Camping del Hum
7 Hotel Marín Annex
9 Hotel El Dragón
17 Hotel Brisas del Hum
20 Hotel San Martín
21 Hotel Marín

▼ PLACES TO EAT

2 Comedor Municipal
   & Club Surubí
19 Restaurant La Churrasquera

OTHER

3 Hospital
4 Plaza Rivera
5 Teatro Municipal
6 Biblioteca Museo Giménez
8 ANTEL
10 ONDA
11 Tourist Office
12 Cambio España
13 Buses Klüver
14 Buses Chadre
15 Plaza Independencia
16 Cathedral
18 ETA/CUT
22 Post Office

Post & Telecommunications The post office is at Rodó 650, corner of 18 de Julio. ANTEL is on 18 de Julio between Roosevelt and Castro y Careaga.

Things to See & Do

The **Biblioteca Museo Giménez**, on Giménez between Sarandí and 25 de Mayo, displays paintings by the local artist. Some distance west of town is the **Museo Paleontológico**, accessible by public transport, with a valuable collection of fossils. It's open daily except Mondays from 7.30 am to 6.30 pm. On Sunday mornings, in Plaza Lavalleja, there is a flea market and crafts fair.

Places to Stay

Camping Only eight blocks from Plaza Independencia, Mercedes' *Camping del Hum* occupies half the Isla del Puerto in the Río Negro, connected to the mainland by a bridge. It is unquestionably one of the best campgrounds in the River Plate region, with excellent swimming, fishing and sanitary facilities. Fees are only US$0.60 per person plus US$0.60 per tent.

Hotels Cheapest accommodation in town is *Hotel San Martín* (☎ 3212), Artigas 305, with singles for US$4 per person with shared bath, US$5 with private bath. The rather gloomy *Hotel El Dragón* (☎ 3204), at Giménez 659 and 18 de Julio, has singles with shared bath for US$4.50, with private bath for US$7.50. Try instead the quiet and friendly *Hotel Marín* (☎ 2987) at Rodó 668, which has singles for US$6; its annex (☎ 2115) at Roosevelt 627, between 18 de Julio and 25 de Mayo, has more character but is slightly more expensive at US$7, plus US$1.50 for air-conditioning.

Despite its depressing exterior, *Hotel Brisas del Hum* (☎ 2740) at Artigas 201 is the closest to a luxury hotel in town. Rates are US$30/40 a single/double plus IVA.

Places to Eat

La Churrasquera, Castro y Careaga 790 at Ituzaingó, is a moderately priced parrilla with large portions and discounts for ACA members. On the Isla del Puerto, near the campground, the *Comedor Municipal* and the *Club Surubí* both have good inexpensive food, including river fish. The outdoor seating is far from luxurious, but very pleasant.

Getting There & Away

Buses Klüver, on Plaza Independencia on the corner of Giménez and Colón, has three buses daily to Palmar and three weekly to Durazno. ONDA, across the street, has three buses daily to Montevideo, three to Fray Bentos, and one to Dolores. For Buses Chadre, Artigas 176, Mercedes is a stopover on the route from Bella Unión to Montevideo (see the Fray Bentos listing for details).

CUT and ETA, with services to Gualeguaychú, Argentina, share offices at Artigas 233. ETA also goes to interior destinations such as Trinidad, Durazno, Paso de los Toros, Tacuarembó and Rivera. CUT, with the most modern buses, has four services daily to Montevideo (US$7).

PAYSANDÚ

Capital of its department and the second-largest city in Uruguay, Paysandú (population 100,000) traces its origins to the mid-18th century, as an outpost of cattle herders from the Jesuit mission at Yapeyú, Corrientes. The first *saladero* was established in 1840, but construction of its late 19th-century frigorífico was a turning point in its industrial history. Today, it is Uruguay's only significant industrial centre outside Montevideo, processing beer, sugar, textiles, leather and other products. For most independent travellers, it will be a stopover en route to or from Argentina.

Orientation

On the east bank of the Río Uruguay, Paysandú is 370 km from Montevideo and 110 km north of Fray Bentos. The Puente Internacional General Artigas, 15 km north of town, connects it with the Argentine city of Colón, Entre Ríos province. With a slightly irregular grid pattern, the centre of activity is Plaza Constitución, while the main

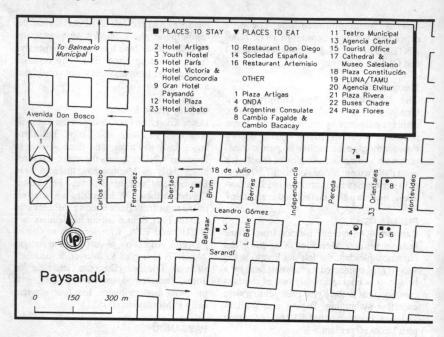

PLACES TO STAY
- 2 Hotel Artigas
- 3 Youth Hostel
- 5 Hotel París
- 7 Hotel Victoria & Hotel Concordia
- 9 Gran Hotel Paysandú
- 12 Hotel Plaza
- 23 Hotel Lobato

PLACES TO EAT
- 10 Restaurant Don Diego
- 14 Socledad Española
- 16 Restaurant Artemisio

OTHER
- 1 Plaza Artigas
- 4 ONDA
- 6 Argentine Consulate
- 8 Cambio Fagalde & Cambio Bacacay
- 11 Teatro Municipal
- 13 Agencia Central
- 15 Tourist Office
- 17 Cathedral & Museo Salesiano
- 18 Plaza Constitución
- 19 PLUNA/TAMU
- 20 Agencia Elvitur
- 21 Plaza Rivera
- 22 Buses Chadre
- 24 Plaza Flores

Paysandú

0   150   300 m

commercial street is 18 de Julio, which runs east-west along the south side of the plaza. Except for a small area around the port, directly west of downtown, the entire riverfront is open parkland because it is subject to flooding, but it provides a welcome refuge from the oppressive summer heat.

Information

Tourist Office The tourist office (☎ 6221) is opposite Plaza Constitución, at 18 de Julio 1226. It has one of the best city maps in Uruguay and a selection of useful brochures.

Money Cambio Fagalde is at 18 de Julio 1004, and Cambio Bacacay next door at 18 de Julio 1008.

Foreign Consulates The Argentine Consulate (☎ 2253) is at Leandro Gómez 1034.

Travel Agencies There are numerous travel agencies. Try Agencia Elvitur (☎ 4449) at Montecaseros 1024.

Medical Services The Hospital Escuela del Litoral (☎ 4836) is at Montecaseros 520.

Things to See

Paysandú has several worthwhile museums, particularly the gauchoesque **Museo de la Tradición** at the Balneario Municipal, north of town. Visit also the **Museo Salesiano**, the Salesian Museum, at 18 de Julio and Montecaseros and the **Museo Histórico** at Zorrilla and Sarandí.

Places to Stay

Camping There is a campground in the Balneario Municipal on the Río Uruguay, two km from the centre, and another at the Parque Sacra. The former has only basic facilities, the latter electricity, but neither has hot water. Neither charges any fee.

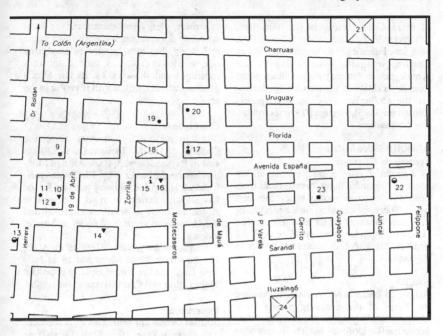

Hostels & Hotels Youth hostel accommodation is available at the *Liga Departamental de Fútbol* (☎ 4247), Baltasar Brum (ex-Gran Bretaña) 872, for about US$1 per person. Other than this, the cheapest lodging in town is *Hotel Victoria* (☎ 4320), 18 de Julio 979, which is also the friendliest. It charges US$4.50 per person with shared bath, US$8 with private bath. Rates at *Hotel Concordia* (☎ 2417), which shares the same address, are about the same. *Hotel Artigas* (☎ 4343), Baltasar Brum 943, is slightly dearer at US$6 per person with shared bath, US$9 with private bath. *Hotel Plaza* (☎ 2022), Leandro Gómez 1121, charges US$7.50 with shared bath, US$10 with private bath.

Several hotels charge about US$12 per person, including *Hotel París* (☎ 3774), Leandro Gómez 1008; *Hotel Rafaela* (☎ 5053), 18 de Julio and Zorrilla; and *Hotel Bulevar* (☎ 2682), outside the centre at Bulevar Artigas 960. At *Hotel Lobato* (☎ 2241), Leandro Gómez 1415,

singles/doubles with private bath cost US$14/22. Acknowledged as the best in town is *Gran Hotel Paysandú* (☎ 3400), 19 de Abril and 18 de Julio.

Places to Eat
Restaurant Don Diego, 19 de Abril 917, has reasonable parrillada, pizza and minutas. Other good eating places include the *Sociedad Española*, Leandro Gómez 1192, and *Restaurant Artemisio*, which is highly recommended, at 18 de Julio 1248 near the tourist office.

Getting There & Away
Air PLUNA (☎ 3071), Florida 1249, sells tickets for TAMU flights to Montevideo, which leave Paysandú on Monday, Thursday, Friday and Saturday at 8.20 am. The fare is US$13.

Bus Paysandú is building a new bus terminal at Montecaseros and Artigas, directly south of Plaza Constitución. In the meantime, ONDA (☎ 3020) is at Leandro Gómez 1000, with four buses daily to Montevideo. Buses Chadre (☎ 5310), Avenida España and Juncal, passes through Paysandú en route from Bella Unión to Montevideo; for details, see the section on Fray Bentos. Agencia Central (☎ 3403), Herrera 873, goes to interior destinations.

AROUND PAYSANDÚ
Termas de Guaviyú

In a soothing yatay palm savannah 60 km north of Paysandú, these thermal baths have been developed to soothe your aches and pains. There are camping sites available, or you can arrange motel accommodation (US$14 a triple for category 'B' or US$25 a triple for category 'A') at the tourist office in Paysandú.

SALTO

Salto, 520 km from Montevideo, is the most northerly of the crossing points from Uruguay into Argentina. There are launches across the Río Uruguay, but it is also possible to take a bus across the enormous Salto Grande dam, north of the city, to Concordia, Entre Ríos province. To visit the dam project, make arrangements at the tourist office (☎ 4096), Uruguay 1052.

There is a youth hostel at the *Club de Remeros* (☎ 3418), César Mayo Gutiérrez and Belén. Otherwise, try *Pensión 33*, Treinta y Tres 269. On the costanera, the *Camping Municipal* is free but has only very basic services. Eight km south of town, at *Termas del Daymán*, there are much better facilities for about US$2 per person. Saunas and other extras are available but not included in the basic price.

TACUAREMBÓ

Capital of its department, Tacuarembó has sycamore-lined streets and attractive plazas which make it one of the most agreeable towns in Uruguay's interior. Since its founding in 1832, authorities have kept sculptors busy on busts and monuments which pay tribute to the usual military heroes but also

to writers, clergy and educators. The local economy depends on livestock, both cattle and sheep, but local producers also grow rice, sunflowers, peanuts, linseed, tobacco, asparagus and strawberries. Its late March gaucho festival merits a visit if you're in the area.

Orientation

Sited in rolling hill country along the Cuchilla de Haedo, Tacuarembó is 230 km east of Paysandú and 390 km north of Montevideo, on the banks of the Río Tacuarembó Chico. It is a major highway junction for the Uruguayan interior, as roads lead west to Argentina, north to Brazil, east to Brazil and the Uruguayan coast, and south to Montevideo.

Centre of the town is Plaza 19 de Abril, but the streets 25 de Mayo and 18 de Julio both lead past the almost equally important Plaza Colón and Plaza Rivera to the south.

Information

Tourist Office The tourist office is at Suárez 215, opposite Plaza 19 de Abril. The staff are friendly and helpful, and can offer a simple map and limited brochures.

Telecommunications ANTEL is at Sarandí 242.

Medical Services The regional hospital (☎ 2955) is at Treinta y Tres and Catalogne.

Museo del Indio y del Gaucho

Tacuarembó's regional museum, at Flores and Artigas, pays romantic tribute to Uruguay's nearly forgotten Indians and gauchos, and their role in the country's rural history.

Festivals

In late March, Tacuarembó hosts the **Fiesta de la Patria Gaucha**, three days of exhibitions featuring traditional gaucho skills, music and other activities. It takes place in Parque 25 de Agosto, at the north end of town.

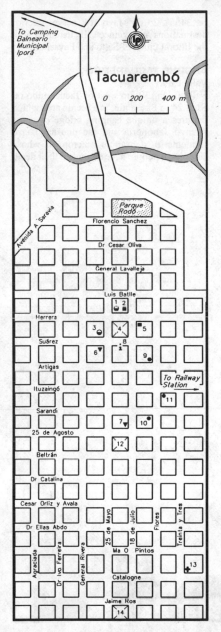

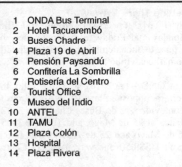

1   ONDA Bus Terminal
2   Hotel Tacuarembó
3   Buses Chadre
4   Plaza 19 de Abril
5   Pensión Paysandú
6   Confitería La Sombrilla
7   Rotisería del Centro
8   Tourist Office
9   Museo del Indio
10 ANTEL
11 TAMU
12 Plaza Colón
13 Hospital
14 Plaza Rivera

Places to Stay

Camping The densely forested *Balneario Municipal Iporá*, seven km north of town, has both free and paying sites near an artificial lake. The free sites have clean toilets but lack showers. For US$1 per person, you may decide that access to showers justifies the costlier alternative.

Buses to the campground leave from near the ONDA terminal on Plaza 19 de Abril.

Pensiones & Hotels The friendly *Pensión Paysandú* (☎ 2453), 18 de Julio 154 opposite Plaza 19 de Abril, offers good, clean but basic accommodation for US$4.50 a single in a shared room, US$6/10 a single/double for a private room with shared bath. *Hotel Tacuarembó* (☎ 2945), 18 de Julio 133, is more comfortable but more impersonal, with rooms for US$15/26 with private bath.

Places to Eat

Hotel Tacuarembó has a good restaurant which serves parrillada, the regional standard, and other dishes; two other parrillas are *La Rueda*, Beltrán and Flores, and *La Cabaña*, 25 de Mayo 217. A reasonable confitería is *La Sombrilla*, 25 de Mayo and Suárez. *Rotisería del Centro*, on 18 de Julio near Plaza Colón, sells an enormous, tasty chivito which is a meal in itself.

Getting There & Away

Air TAMU (☎ 2341), Flores 300, flies Monday and Friday from Montevideo via Artigas to Tacuarembó, then returns directly from Tacuarembó to Montevideo.

Bus ONDA (☎ 2416), at 18 de Julio and Herrera, opposite Plaza 19 de Abril, goes to Montevideo, as do Buses Chadre (☎ 3432), Suárez at 25 de Mayo, and Turil (☎ 3305), 25 de Mayo and 25 de Agosto. The fare is about US$8.50 one way. Agencia Central (☎ 3455), 25 de Mayo 169, serves interior destinations and connects Tacuarembó with the littoral cities of Salto and Paysandú.

AROUND TACUAREMBÓ
Valle Edén

Valle Edén, 30 km west of Tacuarembó on Ruta 24 to Paysandú, is a scenic area which features a unique hanging bridge over the Arroyo Jabonería and the unusual Cerro Cementerio, a granitic outcrop on whose sides local people have entombed their dead.

The Uruguayan Riviera

East of Montevideo, innumerable beach resorts dot the scenic Uruguayan coast, where sandy river beaches, vast dunes and dramatic ocean headlands extend all the way to the Brazilian border. The area attracts hordes of tourists during the summer but relatively few after wealthy Brazilians and Argentines end their holidays in early March. Its showplace is exclusive Punta del Este, where so much happens that Argentina maintains a summer consulate and the Buenos Aires daily *La Nación* opens a temporary bureau. While there is more reasonable accommodation and facilities in nearby Maldonado, other resorts are just as attractive and much more affordable. In early March, after the summer crowds have departed, prices drop considerably and the weather is ideal and the pace much more leisurely.

The present chapter starts with resorts immediately east of Montevideo, following the Ruta Interbalnearia (coastal highway) and works east and then north toward the Brazilian border, describing interior destinations where appropriate. Technically, the beaches west of Punta del Este are river beaches but, except for the gentle surf, most visitors will find little difference with the ocean beaches to the east.

East of Montevideo

ATLÁNTIDA
In the department of Canelones, only 50 km from Montevideo, Atlántida is the first major resort along the coastal highway. The tourist office (☎ 22736) is at the intersection of Calles 14 and 1. There are several reasonably priced residenciales, while just west of town is the highly regarded *Hostería del Fortín de Santa Rosa*, a popular hideaway for well-heeled folks from Montevideo. For the rest of us, there is *Camping El Ensueño*

(☎ 2371), nine blocks from the Playa Brava, Atlántida's most popular beach. Fees are about US$1.75 per person for excellent facilities, including 24-hour hot water and sanitary facilities. COT (☎ 3888), Calle 18 and Avenida Artigas, has regular buses to Montevideo and farther down the coast.

Maldonado Department

PIRIÁPOLIS
Piriápolis, about 100 km from Montevideo, is the westernmost beach resort in the department of Maldonado, less sophisticated but more affordable than Punta del Este. Founded in 1893, it was developed as a tourist resort in the 1930s by the Argentine entrepreneur Francisco Piria, who built its greatest landmark, the imposing Hotel Argentino, and an eccentric residence known as 'Piria's Castle', now part of a city park. At one time Piria's ferries brought tourists directly from Argentina.

In the surrounding countryside there are many interesting features, including Cerro Pan de Azúcar, one of the highest points in Uruguay, and the hill resort of Minas (see below).

Orientation
With a permanent population of only about 6000, Piriápolis is very compact. Almost everything is within reasonable walking distance in an area bounded by the waterfront Rambla de los Argentinos to the south, Bulevar Artigas in the west, Calle Misiones in the north, and Avenida Piria on the east. Almost everything in town is defined by its proximity to the Hotel Argentino.

Information
Tourist Office The tourist office (☎ 2560) is at Rambla de los Argentinos 1348, near the Hotel Argentino. It's open daily from 9.30

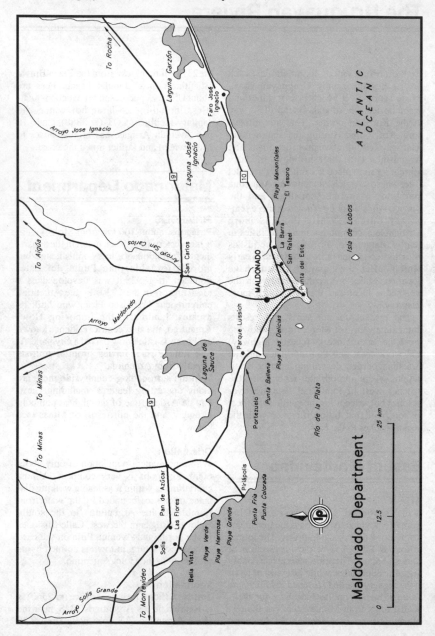

Maldonado Department

am to 1 pm and 3.30 to 9 pm, and has maps, a few brochures, and a listing of current hotel prices.

Money Banco del Uruguay is at Tucumán and Sanabria. You can change cash, but not travellers' cheques, at the Hotel Argentino.

Telecommunications ANTEL is on Calle Tucumán, behind the enormous skyscraper near the corner with Calle Manuel Freire.

Things to See & Do

For a good view of Piriápolis, climb the **Cerro del Inglés** (also known as Cerro San Antonio) at the east end of town. For real lazybones, there is a chairlift to the top.

Swimming and sunbathing are the most popular activities, but there is good fishing from the rocks at the west end of the Playa de Piriápolis.

Places to Stay

In Piriápolis and most of the Uruguayan Riviera, there is abundant accommodation but prices and availability are strongly seasonal. Many places open only between December and April, while nearly all raise their prices dramatically between December 15 and March 1. The best bargains come after March 1, when the weather is delightful but the crowds are gone.

Places to Stay – bottom end

Camping *Camping Piriápolis F C* (☎ 3275) is at Misiones and Niza, 350 metres behind the Hotel Argentino. It has every necessary facility, including electricity and hot showers, for US$2 per person per day, while there are a few rooms with shared bath available for US$10 a double. It's open from mid-December to the end of April.

Hostels, Pensiones & Hotels The youth hostel *Albergue de Piriápolis* (☎ 2157), at Simón del Pino 1136 behind the Hotel Argentino, charges US$1 per person per night with hostel card. It's open all year, but reservations are essential in January and February.

Petite Pensión (☎ 2471) is a tiny (seven-room) but friendly family-run hotel at Sanabria 1084 near Ayacucho, two blocks above the beach. Rates are US$8 off-season, US$12 per person in summer. Winter rates are comparable at *Hotel Centro* (☎ 2516), but summer rates are US$18 per person. Try also *Hotel Alcázar* (☎ 2507), Piria and Tucumán, where singles are US$10 off-season but US$19 in summer.

Places to Stay – middle

There is an abundance of midrange accommodation. *Hotel Sierra Mar* (☎ 2613), Sanabria 1051, has rooms for US$12 per person with breakfast in off-season, US$15 in summer. There are many more in this general price range, including *Hotel San Sebastián* (☎ 2546), Sanabria 942; *Hotel Danae* (☎ 2594) at Rambla and Freire; and the highly recommended *Hotel Colonial*, Balconada de Piria and Talcahuano, which is quieter and a bit more distant from the centre, near the verdant Cerro del Inglés.

Places to Stay – top end

Even if you don't stay at *Hotel Argentino* (☎ 2791), you should visit this elegant, 350-room European-style spa on the Rambla de los Argentinos. Rates are US$50 per person with half-pension, US$60 with full pension, plus IVA. It has thermal baths, a casino, a classic dining room and other luxuries.

Places to Eat

Restaurant La Langosta, Rambla de los Argentinos 1215, has very good seafood and parrillada at moderate prices. There are several other appealing restaurants along the Rambla, including *Viejo Martín* at the corner of Trapani and *Restaurant Delta* at the corner of Atanasio Sierra.

Things to Buy

For artisanal items, go to the Paseo de la Pasiva, an attractive colonnaded gallery along the Rambla.

Getting There & Away

All the bus companies have offices along the

Rambla de los Argentinos. In high season COT (☎ 2259) runs up to 27 buses daily to and from Punta del Este. ONDA has a dozen a day. Díaz has 14 buses daily from Piriápolis to Pan de Azúcar and Minas. The fare to Montevideo is about US$2 one way.

AROUND PIRIÁPOLIS
Pan de Azúcar
West of the highway to the town of Pan de Azúcar, 10 km north, 493-metre **Cerro Pan de Azúcar** is the third-highest point in the country. There is a hiking trail to the top, and a small but well-kept zoo at the nearby **Parque Municipal**. On the opposite side of the highway is the **Castillo de Piria**, Francisco Piria's opulent and outlandish residence.

MINAS
In the Cuchilla Grande hills of the department of Lavalleja, 120 km north-east of Montevideo and 60 km north of Piriápolis, Minas is an agreeable hill town which offers a change of pace from the monotony of the Pampas. It draws its name from the quarries of building materials which are found nearby, but its favourite attraction is **Parque Salus** 10 km west of town, source of Uruguay's best known mineral water and site of a brewery. Every April 19, as many as 70,000 pilgrims visit the **Cerro y Virgen del Verdún**, 6 km west of town.

The tourist office (☎ 4118) is at the bus terminal, but visit also the **Casa de la Cultura** at Lavalleja and Rodó. For inexpensive, but adequate, lodging try *Residencia Minas*, 25 de Mayo 502. At Parque Salus, accommodation is available at *El Parador Salus*.

Camping is possible at woodsy **Parque Arequita**, nine km north of Minas on the road to Polanco (public transport is available from Minas). Sector 'A' is more basic, with cold showers only, but is ridiculously cheap at US$0.35 per person per day. Sector 'B', which has swimming pools and hot showers, costs US$1.50 per day per person. A limited number of two-bed cabañas are available for US$5 per night.

In **Villa Serrana**, 23 km beyond Minas, there is hostel accommodation at *Chalet Las Chafas*, which has kitchen facilities, a swimming pool and a lake. Buses from Minas go no closer than three km from the hostel, so you'll need to walk or hitch. More upscale is the *Mesón de las Cañas* (☎ 1611), which charges US$24 per person with full pension.

MALDONADO
Maldonado, 130 km east of Montevideo and only 30 km from Piriápolis, dates from 1755, when Governor J J de Viana of Montevideo transferred the first settlers to establish an outpost to provision ships at the entrance to the Río de la Plata. Its centre still retains a certain colonial atmosphere, but the town has sprawled because of tourist development associated with exclusive Punta del Este where, ironically, a Jesuit visitor once wrote that 'you see nothing here but a few cabins, the abodes of misery'. British forces occupied the city during the siege of Buenos Aires in 1806.

Orientation
Capital of its department, with room to grow, Maldonado is a more economical alternative to fashionable Punta del Este. Food and accommodation are much cheaper than in Punta del Este, which is easily accessible by public transport. Because the two have grown together, only convenience separates them in this book, and visitors will have to refer back and forth between the two entries.

Maldonado's centre is Plaza San Fernando, from which most points of interest (except the beaches) are within a few blocks. The original city plan is a standard grid, but between Maldonado and Punta del Este it is highly irregular. To the west, along the Río de la Plata, the Rambla Claudio Williman is the main thoroughfare, while to the east Rambla Lorenzo Batlle Pacheco follows the Atlantic coast. Locations along these routes are usually identified by numbered *paradas* (bus stops). There are many attractive beaches along both routes, but the ocean beaches have rougher surf. For more infor-

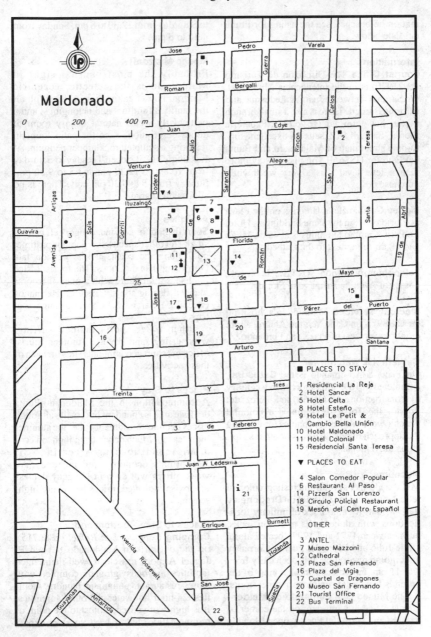

Maldonado

0   200   400 m

■ PLACES TO STAY

1 Residencial La Reja
2 Hotel Sancar
5 Hotel Celta
8 Hotel Esteño
9 Hotel Le Petit &
  Cambio Bella Unión
10 Hotel Maldonado
11 Hotel Colonial
15 Residencial Santa Teresa

▼ PLACES TO EAT

4 Salon Comedor Popular
6 Restaurant Al Paso
14 Pizzería San Lorenzo
18 Círculo Policial Restaurant
19 Mesón del Centro Español

OTHER

3 ANTEL
7 Museo Mazzoni
12 Cathedral
13 Plaza San Fernando
16 Plaza del Vigía
17 Cuartel de Dragones
20 Museo San Fernando
21 Tourist Office
22 Bus Terminal

mation on beaches, see the listing for Punta del Este below.

Information

Tourist Office The Dirección de Turismo (☎ 21920) is in the Intendencia Municipal, on Sarandí between Juan A Ledesma and Enrique Burnett. There is also a small branch at the bus terminal (☎ 25701). Papelería Sienra, Sarandí 812, sells an excellent, up-to-date street map of Maldonado and Punta del Este for US$6. If you plan to stay more than a few days, it is a very worthwhile purchase.

Money Cambio Bella Unión is on the Plaza at Florida 764, in the same building as Hotel Le Petit. Cambio Dominus is at 25 de Mayo and 18 de Julio, next to the Cathedral.

Telecommunications ANTEL is at the corner of Avenida Artigas and Florida.

Medical Services Maldonado's hospital (☎ 25889) is on Calle Ventura Alegre, about eight blocks west of Plaza San Fernando.

Cathedral & Watchtower

On Plaza San Fernando is the **Cathedral**, completed in 1895 after more than a century of construction. At Gorriti and Pérez del Puerto, the **Torre de Vigia** is a colonial watchtower built with peepholes for viewing the approach of hostile forces or other suspicious movements.

Museums

Maldonado has several interesting colonial relics, including the **Cuartel de Dragones y de Blandengues**, a block of military fortifications with stone walls and iron gates, built between 1771 and 1797, located along 18 de Julio and Pérez del Puerto. Currently undergoing restoration, it is open daily from 7 to 11 pm, but you can sneak a view of the grounds from a side entrance at other hours.

The **Museo San Fernando de Maldonado** is a fine arts museum on the corner of Sarandí and Pérez del Puerto, open Monday to Saturday from 12.30 to 8 pm, Sunday from 4.30 to 8 pm.

Museo Mazzoni

Probably the most unusual sight in Maldonado is the eclectic, eccentric Mazzoni house, dating from 1782. With all the family's furniture and belongings, and a particularly weird natural history room, it defies description – see the patio fountain featuring a sculpted rockhopper penguin. At Ituzaingó 789, it's open Tuesday to Saturday from 10 am to 12.30 pm and 5 to 9.30 pm, Sunday from 5 to 9.30 pm only. There is no admission charge.

Activities

Sport fishing for corvina, conger eel, bonito, shark and other species is a popular pastime, both along the coast, at sea, and on Isla Gorriti and Isla de Lobos. The tourist office publishes a brochure with a map of recommended fishing spots. Cassarino Hermanos (☎ 23735), Sarandí 1253, will arrange boat trips.

Other water sports include surfing, windsurfing, and diving. Another tourist office brochure recommends sites for each of these activities.

Places to Stay

Accommodation in the Maldonado/Punta del Este area is abundant but costly, although prices decline considerably after the summer high season. Much depends, though, on economic conditions in Argentina – if Argentina's economy and currency are weak, prices will drop in Uruguay. Unless otherwise indicated, prices below are high-season.

Places to Stay – bottom end

Camping *Camping San Rafael* (☎ 86715), on the outskirts of Maldonado beyond El Jagüel Airport, has clean, well-maintained facilities on woodsy grounds, complete with store, restaurant, automatic laundry facilities, 24-hour hot water and other amenities. It is highly organised, almost to the point of regimentation, but at least you can expect quiet after midnight. Sites cost US$7 for two in January and February, US$6 the rest of the year. It accepts Uruguayan pesos, US dollars, and almost all credit cards. Bus No 5 from Maldonado drops you at the entrance.

Residenciales & Hotels The best bargain is the recently opened *Albergue Juvenil* (youth hostel), across from the Club de Pesca in Manantiales, east of Maldonado, reached by CODESA bus.

In Maldonado proper, check out *Residencial La Reja* (☎ 23712), 18 de Julio 1092 at José Pedro Varela, or *Residencial Santa Teresa* (☎ 25130), Santa Teresa 753 at Pérez del Puerto, where singles/doubles with shared bath cost US$18/20, and with private bath US$25/28. Try also *Residencial Obreros* at 19 de Abril and Pérez del Puerto.

Places to Stay – middle
The recently remodelled *Hotel Celta* (ex-Hospedaje Ituzaingó, ☎ 30139) at Ituzaingó 839, is a popular choice for foreign travellers. Standard rates are US$30 per person, but its gregarious Irish owner Michael Power has budget rooms which are cheaper, especially out of season. Facilities now include international satellite TV in the rooms. *Hotel Esteño* (☎ 25222), Sarandí 881, charges US$14 per person. Prices are similar at *Hotel Maldonado* (☎ 24664), Florida 830, and *Hotel Sancar* (☎ 23563), Juan Edye 597.

Places to Stay – top end
Hotel Colonial (☎ 23346), on 18 de Julio near the Cathedral, charges US$36 a double. *Hotel Le Petit* (☎ 23044), at Florida and Sarandí opposite Plaza San Fernando, charges US$22 per person.

Places to Eat
The modest *Tequila Bar*, Ituzaingó and Román Guerra, is great value for money. Other inexpensive choices include *Salon Comedor Popular* at Dodera and Ituzaingó, and the *Circulo Policial de Maldonado* at Pérez del Puerto 780. *San Lorenzo*, Sarandí 834, is an inexpensive but ordinary pizzería on Plaza San Fernando.

Pricier but good value is *Restaurant Al Paso*, a parrilla at 18 de Julio 888. More upmarket is *Mesón del Centro Español* at Arturo Santana and 18 de Julio, with excellent but pricey Spanish seafood. Another highly regarded place is the Maldonado branch of Montevideo's *Forte di Makale*, on Sarandí near Enrique Burnett.

Getting There & Away
El Jagüel Airport is mainly used by small private craft, but some commercial flights land there. Laguna de Sauce Airport cannot handle aircraft larger than 737s.

The bus terminal is on Avenida Roosevelt and Sarandí, eight blocks south of the plaza. COT (☎ 25026) goes to Piriápolis, Montevideo and Colonia. ONDA (☎ 23581) serves the same destinations, as well as Buenos Aires and Córdoba in Argentina, and Porto Alegre, Brazil. TTL (☎ 69224) serves Montevideo, Porto Alegre and São Paulo from San Carlos.

Transporte Nuñez (☎ 30170) has two buses daily to Montevideo.

Getting Around
CODESA (☎ 23481), Avenida Velásquez, runs local buses to Punta del Este, La Barra, Manantiales and San Carlos. Olivera (☎ 24039) connects Maldonado and Punta del Este with San Rafael, Punta Ballena, Portezuelo and the airport.

AROUND MALDONADO
Casapueblo
At Punta Ballena, a scenic headland 10 km west of Maldonado, the Uruguayan artist Carlos Páez Vilaró (who, amongst other things, has participated in the Cannes film festival) built this unconventional, sprawling, multilevel Mediterranean hillside villa and art gallery with no right angles. For an admission charge of US$1.75, visitors can tour the gallery, view a slide presentation on its creation, and dine or drink at the bar-cafetería. Parts of the building are open to member-patrons only, but you can sneak a view from the outside.

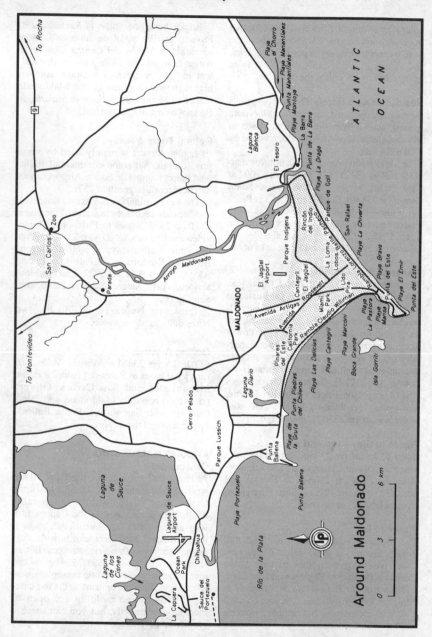

Around Maldonado

PUNTA DEL ESTE

One of South America's most glamourous summer resorts, Punta del Este swarms with upper-class Argentines who disdain Mar del Plata since the latter lost its exclusivity. Strictly speaking, it is part of Maldonado, but economically and socially it is a world apart, with its elegant seaside homes, yacht harbour, and expensive hotels and restaurants. Budget travellers are not likely to lodge here, although there is a small selection of reasonable accommodation.

Orientation

Geographically, the tiny peninsula of Punta del Este is south of Maldonado proper but easily accessible by public transport. The Rambla General Artigas circles the peninsula, passing the protected beach of the Playa Mansa and the yacht harbour on the west side, the exclusive residential zone at its southern tip, and the rugged Playa Brava, open to the South Atlantic, in the east.

Punta del Este has two separate grid systems, dictated by a constricted neck just east of the yacht harbour. The newer, high-rise hotel zone is north of this neck, while the area to the south is almost exclusively residential. Streets in Punta del Este bear both names and numbers; when appropriate, addresses given below refer first to the street name, with the number in parentheses. Avenida Juan Gorlero (22), the main commercial street, is universally referred to as just 'Gorlero'.

Information

Tourist Office The tourist office (☎ 40514) is at the Liga de Fomento (a promontional organisation), at the intersection of the Rambla and Angostura near the west end of Inzaurraga (31). It distributes a simple map of Punta del Este (but none of Maldonado) and a very useful booklet, *Lo Que Hay Que Saber*, which is loaded with information, including a schedule of concerts, theatre, art exhibitions and other summer events. There is also an office (☎ 40512) on Plaza Artigas, which has a list of hotels and restaurants, with up-to-the-minute prices.

Money Nearly all the banks and cambios are along Gorlero. Try Cambio Bella Unión at Gorlero and Las Focas (30) or Banco de la República, also on Gorlero.

Post & Telecommunications The post office is at Gorlero 633. ANTEL is on the corner of Arrecifes and Mesana.

Foreign Consulates During high season, Argentina operates a consulate (☎ 41106) at the Santos Dumont Building, Gorlero between Inzaurraga (31) and Las Focas (30).

Travel Agencies There are many travel agencies along Avenida Gorlero, such as Turalfi (☎ 41853), Gorlero 942, and Turisport (☎ 44657), Gorlero and La Galerna (21).

Beaches

On the west side of Punta del Este, the Rambla Artigas snakes along the calm Playa Mansa on the Río de la Plata, then circles around the peninsula, passing Playa de Los Ingleses and Playa El Emir to the wilder Playa Brava on the Atlantic side. From Playa Mansa, west along Rambla Williman, the main beach areas are: La Pastora, Marconi, Cantegril, Las Delicias, Pinares, La Gruta at Punta Ballena, and Portezuelo, beyond Punta Ballena. Eastward, along the Rambla Lorenzo Batlle Pacheco, the prime areas are: La Chiverta, San Rafael, La Draga and Punta de La Barra. At all these beaches, there are *paradores* (small restaurants) with beach service, which is more expensive than bringing your own goodies. Beach-hopping is a popular activity, depending on local conditions and the general level of action.

Places to Stay

In summer, Punta is jammed with people and prices for accommodation can be astronomical (although the most luxurious places are in ritzy suburbs like Barrio Parque del Golf). Prices below are high-season rates unless otherwise indicated, and include IVA and breakfast.

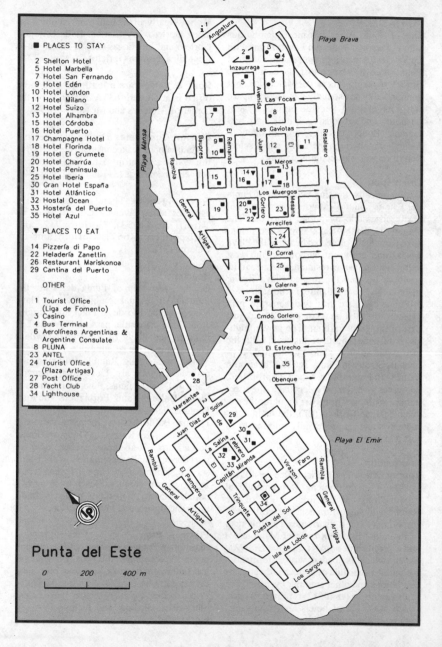

■ PLACES TO STAY

2 Shelton Hotel
5 Hotel Marbella
7 Hotel San Fernando
9 Hotel Edén
10 Hotel London
11 Hotel Milano
12 Hotel Suizo
13 Hotel Alhambra
15 Hotel Córdoba
16 Hotel Puerto
17 Champagne Hotel
18 Hotel Florinda
19 Hotel El Grumete
20 Hotel Charrúa
21 Hotel Peninsula
25 Hotel Iberia
30 Gran Hotel España
31 Hotel Atlántico
32 Hostal Ocean
33 Hostería del Puerto
35 Hotel Azul

▼ PLACES TO EAT

14 Pizzería di Papo
22 Heladería Zanettin
26 Restaurant Mariskonoa
29 Cantina del Puerto

OTHER

1 Tourist Office
  (Liga de Fomento)
3 Casino
4 Bus Terminal
6 Aerolíneas Argentinas &
  Argentine Consulate
8 PLUNA
23 ANTEL
24 Tourist Office
  (Plaza Artigas)
27 Post Office
28 Yacht Club
34 Lighthouse

Punta del Este

0   200   400 m

Places to Stay – bottom end

Modest accommodation is hard to come by in Punta del Este proper, but does exist at *Hostal Ocean* (☎ 43248), La Salina (9) 636, in the quiet, residential part of town. Triples with shared bath costs US$10 per person without breakfast, but ring ahead for reservations. The next cheapest thing you'll find is *Hostería del Puerto* (☎ 45345), Capitán Miranda (7) and Calle 2 de Febrero (10), a pleasant older-style hotel in the older part of town, with singles/doubles for US$20/30 with private bath.

Hotel Marbella (☎ 41814), on Inzaurraga between Gorlero and El Remanso (20), and *Hotel Córdoba* (☎ 40008), Los Muergos (27) 660, cost US$22.50, while *Hotel Puerto* (☎ 40332), Los Muergos 622, and *Hotel El Grumete* (☎ 41009), El Remanso (20) 797, cost US$25 per person.

Places to Stay – middle

Midrange accommodation, such as *Hotel San Fernando* (☎ 40720), Las Focas (30) between Baupres (18) and El Remanso (20), and *Hotel Peninsula* (☎ 41533), Gorlero 761, starts around US$28. Several places charge about US$35, including *Hotel Florinda* (☎ 40022), on Los Muergos (27) between Gorlero and El Mesana (24), *Hotel Milano* (☎ 40039) at El Mesana (24) 880, and *Hotel Charrúa* (☎ 41402), Los Muergos (27) 617.

Hotel Atlántico (☎ 40229), across from the Hostería del Puerto in the residential part of town, charges US$37.50 per person, as does *Hotel Suizo* (☎ 41517), Los Meros (28) 590. *Gran Hotel España* (☎ 40228), La Salina (9) 660, costs US$38 per person in high season, but US$36/45 a single/double off season. At *Hotel Azul* (☎ 40106) Gorlero 540, and *Hotel Edén* (☎ 40505), El Remanso (20) 887, rates are US$40 per person.

Places to Stay – top end

At *Hotel Alhambra* (☎ 40094), Los Meros (28) 573, doubles cost US$44 per person, while *Hotel London* (☎ 41911), El Remanso (20) 877 is slightly dearer. At *Champagne Hotel* (☎ 45276), Gorlero 828, doubles are US$62.50 per person.

Real luxury accommodation is not in Punta del Este proper, but out on the Ramblas and into the suburbs. If you have money to burn, check out *La Posta del Cangrejo* (☎ 70021) in Barra del Maldonado (US$65 per person), *Hotel Solana del Mar* (☎ 78888), Km 126.5, Punta Ballena (US$67), or the truly extravagant *Hotel L'Auberge* (☎ 82601) in Barrio Parque del Golf (US$112).

Places to Eat

If a tidal wave swept over the narrow peninsula of Punta del Este, half the restaurants in Uruguay would disappear, it seems. Most tend to the expensive, but there are several reasonably priced pizzerías and cafés along Gorlero, such as *Di Papo*, Gorlero 841. Another modest but good place is the *Cantina del Puerto*, La Salina (9) and 2 de Febrero (10). *Los Caracoles*, El Remanso (20) and Los Meros (28), is a midrange parrilla.

International restaurants are too numerous for an exhaustive list. Good seafood is available at *Bossangoa*, Capitán Miranda (7) and 2 de Febrero, but many other places serve fish – if you can afford it, try *Mariskonoa*, Resalsero (26) 650. Homesick Australians will find an unexpected bit of home at *La Pomme*, at Solís (11) and Virazón (12), which also serves French food. Another highly regarded French restaurant is *Blue Cheese*, Rambla General Artigas and El Corral (23). Between Punta and Maldonado, *La Bourgogne*, Pedragosa and Avenida Córdoba, is very expensive.

Montevideo's *Bungalow Suizo* has a local branch on the Rambla Batlle at Parada 8, near Avenida Roosevelt. Farther out, at La Barra, *La Posta del Cangrejo*, in the hotel of the same name, has outstanding but costly seafood.

Heladería Zanettin, Gorlero and Arrecifes (25), has first-rate ice cream.

Entertainment

Punta del Este is lively at night, with many

cinemas along Avenida Gorlero and discos along the Rambla Batlle. There is a casino at Gorlero and Inzaurraga (31).

Things to Buy

For souvenirs, visit the Feria Artesanal on Plaza Artigas. In high season, December to March, hours are from 6 pm to 1 am daily, while the rest of the year it's open from 5 pm to midnight weekends only. Manos del Uruguay has an outlet at Gorlero and Las Gaviotas (29).

Getting There & Away

Air PLUNA (☎ 41840) is at Gorlero 940. In summer, it has daily flights to Montevideo except Thursday (where there are none) and Sunday (when there are two). Depending on the day, flights continue to Porto Alegre, São Paulo, Río de Janeiro (all in Brazil), Asunción (Paraguay) and Santiago, Chile.

Aerolíneas Uruguayas (☎ 88844), Bulevar Artigas and Parada 2, flies direct from Aeroparque in Buenos Aires on Friday evening, returning to Buenos Aires on Sunday evening and Monday morning, which allows wealthy Argentines to spend the weekend. The return fare of US$110 includes transportation to and from the airport.

Aerolíneas Argentinas (☎ 43801) is in the Santos Dumont Building on Gorlero between Inzaurraga (31) and Las Focas (30). It flies to Buenos Aires' Aeroparque Jorge Newbery on Thursday, Friday and Sunday.

Bus The Terminal Playa Brava is on the Rambla General Artigas at Inzaurraga. Bus services to Punta del Este are an extension of those to Maldonado; for details on bus services, see Getting There & Away under Maldonado.

Buquebus (☎ 84995) is at Gorlero 732; see the chapter on Montevideo for more detailed information on their services. Transporte Nuñez (☎ 83923), COT (☎ 83558) and ONDA (☎ 86801) have offices at the bus terminal.

Car Rental All major agencies have offices in Punta del Este. Hertz (☎ 42431) is on Los Meros (28) near Gorlero. Budget (☎ 46363) has offices at Los Muergos (27) and Gorlero. Multicar (☎ 43143) is at Gorlero 860.

Getting Around

To/From the Airport Maldonado and Punta del Este have two airports. Aerolíneas Argentinas and PLUNA use Aeropuerto Laguna de Sauce, west of Portezuelo, reached by Buses Olivera (☎ 24039) from Maldonado. Aeropuerto El Jagüel is at the west end of Avenida Aparicio Saravia, five km from downtown Maldonado, also served by Olivera.

Bus Maldonado Turismo (☎ 81725), Gorlero and Inzaurraga (31), connects Punta del Este with La Barra and Manantiales.

AROUND PUNTA DEL ESTE

Isla Gorriti

Boats leave every half-hour or so from the yacht harbour for this nearby island, which has excellent sandy beaches and the ruins of an 18th-century fortress. It also has two restaurants, *Parador Puerto Jardín* and *Playa Onda*.

Isla de Lobos

About six miles offshore, the nature reserve of Isla de Lobos hosts a population of some 300,000 southern fur seals. During the invasion of 1806, British forces stranded numerous prisoners here without food or water, many of whom perished swimming to Maldonado. To arrange trips to the reserve, contact the Unión de Lanchas (☎ 42594) in Punta del Este.

Rocha Department

The modern department of Rocha, between Maldonado and the Brazilian border, was subject to a constant tug-of-war between Portugal and Spain in the colonial era and between Brazil and Argentina up to the middle of the 19th century. This conflict left several valuable historical monuments, such as the fortresses of Santa Teresa and San Miguel, while discouraging rural settlement and sparing some of Uruguay's wildest countryside. No one will compare it to trackless Amazonia, but it does have nearly undeveloped areas like Cabo Polonio, with extensive dunes and a large colony of southern sea lions, and Parque Nacional Santa Teresa (more a cultural than a natural park, however). The interior has a varied landscape of palm savannas and marshes, which are rich in bird life.

ROCHA

Founded in 1793 by Rafael Pérez del Puerto, picturesque Rocha is capital of the department and merits at least an afternoon's visit for those who are staying on the beach at La Paloma. In the narrow alleyways off Plaza Independencia there are a number of interesting houses from the late colonial and early independence eras. Virtually everything of interest, including hotels and transport, is on or near the plaza.

Money exchange is available at Banco de la República or Banco Comercial. Accommodation is very reasonable, but probably not cheap enough to justify staying here rather than in La Paloma. Try the tidy *Hotel Municipal Rocha*, a block off the plaza on 19 de Abril between Ramírez and Presbítero Aquiles, which charges US$7.50/10 a single/double. The modest *Hotel Centro*, Ramírez 152, is slightly dearer. The best in town is *Hotel Plaza*, actually half a block east, with rooms for US$15/25 and a downstairs restaurant-confitería. *Confitería La Candela*, on the plaza, has tasty and visually appealing sweets and pastries.

Rocha is a hub for bus travel between Montevideo and the Brazilian border. Rutas del Sol runs eight buses daily to Montevideo and five daily to Chuy via La Paloma, La Pedrera and Castillos, plus six daily to Barra Valizas (US$3.50). Cynsa has ten daily to La Paloma and nine from La Paloma back to Rocha, where you can catch their service to Chuy.

LA PALOMA

Some 28 km south of Rocha and 250 km from Montevideo, placid La Paloma (population 5000) is less developed, less expensive and much less crowded than Punta del Este, but still has almost every important comfort and amenity except Punta's hyperactive nightlife. As elsewhere on the coast, there are attractive sandy beaches in town and beyond – those to the east are less protected from ocean swells.

Orientation

La Paloma occupies a small peninsula at the south end of Ruta 15. The centre, on both sides of the Avenida Nicolás Solari, is small and very compact. Although the streets are named, the buildings, including hotels and restaurants, lack numbers and are more easily located by their relationship to prominent intersections and other landmarks. At the eastern entrance to town, on the highway to Rocha, is the woodsy Parque Andresito, an appealing camping area with excellent facilities.

Information

Tourist Office The tourist office (☎ 6088) is on the roundabout at the east end of Avenida Nicolás Solari. In summer, it's open from 8 am to 11 pm, but the rest of the year only from 9 am to 9 pm.

Money You can change US dollars cash at Banco de la República, at Avenida Nicolás Solari and Titania.

Post & Telecommunications The post office is on Avenida Nicolás Solari, just east of the ONDA bus terminal. ANTEL is on Avenida Nicolás Solari between Avenida El Navío and De La Virgen.

Lighthouse

In 1874, construction of El Faro del Cabo Santa María, the lighthouse, marked the beginning of La Paloma's growth as a summer beach resort. It's open to the public from 7 to 8 pm in summer, from 6 to 7 pm the rest of the year.

1	Lighthouse
2	Banco de la República
3	ONDA Bus Terminal
4	Post Office
5	Casino/Hotel Santa María
6	Residencial Canopus
7	Hotel Barcelo
8	Residencial La Tuna
9	Hotel Bahía
10	Residencial Trocadero
11	Hotel Embeleco
12	Hotel Viola
13	Tourist Office
14	Restaurant La Marea/ Buses CYNSA
15	Residencial Tirrenia
16	Residencial Puertas del Sol
17	Camping Parque Andresito

Organised Tours

Since public transport doesn't go to some of the more interesting sites on the coast, you may want to look at the alternatives of organised tours. In summer, Rochatur runs trips to Cabo Polonio (US$14), Chuy (US$18, lunch included), and Parque Nacional Santa Teresa.

Places to Stay

Camping *Camping Parque Andresito* (☎ 6107), at the northern entrance to town, has an 'A' sector which has amenities such as hot showers and electricity for US$5 for two persons. For US$1.50 per person, sector 'B' offers a less structured environment, no electricity, cold showers, and the chance to sneak into the sector 'A' hot showers. Both sectors share a supermarket, restaurant and other facilities, and have excellent beach access.

Hostels For budget travellers, the most reasonable accommodation is the youth hostel, *Albergue La Paloma*, in Parque Andresito. Between November and March, make reservations in Montevideo.

Residenciales & Hotels La Paloma has a wider selection of economical alternatives

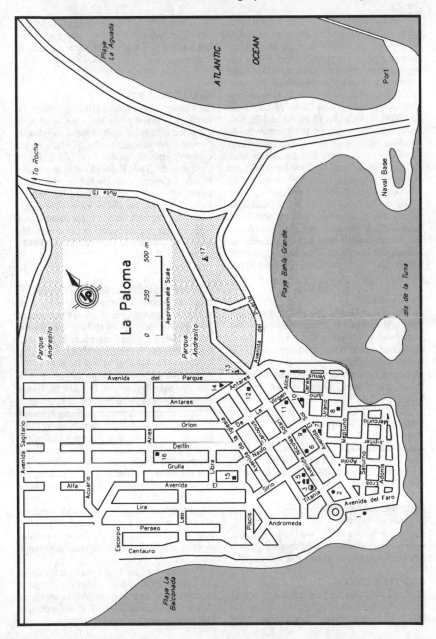

than either Punta del Este or Maldonado, such as *Residencial Puertas del Sol* (☎ 6066), on Delfín near Aries, which charges US$11 per person. Most others are slightly more expensive at around US$14 per person, including *Residencial Tirrenia* (☎ 6230) on Avenida El Navío, *Residencial Trocadero* on Juno near Ceres, *Hotel Bahía* (☎ 6029) at Avenidas El Navío and El Sol, *Residencial Canopus* (☎ 6068) on Avenida Nicoláas Solari near Sirio, and *Hotel Viola* (☎ 6020) on Avenida Nicolás Solari near Antares. *Residencial La Tuna* (☎ 6083), on Neptuno between Juno and Avenida El Navío, charges US$18 per person.

Somewhat more upscale accommodation is available at *Hotel Barcelo* (☎ 6052), on Avenida El Sol at its intersection with Urano and Jupiter, which costs US$22 per person. *Hotel Embeleco* (☎ 6108), at Avenida del Sol and De La Virgen, has rooms for US$30 per person.

Places to Eat
La Marea, on Avenida del Parque, has good, fresh and reasonably priced seafood, but the waiters are overworked and service is slow. *Hotel Bahía* and *Hotel Embeleco* also have restaurants. There are several pizzerías, including *La Currica* on Avenida Nicoláas Solari and *Ponte Vecchio* on La Aguada beach.

Getting There & Away
Buses CYNSA is on Avenida del Parque, next to Restaurant La Marea. ONDA is at Avenida Nicolás Solari and Titania, next to the Banco de la República. The bus to Rocha costs US$0.75.

AROUND LA PALOMA
Laguna de Rocha
Laguna de Rocha, 10 km west of La Paloma, is an ecological reserve. It has populations of black-necked swans, storks and waterfowl.

CABO POLONIO
East of La Paloma on Ruta 10, this is one of the wildest parts of Uruguay, with the possibility of a 10-km trip over dunes to visit a sea

lion colony – near the entrance, many people advertise rides to the reserve, which is a hefty but feasible full day's walk. Dune walking is very tiring, and be sure to take water.

AGUAS DULCES
This quaint, old-fashioned fishing village, 11 km directly south of the town of Castillos, is the place for a *really* quiet seaside holiday. It has one modest accommodation place, *Hotel Gainfor*, and an equally modest municipal campground. Taste the seafood at any of the several restaurants, but do not leave without tasting the messy but flavourful fruit of the *butía* palm, sold by almost every tiny shop.

Nearby Barra de Valizas has a youth hostel with kitchen facilities and hot showers, for which you must make reservations in Montevideo.

PARQUE NACIONAL SANTA TERESA
More an historical than a natural attraction, this coastal park 35 km south of Chuy incorporates the hilltop **Fortaleza de Santa Teresa**, begun by the Portuguese in 1762 but finished by the Spaniards after its capture by Governor Cevallos of Montevideo in 1793. Across Ruta 9, the enormous Laguna Negra and the marshes of the Bañado de Santa Teresa support a large amount of bird life.

By international standards, Santa Teresa is a very humble unit, but it attracts many Uruguayan and Brazilian visitors, offering uncrowded beaches and decentralised camping in forest plantations so irregular that they would seem natural if you didn't know that eucalyptus is native to Australia and pine to the Northern Hemisphere only. Other features include a small zoo, an indoor plant nursery, and a shade nursery. The park gets very crowded during Carnaval, but the most of the time it absorbs visitors without difficulty.

Camping fees are US$4 per site, for up to six people, with basic facilities. At park headquarters, there are abundant services, including phone and post offices, supermarket, bakery, butchery and restaurant.

CHUY

Chuy is the grubby but energetic Uruguayan-Brazilian border town at the terminus of Ruta 9, 340 km from Montevideo. Pedestrians and vehicles cross freely between the Uruguayan and Brazilian sides, which are separated only by a median strip along the main avenue which, interestingly, is Avenida Brasil on the Uruguayan side and Avenida Uruguay on the Brazilian side. There are several exchange houses along Avenida Brasil, although changing travellers' cheques is problematical.

Hotel Plaza (☎ 81), at Avenida Artigas and Arachanes, has singles for US$12, but accommodation should be cheaper on the Brazilian side. Ten km south of Chuy, on the coast, a side road leads to *Camping Chuy* and *De la Barra*, both of which charge US$5 per site for two persons, with all facilities. Local buses from Chuy go directly to both.

If proceeding beyond Chuy into Brazil, you must complete Uruguayan emigration formalities at the border post on Ruta 9, 1 km south of town. If you need a visa, Brasil has a consulate (☎ 49) at Fernández 147.

Entering Uruguay, you will find an extremely helpful and well-informed tourist office which, with a little polite cajoling, will give you a computer printout of anything you need, such as up-to-date hotel and restaurant information, for the whole department. Several bus companies connect Chuy with Montevideo, including ONDA, Avenida Brasil 587, and Rutas del Sol, Numancia 217. There is also a bus service to Treinta y Tres.

Seven km west of Chuy, do not miss the restored **Fuerte San Miguel**, a pink-granite fortress built in 1734 during the hostilities between Spain and Portugal. Its entrance protected by a moat, it overlooks the border from an isolated high point. It is closed on Monday, but you can still glimpse the interior and visit the nearby gaucho museum.

Treinta y Tres & Cerro Largo

TREINTA Y TRES

Little-visited Treinta y Tres (population 30,000) is a gaucho town in the very scenic rolling hill country of the Cuchilla Grande on the Río Olimar, inland 150 km west from Chuy and 290 km north-east of Montevideo. Founded in 1853, it is also the departmental capital. It is on the interior route to Brazil via Melo or Río Branco. The route north to Melo is one of the most beautiful in Uruguay.

Most of the main services are on the Plaza, including ONDA and Nuñez, which have eight buses daily to Melo and to Montevideo via Minas. The simple but clean and friendly, *Hotel Olimar* has singles for US$5 with shared bath, US$9 with private bath. *Restaurant London*, also on the plaza, has good, filling and inexpensive meals.

MELO

Capital of the department of Cerro Largo, 110 km north of Treinta y Tres, Melo is a transport hub for Uruguay's interior, with bus connections to Río Branco, Aceguá, and Rivera, all of which have border crossings to Brazil. Founded in 1795, the town has a few remaining colonial buildings and a stone post house which now houses the **Museo del Gaucho**.

TAMU has inexpensive flights to and from Montevideo on Monday, Thursday, Friday and Saturday. There are Brazilian consulates in Melo (☎ 2084) at Aparicio Saravia 711, in Río Branco (☎ 3) at Lavalleja and Palomeque, and in Rivera (☎ 3278) at Ceballos 1159.

Melo's Parque Rivera has a public campground, while Río Branco has a youth hostel. Look for other inexpensive accommodation around the plaza.

Paraguay

Facts about the Country

Paraguay is South America's 'empty quarter', little known even to its neighbours. For much of its history, sustained by geographical isolation, it has distanced itself from the Latin American mainstream, but economic developments since the 1970s and political developments since the late 1980s appear to have brought about irrevocable changes. Once South America's most notorious and durable police state, the country now welcomes foreign visitors and offers a number of worthwhile sights, including the riverside capital of Asunción and its scenic surroundings, the Jesuit missions of the upper Río Paraná, the massive Argentine/Paraguayan and Brazilian/Paraguayan hydroelectric projects at Itaipú and Yacyretá,

and several national parks, although access is difficult to most of them.

HISTORY

Paraguay's pre-Columbian cultural patterns were more complex than either Argentina's or Uruguay's. At the time of first European contact, Guaraní-speaking people inhabited most of what is now eastern Paraguay, whilst west of the Río Paraguay a multitude of Indian groups, known collectively as 'Guaycurú' to the Guaraní, inhabited overlapping territories in the Chaco. Among these groups were the Tobas, Matacos, Mbayás, Abiponcs and many othcrs, somc of whom are now extinct.

The Guaraní were semisedentary shifting cultivators, whilst groups of hunter-gatherers such as thc Aché (Guayakí) lived in enclaves of dense tropical and subtropical forests ncar thc borders of present-day Brazil. The Chaco Indians were mostly hunter-gatherers, who also fished along the Río Pilcomayo and other permanent watercourses.

Although predominantly a peaceful people, the Guaraní did not always refrain from venturing into Guaycurú territory and battling with them. They even raided the foothills of the Andes, where they obtained gold and silver objects which later aroused the interest of the Spaniards. The Guaycurú, for their part, did not hesitate to fight back, and later Spanish-Guaraní expeditions into the Chaco were frequently violent. Well into this century, Indian hostility deterred settlement of many parts of the region.

European Exploration & Settlement

Europeans first entered the upper Paraná in 1524 when Alejo García, a survivor of Juan de Solís' ill-fated expedition to the Banda Oriental, walked across southern Brazil, Paraguay and the Chaco to the foothills of Bolivia with Guaraní guides. Although he found silver in the Andes, García died on the

PARAGUAYAN NATIONAL PARKS

1 Parque Nacional Defensores del Chaco
2 Parque Nacional Teniente Enciso
3 Parque Nacional Tinfunqué
4 Parque Nacional Cerro Corá
5 Parque Nacional Ybycuí
6 Parque Nacional Caaguazú

Paraguay

0   100   200 km

return journey. His discoveries resulted in the renaming of the Río de Solís as the Río de la Plata (River of Silver).

Sebastián Cabot sailed up the Río Paraguay in 1527, but Pedro de Mendoza's expedition made the major advance; after failing to establish a permanent settlement at Buenos Aires, his men founded a fortress called Nuestra Señora de la Asunción on the east bank of the Río Paraguay. At Asunción, the Guaraní were far more tolerant of the Spanish presence, and made a military alliance with them against the hostile Chaco people.

The Guaraní were more sedentary than the nomadic Chaco tribes, although not as stable as the Indian civilisations of the Andes, so relations between the Indians and the Spaniards took an unusual course: the Guaraní absorbed the 350 Spaniards (and a few other Europeans) into their social system by providing them with women and, therefore, with food, since women bore the major responsibility for Guaraní agriculture. The Spaniards, in effect, became heads of the household, and the *encomienda*, when it was introduced, merely ratified this informal arrangement. The Spaniards adopted

Guaraní food, customs and even language, but cultural assimilation was a two-way process. Gradually there emerged a hybrid, Spanish-Guaraní society in which the Spaniards were politically dominant. The mestizo children of the Spaniards adopted Spanish cultural values, despite their acquisition of the Guaraní language and other local customs.

The Jesuit Missions

In the colonial period, Paraguay comprised a much larger area than it does now, and included large sections of present-day Brazil and Argentina. In part of this area, on both sides of the upper Río Paraná, Jesuit missionaries conducted a remarkable experiment, creating a series of highly organised settlements in which the Guaraní learned many aspects of European high culture as well as new crafts, crops, and methods of cultivation. For more than a century and a half, until their expulsion in 1767 because of local jealousies and Madrid's concern that their power had become too great, Jesuit organisation deterred Portuguese intervention in the region and protected the interests of the Spanish crown. For more information on the missions themselves, see the chapter on Argentine Mesopotamia.

Jesuit influence was less effective among the non-Guaraní peoples of the Chaco, whose resistance to the Spaniards discouraged any proselytising. Martin Dobrizhoffer, an Austrian Jesuit who spent nearly 20 years in the region, wrote about these people:

The savage Guaycurus, Lenguas, Mocobios, Tobas, Abipones, and Mbayas, wretchedly wasted the province with massacres and pillage, without leaving the miserable inhabitants a place to breathe in, or the means of resistance. To elude their designs, little fortlets are every where erected on the banks of the Paraguay, fitted up with a single cannon, which, being discharged whenever the savages come in sight, admonishes the neighbours to fight or fly...

For these Indians, admitted Dobrizhoffer, the Chaco was a refuge 'which the Spanish soldiers look upon as a theatre of misery, and

the savages as their Palestine and Elysium'. There, he wrote, they had 'mountains for observatories, trackless woods for fortifications, rivers and marshes for ditches, and plantations of fruit trees for storehouses...'. Having acquired the horse, groups like the Abipones and Tobas were mobile and flexible in their opposition, while the riverine Payaguá could prey upon riverboats:

These atrocious pirates, infesting the rivers Paraguay and Parana, had for many years been in the habit of intercepting Spanish vessels freighted with wares for the port of Buenos-Ayres...and of massacring the crews...

They have two sorts of canoes; the lesser for fishing and daily voyages, the larger for the uses of war. If their designs be against the Spaniards, many of them join together in one fleet, and are the more dangerous from their drawing so little water, which enables them to lurk within the shelter of the lesser rivers, or islands, till a favourable opportunity presents itself of pillaging loaden vessels, or of disembarking and attacking the colonies...For many years they continued to pillage the Spanish colonies, and all the ships that came in their way, from the city of Asumpcion, forty leagues southwards.

Several Jesuit missionaries, some like Dobrizhoffer being excellent amateur ethnographers and naturalists, managed to live among the Chaco tribes from the mid-17th century, but the area remained an Indian refuge from Europeans even into this century. After secular Spaniards discovered that the Chaco route promised neither gold nor silver, they abandoned the area entirely and the most important political and economic developments occurred east of the Río Paraguay.

Independence & the Reign of El Supremo

When Paraguayans deposed their Spanish governor and declared independence in 1811, the Spanish crown declined to contest the action by its isolated and economically insignificant colony. Within a few years, José Gaspar Rodríguez de Francia emerged as the strongest member of the governing junta. From 1814 to 1840, the autocratic Francia ruled the country as El Supremo.

In the late 16th century, Spanish official López de Velasco wrote that Paraguay had 'all which is necessary for sustenance, but no wealth in money, for...all their wealth is in the agriculture of the country'. Even in 18th-century Asunción, wrote Dobrizhoffer, money was so scarce that the 'want or ignorance of metals may be reckoned among the divine blessings and advantages of Paraguay'. Francia, recognising Paraguay's inability to compete with its neighbours, made a virtue of necessity by virtually sealing off the country's borders to commerce and promoting self-sufficiency – subsistence on a countrywide scale.

To accomplish his goals, Francia expropriated the properties of landholders, merchants and even the Church (converting monasteries into army barracks), establishing the state as the dominant economic as well as political power. The small agricultural surplus – mostly *yerba mate* and tobacco – was state controlled. Like his successors almost to the present day, Francia ruled by fear, confining his opponents in what J P Robertson, who claimed to be the first Englishman to visit Paraguay during the Francia dictatorship, described as 'state dungeons':

They are small, damp vaulted dungeons, of such contracted dimensions that to maintain an upright posture in them is impossible, except under the centre of the arch.

Here it is, that loaded with irons, with a sentinel continually in view, bereft of every comfort, left without the means of ablution, and under a positive prohibition to shave, pare their nails, or cut their hair – here, in silence, solitude and despair, the victims of the Dictator's vengeance...pass a life to which death would be preferable...The wretched, and in most cases innocent victim is left to pine away his hours in darkness and solitude.

In a precocious example of newspeak which anticipated Orwell by more than a century, Francia called his most notorious dungeon the Chamber of Truth.

Francia himself was not immune to the climate of terror. After escaping an assassination attempt in 1820, El Supremo so feared assassination that his food and drink were consistently checked for poison, no one could approach him closer than six paces, the streets were cleared for his carriage, and he slept in a different place every night. In 1840 he died a natural death, and was replaced by Carlos Antonio López. In 1870, political opponents who knew how to keep a grudge disinterred Francia's remains and threw them into the Río Paraguay.

The López 'Dynasty' & the War of the Triple Alliance

With the income from state enterprises, Carlos Antonio López ended Paraguay's extreme isolation, building railways, a telegraph, an iron foundry, a shipyard and – most importantly – an army. He ruled just as autocratically as Francia, leaving Paraguay with a standing army of 28,000 men and another 40,000 reserves by the early 1860s (Argentina, at the time, had only 6000 men in uniform). His son, the megalomaniacal Francisco Solano López, led the country into the catastrophic War of the Triple Alliance against Argentina, Uruguay and Brazil.

Supporting a federalist Blanco faction in Uruguay, Solano López marched his forces across the Argentine territory of Misiones and even captured Corrientes, but Triple Alliance forces destroyed his navy and, after four years, captured Asunción. Solano López retreated into the bush but died, in 1870, at the hands of Brazilian forces at Cerro Corá, near present-day Pedro Juan Caballero.

Paraguay lost 150,000 sq km of territory but, even worse, also lost much of its population through combat, famine and disease – it was often said that only women, children, and burros remained. By some contemporary accounts, women outnumbered men three to one at the end of the war; others said that the country lost more than half its population, but recent research indicates that the total loss may not have exceeded 20%. Still, this was a blow from which the country has never quite recovered.

Reconstruction & the Chaco War

After 1870, despite a new constitution, Paraguay underwent a sustained period of political instability. As borders opened, a trickle of European and Argentine immigrants arrived to resuscitate the agricultural economy, but political life did not stabilise for decades. The Colorado party, formed in 1887, helped re-establish the country as a sovereign state, encouraged agricultural development and brought about reforms in public education. The other major party, the Liberals, took power after the turn of the century.

About this time, tension began to arise between Paraguay and Bolivia over the ill-defined borders of the Chaco, which neither country effectively occupied. As early as 1907, both began to build fortifications, but full-scale hostilities did not erupt until 1932. After a cease-fire in 1935, which left no clear victor, a peace treaty awarded Paraguay three-quarters of the territory in dispute. The country paid dearly, however, both financially and in the loss of another sizable portion of its population.

The reasons underlying the war were unclear. Certainly the Paraguayans, by encouraging Mennonite immigrants to settle in the Chaco, had provoked the Bolivian government. Bolivia's war effort, on the other hand, was rumoured to have been underwritten by oil companies – one Paraguayan tourist brochure remarks that maverick United States Senator Huey Long, for whom a settlement on the Ruta Trans-Chaco (Trans-Chaco highway) is named, was assassinated for attacking Standard's involvement on behalf of Bolivia. In any event, no oil was ever discovered and the region is still a thinly populated backwater.

Modern Developments

After the end of the Chaco war, Paraguay endured more than a decade of disorder until the end of a brief civil war which returned the Colorados to power in 1949. A military coup in 1954 removed the constitutional president and brought to power General Alfredo Stroessner who, despite completely bogus elections ('guided democracy'), ruled the country for 35 years in a manner which,

in the Soviet Union, would have been denounced as a 'cult of personality'.

Since Stroessner's overthrow by General Andrés Rodríguez in 1989, even a concerted effort has been unable to eradicate the thousands of monuments to General Stroessner and his relatives, despite measures such as the renaming of the city of Puerto Presidente Stroessner (now Ciudad del Este). Some Paraguayans even express a certain nostalgia for Stroessner, (now suffering poor health and in Brazilian exile), who has publicly sought permission to return to Asunción. Most, though, appreciate the demise of the Stroessner police state even if sceptical that it will bring any benefits beyond the freedom to say publicly what they have always thought.

For more information on the Stroessner regime and its successor, see the Government section below.

GEOGRAPHY & CLIMATE

Landlocked and isolated in the heart of South America, surrounded by gigantic Brazil, Argentina and Bolivia, Paraguay appears much smaller than it really is. With an area of 407,000 sq km, the country is slightly larger than Germany and almost exactly the size of California. More than half the country is forested, but most of its timber has little commercial value.

The Río Paraguay, which connects the capital of Asunción with the Río Paraná, the rest of the River Plate drainage and the Atlantic Ocean, divides the country into two unequal halves. In the smaller eastern sector, comprising about 40% of the national territory and containing the great majority of the population, a well-watered, elevated plateau of rolling grasslands with patches of subtropical forest separates the valley of the Río Paraguay from the upper Paraná, which forms much of Paraguay's borders with Brazil and Argentina. The Paraná constitutes an outstanding hydroelectric resource whose development may turn Paraguay into an energy colony of its larger neighbours. Mineral resources, including petroleum, are almost nonexistent.

Eastern Paraguay's climate is humid, with rainfall distributed fairly evenly throughout the year. In the east, near the Brazilian border, it averages an abundant 2000 mm per annum, and declines to about 1500 mm near Asunción. Since elevations do not exceed 600 metres, temperatures are almost uniformly hot in summer – the average maximum temperature in December, January and February is 35°C. Winter temperatures are milder, with an average maximum of 22°C in July, the coldest month, although frosts are not unknown. Paraguay is vulnerable to cold fronts known as *pamperos* which work their way north from temperate Argentina in the spring and autumn, causing temperatures to fall dramatically – as much as 20°C in only a few hours.

Paraguay's western sector is an extensive plain, known as the Chaco. Only about 4% of all Paraguayans live in the Chaco, whose principal economic activity is cattle ranching on very large estancias. Temperatures are even higher than in eastern Paraguay, often exceeding 40°C, and rainfall is erratic, as high rates of evaporation make rain-fed agriculture undependable where precipitation does not exceed 1000 mm. German Mennonite immigrants have nevertheless successfully raised cotton and other commercial crops in the region.

FLORA & FAUNA

Paraguay's vegetation correlates strongly with rainfall and diminishes from east to west. Its humid subtropical forest is densest in the moist valleys of eastern Paraguay, near the Brazilian frontier, and more sparse on the thinner upland soils. The most important tree species are *lapacho (Tabebula* species), *trebol (Amburana cearensis), peroba (Aspidosperma polyneuron)* and *guatambú (Balfourodendron riedelanium)*. Between this forest and the Río Paraguay, the dominant vegetation is savanna, with occasional gallery forests along watercourses, while west of the Río Paraguay, palm savanna gradually gives way to scrub and thorn forest, including the valuable *quebracho* tree, a source of natural tannin. Throughout the country, there is a particular abundance of aroid plants (such as philodendrons) and orchids.

Paraguayan wildlife is equally diverse, but the dense human population of rural eastern Paraguay has put great pressure on the region's fauna. Paraguayan mammals in danger of extinction include the giant anteater, maned wolf, river otter, Brazilian tapir, jaguar, and two species of marsh deer. One modest but notable wildlife success has been the rediscovery in the mid-1970s of the Chacoan peccary, thought to be extinct for at

least half a century, and its nurture by a joint effort of Paraguayan and international conservationists.

Bird life is abundant throughout the country, but especially in the Chaco. Paraguay has 21 species of parrots and parakeets, including the stunning hyacinthine macaw and the nearly extinct spix macaw in the eastern forests, a southerly extension of the Brazilian Pantanal. The most visible and impressive species are the jabirú and wood storks of the Chaco, among others. In the riverine lowlands, there are numerous reptiles, including two species of caiman, anaconda and boa constrictor. Short-term visitors are unlikely to see the truly rare species, but have a good chance of seeing many reptiles which they have never seen before.

National Parks

Paraguay has half a dozen national parks and several lesser reserves protecting a variety of habitats throughout the country. The three largest parks are in the Chaco, while the three smaller and more biologically diverse units are in eastern Paraguay. For more detailed information on Paraguayan parks or reserves, contact the Fundación Moisés Bertoni (☎ 21-2386), 25 de Mayo 2140 in Asunción, which operates convenient and reasonably priced tours.

Unfortunately, because of corruption, economic pressure, and traditionally weak political commitment, some of Paraguay's parks have experienced serious disruption in a country whose natural diversity is impressive. Despite these difficulties, organisations like the Fundación Moisés Bertoni have accomplished a great deal by publicising environmental issues both locally and abroad and facilitating visits to the parks.

Parque Nacional Defensores del Chaco

In the semi-arid north-west Chaco, 830 km from Asunción, this 780,000-hectare park is by far the country's largest, although direct protective activities are minimal over most of the area. Its dominant vegetation is thorn forest of *quebracho*, *algarrobo* and *palo*

santo, and large mammals include jaguar, puma, tapir, peccary and monkeys. Access is very difficult but not impossible.

Parque Nacional Tinfunqué

On the Río Pilcomayo, 300 km from Asunción, this 280,000-hectare unit of savanna and marshlands is the second-largest park in the country. Consisting entirely of private estancias, it is effectively a paper park, with neither a management plan nor direct protective activities, but landowners do not object to visitors. Wildlife includes capybara, swamp deer, caiman, and a great variety of bird life.

Parque Nacional Teniente Enciso

In the semi-arid upper Chaco, 665 km from Asunción on the Ruta Trans-Chaco, 40,000-hectare Teniente Enciso features low, dense thorn forest and wildlife similar to that of the larger and less accessible Defensores del Chaco. Managed jointly by the Ministry of Defence and the Ministry of Agriculture and Livestock, it has park rangers and some visitor facilities.

Parque Nacional Caaguazú

Tripled in size by recent acquisitions, 18,000-hectare Caaguazú is an area of mixed secondary Brazilian rainforest with considerable historical and anthropological interest, situated 250 km south-east of Asunción in the department of Caazapá. There are several cave sites with aboriginal inscriptions. The most common wildlife species are the coatimundi, deer and reptiles. Because of pressure from colonists, its size has been reduced from an original 200,000 hectares and direct protective activities are few.

Parque Nacional Cerro Corá

In the department of Amambay, 500 km from Asunción, 22,000-hectare Cerro Corá is probably the most scenic of Paraguay's parks, with transitional humid subtropical forest among isolated peaks up to 450 metres. It also features numerous cave sites and was the scene of a famous battle at which Marshal López died during the War of the Triple Alliance.

Paraguay
Departments & Capitals

0   100   200 km

The park has a visitor centre, camping area, and several *cabañas* (cabins) where visitors can lodge.

Parque Nacional Ybycuí In the department of Paraguarí only 150 km from Asunción, 5000-hectare Ybycuí, with its humid subtropical forest, is the most accessible and probably best managed of Paraguay's parks, despite the presence of illegal colonists and problems with timber poachers. There are several self-guided nature trails, a longer backpack trail, a visitor centre and a campground, plus the ruins of Paraguay's first iron

foundry. A small restaurant serves meals on weekends.

GOVERNMENT

On paper, Paraguay is a republic whose 1967 constitution establishes a strong president, popularly elected for a five-year term, who in turn appoints a 10-member cabinet to assist in governing. Congress consists of a 60-member Chamber of Deputies and a 30-member Senate, elected concurrently with the president. Administratively, the country comprises 19 departments governed by delegates appointed by the president.

In practice, Paraguay has been one of the western hemisphere's most odious and durable dictatorships. Electoral politics has been extremely corrupt and is controlled by the government, which has permitted only token opposition. Lack of any limitation to presidential or congressional terms helped solidify the Stroessner dictatorship for 35 years until Stroessner was overthrown in early 1989.

Historically, the electoral system is simple and unrepresentative. The party with the most votes automatically gains two-thirds of the seats in Congress, effectively marginalising the opposition. Controlling the machinery of government, the Colorado Party has been the dominant formal organisation in Paraguayan political life since the civil war of 1947, when it defeated the forces of the Liberal Party and the Revolutionary Febreristas. For most of this period, the Colorados have depended on Stroessner and the Paraguayan military for their privileged status.

Both the Liberals and the Febreristas, a moderate labour-oriented party, have continued to operate within the stringent bounds of acceptable public dialogue, but others, including Liberal and Colorado factions, have boycotted bogus elections. With the Liberals and Febreristas, the Christian Democrats and MOPOCO (a dissident Colorado faction) have constituted the Acuerdo Nacional (national accord) of political opposition. Radical leftist opponents of the Stroessner government have been tortured to death.

Shortly after deposing Stroessner in 1989, General Andrés Rodríguez won the presidency, unopposed, in an election in which the entire spectrum of opposition parties obtained a larger percentage of congressional seats than ever before. In December 1991, in what was probably the fairest election ever held in Paraguay (which may be faint praise), General Rodríguez's Colorado Party won a legislative majority.

Even before the 1991 election, however, political activity and dialogue had flourished on a scale unprecedented in Paraguayan history. Whether these promising developments will result in an enduring democracy is still uncertain because of Paraguay's authoritarian tradition and continuity among the entrenched Colorado elite. One of the great ironies of Stroessner's overthrow was Rodríguez's triumphant appearance on Paraguayan television with his daughter and grandchildren – also Stroessner's grandchildren, since Rodríguez's daughter is married to Stroessner's son, Gustavo. So far, Paraguayans have managed to keep it in the family.

ECONOMY

Historically, Paraguay's economy has depended on agriculture and livestock. Its principal exports have been beef, maize, sugar cane, soybeans, lumber and cotton, but a large proportion of the rural populace cultivates subsistence crops on small landholdings, selling any surplus on local markets and labouring on large estancias and plantations to supplement the household income. High transport costs, due primarily to Paraguay's landlocked isolation, have driven the cost of its exports up in comparison with other Latin American countries.

While Paraguay lacks mineral energy resources, it has begun to develop its abundant hydroelectric potential over the past 15 years through its participation with Brazil and Argentina in enormous dam projects. Brazil takes most of the electricity from Itaipú, located on the upper Paraná above Ciudad del Este, while corruption-plagued Yacyretá, on the border with the Argentine province of Corrientes, may never be finished (see the chapter on Argentine Mesopotamia). While Paraguay has benefited from playing off South America's major economic and military powers against each other, it risks becoming an energy colony, especially if the price of competing sources of energy drops and Paraguay cannot repay its share of capital costs, which Brazil and Argentina have already paid, and maintenance.

Paraguayan industry, which consists for the most part of the processing of agricultural products, benefits little from this enormous hydroelectric capacity. The slowdown in construction with the completion of Itaipú and Yacyretá's continuing problems have nearly eliminated the economic growth of the 1970s. In fact, Paraguay's major industry is contraband, most of which passes through Ciudad del Este to or from Brazil. According to Brazilian estimates, US$1 billion of electronic equipment was smuggled from Paraguay in 1987, whilst Brazilian soybean and coffee producers have sold their crops illegally in Paraguay because of advantageous exchange rates and avoidance of Brazilian taxes. Paraguayan importers, including high-ranking military officials, have re-exported these commodities to Brazil. Stolen cars and illegal drugs, including cocaine, are other unfortunate goods which pass into or through Paraguay.

POPULATION & PEOPLE

Paraguay has a population of 4.8 million, approximately one-seventh that of California, with which it shares almost the same geographical size. With 800,000 residents, Asunción is by far the largest city, but only 43% of Paraguayans live in cities, compared with more than 80% in Argentina and Uruguay. Many Paraguayans are peasant cultivators who produce a small surplus for sale.

By world and even South American standards of welfare, Paraguayans rank relatively low. Infant mortality rates are higher than any other South American country except Colombia, Bolivia and Peru, and the life expectancy of 65 years is lower than any other country in South America except Bolivia and Peru. For both political and economic reasons, many Paraguayans live outside the country, mostly in Brazil and Argentina – between 1950 and 1970, more than 350,000 Paraguayans sought work in Argentina. Many political exiles have returned since the overthrow of the Stroessner dictatorship.

More than 75% of Paraguayans are mestizos, of mixed Spanish-Guaraní heritage. Almost all of these are bilingual, speaking

Guaraní by preference, although Spanish is the language of government and commerce. Even upper-class Paraguayans speak Guaraní, however.

About 20% of Paraguayans are descendants of European immigrants. Since the 1930s, agricultural settlement by German Mennonites, who have prospered in the difficult environment of the central Chaco, has caused ethnic friction and continuing problems with some Indian groups. Japanese immigrants have settled in parts of eastern Paraguay, along with Brazilian agricultural colonists, many of German origin, who have moved across the border in recent years. Asunción has seen a substantial influx of Koreans, who are mostly involved in commerce.

In the Chaco and in scattered areas of eastern Paraguay, there are small but significant populations of indigenous people, some of whom, until very recently, still relied on hunting and gathering for their livelihood.

According to many credible accounts, the Stroessner dictatorship conducted an active campaign of genocide against the Aché (Guayakí) Indians of eastern Paraguay in the 1970s.

Most of Paraguay's Indians are in the Chaco, where isolated groups such as the Ayoreo lived almost untouched by European civilisation until very recently. The largest groups are the Nivaclé and Lengua, both of whom number around 10,000. Many of them have become dependent labour for the region's agricultural colonists. In total, Indians comprise only about 3% of the population.

EDUCATION

Education is compulsory to the age of 12 only. In the country as a whole, literacy is only 81%, the lowest of the River Plate republics but higher than all the Andean countries except Ecuador. Higher education is the province of the Universidad Nacional and the Universidad Católica in Asunción.

ARTS

Novelist and poet Augusto Roa Bastos recently put Paraguay on the international literary map by winning the Spanish government's Cervantes Prize, but very little Paraguayan literature is available to English-speaking readers; for more details, see the Books & Maps section in the Paraguay Facts for the Visitor chapter.

As in Buenos Aires and Montevideo, theatre is a popular medium, with occasional offerings in Guaraní as well as Spanish. In 1933, during the Chaco war, Asunción theatregoers swarmed to see the Guaraní dramatist Julio Correa's *Guerra Ayaa*. The visual arts are very important and popular; Asunción has numerous galleries, most notably the Museo del Barro, which emphasises modern, sometimes very unconventional, works. Both classical and folk music are performed at venues in Asunción.

Paraguay's most famous traditional craft is the production of multicoloured ñandutí lace in the Asunción suburb of Itauguá.

Paraguayan harps and guitars are made in the village of Luque, while other high-calibre artisanal goods come from the Indian communities of the Chaco. While production for sale rather than for use may have debased the quality of certain items, such as spears and knives, wood carvings are truly appealing.

CULTURE

English-speaking visitors will find Paraguay more 'exotic' than either Argentina or Uruguay because of its unique racial and cultural mix; however, Paraguayans in general are eager to meet and speak with foreign visitors. Take advantage of any invitation to drink *mate*, often in the form of ice-cold *tereré*, which can be a good introduction to Paraguay and its people.

In the Mennonite colonies of the Chaco, an ability to speak German will quickly dissolve barriers in this culturally insular community. It is much more difficult, however, to make contact with the indigenous people of the region, and it is undiplomatic to probe too quickly into the relations between the two, which are a controversial subject. From regular contact with the Mennonites, many Chaco Indians speak German rather than Spanish as a second language.

Paraguayans in general are very sports-minded; the most popular soccer team, Olímpia, has beaten the best Argentine sides. Tennis and basketball have also become popular spectator sports, but golf and squash are exclusively the province of the elite.

RELIGION

Roman Catholicism is Paraguay's official religion, but folk variants are important and the Church is weaker and less influential than in most other Latin American countries. One 19th-century visitor, undoubtedly a Protestant, wrote that:

Paraguayans were steeped in religious ignorance and floundering in idolatry...The priests were ignorant and immoral, great cockfighters and gamblers, possessing vast influence over the women, a power which they turn to the basest of purposes.

Traditionally, Paraguay's isolation and the state's indifference to religion have resulted in a wide variety of irregular religious practices – according to one anthropologist, rural Paraguayans view priests more as healers or magicians than spiritual advisers. It is also true that women are far more religious than men.

Protestant sects have made fewer inroads in Catholic Paraguay than in some other Latin American countries, although fundamentalist Mennonites have proselytised amongst Chaco Indians since the 1930s. Other evangelical groups, including the highly controversial New Tribes Mission, have operated with the collusion and, some say, active support, of the Stroessner dictatorship. This regime was no friend to the country's indigenous people, who, of course, have their own religious beliefs, many of which they have retained or only slightly modified, despite nominal allegiance to Catholicism or evangelical Protestantism.

LANGUAGE

Paraguay is officially bilingual in Spanish and Guaraní, a legacy of the early colonial period when the outnumbered Spaniards had no alternative but to interact with the indigenous population. Guaraní has undoubtedly been influenced by Spanish, but it has also modified Spanish in its vocabulary and pattern of speech. During the Chaco war of the 1930s, Guaraní enjoyed resurgent popularity for both practical and nationalist reasons when, for security purposes, field commanders prohibited the use of Spanish on the battlefield.

Several other Indian languages are spoken in the Chaco and isolated parts of eastern Paraguay, including Lengua, Nivaclé, and Aché.

Common Guaraní Words & Phrases

The following is a small sample of Guaraní words and phrases which many travellers may find useful, if only to break the ice.

Those given are not so consistently phonetic as Spanish, but are still fairly easy to pronounce. A few, it will be obvious, have been adapted from the Spanish.

I	*she*
you	*nde*
we	*ñande*
this	*péva*
that	*amóa*
no	*nahániri*
all	*entéro*
many	*hetá*
big	*guazú*
small	*mishí*
one	*peteí*
two	*mokoi*
eat	*okarú*
drink	*hoiú*
water	*i*
meat	*soó*
hot	*hakú*
cold	*roí*
woman	*kuñá*
man	*kuimbaé*
person	*hente*
road	*tapé*
rain	*amá*
cloud	*araí*
mountain	*sero*
new	*piahú*
good	*porá*
name	*héra*

How are you?
   kuñakarai?
Fine, and you?
   Iporãiterei...ha nde?
I'm fine, too.
   Iporãiterei avei.
Where are you from?
   Moõguápa nde?
I'm from Australia.
   Che Australia gua.
How are you?
   Moõpa reiko?
I live in California.
   Che aiko California pe.

Facts for the Visitor

Travellers will find Paraguay similar to Argentina and Uruguay in some respects, but very different in others. Only facts for the visitor which differ significantly from the other River Plate republics are mentioned below.

VISAS & EMBASSIES

Paraguay requires visas of all foreigners, except those from neighbouring countries (who need only national identification cards) and nationals of most Western European countries and the USA. According to the Paraguayan Consulate in Washington, DC, Canadians, Australians and New Zealanders need a clean police record and a bank statement and must pay a fee of US$10 for a visa. Canadians should do this through the Paraguayan Consulate in New York. French visitors also require visas.

All visitors need a tourist card, valid for 90 days, which is obtained at the airport or overland border crossing and costs US$3. At some overland crossings, officials will accept local currency only.

Paraguayan Embassies & Consulates

Paraguay has diplomatic representation in neighbouring countries and overseas, although its network is not so extensive as Argentina's.

Argentina
  Maipú 464, Buenos Aires (☎ 322-6536)
Australia
  Paraguay does not have diplomatic representation in Australia.
Bolivia
  Avenida Arce, Edificio Venus, La Paz (☎ 322-018)
Brazil
  No 1208, Rua do Carmo 20, Centro, Río de Janeiro (☎ 242-9671)
  10th floor, Avenida São Luis 112, São Paulo (☎ 255-7818)
Chile
  Huérfanos 896, Santiago (☎ 39-4640)

UK
  Braemar Lodge, Cornwall Gardens, London SW7 4AQ (☎ (071) 937-1253)
USA
  2400 Massachusetts Ave NW, Washington, DC (☎ 483-6960)
  7205 NW 19th St, Miami, Fl (☎ 477-4002)
  Suite 1947, 1 World Trade Center, New York, NY (☎ 432-0733)
  8322 Seaport Drive, Huntington Beach, Ca (☎ 969-2955)

Foreign Embassies & Consulates in Paraguay

South American countries, the USA and most Western European countries have diplomatic representation in Asunción, but Australians and New Zealanders must depend on their consulates in Buenos Aires or upon the British Consulate.

Both Argentina and Brazil have consulates in border towns. These are mentioned in the appropriate chapters of the text.

Argentina
  cnr Avenidas España & Perú (☎ 21-2320/5)
Belgium
  5th floor, Juan O'Leary 409 (☎ 44-4075)
Bolivia
  Calle Eligio Ayala 2002 (☎ 20-3654)
Brazil
  3rd floor, General Díaz 523 (☎ 44-8084)
Canada
  Avenida Artigas 2006 (Honorary Consul) (☎ 29-3301)
Chile
  Guido Spano 1687 (☎ 60-0671)
France
  Avenida España 676 (☎ 23111)
Germany
  Venezuela 241 (☎ 24006)
Israel
  3rd floor, Cnr Juan O'Leary & General Díaz (☎ 49-5097)
Italy
  Avenida Mariscal López 1104 (☎ 25918)
Japan
  Avenida Mariscal López 2364 (☎ 60-4616)
Peru
  Avenida Mariscal López 648 (☎ 20-0949)
Spain
  3rd floor, 25 de Mayo 171 (☎ 49-0686)

UK
>   4th floor, Presidente Franco 706 (☎ 44-4472)
Uruguay
>   Cnr Avenida Brasilia & Siria (☎ 25022)
USA
>   Avenida Mariscal López 1776 (☎ 20-1041)

DOCUMENTS

Passports are necessary for many everyday transactions, such as cashing travellers' cheques, checking into hotels, and passing the various military and police checkpoints in the Chaco. Paraguay requires that foreign drivers possess the International Driving Permit, although document checks are perfunctory.

CUSTOMS

Paraguayan customs officially admit 'reasonable quantities' of personal effects, alcohol and tobacco; since contraband is the national sport, however, officials at overland crossings wink at anything which is not flagrantly illegal. At Ciudad del Este, customs officials declined even to look at our car, let alone process its papers (although our Argentine number plates may have been a factor in our being treated so routinely).

MONEY

The unit of currency is the *guaraní* (plural guaraníes), indicated by a capital letter 'G' with a forward slash (₲). Banknote values are 100, 500, 1000, 5000 and 10,000 guaraníes, and there are coins for 1, 5, 10, 20, 50 and 100 guaraníes.

Inflation in Paraguay is much less serious than in Argentina, and prices in general are slightly lower than in Uruguay. Money is readily exchanged at casas de cambio in Asunción, Ciudad del Este, Encarnación and Pedro Juan Caballero, but banks are the rule in the interior. Street changers give slightly lower rates than cambios, but can be helpful on weekends or in the evening, when cambios are closed.

Most better hotels, restaurants and shops in Asunción accept credit cards, but their use is less common outside the capital.

Exchange Rates

Exchange houses accept travellers' cheques at slightly lower rates than cash dollars, and sometimes charge commissions, although these are not as high as those levied in Argentina. German marks are more welcome in Asunción than in other South American capitals, although prices are given in US dollars, still the most popular foreign currency. There is no black market.

A$1	=	₲971.36
US$1	=	₲1281.48
UK£1	=	₲2202.63
FFr1	=	₲228.02
It£1	=	₲1.03
DM1	=	₲769.09
UrgN$1	=	₲0.53
BraCr1	=	₲0.72
Arg$1	=	₲1296.87
Bol$1	=	₲340.82

WHEN TO GO & WHAT TO BRING

Because of Paraguay's intense summer heat, most visitors from midlatitudes will prefer the winter months from, say, May to August or September, when the country will seem positively spring-like. Days will normally be warm, but nights can be very cool, and frosts are not unusual.

Because of the heat, Paraguayans dress very informally. Light cotton clothing will suffice for almost all conditions except in winter, but a sweater or light jacket is advisable for changeable spring weather. If spending any time outdoors in the brutal tropical sun, do not neglect a wide-brimmed hat or baseball cap, a lightweight long-sleeved shirt, and sunblock. Mosquito repellent is imperative in the Chaco and many other places.

TOURIST OFFICES

There are fewer tourist offices in Paraguay than in Argentina or Uruguay, and they are less well organised. They can be found in Asunción, Encarnación, Ciudad del Este and a few other places.

Foreign Representatives

The larger Paraguayan consulates, such as in New York and Los Angeles (see the list above), usually have a tourist representative in their delegation.

Líneas Aéreas Paraguayuas

In many countries, local representatives of Líneas Aéreas Paraguayas (LAP) serve as Paraguay's de facto tourist representative, and distribute an excellent information package which, at least in the United States, they will send free on request. This includes their glossy in-flight magazine, *Dimensión*, and also a thick multicolour brochure on Paraguayan natural history, with informative text as well as photographs.

Besides the regular numbers below, LAP has toll free numbers for Florida (☎ 1-800-432-1934); California (☎ 1-800-832-8388); and the rest of the United States (☎ 1-800-327-3551).

Belgium
    Blvd de L'Imperatrice 66/68, Brussels (☎ 513-6190)
France
    25 Rue de Ponthieu, Paris (☎ 891-934)
Germany
    Kaiserstrasse 33, Frankfurt (☎ 233-751)
Spain
    Plaza de los Mostenses s/n, Madrid (☎ 241-9253)
Switzerland
    4, Rue Winkelrield, Geneva (☎ 325-686)
USA
    Suite 920, 510 W Sixth St, Los Angeles, Ca (☎ 627-7681)
    Suite 875, 7270 NW 12th St, Miami, Fl (☎ 591-1916)
    Suite 576, 3834 Peachtree Rd, Atlanta, Ga (☎ 233-2717)
    Suite 1007, 11 E Adams, Chicago Il (☎ 922-6576)
    Suite 1919, 342 Madison Ave, New York, NY (☎ 972-3830)
    Suite 1264, 3701 Kirby Drive, Houston, Tx (☎ 524-0885)

USEFUL ORGANISATIONS

For visitors interested in natural history and conservation, the Fundación Moisés Bertoni (☎ 21-2386), 25 de Mayo 2140, Asunción, is an indispensable organisation which welcomes foreign visitors. Named after a 19th-century Swiss-Paraguayan naturalist, it sponsors projects which encourage biological diversity and restoration of degraded ecosystems, cooperates with the state in strengthening national parks and other reserves, promotes environmental education and research, and tries to involve Paraguayan citizens and private enterprise in conservation. It also offers reasonably priced tours to Paraguayan reserves which are otherwise difficult to reach.

The governmental organisation in charge of Paraguay's national parks, working in concert with the Fundación Moisés Bertoni and the US Peace Corps, is the Ministry of Agriculture's Servicio Forestal Nacional (☎ 44-5214), 12th floor, 25 de Mayo 640, Asunción.

For motorists, the Touring y Automóvil Club Paraguayo is less widespread and useful than its Argentine equivalent, but has some maps and useful booklets. Contact its Asunción office (☎ 24366) on the corner of Calle Brasil and 25 de Mayo.

BUSINESS HOURS & HOLIDAYS

Most shops are open weekdays and Saturdays from 7 am to noon, then close until midafternoon and stay open until 7 or 8 pm. Banking hours are usually 7.30 to 11 am weekdays, but exchange houses keep longer hours.

Because of the summer heat, Paraguayans go to work very early – in summer, from mid-November to mid-March, government offices open as early as 6.30 am and usually close before noon.

1 January
    Año Nuevo (New Year's Day)
3 February
    Día de San Blas (Patron Saint of Paraguay)
1 March
    Cerro Corá (Death of Marshal López)
March/April (dates vary)
    Viernes Santo/Pascua (Good Friday/Easter)
1 May
    Día de los Trabajadores (Labour Day)
15 May
    Independencia Patria (Independence Day)

12 June
> *Paz del Chaco* (End of Chaco War)

15 August
> *Fundación de Asunción* (Founding of Asunción)

29 September
> *Victoria de Boquerón* (Battle of Boquerón)

8 December
> *Día de la Virgen* (Immaculate Conception)

25 December
> *Navidad* (Christmas Day)

POST & TELECOMMUNICATIONS

Postal rates are cheaper in Paraguay than in Argentina or Uruguay but, as elsewhere in Latin America, truly essential mail should be registered. Antelco is the state telephone monopoly, with central long-distance offices which resemble those of ENTel in Argentina and ANTEL in Uruguay. Central offices in Asunción have fibre optic lines with direct connections to operators in the USA and Japan. Credit card or collect calls to the United States and other overseas destinations are cheaper than paying locally. For local calls, public phone boxes are few and far between.

TIME

Paraguay is three hours behind GMT except in summer, when daylight saving time adds an extra hour.

BOOKS & MAPS

Paraguay's pre-eminent literary figure is poet-novelist Augusto Roa Bastos, winner of the Spanish government's Cervantes Prize for literary excellence in 1990. Although he has spent much of his adult life in exile from the Stroessner dictatorship, Roa Bastos has focused on Paraguayan themes and history in the larger context of politics and dictatorship.

Some of his best work is available in English. *Son of Man* (New York, Monthly Review Press, 1988), originally published in 1961, is a novel tying together several episodes in Paraguayan history, including the Francia dictatorship and the Chaco War. *I the Supreme* (New York, Knopf, 1986), is an historical novel about the paranoid dictator, Francia.

Works by other important Paraguayan writers, such as novelist Gabriel Casaccia and poet Elvio Romero, are not readily available in English.

History

Despite a slightly misleading title, J Richard Gorham's edited collection *Paraguay: Ecological Essays* (Miami, Academy of the Arts and Sciences of the Americas, 1973), contains excellent material on pre-Columbian and colonial Paraguayan history and geography. For a standard account of rural Paraguay in historical context, see Elman and Helen Service's *Tobatí: Paraguayan Town* (University of Chicago, 1954). Harris Gaylord Warren's *Rebirth of the Paraguayan Republic* (University of Pittsburgh, 1985) tells the story of Paraguay's incomplete recovery, under the direction of the Colorado party, from the disaster of the War of the Triple Alliance.

The Stroessner Era For a general account of human rights abuses under Stroessner, see *Rule by Fear: Paraguay After Thirty Years Under Stroessner* (New York, Americas Watch, 1985). Richard Arens' edited collection *Genocide in Paraguay* (Philadelphia, Temple University Press, 1976) is an account of the Paraguayan government's role in the attempted extermination of the Aché Indians. Carlos Miranda's *The Stroessner Era* (Boulder, Colorado, Westview Press, 1990) is a thoughtful, nonpolemical analysis of Stroessner's rise and consolidation of power, plus a short political obituary.

Travel Guides & Maps

Although the maps available of Asunción are adequate, those representing places outside the capital are not even mediocre. The best country map comes from the Instituto Geográfico Militar on Avenida Artigas, but they're not giving away any secrets. The Touring y Automóvil Club Paraguayo sells an *Hoja de Rutas* booklet which, despite serious cartographic shortcomings, has much useful information. In Filadelfia, it is possible to purchase an excellent, detailed map of the Mennonite colonies.

Conozca Paraguay, also known as the *Guía Turística Márquez*, is a regularly updated guidebook in Spanish, Portuguese and somewhat fractured English. It's as loaded with advertisements as it is with text, but if you're spending more than a week or so in the country it can be a useful resource. It costs about US$8 at most downtown bookshops. For amusement, read the bizarre theory of the Director of the Instituto Paraguayo de Ciencias del Hombre, who maintains that some groups of Guaraní were descendants of Vikings who crossed into Paraguay from Perú in the 13th century! This section appears only in the Spanish and Portuguese texts, however.

MEDIA

Historically, the Stroessner dictatorship severely punished press criticism, closed opposition papers, jailed editors and reporters, and monitored foreign press agencies.

Nevertheless, Asunción's daily *ABC Color* made its reputation as nearly the sole opposition to Stroessner, despite being subject to severe restrictions. An independent radio station, Radio Ñandutí, also criticised the Stroessner regime. The newspaper *Ultima Hora* is relatively independent, but *Hoy* and *Patria* (the official Colorado party newspaper) are controlled by Stroessner relatives. *El Pueblo*, a small circulation organ of the Revolutionary Febrerista party, is independent of the government, but has had little impact

The German community in Asunción publishes a twice-monthly newspaper, *Neues für Alle*, which is widely distributed among German speakers throughout the country. The *Buenos Aires Herald* and other Argentine newspapers are available in Asunción, at a kiosk on the corner of Chile and Calle Palma.

FILM & PHOTOGRAPHY

Asunción is one of the best places in South America to buy film, with Fujichrome 100 slide film readily available for about US$5 per roll without developing. This is suitable for Paraguay's tropical light conditions and verdant greens, although in the dense subtropical rainforests of eastern Paraguay it would be useful to have high-speed film, which is much more expensive and best brought from overseas.

HEALTH

According to US Peace Corps volunteers, Paraguay presents few health problems for travellers. In 1990, it was feared that a volunteer had contracted Chagas' disease. This is an ailment transmitted by the *vinchuca*, a biting insect which frequents dwellings with thatched roofs and dirt floors. It's a particularly nasty disease, with an incubation period of many years. When it finally manifests itself, the heart virtually explodes and the victim dies suddenly. There is no effective cure. However, it was later realised that the volunteer's original diagnosis was wrong, so hopefully Chagas' disease won't be a problem in Paraguay.

Peace Corps officials recommend that volunteers follow the '20-metre rule' with respect to drinking water in rural areas – if the water source is within 20 metres of a latrine, do not drink it. Wayne drank tap water in Paraguay from Ciudad del Este all the way to Filadelfia with no ill effects, but if you have any doubts, stick to mineral water, which is readily available. If the South American cholera epidemic of 1991 spreads to Paraguay, take extra precautions.

Malaria is no longer a major threat in Paraguay, but the monstrous Itaipú hydro-electric project on the Brazilian border appears to have created a habitat for mosquito vectors. Other causes for concern, but not hysteria, are tuberculosis, typhoid, hepatitis, and hookworm *(susto)* – avoid going barefoot. Cutaneous leishmaniasis *(ura)*, a malady transmitted by biting sandflies which results in open sores, is very unpleasant and is dangerous if untreated.

WOMEN TRAVELLERS
Paraguay is generally safe for women travellers, but modesty is important and women should, in general, avoid eye contact with unfamiliar males, especially in the countryside. Single women should avoid even 'friendly' conversation with men on buses.

DANGERS & ANNOYANCES
In the Chaco, especially, watch for poisonous snakes. As elsewhere in the world, you're not likely to find them unless you go looking, but the consequences of snakebite are so serious that you won't care to chance it. Differing from its northern counterparts, the Brazilian rattlesnake *(Crotalus durissus)* transmits a highly potent neurotoxin which can cause paralysis so severe that neck muscles cannot hold up the head, and the neck appears broken. However, you are more likely to be troubled by mosquitos, so bring repellent, lightweight long-sleeved shirts, and a hat to protect yourself from both them and the sun.

Since the end of the Stroessner dictatorship, the police operate with less impunity than formerly, although it is wise not to aggravate either them or the military. Surprisingly, highway police appear less arbitrary than in Argentina; however, at Chaco highway checkpoints you will encounter teenage conscripts with automatic rifles as big as they are – although the rumour is that officers don't dare issue them ammunition for fear of being turned upon. Be polite, show your papers, and you are unlikely to be seriously inconvenienced. There is tension between the pacifist Mennonites and the Paraguayan military and police in the Chaco.

HIGHLIGHTS
For independent travellers with an open mind, little-visited Paraguay has much to offer. As one of Latin America's oldest cities, Asunción's historical significance is considerable, even though it has relatively few colonial remains. South-eastern Paraguay, between Asunción and Encarnación, has important colonial remains, including those of Jesuit missions such as Trinidad. This site in some ways surpasses that of Argentina's San Ignacio Miní. Fishing along the Río Paraná and the Río Paraguay is, obviously, similar to that in Argentina.

On the Brazilian frontier, the massive binational hydroelectric complex at Itaipú deserves a visit, if only to mourn Sete Quedas, a series of falls which surpassed even Iguazú before their disappearance under a massive reservoir. Iguazú itself is easily visited from Ciudad del Este (ex-Puerto Presidente Stroessner), but Paraguay has important natural assets of its own in several widely dispersed national parks. The most accessible of these is Ybycuí, which preserves a representative sample of subtropical rainforest. Other reserves can be found both in eastern Paraguay and the nearly vacant Chaco region, one of South America's great wildernesses. Paraguay's bird life is exceptionally rich both in eastern Paraguay and the Chaco, although mammals and reptiles have suffered by comparison.

FOOD & DRINKS
Paraguayan food resembles in some aspects

that of Argentina and Uruguay, but differs in others. On balance, meat consumption is much lower than in either of the other River Plate republics, although *parrillada* (grilled meat) is a restaurant standard. Tropical and subtropical foodstuffs play a much greater role in the Paraguayan diet and have their origins in the country's indigenous Guaraní heritage.

Grain, particularly maize, and tubers such as *mandioca* (manioc or cassava) are part of almost every meal. *Locro* is a maize stew which resembles its Argentine equivalent, while *mazamorra* is a corn mush. *Sopa paraguaya*, the national dish and a dietary staple, is not soup but rather a cornbread with cheese and onion. *Chipa guazú*, a recommended choice, is a variant of sopa paraguaya – it's a sort of cheese soufflé. *Mbaipy so-ó* is a hot maize pudding with chunks of meat, while *bori-bori* is a chicken soup with cornmeal balls. *Sooyo sopy* is a thick soup of ground meat, accompanied by rice or noodles, while *mbaipy he-é* is a dessert of corn, milk and molasses.

Manioc dishes are the province of the rural poor, since the crop yields abundantly on poor to mediocre soils. *Chipa de almidón* resembles chipa guazú, but manioc flour dominates instead of cornmeal. *Mbeyú*, also known as *torta de almidón*, is a plain grilled manioc pancake which in some ways resembles the Mexican tortilla. During Holy Week, the addition of eggs, cheese and spices transforms ordinary food into a holiday treat.

Like Argentines and Uruguayans, Paraguayans consume enormous amounts of *mate*, but do it more commonly in the form of *tereré*, served refreshingly ice-cold in the withering summer heat. A common story says that tereré became popular among soldiers during the Chaco War, when it was used to filter the region's muddy water, but as early as the 18th-century, a Jesuit writer noted that *mate* 'assuages both hunger and thirst, especially if...drunk with cold water without sugar'. Throughout eastern Paraguay, roadside stands offer *mosto* – sugar-cane juice. *Caña*, cane alcohol, is a popular alcoholic beverage.

ENTERTAINMENT

Cinema and live theatre are popular in Asunción, and the capital's cultural life is much livelier since the overthrow of Stroessner. As elsewhere, soccer is the most popular spectator and participant sport: Asunción's most popular team, Olímpico, is competitive with the best Argentine and Uruguayan sides.

THINGS TO BUY

Paraguay's most well-known handicraft is its ñandutí lace, which ranges in size from doilies to bedspreads. The women of Itauguá, a village east of Asunción, are the best known weavers. In the town of Luque, artisans produce stunningly beautiful handmade musical instruments, particularly guitars and harps, for surprisingly reasonable prices.

Paraguayan leather goods are excellent, and bargains are more readily available than in either Argentina or Paraguay. Chaco Indians produce carvings of animals from the aromatic wood of the palo santo, replicas of spears and other weapons, and traditional string bags *(yiscas)*.

Asunción and Ciudad del Este are good places to look for electronics, particularly to replace a lost or stolen camera. The selection is not so great as the *zona franca* (free zone) of Iquique, Chile, but prices are very reasonable.

Getting There & Away

Paraguay is a hub of sorts for Southern Cone air traffic, but overland travellers to destinations other than the Iguazú Falls and Posadas will find it a bit out of the way. There is a difficult but intriguing land crossing from Bolivia.

AIR

To/From the USA

Líneas Aéreas Paraguayas (LAP), also known as Air Paraguay, has traditionally been a discount carrier, but its fares no longer differ from those of other IATA (International Air Transport Association) airlines. It has flights from Miami to Asunción on Monday, Wednesday and Friday, with connections to Río de Janeiro, São Paulo, Buenos Aires, Montevideo and Santiago de Chile.

American Airlines flies three times weekly from Miami via Lima and La Paz, while Varig makes connections in Río de Janeiro for Miami and New York. On Wednesday and Friday, Varig has flights to Los Angeles via Río de Janeiro. Lloyd Aéreo Boliviano (LAB) has a Friday flight to Miami via Santa Cruz and Panamá.

To/From Europe

LAP has three weekly flights from Europe to Asunción: Monday from Brussels via Madrid, and Dakar (Senegal) (for refuelling – stopovers are not permitted; Wednesday from Frankfurt via Madrid and Dakar; and Friday from Frankfurt via Brussels and Dakar. Iberia also has a flight via Madrid, Río de Janeiro and São Paulo, while Varig has connections via the same Brazilian cities. Return services to Europe are similar.

To/From Neighbouring Countries

LAP flies to Río de Janeiro and São Paulo on Tuesday, Thursday (two flights) and on Saturday. Varig provides similar services. LAP also flies on Tuesdays to Santa Cruz, Bolivia, continuing to Lima, and five times weekly to

Ezeiza Airport, Buenos Aires. Lloyd Aéreo Boliviano also flies to Santa Cruz, and Aerolíneas Argentinas has flights to Ezeiza.

To/From Other South American Countries

LAP and PLUNA (Uruguay's national carrier) fly from Asunción to Montevideo via Ezeiza weekly, while LAP and Ladeco (Líneas Aéreas del Cobre) both fly to Santiago, Chile, three times weekly. LAP and American connect Asunción with Lima.

LAND

Paraguay's relatively few overland crossings underscore the country's geographical isolation. There are only three legal border crossings from Argentina, two from Brazil, and one from Bolivia.

To/From Argentina

There are two direct border crossings between Paraguay and Argentina, plus one requiring a brief detour through Brazil. If the corruption-plagued Yacyretá hydroelectric project on the Río Paraná is ever completed, another will open from Ayolas to Ituzaingó, Corrientes, via a bridge over the top of the dam.

Asunción to Clorinda There is a frequent bus service via the Puente Internacional Ignacio de Loyola between Asunción and Clorinda, in the Argentine province of Formosa, which is renowned for ferocious customs checks.

Encarnación to Posadas Frequent bus services across the Paraná have facilitated this crossing on the new international bridge to Posadas, in the Argentine province of Misiones. It is still possible to take a launch between the river docks, at least until the Yacyretá dam floods the low-lying parts of both cities. There is also a rail service from

Asunción to Buenos Aires, although it is much slower than the bus.

Ciudad del Este to Puerto Iguazú Frequent buses connect Ciudad del Este (formerly Puerto Presidente Stroessner) to the Brazilian city of Foz do Iguaçu, with easy connections to Puerto Iguazú in the Argentine province of Misiones. Alternatively, you can cross by launch from Puerto Presidente Franco, a few km south of Ciudad del Este, directly to Puerto Iguazú across the Paraná without passing through Brazil.

To/From Brazil
Ciudad del Este to Foz do Iguaçu This is the most frequently used overland border crossing between the two countries. Vehicles and pedestrian traffic move freely across the Puente de la Amistad (Friendship Bridge) which connects the two cities across the Paraná, but if you are planning to spend more than a day in either country, you should complete immigration procedures.

Pedro Juan Caballero to Ponta Porã Pedro Juan Caballero is a small town on the Paraguayan/Brazilian border, while Ponta Porã is its Brazilian counterpart. Each town has a consulate of the neighbouring country. There is a regular bus service from Asunción to Pedro Juan Caballero, although the route is unpaved and can be impassable in very bad weather. From the Brazilian city of Campo Grande, there are several buses and two trains daily.

To/From Bolivia
This is one of the most difficult overland border crossings in South America, as there is no regular public transport between Colonia La Patria, on the Ruta Trans-Chaco, 85 km from the border, and the Bolivian town of Boyuibe, a further 135 km west. Beyond Filadelfia, the road is dirt, and is subject to long delays in the event of heavy, if infrequent, rains. Before attempting the crossing, ask the Bolivian Consulate in Asunción for permission.

There are countless military checkpoints where you can wait for days in hope of a truck to Bolivia. Your best bet is to take the NASA bus from Asunción to Colonia La Patria and ask there about the possibility of getting a lift with a truck, although Mariscal Estigarribia, where there is a petrol station, would be a more comfortable place to wait. To the amazement of the Paraguayans, a friend of ours did the trip from Bolivia on a bicycle, despite the heat and lack of water in the area.

RIVER
This is not a conventional means of travel to Paraguay, but it is possible. In winter, there are occasional tour boats from Buenos Aires to Asunción, although there is no ordinary passenger service. From Asunción, the Flota Mercantil del Estado (State Merchant Fleet) does carry passengers on its irregular trips to and from the Brazilian city of Corumbá. For details, see the chapter on Asunción.

LEAVING PARAGUAY
Departure Tax
A departure tax of US$5 is collected at Aeropuerto Silvio Pettirossi for international flights.

Getting Around

Public transport in Paraguay is generally cheap and efficient, if not always quite as comfortable as in Argentina or Uruguay. Travellers spending more than a week or two in the country may find it useful to acquire Alberto D Hoffman's *Horarios de Transportes del Paraguay*, an exhaustive listing of all forms of public transport, published privately in Ciudad del Este, but available at general bookshops throughout the country. For about US$3 it is an amazing bargain.

AIR

Domestic air services in Paraguay are limited. LAP has only international flights, but Líneas Aéreas de Transporte Nacional (LATN) and Transportes Aéreo Militar (TAM), the Air Force's passenger service, fly to interior destinations such as Concepción, Pedro Juan Caballero, and a very few isolated parts of the Chaco. Fares are not as cheap as in Uruguay, but are still reasonable – a ticket to Pedro Juan Caballero, more than 500 km from Asunción, costs about US$28. For further details, see appropriate sections of the text.

BUS

The quality of bus services in Paraguay varies considerably, depending on whether you take *servicio removido*, which picks up passengers at every shady tree on the highway, or *servicio directo*, which stops only at fixed locations in each city or town. Other common terms are *regular* (buses which stop at every shady spot along the highway), *común* (a basic bus that stops in only a limited number of places), and *ejecutivo* (a faster deluxe bus with toilets, tea and coffee service and other facilities). Larger Paraguayan cities have central bus terminals, but in those cities which do not, bus companies are within easy walking distance of each other, and are usually found around the central plaza.

Buses run very frequently to destinations all around the country, and only on or near holidays should reservations be necessary. Fares are very cheap – for example, Asunción to Filadelfia, a distance of about 450 km, costs only about US$7 removido or US$10 directo.

TRAIN

Paraguay's antique, wood-burning trains are more interesting than practical. Visitors to Asunción should not miss the short ride to Aregua, on the shores of Lago Ypacaraí, but the slow, dusty ride to Encarnación for the connection to Buenos Aires at Posadas will test the endurance of all but the most devoted railroad fanatics. It averages barely 20 km per hour and travels at night, even depriving you of the landscape, although one return trip from Encarnación does travel during the daytime. The inconvenience and discomfort are compensated, however, by the absurdly cheap fares.

CAR

Driving in Paraguay presents some hazards which are not common to either Argentina or Uruguay, the most notable being the presence of high-wheeled wooden oxcarts and livestock on the road. For the most part, carts stick to tracks which parallel the highway, but on occasion they must cross. Everywhere in the country, but especially in the Chaco, you must watch for cattle on the road. Because of these hazards, driving at night is not advisable.

Paraguay formally requires the International Driving Permit, in addition to a state or national driver's licence, but cars with foreign number plates are rarely stopped except at military checkpoints in the Chaco. Car theft is very common in Paraguay, and many vehicles are imported illegally from Argentina, with authorities turning a blind eye. If your vehicle is conspicuous, be especially certain it is secure.

Operating a car in Paraguay is more economical than either Argentina or Uruguay because the price of petrol is slightly cheaper and there has been a flood of cheap spares – if you need to purchase tyres, for example, Asunción is the place to do so. If you need repairs, Paraguayan mechanics are very competent and labour is much cheaper than in Argentina.

The Touring y Automóvil Club Paraguayo (☎ 24366), corner of Brasil and 25 de Mayo in Asunción, is the equivalent of Argentina's ACA, but its road maps are seriously inferior. Less widespread than the ACA, they are nonetheless friendly and helpful.

BOAT

The Flota Mercantíl del Estado operates passenger services from Asunción up the Río Paraguay to Concepción and other river ports, as far as Corumbá, Brazil. For more details, see the appropriate chapters.

LOCAL TRANSPORT
To/From the Airport

Except in Asunción, air travel is infrequent in Paraguay, but Asunción city buses go to Silvio Pettirossi Airport. For details, see the chapter on Asunción. LAP and TAM have airport buses for their own passengers, while the taxi fare is about US$10.

Bus & Tram

Asunción has an extensive public transport system, but late-night buses are less frequent than in Buenos Aires. As in Argentina, the driver or conductor will ask your destination. Retain your ticket, since an inspector may check it. The standard fare is about US$0.25.

Buses to Asunción suburbs such as San Lorenzo, Villa Hayes and Aregua leave from the centre as well as from the bus terminal.

In downtown Asunción, a single relic tramline runs to Defensa Nacional and Padre Cardozo, a distance of only a few kilometres.

Taxi

Unlike cabs in Argentina and Uruguay, those in Paraguay operate on the basis of direct metre readings. Fares are comparable to Argentina and Uruguay, but after midnight drivers are likely to levy a surcharge. There is often a small surcharge for luggage as well.

Asunción

From its central location on the Río Paraguay, Asunción has always been the landlocked country's link to the outside world and the pivot of its political, economic and cultural life. Even though only about 20% of the country's population lives in the capital, most of the remainder lives within about 150 km. Unlike Buenos Aires and other Latin American metropolises, Asunción has sprouted relatively few skyscrapers, so the sun still reaches the sidewalks of narrow downtown streets – a mixed blessing in summer's overpowering heat, which is relieved only by shady plazas and streets. Although Asunción has some limited industry on its outskirts, mostly the processing of agricultural materials, its economy is really administrative and commercial.

History

Founded in 1537 by Juan de Salazar, an officer from Mendoza's failed colony at Buenos Aires, Asunción proved more attractive to early Spaniards with its abundant food supplies and the hospitable Guaraní. By 1541, its European population was about 600 and, for more than 40 years until the refounding of Buenos Aires in 1580, it was the most important settlement in the River Plate region. Spaniards initially expected Asunción to be the gateway to Perú, but the hot, dry Chaco, with its many hostile Indians, proved to be an insuperable barrier to travel and was superseded by the route down the eastern side of the Andes to Salta, Tucumán, Córdoba, and Buenos Aires.

By European standards, colonial Asunción was a stagnant backwater. The Austrian Jesuit missionary Martin Dobrizhoffer, visiting in the mid-18th century, was not impressed with either the city or its society:

Neither splendid edifices nor city fortifications are here to be found. Many of the houses are of stone or brick, and roofed with tiles, but none of them are above one story high. The monasteries are nearly of the same description, possessing nothing by which you could recognise the church. The streets are crooked, and impeded with ditches and stones thrown out of their places, to the imminent peril of both men and horses. It has but one market-place, and that covered with grass. The governor and bishop have resided here since the time of Charles V, though neither has any proper seat...Even matrons of the higher rank, boys, girls, and all the lower orders speak Guarany, though the generality have some acquaintance with Spanish. To say the truth, they mingle both, and speak neither correctly...The Spanish miserably corrupted the Indian, and the Indian the Spanish language.

After independence, little changed during the isolationist dictatorship of Francia. Englishman J P Robertson, during a visit near the end of Francia's rule, also saw the capital through European eyes, but thought more highly of its residents:

In extent, architecture, convenience, or population, it does not rank with a fifth-rate town in England...Its government-house, with the title of palace, is a mean, low, whitewashed, though extensive structure. Its largest buildings – though anything but sumptuous – are the convents...while the great bulk of the dwellings were simple huts, constituting narrow lanes, or standing apart, surrounded by a few orange-trees. There could not be said to be more than one street in the town, and that was unpaved...

The inhabitants of Assumption and its suburbs amounted...to ten thousand...The great bulk of the population was of a breed between Spaniards and Indians, so attenuated...as to give the natives the air and appearance of descendants from Europeans. The men were generally well made and athletic; the women almost invariably pretty.

Only with the death of Francia did Asunción's isolation end, as Carlos Antonio López opened the country to foreign influence and nearly obliterated the city's colonial remains in the process. López and his son, Francisco Solano López, built Asunción's major public buildings, including the Palacio de Gobierno (now the Congress), the Panteón de los Héroes, the train station, Francisco Solano López's residence (now the Palacio de Gobierno), and an opera house modelled on La Scala (now the internal revenue building). But Francisco Solano López effectively ended this brief era of material progress by foolishly plunging Paraguay into the War of the Triple Alliance.

Ten years after the war, in 1880, a British journalist commented that these López family legacies were nothing more than 'extravagant luxuries' which stuck out like sore thumbs among their surroundings:

These ruins of past greatness, glaring at the wretched buildings all around, looking down on the poverty-stricken people that wander under their rumbling pillars, tottering arcades, and dangling rafters, are unique. They are not grand, rather the reverse, but they must have appeared colossal to a people living in primitive dwellings.

Public improvements were indeed slow to come in the capital. Well into the 20th century, even the central areas of Asunción went unpaved, although from 1873 a horse-drawn tramway, later upgraded to a steam locomotive, operated into Villa Morra and and the north-east of the city. As European immigrants trickled in, the city gradually improved its appearance and developed exclusive residential suburbs to the east.

Progress was further retarded by the Chaco war of the 1930s, but the city has sprawled to encompass ever more distant areas such as the university centre of San Lorenzo. In recent decades, there has been a minor boom in high-rise office and hotel construction in the centre, but the city still retains much of its 19th-century structure of low buildings lining narrow streets. At the same time, the influx of people from the impoverished countryside has resulted in the growth of enormous shantytowns along the riverfront, the railway, or anywhere else there happens to be a vacant lot.

Orientation

Asunción sits on a bluff above the east bank of the Río Paraguay. Like most colonial cities, it features a conventional grid pattern, refashioned by the irregularities of a river-side location and some modern developments. Most of the city's key sights and inexpensive hotels and restaurants are located within a slightly larger area bound by the riverfront, Avenida Colón in the west, Calles Haedo and Luis A Herrera in the south, and Estados Unidos to the east. There are few colonial remains.

The city centre is the Plaza de los Héroes, bound by Independencia Nacional in the east, Calle Palma on the north side, Chile in the west, and Calle Oliva to the south. Street names change on either side of Independencia Nacional. The city's commercial and financial institutions are concentrated along Calle Palma and its eastward extension, Mariscal Estigarribia, which is interrupted by Plaza Uruguay. This plaza is bound by Calle Eligio Ayala on the north, México in the west, 25 de Mayo in the south, and Antequera to the east (do not confuse Calle Eligio Ayala with Eusebio Ayala, a major arterial which heads east out of town). Although Plaza Uruguay is an attractive, shady refuge from the midday heat, prostitutes frequent the area at night and single women will probably prefer to avoid it.

To the north, along the riverfront, the irregular Plaza Constitución is bound by Independencia Nacional to the east, El Paraguayo Independiente in the south, and 14 de Mayo in the west. It contains the Congreso Nacional (Congress building). Below the bluff, subject to flooding, lie the so-called *viviendas temporarias*, Paraguay's shantytown equivalent of Argentina's *villas miserias*. El Paraguayo Independiente, a diagonal, leads west to the Palacio de Gobierno, the presidential palace.

Asunción's most prestigious residential areas are east of downtown, out on the Avenidas España and Mariscal López toward Silvio Pettirossi Airport (ex-Aeropuerto Presidente Stroessner). Most of the capital's embassies and its best restaurants are here, in neighbourhoods like Villa Morra. North- east of downtown, at the end of Avenida Artigas, is the Jardín Botánico, once the López family estate and now the city's

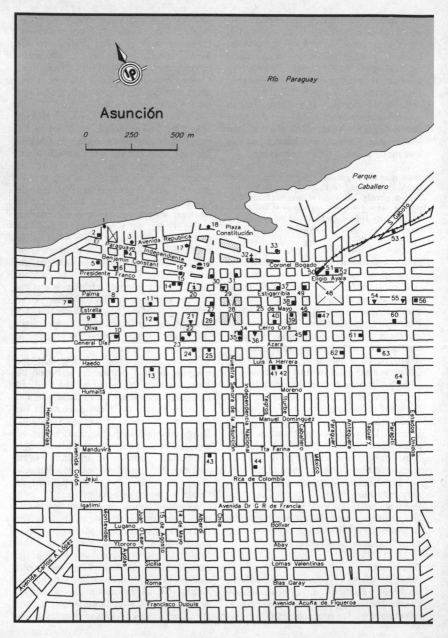

Asunción

Río Paraguay

Parque Caballero

0   250   500 m

Plaza Constitución
El Paraguayo
Avenida República
Independiente
Benjamin Constant
Presidente Franco
Palma
Estrella
Oliva
General Díaz
Haedo
Humaitá
Manduvirá
Jejui
Igatimi
Coronel Bogado
Eligio Ayala
Estigarribia
25 de Mayo
Cerro Corá
Azara
Luis A Herrera
Moreno
Manuel Domínguez
Tta Farina
Rca de Colombia
Avenida Dr G R de Francia
Bolívar
Abay
Lomas Valentinas
Blas Garay
Avenida Acuña de Figueroa
Francisco Dupuis
Roma
Sicilia
Ytororó
Lugano
Montevideo
Juan O'Leary
15 de Agosto
14 de Mayo
Alberdi
Chile
Nuestra Señora de la Asunción
Independencia Nacional
Yegros
Iturbe
Caballero
México
Paraguari
Antequera
Iacuary
Parapiti
Estados Unidos
Hernandarias
Avenida Colón
Avenida Carlos A López
S Caboto

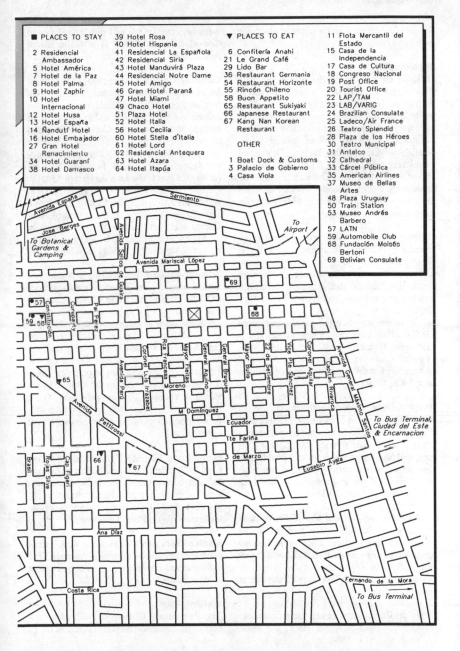

■ PLACES TO STAY

- 2 Residencial Ambassador
- 5 Hotel América
- 7 Hotel de la Paz
- 8 Hotel Palma
- 9 Hotel Zaphir
- 10 Hotel Internacional
- 12 Hotel Husa
- 13 Hotel España
- 14 Ñandutí Hotel
- 16 Hotel Embajador
- 27 Gran Hotel Renacimiento
- 34 Hotel Guaraní
- 38 Hotel Damasco
- 39 Hotel Rosa
- 40 Hotel Hispania
- 41 Residencial La Española
- 42 Residencial Siria
- 43 Hotel Manduvirá Plaza
- 44 Residencial Notre Dame
- 45 Hotel Amigo
- 46 Gran Hotel Paraná
- 47 Hotel Miami
- 49 Chaco Hotel
- 51 Plaza Hotel
- 52 Hotel Italia
- 56 Hotel Cecilia
- 60 Hotel Stella d'Italia
- 61 Hotel Lord
- 62 Residencial Antequera
- 63 Hotel Azara
- 64 Hotel Itapúa

▼ PLACES TO EAT

- 6 Confitería Anahí
- 21 Le Grand Café
- 29 Lido Bar
- 36 Restaurant Germania
- 54 Restaurant Horizonte
- 55 Rincón Chileno
- 58 Buon Appetito
- 65 Restaurant Sukiyaki Japanese Restaurant
- 66 Japanese Restaurant
- 67 Kang Nan Korean Restaurant

OTHER

- 1 Boat Dock & Customs
- 3 Palacio de Gobierno
- 4 Casa Viola
- 11 Flota Mercantil del Estado
- 15 Casa de la Independencia
- 17 Casa de Cultura
- 18 Congreso Nacional
- 19 Post Office
- 20 Tourist Office
- 22 LAP/TAM
- 23 LAB/VARIG
- 24 Brazilian Consulate
- 25 Ladeco/Air France
- 26 Teatro Splendid
- 28 Plaza de los Héroes
- 30 Teatro Municipal
- 31 Antelco
- 32 Cathedral
- 33 Cárcel Pública
- 35 American Airlines
- 37 Museo de Bellas Artes
- 48 Plaza Uruguay
- 50 Train Station
- 53 Museo Andrés Barbero
- 57 LATN
- 59 Automobile Club
- 68 Fundación Moisés Bertoni
- 69 Bolivian Consulate

largest open space, and a popular place for weekend outings.

Information

Tourist Office The tourist office, at Calle Palma 468 between Alberdi and 14 de Mayo, is friendly but not especially knowledgeable or helpful, although it supplies a good city centre map/brochure and has several looseleaf notebooks full of tourist information which you can consult. It's open weekdays from 7 am to 8 pm and Saturday from 8 to 11.30 am. Do pick up *Fin de Semana*, a weekly calendar of entertainment and cultural events, which is widely distributed throughout the city.

Money Cambios Guaraní, purportedly owned by General Rodríguez, is at Calle Palma 449. According to some accounts, General Stroessner's closure of foreign exchange houses and grant of a foreign exchange concession to his own son precipitated the Rodríguez coup.

There are several other exchange houses on Calle Palma and nearby side streets: Internacional Cambios at Calle Palma 364, Yguazú Cambios at Calle Palma 547, and Amambay Cambios, on the corner of Estrella and 14 de Mayo.

Post & Telecommunications The main post office is on the corner of Alberdi and El Paraguayo Independiente, and is open weekdays from 7.30 am to noon and 2.30 to 7.30 pm, and Saturday from 8 am to 1 pm. It also has an attractive patio garden, a museum (worthwhile if you're already in the building or nearby), and good views of downtown Asunción from the roof.

Antelco, on the corner of Presidente Franco 198 and Nuestra Señora de la Asunción, has a direct fibre optic line to connect with operators in the USA and Japan for collect or credit card calls. There is another office, much less state-of-the-art, at the bus terminal.

Foreign Consulates Brazil has a consulate at General Díaz 523, 3rd floor; it's open

weekdays from 8 am to 1 pm. The Bolivian Consulate (☎ 20-3654) is at Calle Eligio Ayala 2002.

Cultural Centres Asunción has several international cultural centres, all of which frequently offer films at little or no cost, plus artistic and photographic exhibitions. These include the Casa de la Cultura Paraguaya (formerly the Colegio Militar), on the corner of 14 de Mayo and El Paraguayo Independiente; the Centro Juan de Salazar (☎ 44-9221) at Calle Luis A Herrera 834; the Centro Anglo-Paraguayo (☎ 25525) at Avenida España 457; the Centro Paraguayo Japonés (☎ 60-7276), on the corner of Julio Correa and Portillo; the Alliance Française at Mariscal Estigarribia 1039; and the Instituto Alemán (☎ 26642) at Salazar 310.

Travel Agencies The Touring y Automóvil Club Paraguayo (☎ 24366) is on the corner of Calle Brasíl and 25 de Mayo. Asunción has a multitude of other downtown travel agencies, such as Exprinter (☎ 44-4639) at 25 de Mayo and Yegros, Guaraní Turismo (☎ 44-8379) at Calle Palma 449, and the Mennonite-operated Menno Travel (☎ 44-1210) at Azara 532, an especially good source for information on the Chaco. Paula Braun at Ypacaraí Turismo (☎ 49-0474), on the corner of General Díaz and 15 de Agosto, is an English-speaking Mennonite travel agent.

Bookshops Librería Comuneros, at Cerro Corá 289, offers a good selection of historical and contemporary books on Paraguay. Another good shop is Librería Internacional, at Caballero 270. There are interesting open-air bookstalls on Plaza Uruguay.

Medical Services The Hospital de Clínicas (☎ 80982) is on the corner of Avenida Dr J Montero and Lagerenza, about one km west of downtown.

Walking Tour

The **Palacio de Gobierno**, built as a residence for Francisco Solano López, is on El

Paraguayo Independiente between Ayolas and Juan O'Leary. Since the ousting of Stroessner, it is safe to approach it to take photographs. This is a major improvement over the situation which was in effect during the regimes of both Stroessner and Francia – according to J R Robertson, El Supremo once ordered that 'every person observed gazing at the front of his palace should be shot in the act'. There is a flag ceremony daily at sunset.

One of the few colonial buildings to survive the Francia years is the nearby **Casa Viola**, on Ayolas and El Paraguayo Independiente, which is currently undergoing restoration; by the time this book appears, it should be open to the public. Two blocks east, at 14 de Mayo, is the **Casa de Cultura Paraguaya**, formerly the Colegio Militar. Overlooking the river, on Plaza Constitución at the foot of Alberdi, is the **Congreso Nacional**.

At the east end of Plaza Constitución is the mid-19th century **Cathedral**. It has a museum which is open daily except Sunday from 8 to 11 am. South of the Plaza, on the corner of Chile and Presidente Franco, is the **Teatro Municipal**, while a block to the west, on the corner of Presidente Franco and 14 de Mayo, is the **Casa de la Independencia**, dating from 1772. This is where Paraguayan independence was declared in 1811. The Casa de la Independencia is the oldest remaining building in Asunción, and has its own museum.

On the Plaza de los Héroes, on the corner of Chile and Calle Palma, is the **Panteón de los Héroes** (see below). Four blocks east, the small **Museo de Bellas Artes**, on the corner of Iturbe and Mariscal Estigarribia, is a disappointment. It's open weekdays from 7 am to 1 pm and 2 to 9 pm. Next door, the **Archivo Nacional** has fabulous woodwork and an interesting spiral staircase. At the foot of Iturbe are the remains of the **Cárcel Pública**, one of the dungeons in which Dr Francia kept his political enemies such as Pedro Juan Caballero, who committed suicide here.

Political activists with a macabre sense of history may want to visit the site of the assassination of former Nicaraguan dictator Anastasio Somoza, on Avenida España between América and Venezuela. Interestingly and perhaps fittingly, this segment of Avenida España is officially called 'Generalísimo Franco', perhaps the only street in Latin America named for the late Spanish dictator. The name itself may fall victim to the de-Stroessnerization process, since most people prefer and continue to use 'Avenida España'.

Panteón de los Héroes

On the Plaza de los Héroes, on the corner of Chile and Calle Palma, a sombre honour guard protects the remains of Carlos Antonio López, his son Francisco Solano López, Bernardino Caballero, Marshal José Félix Estigarribia, and other heroes of Paraguay's catastrophic wars. Originally intended to be a religious shrine, work commenced on the Panteón during the rule of Carlos López, and was not finished until 1936, after the end of the Chaco war.

Jardín Botánico

Once the estate of the López family, Asunción's botanical gardens are the city's largest open space and are a popular area for weekend outings. At the entrance to the gardens is the house of José Artigas, the Uruguayan hero who spent his later years in exile here. There is a small admission charge to the park, which includes a rather pathetic zoo (home to exotic rather than Paraguayan species). The park is also home to the displaced Maká Indians of the Chaco, for whose plight no one seems to take responsibility. The municipal campground is also here.

Within the park, the **Museo de Historia Natural** is a vintage building which houses an impressive collection of specimens. Unfortunately, however, the exhibits are poorly labelled and displayed, with no attempt to place them in any ecological context. Nevertheless, the collection is worth seeing for the spectacular display of insects – one Paraguayan butterfly has a wingspan of 274 mm – some visitors, however, may think the variety which can be found out-doors nearly as impressive. The museum is open Monday to Saturday from 7.30 to 11.30 am and 1 to 5 pm, Sundays and holidays from 8 am to 1 pm. From the centre, the most direct bus is the No 44 ('Artigas') from the corner of Calle Oliva and 15 de Agosto, which goes directly to the gates of the park. Alternatively, take Nos 23 or 35.

Museo Etnográfico Andrés Barbero

Founded by and named for the former president of the Sociedad Científica del Paraguay, this anthropological and archaeological museum displays Paraguayan Indian tools, ceramics, weavings and a superb collection of photographs, plus good maps which indicate where everything comes from. For US$1.75, you can purchase an excellent illustrated guide to accompany your tour. One of Asunción's best, the museum is at Avenida España 217, and is open weekdays from 8 am to 11 am, and on Saturdays by request only. The museum library is open weekdays from 7.30 to 11 am and from 3 to 7.30 pm.

Museo del Barro

This is Asunción's foremost modern art museum, and some very unconventional work is on display. There are also other interesting exhibits from the 18th century to the present, including political caricatures of prominent Paraguayans. If you should be as fortunate as we were and stumble onto the opening of an exhibition, the food and wine are excellent.

To get there, take any No 30 bus beyond the end of Avenida San Martín and look for the prominent sign – otherwise it's difficult to locate. It occupies a new facility just off the Avenida Aviadores del Chaco, on Calle 1 between Emeterio Miranda and Molas López in the newly developed area of Isla de Francia, and is open daily except Sunday from 5 to 8 pm.

Museo Boggiani

From 1887 to the turn of the century, Guido Boggiani, an Italian ethnographer, con-ducted fieldwork among the Chamacoco Indians of the upper Río Paraguay. After he declined to marry one of their women, the Chamacoco, fearing that he would live with another faction of their tribe or with their traditional enemies, the Caduveo, consequently killed him.

Before his death, Boggiani assembled an impressive collection of feather art, much of which was forwarded to the Museum für Volkerkunde in Berlin. However, some of his collection remains on exhibit in this new and well-organised museum, at Coronel Bogado 888 in the suburb of San Lorenzo. Expansion is planned for the near future. The museum is open Tuesday to Saturday from 10 am to noon and from 3 to 6 pm, and it's well worth the 45-minute bus ride out Avenida Mariscal López.

Art Galleries

In addition to the cultural centres and museums listed above, Asunción's arts community displays its work in numerous private galleries, including Artesanos, on the corner of Cerro Corá and 22 de Setiembre; Fabrica, at Mariscal Estigarribia 1384; Belmarco, at Calle Brasíl 265; the Sala Agustín Barros, at Avenida España 352; Forum Galería de Arte at Calle Eligio Ayala 1184; Pequeña Galería in the Villa Morra Shopping Centre; Michele Malingue at República Francesa 190; Chini Galería de Arte at Cerro Corá 1539; Liliana Boccia at Mayor Bullo 970; Cristina Osnaghi-Atelier at Manduvirá 120; and José Leonard Miró, at R Peña 288.

Mercado Pettirossi

This lively Saturday morning market, occupying several blocks east along Avenida Pettirossi from its beginning at Calle Brasíl, deserves a visit, but don't make the mistake of trying to drive through it or, even worse, attempting to park.

Organised Tours

For city tours, day or night, as well as excursions to outlying areas such as San Bernardino, Iguazú Falls, and the Jesuit missions, contact Lions Tur (☎ 49-0591), Alberdi 454.

The Fundación Moisés Bertoni (☎ 21-2386), 25 de Mayo 2140, arranges eco-tourism excursions to Paraguay's national parks and other reserves at regular intervals.

Places to Stay – bottom end

Camping Asunción's campground is in the shady Jardín Botánico, the city's botanical gardens, about five km from the city centre. It is generally quiet and secure, and the staff are friendly, but the animals in the nearby zoo may keep you awake. There are lukewarm showers and adequate toilet facilities, but take care not to pitch your tent over an ant colony – their bites are quite painful. Bring mosquito repellent.

Fees are negligible at US$0.40 per vehicle or tent, plus US$0.10 per person for admission to the gardens. When returning to your site at night, tell the watchman at the entrance on Avenida Artigas that you are staying in the campground.

From the centre, the most direct bus is the No 44 ('Artigas') from the corner of Calle Oliva and 15 de Agosto. Alternatively, take Nos 23 or 35.

Hospedajes, Residenciales & Hotels

Asunción has loads of inexpensive accommodation, much of it Korean-owned after heavy immigration over the past decade or so. Most of these hotels are clean and basic, though at the upper end of the range some have air-conditioning, a welcome feature in steamy Asunción.

Probably the cheapest acceptable place is *Residencial Ambassador* (☎ 44-5901), on the corner of Calle Montevideo 110 and El Paraguayo Independiente, only a stone's throw from the Palacio de Gobierno. It's very basic and a bit musty, but friendly. There are fans on the ceiling and it costs only US$2.50 per person. Up the block, at Calle Montevideo 160, is the *Hotel América* (☎ 49-3251), where singles/doubles with shared bath cost US$3.50/6, or with private bath, US$6.50 a single.

Hotel Damasco (☎ 44-1248), Caballero 290, costs only US$3/4 with shared bath, while *Hotel Nueva Aurora* (☎ 44-5625), Mariscal Estigarribia 442, charges US$4 per person with shared bath. Rates are similar at *Residencial Notre Dame* (☎ 44-9723), Independencia Nacional 1076. Try also the recommended *Hospedaje Oasis*, Azara 736, and *Residencial Antequera*, Antequera 630.

Hotel Hispania (☎ 44-4108), Cerro Corá 265, has been a popular budget alternative for many years, with clean but rather gloomy downstairs rooms for US$4/6 with shared bath, US$6/8 with private bath. At *Hotel Lord* (☎ 44-6087), Tacuary 576, rates are US$4 per person with shared bath. *Hotel Palma* (☎ 49-0150), at Calle Palma 873, charges US$4/7 with shared bath. *Hotel Itapúa* (☎ 44-5121), Moreno 943, costs about US$5/8, as does *Residencial Siria* (☎ 44-7258), at Calle Luis A Herrera 166.

The Korean-run *Hotel Amigo* (☎ 49-1987), on the corner of Caballero 521 and Cerro Corá, charges US$7/12 for rooms with air-conditioning, and has a restaurant downstairs. *Hotel Embajador* (☎ 49-3393), on the corner of Presidente Franco 514 and 14 de Mayo, has singles with shared bath for US$7, and with private bath, US$10. At *Hotel Miami* (☎ 44-4950), México 449, rates are US$10/15 with private bath, breakfast and air-conditioning.

If you're catching an early bus, you may prefer to stay at a place across from the terminal. Try *Hotel Familiar Yasy* (☎ 55-1623), Fernando de la Mora 2390, which is friendly and quiet, with rates of US$4.50 per person with private bath. Next door there's an anonymous restaurant which has outstanding chicken empanadas. Nearby is the *Hotel 2000* (☎ 55-1628), which charges US$10/17.

Places to Stay – middle

Excellent value, and very clean and friendly, the *Ñandutí Hotel* (☎ 44-6780), has rates of US$10/15 with shared bath, US$13/18 with private bath.

Hotel Azara (☎ 44-9754), Azara 850, has doubles with private bath, fridge and air-conditioning for US$17. The *Plaza Hotel* (☎ 44-8834), next to the train station on the corner of Calle Eligio Ayala and Paraguarí, is quiet and friendly, and has rooms with private bath for US$12/17.50. *Hotel Stella d'Italia* (☎ 44-8731), Cerro Corá 933, is clean and attractive, with rates of US$11/15 with shared bath. *Hotel España* (☎ 44-3192), Haedo 667, is slightly more expensive at US$13/15, as is *Residencial La Española* (☎ 44-9280), Calle Luis A Herrera 142.

Hotel Asunción Palace (☎ 49-2151), Avenida Colón 475, is more modest than its name suggests, charging US$15/25. *Hotel Amalfi* (☎ 44-1 162), Caballero 877, and the *Hotel Manduvirá Plaza* (☎ 44-7533), at Manduvirá 345, are a bit more expensive. *Gran Hotel Paraná* (☎ 44-4545), on the corner of 25 de Mayo and Caballero, has standard rooms for US$21/28, and 'luxury' rooms for US$34/42. *Hotel de la Paz* (☎ 49-0786), Avenida Colón 350, costs US$23/29. Try also the *Hotel Zaphir* (☎ 49-0025), Estrella 955, which charges about US$27/32.

Places to Stay – top end

One of the older hotels in central Asunción, *Gran Hotel Renacimiento* (☎ 44-5165), Chile 388 opposite the Plaza de los Héroes, has more personality than most of the others. Rates are US$35/45 with breakfast, television, telephone and other amenities. The *Husa Asunción* (☎ 49-3760), 15 de Agosto 420, is comparably priced, while the modern *Chaco Hotel* (☎ 49-2066), Caballero 285, has rooms for US$57/73 with breakfast, plus a rooftop swimming pool. *Hotel Internacional* (☎ 49-6587), Ayolas 520, and *Hotel Cecilia* (☎ 44-1637) Estados Unidos 341, are another step up. The high-rise *Hotel Guaraní* (☎ 49-1131), Cerro Corá, has standard rooms for US$60/70, with suites for US$95/110.

Downtown, the top of the line is the extravagant *Hotel Excelsior* (☎ 49-5632), Chile 980, which charges US$105/115. Asunción's very best is the *Yacht y Golf Club Paraguayo* (☎ 36117), whose very name should give you an indication of what you'll expect to pay: US$133/145. It's in the ritzy suburb of Lambaré, west of town.

Places to Eat

From modest snack bars to high-class international cuisine, Asunción has a surprising variety of quality food. The best dining areas are downtown and the neighbourhoods to the east, around Avenidas Mariscal López and España.

One of Asunción's best breakfast and lunch places is the *Lido Bar*, on the corner of Chile and Calle Palma, which offers a variety of tasty Paraguayan specialities at reasonable prices. Packed with locals, it is good for a fast food snack at any hour. *Anahi*, on the corner of Presidente Franco and Ayolas, is an outstanding *confitería* with good food and ice cream at moderate prices. It's also open on Sunday, when most downtown restaurants are closed. A few doors away, toward Calle Montevideo, is an outstanding German bakery.

Another worthwhile stop is *Confitería El Molino*, with branches at Calle Palma 488 and Avenida España 382. *Restaurant Periplo*, Presidente Franco 583, has a fixed-price lunch for US$1.75 which is good enough to overlook the atrocious service, but you would expect better service for the more expensive dinner. It is known for a delicious Spanish paella, however.

Rincón Chileno, on the corner of Estados Unidos 314 and 25 de Mayo, has good, moderately priced Chilean food, and is popular with Peace Corps volunteers, who are a good source of information on the country. The owner, though, can be hostile if you question his mathematics. One block above, at Estados Unidos 422, is *Chopperría Vieja Bavaria*, which has good beer and fast food. It's a hangout for German visitors, but everyone is welcome.

Restaurant Germania, Cerro Corá 180, comes highly recommended, as does *Restaurant Munich*, Calle Eligio Ayala 163. *Gauchao*, Calle Luis A Herrera 1568, serves Brazilian cuisine, as does *Do Gaúcho*, on the corner of Avenida Colón and Manduvirá.

As elsewhere in the River Plate republics,

parrillas (grills) are the standard. There are several along the Avenida Brasilia, north of Avenida España: *La Paraguaya*, Avenida Brasilia 624, *Maracaná*, on the corner of Avenida Brasilia and Salazar, and *Anrejó* (also a pizzería), Avenida Brasilia 572. *Baby Beef*, Avenida Brasilia 632, is not, in spite of its name, only a parrilla – it also serves Brazilian food.

Moving upscale, *Talleyrand*, Mariscal Estigarribia 932, is one of Asunción's most highly regarded French/international restaurants – it's expensive, but good for a special occasion. *La Maison des Alpes*, on the corner of Bruselas and Viena, and *La Preferida*, a German restaurant at 25 de Mayo 1005, are also worth a visit. Another attractive dinner place is *La Pergola Jardín*, Avenida Perú 240. Spanish food is available at *El Antojo*, Ayolas 631.

For Italian food, try *Il Capo*, at Avenida Perú 291, or the *Spaghettoteca*, on the corner of Avenida San Martín and Austria in Villa Morra. Peace Corps volunteers have enthusiastically recommended *Buon Appetito*, on the corner of 25 de Mayo 1199 and Constitución. *Pizzometro*, Bruselas 1789 in the Luis Herrera neighbourhood, has all-you-can-eat pizza.

Asunción probably has better Asian food than either Buenos Aires or Montevideo, and greater variety to boot because of the influx of Koreans – try *Kang Nan*, Avenida Perú 1129. For Japanese food, check out *Restaurant Sukiyaki*, on the corner of Constitución 763 and Avenida Pettirossi. Chinese food is still the most common, at places like *Formosa* at Avenida España 780, *Celestial* at Calle Luis A Herrera 919, and *Taipei* at Calle Brasíl 976.

Asunción's most exquisite ice cream can be found at *4-D*, an Italian-style place on the corner of Avenida San Martín and Olegario Andrade, reached by bus Nos 12, 16, 28 or 30 (red). As good as the best of Buenos Aires, it has a remarkable selection of premium flavours.

Entertainment

Cinemas Sadly, Asunción's downtown cinemas rarely offer anything more challenging than cheap porno or the latest Arnold Schwarzenegger flick, but the capital's many cultural centres (see above) offer the best of foreign cinema. Check *Fin de Semana* for current listings.

Discos Downtown, try Piano Bar at the Hotel Internacional, Ayolas 520; La City, on the corner of Presidente Franco and 15 de Agosto; and Alcatraz, at Caballero 1. Others are mostly in the residential neighbourhoods east of downtown, such as Muzak Mall, on the corner of Ocampos and Bertoni in Villa Morra.

Theatre While it lacks quality cinemas other than those at its cultural centres, Asunción compensates with numerous venues for live theatre and music. These include the Casa de la Cultura Paraguaya (see the Cultural Centres section, above); the Teatro Arlequín (☎ 60-5107), on the corner of De Gaulle and Quesada in Villa Morra; Escuela de Teatro Arlequín, on the corner of Salazar and Avenida Artigas; Teatro de las Américas (☎ 24772), José Berges 297; Placita Ayolas, on the corner of Ayolas and Humaitá; and the Teatro Show del Hotel Excelsior (☎ 49-5632), Chile 980. The season generally runs from March to October.

Things to Buy

Artesanía Viva, at José Berges 993, features Chaco Indian crafts, including ponchos, hammocks and bags, plus books and information on Chaco Indian groups. Artesanía Hilda, on the corner of Presidente Franco and O'Leary, sells ñandutí lace and other Paraguayan handicrafts. Casa Over-all, at Mariscal Estigarribia 397 near Caballero, has a good selection of ñandutí and leather goods.

In the suburb of San Lorenzo, visit the Centro de Promoción de Artesanía Indígena (☎ 2870), on the corner of Coronel Bogado and Mariscal López, which has an outstanding collection of Chaco Indian artefacts –

baskets, wood carvings, spears, weavings – all of very fine quality at very low prices. Note especially the animal carvings from the aromatic *palo santo*. It's open Tuesday to Friday from 8.30 am to noon and 2 to 6 pm, Saturdays from 8.30 am to 6 pm.

Getting There & Away
Air Because of its central location on the South American continent, Asunción is a good place to catch flights to neighbouring countries, Europe and the USA.

Aerolíneas Argentinas
    Independencia Nacional 1365 (☎ 49-1012)
Aéroperú
    Benjamín Constant 536 (☎ 49-3122)
Air France
    Calle Oliva 393 (☎ 49-8768)
American Airlines
    Independencia Nacional 557 (☎ 43-3330)
Iberia
    25 de Mayo 161 (☎ 49-3351)
Líneas Aéreas del Cobre (Ladeco)
    General Díaz 347 (☎ 44-7028)
Líneas Aéreas Paraguayas (LAP)
    Calle Oliva 467 (☎ 49-1046)
Lloyd Aéreo Boliviano (LAB)
    Cnr 14 de Mayo & Calle Oliva (☎ 49-4715)
Lufthansa
    3rd floor, Cnr Estrella & Chile (☎ 44-7964)
PLUNA
    Alberdi 513 (☎ 49-0128)
Varig
    Cnr General Díaz & 14 de Mayo (☎ 49-7351)

TAM, the military airline (☎ 44-5843), is next door to LAP at Calle Oliva 471. It serves many off-the-beaten-track destinations in the Chaco and along the northern Río Paraguay.

LATN (☎ 21-2277), Calle Brasíl and Mariscal Estigarribia, flies daily to Concepción (US$22) and San Pedro (if necessary), and daily except Sunday to Juan Pedro Caballero (US$28). It also serves the upper Río Paraguay destinations of Puerto Pinasco, Puerto Casado and Valle Mí (US$28) on Monday and Wednesday. Thursday and Saturday it flies to the Río Pilcomayo outposts of Fortín Caballero, Fortín Teniente Martínez, and Fortín Rojas

Silva (US$28), the best access to Parque Nacional Tinfunqué.

Bus The new bus terminal (☎ 55-1732) is on the corner of Fernando de la Mora and República Argentina, and can be reached from the centre by bus Nos 8, 10, 25, 31 or 38 from Calle Oliva. Some companies continue to operate ticket offices on Plaza Uruguay, enabling you to avoid an unnecessary trip. Asunción has excellent and frequent international as well as national connections; fares vary depending on the quality of the service. Travelling into Argentina or Brazil, it is generally cheaper to take a local bus across the border (for example, Asunción to Clorinda or Encarnación to Posadas) and then to purchase a long-distance bus ticket.

Nuestra Señora de la Asunción (☎ 55-1667) and Expreso Brújula (☎ 55-1662) operate buses to Falcón, on the Argentine border, from downtown Asunción. These leave hourly, from the corner of Presidente Franco and Avenida Colón, between 5 and 11 am, and 12.30 to 5.30 pm. Nuestra Señora, Brújula and Empresa Godoy leave from the terminal directly to Clorinda at 5, 6, 8 and 9 am, and at 12.30, 2.30, 4.30 and 6 pm. The fare to Clorinda is US$1.75.

Nuestra Señora de la Asunción also has a frequent service to Posadas (four hours), Buenos Aires (US$50, 20 hours), and Foz do Iguaçu (five hours), and one service weekly to Rosario, Argentina. Chevalier Paraguaya (☎ 55-1660) has buses to Buenos Aires via Formosa and Santa Fe. Expreso Brújula also serves Resistencia and Buenos Aires frequently, and Montevideo and São Paulo less often. Singer (☎ 55-1763) has daily buses to Posadas, with connections to Buenos Aires, while La Internacional (☎ 55-1662) goes to Buenos Aires via Formosa.

Expreso Río Paraná (☎ 55-1733) also has a service to Buenos Aires. Empresa Godoy (☎ 55-1662) serves Resistencia via Formosa, and Buenos Aires via both Formosa and Encarnación. La Encarnaceña (☎ 50-4093) also has a regular service to Buenos Aires, while Cacorba (☎ 55-1662)

has buses to Córdoba (18 hours) Tuesday and Friday. Expreso Pullman Sur operates the only buses to Santiago, Chile (30 hours), on Monday and Thursday.

COIT (☎ 55-1738) goes to Río de Janeiro on Monday, Wednesday and Saturday evenings, and to Montevideo on Wednesday and Saturday mornings. Nacional Expreso (☎ 55-1662) goes to Brasilia twice weekly. Pluma (☎ 55-1618) frequently connects Asunción with Foz, São Paulo (18 hours), Río de Janeiro (22 hours), Curitibá (14 hours), and Paranaguá (16 hours). RYSA (☎ 55-1618) also goes to Foz and São Paulo. Unesul goes to Porto Alegre, and Catarinense (☎ 50-4192) provides a service to Florianópolis via Blumenau.

Asunción is the major hub for bus travel throughout Paraguay. There are countless buses to Ciudad del Este (US$4 regular, US$8 común, US$16 cjecutivo, 4½ hours) with Rápido Caaguazú (☎ 55-1665), RYSA and Nuestra Señora. Nuestra Señora, RYSA, Alborada (☎ 55-1612), La Encarnaceña and Flecha de Oro (☎ 55-1641) all serve Encarnación (US$8, five hours).

For Pedro Juan Caballero, try San Jorge (☎ 55-1647), Empresa Amambay (☎ 55-2175), Santaniana (☎ 55-1580), and La Ovetense (☎ 55-1747). Connections between Asunción and Concepción are offered by NASA (☎ 55-1731), La Ovetense, San Jorge (☎ 55-1647), and Ciudad de Concepción (55-1912).

La Chaqueña serves nearby Chaco destinations such as Presidente Hayes and Benjamín Aceval. Long-distance Chaco carriers are NASA (☎ 55-1731), Stel Turismo, and Ecmetur (☎ 55-2401), with services to Pozo Colorado and Concepción (weather permitting on the dirt road from Pozo), Filadelfia (US$11, eight hours), Neuland, Mariscal Estigarribia (US$13), and Colonia La Patria, the last stop on the Ruta Trans-Chaco.

Other destinations near Asunción, such as San Bernardino and Caacupé, have such frequent services that it would be inconvenient to list them all here; instead, refer to the destination itself for such information.

Train Built in 1856, the train station is on Plaza Uruguay, on the corner of Calle Eligio Ayala and México. Daily except Sundays, the steam train to Lago Ypacaraí leaves at noon, passing through the backyards of Asunción's shantytowns en route to the botanical gardens, Luque, Isla Valle and Areguá. The fare to Areguá, a US Peace Corps training centre, is US$0.35 single.

To Encarnación, the snail's pace steam locomotive takes 16 hours (compared to five hours on the bus), but costs only US$3. You can buy a through ticket to Lacroze Station in Buenos Aires for US$29, but most people take the bus to Encarnación, cross the bridge to Posadas and purchase their train tickets there.

Car Rental Asunción has several car rental agencies: Hertz (☎ 60-5708) at Eusebio Ayala, km 4.5 or at Silvio Pettirossi Airport (☎ 20-6195); National (☎ 49-1379) at Yegros 501; Rent-A-Car (☎ 49-2733) at Calle Palma 503; and Touring Car (☎ 44-7945) at Iturbe 682.

River An alternative way of crossing to Argentina is the launch from Puerto Itá Enramada, west of the capital, to Puerto Pilcomayo, Formosa. These leave every half hour on weekdays between 7 am and 5 pm, and Saturdays irregularly from 7 to 10 am. It is possible to return by bus from Clorinda.

For long-distance boat services up the Río Paraguay, visit the Flota Mercantil del Estado (☎ 44-8544) at Estrella 672. Although getting hard information from them is like pulling wisdom teeth, both the *Presidente Carlos Antonio López* and the *Bahía Negra* supposedly sail twice monthly from Asunción to Concepción (310 km, 26 hours), continuing to Corumbá, Brazil (another 830 km, 72 hours more), if river conditions permit. By the current schedule, boats depart Fridays at 8 am and return from Concepción at noon on Sunday, but this can change. Passages to Concepción are: US$10 1st-class, US$6 tourist; to Corumbá, US$35 tourist, US$25 with deck space.

As many as a dozen naval supply boats per

week also take passengers up the Río Paraguay as far as Concepción; inquire at the port at the river end of Calle Montevideo.

Getting Around
To/From the Airport
From downtown, bus No 30A takes 50 to 60 minutes to Silvio Pettirossi Airport. Taxis cost about US$10.

Bus
Asunción city buses go almost everywhere for around US$0.20, but Paraguayans are less nighttime people than Argentines or Uruguayans and buses are few after about 10 or 11 pm, so plan your late night trip well or else take a cab. On the other hand, buses start running very early in the morning, since Paraguayans start work around 6.30 or 7 am. Around noon, buses are jammed with people going home for an extended lunch, so avoid travel into the neighbourhoods or suburbs at this hour.

Taxi
Asunción's cabs are metred and reasonable, but may tack on a surcharge late at night.

Eastern Paraguay

East of the Río Paraguay and beyond Asunción is the nucleus of historical Paraguay, the homeland of the Guaraní people among whom the Spaniards began to settle in the 16th century. More than 90% of the country's population now lives here, mostly within 100 km of Asunción, but the border towns of Encarnación, across the Río Paraná from the Argentine city of Posadas, and Ciudad del Este (ex-Puerto Presidente Stroessner), across the Paraná from the Brazilian city of Foz do Iguaçu, have grown dramatically because of the enormous binational hydroelectric projects at Itaipú and Yacyretá.

Many of Paraguay's finest cultural, historical and natural attractions are within a short distance of Asunción, on a convenient and popular circuit from the capital. These include the weaving centre of Itauguá, the lakeside resorts of San Bernardino and Areguá, the celebrated shrine of Caacupé, colonial villages like Piribebuy and Yaguarón, and, a bit farther, the Parque Nacional Ybycuí. On and near the highway between Asunción and Encarnación, numerous Jesuit ruins are in equal or better repair than those in the Argentine province of Misiones. Fast-growing Ciudad del Este is Paraguay's gateway to the Iguazú Falls and the gigantic Itaipú hydroelectric project, itself a tourist attraction of sorts.

The Circuito Central

With typical hyperbole, Paraguayan tourist brochures label this itinerary, roughly a 200 km round trip from Asunción, the Circuito de Oro (Golden Circuit), but its lack of truly glittering attractions should not deter you from making day trips, weekend excursions or even longer outings from the capital.

In most of these towns and villages, people pay little attention to street names, if indeed there are any.

AREGUÁ

On the south shore of Paraguay's largest lake, Lago Ypacaraí, Areguá is a resort town, and is slightly higher and cooler than Asunción. Just 28 km from the capital, it is also a US Peace Corps training centre, but volunteers warn that pollution from a nearby fertilizer plant has made the lake undesirable for swimming. On the main avenue from the train station to the lake, *Hospedaje Ozli* has rooms with fan for US$4 per person. This place has pleasant gardens and good food is available at reasonable prices.

Most visitors arrive by the antique steam train, which leaves downtown Asunción around noon, and return by bus. From Asunción's bus terminal, Transporte Ypacaraiense (Línea 242) leaves almost every half hour during the day. For a longer excursion, there is a launch across the lake to San Bernardino from the pier at the Balneario Municipal. It departs every half hour from 10.15 am to 2.15 pm.

ITAUGUÁ

Founded in 1728 and only 30 km from Asunción, Itauguá is the home of Paraguay's famous ñandutí lace, a cottage industry which is practised by skilled women from childhood to old age. Outdoors, on both sides of Ruta 2, the main highway to Ciudad del Este, weavers display their multicoloured merchandise, ranging in size from doilies to bedspreads. You can bargain with the shopkeepers – the smaller pieces cost only a few dollars, but the larger ones range from US$50 upward. It is possible to visit many of these houses, where you can see the women working on their latest project.

Two blocks south of the highway, the **Museo Parroquial San Rafael** displays Franciscan and secular relics from the colonial era to the present day, including

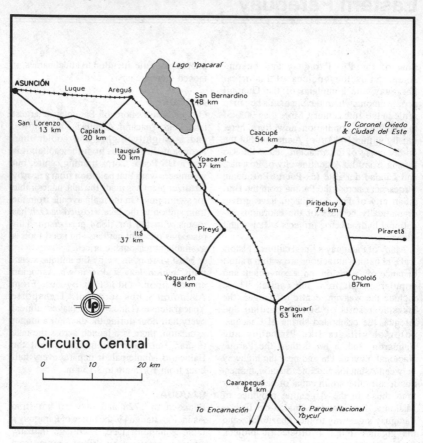

Lago Ypacaraí

ASUNCIÓN   Luque   Areguá

San Bernardino
48 km

San Lorenzo
13 km

Capiatá
20 km

Itauguá
30 km

Ypacaraí
37 km

To Coronel Oviedo
& Ciudad del Este

Caacupé
54 km

Piribebuy
74 km

Itá
37 km

Pireyú

Piraretã

Yaguarón
48 km

Chololó
87km

Paraguarí
63 km

Circuito Central

0   10   20 km

Caarapeguá
84 km

To Encarnación

To Parque Nacional
Ybycuí

Franciscan-influenced indigenous artwork, as well as very early examples of ñandutí. Although it is dark and the exhibits are kept under less than ideal conditions, it definitely justifies a visit. It is open daily from 7 to 11 am and from 3 to 5 pm.

From the Asunción bus terminal, Transporte Ñandutí (Línea 165) leaves for Itauguá every 15 minutes between 5 am and 11 pm.

SAN BERNARDINO
San Bernardino, on the eastern shore of Lago Ypacaraí and 48 km from Asunción on a northern spur off Ruta 2, was settled by German colonists in the late 19th century. It is now a weekend resort for Asunción's elite, and has a wide selection of restaurants, cafés and hotels along its shady streets and the lakeshore, but there are still reasonable budget alternatives. The lake is cleaner than at Areguá.

Restaurant Las Palmeras and the German bakery on Calle Colonos Alemanes are good places to eat, while the *Hotel Santa Rita* (☎ 258) is probably the best bargain for accommodation, with singles around US$6. *Hotel del Lago* (☎ 201) has doubles for US$16, while more upscale lodging is available at *Acuario San Bernardino* (☎ 371), at US$20/25 a single/double, and the *Casino San Bernardino* (☎ 301), at US$40/45.

From the Asunción terminal, Transporte Villa del Lago (Línea [line] 210) has buses to San Bernardino every 20 to 30 minutes for most of the day. Transporte Cordillera de los Andes (Línea 103) has a slightly less frequent service.

CAACUPÉ

Every 8th of December since the mid-18th century, hordes of pilgrims have descended upon Caacupé for the **Día de la Virgen**, or Immaculate Conception, but even at other times of the year it is an important resort and Paraguay's most important religious centre. Often, after ending their tour of duty in the Chaco, military conscripts from eastern Paraguay walk the length of the Ruta Trans-Chaco and the last 54 km across Asunción to the famous Basílica de Nuestra Señora de Los Milagros, which dominates the townscape. It is situated on a huge cobblestone plaza, which easily accommodates the 300,000 faithful who often gather here. Opposite the plaza is a block of cheap restaurants and tacky souvenir stands.

Hospedaje Uruguayo, midway between Ruta 2 and the Basílica, has very comfortable rooms in an attractive tropical garden setting for US$7 single with private bath and fan, US$12 with air-conditioning. *Hotel La Giralda*, on the corner of Alberdi and 14 de Mayo, has singles for US$8. *Hospedaje San Blas I*, north of the highway but still only 1½ blocks from the Basílica, has singles/doubles for US$4/7 with shared bath. *Hospedaje Ideal* is comparably priced. *Camping Melli* appears virtually abandoned, although there is a caretaker.

From Asunción, Transporte La Caacupeña (Línea 119) and Transporte Villa Serrana (Línea 110) run buses almost every 10 minutes between 5 am and 10 pm.

PIRIBEBUY

During the War of the Triple Alliance, the village of Piribebuy briefly served as the national capital and also saw serious combat.

Founded in 1640, it features a mid-18th century church in excellent repair, which retains some of the original colonial woodwork and sculpture. The **Museo Histórico Comandante Pedro Juan Caballero**, opposite the church on the plaza, has interesting exhibits in a deteriorating condition. It is opened on request – ask at Don Alfredo Bernal's house at Maestro Fermín López 1048, a block off the plaza. Don Alfredo himself is a Chaco War veteran, wounded three times by Bolivian bullets, and will show you his own uniform on display.

Only 74 km from Asunción, on a southern branch off Ruta 2, Piribebuy is a good place for a glimpse of rural Paraguay. At its northern entrance is the government's experimental sugar cane plantation, with a nearby mill, while across the highway peasants grow maize, beans, and manioc. At the south end of town, a skilled carpenter produces up to five traditional wooden-wheeled oxcarts per year. Still common along Paraguay's highways, these carts of hard lapacho wood last up to 25 years and cost from US$400 to US$600 apiece.

Restaurant Hotel Rincón Viejo, across the street from Don Alfredo's house, has doubles with private bath for US$12, but bargaining may lower the price to US$8. Transporte Piribebuy (Línea 197) has buses from Asunción every half-hour between 5 am and 9 pm.

AROUND PIRIBEBUY

Chololó

South of Piribebuy, the narrow, scenic paved road leads to Chololó, less a village than a series of riverside campgrounds; there is a branch road to the modest waterfall at Piraretá.

Paraguarí

At Paraguarí, the road connects with Ruta 1, leading back to Asunción. The landscape around Paraguarí is very attractive hill country, but the town itself is notable only for having expunged 'Presidente Stroessner' as a street name, although the children's playground still bears a plaque honouring

Stroessner's wife Eligia. *Hotel Chololó* (☎ 242) offers reasonable accommodation for around US$8 single. Transporte Ciudad Paraguarí (Línea 193) has buses to Asunción every 15 minutes between 5 am and 8 pm.

YAGUARÓN

Yaguarón's pride is its 18th-century Franciscan church, a wooden structure 70 metres long and 30 metres wide and a landmark of colonial architecture, although its bell tower is a 20th-century reconstruction. It is also the home of the **Museo del Doctor Francia**, 2½ blocks from the church in a well-preserved colonial house in which Francia was appointed colonial administrator. It contains some good colonial and early independence portraiture, including likenesses of El Supremo at different ages. It's open Tuesday, Thursday and Saturday from 3 to 5 pm and Sunday and holidays from 9.30 to 11.30 am and 3 to 5 pm.

Across Ruta 1 from the church is an inexpensive, unnamed restaurant which has mediocre food except for its excellent, fresh, home-made ice cream. It also has basic accommodation for US$2.50 per person. From Asunción, 48 km north, Transporte Ciudad Paraguarí (Línea 193) has buses every 15 minutes between 5 am and 8.15 pm.

ITÁ

Founded in 1539 by Domingo Martínez de Irala, Itá is known for its *gallinita* pottery, made of local black clay. There are very frequent buses to and from Asunción, 37 km away, with Transporte 3 de Febrero (Línea 159) and Transporte Cotrisa SRL (Línea 159).

South-Eastern Paraguay

PARQUE NACIONAL YBYCUÍ

In the department of Paraguarí, 5000-hectare Parque Nacional Ybycuí is the most accessible unit in the Paraguayan system. Created in 1973, it preserves one of the last remaining stands of Brazilian rainforest in eastern Paraguay. Its rugged topography consists of steep hills, reaching up to 400 metres, dissected by creeks which form a number of attractive waterfalls and pools. In structure and species composition, the forests resemble those of Argentina's Parque Nacional Iguazú. Wildlife, though abundant, is rarely seen because the forest is so dense; animals are so difficult to see that they usually hide rather than run. Annual rainfall is about 1500 mm, while temperatures average around 22°C to 24°C.

Things to See & Do

Ybycuí is remarkably tranquil and undeveloped, although the influx of weekenders from Asunción can disrupt its peacefulness. When this happens, you can take refuge on any of several hiking trails, which are more extensive and accessible than those at Iguazú. There is a ranger on duty at park headquarters, as well as two Peace Corps volunteers assigned to park improvement projects, who are good sources of information.

Mirador Trail West of the campground, on the opposite side of the road from the ranger's house, this short but steep trail to an overlook doesn't quite repay the climb, since the forest is so dense it's hard to see out. There is wildlife, but you are more likely to hear it than see it.

Salto Guaraní Below this waterfall near the campground, there is a bridge to a pleasant creekside trail which leads to the old iron foundry at La Rosada. You will see a wealth of butterflies, including the large metallic blue morpho. Watch out for poisonous snakes, but bear in mind that the rattler and coral snake are not aggressive and the very aggressive yarará is generally nocturnal.

La Rosada The first of its kind in South America, this iron foundry was built during the government of Carlos Antonio López, but was destroyed by Brazilian forces during the War of the Triple Alliance. The old waterwheel is of special interest. Located at the park entrance, two km west of the campground, it has an adjacent museum which keeps irregular hours.

Much of Ybycuí's forest is secondary, having recovered from overexploitation during the years when the foundry operated on wood charcoal, two tonnes of which were required to produce a single tonne of iron. Engineers dammed Arroyo Mina to provide water and power for the bellows, while oxcarts brought the ore from several different sites, more than 25 km away.

Places to Stay

There are no hotels in the park, so your only alternative is to camp at Arroyo Mina, which has adequate sanitary facilities, cold showers, and a confitería which serves meals on weekends. Level sites are relatively few. Fortunately, mosquitos are also few, but swarming moths and flea-like insects are a nighttime nuisance, even though they do not bite.

At the cotton-mill village of Ybycuí, *Hotel Pytu'u Renda* (☎ 264) charges US$10 for a single.

Getting There & Away

Parque Nacional Ybycuí is 151 km southeast of Asunción. Ruta 1, the paved highway to Encarnación, leads 84 km south to Carapeguá, where there is a turnoff to the park, a further 67 km, via the villages of Acahay and Ybycuí. From Asunción, Transporte Emilio Cabrera has eight buses daily to Acahay, where it is necessary to make local connections to the village of Ybycuí – a bus leaves daily at noon for the park entrance, returning to the village every morning at 7 am. There are also covered lorries which continue through the park to the village of Sargento Barrientos.

If driving, do not mistake Parque Nacional Bernardino Caballero, an historical monument with a semi-abandoned museum, for Parque Nacional Ybycuí, which is several km farther down the road.

The Fundación Bertoni (☎ 21-2386), 25 de Mayo 2140 in Asunción, runs occasional full-day excursions to the park, including transportation, guides and a picnic lunch, for US$20.

VILLA FLORIDA

On the banks of the Río Tabicuary, 161 km south-east of Asunción, Villa Florida is a popular but relatively expensive *balneario* (bathing resort) and fishing and camping spot. *Hotel La Misionera*, while spotlessly clean, is very basic for US$12 per person, although it does have a good, reasonably priced restaurant with fish dishes.

ENCARNACIÓN

The city of Encarnación, opposite the Argentine city of Posadas, was the site of the early Jesuit *reducción* (mission) of Itapúa, and is now the southern gateway to Paraguay. Nothing now remains of the original mission.

Encarnación, a lively town of 50,000, is a town in limbo – if and when the Yacyretá dam is completed, the resulting 'lake' will inundate the oldest part of the city. In the meantime, most established businesses have moved onto high ground, leaving the old town centre as a rather tawdry but vibrant bazaar of cheap imported trinkets – digital watches, personal cassette players and other electronic goodies which Argentines swarm to buy – and decaying public buildings and housing. See it before it drowns.

Orientation

Encarnación sits on the north bank of the Río Paraná, directly opposite the much larger city of Posadas, Argentina. It is connected to Posadas by a new international bridge, built by Argentina at Paraguay's insistence as part of the Yacyretá agreement. Encarnación now comprises two very different parts: an older, colonial quarter along the flood-prone river front, and a newer section on the bluff overlooking the river. From the riverside, Avenida Mariscal J F Estigarribia leads from the old commercial centre to the new one around the Plaza Artigas, which was the site of the original Jesuit mission. Most government offices and businesses have relocated to higher ground, but a few hang on.

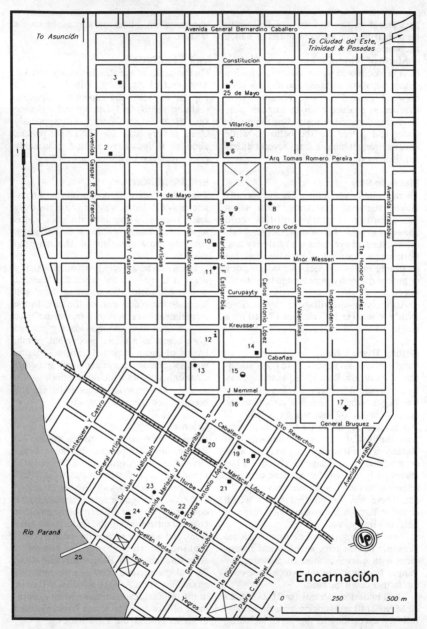

To Asunción

Avenida General Bernardino Caballero

To Ciudad del Este,
Trinidad & Posadas

Constitucion

3

4

25 de Mayo

Villarrica

5

6

Arq Tomas Romero Pereira

Avenida Gaspar R de Francia

Avenida Irrazabau

2

7

14 de Mayo

Antequera Y Castro

General Artigas

Dr Juan L Mallorquin

Avenida Mariscal J F Estigarribia

9

8

Cerro Corá

10

Mnor Wiessen

11

Carlos Antonio López

Lomas Valentinas

Independencia

Tte Honorio Gonzalez

Curupayty

Kreusser

12

14

Cabañas

13

15

J Memmel

16

17

General Bruguez

Antequera Y Castro

General Artigas

Dr Juan L Mallorquin

Avenida Mariscal J F Estigarribia

J Caballero

P

Sto Reverchon

Avenida Irrazabal

20

19 18

Iturbe

Carlos Antonio López

Mariscal López

21

23

22

Avenida General Gamarra

24

Capellán Molas

General Escobar

Rio Paraná

Yegros

25

Yegros

te Gonzalez

Padre C Winquel

Encarnación

0   250   500 m

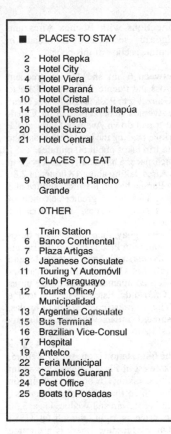

■ PLACES TO STAY

2 Hotel Repka
3 Hotel City
4 Hotel Viera
5 Hotel Paraná
10 Hotel Cristal
14 Hotel Restaurant Itapúa
18 Hotel Viena
20 Hotel Suizo
21 Hotel Central

▼ PLACES TO EAT

9 Restaurant Rancho Grande

OTHER

1 Train Station
6 Banco Continental
7 Plaza Artigas
8 Japanese Consulate
11 Touring Y Automóvil Club Paraguayo
12 Tourist Office/ Municipalidad
13 Argentine Consulate
15 Bus Terminal
16 Brazilian Vice-Consul
17 Hospital
19 Antelco
22 Feria Municipal
23 Cambios Guaraní
24 Post Office
25 Boats to Posadas

Information

Tourist Office The Sección de Cultura at the Municipalidad, on the corner of Avenida Mariscal J F Estigarribia and Kreusser, is helpful but has almost no printed matter. It's open weekdays from 7 am to 12.30 pm.

Money In the old city, try Cambios Guaraní at Avenida Mariscal J F Estigarribia 307. In the newer part of town, you can change at the Banco Continental, Avenida Mariscal J F Estigarribia 1418, or the nearby branch of Citlbank. Outside regular hours and on weekends, the bus terminal is loaded with money changers.

Post & Telecommunications The post office is at Capellán Molas 337, in the old city. Antelco is on the corner of P J Caballero and Carlos Antonio López, next door to the Hotel Viena.

Foreign Consulates The Argentine Consulate is on the corner of Dr Juan L Mallorquín 788 and Cabañas. It's open weekdays from 7.30 am to 1.30 pm. The Brazilian Vice-Consulate is at Memmel 452, directly across from the bus terminal, and is open weekdays from 8 am to noon. Japan has a consulate at Carlos Antonio López 1290.

Travel Agencies The Touring y Automóvil Club Paraguayo, on the corner of Avenida Mariscal J F Estigarribia and Mnor Wicssen, has poor country maps, but these may be the only ones available in town.

Medical Services The Hospital Regional is on the corner of Independencia and General Bruguez.

Film Developing Serpylcolor, on the corner of Avenida Mariscal J F Estigarribia and Curupayty, has very cheap Fujichrome film. Travellers in Posadas may want to cross the border to load up before continuing to Iguazú or Buenos Aires.

Feria Municipal

On the corner of Carlos Antonio López and General Gamarra, the municipal market is a warren of stalls belonging to petty merchants intent on milking every last peso out of visiting Argentines before the flood. This description may sound pejorative, but in reality the place has a liveliness which transcends the dubious quality of the baubles and gadgets which change hands here. It is also a good, inexpensive place to eat.

Places to Stay

Camping There is a public campground at the entrance to the Jesuit ruins at Trinidad, 28 km from Encarnación, but it was not in operation at the time of writing.

Hotels Encarnación does not lack reasonable accommodation, and visitors to Posadas may find it almost as convenient and much cheaper to stay on the Paraguayan side. Undoubtedly the cheapest is the homey *Hotel Repka* (☎ 3546), at Tomas Romero Pereira 44 near the train station, which has singles/doubles with shared bath for US$2/3.50. *Hotel Itapúa* (☎ 3346), directly across from the bus terminal on the corner of Cabañas and Carlos Antonio López, has singles for US$3 with shared bath, US$5 with private bath. *Hotel Suizo* (☎ 3692), Avenida Mariscal J F Estigarribia 562 between P J Caballero and Mariscal López, charges US$3.50/6 single/double. At *Hotel Central* (☎ 3454), Carlos Antonio López 542, and *Hotel City* (☎ 2432), Antequera Y Castro 1659, rates are around US$4/7.

The clean, quiet *Hotel Viena* (☎ 3486), P J Caballero 568, is excellent value, with singles with private bath for US$6.50 – German speakers may get a small discount and special attention. Do not confuse it with the *Hotel Viera* (☎ 2038), 25 de Mayo 413, which is pricier at about US$12 per person. *Hotel Paraná* (☎ 4480), Avenida Mariscal J F Estigarribia 1414, has singles/doubles with private bath for US$15/21, while *Hotel Cristal* (☎ 2371), Avenida Mariscal J F Estigarribia 1157, is the best in town at US$20/30. Just outside town, the *Novotel* (☎ 5120), in Villa Quitéria at Ruta 1, km 361, has 1st-class accommodation for US$32/40.

Places to Eat

Restaurant Cuarajhy, on Plaza Artigas at the corner of Avenida Mariscal J F Estigarribia and Arq T R Pereira, is a good, moderately priced parrilla, packed with locals and Argentines. *Restaurant Rancho Grande*, on the corner of Avenida Mariscal J F Estigarribia and Cerro Corá, is a large pleasant parrilla under a thatched roof, and is very popular with locals; at night, Paraguayan folk musicians perform, including harpists.

Getting There & Away

Air There are no air services to Encarnación itself, but Posadas on the Argentine side has air connections with Buenos Aires and Puerto Iguazú – see the entry for Posadas in the Argentine section of this book.

Bus Between 6 am and 11 pm, frequent buses cross the Puente Internacional Beato Roque González to Posadas for US$1. These begin at Avenida General Bernardino Caballero and travel down Avenida Mariscal J F Estigarribia, passing the bus terminal and the port. The trip takes about 50 minutes.

La Encarnaceña has a daily bus service to Buenos Aires, taking about 18 hours, at 2.30 pm. Río Paraná has an identical service at 3 pm. There is a much greater selection of departures from Posadas, and prices are slightly lower.

Within Paraguay, there are 27 daily buses to Asunción, with Flecha de Oro, La Encarnaceña, Nuestra Señora, Alborada and RYSA (all for US$8, taking five to six hours). Ten companies run some 30 buses daily to Ciudad del Este (US$6, four to five hours). There are also connections to Ayolas, San Cosme y Damián, Villarrica, and many lesser destinations.

Train The train station is on Arq T R Pereira, six blocks west of Plaza Artigas. The steam locomotives, taking 16 hours to Asunción (more than three times as long as the bus), leave Sunday at 5 am and Wednesday at 3.30 pm. The price is right, though, at US$3 single. On Wednesdays, there is a through train to Buenos Aires, but most travellers catch this in Posadas.

River For the time being, launches still cross the Paraná to Posadas every half-hour on weekdays from 6.30 am to 5 pm, Saturdays and 'semi-holidays' from 7 am to 10.15 am and 1 to 4.30 pm, and Sundays and holidays from 8.15 to 9.15 am and 3.30 to 4.30 pm. The trip takes 30 minutes and costs US$1.

Getting Around

Encarnación has a good local bus system, but for all practical purposes, your feet should get you around town. If you need to make a quick connection from the bus terminal to the train station, or vice versa, there are both horse-drawn and petrol-powered cabs.

TRINIDAD

South-eastern Paraguay was the province of the Jesuits until their expulsion in 1767 and shares the history of the Argentine province of Misiones. The missions stretched as far north as San Ignacio Guazú and Santa María de Fe, on the road to Asunción. For more details on the history of the Jesuit missions, see the chapter on Argentine Misiones.

Paraguay's best preserved Jesuit reducción, Trinidad occupies an imposing hilltop site 28 km from Encarnación. Though its church is not as large and its grounds not as extensive as those at San Ignacio Miní, Trinidad is in many ways its equal. No visitor to Argentine Misiones and Iguazú Falls should neglect to cross the border to visit the ruins of Trinidad. From its bell tower the Jesuit mission at Jesús, 10 km north, is easily visible – Jesús is strictly speaking not ruins but rather an incomplete construction project, interrupted by the Jesuits' expulsion in 1767.

Founded only in 1706, Trinidad was one of the later Jesuit establishments, but by

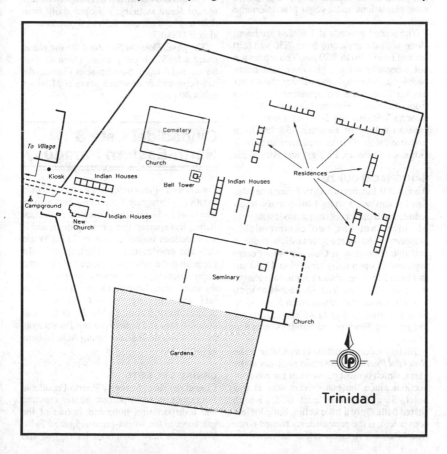

Trinidad

1728 it boasted a Guaraní population of more than 4000. Designed by the Italian Jesuit architect Juan Bautista Prímoli, who spent 12 years on the project, it was not finished until 1760, only a few years before the Jesuit expulsion. Its church, whose truly elaborate pulpit, frescos, statues and other adornments still remain in an excellent state of repair, was the centrepiece of the reducción.

As elsewhere, the Jesuits introduced European crafts and industry, so that Trinidad became famous for the manufacture of bells, organs, harps and statuary. It also operated three cattle estancias, two large *yerba mate* plantations and a sugar plantation and mill.

The fenced grounds at Trinidad are open, along with the museum, from 7.30 to 11.30 am and from 1.30 to 5.30 pm. The fences are not especially secure, however, and many people climb through and wander about after closing time, with no apparent complaint from the staff. Fifteen buses daily pass through Trinidad and Jesús en route to the German colony of Hohenau, 38 km from Encarnación. The companies are B R Gonzáles, Pastoreo, El Tigre and Alto Verá.

SAN IGNACIO GUAZÚ

About 100 km north-west of Encarnación, San Ignacio was also an 18th-century Jesuit reducción. It preserves only a modest sample of ruins, but has two commendable museums. The **Museo Jesuítico** holds a valuable collection of Guaraní Indian carvings, and is open daily from 8 to 11.30 am and from 2 to 5 pm, with an admission charge of about US$0.40. The **Museo Histórico Semblanza de Héroes** is open Monday to Saturday from 7.45 to 11.45 am and from 2 to 5 pm, and Sundays and holidays from 8 to 11 am.

Budget accommodation is available at the *Hotel del Puerto*, on the main highway at the plaza, which is most convenient for bus connections since the bus drivers stay at this hotel. Singles/doubles cost US$3/5 with shared bath. Only a little better, but a lot less convenient, is the pretentiously named *Gran Hotel Parador Arapizandú*, at the turnoff to

Ayolas at the north end of town, which charges US$4 per person with private bath.

There are more than 30 buses per day to Asunción (3½ hours), 20 to Encarnación, 20 to the departmental capital of San Juan Bautista, and 15 to the Río Paraná port of Ayolas. There are also five buses daily to the village of Santa María.

SANTA MARÍA

Twelve km from San Ignacio off Ruta 1, Santa María is an ancient Jesuit reducción with dirt roads and a shady plaza.

The **Museo Jesuítico** has a superb collection of Jesuit statuary; it's open daily from 8.30 to 11.30 am and 1.30 to 5 pm. Admission is US$0.75.

The basic *Pensión San José*, on the plaza, charges US$2.50 per person. There are five buses daily from San Ignacio Guazú, the most convenient of which leave at 11.30 am and 4.30 pm.

Ciudad del Este & North-Eastern Paraguay

Easternmost Paraguay, along the Brazilian frontier, is Paraguay's economic boom zone. The world's largest hydroelectric project, at Itaipú, has spurred this development, and is a marvellous object lesson in Third World debt and environmental catastrophe, whilst propelling the town of Ciudad del Este into unprecedented, if temporary, prosperity. At the same time, Brazilian agricultural colonists are moving across the border, deforesting the countryside for coffee and cotton farms and squeezing out Paraguayan peasants and the few remaining Aché Indians of the region.

CIUDAD DEL ESTE

Ciudad del Este, formerly Puerto Presidente Stroessner, is an important border crossing and transportation hub, and is one of the gateways to the world-famous Iguazú Falls. While it is hard to ignore its ragged and undisciplined squalor, Ciudad del Este still has a certain infectious boom-town vitality, and it makes an interesting stopover for a day or so. Brazilian and Argentine shoppers jam the sidewalks at night in search of low prices for consumer electronics, a sector in which Asian immigrants are pre-eminent.

Orientation

Ciudad del Este sits on the west bank of the Río Paraná, and is connected to the Brazilian city of Foz do Iguaçu by the Puente de la Amistad (Bridge of Friendship). Created only in 1957, the town has a somewhat irregular plan. The main street is the Avenida San Blas, the westward extension of the Puente de la Amistad, which becomes Ruta 2 to Caaguazú, Coronel Oviedo and Asunción. Whilst a bit complex and irregular, the centre is very compact and can easily be managed on foot.

Information

Tourist Office For information, ask at the Municipalidad, on Avenida Alejo García, which opens very early but closes before noon. Many places around town distribute a brochure entitled *Guía Turística y Comercial Ciudad del Este* which contains some useful information and a map.

Money Money changers are everywhere, especially at the border, but they give poorer rates than the banks or cambios. Guaraní Cambios is on the corner of Avenida Monseñor Rodríguez and Tte Coronel Pampliega.

Telecommunications Antelco is on the corner of Avenida Alejo García and Pai Pérez, directly alongside the Municipalidad.

Foreign Consulates The Brazilian Consulate, on the corner of Tte Coronel Pampliega 337 and Pai Pérez, is open weekdays from 8 am to 6 pm.

Travel Agencies The Touring y Automóvil Club Paraguayo (☎ 2340) is on Avenida San Blas, about one km west of Plaza Madame

Lynch on the road to Asunción. It is friendly and helpful, selling a road atlas which, unfortunately, suffers from truly atrocious cartography.

Places to Stay

Accommodation is abundant in Ciudad del Este, but costlier than in other Paraguayan cities. The most reasonably priced place is the *Hotel Paraná* (☎ 2568), Camilo Recalde 128, where singles/doubles cost US$10/13. The cozy, friendly *Hotel Mi Abuela* (☎ 2373), with an attractive garden courtyard, has singles/doubles with private bath and ceiling fans for US$10/15; for air-conditioning, add about US$2 per person. Also good value is the German-run *Hotel Munich* (☎ 2371), on the corner of Emilio R Fernández and Capitán Miranda, where singles/doubles with private bath, breakfast and air-conditioning cost US$12/15.

Convair Hotel (☎ 2349), on the corner of Avenida Adrián Jara and Avenida Alejo García, has several categories of accommodation, ranging from basic 'C' with ceiling fans (US$12/15); 'B' with air-conditioning and television (US$22/27); and 'A', with air-conditioning, television, telephone and other amenities (US$25/35).

At the modern *Hotel Puerta del Sol* (☎ 8081), Avenida Boquerón 111, rates are US$16/21 with private bath and air-conditioning. *Hotel San Rafael* (☎ 8105), on the corner of Avenida Adrián Jara and Abay, charges US$21/30 for rooms with breakfast and air-conditioning, while the modernistic *Executive Hotel* (☎ 8981) is dearer at US$30/35.

Places to Eat

In spite of its misleading name, *Restaurant Seoul*, a sidewalk café on the corner of Curupayty and Avenida Adrián Jara, is a parrillada, offering a good, complete meal for around US$3 with surprisingly good live entertainment (Paraguayan folk music) at no additional charge.

Getting There & Away

Air A new international airport is being built

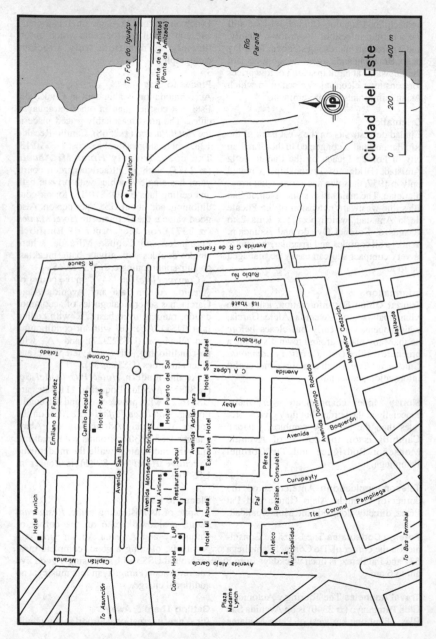

Ciudad del Este

near Ciudad del Este, but there are also major airports at both Foz do Iguaçu in Brazil, and Puerto Iguazú in Argentina. From Foz, Varig and other Brazilian airlines have flights to São Paulo, Curitibá, Río de Janeiro and Asunción; from Puerto Iguazú, Aerolíneas and Austral have regular services to Aeroparque in Buenos Aires.

LAP (☎ 4340) is on the corner of Adrián Jara and Tte Coronel Pampliega. The military airline TAM (☎ 8352), in the Edificio SABA just off Monseñor Rodríguez, has recently commenced flights to Asunción from the airstrip at Itaipú. These leave Monday at 8 am and Saturday at noon.

Bus Buses leave Ciudad del Este for Foz do Iguaçu every 10 minutes on weekdays and Saturdays, and every half-hour on Sundays and holidays. Catch them at the entrance to the bridge over the Paraná after going through Paraguayan immigration. On the other side, disembark to go through Brazilian immigration (unless you are just crossing for the day); if you hold on to your ticket, any following bus will take you to the terminal at Foz.

There are half a dozen international services daily to São Paulo (18 hours), Río de Janeiro (25 hours), Florianópolis (15 hours) and Curitibá (13 hours) with PLUMA, RYSA, Catarinense and La Paraguaya. There is, of course, a wider selection of Brazilian bus services in Foz proper.

From Ciudad del Este to Asunción (US$8, five hours), there are 34 buses daily with RYSA, Rápido Caaguazú, and Nuestra Señora. There are nearly as many to Encarnación, with Nuestra Señora, Transporte Paraná, RYSA, Empresa Ciudad del Este and others. Salto Cristal has two per day via Villarrica to Ybycuí, convenient for Parque Nacional Ybycuí, while Piribebuy and La Guaireña also go to Villarrica several times daily.

River If you prefer to bypass Brazil, there are launches from Puerto Presidente Franco to Puerto Iguazú, Argentina, from 7.30 am to 2 pm, at intervals of half an hour to one hour.

Getting Around

Ciudad del Este's public transport system has been able to keep pace with the city's rapid development, but for most travellers the central area is compact enough that it will not be necessary to use it. The exception is the bus terminal, south of town; take the No 8 bus (red) from Avenida Alejo García.

AROUND CIUDAD DEL ESTE
Itaipú Dam

With an installed capacity of 12.6 million kilowatts, the bi-national Itaipú dam is the world's largest hydroelectric project and an extraordinary illustration of the ways in which massive development projects have put countries such as Brazil many billions of dollars into debt with no hope of repayment. Paraguay, though, has benefited economically from the Itaipú project because of the construction boom, its own low domestic demand, and Brazil's need to purchase the Paraguayan surplus. It risks, however, becoming an energy colony of its mammoth neighbour. At the same time, should the price of competing sources of energy drop, reduced Brazilian demand could saddle Paraguay with the repayment of an unexpected share of the project's enormous capital and maintenance costs.

Project propaganda omits any reference to the costs of the US$25 billion project, and environmental concerns figured not at all in the Itaipú equation. The dam created a reservoir covering 1350 sq km, 220 metres deep, which drowned the falls at Sete Quedas, a larger and even more impressive natural feature than Iguazú. Recent research indicates that stagnant water created by the reservoir has provided a new habitat for anopheline mosquitos, posing an increased malaria risk in an area where the disease had nearly been eradicated.

On both sides of the border, there are free tours, led by well-rehearsed guides, which stop long enough for visitors to take photographs. On the Paraguayan side, these leave from the Centro de Recepción de Visitas, north of Ciudad del Este near the town of Hernandarias. Hours are Monday to Saturday at 8.30, 9.30 and 10.30 pm, and at 2, 3 and 4 pm, and Sundays at 8.30, 9.30 and 10.30 am. Passports are required. There is a documentary film half an hour before the tour departs.

From Ciudad del Este, take any Hernandarias Transtur or Tacurú Pucú bus from the roundabout on the intersection of Avenida San Blas and Avenida Alejo García. These leave every 10 to 15 minutes throughout the day – ask to be dropped at the entrance to the unmistakably conspicuous project.

Salto Monday

They're not Sete Quedas, but these falls on the Río Monday, near Puerto Presidente Franco, are the best Paraguay now has to offer. They're only 10 km from Ciudad del Este, but there is no scheduled public transport, so taxi is the best alternative. Otherwise it should be possible to catch one of the frequent buses from Ciudad del Este to Puerto Presidente Franco, and walk to the falls from there.

Colonia Iguazú

Forty km west of Ciudad del Este on the highway to Asunción, Colonia Iguazú is a Japanese agricultural colony, established in 1960 with the assistance of the Japanese government, which specialises in cotton. Buses from Ciudad del Este stop at the Esso Servicentro, where the restaurant serves excellent Japanese food along with Paraguayan dishes.

CORONEL OVIEDO

Midway between Asunción and Ciudad del Este, Coronel Oviedo is a major crossroad in eastern Paraguay – long-distance buses pass through town at least every 15 minutes all day. Roads go north to Saltos del Guairá and Pedro Juan Caballero (with a branch to Concepción), and south to Villarrica, centre of an area of German colonisation on the Asunción-Encarnación railway.

Hotel Alemán, at the crossroads, is a rea-sonable place to stay, while the nearby *Parador La Tranquera* has good food. In the town proper, three km north of the cross-roads, the highly recommended *Hotel Colonial* has singles for US$10. *Hotel del Rey*, Avenida Mariscal J F Estigarribia 261, is slightly cheaper.

Between Coronel Oviedo and San José, a branch road leads to the frequently renamed **Nueva Australia**, a short-lived socialist experiment populated by the descendants of late 19th-century Australian immigrants. Named Hugo Stroessner, for Alfredo's immigrant father, on some maps, the dissension-ridden agricultural colony attracted its earliest participants with exaggerated propaganda on the area's economic potential, until it finally broke apart in 1896. Colonia Cosme, an offshoot south of Villarrica, struggled on a few years more.

PEDRO JUAN CABALLERO

Pedro Juan Caballero, capital of the department of Amambay, is the Paraguayan counterpart of the Brazilian town of Ponta Porã. There is no clearly marked border, and locals cross from one side to the other at will. You can do the same, but if you want to continue any distance into either country, you have to visit immigration at Calle General Bruguez 1247. There are reports of contraband drug traffic in the area, so beware of unsavoury characters.

Guaraní Cambios is on Dr Francia, but there are several other cambios. The Brazilian Consulate (open weekdays, 8 am to noon and 2 to 6 pm) is in the *Hotel La Siesta*, on the corner of Alberdi and Dr Francia. This hotel has singles/doubles for US$17/22. More economical accommodation is available at several hotels along Mariscal López: *Hotel La Negra*, Mariscal López 1342; (US$2.50/3.50); *Hotel Cerro Corá*, Mariscal López 1511 (US$4/7); *Hotel Guavirá*, Mariscal López 1325 (US$4/7); *Hotel del Paraguay*, Mariscal López 1185 (US$4/8); and *Hotel Peralta*, Mariscal López 1257 (US$5 a single). *Hotel Eiruzú*, Avenida Mariscal J F Estigarribia 48, charges US$22/31.

Getting There & Away
TAM and LATN have a dozen flights a week to Asunción at very reasonable fares.

Ten buses daily connect Pedro Juan Caballero with Asunción via Coronel Oviedo; the 532-km trip can take as little as eight hours or as many as 12, depending on the weather and the condition of the road, half of which is not paved.

There are also 10 buses daily to Concepción, where it is possible to travel downriver to Asunción, and one per day to Ciudad del Este. NASA goes daily to Campo Grande, Brazil, but there are more bus services across the border in Ponta Porã and two trains per day.

PARQUE NACIONAL CERRO CORÁ
If you pass through north-eastern Paraguay you should not bypass 22,000-hectare Parque Nacional Cerro Corá, only 40 km west of Pedro Juan Caballero. This park protects an area of dry tropical forest and savanna grasslands in a landscape of steep, isolated hills which rise above the central plateau. Besides a representative sample of Paraguayan flora and fauna, the park also has cultural and historical significance, with pre-Columbian caves and petroglyphs. It was also the site of the battle in which a Brazilian soldier killed Francisco Solano López at the end of the War of the Triple Alliance.

The park has nature trails, a camping area, and a few basic cabañas where travellers can lodge. There are rangers, but there is no formal visitor centre.

CONCEPCIÓN
On the east bank of the Río Paraguay, 310 km upstream from Asunción, Concepción is a small provincial town with an interesting market. It conducts considerable river trade with Brazil. Concepción has two inexpensive hotels, one a new annex of the other: *Hotel Victoria* at Presidente Franco 902, and *Hotel Victoria* at Presidente Franco 693. Both charge around US$4/7.50 for singles/doubles with shared bath.

Getting There & Away
For details of boat traffic from Asunción to Corumbá, Brazil, see the Getting There & Away entry under Asunción.

If you take the boat from Asunción to get a taste of life on the river, you can return by air or bus. TAM and LATN have 15 flights weekly to Asunción, while bus services, subject to suspension due to the condition of the roads, can go either via Pozo Colorado in the Chaco or via Coronel Oviedo, the latter being a nine-hour trip. There are daily buses to Pedro Juan Caballero (continuing to Campo Grande, Brazil), and to Ciudad del Este.

The Chaco

With more than 60% of the country's territory and only a handful of its population, the Chaco is the Paraguayan frontier. Except in the immediate area around Asunción, great distances separate tiny settlements. Its only paved highway, the Ruta Trans-Chaco, leads 450 km to the town of Filadelfia, centre of an area colonised by Mennonite immigrants from Europe since the late 1920s. Beyond Filadelfia, the pavement ends but the highway continues to the Bolivian border at Eugenio Garay, another 300 km north-west.

Geographically, the Paraguayan Chaco is the northernmost segment of an almost featureless plain which rises slowly from south-east to north-west, its surface consisting of soils eroded from the Andes. It comprises three rather distinct zones which emerge gradually as one travels from east to west. Immediately west of the Río Paraguay, the landscape of the Low Chaco becomes a soothing, verdant savanna of caranday palms with scattered islands of thorny scrub, known as *monte*. In this poorly drained area, ponds and marshes shelter large numbers of colourful birds, including the ungainly South American storks. Peasant cultivators build picturesque houses of palm logs, but the primary industry is cattle ranching on estancias even larger than those in Argentina or Uruguay. On both sides of the highway, Paraguayan gauchos gather scrawny cattle.

As the Ruta Trans-Chaco continues northwest, rainfall declines and the drought-tolerant monte expands, with substantial groves of quebracho, palo santo, and the unique *palo borracho*, which conserves water in its bulbous trunk. Despite erratic environmental conditions, Mennonite colonists have built successful agricultural communities in the Middle Chaco, but no one has yet established anything but army bases and cattle estancias in the High Chaco beyond Mariscal Estigarribia, where the thorn forest is denser and rainfall even more undependable.

Historically, the Chaco has been the last refuge of Paraguay's Indian people, such as the Ayoreo and Nivaclé, who managed an independent subsistence until very recently by hunting, gathering and fishing. Later industries included cattle ranching and extraction of the tannin-rich quebracho. It was the Mennonite colonists from Europe, arriving from 1927, who first proved that parts of the Chaco were suitable for more intensive agriculture and permanent settlement. The first Mennonite settlers arrived in the heart of the Chaco not by the Ruta Trans-Chaco (not completed until 1964 and not paved until very recently), but rather by a railway from Puerto Casado, on the upper Río Paraguay.

A glance at the map reveals an inordinate number of Chaco place names which begin with the word *Fortín*. These were the numerous fortifications and trenches, many of which remain in a nearly unaltered state, from the Chaco War of 1932 to 1935. Most of these sites are abandoned, but small settlements have grown up near a few. The Paraguayan military still retains a visible presence throughout the Chaco.

The Chaco War gave Paraguay the incentive to build a network of dirt roads, most of which have deteriorated since the end of hostilities. This generality does not apply in the Mennonite communities, which have done an outstanding job of maintaining those roads within their autonomous jurisdiction. Most of the others are impassable except to 4WD vehicles.

Travel in the Chaco can be rough, and there is very little accommodation outside the few main towns, although it is possible to camp almost anywhere – but beware of snakes. In a pinch, the estancias or the *campesinos* (country people) along the Ruta Trans-Chaco will put you up in a bed with a mosquito net if they have one. Otherwise, you're on your own.

VILLA HAYES

Only a short distance from Asunción across the Puente Remanso, Villa Hayes is an historical curiosity which merits at least a quick visit from the capital. It takes its name from one of the United States' most obscure and undistinguished presidents who, strangely, is considered a hero by Paraguayans.

Rutherford B Hayes (pronounced 'eye-zhess' in the River Plate accent of Paraguay), was president of the United States from 1877-81, leaving office without even seeking a second term. In his hometown of Delaware, Ohio, the only monument to his memory is a plaque on the site of his birthplace, now a petrol station. In Paraguay, by contrast, he is commemorated by the Club Presidente Hayes, which sponsors the local soccer team, a Rutherford B Hayes School, and a monument outside the school. In 1928 and 1978, the town held major festivities to honour Hayes. Some consider him an honourary Paraguayan.

Why this homage to a man almost forgotten in his own country, who never even set foot in Paraguay, 7400 km to the south? At the end of the War of the Triple Alliance, Argentina claimed the whole of the Chaco but, after delicate negotiations, both countries agreed to submit claims over a smaller area, between the Río Verde and the Río Pilcomayo, to arbitration. In 1878, Argentine and Paraguayan diplomats travelled to Washington to present their cases to Rutherford B Hayes, who decided in Paraguay's favour. In gratitude, the Congress in Asunción immortalised the American President by renaming the territory's largest town, Villa Occidental, Villa Hayes in his honour.

To attend the Hayes sesquicentennial in 2028, take bus No 46 from Calle Eligio Ayala in downtown Asunción. It leaves every half-hour between 5.30 am and noon, and every 45 minutes from noon to 9 pm.

POZO COLORADO

Pozo Colorado, 274 km north-west of Asunción, has little to commend it, but it is situated on the only important crossroad in the entire Chaco. From here, a dry-weather road goes east to Concepción, where it is possible to catch a bus back to Asunción or on to the Brazilian border at Pedro Juan Caballero. There is a military checkpoint just before arriving at Pozo.

The unnamed restaurant on the north side of the highway has decent food and very cold beer; it may be able to offer a bed for the night, but if not, try the Shell station across the road. From Concepción, NASA has two buses daily to Asunción via Pozo Colorado, at 7.30 am and 11 pm. These should arrive 2½ to three hours later in Pozo. There are several other buses which continue from Pozo on to the Mennonite settlements at Filadelfia, Loma Plata and Neu-Halbstadt.

The Mennonite Colonies

Mennonites are Anabaptists, believing in adult rather than infant baptism. This might sound pretty harmless today, but in 16th-century Holland and Switzerland it was enough to get them in serious trouble with both Catholics and other Protestants. Pacifists, they also believed in separation of church and state and rejected compulsory military service, making the situation even worse and causing them to flee to Germany, Russia and Canada. By the early 20th century, political upheaval once again caused them to seek new homes, this time in Latin America. Their primary destinations were Mexico and Paraguay.

For Mennonites, the attractions of Paraguay were large amounts of nearly uninhabited land, in which they could follow their traditional agricultural way of life, and the government's willingness to grant them political autonomy under a Privilegium, with responsibility for their own schools with German-language instruction, community law enforcement, separate economic organisation and freedom from taxation, religious liberty and exemption from military service. The first group to arrive in Paraguay, in 1927, were *Sommerfelder* (Summerfield)

Mennonites from the Canadian prairies, who left after Canadian authorities failed to live up to their promise of exemption from military service. These Sommerfelder formed Menno colony, the first of three distinct but territorially overlapping Mennonite groups. Centred around the town of Loma Plata, it is still the most conservative and traditional of the colonies.

Only a few years after the founding of Menno colony, refugees from the Soviet Union established Fernheim (Distant Home), with its 'capital' at Filadelfia. Neuland (New Land) was founded in 1947 by Ukrainian German Mennonites, many of whom had served unwillingly in the German army in WW II and managed to stay in the west after being released from prisoner-of-war camps. Its largest settlement is Neu-Halbstadt.

Mennonite immigrants obtained major concessions under the Privilegium, but soon found that the Paraguayans had exploited their desire to live in peaceful isolation by granting them land in the midst of a potential war zone. Since the early part of the century, Paraguay and Bolivia had been building fortifications in anticipation of armed conflict over an area which had been a cause of antagonism since colonial days. In 1932, this erupted into open warfare, with Mennonite settlements the scene of ground fighting and even Bolivian air attacks.

Because of their isolation, the Mennonites saw Paraguayans only infrequently, but regularly came into contact, and sometimes conflict, with Chaco Indians. During the war nomadic Indians, who felt allegiance to neither country, were targets for both the Bolivians and Paraguayans and sometimes found refuge with the Mennonites. Some, however, so strongly resented the Mennonite intrusion that they resisted violently. As late as the 1940s, Ayoreo hunter-gatherers attacked and killed members of a Mennonite family in the north-western Chaco, although it is not clear who was at fault.

Such extreme cases were unusual, but more than a few Indians felt that the Mennonites were invaders and did not hesitate to let their domestic animals graze on Mennonite crops. From motives which were both religious and expedient, Mennonites encouraged the Indians to become settled cultivators, following their own example but they also distanced themselves from the Indians – those who adopted the Mennonite religion were encouraged to form their own church, and to integrate more closely into Paraguayan than Mennonite society. Over time, many Lengua and Nivaclé (Chulupí) Indians became seasonal labourers on Mennonite farms, but this opportunistic exploitation and some Mennonites' patronising attitudes alienated many Indians whose cultural system was more egalitarian and reciprocal. There is no doubting the sincerity of the Mennonites' Christian convictions and their pacifism but, as one member of the community said, 'Not all of us live up to our ideals'.

As more Paraguayans settle in the Chaco, the Mennonite communities have come under pressure from authorities, and there is concern that the government may abrogate the Privilegium. Few Mennonites are reinvesting their earnings in Paraguay, and some are openly looking for alternatives elsewhere. Others are disgruntled with developments in Filadelfia, whose material prosperity has contributed to a generation more interested in motorbikes and videos than traditional Mennonite values. Beer and tobacco, once absolutely *verboten* in Mennonite settlements, are now sold openly, although only non-Mennonites would normally consume them in public.

There are perhaps 10,000 Mennonites and a slightly larger number of Indians in the Mennonite region. Among themselves, Mennonites prefer to speak *Plattdeutsch* (Low German) dialect, but they readily speak and understand *Hochdeutsch* (High German), which is the language of instruction in the schools. Most adults now speak Spanish and a number speak passable English. Indians are as likely to speak German as Spanish, although most prefer their native languages.

FILADELFIA

Filadelfia is the administrative and service centre for Mennonite farmers of Fernheim colony. It is the most visited of the three colonies, with the most reasonable accommodation and outgoing people. In some ways, it resembles the cattle towns of the Australian outback or the American West, but dairy products and cotton are the primary products rather than beef. Just as aboriginal people work the cattle stations of Australia, so Nivaclé, Lengua, Ayoreo and other indigenous people work the Mennonite farms.

Filadelfia is still a religious community and shuts down almost completely on Sundays. On weekday mornings, you will see Mennonite farmers drive to town in their pickup trucks in search of Indians for day labour, returning with them in the afternoon. At noon, when the heat can be overpowering, the town is exceptionally quiet, as the Mennonites have adopted the custom of the tropical siesta.

Orientation

Filadelfia is about 450 km north-west of Asunción via the Ruta Trans-Chaco. The town itself lies about 20 km north of the Trans-Chaco, on a spur whose pavement ends about one km south of town. Its dusty, unpaved streets form a very orderly grid. The *Hauptstrasse* (main street) is north-south Hindenburg, named after the German general and president whose government helped the Fernheim refugees escape the Soviet Union. The other main street is Calle Trébol, which leads east to Loma Plata, the centre of Menno colony, and west to the Trans-Chaco and Fortín Toledo. Nearly every important public service is on or near Hindenburg.

Information

Tourist Office Filadelfia's de facto tourist office is the Reisebüro, the travel agency on Hindenburg between Calle Trébol and Unruh.

Money Try the Reisebüro or the Mennonite cooperative supermarket, near the corner of Unruh and Hindenburg.

Post & Telecommunications The post office is in the headquarters of the Mennonite cooperative, near the corner of Hindenburg and Unruh. Antelco is across the street, on the east side of Hindenburg.

Medical Services Filadelfia has a modern hospital, on the corner of Hindenburg and Calle Trébol.

Unger Museum

This well-arranged museum, opposite the Hotel Florida on Hindenburg, tells the story of Fernheim colony from its foundation in 1930 to the present, and also contains ethnographic materials on the Chaco Indians. It keeps no regular schedule but Hartmut Wohlgemuth, manager of the Hotel Florida, will happily provide a guided tour in Spanish or German when his schedule permits. There is an admission charge of about US$1.

Places to Stay

Camping Camping is possible free of charge in shady Parque Trébol, five km east of Filadelfia, but there is no water and only a single pit toilet. While camping there one evening, we saw a highly poisonous (but timid) coral snake.

Hotels Filadelfia's only formal accommodation is the *Hotel Florida*, on the corner of Hindenburg and Unruh. It has motel-style rooms with private bath and air-conditioning for US$25 a double, but its budget annex is an excellent bargain at US$3 per person with comfortable beds, shared bath with cold showers (not a bad idea here), and fans.

Places to Eat

The *Hotel Florida* has a very decent restaurant, and there are several shops which offer snacks and home-made ice cream along Hindenburg. Try also the parrillada at *La Estrella*, around the corner from the Hotel Florida on Unruh, which has a shady outdoor dining area.

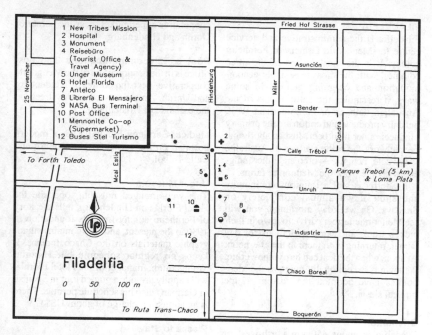

Key to map:
1 New Tribes Mission
2 Hospital
3 Monument
4 Reisebüro (Tourist Office & Travel Agency)
5 Unger Museum
6 Hotel Florida
7 Antelco
8 Librería El Mensajero
9 NASA Bus Terminal
10 Post Office
11 Mennonite Co-op (Supermarket)
12 Buses Stel Turismo

Fried Hof Strasse
Asunción
Bender
Calle Trébol
Unruh
Industrie
Chaco Boreal
Boquerón
25 November
Hindenburg
Miller
Gondra
Meal Estig
To Fortín Toledo
To Parque Trebol (5 km) & Loma Plata
To Ruta Trans-Chaco

Filadelfia

0   50   100 m

Things to Buy

Librería El Mensajero, behind Antelco and across from the Mennonite cooperative, is an evangelical bookshop which, however, also offers a good selection of Chaco Indian crafts. There is a better selection of crafts available at Neu-Halbstadt.

Getting There & Away

Bus The NASA bus terminal is on Hindenburg, just north of Industrie. NASA's Sunday, Wednesday and Friday service to Asunción, at 8 am, is an 11-hour milk run which stops at every wide spot on the road. It only costs US$7, however. A better bet would be their direct weekday service at 10 pm, which takes only seven hours to the capital, although it's dearer at US$11. NASA also offers direct buses at noon on Saturday and 8.30 pm on Sunday. On Friday, at 6 am, it goes to Mariscal Estigarribia (two hours) and Colonia La Patria (five hours), the last stop for public transport on the Ruta Trans-Chaco before the Bolivian border.

Stel Turismo, with offices in a warehouse on the west side of Hindenburg just south of Industrie, connects Filadelfia with Asunción daily except Saturday at 7 pm. Ecmetur has buses to the capital on Saturday at 1.30 pm and Sunday, Tuesday and Thursday at 8.30 pm.

Expreso CV, the local bus line, connects Filadelfia with Loma Plata (25 km) daily at 8 am, returning at 9 am. Buses to Asunción also stop at Loma Plata and most continue to Neu-Halbstadt. Hitching or asking for lifts is worth a try if you plan to go anywhere else, like Fortín Toledo, Neu-Halbstadt or Loma Plata at odd hours.

AROUND FILADELFIA
Fortín Toledo

About 40 km west of Filadelfia, Fortín Toledo is an area of both natural and historical interest. It was the site of trench warfare during the Chaco conflict, and is also the site of the **Proyecto Taguá**, a small reserve which is nurturing a population of the Chaco or Wagner's peccary *(Catagonus wagneri)*, thought extinct for nearly half a century until its rediscovery in a remote area in 1975. Jakob and María Unger, the local project managers, speak German, Spanish and English, and welcome visits if their schedules permit. Jakob's grandfather was a founder of the Fernheim colony.

The peccaries are confined within a large fenced and forested area, with a large pond which attracts many Chaco birds. Directors of the project, sponsored in part by the San Diego zoo, hope to be able to expand the reserve, but there are legal problems with acquisition of adjacent property which is part of an inheritance dispute. Nearby you can visit the fortifications of Fortín Toledo, some of which are still in excellent repair, and a Paraguayan military cemetery. Try to imagine yourself in the dusty or muddy trenches, awaiting the charge of the Bolivians.

To get to Fortín Toledo from Filadelfia, hitch or take a bus (such as the NASA bus to Colonia La Patria) out on Calle Trébol to the intersection with the Ruta Trans-Chaco. From there, cross the highway and continue about three km to an enormous tyre on which are painted the words 'pasar prohibido'. Continue on the main road another seven km, passing several buildings occupied by squatters on an old estancia, before taking a sharp right which leads to a sign reading 'Proyecto Taguá' (if walking, try to do so before the midday heat).

You may be able to hitch this segment as well, but you can also contact Jakob and María through the Mennonite radio station in Filadelfia (there is no telephone in Fortín Toledo). If they happen to be in Filadelfia, they will give you a lift to the reserve; if they're not, they will come to Filadelfia to pick you up but will charge you for their expenses (petrol is not cheap in Paraguay).

LOMA PLATA

Loma Plata, 25 km east of Filadelfia, is the administrative and service centre of Menno colony, and is the oldest and most traditional of the Mennonite settlements. It has an excellent museum with an outdoor exhibit of early farming equipment and a typical pioneer house, plus an outstanding photographic exhibit on the colony's history. Ask for the key at the Secretariat, the large building next door to the museum.

Accommodation is available at *Hotel Loma Plata* for about the same price as the Hotel Florida in Philadelphia, but with no budget annex, so it is probably better to make a day trip from Filadelfia from where there are daily connections by bus. Buses from Filadelfia to Asunción stop half an hour later in Loma Plata. Likewise, buses from Asunción to Filadelfia stop first in Loma Plata.

NEU-HALBSTADT

Neu-Halbstadt is the service centre of Neuland colony, 33 km south of Filadelfia. Founded in 1947 by Ukrainian German Mennonites, it resembles Filadelfia and Loma Plata. *Hotel Boquerón* has singles/doubles for US$15/22, with a good restaurant as well. Nearby Fortín Boquerón preserves a sample of the trenches of the Chaco war. There is a campground north of Neu-Halbstadt, but at the time of writing it was locked up.

South of Neuland are the largest Indian reserves, where many Lengua and Nivaclé have settled with the assistance of the Asociación del Servicio de Cooperación Indígena Menonita (ASCIM) and become farmers. Neu-Halbstadt is a good place to obtain Indian handicrafts, including bags and hammocks, and woven goods, including belts and blankets coloured with natural dyes. For excellent information on local Indians and access to a great selection of crafts, contact Walter and Verena Regehr in Neu-Halbstadt, who distribute Indian crafts on a non-profit basis. You can also see these goods at Artesanía Viva in Asunción.

Several buses from Asunción to Filadelfia continue to Neu-Halbstadt, while others come directly from Asunción. NASA has

Tuesday and Thursday buses to Asunción at 6.30 pm, while Stel Turismo leaves for the capital daily except Monday at the same hour.

The High Chaco

PARQUE NACIONAL DEFENSORES DEL CHACO

Created in 1980, the High Chaco park of Defensores del Chaco is Paraguay's largest (780,000 hectares) and most remote unit. Once the exclusive province of nomadic Ayoreo hunter-gatherers, it is mostly a forested alluvial plain about 100 metres in elevation, but the isolated 500-metre peak of Cerro León is the park's greatest landmark, looming above the surrounding area.

Quebracho, algarroba, palo santo and cactus are the dominant species in the dense thorn forest, which harbours populations of important animal species despite the pressures of illicit hunting, which has proved difficult to control over such a large area with limited staff. This is the most likely place in Paraguay to view large cats such as jaguar, puma, ocelot, and Geoffroy's cat, plus other unique species although, as everywhere, such species are only rarely seen.

Defensores del Chaco is 830 km from Asunción over roads which are impassable to most ordinary vehicles, especially after rain. Park headquarters are reached by a road north from Filadelfia to Fortín Teniente Martínez and then to Fortín Madrejón, another 213 km north. Further facilities are at Aguas Dulces, 84 km beyond Madrejón.

As there is no regular public transportation to Defensores del Chaco, access is difficult, but not impossible. Inquire at the Fundación Moisés Bertoni in Asunción, which conducts four-day excursions in 4WD vehicles, stopping at points of interest, such as Fortín Toledo, en route. In the past, these have been held in the normally dry and comfortable month of August. Alternatively, the Fundación may be able to put you in contact with rangers who must occasionally travel to Asunción and will, if space is available, take passengers on the return trip. Getting away may present some difficulty, but have patience – you are unlikely to be stranded forever.

MARISCAL ESTIGARRIBIA

Mariscal Estigarribia, 540 km from Asunción, is the last sizable settlement on the Ruta Trans-Chaco before the Bolivian border. There is accommodation at the *Hotel Alemán*, a police checkpoint, and a petrol station which is a good place for trying to catch a lift into Bolivia. If driving, bear in mind that there is no dependable source of petrol beyond Mariscal Estigarribia, so be sure to fill up here, and carry extra petrol, food and water.

Every Friday at 8 am, there is a NASA bus to Colonia La Patria (three hours), the last Trans-Chaco outpost accessible by public transport. To Asunción (10 hours), buses leave daily, with two departures on Sundays. The fare to the capital is US$12.50.

COLONIA LA PATRIA

Only 85 km from the Bolivian border, Colonia La Patria is being developed as a rural service centre for the estancias of the High Chaco, with running water, a power station, school, hospital, phone system, motel and petrol station. Every Friday at 2 pm, there are buses to Mariscal Estigarribia (three hours), Filadelfia (five hours), and Asunción (14 hours).

Glossary

Unless otherwise indicated, the terms below apply to all three River Plate countries of Argentina, Uruguay and Paraguay. Terms specific to the Falkland Islands are also noted. The list includes common geographical and biological terms as well as slang terms from everyday speech. The latter includes *lunfardo*, the street slang of Buenos Aires.

AAA – Argentine Anti-communist Alliance, a right-wing death squad probably organised by Peron's mysterious advisor José López Rega.

ACA – Automóvil Club Argentino, the automobile club which provides maps, road service, insurance and other services, and operates hotels, motels and campgrounds throughout the country. A valuable resource even for travellers without motor vehicles.

acequia – irrigation canal, primarily in the Cuyo region.

Acuerdo Nacional – in Paraguay, a broad coalition of opponents of the Stroessner dictatorship.

aerosilla – chairlift.

alameda – street lined with poplar trees.

alerce – large coniferous tree, resembling California redwood, for which Argentina's Parque Nacional Los Alerces is named.

alfajores – biscuit sandwiches with chocolate, dulce de leche or fruit.

alíscafo – hydrofoil, from Buenos Aires across the Río de la Plata to Colonia, Uruguay.

altiplano – high Andean plain, often above 4000 metres, in the north-western Argentine provinces of Jujuy, Salta, La Rioja and Catamarca.

apunamiento – altitude sickness.

argentinidad – rather nebulous concept of Argentine national identity, often associated with extreme nationalistic feelings.

arrayan – tree of the myrtle family, for which Argentina's Parque Nacional Los Arrayanes is named.

arroyo – creek, stream.

asado – barbecue, usually a family outing in summer.

autopista – freeway or motorway.

balneario – bathing resort or beach.

balsa – a launch or raft.

bañado – marsh or seasonally flooded zone on the rivers of northern Argentina. Bañados are good habitat for migratory birds, but are also often used for temporary cultivation.

banda negativa – low-cost air tickets in Argentina, where limited seats on particular flights are available for up to 40% less than the usual price.

baqueano – back-country tracker.

barrio – neighbourhood.

bencina – white gas, used for campstoves. Also known as *nafta blanca*.

BFFI – British Forces Falkland Islands.

bicho – any small creature, from insect to mammal.

biota – the fauna and flora of a region.

boleadoras – heavily weighted thongs, used by Pampas and Patagonian Indians for hunting guanaco and rhea. Also called *bolas*.

boga – tasty river fish from the rivers of Argentine Mesopotamia.

bonos – bonds used as legal currency in the provinces of Jujuy, Salta and Tucumán, but worthless outside the province of issue. Bonos usually have a date of expiration beyond which they have no value.

Cabildo – colonial town council.

cachila – in Uruguay, an antique automobile, often beautifully maintained.

cacique – Indian chief.

caldén – *Prosopis caldenia*, a characteristic tree of the Dry Pampa.

calle – street.

Camp, The – in the Falkland Islands, the area beyond Stanley, i.e. the countryside. Anglo-Argentines use the same term to refer to the countryside, but it can also mean a given field or paddock, in both Falklands or Anglo-Argentine usage.

campo – the countryside. Alternately, a field or paddock.

caracoles – a winding road, usually in a mountainous area.

carapintada – in the Argentine military, extreme right-wing, ultranationalist movement of disaffected junior officers, responsible for several attempted coups during the Alfonsín and Menem administrations.

carpincho – capybara, a large aquatic rodent which inhabits the Paraná and other subtropical river areas.

casa de familia – modest family accommodation, usually in tourist centres.

casa de gobierno – literally 'government house', a building now often converted to a museum, offices etc.

casco – 'big house' of a cattle or sheep estancia.

cataratas – waterfalls.

caudillo – in 19th-century Argentine politics, a provincial strongman whose power rested more on personal loyalty than political ideals or party organisation.

cerro – mount, mountain.

chachacoma – Andean shrub whose leaves produce a herbal tea which relieves symptoms of altitude sickness.

chacra – small, independent farm.

chivito – Uruguayan steak sandwich.

chusquea – solid bamboo of the Valdivian rain forest in Patagonia.

ciervo – deer.

coima – a bribe. One who solicits a bribe is a *coimero*.

comedor – basic cafeteria or dining room in a hotel.

confitería – café which serves coffee, tea, desserts and simple food orders. Many confiterías are important social centres in Argentina.

congregación – in colonial Latin America, the concentration of dispersed native populations in central settlements, usually for purposes of political control or religious instruction (see also *reducción*).

congrio – conger eel, a popular and delicious Chilean seafood.

conventillo – tenements which housed immigrants in older neighbourhoods of Buenos Aires and Montevideo. On a reduced scale, these still exist in the San Telmo area of Buenos Aires and the Ciudad Vieja of Montevideo.

cordobazo – 1969 uprising against the Argentine military government in the city of Córdoba, which eventually paved way for the return of Juan Perón from exile.

cospel – token used in Argentine public telephones in lieu of coins. There are different cospeles for local and long-distance phones.

costanera – seaside, riverside or lakeside road.

criollo – in colonial period, an American-born Spaniard, but the term now commonly describes any Argentine of European descent. The term also describes the feral cattle of the Pampas.

cuatrerismo – cattle rustling.

curanto – Chilean seafood stew.

dique – reservoir used for recreational purposes.

Dirty War – see *Guerra Sucia*.

dulce de leche – caramelised milk, an Argentine invention and obsession, often spread on bread or crackers and stuffed in pastries.

dorado – large river fish in the Paraná drainage, known among fishing enthusiasts as the 'Tiger of the Paraná' for its fighting spirit.

encomienda – colonial labour system, under which Indian communities were required to provide workers for Spaniards (*encomenderos*), in exchange for which the Spaniard was to provide religious and language instruction. In practice, the system benefited Spaniards far more than native peoples.

ERP – Ejército Revolucionario Popular, revolutionary leftist group which mimicked Cuban-style revolution in the sugar-growing areas of Tucumán in 1970s. Wiped out by the Argentine army during the Dirty War.

estancia – extensive grazing establishment, either for cattle or sheep, with dominating owner or manager and dependent resident labour force.
estanciero – owner of an estancia.

facturas – pastries.
ficha – token used in the Buenos Aires subway system (Subte) in lieu of coins.
FIBS – Falkland Islands Broadcasting Service.
FIC – Falkland Islands Company.
FIDC – Falkland Islands Development Corporation.
FIG – Falkland Islands Government.
FIGAS – Falkland Islands Government Air Service.
frigorífico – meat freezing factory.

Gardeliano – fan of the late tango singer Carlos Gardel.
gas-oil – diesel fuel.
gasolero – motor vehicle which uses diesel fuel, which is much cheaper than ordinary petrol in Argentina.
guapoy – strangler fig of subtropical forests.
Guerra Sucia – in the 1970s, the Dirty War of the Argentine military against left-wing revolutionaries and anyone suspected of sympathising with them.
guita – in lunfardo, money.
gurí – Guaraní word meaning 'child' which has been adopted into regional speech in Argentine Mesopotamia and Paraguay.

hacienda – in the Andean North-West, a large but often underproductive rural landholding, with a dependent resident labour force, under a dominant owner. In Argentina, a less common form of *latifundio* than in other Latin American countries.

ichu – bunch grass of the Andean steppe (altiplano).
iglesia – church.
indigenismo – movement in Latin American art and literature which extolls aboriginal traditions, usually in a romantic or patronising manner.
ingenio – industrial sugar mill.

IVA – *impuesto de valor agregado*, value added tax (VAT), often added to restaurant or hotel bills in Argentina and Uruguay. If there is any question, ask whether IVA is included in the bill.

jabalí – wild European boar, a popular game dish in Argentine Patagonia.
jineteada – any horseback riding competition, as in a rodeo.

lapacho – important timber tree in subtropical northern Argentina.
latifundio – large landholding, such as a cattle or sheep estancia.
lunfardo – street slang of Buenos Aires, with origins in immigrant neighbourhoods at the turn of the century.

manta – a shawl or bedspread.
mara – Patagonian hare.
mazamorra – thickish maize soup, typical of the North-West Andean region.
mazorca – political police of 19th-century Argentine dictator Juan Manuel de Rosas.
mediero – sharecropper, a tenant who farms another's land in exchange for a percentage of the crop.
meseta – interior steppe of eastern Patagonia.
mestizo – a person of mixed Indian and Spanish descent.
minifundio – small landholding, such as a peasant farm.
minuta – in restaurant or confitería, a short order such as spaghetti or milanesa.
mirador – viewpoint, usually on a hill but often in a building.
Montoneros – left-wing faction of the Peronist party, which became an underground urban guerrilla movement in 1970s.
monte – scrub forest. The term is often applied to any densely vegetated area.
municipalidad – city hall.
museo – museum.

nafta – gasoline or petrol.
novela – television soap opera.

ñandú – large, flightless bird, resembling the ostrich. There are two Argentine species.

ñandutí – delicate 'spider-web' lace woven by the women of Itauguá, a small town near Asunción, Paraguay.

ñoqui – a public employee whose primary interest is collecting a monthly paycheck. So-called because potato pasta, or ñoquis (from the Italian *gnocchi*), are traditionally served in financially strapped Argentine households on the 29th of each month, the implication being that the employee makes his or her appearance at work around that time.

oligarquía terrateniente – derogatory term for the Argentine landed elite.

onces – 'elevenses', Chilean afternoon tea.

pampero – South Atlantic cold front which brings dramatic temperature changes to Uruguay, Paraguay and the interior of northern Argentina.

parada – bus stop.

parrillada, parrilla – respectively, a mixed grill of steak and other beef cuts, and a restaurant specialising in such dishes.

pasarela – catwalk across a stream or bog.

paseo – an outing, such as a walk in the park or downtown.

peatonal – pedestrian mall, usually in the downtown area of major Argentine cities.

pehuén – Araucaria, or 'monkey puzzle' tree of southern Patagonia.

peña – club which hosts informal folk music gatherings.

peones golondrinas – 'swallows', term frequently applied to seasonal labourers from Bolivia in the Tucumán sugar harvest, but also used in similar contexts elsewhere in Argentina.

pingüinera – penguin colony.

piropo – sexist remark, ranging from complimentary and relatively innocuous to rude and offensive.

Porteño – inhabitant of Buenos Aires, a 'resident of the port'

precordillera – foothills of the Andes.

primera – 1st-class on a train.

Privilegium – agreement between the government of Paraguay and Mennonite agricultural colonists, granting the latter land and political autonomy, including the right to German-language schools, freedom of religion, exemption from military service, cooperative economic organisation, and independent law enforcement.

Proceso – in full, 'El Proceso de Reorganización Nacional', a military euphemism for its brutal attempt to remake Argentina's political and economic culture between 1976 and 1983.

propina – a tip, eg in a restaurant or cinema.

pucará – in the Andean North-West, an indigenous fortification, generally on high ground commanding an unobstructed view in several directions.

puchero – soup combining vegetables and meats, served with rice.

puesto – 'outside house' on cattle or sheep estancia.

pucho – in lunfardo, a cigarette or cigarette butt.

pulpería – rural shop or 'company store' on cattle or sheep estancia.

puna – Andean highlands, usually above 3000 metres.

quebracho – literally, the 'axe-breaker' tree (*Quebrachua lorentzii*) of the Chaco, a natural source of tannin for the leather industries of the River Plate.

quilombo – in lunfardo, a mess. Originally a Brazilian term describing a settlement of runaway slaves, it came to mean a house of prostitution in Argentina.

quinoa – a native Andean grain, the dietary equivalent of rice in the pre-Columbian era.

rambla – avenue or shopping mall.

rancho – a rural house, generally of adobe, with a thatched roof.

recargo – additional charge, usually 10%, which many Argentine businesses add to credit card transactions because of high inflation and delays in payment.

reducción – like congregación, the concentration of native populations in towns modelled on the Spanish grid pattern, for purposes of political control or religious instruction. The term also refers to the settlement itself.

refugio – a usually rustic shelter in a national park or remote area.

río – river.

ruta – route or highway. In Argentina, these are either national or provincial.

sábalo – popular river fish in the Paraná drainage.

saladero – establishment for salting meat and hides.

salar – salt lake or salt pan, usually in the high Andes or Argentine Patagonia.

siesta – lengthy afternoon break for lunch and, occasionally, a nap.

s/n – 'sin número', indicating a street address without a number.

smoko – in the Falkland Islands, midmorning tea or coffee break, usually served with cakes and other homemade sweets.

sobremesa – after-dinner conversation.

soroche – altitude sickness.

Southern Cone – in political geography, the area comprising Argentina, Chile, Uruguay and parts of Brazil and Paraguay. So-called after the area's shape on the map.

squaddies – British enlisted men on four-month tours-of-duty in the Falkland Islands.

Subte – the Buenos Aires underground.

surubí – popular river fish in Argentine Mesopotamia and elsewhere in the River Plate drainage. Frequently served in restaurants.

taguá – Wagner's peccary, a species of wild pig thought extinct but recently rediscovered in the Paraguayan Chaco.

tapir – large hoofed mammal of subtropical forests in northern Argentina and Paraguay, a distant relative of the horse.

teleférico – gondola cable-car.

tenedor libre – 'all-you-can-eat' restaurant.

tereré – cold mate, as consumed by Paraguayans.

todo terreno – mountain bike.

tola – high-altitude shrubs in the altiplano of north-western Argentina.

trapiche – antique sugar mill.

trasnochador – one who stays up very late or all night, as do many Argentines.

trucho – bogus, a term widely used by Argentines to describe things which are not what they appear to be.

turco – 'Turk', an often derogatory term for any Argentine of Middle Eastern descent.

turismo aventura – term used to describe non-traditional forms of tourism, such as trekking and river rafting.

turista – 2nd-class on a train, usually not very comfortable.

tuteo – use of the pronoun *tu* in Spanish and its corresponding verb forms.

two-nighter – in the Falkland Islands, a traditional party for visitors from distant sheep stations, who would invariably stay the weekend.

vicuña – wild relative of domestic llama and alpaca, found only at high altitudes in Argentina's Andean North-West.

villas miserias – shantytowns on the outskirts of Buenos Aires and other Argentine cities.

vinchuca – biting insect, living in thatched dwellings with dirt floors, which is a vector for Chagas' disease (American trypanosomiasis).

viviendas temporarias – riverfront shantytowns of Asunción, Paraguay.

vizcacha – wild relative of the domestic chinchilla. There are two common species in Argentina, the mountain vizcacha *(Lagidium vizcacha)* of the Andean highlands and the plains vizcacha *(Lagostomus maximus)* of the subtropical lowlands. Some regard the latter as a pest.

voseo – use of the pronoun *vos* and its corresponding verb forms in the River Plate republics of Argentina, Uruguay and Paraguay.

warrah – the now extinct but possibly domesticated Falklands fox or wolf, *Dusicyon australis*, presumptive evidence of Yahgan Indian presence on the Falklands.

yacaré – South American alligator, found in

humid, subtropical parts of Argentina, Uruguay and Paraguay.

yerba mate – 'Paraguayan tea' *(Ilex paraguariensis)*, which Argentines consume in very large amounts, but Paraguayans, Uruguayans and Brazilians also use regularly. Taking *mate* is an important everyday social ritual.

yisca – bag made of vegetable fibre, traditional among the Toba Indians of the Chaco.

yungas – in north-western Argentina, transitional subtropical lowland forest.

yuyos – 'herbs', mixed with *yerba mate* in northern Argentina.

zafra – sugar harvest.

Zonda – in the central Andean provinces, a powerful, dry north wind like the European *Föhn* or the North American *Chinook*.

Index

TEXT

Thanks

Our thanks to readers and travellers who wrote in with information:

Julia Arias (AUS), Azevedo, Stuart W Bander, New York (USA), Isabel Barutta (Arg), Brigitte Beller (F), Ian Bourne (USA), Juan Brambati (Arg), Paul Bruthiaux, Culver City (USA), David Butler (AUS), Sue & Peter Chetwood (AUS), James M Clausing (AUS), Edith D'Esposito (USA), Mrs Marion Davies (UK), Kerndall Dtovrerel (USA), David Epperson, John D Farr (USA), Mario Feldman (Arg), Jose Luis Fonrouge (Arg), Tony Gass (USA), Cathe Giffuni (USA), Gustavo Giorgis (Arg), Wolf Gotthilf, Braunschweig (D), Martin Jose Guzman (Arg), Michael Hawley (USA), Ian Henderson, London (UK); Ben Herman, San Francisco (USA); Jim Hermann (USA), Mrs H D Holladay (UK); Louisa Holgersson (S), T P Hunt (UK), Winslow Robert Hunt & Kathleen King, Pocatello (USA), Katty Kauffman, Frederic Klopp (F), Daniel Alberto Korman (Arg), Pete Larrett (USA), Francisco J S Lukman (Arg), Manel Roca Marco, Barcelona (Sp), Federico Luis Martin (Arg), Ira Meyer (USA), John Moynihan, New York (USA), G Navarro, Rijen (NL), Ms Jill Norman (UK), Dana Ott, Washington DC (USA), Rachel Panckhurst, Montreal (C), Giancarlo Perlo (I), Christian Personat, St Michel/Orge (F), R Rattur, David Rawson-McKenzie, Hamilton (Bermuda), Cathy Reid (AUS), Brian Robinson (UK), Harry Sansen, San Antonio (USA), John C Schaumburg (USA), Tony Schirato, Trieste (I), Jorge Antolin Solache (Arg), Martin Spencer (AUS), Mrs V Tauras (AUS), Ian Turland (AUS), Mike Wall (USA), Russell Willis, Millner (AUS); Graham Youdale, Killara (AUS), Werner Zwick (D).

Arg – Argentina, AUS – Australia, C – Canada, D – Germany, F – France, I – Italy, NL – Netherlands, S – Sweden, Sp – Spain, UK – United Kingdom, USA – United States

Keep in touch!

We love hearing from you and think you'd like to hear from us.

The Lonely Planet Newsletter covers the when, where, how and what of travel. (AND it's free!)

When...is the right time to see reindeer in Finland?
Where...can you hear the best palm-wine music in Ghana?
How...do you get from Asunción to Areguá by steam train?
What...should you leave behind to avoid hassles with customs in Iran?

To join our mailing list just contact us at any of our offices. (details below)

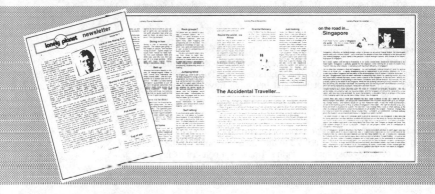

Every issue includes:

- a letter from Lonely Planet founders Tony and Maureen Wheeler
- travel diary from a Lonely Planet author - find out what it's really like out on the road
- feature article on an important and topical travel issue
- a selection of recent letters from our readers
- the latest travel news from all over the world
- details on Lonely Planet's new and forthcoming releases

Also available Lonely Planet T-shirts. 100% heavy weight cotton (S, M, L, XL)

LONELY PLANET PUBLICATIONS
Australia: PO Box 617, Hawthorn, 3122, Victoria (tel: 03-819 1877)
USA: Embarcadero West, 155 Filbert Street, Suite 251, Oakland, CA 94607 (tel: 510-893 8555)
UK: Devonshire House, 12 Barley Mow Passage, Chiswick, London W4 4PH (tel: 081-742 3161)

Guides to the Americas

Alaska – a travel survival kit
Jim DuFresne has travelled extensively through Alaska by foot, road, rail, barge and kayak. This guide has all the information you'll need to make the most of one of the world's great wilderness areas.

Baja California – a travel survival kit
For centuries, Mexico's Baja peninsula – with its beautiful coastline, raucous border towns and crumbling Spanish missions – has been a land of escapes and escapades. This book describes how and where to escape in Baja.

Bolivia – a travel survival kit
From lonely villages in the Andes to ancient ruined cities and the spectacular city of La Paz, Bolivia is a magnificent blend of everything that inspires travellers. Discover safe and intriguing travel options in this comprehensive guide.

Brazil – a travel survival kit
From the mad passion of Carnival to the Amazon – home of the richest and most diverse ecosystem on earth – Brazil is a country of mythical proportions. This guide has all the essential travel information.

Canada – a travel survival kit
This comprehensive guidebook has all the facts on the USA's huge neighbour – the Rocky Mountains, Niagara Falls, ultramodern Toronto, remote villages in Nova Scotia, and much more.

Central America on a shoestring
Practical information on travel in Belize, Guatemala, Costa Rica, Honduras, El Salvador, Nicaragua and Panama. A team of experienced Lonely Planet authors reveals the secrets of this culturally rich, geographically diverse and breathtakingly beautiful region.

Chile & Easter Island – a travel survival kit
Travel in Chile is easy and safe, with possibilities as varied as the countryside. This guide also gives detailed coverage of Chile's Pacific outpost, mysterious Easter Island.

Colombia – a travel survival kit
Colombia is a land of myths – from the ancient legends of El Dorado to the modern tales of Gabriel Garcia Marquez. The reality is beauty and violence, wealth and poverty, tradition and change. This guide shows how to travel independently and safely in this exotic country.

Costa Rica – a travel survival kit
This practical guide gives the low down on exceptional opportunities for fishing and water sports, and the best ways to experience Costa Rica's vivid natural beauty.

Ecuador & the Galápagos Islands – a travel survival kit
Ecuador offers a wide variety of travel experiences, from the high cordilleras to the Amazon plains – and 600 miles west, the fascinating Galápagos Islands. Everything you need to know about travelling around this enchanting country.

Hawaii – a travel survival kit
Share in the delights of this island paradise – and avoid its high prices – both on and off the beaten track. Full details on Hawaii's best-known attractions, plus plenty of uncrowded sights and activities.

La Ruta Maya: Yucatán, Guatemala & Belize – a travel survival kit
Invaluable background information on the cultural and environmental riches of La Ruta Maya (The Mayan Route), plus practical advice on how best to minimise the impact of travellers on this sensitive region.

Mexico – a travel survival kit
A unique blend of Indian and Spanish culture, fascinating history, and hospitable people, make Mexico a travellers' paradise.

Peru – a travel survival kit
The lost city of Machu Picchu, the Andean altiplano and the magnificent Amazon rainforests are just some of Peru's many attractions. All the travel facts you'll need can be found in this comprehensive guide.

South America on a shoestring
This practical guide provides concise information for budget travellers and covers South America from the Darien Gap to Tierra del Fuego. The *New York Times* dubbed the author 'the patron saint of travellers in the third world'.

Trekking in the Patagonian Andes
The first detailed guide to this region gives complete information on 28 walks, and lists a number of other possibilities extending from the Araucanía and Lake District regions of Argentina and Chile to the remote icy of South America in Tierra del Fuego.

Also available:
Brazilian phrasebook, **Latin American Spanish** phrasebook and **Quechua** phrasebook.

Lonely Planet Guidebooks

Lonely Planet guidebooks cover every accessible part of Asia as well as Australia, the Pacific, South America, Africa, the Middle East, Europe and parts of North America. There are five series: *travel survival kits*, covering a country for a range of budgets; *shoestring guides* with compact information for low-budget travel in a major region; *walking guides*; *city guides* and *phrasebooks*.

Australia & the Pacific
Australia
Bushwalking in Australia
Islands of Australia's Great Barrier Reef
Fiji
Melbourne city guide
Micronesia
New Caledonia
New Zealand
Tramping in New Zealand
Papua New Guinea
Bushwalking in Papua New Guinea
Papua New Guinea phrasebook
Rarotonga & the Cook Islands
Samoa
Solomon Islands
Sydney city guide
Tahiti & French Polynesia
Tonga
Vanuatu
Victoria

South-East Asia
Bali & Lombok
Bangkok city guide
Myanmar (Burma)
Burmese phrasebook
Cambodia
Indonesia
Indonesia phrasebook
Malaysia, Singapore & Brunei
Philippines
Pilipino phrasebook
Singapore city guide
South-East Asia on a shoestring
Thailand
Thai phrasebook
Vietnam, Laos & Cambodia
Vietnamese phrasebook

North-East Asia
China
Mandarin Chinese phrasebook
Hong Kong, Macau & Canton
Japan
Japanese phrasebook
Korea
Korean phrasebook
Mongolia
North-East Asia on a shoestring
Seoul city guide
Taiwan
Tibet
Tibet phrasebook
Tokyo city guide

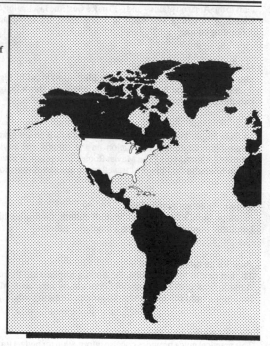

West Asia
Trekking in Turkey
Turkey
Turkish phrasebook
West Asia on a shoestring

Middle East
Arab Gulf States
Egypt & the Sudan
Egyptian Arabic phrasebook
Iran
Israel
Jordan & Syria
Yemen

Indian Ocean
Madagascar & Comoros
Maldives & Islands of the East Indian Ocean
Mauritius, Réunion & Seychelles

Mail Order

Lonely Planet guidebooks are distributed worldwide. They are also available by mail order from Lonely Planet, so if you have difficulty finding a title please write to us. US and Canadian residents should write to Embarcadero West, 155 Filbert St, Suite 251, Oakland CA 94607, USA; European residents should write to Devonshire House, 12 Barley Mow Passage, Chiswick, London W4 4PH; and residents of other countries to PO Box 617, Hawthorn, Victoria 3122, Australia.

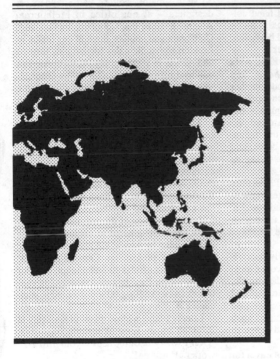

Indian Subcontinent
Bangladesh
India
Hindi/Urdu phrasebook
Trekking in the Indian Himalaya
Karakoram Highway
Kashmir, Ladakh & Zanskar
Nepal
Trekking in the Nepal Himalaya
Nepal phrasebook
Pakistan
Sri Lanka
Sri Lanka phrasebook

Africa
Africa on a shoestring
Central Africa
East Africa
Trekking in East Africa
Kenya
Swahili phrasebook
Morocco, Algeria & Tunisia
Moroccan Arabic phrasebook
South Africa, Lesotho & Swaziland
Zimbabwe, Botswana & Namibia
West Africa

Central America
Baja California
Central America on a shoestring
Costa Rica
La Ruta Maya
Mexico

North America
Alaska
Canada
Hawaii

South America
Argentina, Uruguay & Paraguay
Bolivia
Brazil
Brazilian phrasebook
Chile & Easter Island
Colombia
Ecuador & the Galápagos Islands
Latin American Spanish phrasebook
Peru
Quechua phrasebook
South America on a shoestring
Trekking in the Patagonian Andes

Europe
Dublin city guide
Eastern Europe on a shoestring
Eastern Europe phrasebook
Finland
Iceland, Greenland & the Faroe Islands
Mediterranean Europe on a shoestring
Mediterranean Europe phrasebook
Poland
Scandinavian & Baltic Europe on a shoestring
Scandinavian Europe phrasebook
Trekking in Spain
Trekking in Greece
USSR
Russian phrasebook
Western Europe on a shoestring
Western Europe phrasebook

The Lonely Planet Story

Lonely Planet published its first book in 1973 in response to the numerous 'How did you do it?' questions Maureen and Tony Wheeler were asked after driving, bussing, hitching, sailing and railing their way from England to Australia.

Written at a kitchen table and hand collated, trimmed and stapled, *Across Asia on the Cheap* became an instant local bestseller, inspiring thoughts of another book.

Eighteen months in South-East Asia resulted in their second guide, *South-East Asia on a shoestring*, which they put together in a backstreet Chinese hotel in Singapore in 1975. The 'yellow bible' as it quickly became known to backpackers around the world, soon became *the* guide to the region. It has sold well over half a million copies and is now in its 7th edition, still retaining its familiar yellow cover.

Today there are over 120 Lonely Planet titles in print – books that have that same adventurous approach to travel as those early guides; books that 'assume you know how to get your luggage off the carousel' as one reviewer put it.

Although Lonely Planet initially specialised in guides to Asia, they now cover most regions of the world, including the Pacific, South America, Africa, the Middle East and Europe. The list of *walking guides* and *phrasebooks* (for 'unusual' languages such as Quechua, Swahili, Nepalese and Egyptian Arabic) is also growing rapidly.

The emphasis continues to be on travel for independent travellers. Tony and Maureen still travel for several months of each year and play an active part in the writing, updating and quality control of Lonely Planet's guides.

They have been joined by over 50 authors, 54 staff – mainly editors, cartographers, & designers – at our office in Melbourne, Australia, 10 at our US office in Oakland, California and another three at our office in London to handle sales for Britain, Europe and Africa. In 1992 Lonely Planet opened an editorial office in Paris. Travellers themselves also make a valuable contribution to the guides through the feedback we receive in thousands of letters each year.

The people at Lonely Planet strongly believe that travellers can make a positive contribution to the countries they visit, both through their appreciation of the countries' culture, wildlife and natural features, and through the money they spend. In addition, the company makes a direct contribution to the countries and regions it covers. Since 1986 a percentage of the income from each book has been donated to ventures such as famine relief in Africa; aid projects in India; agricultural projects in Central America; Greenpeace's efforts to halt French nuclear testing in the Pacific and Amnesty International. In 1993 $100,000 was donated to such causes.

Lonely Planet's basic travel philosophy is summed up in Tony Wheeler's comment, 'Don't worry about whether your trip will work out. Just go!'